Human Rights

The International Library of Essays in Law and Legal Theory
Second Series
Series Editor: Tom D. Campbell

Titles in the Series:

Freedom of Speech, Volumes I and II
Larry Alexander

Law and Legal Interpretation
Fernando Atria and D. Neil MacCormick

Privacy
Eric Barendt

Comparative Legal Cultures
John Bell

Contract Law, Volumes I and II
Brian Bix

Corporate Law
William W. Bratton

Law and Democracy
Tom Campbell and Adrienne Stone

Legal Positivism
Tom D. Campbell

Administrative Law
Peter Cane

International Trade Law
Ronald A. Cass and Michael S. Knoll

Sociological Perspectives on Law, Volumes I and II
Roger Cotterrell

Intellectual Property
Peter Drahos

Family, State and Law, Volumes I and II
Michael D. Freeman

Natural Law
Robert P. George

The Creation and Interpretation of Commercial Law
Clayton P. Gillette

Competition Law
Rosa Greaves

Chinese Law and Legal Theory
Perry Keller

Constitutional Law
Ian D. Loveland

Human Rights
Robert McCorquodale

Anti-Discrimination Law
Christopher McCrudden

Medical Law and Ethics
Sheila McLean

Mediation
Carrie Menkel-Meadow

Environmental Law
Peter S. Menell

Criminal Law
Thomas Morawetz

Law and Language
Thomas Morawetz

Law and Anthropology
Martha Mundy

Gender and Justice
Ngaire Naffine

Law and Economics
Eric A. Posner

Japanese Law
J. Mark Ramseyer

Restorative Justice
Declan Roche

Constitutional Theory
Wojciech Sadurski

Justice
Wojciech Sadurski

The Rule of Law
Frederick Schauer

Regulation
Colin Scott

War Crimes Law
Gerry Simpson

Restitution
Lionel D. Smith

Freedom of Information
Robert G. Vaughn

Tort Law
Ernest J. Weinrib

Rights
Robin West

Welfare Law
Lucy A. Williams

Human Rights

Edited by

Robert McCorquodale

University of Nottingham, UK

Published by
Dartmouth Publishing Company
Ashgate Publishing Limited
Gower House
Croft Road
Aldershot
Hants GU11 3HR
England

Ashgate Publishing Company
Suite 420
101 Cherry Street
Burlington, VT 05401-4405
USA

Ashgate website: http://www.ashgate.com

British Library Cataloguing in Publication Data
Human rights. – (International library of essays in law and legal theory. Second series)
1. Human rights
I. McCorquodale, Robert
342'.085

Library of Congress Cataloging-in-Publication Data
Human rights / edited by Robert McCorquodale.
p. cm. — (International library of essays in law and legal theory. Second series)
Includes bibliographical references.
ISBN 0-7546-2159-6 (alk. paper)
1. Human rights. I. McCorquodale, Robert. II. Series.

K3240 .H8463 2002
341.4'81—dc21

2002074716

ISBN 0 7546 2159 6

Printed in Great Britain by The Cromwell Press, Trowbridge, Wiltshire

Contents

Acknowledgements

The editor and publishers wish to thank the following for permission to use copyright material.

Australian Yearbook of International Law for the essays: Dianne Otto (1997), 'Rethinking Universals: Opening Transformative Possibilities in International Human Rights Law', *Australian Year Book of International Law*, **18**, pp. 1–36; Hilary Charlesworth (1992), 'The Public/Private Distinction and the Right to Development in International Law', *Australian Year Book of International Law*, **12**, pp. 190–204.

Upendra Baxi (1999), 'Voices of Suffering, Fragmented Universality, and the Future of Human Rights', in Burns H. Weston and Stephen P. Marks (eds), *The Future of International Human Rights*, Ardsley, NY: Transnational Publishers, Inc., pp. 101–56. Copyright © 1999 Upendra Baxi.

Blackwell Publishing Limited for the essay: David Beetham (1995), 'What Future for Economic and Social Rights?', *Political Studies*, **43**, pp. 41–60. Copyright © 1995 Political Studies Association.

Brooklyn Journal of International Law for the essays: Joy Gordon (1998), 'The Concept of Human Rights: The History and Meaning of its Politicization', *Brooklyn Journal of International Law*, **23**, pp. 689–791. Copyright © 1998 Brooklyn Journal of International Law; Frank J. Garcia (1999), 'The Global Market and Human Rights: Trading Away the Human Rights Principle',, *Brooklyn Journal of International Law*, **25**, pp. 51–97. Copyright © 1999 Brooklyn Journal of International Law.

Comité International De La Croix-Rouge for the essay: Louise Doswald-Beck and Sylvain Vité (1993), 'International Humanitarian Law and Human Rights Law', *International Review of the Red Cross*, **293**, pp. 94–119. Copyright © 1993 Comité International De La Croix-Rouge.

Fordham University for the essay: Ruti Teitel (1997), 'Human Rights Genealogy', *Fordham Law Review*, **66**, pp. 301–17. Copyright © 1997 Fordham Law Review.

Johns Hopkins University Press for the essays: Jerome J. Shestack (1998), 'The Philosophic Foundations of Human Rights', *Human Rights Quarterly*, **20**, pp. 201–34. Copyright © 1998 The Johns Hopkins University Press. Reprinted with permission of The Johns Hopkins University Press; Peter Jones (1999), 'Human Rights, Group Rights, and Peoples' Rights', *Human Rights Quarterly*, **21**, pp. 80–107. Copyright © 1999 The Johns Hopkins University Press. Reprinted with permission of The Johns Hopkins University Press; Audrey R. Chapman (1996), 'A "Violations Approach" for Monitoring the International Covenant on Economic, Social and Cultural Rights', *Human Rights Quarterly*, **18**, pp. 23–66. Copyright © 1996 The Johns Hopkins University Press. Reprinted with permission of The Johns Hopkins University Press.

Michael Ignatieff (2001), 'The Attack on Human Rights', *Foreign Affairs*, **80**, pp. 102–16. Copyright © 2001 Michael Ignatieff.

Lucius und Lucius Verlagsgesellschaft mbH for the essay: Boaventura de Sousa Santos (1997), 'Toward a Multicultural Conception of Human Rights', *Zeitschrift für Rechtssoziologie*, **18**, pp. 1–15.

Amartya Sen (1994), 'Freedoms and Needs', *New Republic*, January, pp. 1–11 (original pp. 31–36, 38). Copyright © 1994 Amartya Sen.

Sweet & Maxwell Limited for the essay: David Kennedy (2001), 'The International Human Rights Movement: Part of the Problem?', *European Human Rights Law Review*, **3**, pp. 245–67. Copyright © 2001 David Kennedy.

University at Buffalo School of Law for the essay: Joseph Oloka-Onyango (2000), 'Human Rights and Sustainable Development in Contemporary Africa: A New Dawn, or Retreating Horizons?', *Buffalo Human Rights Law Review*, **6**, pp. 39–76.

University of Nottingham, Human Rights Law Centre for the essay: Sigrun I. Skogly (2002), 'Is There a Right Not to be Poor?', *Human Rights Law Review*, **2**, pp. 59–80.

Virginia Journal of International Law for the essay: Makau Wa Mutua (1995), 'The Banjul Charter and the African Cultural Fingerprint: An Evaluation of the Language of Duties', *Virginia Journal of International Law*, **35**, pp. 339–80.

Every effort has been made to trace all the copyright holders, but if any have been inadvertently overlooked the publishers will be pleased to make the necessary arrangement at the first opportunity.

Preface to the Second Series

The first series of the International Library of Essays in Law and Legal Theory has established itself as a major research resource with fifty-eight volumes of the most significant theoretical essays in contemporary legal studies. Each volume contains essays of central theoretical importance in its subject area and the series as a whole makes available an extensive range of valuable material of considerable interest to those involved in research, teaching and the study of law.

The rapid growth of theoretically interesting scholarly work in law has created a demand for a second series which includes more recent publications of note and earlier essays to which renewed attention is being given. It also affords the opportunity to extend the areas of law covered in the first series.

The new series follows the successful pattern of reproducing entire essays with the original page numbers as an aid to comprehensive research and accurate referencing. Editors have selected not only the most influential essays but also those which they consider to be of greatest continuing importance. The objective of the second series is to enlarge the scope of the library, include significant recent work and reflect a variety of editorial perspectives.

Each volume is edited by an expert in the specific area who makes the selection on the basis of the quality, influence and significance of the essays, taking care to include essays which are not readily available. Each volume contains a substantial introduction explaining the context and significance of the essays selected.

I am most grateful for the care which volume editors have taken in carrying out the complex task of selecting and presenting essays which meet the exacting criteria set for the series.

TOM CAMPBELL
Series Editor
Centre for Applied Philosophy and Public Ethics
Charles Sturt University

Introduction

> [F]or the historically disempowered, the conferring of rights is symbolic of all the denied aspects of their humanity: rights imply a respect that places one in referential range of self and others, that elevates one's status from human body to social being . . . 'Rights' feels new in the mouths of most black people. It is still deliciously empowering to say. It is the magic wand of inclusion and exclusion, of power and no power. The concept of rights, both positive and negative, is the maker of citizenship, our relation to others. (Williams, 1991, p. 164)

The Context

Human rights are much more than ideas and are beyond the limits of law. Human rights are both lived dreams and denied realities. The theories of human rights, as Patricia Williams makes clear in the statement quoted above, are founded on our relation to others. Those others can be our social and cultural communities, our economic and political structures and those whom we encounter in our daily lives. A key aspect of human rights is the perspective taken:

> The modern vocabulary and grammar of rights is a many-faceted instrument for reporting and asserting the requirements or other implications of a relationship of justice *from the point of view of the person(s) who benefit(s)* from that relationship. It provides a way of talking about 'what is just' from a special angle: the viewpoint of the 'other(s)' to whom something . . . is owed or due, and who would be wronged if denied that something. (Finnis, 1980, p. 205, emphasis in original)

Very often, the relationship is one of power and no power, or of inequality of powers. As Vaclav Havel noted, '[t]he exercise of power is determined by thousands of interactions between the world of the powerful and that of the powerless, all the more so because these worlds are never divided by a sharp line: everyone has a small part of himself in both' (Havel, 1990, p. 182). It is in these contexts of powers, justice and of relations to others that theories of human rights have been shaped, moulded and debated.

Theories of human rights are not easily reduced to a few essential essays. This is partly because a significant amount of the literature on this area is found in monographs or in chapters in edited books. It is also partly because there is a vast array of writing on human rights and to find the few essential essays is no easy task. Philip Alston managed to achieve it with his *Human Rights Law* (1996), which forms part of the first series of the International Library of Essays in Law and Legal Theory, by emphasizing certain themes. This volume is intended as a supplement to his, and therefore does not include essays that deal with the main themes that he considered. There are, as a consequence, no essays in this volume that directly deal with the issues of universality in a cultural perspective (to use his term) or about rights in relation to political participation, although these issues continue to engage many scholars.

Instead, the focus here is on essays that take a specifically philosophical approach to human rights – that is, those that explore the concepts of what are human rights. 'Human rights theories' in this volume are, as in Alston's volume, considered to be those theories developed in relation to the international community, as against national theories of rights.[1] The latter are dealt with expertly by two volumes on *Rights* (Nino, 1991; West, 2002), which are also part of this Library (and see also Leiser and Campbell, 2001). The essays included in this volume are divided into two broad categories: those essays that explore the nature of human rights and those that seek to apply human rights theories to other fields; although it is recognized that these two categories do overlap. The intention is to include a diversity of essays that challenge the dominant theories of human rights and offer different perspectives on their application, and to include primarily essays that were published after the completion of Alston's volume in 1994 until 2001/2002.

Is there is a need for theoretical understandings of human rights? Hersch Lauterpacht observed in 1950 that human rights 'largely remain in the realm of theory unless they are made secure in the firm anchorage of the international legal order' (Lauterpacht, 1950, p. 126). International human rights law now has a definite anchor in the international legal order. It was accepted by states in the Vienna Declaration and Programme of Action on Human Rights 1993 that 'human rights are a legitimate concern of the international community' (Vienna, 1993, para. 4). Indeed, it is an extraordinary fact that states are now prepared to accept limitations on their sovereignty in relation to human rights issues and to enter binding treaties to this effect. The development of international human rights law has been so rapid that Philip Alston has called for a quality control of new human rights (Alston, 1984). There does remain continuing pressure from parts of the international community, including non-governmental organizations, to ensure that there is a firmer anchorage for the protection of human rights. There is also a move to incorporate a 'global ethic', which would include human rights, into international relations (Booth, 1995; Chandler, 2001).

Yet these developments in international human rights law remain almost exclusively under states' control, and this has an effect on the concept of human rights, as Philip Allott has noted:

> Human rights [have been] quickly appropriated by governments, embodied in treaties, made part of the stuff of primitive international relations, swept up into the maw of an international bureaucracy. The reality of the idea of human rights has been degraded. From being a source of ultimate anxiety for usurping holders of public social power, they were turned into bureaucratic small-change. Human rights, a reservoir of unlimited power in all the self-creating of society, became a plaything of governments and lawyers. The game of human rights has been played in international statal organisations by diplomats and bureaucrats, and their appointees, in the setting and the ethos of traditional international relations . . . [and so] the potential energy of the idea [of human rights] has been dissipated. (Allott, 1990, p. 288)

The potential of human rights is also limited by the process of drafting international human rights law, as particularization often leads to a limiting of the concept of rights, as compromises, exceptions and restrictions are made to these rights (Campbell, 1986). In addition, because the volume of international human rights law has become so vast and diverse, the theoretical foundations are easily neglected in the desire to clarify and explore the substantive, procedural and institutional aspects of this system. Yet, without some clear conceptual bases, human rights law becomes even more subject to the whims of states and the vagaries of international events. As Jerome Shestack observed:

> How we understand the meaning of human rights will influence our judgments on such issues as which rights are regarded as absolute, which are universal, which should be given priority, which can be overruled by other interests, which call for international pressures, which can demand programs for implementation, and which will be fought for. (Shestack, 1984, p. 70)

So there remains a requirement for a constant reminder of, and debate about, theories of human rights.

Human rights are important not just for the person, group or community whose rights are violated but also for those who violate human rights, as they can no longer act as they wish against those under their jurisdiction without risking an international response. All of humanity is demeaned when human rights are violated, and we are all challenged to act in a way that protects, promotes and ensures human rights. Our responses to this challenge can be dependent on our conceptual understanding of human rights, and this volume explores some of these conceptual understandings.

Challenging Human Rights Concepts

It is appropriate to begin this volume with an essay by Jerome Shestack (Chapter 1), as its purpose is to provide an analytical survey of many of the key philosophical justifications for human rights. As new theories of human rights usually offer critiques of older theories, it can be difficult to find an insightful commentary on these older theories. Shestack's essay offers that commentary, as well as a valuable summary of a substantial proportion of the older theories. It also reminds us that the term 'human rights' does not automatically mean a legal claim by an individual against another who has a duty to uphold that entitlement (MacCormick, 1982). As Hohfeld (1913) demonstrated, (human) rights is a term with much ambiguity, as it can mean an immunity, a privilege (liberty), a power or a claim-right (or a number of these at once).

Shestack's survey is complemented by Ruti Teitel's essay (Chapter 2), in which she undertakes a search into the history of international human rights theory. This is a 'genealogical' search in that she explores the historical and political legacies, and the founding structures and rhetoric, of contemporary theories of human rights in order to find a 'family tree' of human rights theories. By this means, she weeds out those theorists who see the roots as purely post-Second World War and measured only by judicial enforcement. She also prunes away the limited dualisms, such as realism versus idealism, found in many theories. Instead, she nurtures the 'human' part of human rights and the importance of human rights discourse in developing a strong and enduring human rights theory.

In the next essay, Joy Gordon (Chapter 3) provides a detailed examination of human rights, in which she offers a critique of the current dominant (liberal) theory (or theories) of human rights. She traces this theory to Augustine's notion of a just war and to the Enlightenment's desire for the good life, in which rights were political, abstract and narrowly conceived. Her argument is that this theory, by impliedly asserting an absolute good, suppresses alternative moral discourses and can increase human suffering. Her examples from the Nuremberg trials and recent practices show that the dominant theory places the protection from atrocities in the same category as political and intellectual activities, and that these latter activities are deemed to be more essential and immediate than economic needs. This leads to a position where there is no distinction between the concept of human rights and the action to protect human rights as 'the moral content of the conception of human rights is . . . inseparable from the [political] agenda' (p. 154). Rather, she argues that human rights should not be abstract notions but should be directly related to concrete life activities and applied as such.

Gordon sets a high standard in her expectation that human rights theories must be applied consistently and coherently in all political (and economic) practice. In fact, it is the very inconsistency and incoherence of state practice that often demands a human rights theory to be beyond the limitations of state practice. Crucially, though, she makes the point about the need for human rights theories to address the needs of people in their daily lives. She also highlights the appalling inconsistency in the dominant human rights theory. For example, under this theory, voting once every four years for a person who rarely meets the voters is upheld as a human right, whilst those who freeze to death for lack of heat or die because a doctor could not be afforded are not considered to have had their human rights violated. Gordon offers a three-part theory of human rights. First, it includes the most minimal and urgent conditions for human life and so protects against extreme physical violence, such as torture, genocide and slavery. Second, it includes everything necessary for human beings to live and so protects essential economic and physical needs, such as the provision of food, shelter, water, employment and medical care. Third, it includes everything necessary for both a full and good life and those things indirectly necessary to protect the essential economic and physical needs, and so protects expression, association, movement and political participation. This is a broad definition that seeks to provide an alternative to the narrow human rights concepts of the dominant liberal theory.

In Chapter 4 Upendra Baxi also critiques the narrowness of the dominant human rights theories, taking a broad and expansive approach to the human rights theories, both current and in the future. Taking as his starting point the power of human rights languages (see also Leuprecht, 1988 and Williams' quote at the beginning of this Introduction), Baxi considers that human rights are the 'common language of humanity . . . as [human rights] are all that we have to interrogate the barbarism of power, even when these remain inadequate to humanize fully the barbaric practices of politics' (p. 160). He is very aware of the limitations of this language for the 'wretched of the earth', not least because the term 'human rights' itself shelters diversity and exclusions, and seems to be constantly expanding in content, often without conceptual support. Baxi critically reviews contemporary human rights theories and practices, and finds them removed from the experiences of the oppressed. In turn, he seeks to provide a social theory of human rights, in which he considers human rights movements as social movements that are threatened by being conceived in economic market terms, which leads to the protection of global capital rather than the symbolic capital of human dignity (see also Stammers, 1995). In this essay, he argues for a conceptual approach that permits the voices of the suffering to be heard and so offers a future for human rights.

Both Gordon and Baxi's theories place considerable stress on economic, social and cultural rights, which have traditionally had much less emphasis in the international community. This lack of emphasis is seen in, for example, the lack of any initial provision for a supervisory body within the International Covenant on Economic, Social and Cultural Rights (although such a provision was created later) and the small number of non-governmental organizations committed to pursuing these rights – as rights – at the international level. Indeed, the debate about whether these areas of human life can be considered to be human rights is a long-running one.

David Beetham (Chapter 5) offers a cogent and compelling argument for treating economic and social rights as human rights, defining and justifying these rights in a context where the basic means for sustaining life are vulnerable to constant threat. He considers that human rights theories all embody a notion of justice, an account of obligations and of duties corresponding to the rights claimed, and a presupposition of both human needs and human development. In his theory he relies on Henry Shue's clarification of the different types of duty that are required to make human rights effective (Shue, 1996) – namely, 'the duty to *avoid* depriving a person of some necessity; the duty to *protect* them from deprivation; and the duty to *aid* them when deprived' (p. 225, emphasis in original). These duties, he argues are assignable, delimited and practical. States have the primary duty to use society's resources when individuals, families and communities are unable to provide these resources, and the international community of states must assist those states whose national resources prove insufficient.

Beetham's theory unearths some of the interactions between human rights and duties. This issue is addressed directly by Makau Wa Mutua (Chapter 6) as he aims to provide a human rights theory that would be a basis for social and political reconstruction in Africa. He places traditional human rights theories within the European idea of the state and the individual, and shows how this has limited utility in Africa. This lack of applicability has created in Africa 'a crisis of cultural and philosophical identity: the delegitimation of values, notions, and philosophies about the individual, society, politics, and nature developed over centuries' (p. 239). Mutua seeks to legitimize these values and philosophies, especially the pre-colonial African notion that the individual social being was the bearer of both rights and duties. He does not see this as being a culturally relativist argument or an attempt to deny the Western liberal concepts of human rights. Rather, he offers a complementary concept of human rights in which rights are not set solely within the context of an individual claim against the state that owes a duty to the individual, but are a means to balance the intertwined claims of both the individual's and the community's rights and duties. These intertwined claims are more apparent in societies in which the state, and its interaction with the individual, is not the same as in Europe. Mutua sees the inclusion of both rights and duties within the African Charter of Human and Peoples' Rights as important because it could strengthen community ties and social cohesiveness and so act as a 'glue to reunite individuals and different nations within the modern state, and at the same time set the proper limits of conduct by state officials' (p. 264).

Mutua's view is an important reminder of the relationship between rights and duties. As one of the participants in the United Nations debates leading to the adoption of the Universal Declaration of Human Rights, Mrs Menon of India, said:

> Mahatma Gandhi had said, all rights were born of obligations, and no man could claim the rights to live unless he fulfilled his duties as a citizen of the world. From the very fact that it proclaimed rights, therefore, the Declaration was a declaration of obligations.[2]

As she makes clear, the UDHR, and all subsequent international human rights instruments, are premised on the concept that each person or group, in the exercise of her/his/their rights, has duties to others. This concept of human rights encompasses the notion of duties or responsibilities,[3] so this means that rights and duties/responsibilities are a part of a multifaceted, integrated relationship and are not separate or opposing ideas.

This interrelationship between rights and duties/responsibilities is important for another aspect of human rights: the limitations on their exercise. Human beings do not exist in a vacuum but are part of a community and communities, and their rights are exercised in that context. Thus the exercise of nearly all human rights is necessarily limited[4] in order to protect the rights of other individuals and of the general community. This practical and legal consequence of human rights theories does mean that, sometimes, rights can seem to be in conflict and a determination is needed as to the method to provide for the greatest protection of all rights. This has been especially the case in regard to groups or collectives, where the unjust priority of a particular collective (the state) over other forms of collective has led to many of the conflicts within states.

The issue of whether groups or collectives can have human rights is the focus of Peter Jones' essay (Chapter 7). The role of groups in society is important for human rights concepts as 'groups and communities, and not isolated individuals, transmit culture from one generation to the next [and] embody and give cultural and social differences in society' (Steiner, 1991, p. 1541). Historically, the rights of some groups, such as minorities and corporations, have been protected. In fact, most human rights theories give special status to the individual within a particular collective – the collective of the 'nation-state'. However, a right is a group right if it is borne by a group as a group, rather than by an exercise of an individual right that may directly or indirectly benefit the group (such as the individual rights of freedom of assembly and association). Indeed, it has been shown that not only is the purpose of a group right to protect a group, as a group, from oppression and to empower them (McCorquodale, 1994), but also that the right to equal concern and respect is grounded on the interest which every person has in the quality of her or his own life and that this can be applied equally to collectives (Freeman, 1995; Yasuaki, 1997). Jones considers that groups can be conceived as shared interest collectives or as a corporate unitary entity and argues that only the former have group rights because the latter are not held by human beings as such, but by a corporate entity. He demonstrates this by reference to the right of self-determination.

The right of self-determination, from its definition and exercise to its philosophical basis and status, is one of the most contentious ideas in the international community. Much of the language of self-determination is distorted by the political, economic, social and cultural objectives of those who seek power, and consequently its nexus with any theoretical foundation of human rights is often lost. Although the right includes political, economic, social and cultural elements (McCorquodale, 2000), Jones deliberately limits his examination of the right of self-determination in relation to political development. He shows that, by adopting a collective concept of group rights, a more flexible and less territorial definition of 'self', and wider choices of exercises of the right, are all available. This approach may open possibilities for dialogue that are often submerged by the oppositional stances of those involved.

Issues of oppositions, the limited understanding of the role of the community, the restrictiveness of much human rights discourse and much more are dealt with in the essay by Dianne Otto (Chapter 8). Otto reviews the universalist nature of human rights concepts, not from a universal versus cultural relativist angle but from a deeper analysis of the universalist tradition of human dignity as a foundation for human rights theories. She shows how the construction of 'human dignity' – a term widespread in international human rights documents and philosophical justifications for human rights (for example, Schachter, 1983) – within the relationship of the individual and her/his society erases alternative experiences, particularly for those having communitarian traditions and for women. For example, she examines the Universal Declaration of Human Rights and sees that it is premised 'on modernity's assumption that the preconstituted, autonomous, self-interested individual is the foundational unit of society and the sole subject of international human rights law' (p. 315). This premise creates boundaries of inclusion and exclusion so that human rights becomes, to use Otto's term, 'a technology of difference'. She demonstrates this in a number of ways, such as by showing the destructive, hierarchical nature of the generational view of human rights (where civil and political rights are 'first generation', economic, social and cultural rights are 'second generation', and so on) and pointing out that human rights discourse at the international level is confined to being primarily a discourse between elites.

Otto effectively uses Foucault's concepts of power (Foucault, 1980) to show how international human rights law is focused on protecting human rights against a centralized state, where the state is meant to be the only relevant identity for the inhabitants of a territory. Indeed, the history of internal conflicts is replete with examples of states' repression of groups that have sought to assert their separate identity from the state, most notably involving claims to the right of self-determination.[5] This limited focus of human rights has created a legal institutional framework that privileges some knowledge and forces claimants to fit within certain restrictive legal parameters. For example, some groups are compelled to 'go ethnic . . . [to defend their rights by] staging a collective identity and demanding rights in the name of that identity' (Cheah, 1997, p. 256). Despite the problems of the dominant universalist theories of human rights, Otto sees transformative possibilities in human rights by the forging of alliances and coalitions between local and global knowledge and fostering discourses across apparently dualistic divisions.

Boaventura de Sousa Santos (Chapter 9) also sees dialogue as important. He considers that a theory of human rights can be applied universally by means of 'diatopical hermeneutics'. By this he means that each culture, no matter how strong it is, is incomplete and so his aim is 'to raise the consciousness of reciprocal incompleteness to its possible maximum by engaging in the dialogue, as it were, with one foot in one culture and the other in another' (p. 349). He argues that this allows human rights to perform a progressive, emancipatory service in the international community and overcome some of its historical bias and restrictive presuppositions. He places this in the context of globalization, arguing that human rights have been used as a form of globalization from above, when they should be conceived as a multicultural (counter-hegemonic) globalization from below (Falk, 1993).

Applying Human Rights Concepts

Globalization is 'an economic, political, social, and ideological phenomenon which carries with it unanticipated, often contradictory and polarising consequences' (Sjolander, 1996, p. 604). A matter of increasing concern to human rights scholars (for example, Orford, 1998; Muchlinski, 2001) has been the impact of the processes of globalization on human rights protections. Explorations of the role of institutional economic organizations, such as the World Bank, International Monetary Fund (IMF) and the World Trade Organization (WTO), and of transnational corporations, in relation to their impact on human rights have found that it both offers opportunities and raises dangers for the protection of human rights (McCorquodale with Fairbrother, 1999).

Frank Garcia's essay (Chapter 10) acknowledges these different consequences of globalization and focuses on the conceptual contrasts between international economic law and international human rights law. He notes that:

> The regulatory framework which international economic law provides for globalization operates according to a view of human nature, human values and moral decision-making fundamentally at odds with the view of human nature, human values and moral decision-making which underlies international human rights law. The human rights movement could thus find in market globalization the ultimate victory of a regulatory system that, by nature and operation, cannot properly take into account what the human rights movement holds most dear: that underlying positive human rights laws are moral entitlements that ground moral, political, and legal claims of special force, claims which must be morally and legally prior to society and the state. (pp. 361–62)

Garcia shows how global economic decisions, illustrated by the World Trade Organization (WTO) dispute settlement mechanism, involve the allocation of social benefits and burdens that may operate contrary to the forms of social justice envisaged by human rights theories. In a number of areas the regulatory systems of international economic law and international human rights law overlap and compete. According to Garcia, when this happens human rights principles tend to be overridden.

Whilst the economic theory underpinning globalization has an impact on human rights theory, it is also part of a broader challenge to human rights: how to take account of non-state actors. One area in which human rights law and theory has been largely absent is in relation to the actions of non-state actors, such as transnational corporations, armed opposition groups and terrorists. Some international human rights supervisory bodies have been alert to this and have sought to clarify the state's responsibilities in this regard. For example, in *Vélásquez Rodriguez* v. *Honduras*, the Inter-American Court of Human Rights held that:

> The State is obligated to investigate every situation involving a violation of rights under the Convention. If the State apparatus acts in such a way that the violation goes unpunished and the victim's full enjoyment of such rights is not restored as soon as possible, the State has failed to comply with its duty to ensure the free and full exercise of those rights to persons within its jurisdiction. The same is true when the State allows private persons or groups to act freely and with impunity to the detriment of the rights recognised in the Convention.[6]

So, where a state is not directly responsible for the actual violation (such as when it is caused by a non-state actor) or when the state acquiesces in allowing the act to occur, then the state can still be held responsible for a lack of positive action in responding to, or preventing, the violation. Yet these obligations remain on the state itself, due to the state-centric framework and conceptual foundations of the international human rights regime, and there are still few direct human rights obligations on non-state actors (Jochnick, 1999; McCorquodale and La Forgia, 2001).

This silence of international human rights law was seen most starkly in the events of 11 September 2001 in the United States of America and the response to those events. Michael Ignatieff (Chapter 11) looks at these events and responses in his essay, and sees the dangers in a limited concept of human rights. He defends the moral universality of human rights as a means to challenge powerful religions, family structures, authoritarian states and tribes, but contends that the ability of the powerless to exercise human rights requires a close cultural understanding of the frameworks that can constrain freedoms and choices. His plea is for a use of human rights vocabulary as a basis for deliberation and dialogue rather than purely as what Dworkin (1977) terms as 'trumps'.

One area where non-state actors have been directly affected by international human rights law has been that of international criminal responsibility. This has become a rapidly developing area of international law, especially with the two International Criminal Tribunals and the uniform agreement for an International Criminal Court. Whilst this development has occurred with a minimum of theoretical argument in terms of human rights, international criminal law has been seen as drawing from the conceptual foundations of both international human rights law and international humanitarian law (Roberts, 2002). As Louise Doswald-Beck and Sylvain Vité explain in Chapter 12, international human rights law has traditionally been conceptually limited to dealing with the protection of human rights in times of peace, and international humanitarian law has dealt with the protection of humans during armed conflicts. Each has its own separate theoretical foundations. However, the strict division between them has now become difficult to defend. This was most evident during the conflicts in the former Yugoslavia at the end of the twentieth century. Doswald-Beck and Vité show the degree to which the different theoretical bases of international humanitarian law and international human rights law intersect and diverge, and how they are increasingly mutually influencing each other.

This mutual influence could have an effect on the enforcement of both areas of international law. There are now a multitude of international human rights supervisory mechanisms, which use a variety of methods to ensure that states comply with their human rights obligations. In addition, the broader international community, including non-governmental organizations, uses other measures to ensure that states are alerted to violations of human rights and the consequences of non-compliance. National human rights institutions and the use of truth and reconciliation commissions have increased the methods of supervision (Landsman, 2001). However, there has not been a great deal of literature on the conceptual aspects of enforcement of international human rights law (Mutua, 1998).

Audrey Chapman's essay (Chapter 13) offers such a conceptual analysis in relation to one of the international supervisory bodies. She argues that a change is needed in the paradigm for evaluating compliance with the rights protected under the International Covenant on Economic, Social and Cultural Rights, if those rights are to be taken seriously. Process and procedures are an essential element in both the protection of human rights and the development of an effective international human rights system (Higgins, 1994). However, the issues discussed in Beetham's essay (Chapter 5) resurface here as a result of the questions about the nature of economic, social and cultural rights. This creates great difficulty in monitoring compliance with these rights, particularly the notion of the 'progressive realization' of these rights under Article 2 of the International Covenant on Economic, Social and Cultural Rights. Rather than trying to assess progressive realization, Chapman suggests that the Committee on Economic, Social and Cultural Rights should adopt a 'violations approach' in which violations of these rights are identified and declared as such. She demonstrates how this approach is both possible and desirable by reference to both the Committee's practice and the rights protected.

Chapman's approach would mean that the method of dealing with compliance was similar with regard to all human rights. A different approach, though with potentially the same effect, is that taken by Amartya Sen (Chapter 14). Sen is a Nobel Prize-winning economist who has written widely on issues that pertain to human rights, including a book, *Development as Freedom* (Sen, 1999). In this short essay, he explains the extensive interconnections, both instrumental and constitutive, between political rights and economic needs. Whilst the interdependence of human rights has been a long-term formal stance of the United Nations (for example, Vienna, 1993, para. 5), this has not been reflected in practice. Sen argues that there is a political significance in having rights that can exceed their personal utility and that having civil and political rights can have a direct impact on government economic decision-making. He uses famine as an example to show, he claims, that no state that substantially protects civil and political rights has experienced a famine. Whilst recognizing the limits of political rights – especially in a democracy where the rights of minorities can be overcome in the supposed desire to protect the interests of the majority – he argues that they nevertheless have the additional benefit of enabling the conceptualization, formulation and expression of economic needs.

One particular economic need is development, the right to which remains a very contentious right in international law (Rich, 1988) and a fuller consideration of which is provided in another volume in this series (Carty, 1992). In Chapter 15 Hilary Charlesworth, a leading feminist legal philosopher, considers this right. She begins by setting out some of the central aspects of feminist legal theory, such as the false dichotomy between private and public activities. She then shows how the structure of international human rights law effectively excludes actions occurring in the private sphere, such as domestic violence, and excludes violations that are occasioned by non-state actors, finally proving that the right to development, as currently conceived, reinforces this structure. The right is based on the notion that 'development' means industrialization, Westernization and economic growth. Despite the fact that women are responsible for as much as 80 per cent of food production in developing states, as well as nearly all 'domestic' work, they are not seen as 'economically productive' workers, sufficient to be counted in measures of economic growth (such as the UN System of National Accounts), because their actions take place in the 'private' sphere. One consequence of this is that they are overlooked by international institutions and states when making decisions about the provision of aid and other financial assistance, except in their role as 'mothers'. Charlesworth seeks to change this position through a reconceptualization and restructuring of the international legal system.

Joe Oloka-Onyango (Chapter 16) also considers women's rights, as well as the rights of other groups, such as refugees. He examines these issues within the context of the extent to which the enjoyment of human rights 'ensures that daily physical existence is not under a threat of predictable extermination by hunger, disease, or conflict' (p. 526). This approach he calls 'sustainable human development' and he explores how this is applied and enforced in Africa, recognizing the diversity of experiences within that continent. After calling for more education, both generally and about human rights, he finally notes the clarification of the justiciability of economic, social and cultural rights in a series of South African cases.[7]

The issue of how human rights are part of sustaining daily life is taken further by Sigrun Skogly (Chapter 17). The context of her essay is the reality of poverty for so many people in the world and she asks whether or not it is helpful to think of poverty in terms of human rights. In seeking to answer this question, she relies on the conceptual work of Amartya Sen (see Chapter 14) and others, applies the variety of rights set out in human rights treaties and sets these within the framework of the daily existence of those who are in poverty. Whilst concluding that there is no express right not to be poor, she argues that, if the guarantees within international human rights treaties were fulfilled, it would result in changes that would lift people out of poverty. Moreover, she notes that there are distinct and important advantages to a human rights-based approach to poverty, including the use of legal standards and obligations, international supervisory mechanisms and valuable analytical tools that can ensure that poverty is not seen as a fault or an inevitability but, rather, as an affront to human dignity. Such an approach might also lead to more effective political and social pressure, by non-governmental organizations among others, to alleviate poverty.

The final essay also seeks a change in the approach to human rights. David Kennedy has been the catalyst for much of the 'Newstream' of international legal scholarship, which has offered a refreshing critique, often using critical legal theory and feminism, of the dominant international legal concepts. In his essay (Chapter 18), Kennedy deals with problems in the international human rights movement, by which he includes all who deal in some way with the international human rights system. He sees the power in the social construct of human rights irrespective of whether their existence can be coherently explained (as Rorty (1993) has argued). His concern is the lack of recognition of the harmful effects of the articulation, institutionalization and enforcement of human rights (both in its vocabulary and its practice), and so he offers a 'more pragmatic attitude to human rights' (p. 582).

Kennedy examines the problems of human rights hegemony by which it pretends to occupy the entire field of emancipatory possibilities, but argues that it is both narrow in scope and general in vocabulary, and that it largely expresses the ideology and practice of a specific form of liberalism. It also creates a binary opposition between the individual as a right-holding identity and the state (see Otto, Chapter 8). One consequence of these problems is that human rights promise much more than they can deliver, and this has been a long-standing criticism of human rights law by critical legal scholars:

> Without even knowing it, [people] start talking as if 'we' were rights-bearing citizens who are 'allowed' to do this or that by something called 'the state', which is a passivizing illusion – actually an hallucination which establishes the presumptive political legitimacy of the status quo . . . It may be necessary to use the rights argument in the course of political struggle, in order to make gains. But the thing to be understood is the extent to which it is enervating to use it . . . [It is] an hallucination that as long as people believe in it, they will disempower themselves. (Gabel and Kennedy, 1984)

Kennedy adds to his critique a perceptive comment on the international human rights regime and bureaucracy, which has degraded and limited the idea of human rights. His hope is that, by articulating these concerns, they can be addressed, overcome and/or avoided. Certainly his contribution will be an important element in the response.

Conclusions

There remain a number of important contributions to human rights theory that have not been included, as is inevitable in a volume of this nature. For example, there have been significant advances in recent years in the application of human rights theories to a number of different areas that are not represented here. These include: human rights within international environmental law (for example, Brown Weiss, 1996; Pevato, 1999); indigenous peoples' rights (for example, Anaya, 1996; Kingsbury, 1998; Weissner, 1999); and human rights as a basis for intervention in a state, usually known as humanitarian intervention (for example, Kritsiotis, 1998; Henkin *et al.*, 1999; White, 2000).

These advances show the transformative potential of human rights theories. By providing a coherent, conceptual approach to international human rights law, human rights theories can be a means to challenge vested, entrenched and oppressive power (Robinson, 1997). Part of this challenge is in changing the location and nature of power and, as Williams' quote at the beginning of this Introduction made clear, there is now a power in the language of human rights and in its theories.

Notes

1 The distinction between 'rights' as being national human rights theories and 'human rights' as being international human rights theories is generally found in philosophy: see Martin and Nickel (1980).
2 General Assembly Official Records, Third Session, Part 1, Plenary Meetings, 1948, at p. 894.
3 Contrary to the unsustainable position of the Inter-Action Council's draft Universal Declaration of Human Responsibilities.
4 Rights that protect the personal or physical integrity of an individual or of a group, such as the right of freedom from torture, cruel, inhuman or degrading treatment or punishment, and the prohibition on genocide, do not include limitations on their exercise.
5 'Many peoples today are deprived of their right of self-determination, by elites of their own countrymen and women: through the concentration of power in a particular political party, in a particular ethnic or religious group, or in a certain social class' – statement by the UK representative to the Third Committee of the General Assembly on 12 October 1984, *British Yearbook of International Law*, **55** (1984), p. 432.
6 *Vélásquez Rodriguez* v. *Honduras*, 28 ILM 294 (1989) para. 176.
7 See, for example, *Soobramoney* v. *Minister for Health* (Constitutional Court 1997) and *Minister of Health* v. *Treatment Action Campaign* (Constitutional Court 2002).

References

Allott, Philip (1990), *Eunomia: New Order for a New World*, Oxford: Oxford University Press.
Alston, Philip (1984), 'Conjuring up New Human Rights: A Proposal for Quality Control', *American Journal of International Law*, **78**, p. 607.
Alston, Philip (1996), *Human Rights Law*, Aldershot: Dartmouth.
Anaya, James (1996), *Indigenous Peoples in International Law*, Oxford: Oxford University Press.
Booth, Ken (1995), 'Human Wrongs and International Relations', *International Affairs*, **71**, p. 110.
Brown Weiss, Edith (1996), *In Fairness to Future Generations: International Law, Common Patrimony, and Intergenerational Equity*, Ardsley, NY: Transnational Publishers.
Campbell, Tom (1986), 'Introduction: Realizing Human Rights', in T. Campbell *et al.* (eds), *Human Rights: From Rhetoric to Reality*, Oxford: Blackwell, p. 1.
Carty, Anthony (1992), *Law and Development*, Aldershot: Dartmouth.
Chandler, David (2001), 'Universal Ethics and Elite Politics: The Limits of Normative Human Rights Theory', *International Journal of Human Rights*, **5**, p. 72.
Cheah, Pheng (1997), 'Posit(ion)ing Human Rights in the Current Global Conjuncture', *Public Culture: Society for Transnational Studies*, **9**, p. 233.
Dworkin, Richard (1977), *Taking Rights Seriously*, Cambridge, MA: Harvard University Press.
Falk, Richard (1993), 'The Making of Global Citizenship', in J. Brecher, J. Childs and J. Cutler (eds), *Global Visions: Beyond the New World Order*, Cambridge, MA: South End Press, p. 39.
Finnis, John (1980), *Natural Law and Natural Rights*, Oxford: Clarendon Press.
Foucault, Michel (1980), 'Two Lectures', in C. Gordon (ed.), *Power/Knowledge*, Brighton: Harvester, p. 78.
Freeman, Michael (1995), 'Are there Collective Human Rights?', *Political Studies*, **43**, p. 25.
Gabel, Peter and Kennedy, Duncan (1984), 'Roll Over Beethoven', *Stanford Law Review*, **36**, p. 1
Havel, Vaclav (1990), *Disturbing the Peace*, London: Faber.
Higgins, Rosalyn (1994), *Problems and Process: International Law and How We Use It*, Oxford: Oxford University Press.
Henkin, Louis, Wedgwood, Ruth, Charney, Jonathan, Chinkin, Christine, Falk, Richard, Franck, Thomas and Reisman, Michael (1999), 'NATO's Kosovo Intervention', *American Journal of International Law*, **93**, pp. 824–62.
Hohfeld, Wesley (1913), 'Fundamental Legal Conceptions as Applied to Judicial Reasoning', *Yale Law Journal*, **23**, p. 16.

Jochnick, Chris (1999) 'Confronting the Impunity of Non-State Actors: New Fields for the Promotion of Human Rights', *Human Rights Quarterly*, **21**, p. 56.

Kingsbury, Benedict (1998), 'Indigenous Peoples in International Law: A Constructivist Approach to the Asian Controversy', *American Journal of International Law*, **92**, p. 414.

Kritsiotis, Dino (1998), 'Reappraising Policy Objections to Humanitarian Intervention', *Michigan Journal of International Law*, **19**, p. 1005.

Landsman, Todd (2001), 'Publish Not Punish: The Contested Truth of the South African Truth and Reconciliation Commission', *Human Rights and Human Welfare*, **1** (3)

Lauterpacht, Hersch (1950), *International Law and Human Rights*, New York: Praeger.

Leiser, Burton and Campbell, Tom (eds) (2001), *Human Rights in Philosophy and Practice*, Aldershot: Ashgate.

Leuprecht, Peter (1988), 'Reflections on Human Rights', *Human Rights Law Journal*, **9**, p. 163.

Martin, Rex and Nickel, James (1980), 'Recent Work on the Concept of Rights', *American Philosophical Quarterly*, **17**, p. 165.

MacCormick, Neil (1982), *Legal Right and Social Democracy*, Oxford: Clarendon Press.

McCorquodale, Robert (1994), 'Self-Determination: A Human Rights Approach', *International and Comparative Law Quarterly*, **43**, p. 857.

McCorquodale, Robert (2000), *Self-Determination in International Law*, Aldershot: Ashgate.

McCorquodale, Robert with Fairbrother, Richard (1999), 'Globalization and Human Rights', *Human Rights Quarterly*, **21**, p. 735.

McCorquodale, Robert and La Forgia, Rebecca (2001), 'Taking off the Blindfolds: Torture by Non-State Actors', *Human Rights Law Review*, **1**, pp. 189–218.

Muchlinski, Peter (2001), 'Human Rights and Multinationals: Is There a Problem?', *International Affairs*, **77**, p. 31.

Mutua, Makau Wa (1998), 'Looking Past the Human Rights Committee: An Argument for De-Marginalizing Enforcement', *Buffalo Human Rights Law Review*, **4**, p. 211.

Nino, Carlos (1991), *Rights*, Aldershot: Dartmouth.

Orford, Anne (1998) 'Contesting Globalization: A Feminist Perspective on the Future of Human Rights', *Transnational Law and Contemporary Problems*, **8**, p. 171.

Pevato, Paula (1999), 'A Right to Environment in International Law: Current Status and Future Outlook', *Review of European Community and International Environmental Law*, **8**, p. 309.

Rich, Roland (1988), 'The Right to Development as an Emerging Human Right', *Virginia Journal of International Law*, **23**, p. 287.

Roberts, Paul (2002), 'Restoration and Retribution in International Criminal Justice: An Exploratory Analysis', in A. von Hirsch, J. Roberts, A. Bottoms, K. Roach and M. Schiff (eds), *Restorative Justice and Criminal Justice*, Oxford: Hart.

Robinson, Mary (1997), 'Realising Human Rights: Take Hold of It Boldly and Duly', Romanes Lecture, <www.unhchr.ch>.

Rorty, Richard (1993), 'Human Rights, Rationality, and Sentimentality', in S. Shute and S. Hurley (eds), *On Human Rights*, New York: Basic Books, p. 111.

Schachter, Oscar (1983), 'Human Dignity as a Normative Concept', *American Journal of International Law*, **77**, p. 848.

Sen, Amartya (1999), *Development as Freedom*, New York: A.A. Knopf.

Shestack, Jerome (1984), 'The Jurisprudence of Human Rights', in T. Meron (ed.), *Human Rights in International Law: Legal and Policy Issues*, Oxford: Clarendon Press.

Shue, Henry (1996), *Basic Rights*, 2nd edn, Princeton, NJ: Princeton University Press.

Sjolander, Claire Turenne (1996), 'The Rhetoric of Globalization: What's in a Wor(l)d?', *International Journal*, **LI** (4), p. 603.

Stammers, Neil (1995), 'A Critique of Social Approaches to Human Rights', *Human Rights Quarterly*, **17**, p. 488.

Steiner, Henry (1991), 'Ideals and Counter-Ideals in the Struggle over Autonomy Regimes for Minorities', *Notre Dame Law Review*, **64**, p. 1539.

Vienna Declaration and Programme of Action on Human Rights (1993), *International Legal Materials*, **32**, p. 1661.

Weissner, Seigfried (1999), 'The Rights of Indigenous Peoples: A Global and Comparative International Legal Analysis', *Harvard Human Rights Journal*, **12**, p. 57.
West, Robin (2002), *Rights*, Aldershot: Dartmouth.
White, Nigel (2000), 'The Legality of Bombing in the Name of Humanity', *Journal of Conflict and Security Law*, **5**, p. 29.
Williams, Patricia (1991), *The Alchemy of Race and Rights*, Cambridge, MA: Harvard University Press.
Yasuaki, Onuma (1997), 'Towards an Intercivilizational Approach to Human Rights', *Asian Year Book of International Law*, **7**, p. 21.

Part I
Challenging Human Rights Concepts

[1]

The Philosophic Foundations of Human Rights

*Jerome J. Shestack**

I. INTRODUCTION

Today, through the United Nations and its half century of enactments, an impressive body of human rights doctrine is embodied in international law. This is in sharp contrast to the situation fifty years ago when there was no body of international human rights law.

Having come this far legally, why then should one still be concerned with the philosophic foundations of such international human rights law? To philosophize, Plato taught, is to come to know oneself. Others say that the special function of philosophy is to deepen our understanding of truth. Still others see the philosopher as a judge, assessing the varieties of human experience and pronouncing on the claim to knowledge.[1] Yet, still more reasons exist for exploring the philosophic underpinnings of human rights law.

First, one's own attitudes toward the subject of international human rights law are likely to remain obscure unless one understands the philosophies that shape them.[2] Piaget's statement that "morality is the logic of action" contains a striking insight.

---

* *Jerome J. Shestack* is President of the American Bar Association. He is a past United States Ambassador to the United Nations Commission on Human Rights.

1. The term "justification of moral principles" is used here in the sense of "warranted assertions" containing qualities that go beyond local and transient rightness. I believe that most of what passes for discussion of "truth" in philosophy is such justification. *See* Hilary Putnam, *Are Legal Values Made or Discovered,* 1 Legal Theory 5 (1995) (analyzing truth and warranted assertions).
2. A familiar anecdote is that of Gertrude Stein, who, on her deathbed, asked of her friends: "What is the answer? What is the answer?" A philosopher friend leaned over and spoke gently in her ear. Gertrude Stein closed her eyes and whispered: "Then, what is the question? What is the question?" Identifying the pertinent questions is a large measure of the philosophic enterprise.

Second, if one understands the law addressed, one is more amenable to the authority of the international law of human rights. That trait is particularly valuable for an arena that still lacks formal enforcement mechanisms. Stated another way, one furthers fidelity to human rights law by understanding the moral justifications that underlie that law.

Third, understanding the philosophic foundations of the law helps one devise a translation formula that will permit men and women to speak to each other across the gulfs of creed and dogma, a necessary exercise for universal recognition of international law principles.

What then is the segment of philosophy examined when delving into human rights? The answer is that human rights are a set of moral principles and their justification lies in the province of moral philosophy. This article explores that field.[3]

This article will first address the historical sources of human rights justifications, next survey key modern human rights theories, and then analyze some of the current conflicts in human rights theory. At best, it can only touch on the teachings in a field that is complex, vast, and too often obscure.[4]

II. THE NATURE OF HUMAN RIGHTS

One of the initial questions in any philosophic inquiry is what is meant by human rights. The question is not trivial. Human beings, as Sartre said, are "stalkers of meaning." Meaning tells one "why." Particularly in the international sphere, where diverse cultures are involved, where positivist underpinnings are shaky, and where implementation mechanisms are fragile, definition can be crucial. Indeed, some philosophic schools assert that the entire task of philosophy centers on meaning. How one understands the meaning of human rights will influence one's judgment on such issues as which rights are regarded as universal, which should be given priority, which can be overruled by other interests, which call for international

3. It bears emphasis that while the modern human rights theories discussed below have been articulated largely by Western philosophers, the moral concepts are not exclusively Western and find counterparts in non-Western thought as well. Of course, the truth of a philosophical principle should not depend on its geography but instead on the soundness of its foundation. Self-determination, for example, is a Western-originated concept.

4. The last fifteen years alone have produced numerous volumes and articles on moral philosophy, though surprisingly few have dealt directly with human rights. The dense, specialized lexicon that most theorists use unfortunately means that they fail to reach the wide audience that they should seek.

pressures, which can demand programs for implementation, and for which one will fight.

What is meant by *human* rights? To speak of *human* rights requires a conception of what rights one possesses by virtue of being human. That does not mean human rights in the self-evident sense that those who have them are human, but rather, the rights that human beings have simply because they are human beings and independent of their varying social circumstances and degrees of merit.

Some scholars identify human rights as those that are "important," "moral," and "universal." It is comforting to adorn human rights with those characteristics; but, such attributes themselves contain ambiguities. For example, when one says a right is "important" enough to be a *human* right, one may be speaking of one or more of the following qualities: (1) intrinsic value; (2) instrumental value; (3) value to a scheme of rights; (4) importance in not being outweighed by other considerations; or (5) importance as structural support for the system of the good life. "Universal" and "moral" are perhaps even more complicated words. What makes certain rights universal, moral, and important, and who decides?[5]

Intuitive moral philosophers claim that definitions of human rights are futile because they involve moral judgments that must be self-evident and that are not further explicable. Other moral philosophers focus on the consequences of human rights and their purpose. The prescriptivist school says that one should not be concerned with what is *sought* to be achieved by issuing a moral (human rights) utterance but with that which is actually accomplished.

The definitional process is not easier when examining the term *human rights*. Certainly "rights" is a chameleon-like term that can describe a variety of legal relationships.[6] Sometimes "right" is used in its strict sense of the right holder being *entitled* to something with a correlative duty in another. Sometimes "right" is used to indicate an *immunity* from having a legal status altered. Sometimes it indicates a *privilege* to do something. Sometimes it refers to a *power* to create a legal relationship. Although all of these terms have been identified as rights, each invokes different protections.

For example, when speaking of an *inalienable* right, does one mean a right to which no expectations or limitations are valid? Or does one mean a *prima facie* right with a special burden on the proponent of any limitation? Or is it a principle that one must follow unless some other moral principle weighty enough to allow abridgment arises?

---

5. For a discussion of the difficulties in determining the universality of a proposition, see Richard Mervyn Hare, Freedom and Reason 10–13, 30 (1963).

6. *See* Wesley Newcomb Hohfeld, Fundamental Legal Conceptions as Applied in Judicial Reasoning (Yale Univ. Press, 1923).

If one classifies a right as a *claim* against a government to refrain from certain acts, such as not to torture its citizens or deny them freedom of speech, religion, or emigration, then other complexities arise. If a particular claim stems from a metaphysical concept such as the nature of humanity, or from a religious concept such as the divine will, or from some other *a priori* concept, then the claim may really be an immunity to which normative judgments should not apply. If, however, the claim is based on certain interests such as the common good, other problems arise such as the need to determine what constitutes the common good, or the need to balance other societal interests, that may allow a wide variety of interpretations not supportive of individual human rights demands.

If speaking of the "rights" in the International Covenant on Economic, Social and Cultural Rights,[7] such as the right to social security, health, education, fair wages, a decent standard of living, and even holidays with pay, what does one intend? Are these rights that individuals can realistically assert, or are they only aspirational goals? Assuming they are rights as intended, on whom are the correlative duties imposed?

If one speaks of *privileges*, other concerns arise. If the privileges are granted by the state, then presumably the state is entitled to condition them. Does the right of a state to derogate from rights in an international covenant mean that the rights are, in fact, only privileges? Here too, the answer is connected to the moral strength and inviolability of the "right" or "privilege" that is involved.

The definitional answers to these questions are obviously complex.

To summarize, even where international law has established a conventional system of human rights, a philosophic understanding of the nature of rights is not just an academic exercise. Understanding the nature of the "right" involved can help clarify one's consideration of the degree of protection available, the nature of derogations or exceptions, the priorities to be afforded to various rights, the question of the hierarchical relationships in a series of rights, the question of whether rights "trump" competing claims based on cultural rooting, and similar problems. To be sure, the answers to these questions may evolve over time through legal rulings, interpretations, decisions, and pragmatic compromises. But how those answers emerge will be influenced, if not driven by, the moral justifications of the human rights in issue.

A starting point in understanding the moral foundations of human rights law is to examine the *sources* of human rights claims. From where does one

7. International Covenant on Economic, Social and Cultural Rights, *adopted* 16 Dec. 1966, 993 U.N.T.S. 3, G.A. Res. 2200 (XXI), U.N. GAOR, 21st Sess., Supp. No. 16, U.N. Doc. A/6316 (1966) (*entered into force* 3 Jan. 1976).

derive the moral justifications that can be urged for or against human rights law? What is their scope or content, and how compelling are they?

III. SOURCES OF HUMAN RIGHTS

A. Religion

To be sure, the term "human rights" as such is not found in traditional religions. Nonetheless, theology presents the basis for a human rights theory stemming from a law higher than that of the state and whose source is the Supreme Being.

If one accepts the premise of the Old Testament that Adam was created in the "image of God," this implies that the divine stamp gives human beings a high value of worth.[8] In a similar vein the Quran says, "surely we have accorded dignity to the sons of man." So too, in the Bhagavad-Gita, "Who sees his Lord/Within every creature/Deathlessly dwelling/Amidst the mortal: That man sees truly . . . ."

In a religious context every human being is considered sacred. Accepting a universal common father gives rise to a common humanity, and from this flows a universality of certain rights. Because rights stem from a divine source, they are inalienable by mortal authority. This concept is found not only in the Judeo-Christian tradition, but also in Islam and other religions with a deistic base.[9]

Even if one accepts the revealed truth of the fatherhood of God and the brotherhood of all humans, the problem of which human rights flow therefrom remains. Equality of all human beings in the eyes of God would seem a necessary development from the common creation by God, but freedom to live as one prefers is not. Indeed, religions generally impose severe limitations on individual freedom. For most religions, the emphasis falls on duties rather than rights. Moreover, revelation is capable of differing interpretations, and some religions have been quite restrictive toward slaves, women, and nonbelievers, even though all are God's creations. Thus, at least as practiced, serious incompatibilities exist between various

---

8. An appealing expression of this comes from the Talmud:

> A man may coin several coins with the same matrix and all will be similar, but the King of Kings, the Almighty, has coined every man with the same matrix of Adam and no one is similar to the other. Therefore, every man ought to say the whole world has been created for me.

Sanhedrin 38:1 (Adin Steinsaltz ed., Random House 1989).

9. *See generally* SIMON GREENBERG, FOUNDATIONS OF A FAITH (1967); LEONARD SWIDLER, RELIGIOUS LIBERTY AND HUMAN RIGHTS: IN NATIONS AND IN RELIGIONS (1986); ANN ELIZABETH MAYER, ISLAM AND HUMAN RIGHTS (1991).

religious practices and the scope of human rights structured by the United Nations.

However, religious philosophers of all faiths are engaged in the process of interpreting religious doctrines toward the end of effecting a reconciliation with basic human rights prescriptions. This process is largely via hermeneutic exercise, namely reinterpretation of a religion's sacred texts through both historical explication and a type of prophetic application to modern conditions.

Thus, religious doctrine offers a promising possibility of constructing a broad intercultural rationale that supports the various fundamental principles of equality and justice that underlie international human rights. Indeed, once the leap to belief has been made, religion may be the most attractive of the theoretical approaches. When human beings are not visualized in God's image then their basic rights may well lose their metaphysical *raison d'être*. On the other hand, the concept of human beings created in the image of God certainly endows men and women with a worth and dignity from which the components of a comprehensive human rights system can flow logically.

B. Natural Law: The Autonomous Individual

Philosophers and jurists did not leave human rights solely to theologians. In their search for a law that was higher than positive law, they developed the theory of natural law. Although natural law theory has underpinnings in Sophocles and Aristotle, it was first elaborated by the stoics of the Greek Hellenistic period, and later by those of the Roman period. Natural law, they believed, embodied those elementary principles of justice which were right reason, *i.e.*, in accordance with nature, unalterable, and eternal. A classic example is that of Antigone who defied Creon's command not to bury her slain brother by claiming that she was obeying immutable laws higher then the ruler's command.

Medieval Christian philosophers, such as Thomas Aquinas, put great stress on natural law as conferring certain immutable rights upon individuals as part of the law of God.[10] However, critical limitations in the medieval concepts that recognized slavery and serfdom excluded central ideas of freedom and equality.

As feudalism declined, modern secular theories of natural law arose, particularly as enunciated by Grotius and Pufendorf. Their philosophy detached natural law from religion, laying the groundwork for the secular,

10. St. Thomas Aquinas, Summa Theologica Lib. II, pt. II (1475).

rationalistic version of modern natural law. According to Grotius, a natural characteristic of human beings is the social impulse to live peacefully and in harmony with others. Whatever conformed to the nature of men and women as rational, social beings was right and just; whatever opposed it by disturbing the social harmony was wrong and unjust. Grotius defined natural law as a "dictate of right reason."[11] He claimed that an act, according to whether it is or is not in conformity with rational nature, has in it a quality of moral necessity or moral baseness.

Grotius was also a father of modern international law. He saw the law of nations as embodying both laws that have as their source the will of man and laws derived from the principles of the law of nature. This theory, of course, has immense importance for the legitimacy of international law.

Natural law theory led to natural rights theory—the theory most closely associated with modern human rights. The chief exponent of this theory was John Locke, who developed his philosophy within the framework of seventeenth century humanism and political activity, known as the Age of Enlightenment.[12] Locke imagined the existence of human beings in a state of nature. In that state men and women were in a state of freedom, able to determine their actions, and also in a state of equality in the sense that no one was subjected to the will or authority of another. However, to end the hazards and inconveniences of the state of nature, men and women entered into a "social contract" by which they mutually agreed to form a community and set up a body politic. Still, in setting up that political authority, individuals retained the natural rights of life, liberty, and property. Government was obliged to protect the natural rights of its subjects, and if government neglected this obligation, it forfeited its validity and office.[13]

Natural rights theory was the philosophic impetus for the wave of revolt against absolutism during the late eighteenth century. It is visible in the French Declaration of the Rights of Man,[14] in the US Declaration of Independence,[15] in the constitutions of numerous states created upon liberation from colonialism, and in the principal UN human rights documents.

---

11. Hugo Grotius, De Jure Belli et Pacis (Book 1, 1689). *See also* Heinrich Albert Rommen, The Natural Law: A Study in Legal and Social History and Philosophy (1948).
12. John Locke, The Second Treatise of Government (1952).
13. Nearly a century later, Rousseau refined the concept of a social contract. He saw the first virtue of the social contract as its capacity to organize in collective defense of liberty and order. Second, the social contract establishes a community with potential for doing justice, thereby giving the citizens the morality that had been wanting in the state of nature. Jean-Jacques Rousseau, On the Social Contract (Judith R. Masters trans., St. Martin's Press 1978) (1762).
14. Declaration of the Rights of Man and of Citizens (France 1789).
15. The Declaration of Independence (US 1776).

Natural rights theory makes an important contribution to human rights. It affords an appeal from the realities of naked power to a higher authority that is asserted for the protection of human rights. It identifies with and provides security for human freedom and equality, from which other human rights easily flow. It also provides properties of security and support for a human rights system, both domestically and internationally.

From a philosophical viewpoint, the critical problem that natural rights doctrine faced is how to determine the norms that are to be considered as part of the law of nature and therefore inalienable, or at least *prima facie* inalienable.

Under Locke's view of human beings in the state of nature, all that was needed was the opportunity to be self-dependent; life, liberty, and property were the inherent rights that met this demand. But what about a world unlike the times of Locke, in which ample resources are not available to satisfy human needs? Does natural law theory have the flexibility to satisfy new claims based on contemporary conditions and modern human understanding? Perhaps it does, but that very potential for flexibility has formed the basis for the chief criticism of natural rights theory. Critics pointed out that most of the norm setting of natural rights theories contain *a priori* elements deduced by the norm setter. In short, the principal problem with natural law is that the rights considered to be natural can differ from theorist to theorist, depending upon their conceptions of nature.

Because of this and other difficulties, natural rights theory became unpopular with legal scholars and philosophers.[16] However, in revised form, natural rights philosophy had a renaissance in the aftermath of World War II, as discussed below.

C. Positivism: The Authority of the State

The assault upon natural law intensified during the nineteenth and twentieth centuries. John Stuart Mill claimed that rights are founded on utility. Karl von Savigny in Germany, and Sir Henry Maine in England, claimed that rights are a function of cultural variables. However, the most serious attack on natural law came from a doctrine called legal positivism. This philosophy came to dominate legal theory during most of the nineteenth century and commands considerable allegiance in the twentieth.

16. *See, e.g.*, Jeremy Bentham, The Book of Fallacies (1824) (discussing natural rights as so much "bawling on paper"). Oft-quoted is his colorful attack: "Right is a child of law; from real laws come real rights, but from imaginary law, from laws of nature, come imaginary rights. . . . Natural rights is simple nonsense: natural and imprescriptible rights, rhetorical nonsense,—nonsense upon stilts." *Id.*

Classical positivist philosophers deny an *a priori* source of rights and assume that all authority stems from what the state and officials have prescribed. This approach rejects any attempt to discern and articulate an idea of law transcending the empirical realities of existing legal systems. Under positivist theory, the source of human rights is found only in the enactments of a system of law with sanctions attached to it. Views on what the law "ought" to be have no place in law and are cognitively worthless. The theme that haunts positivist exponents is the need to distinguish with maximum clarity law as it is from law as it ought to be, and they condemned natural law thinkers because they had blurred this vital distinction. In its essence, positivism negates the moral philosophic basis of human rights.[17] By divorcing a legal system from the ethical and moral foundations of society, positive law encourages the belief that the law must be obeyed, no matter how immoral it may be, or however it disregards the world of the individual. The anti-Semitic edicts of the Nazis, although abhorrent to moral law, were obeyed as positive law. The same is true of the immoral apartheid practices that prevailed in South Africa for many years. The fact that positivist philosophy has been used to justify obedience to iniquitous laws has been a central focus for much of the modern criticism of that doctrine. Critics of positivism maintain that unjust laws not only lack a capacity to demand fidelity, but also do not deserve the name of law because they lack internal morality.

Even granting the validity of the criticism, the positivist contribution can still be significant. If the state's processes can be brought to bear in the protection of human rights, it becomes easier to focus upon the specific implementation that is necessary for the protection of particular rights. Indeed, positivist thinkers such as Jeremy Bentham and John Austin were often in the vanguard of those who sought to bring about reform in the law. Always under human control, a positivist system also offers flexibility to meet changing needs.

The *methodology* of the positivist jurists in the technical building of legal conceptions is also pragmatically useful in developing a system of rights in international law. For example, the UN human rights treaties, being rules developed by the sovereign states themselves and then made part of a system of international law, reflect a positive set of rights. While many states may differ on the theoretical basis of these rules, the rules provide a legal grounding for human rights protection. On the other hand, in theory, positivism tends to undermine an international basis for human rights

17. *See, e.g.*, Herbert Lionel Hart, *Positivism and the Separation of Law and Morals*, 71 Harv. L. Rev. 593 (1955); John Austin, The Province of Jurisprudence Determined (Wilfrid E. Rumble ed., 1985).

because of the emphasis positivists place on the supremacy of *national* sovereignty without accepting the restraining influence of an inherent right above the state. Under this view, rules of international law are not law but merely rules of positive morality set or imposed by opinion. Furthermore, by emphasizing the role of the nation state as the source of law, the positivist approach produces the view that the individual has no status in international law.

D. Marxism: Man as a Specie Being

Marxist theory, like natural law, is also concerned with the nature of human beings. However, in Marxism, the view of men and women is not one of autonomous individuals with rights developed from either a divine or inherent nature, but of men and women as "specie beings."[18]

While Marxism fell along with the fall of Communism in Eastern Europe, it was a dominant philosophy in much of the world for many years; in variant forms, Marxism has residual influence, particularly in assigning values to social and economic rights.

Marx regarded the law of nature approach to human rights as idealistic and ahistorical. He saw nothing natural or inalienable about human rights. In a society in which capitalists monopolize the means of production, Marx regarded the notion of individual rights as a bourgeois illusion. Concepts such as law, justice, morality, democracy, freedom, etc., were considered historical categories, whose content was determined by the material conditions and the social circumstances of a people. As the conditions of life change, so the content of notions and ideas may change.

Marxism sees a person's essence as the potential to use one's abilities to the fullest and to satisfy one's needs.[19] In capitalist society, production is controlled by a few. Consequently, such a society cannot satisfy those individual needs. An actualization of potential is contingent on the return of men and women to themselves as social beings, which occurs in a communist society devoid of class conflict. However, until that stage is reached, the state is a social collectivity and is the vehicle for the transformation of society. Such a conceptualization of the nature of society precludes the existence of individual rights rooted in the state of nature that are prior to the state. The only rights are those granted by the state, and their exercise is contingent on the fulfillment of obligations to society and to the state.

18. *See* Sir Isaiah Berlin, Two Concepts of Liberty (1958).
19. Karl Marx, The Economic and Philosophic Manuscripts of 1844 (Martin Milligan trans., Dirk J. Struik ed., 1969).

The Marxist system of rights has often been referred to as "parental," with the authoritarian political body providing the sole guidance in value choice. The creation of such a "specie being" is a type of paternalism that not only ignores transcendental reason, but negates individuality.[20] In practice, pursuit of the prior claims of society as reflected in the interests of the Communist state has resulted in systematic suppression of individual civil and political rights.

On an international level, Marxist theory proved incompatible with a functioning universal system of human rights. The prior claims of a Communist society do not recognize overruling by international norms. While Communist governments admitted a theoretical recognition of the competence of the international community to establish transnational norms, the application of those norms was held to be a matter of exclusive domestic jurisdiction. Communist states repeatedly asserted in international fora that their alleged abuse of human rights was a matter of exclusive *domestic* jurisdiction, not just as a matter of protecting sovereignty or avoiding the embarrassment of international examination, but the assertions reflected communist theory of the unlimited role of the state to decide what is good for the specie beings.[21] Be that as it may, Marxism itself now ironically has become a past historical category.

E. The Sociological Approach: Process and Interests

To many scholars, each of the theories of rights discussed thus far is deficient. Moreover, the twentieth century is quite a different place from the nineteenth. Natural and social sciences have developed and begun to increase understanding about people and their cultures, their conflicts, and their interests. Anthropology, psychology, and other disciplines lent their insights. These developments inspired what has been called the sociological school of jurisprudence. "School" is perhaps a misnomer, because what has evolved is a number of disparate theories that have the common denominator of trying to line up the law with the facts of human life in society. Sociological jurisprudence tends to move away from both *a priori* theories and analytical types of jurisprudence. This approach, insofar as it relates to human rights, sometimes directs attention to the questions of institutional development, sometimes focuses on specific problems of public policy that

20. No attempt is made here to deal with some of the substantial reinterpretation and modification of Marxist theory utilized by various Third World Socialist countries. *See* Julius Nyerere, Ujamaa: Essays on Socialism (1968).

21. *See, e.g.*, Valerii Chalidze, To Defend These Rights: Human Rights and the Soviet Union (Guy Daniels trans., 1974).

have a bearing on human rights, and sometimes aims at classifying behavioral dimensions of law and society. In a human rights context, the approach is useful because it identifies the empirical components of a human rights system in the context of the social process.[22]

A primary contribution of the sociological school is its emphasis on obtaining a just equilibrium of interests among prevailing moral sentiments and the social and economic conditions of time and place. In many ways this approach can be said to build on William James' pragmatic principle that "the essence of good is simply to satisfy demand."[23] This approach also was related to the development in twentieth century society of increased demands for a variety of wants beyond classical civil and political liberties—such matters as help for the unemployed, the handicapped, the underprivileged, minorities, and other elements of society.

It is not possible here to outline the particular approaches of the leading sociological thinkers, but Roscoe Pound's analysis merits special reference. Pound pointed out that during the nineteenth century, the history of the law was written largely as a record of an increasing recognition of individual rights.[24] In the twentieth century, however, this history should be written in terms of a continually wider recognition of human wants, human demands, and social interests. Pound catalogued the interests as individual, public, and social. He did not try to give value preferences to these interests. His guiding principle was one of "social engineering," that is, the ordering of human relations through politically organized society so as to secure all interests insofar as possible with the least sacrifice of the totality of interests.

The approach of Pound and his progeny usefully enlarges one's understanding of the scope of human rights and their correlation with demands. His identification of the interests involved takes into account the realities of the social process; he shows one how to focus on rights in terms of what concerns people and what they want. He makes one "result-minded, cause-minded and process-minded."[25]

However, an approach that merely catalogues human demands is deficient in failing to focus on how rights are interrelated or what the priorities should be. The sociological school does not answer the logical question of how a normative conclusion about rights can be derived empirically from factual premises such as having interests. A descriptive science in the social human rights field is helpful, "but is not enough" to satisfy the need of goal identification.[26] The sociological approach thus provides a useful method, but a method in need of a philosophy. Nonethe-

---

22. *See* Karl Llewellyn, Jurisprudence: Realism in Theory and Practice (1962).
23. William James, Pragmatism (1975).
24. 1 Roscoe Pound, Jurisprudence § 8 (1959).
25. 3 Roscoe Pound, Jurisprudence (1959).
26. *See* Karl Llewellyn, *Book Review,* 28 U. Chi. L. Rev. 174 (1960).

less, by providing a quantitative survey of the interests that demand satisfaction, this school sharpens perceptions of the values involved and the policies necessary to achieve them.

F. Rights Based on the Value of Utility

Another theory that has played a commanding role in political and moral philosophy is utilitarianism.

Utilitarianism is a *maximizing* and *collectivizing* principle that requires governments to maximize the total net sum of the happiness of all their subjects. This principle is in contrast to natural rights theory, which is a *distributive* and *individualizing* principle that assigns priority to specific basic interests of each individual subject.

Classic utilitarianism, the most explored branch of this school, is a moral theory that judges the rightness of actions affecting outcomes in terms of securing the greatest happiness to all concerned. Utilitarian theory played a commanding role in the philosophy and political theory of the nineteenth century and continues with some vigor in the twentieth.

Jeremy Bentham, who expounded classical utilitarianism, believed that every human decision was motivated by some calculation of pleasure and pain. He thought that every political decision should be made on the same calculation, that is, to maximize the net produce of pleasure over pain. Hence, both governments and the limits of governments were to be judged not by reference to abstract individual rights, but in terms of what tends to promote the greatest happiness of the greatest number. Because all count equally at the primary level, anyone may have to accept sacrifices if the benefits they yield to others are large enough to outweigh such sacrifices.

Bentham's happiness principle enjoyed enormous popularity and influence during the first half of the nineteenth century when most reformers spoke the language of utilitarianism. Nonetheless, Bentham's principle met with no shortage of criticism. His "felicific calculus," that is, adding and subtracting the pleasure and pain units of different persons to determine what would produce the greatest net balance of happiness, has come to be viewed as a practical, if not a theoretic, impossibility.

Later utilitarian thinkers have restated the doctrine in terms of "revealed preferences."[27] Here, the utilitarian guide for governmental conduct would

---

27. *See* Joseph Raz, The Morality of Freedom 267–87 (1986). "Consequentialism" is a school of modern moral philosophy that embraces the family of utilitarian theories, some egoistic in principle, some altruistic, some benevolent, etc. Generally, it may be described as holding that actions and other objects of moral assessment are justified only if their consequences have more intrinsic value than alternate actions. The term "consequentialism" was introduced into technical philosophy in 1958 by G.E.M. Anscombe. Consequentialist theorists are often at odds with each other.

not be pleasure or happiness, but an economically focused value of general welfare, reflecting the maximum satisfaction and minimum frustration of wants and preferences. Such restatements of utilitarian theory have an obvious appeal in the sphere of economic decision making. Even then, conceptual and practical problems plague utilitarian value theory: the ambiguities of the welfare concept, the nature of the person who is the subject of welfare, the uncertain basis of individual preference of one whose satisfaction is at issue, and other problems inherent in the process of identifying the consequences of an act and in estimating the value of the consequences.

The approach to the problem of rights through theories of values has an obvious attraction. Utilitarian theories have a teleological structure, that is, they seek to define notions of right solely in terms of tendencies to promote certain specified ends. An ontological commitment may not be necessary here (at least, it is not so evident) because values (equality, happiness, liberty, dignity, respect, etc.) concern behavior and are not known in a metaphysical sense but rather are accepted and acted upon.

The essential criticism of utilitarianism is that it fails to recognize individual autonomy; it fails to take rights seriously.[28] Utilitarianism, however refined, retains the central principle of maximizing the aggregate desires or general welfare as the ultimate criterion of value. While utilitarianism treats persons as equals, it does so only in the sense of including them in the mathematical equation, but not in the sense of attributing worth to each individual. Under the utilitarian equation, one individual's desires or welfare may be sacrificed as long as aggregate satisfaction or welfare is increased. Utilitarianism thus fails to treat persons as equals, in that it literally dissolves moral personality into utilitarian aggregates. Moreover, the mere increase in aggregate happiness or welfare, if abstracted from questions of distribution and worth of the individual, is not a real value or true moral goal.

Hence, despite the egalitarian pretensions of utilitarian doctrine, it has a sinister side in which the well-being of the individual may be sacrificed for what are claimed to be aggregate interests, and justice and right have no secure place. Utilitarian philosophy thus leaves liberty and rights vulnerable to contingencies, and therefore at risk.[29] In an era characterized by inhumanity, the dark side of utilitarianism made the philosophy too suspect

28. An oft-quoted criticism is Rawls' observation that "[u]tilitarianism does not take seriously the distinction between persons." JOHN RAWLS, A THEORY OF JUSTICE 187 (1971).

29. Some utilitarians, notably John Stuart Mill, allow that in moral and legal practice, justice and rights may be considerations superior to interests and to the liberty to pursue the satisfaction of interests. But they insist that justice and rights are derivative of interests and desires and are to be given context by determining what is necessary to maximize the satisfaction of the latter. That, of course, makes justice and rights contingent and does not satisfy the theories that assign rights superior moral standing. In other words, so long

to be accepted as a prevailing philosophy. Indeed, most modern moral theorists seem to have reached an antiutilitarian consensus, at least in recognizing certain basic individual rights as constraints on any maximizing aggregative principle. In Ronald Dworkin's felicitous phrase, rights must be "trumps" over countervailing utilitarian calculations.

IV. MODERN HUMAN RIGHTS THEORIES

A. Rights Based on Natural Rights: Core Rights

The aftermath of World War II brought about a revival of natural rights theory. Certainly, this was due in part to the revulsion against Naziism and the horrors that could emanate from a positivist system in which the individual counted for nothing. It was not surprising that a renewed search for immutable principles to protect humanity against such brutality emerged.

Of course, a large variety of presentations and analyses among scholars exist addressing theories of moral philosophy.[30] While the new rights philosophers do not wear the same metaphysical dress as the early expounders of the Rights of Man, most adopt what may be called a qualified natural law approach in that they try to identify the values that have an eternal and universal aspect. They agree that only a positive legal system that meets those values can function as an effective legal system. In a larger sense, the object of much of revived natural rights thought can be viewed as an attempt to work out the principles that might reconcile the "is" and the "ought" in law.

The common theme emerging from a huge family of theories is that a minimum absolute or core postulate of any just and universal system of rights must include some recognition of the value of individual freedom or autonomy.

Western? Core HR Theory

---

as utility is what Mill said it is, namely, "the ultimate appeal on all ethical questions," individual rights can never be secure. JOHN STUART MILL, ON LIBERTY (Appleton-Century-Crofts & Co. 1947) (1959).

30. Modern rights theorists display a number of common characteristics. First, they are eclectic, borrowing from each other's insights so that it is somewhat imprecise to characterize their theories as simply utilitarian, naturalist, positivist, or any of the other classifications that philosophers use. Second, most rights theorists recognize the need to identify the justifications that can validate the moral principles of human rights. Third, they acknowledge the benefits of constructing an entire system of rights that can satisfy all morally relevant actions and institutions in consistent and conflict-resolving ways. Unfortunately, many theorists also get caught up in the distinctions and fine tunings of contractualism, consequentialism, value neutrality, objectivity, relativism, pluralism, and other branches of epistemological, metaphysical, or ethical philosophy without advancing our understanding of the moral foundations of human rights much beyond the classic theories. In the discussion that follows, there is space to address only the more influential modern theories, and then only in bare bones outline.

Underlying such foundational or core rights theory is the omnipresence of Immanuel Kant's compelling ethic. Kant's ethic maintains that persons typically have different desires and ends, so any principle derived from them can only be contingent. However, the moral law needs a categorical foundation, not a contingent one. The basis for moral law must be *prior* to all purposes and ends. The basis is the individual as a transcendental subject capable of an autonomous will. Rights then flow from the autonomy of the individual in choosing his or her ends, consistent with a similar freedom for all.

In short, Kant's great imperative is that the central focus of morality is personhood, namely the capacity to take responsibility as a free and rational agent for one's system of ends. A natural corollary of this Kantian thesis is that the highest purpose of human life is to will autonomously. A person must always be treated as an end, and the highest purpose of the state is to promote conditions favoring the free and harmonious unfolding of individuality. Kant's theory is transcendental, *a priori*, and categorical (all amount to the same thing), and thus overrides all arbitrary distinctions of race, creed, and custom, and is universal in nature.[31]

In variant forms, modern human rights core theories seem to be settling for concepts of natural necessity. By necessity one means prescribing a minimum definition of what it means to be human in any morally tolerable form of society. Put another way, some modes of treatment of human beings are so fundamental to the existence of anything that one would be willing to call a society that it makes better sense to treat an acceptance of them as constitutive of man or woman as a social being, rather than as an artificial convention. This view does not entail verified propositions as science requires. Rather, it views human life as encompassing certain freedoms and sensibilities without which the designation "human" would not make sense. To use a linguistic metaphor, humanity has a grammatical form of which certain basic human rights are a necessary part. This concept of what one views human beings to be is a profound one, even if it is deemed self-evident.

To be sure, many of the new individualist theories possess a certain vindication aspect. They can be viewed as saying that if one adopts certain human rights as norms (*e.g.*, freedom of thought, equality), one can produce

31. Even most positivist and utilitarian philosophers now seem to concede that unless the idea of Kantian's moral, nonlegal right is admitted, no account of justice as a distinct segment of morality can be given. Put simply, any society which uses the vocabulary of rights presupposes that some justification is required to interfere with a person's freedom. Without that minimal right of freedom, an important segment of our moral scheme (but not all of it) would have to be relinquished, and the various political rights and responsibilities about which we talk could not exist. *See* H.L.A. Hart, The Concept of Law (1994); *see also* Jules L. Coleman, Markets, Morals and the Law (1988) (exemplifying a modern positivist philosopher's view).

a certain kind of society; and if one finds that kind of society desirable, one should adopt the norms and call them absolute principles. This reasoning is of course a type of tautology. Then again, tautologies can be significant if society is willing to accept them.

The renaissance of qualified or modified natural rights or core theories has seminally influenced conventional international human rights norms. The Universal Declaration of Human Rights[32] reflects that influence, as seen in the Declaration's opening statement: "Whereas recognition of the inherent dignity and of the equal and inalienable rights of all members of the human family is the foundation of freedom, justice and peace in the world."[33] In a similar vein, Article 1 provides: "All human beings are born free and equal in dignity. They are endowed with reason and conscience and should act toward one another in a spirit of brotherhood."[34] The debt that "inherent dignity" and "inalienable rights" owe to natural law philosophy is obvious. The key human rights treaties also reflect quite directly the moral universalist foundations discussed above.

The philosophic justification and affirmance of the core principles of human rights as universal principles are highly significant and reassuring for the vitality of human rights in rules for the world of nations. Rights that preserve the integrity of the person flow logically from the fundamental freedom and autonomy of the person. So does the principle of nondiscrimination that must attach to any absolute concept of autonomy. However, affirming such basic or core principles is one thing; working out all the other elements of a complete system of rights such as international law seeks to provide is something else. What rights derive from those deemed core rights? How are they developed with generic consistency? By what theory does one test the legitimacy of an overall system? The next sections discuss some of the leading rights theories that have wrestled with the methodology and justification of an *overall* system of rights.

B. Rights Based on Justice

The monumental thesis of modern philosophy is John Rawls' *A Theory of Justice*.[35] "Justice is the first virtue of social institutions," says Rawls.[36]

---

32. Universal Declaration of Human Rights, *adopted* 10 Dec. 1948, G.A. Res. 217A (III), U.N. GAOR, 3rd Sess., (Resolutions, part 1), at 71, U.N. Doc. A/810 (1948), *reprinted in* 43 Am. J. Int'l L. Supp. 127 (1949).
33. *Id.*
34. *Id.* art. 1.
35. John Rawls, Theory of Justice §§ 1–4, 9, 11–17, 20–30, 33–35, 39–40 (1971) (explaining the essence of Rawls' theory).
36. *Id.* § 1 at 3.

Human rights, of course, are an end of justice; hence, the role of justice is crucial to understanding human rights. No theory of human rights for a domestic or international order in modern society can be advanced today without considering Rawls' thesis.

Principles of justice, according to Rawls, provide a way of assigning rights and duties in the basic institutions of society. These principles define the appropriate distribution of the benefits and burdens of social cooperation. Rawls' thesis is that

> [e]ach person possesses an inviolability founded on justice that even the welfare of society as a whole cannot override. . . . Therefore in a just society the liberties of equal citizenship are taken as settled; the rights secured by justice are not subject to political bargaining or to the calculus of social interests.[37]

But what are the rights of justice? Put another way, what are the principles of morality or the foundation of rules that would be agreed upon by all members of a society? To set the stage for ascertaining the principles of justice, Rawls imagines a group of men and women who have come together to form a social contract. Rawls conceives the contractors in an original position.

The original position is one of equality of the contractor with respect to power and freedom. It is taken for granted that all know the general principles of human psychology, sociology, economics, social organization, and the theory of human institutions. However, the contractors are under a "veil of ignorance" as to the particular circumstances of their own society or of their individual race, sex, social position, wealth, talents, opinions, aspirations, and tastes.[38] Therefore, they are prevented from making a self-interested decision that otherwise would corrupt the fairness of their judgment. In that hypothetical original position, all of the contractors would consider only their own self-interest, which is to acquire a sufficiency of primary human goods, namely fundamental liberties, rights, and opportunities of income and wealth as social bases of self-esteem. Hence, in the original position, contractors would choose a basic structure for society *fairly* because they would be abstracted from knowing the detailed facts about their own condition in the real world.

Rawls then tries to show that if these men and women were rational and acted only in their self-interest under a "veil of ignorance," they would choose principles that would be good for all of the members, not simply to the advantage of some. The answers given by those in the original position may then be taken as a blueprint, or as a pattern for the establishment of laws that are worthy of the universal assent of citizens everywhere. In other

37. *Id.* § 1 at 3–4.
38. *Id.* § 2 at 12.

words, their choices would be the basis for the ordering of a just society in any time or place. Rawls' system thus allows us to derive universal principles of justice (morality) acceptable to all rational human beings.

What particular principles would be chosen? Rawls claims that the contractors, who are in the original position of choosing their own status and prospects, will choose two principles of justice.

Rawls' First Principle is that "each person is to have an equal right to the most extensive total system of equal basic liberties compatible with a similar system of liberty for all."[39] Rawls' principles of justice are arranged in a hierarchy. The first priority is that of liberty. "[L]iberty can be restricted only for the sake of liberty. There are two cases: (a) a less extensive liberty must strengthen the total system of liberty shared by all; (b) a less than equal liberty must be acceptable to those [citizens] with the lesser liberty."[40]

The First Principle focuses on the basic *liberties*. Rawls does not enumerate them precisely, but indicates, roughly speaking, that they include political liberty, freedom of speech and assembly, liberty of conscience and thought, freedom of the person (along with the right to hold personal property), and freedom from arbitrary arrest and seizure. The First Principle requires that these liberties be equal because citizens of a just society are to have the same basic rights. Rawls applies a value criteria in determining basic liberties. He believes that a liberty is more or less significant depending on whether it serves the full, informal, and effective exercise of the moral powers.

Rawls' Second Principle deals with distributive justice. It holds that: "Social and economic inequalities are to be arranged so that they are both: (a) to the greatest benefit of the least advantaged, consistent with the just savings principle, and (b) attached to offices and positions open to all under conditions of fair equality of opportunity."[41] The general conception of justice behind these two principles reached in the original position, is one of "fairness."[42]

Rawls' Second Principle is a strongly egalitarian concept which holds that unless there is a distribution that makes both groups better off, an equal distribution is preferred. Thus, the higher expectations of those better situated are just only if they are part of a scheme that improves the expectations of the least advantaged. In Rawls' theory, the Difference

---

39. *Id.* § 46 at 302.
40. *Id.* (giving examples of restrictions on the scope of majority rule imposed by a bill of rights and restrictions on the freedom to speak imposed by a system of rules of order).
41. *Id.* Rawls' savings principle is a complex restraint on distribution to any one generation by allowing for accumulation of savings to improve the standard of life of later generations of the least advantaged. *Id.* § 44.
42. *Id.* § 11 at 63.

Principle is the most egalitarian principle that would be rational to adopt among the various available alternatives.

Rawls recognizes that a person may be unable to take advantage of rights and opportunities as a result of poverty and ignorance and a general lack of means. These factors, however, are not considered to be constraints on liberty; rather, they are matters that affect the "worth" or "value" of liberty. Liberty is represented by the complete system of the liberties, while the worth of liberty to persons and groups is proportional to their capacity to advance their ends within the framework that the system defines. The basic liberties must be held equally. However, the worth of liberty may vary because of inequality in wealth, income, or authority. Therefore, some have greater means to achieve their aims than others. However, the lesser worth of liberty is compensated for by the Difference Principle discussed above. Rawls, in short, builds a two-part structure of liberty that allows a reconciliation of liberty and equality.[43]

This philosophy, of course, is highly abstract and not easily digested. When one tries to apply Rawls' principles to the nonmetaphorical world, some difficult empirical questions arise.

Consider, for example, the basic civil and political liberties identified by Rawls that involve recognition of individual autonomy. The demands made are of a negative sort; they principally involve noninterference with the equal sharing of basic liberties by individuals. Rawls' overriding principle of justice requires that all citizens share these liberties equally (as indeed, international law provides: here, the respective positions of modern utilitarian, egalitarian, and natural rights philosophy seem to be in general agreement). Moreover, groupings are not empirically difficult. The inclusion of all persons in these liberties does not negate or reduce the share of any and causes the least chance of a clash with other values. In constructing a rights system, it is therefore appropriate to impose a heavy burden on those who would treat persons unequally by denying any of them basic liberties.

However, in the real world, will clashes not occur between liberty and other interests, such as public order and security, or efficient measures to ensure public health and safety? To solve this conflict, Rawls suggests a Principle of Reconciliation under which basic liberties may be restricted only when methods of reasoning acceptable to all make it clear that unrestricted liberties will lead to consequences generally agreed to be harmful for all. This Principle of Reconciliation is that of the common interest. A basic liberty may be limited *only* in cases where there would be an advantage to the total system of basic liberty.

With respect to Rawls' Second Principle, the problems are more

43. *Id.* at 204.

complex. Here, Rawls holds that a condition of distributive justice is fair equality of opportunity. Opportunity, stated as a principle of nondiscrimination, is easy to put into a legal precept, and international human rights covenants and many domestic constitutions do prohibit discrimination by virtue of sex, race, religion, or national origin. However, empirical knowledge tells one that equality of opportunity is not enough because society creates the conditions of the pursuit, thereby affecting the outcome.

For example, a person who grows up under conditions of discrimination and deprivation has less opportunity to get into a college than someone from the mainstream of society with a good elementary and secondary education. Hence, to provide equality of opportunity one must compensate for unequal starting points. However, the opportunities of others also should be protected. The object, therefore, is to give those who have had an unequal start the necessary handicap points and yet not denigrate the opportunities of others. Whether one utilizes subsidies, special courses, quotas, or affirmative action programs depends on how compelling a society views the obligation to provide equality of opportunity. Here, a utilitarian and egalitarian approach may differ substantially. In some democratic states, for example, affirmative action programs for minorities have met a utilitarian backlash. It is not easy to resolve the differences, but understanding the moral conceptions enables one to focus on reconciliation of competing views.

With respect to a more equal apportionment of economic benefits derived under Rawls' Second Principle and the Difference Principle, even more difficult problems arise because the demands on society are heavier. Economic benefits may range from modest ones such as free education, aid to the elderly, aid to the handicapped, social security, etc., to major redistributions of wealth. Obviously such benefits are not achieved merely by a negative restraint on government; they require tinkering with distribution.

But *how much* tinkering with the distribution system is suitable, and to *what* desirable ends? Reasonable moral persons interested both in the well-being of the individual and the common good might recognize that certain economic needs of those at the bottom strata of society present so imperative a claim for relief that they outweigh a larger aggregate of benefits to those higher on the economic scale.[44] One's moral theory affects what one is willing to accept as relevant facts, as well as the degree of sacrifice one is willing to accept to further egalitarian goals. Rawls' Difference Principle addresses this issue. However, if one acknowledges the claims for

---

44. Thus, one would hardly dispute that higher taxation of the upper end of the population is desirable in order to provide for the needs of those at the lower end.

more equitable distribution of economic benefits, one must still decide at what point on the spectrum one draws the line and says that the claims for equality do not outweigh the competing values of liberty or the utilitarian aggregate benefits that will be decreased by meeting the claims. It may be that in any particular social structure the inequalities allowed under the Difference Principle would produce a minimum distribution of goods and benefits too small to satisfy the reasonable demands of the least advantaged, or too large to command acceptance by the advantaged.

Rawls' thesis presents still more difficult moral issues of distributive justice in the international context. For example, many developing nations are economically disadvantaged and their disadvantages can only be redressed by substantial transfer to them of resources, technology, and other benefits from developed countries. The sources of those inequalities compete for dominance in determining the appropriate moral response.

One basis put forward for the disadvantages suffered by developing nations is that developed countries caused the disadvantages through colonialism, imperialism, racism, and other exploitation. If developed states accept that claim, then the moral response should be that the entity that caused the harm should remedy it or, at least, contribute substantially to the remedy. If, however, the accusation is rejected (as unfair, too old, inaccurate, etc.) the moral justification for a response is different. The developed countries may still be willing to help lessen international economic inequality, but that task may be undertaken not out of guilt or the need to make reparations, but out of a utilitarian calculus that includes such values as increasing markets, creating alliances, lessening tension, etc. However, the utilitarian calculation may not warrant any substantial reallocation. Or the response may be elicited through the moral obligation to advance a just world order along the Rawlsian Difference Principle. However, here the Rawlsian concept may impose conditions: for example, in the latter case, donor states may require the donees to accommodate certain civil and political liberties that are part of the donors' concept of justice, as a reciprocal element of (or the price for) a more just international system.[45]

These issues are obviously quite complicated with numerous considerations of *real politik* intersecting, but even this short discussion shows that one cannot divorce the tough issues of fulfilling economic and social rights on both a domestic and international level from the moral issues.

---

45. *See, e.g.*, Felix E. Oppenheim, The Place of Morality in Foreign Policy ch. 3 (1991) (discussing how twenty-four industrial nations decided in Brussels on 4 July 1980 to grant economic aid to less developed nations on the basis of a series of criteria, including adherence to the rule of law and "respect for human rights"). Another condition for transfer of resources from developed to less developed states might be that the receiving states use the resources to increase distributive justice among their own citizens and thereby benefit the poor in those states (extending the lines of Rawls' Difference Principle).

Critics of Rawls' theory maintain that it was designed to support the institutions of modern democracy in a *domestic* state context. But even if that were the case, the criticism does not refute his moral thesis, nor an international extension of it.[46]

Indeed, even if Rawls' theory was intended as a model for domestic states, its application can further an international just order. This is because in the real world, state parties only reach questions of international justice *after* dealing first with the basic structure of the state's institutions, and second with the rights and duties of individual members. If Rawls' moral principles produce justice for individuals in a *domestic* state, that achievement takes a long step toward gaining the domestic state's endorsement and adherence to *international* human rights principles. In this regard, the international world order is no greater than the sum of its state parts. Hence, if the Rawlsian moral schemata contributes to a realization of domestic justice by the various state parts, the prescriptions of international human rights will invariably be served.

Rawls himself has suggested that his model can be applied to a world order if one extends the concept of the original position and thinks of the parties as representatives of different states who together must choose the fundamental principles to adjudicate claims among states. But as Thomas M. Franck has pointed out, once the actors in the original position are *representatives of states*, the dynamic changes, and it is not clear that these actors would opt for moral principles that further human rights unless they themselves are representatives of *just* states.[47] It is a fair point that the implications of Rawls' model on an international level still need to be worked through. In any event, Rawls' moral structure—showing how the values of liberty and equality underlying the nature of the autonomous human can be realized in open institutional forms—should at least be morally compelling for a world in which large segments of humanity suffer oppression, poverty, and deprivation of civil, political, social, and economic rights.

One cannot cover Rawls' highly complex neo-Kantian theory or deal with the considerable critical analysis of it in a few pages,[48] but even brief

46. *See* John Rawls, Kantian Constructivism in Moral Theory: The Dewey Lectures (1980) (conceding this point). But Rawls' later writings do not diminish the force of his theory of justice.

47. Thomas M. Franck, The Power of Legitimacy Among Nations 213–33, 285 n.8 (1990).

48. The literature dealing with Rawls' thesis, pro and con, is vast. *See, e.g.*, Thomas M. Scanlon, Jr., *Rawls' Theory of Justice*, 121 U. Pa. L. Rev. 1020 (1973); Robert Wolff, Understanding Rawls (1977); Reading Rawls (Norman Daniels ed., 1975); Michael J. Sandel, Liberalism and the Limits of Justice (1982); Thomas W. Pogge, Realizing Rawls (1989). The best of these are Chandran Kukathas & Phillip Petit, Rawls: A Theory of Justice and its Critics (1990), and the excellent collection of essays in Communitarianism and Individualism (Shlomo Avineri & Avner de-Shalit eds., 1992).

discussion shows the importance of his theory for the moral justification of a rights-based system of government under a participatory structure. Rawls effects a reconciliation of tensions between egalitarianism and noninterference, as well as between demands for freedom by the advantaged and demands for equality by the less advantaged.[49] His structure of social justice maximizes liberty and the worth of liberty to both groups. One may also consider whether Rawls' thesis is reflected in the consensus on human rights found in the international human rights covenants, and whether, in fact, most of the nations have tacitly agreed to a social contract in this area. Rawls' theory is obviously comforting for the construct of constitutional democracy as well as for the concept of the universality of human rights.

C. Rights Based on Reaction to Injustice

At least brief mention should be made of Professor Edmund Cahn's theory of justice. While Cahn's theory no longer has the influence it once enjoyed, it has a particular appeal to human rights activists. Cahn asserts that although there may be universal *a priori* truths concerning justice from which one may deduce rights or norms, it is better to approach justice from its negative rather than its affirmative side.[50] In other words, it is much easier to identify *injustice* from experience and observation than it is to identify *justice*. Furthermore, says Cahn, where justice is thought of in the customary manner as an ideal mode or condition (*e.g.*, Rawls), the human response will be contemplative, and "contemplation bakes no loaves."[51] But the response to a real or imagined instance of injustice is alive with movement and warmth, producing outrage and anger. Therefore, he concludes, "'[j]ustice' . . . means the active process of remedying or preventing what would arouse the sense of injustice."[52] An examination of the instances that will be considered as effecting an injustice thereby allows a positive formulation of justice.

This concept of the need to right wrong has the capacity to produce action. The practical starting point may well be the strongly felt response to words that move one with emotional force and practical urgency to press for the satisfaction or repair of some need, deprivation, threat, or insecurity.

49. One might contrast Rawls' fertile moral landscape with theories in ROBERT NOZICK, ANARCHY, STATE AND UTOPIA 321–22 (1974). Nozick's system, which he calls "libertarian capitalism," is a radical extension of classical laissez-faire theory. *See* Jerome Shestack, *The Jurisprudence of Human Rights, in* INTERNATIONAL HUMAN RIGHTS (Theodor Meron ed., 1983).

50. EDMOND CAHN, THE SENSE OF INJUSTICE (1949).

51. *Id.* at 13.

52. *Id.* at 13–14 (emphasis omitted).

Such an approach obviously will find a response in human rights advocates anxious to focus public attention on the injustice of the wide variety of egregious human rights abuses that remain prevalent.

However, with the more sophisticated kinds of entitlements arising from considerations of social justice, there is less agreement on what constitutes injustice, and Cahn's insight offers less help. Here one needs an overall structure of the type presented by moral philosophers such as Rawls, Ackerman, or Gewirth.[53] Still, Cahn's insight is useful; in the end it may well be that society will secure only those rights for which its members are aroused to fight.

D. Rights Based on Dignity

A number of human rights theorists have tried to construct a comprehensive system of human rights norms based on a value-policy oriented approach focused on the protection of human dignity.[54] Some religious philosophers, holding dignity to be the inherent quality of the sacredness of human beings, believe that an entire rights system can flow from that concept. A secular exposition of that theory is best presented by Professors McDougal, Lasswell, and Chen.

McDougal, Lasswell, and Chen proceed on the premise that demands for human rights are demands for wide sharing in all the values upon which human rights depend and for effective participation in all community value processes. The interdependent values, which can all fall under the rubric of human dignity, are the demands relating to (1) respect, (2) power, (3) enlightenment, (4) well-being, (5) health, (6) skill, (7) affection, and (8) rectitude. McDougal, Lasswell, and Chen assemble a huge catalogue of the demands that satisfy these eight values, as well as all of the ways in which they are denigrated.

McDougal, Lasswell, and Chen find a great disparity between the rising common demands of people for values of human dignity and their achievement. This disparity is due to "environmental factors," such as "population, resources, and institutional arrangements,"[55] and also to

53. Alan Gewirth is another influential neo-Kantian philosopher who merits study. Gewirth holds that in reasoning ethically, an agent abstracts from his or her particular ends and thinks in terms of what generic rights for rational autonomy the agent would demand on the condition of a like extension to all other agents. These rights are those of freedom and well-being, that Gewirth calls generic rights. He frames his moral thesis on the Principle of Generic Consistency: "Act in accord with the generic rights of your recipients as well as yourself." From these generic rights flow an entire structure of civil, political, economic, and social rights. Alan Gewirth, Reason and Morality (1978).

54. *See, e.g.*, Myres S. McDougal et al., Human Rights and World Public Order (1980).

55. *Id.* at 38.

"predispositional factors," such as special interests seeking "short-term payoffs . . . in defiance of the common interests that give expression to human dignity values."[56] The ultimate goal, as they see it, is a world community in which a democratic distribution of values is encouraged and promoted, all available resources are utilized to the maximum, and the protection of human dignity is regarded as a paramount objective of social policy. While they call their approach a policy-oriented perspective, their choice of human dignity as the *super value* in the shaping and sharing of all other values has a natural rights ring to it.

Their approach also has been criticized as having a Western orientation, which it does, but that does not mean it is wrong. A more telling criticism is the difficulty in making use of their system. Their list of demands is huge; no hierarchical order exists; both trivial and serious claims are intertwined; and it has a utopian aspect that belies reality. Still, McDougal, Lasswell, and Chen have shown how a basic value such as dignity—a value on which most people would agree—can be a springboard for structuring a rights system. Even if one disagrees with their formulation, they have opened the door for a simpler and more useful construction to be built on their insights.

E. Rights Based on Equality of Respect and Concern

A striking aspect of modern theorists is their pronounced effort to reconcile different theories of rights. In this regard, in the discussion of modern theories, one must consider the work of Ronald Dworkin, who offers a promising reconciliation theory between natural rights and utilitarian theories.[57] Dworkin proceeds from the postulate of political morality, *i.e.*, that governments must treat all their citizens with equal concern and respect. No basis for any valid discourse on rights and claims exists in the absence of such a premise.

Dworkin next endorses the egalitarian character of the utilitarian principle that "everybody can count for one, nobody for more than one."[58] Under this principle he believes that the state may exercise wide interventionist functions in order to advance social welfare.

Dworkin believes that a right to liberty in general is too vague to be

56. *Id.* at 45.
57. Ronald Dworkin, Taking Rights Seriously (1977). *See* Jules L. Coleman, *Truth and Objectivity in Law*, 1 Legal Theory 33, 51 (1995) (finding that Dworkin's perspective changed between 1977, when he wrote Taking Rights Seriously, *supra*, and 1986, when he wrote *Law's Empire*, Ronald Dworkin, Law's Empire (1986), in order to deal with the value of community).
58. A practical political application of this principle is participatory democracy.

meaningful. However, certain specific liberties such as freedom of speech, freedom of worship, rights of association, and of personal and sexual relations, do require special protection against governmental interference. This is not because these preferred liberties have some special substantive or inherent value (as most rights philosophers hold), but because of a kind of procedural impediment that these preferred liberties might face. The impediment is that if those liberties were left to a utilitarian calculation, that is, an unrestricted calculation of the general interest, the balance would be tipped in favor of restrictions.

Why is there such an impediment? Dworkin says that if a vote were truly utilitarian, then all voters would desire the liberties for themselves, and the liberties would be protected under a utilitarian calculation. However, a vote on these liberties would not be truly utilitarian nor would it afford equal concern about and respect for liberties solely by reflecting personal wants or satisfactions of individuals and affording equal concerns to others. This is because external preferences, such as prejudice and discrimination against other individuals deriving from the failure to generally treat other persons as equals, would enter into the picture. These external preferences would corrupt utilitarianism by causing the individual to vote against assigning liberties to others.

Accordingly, the liberties that must be protected against such external preferences must be given a preferred status. By doing so, society can protect the fundamental right of citizens to equal concern and respect because it prohibits "decisions that seem, antecedently, likely to have been reached by virtue of the external components of the preferences democracy reveals."[59]

The argument is attractive because Dworkin (like Rawls, but in a different way) has minimized the tension between liberty and equality. Dworkin does so not by conceding a general right to liberty (which might exacerbate the tension), but by specifying particular basic liberties that society must protect to prevent corruption of a government's duty to treat persons as equals.

Dworkin's theory seems to retain both the benefits of natural rights theory without the need for an ontological commitment, and the benefits of utilitarian theory without the need to sacrifice basic individual rights. Dworkin's resplendent universe thus seems to accommodate the two major planets of philosophic thought. Dworkin's theory is also valuable in focusing on the relational rather than the conflicting aspects of liberty and equality. Even if one is not fully convinced at this stage by Dworkin's analysis, one has the feeling that his reconciling approach should work within the institutions of a participatory democracy.

---

59. DWORKIN, TAKING RIGHTS SERIOUSLY, *supra* note 57, at 180.

F. Theory Based on Cultural Relativism (versus Universalism)

The clash between those who evaluate human rights from the perspective of cultural relativism and those who view human rights from the universalist or individualist perspective impacts the moral foundations of human rights. This clash immerses one in the vortex of contemporary human rights politics.

Cultural relativism, as a concept to justify departure from human rights standards in international law on cultural grounds, has scant claim to moral validity. Still, because cultural relativism has been given the trappings of philosophic credentials even in UN circles, it must be addressed.

Cultural relativism is essentially an anthropological and sociological concept loosely grounded in the theory of moral relativism. The notion is that cultures manifest so wide and diverse a range of preferences, morality, motivations, and evaluations that no human rights principles can be said to be self-evident and recognized in all times and all places. Moral relativism is not very influential in modern philosophy, but cultural relativism has been used frequently as an argument against the universality of human rights.

Cultural relativists,[60] in their most aggressive conceptual stance, argue that no human rights are absolutes, that the principles that one may use for judging behavior are relative to the society in which one is raised, that there is infinite cultural variability, and that all cultures are morally equal or valid.[61] Put into a philosophical calculus, the relativist says that "truth is just for a time or place" identified by the standards of one's cultural peers.[62] Relativism thus shifts the touchstones by which to measure the worth of human rights practice. To suggest that fundamental rights may be overridden or adjusted in light of cultural practices is to challenge the underlying moral justification of a universal system of human rights, reflecting the autonomous individual nature of the human being.

What are the sources of cultural relativism? Is it a philosophy at all? How should one analyze cultural relativism in the context of international human rights?[63]

---

60. This term, as used here, includes a broad spectrum of relativist theories (cultural, ethnic, particularist, moral). The various relativist schools vary considerably.

61. *See* Rhoda E. Howard, Human Rights and the Search for Community (1995); *see also* Rhoda E. Howard, *Cultural Absolutism and the Nostalgia for Community,* 15 Hum. Rts. Q. 315 (1993); Rhoda E. Howard, *Dignity, Community and Human Rights, in* Human Rights in Cross-Cultural Perspectives: A Quest for Consensus (Abdullahi Ahmed An-Na'im ed., 1995) (pointing out that "cultural relativists" convert to "cultural absolutists" when they maintain that there is one universal principle, acting in accordance with the principles of one's own group).

62. In many ways, the conflict builds on Hegel's distinction between *moralität* (abstract or universal rules of morality) and *sittlichkeit* (ethical principles specific to a certain community).

63. It is not within the scope of this article to cover the way in which relativism versus individualism plays out in domestic politics, except for a brief note. In some Western

Moral relativism, the normative basis of cultural relativism, is said to derive from the famous aphorism (of dubious meaning) by the Greek philosopher Protagoras that "[m]an is the measure of all things." Plato's Theaetus states the Protagorean thesis in terms of the community (not the individual) as the measure of all things, and Plato fairly decimates the concept. The Protagorean view had, at most, a feeble foothold in philosophic thought until the late eighteenth century when Johan Gottfried von Herder, dissenting from Enlightenment philosophy, claimed that all nations had a unique way of being; only regional and contingent principles existed. Condemning universal values, he introduced the concept of *Volksgeist,* the spirit of the people. Von Herder's view influenced German romanticism and French counterrevolutionary writers who glorified the aggregate of local customs and prejudices under an umbrella called "culture."

From time to time during the nineteenth and early twentieth centuries, the claims of *Volksgeist* arose mostly in the European political context of ultranationalism versus universalist principles of Enlightenment philosophy. In time, with the rise of Pan-Germanism, culture was reduced to the cult of origins. During the Nazi period, the *Volksgeist* theme revealed and realized its stark and tragic totalitarian potential.[64]

During the nineteenth century colonial period, many anthropologists, imbued with feelings of Western superiority, viewed other cultures as "native," "primitive," or "barbaric," relegating those cultures to an inferior status. During the post–World War II period, Western anthropologists and sociologists confessed error and embraced a concept of cultural relativism as a counterpoint to colonialization. In combating colonialization with its implications of superiority over the colonists, the French anthropologist Claude Lévi-Strauss and others of his school argued for the separate, independent value of all cultures, stating that the West should stop extending its culture to the rest of the world. The goal of bringing about independence from colonialism was certainly worthy, but the anthropologists and sociologists went further and gave cultural relativism a moral or

---

states, in particular, a communitarian movement has developed during the past several decades, largely in opposition to political liberalism. Normatively, communitarians ally themselves with moral relativism. The liberal individualist response accuses the communitarians of a conservative political ideology that denigrates individual autonomy and freedom of choice. *See* Communitarianism and Individualism, *supra* note 48 (exemplifying the debate on relativism versus individualism).

64. *See* Alain Finkielkraut, La Defaite de la Pensee (Judith Friedlander trans., Columbia Univ. Press 1995) (1987). In France, for example, the defenders of Albert Dreyfus, in the spirit of the Enlightenment, maintained that "man is not the slave of his race, language or religion, nor of the course of rivers, or the direction of mountain races." The Anti-Dreyfusards found Dreyfus guilty by virtue of his ethnicity, which they regarded as at odds with the true ethnically pure French character. France, as it turned out, by rehabilitating Dreyfus, then opted for a society constituted by a social contract and universal principles rather than one based on the idea of a collective spirit.

ethical stance. In restoring the dignity stolen from other cultures through Western imperialism, they argued that all cultures were morally equal and that universalist values (such as universal human rights) were dead.[65]

For the new states, the theme of cultural identity was appealing; it helped them break with Western imperialism, and it permitted the colonialized to affirm their cultural differences, and to turn what colonizers had mocked into a subject of pride. It was logical that most new states wanted to make their own cultural traditions part of national life and to bind individuals to the integrity and cohesion of the socially-minded spirit. In some states, however, pursuit of cultural identity had deleterious effects. While such pursuit provided a means of resistance under colonial rule, afterwards it turned out to have a repressive side by creating an obligatory homogeneity and diminishing the place of the individuals in the calculus of identity politics.

With this background, this article examines the tenets of cultural relativism, particularly in the context of international human rights. What are the objectives of cultural relativism compared to those of universalism? What are the respective camps defending? A universal moral philosophy affirms principles that protect universal, individual human rights of liberty, freedom, equality, and justice everywhere, giving them a nontransient, nonlegal foundation. The relativists defend a cultural conditioning that supposedly reflects a set of wants and goods that members of disparate cultural groups share (and that may include various human rights goods), but are not wants and goods arrived at through individual choices or preserved for individuals in the community as a matter of right.[66]

Posing the contrast this way should deflate the cultural relativist position in any objective value comparison with universalist principles. But

---

65. Alain Finkielkraut's satirical but insightful account of how cultural relativism has played out is summarized in a recent review of Finkielkraut by Paul Berman:

> In our eagerness to repudiate anything smacking of old-fashioned imperialism, we seize on the principles of modern anthropologists, who insist on regarding the culture of one society as fully equivalent to the culture of another. We applaud ourselves for discovering that our own culture is merely one among many, and is not to be seen as anything superior. But, having set out in the morning along that admirably egalitarian path, we find by about noon that we are obliged to describe the democratic notions of human rights and freedom as merely anthropological traits peculiar to our own culture, and, not wishing to impose our local customs on anyone else, we are obliged by nightfall to conclude that human rights and democracy are fine for us and other customs are fine for other people. Freedom for us, oppression for others (for such is their culture, and we must respect it).

Paul Berman, *In Defense of Reason*, New Yorker Mag., 4 Sept. 1995, at 94 (reviewing Finkielkraut, *supra* note 64).

66. One should mention a basic classic dilemma that relativists face. Relativism holds that all cultures are valid and none absolute or false. Universalism holds that its principles are absolute. If that universalist thesis is *false* then relativism is refuted. If that thesis is *true*, then relativism is refuted. A theory that justifies its own rejection is not a strong contender for acceptance.

cultural relativism cannot be dismissed so readily, if only because in the real world, repressive rulers utilize the relativist claim as justification for their ruling practices. Many examples illustrate repressive rulers who seek to rationalize repressive practices by claiming that the culture of their society accepts those practices over universalist international human rights prescriptions, and that to criticize their society's human rights practices is to impose Western cultural imperialism over their local culture. Thus, rulers use cultural relativist arguments to justify limitations on speech, subjugation of women, female genital mutilation, amputation of limbs and other cruel punishment, arbitrary use of power, and other violations of international human rights conventions. It is no wonder that the doctrine that human rights are contingent on cultural practice has been called the "gift of cultural relativists to tyrants."

Does the cultural relativist thesis withstand scrutiny? The reason it does not has several levels.

First, John Finnis has cogently shown that those philosophers who have surveyed modern anthropological literature have found the basic assumption underlying the relativist approaches unwarranted:

> All human societies show a concern for the value of human life; . . . in none is the killing of other human beings permitted without some fairly definite justification. . . . [I]n all societies there is some prohibition of incest, some opposition to boundless promiscuity and to rape, some favour for stability and permanence in sexual relations. All human societies display a concern for truth, [and] all societies display a favour for the values of co-operation, of common over individual good, of obligation between individuals, and of justice within groups. All know friendship. All have some conception of *meum* and *tuum*, title or property, and of reciprocity. . . . All display a concern for powers or principles which are to be respected as suprahuman; in one form or another, religion is universal.[67]

Here, in short, is a universality of basic moral requirements manifested in value judgments.

One, therefore, should not have to probe deeply to conclude that there is a universal cultural *receptivity* to such fundamental rights as freedom from torture, slavery, arbitrary execution, due process of law, and freedom to travel. Moreover, any observer of state practice can cite example after example where repression that one authoritarian government excuses as cultural identity, turns out *not* to be a cultural tradition at all when a democratic government replaces the authoritarian one. Further, many examples of peoples of like cultures living virtually side by side, where one

67. John Finnis, Natural Law and Natural Rights 83–84 (1980). *See generally* Alison D. Renteln, International Human Rights: Universalism Versus Relativism (1990).

state condemns human rights abuses and a counterpart state creates abuses, illustrate this point. Thus, most human rights abuses are not legitimately identified with the authentic culture of any society, only with authoritarian rulers of that society.[68]

Indeed, even most confirmed relativist scholars are repulsed at practices that are highly coercive and abusive and accept that at least some human rights values are absolute. This is no more than a recognition, grudging or not, that suffering and abuse are not culturally authentic values and cannot be justified in the name of cultural relativism. In short, it is wrong to say that all cultures are equally valid; some cultures contain evil elements which have no rational, intuitive, or empirical claim to moral equivalence with nonabusive cultures.

Second, cultural relativists often incorrectly perceive the attributes of cultural communities. Cultural relativists tend to look at cultures from a static, romanticized perspective in which traditional societies are defined as unchanging, holistic entities, unaffected by human history or the dynamics of cultural change.[69] However, this view fails to take into account the dynamism of culture that normally offers its members a range of development options, or is willing to accommodate varying individual responses to its norms, while preserving legitimate values of authentic tradition. Anthropologists acknowledge that culture is flexible and holds many possibilities of choice within its framework. To recognize the values held by a given people at a given time in no wise implies that these values are a constant or static factor in the lives of current or succeeding generations of the same group.

Third, the dynamics of change have been accelerated in this technological, communicative age with the result that many closed societies, once exposed to individualist benefits, seek to incorporate those values and interests into their culture. In fact, individualist values have a great deal of appeal to all cultures once the values are perceived. Of course, a necessary element of bringing about such change is free discourse between cultures so that the human rights benefits can be known. It is telling that authoritarian

---

68. Related to whether cultural attributes are real or pretextual is the fact that cultural norms are often subject to different interpretations and to manipulation by individuals or groups. For example, male chauvinism of the early nineteenth century made the concept of women's place being in the home a cultural attribute of that time in Victorian England. *See* Carlos Santiago Nino, The Ethics of Human Rights (1991) (discussing the moral foundations of human rights).

69. *See* Howard, *Cultural Absolutism and the Nostalgia for Community*, *supra* note 61, at 326–28. Rhoda Howard points out the tendency of many cultural relativists to present traditional societies in mystical or aggregative terms that ignore or belittle individual preferences. Yet, as communitarian societies have changed, they approach the individualist model in culture as well as politics and economics. *Id.* at 329–32.

rulers try to prevent such discourse; that, at the least, reveals a lack of faith in their normative position.

Fourth, another approach still exists that, in part, renders moot the conflict between universalist and relativist theory. This approach consists of appreciation of what has transpired in international law. Even as theorists have continued to quarrel with each other, fundamental human rights principles have become *universal* by virtue of their entry into international law as *jus cogens*, customary law, or by convention. In other words, the relativist argument has been overtaken by the fact that human rights have become hegemonic and therefore universal by fiat.

The relativist, of course, may reply that international law is not a decisive foundation for the relativist any more than an iniquitous positive law is for the universalist. However, one can counter this argument in relativist terms. Law creates societal pressure for adherence; adherence creates habit; habit creates custom; custom becomes a cultural attribute. Thus, the legal standards convert to the very cultural standard that the cultural relativist advocates. To be sure, the normal process is for theory to turn into law. But conversely, law creates the cultural attributes of a society.[70] In any event, the broad acceptance by many nations across the globe of the principal human rights treaties can be taken, at least on the legal level if not yet in practice, as a triumph of universalism over relativism.

Finally, it is revealing that the implications of the relativist position for human rights has obviously been troubling to many relativist theorists who, in personal terms, would like to see human rights values firmly ensconced in world affairs. They search for justifications other than the universalist theories to affirm human rights, a search which in itself speaks for the flimsy, if not spurious foundations of cultural relativism.

For example, Joseph Raz grounds rights in interests that are themselves grounded in values.[71] Richard Rorty argues that human rights activists should rely not on reason and theory but on passion and the courage of their convictions.[72] Other theorists produce other rationales. Whether at the end of the day individualists and relativists will recommend the same policies on different moral grounds is still an open question among some theorists. While such reconciliation may not satisfy the universalist thesis, human rights proponents should take comfort from the moral compulsion a good person feels to combat evil and to vindicate human rights. If enough feel that moral compulsion, the universalist goals then will have been fulfilled.

70. For example, in the United States in the South, opponents of civil rights laws argued that these laws were against the Southern "way of life." But the enactment of the civil rights laws brought about a change in the way of life and the cultural pattern of Southern society in a fairly short period of time.

71. Raz, *supra* note 27.

72. Richard Rorty, Philosophy and the Mirror of Nature (1979).

V. CONCLUSION

This brief description of modern theories of rights does not even begin to exhaust the elaborate and daunting literature and complexities of the subject. Moreover, the development of rights theory will certainly benefit from flourishing new philosophic and scientific exploration. Scholars such as Rawls, Ackerman, Coleman, Donagan, Donnelly, Dworkin, Finnis, Gewirth, Heller, Howard, Michelman, Nagel, Nino, Nozick, Raz, Richards, Rorty, Sumner, and others in many nations and from diverse backgrounds are still adding insights to classic moral philosophy and developing or refining their own theories both in domestic and international contexts. It is the natural bent of theory analysis to raise queries and articulate doubts. The field is stirring, and the potential for new insight remains large.

Long ago, Hume asked what authority any moral reasoning can have that leads into opinions that are wide of mankind's general practice. It remains a haunting point as one views the gap between the international law of human rights and contemporary practice. A more promising question may be whether moral reasoning can narrow the gap between moral principle and practice. Hopefully, the discussion here, albeit with all the questions it raises, will affirm faith in the meaningfulness and rationality of a quest for a humane society.

[2]

HUMAN RIGHTS GENEALOGY

*Ruti Teitel**

Introduction

As the century draws to an end, this Article explores the status and future directions of contemporary human rights theory. It begins with the puzzle that, despite its conceded normative force, contemporary human rights theory is said to be fundamentally flawed, lacking a center, organizing structure, or unifying value. The puzzle is varyingly attributed to incoherence in international human rights theory and to irreconcilable dualisms pervading the theory.[1] This Article critiques the prevailing understanding by elaborating on the implications of theorizing in these oppositional terms, proposing a genealogical perspective to human rights theory. Such a perspective explores international human rights theory's historical and political legacies, its founding structures and rhetoric, with an eye toward a better understanding of the contemporary international human rights movement, its place in history, and its future potential. International human rights theory is reconsidered in light of its historical and political engendering circumstances. This Article will use "genealogy"[2] in a number of senses: first, as the exploration of the organizing structures, logic, and language that comprehend the domain of contemporary human rights theory; second, as the historical and political circumstances of the international human rights movement; and third, as the connection between the relationship of international human rights theory and other philosophical, political, and legal rights theorizing.

The Article attempts to illuminate the status of prevailing international human rights theory by contributing a genealogical perspective to the contemporary theorizing. Part I examines the origins of the reigning theoretical framework by considering the historical and political circumstances that attended the development of the theory. Part

* Professor of Law, New York Law School; J.D., 1980, Cornell Law School. My gratitude to Camille Broussard, Brenda Davis-Lebron, and Sabrina Bagdasarian for their research and other assistance.

1. Thus, introductions to texts on human rights law often begin with caveats about the subject area's incoherence. *See* Louis Henkin, International Law: Politics and Values 184-85 (1995); Human Rights Law xiii (Philip Alston ed., 1996); *see also* Martti Koskenniemi, *The Pull of the Mainstream*, 88 Mich. L. Rev. 1946, 1961-62 (1990) (reviewing Theodor Meron, Human Rights and Humanitarian Norms as Customary Law (1989)) (observing that international lawyers have not succeeded in developing any compelling theory on the place of human rights within any grand design of international law and that "the justifying rhetoric" of mainstream international lawyers is in "disarray").

2. On the genealogical perspective, see Michel Foucault, Power/Knowledge: Selected Interviews and Other Writings, 1972-1977 (Colin Gordon ed. & Colin Gordon et al. trans., 1980).

II explains how a genealogical approach clarifies problems in the reigning paradigm. Part III explores further the dichotomies in the prevailing theory, thereby clarifying the puzzling status of contemporary human rights theory. Part IV examines the international human rights movement today, incorporating a genealogical perspective and clarifying the contemporary movement's intimate and uneasy relation to its original historical and political circumstances. This part also proposes a more coherent view of the existing international human rights normative apparatus.

I. Rights Genesis

Consider international human rights theory and its engendering circumstances. The founding is said to go like this: Genesis of the human rights movement, by its own description, begins in postwar Europe. This point of departure for contemporary human rights theory is definitional—the international human rights movement is birthed in the war and the postwar experience. Told this way, international human rights creation, like the war itself, gave rise to a new, paradigmatic view of rights as extraordinary and discontinuous from prior expectations.

As a paradigm supported and engendered by the immediate circumstances of the postwar period, international human rights implies an utterly transformed model regarding individual/state responsibility and relations. International human rights, as both a postwar and post-totalitarian movement, was a radical departure from the prevailing rights theorizing assumptions about the state. A creature of postwar circumstances, the new paradigm was said to mean new rights and a departure from the contractarian tradition associated with pre-existing rights theorizing. International human rights drew their normative force, at the time, not necessarily from social consensus, but rather from the exercise of judicial power. This alternative normative vision is instantiated by the Nuremberg Tribunal, the extraordinary Allied justice brought to bear against human rights abusers.

Later, these norms were ratified in various international charters and conventions as merely the institutionalization of preexisting universal norms. The human rights movement, which blossomed in the war's aftermath, was a phenomenon that largely developed within a newly created international legal system.[3] The postwar construction of international human rights appeared in transnational form: initially, in the Nuremberg Charter, then in the United Nations Charter and other United Nations instruments, and in multilateral treaties and conventions.[4] These alternative conceptions of human rights ulti-

3. For an excellent account, see Henkin, *supra* note 1.

4. On transnationalism, see Harold Hongju Koh, *Why Do Nations Obey International Law?*, 106 Yale L.J. 2599 (1997) (book review); *see also* Lawrence G. Helfer &

mately meant a new system of rights protection—inhering outside of social contract—vindicating a view of human rights within an adjudicatory model and an emerging international legal system. At Nuremberg, after the war, international human rights appeared to have ultimate normative power. Human rights seemingly were protectable, with or without the state, as the massive postwar codification projects made rights with normative force positive.

The postwar paradigm implied a reconceptualization of core rights concepts. First, rights were understood to be protected within a conception of rule of law which was largely conceived as legal accountability, indeed as criminal accountability. While this view of rule of law suffers from being *ex post*, it is best understood in its historical postwar context. After the grave atrocities of the war, the human rights project was largely the ascribing of individual responsibility. Next, and relatedly, the understanding of individual responsibility for rights protection under international law changed, particularly the balance between the individual and the state. These changed understandings implied changes in the content of human rights values. The postwar normative scheme that defined human rights in terms of political persecution was a response to the war and to totalitarianism. As such, postwar justice reflected its engendering circumstances.

The new arrangements forced a rethinking of the meaning of rights. This reconsideration included the extent to which these rights appertained to a corresponding system of duties. The change in the prior expectations, which were the legacy of social contract theory,[5] transformed the human rights paradigm entirely. Whereas in earlier rights theory, individuals were entitled to the contractual rights that the state agreed to protect, these assumptions fell away in the postwar paradigm. Individual rights bore no particular relation to the state's assumption of duties. Indeed, the previous formulation of rights appeared unavailable and the state instead a potential source of evil. Accordingly, rights protection moved to alternative sites and systems, to international human rights conventions, mechanics, and processes.

The human rights movement was nurtured by the concomitant development of a new international legal system, as well as by the parallel explosion of constitutionalism.[6] The notion of rights as judicial in nature is supported by the postwar explosion of constitutionalism and judicial review. As time passed, the postwar paradigm and its ad hoc blend of laws of war and the laws of peace become normalized, despite the absence of political circumstances similar to those that at-

Anne-Marie Slaughter, *Toward a Theory of Effective Supranational Adjudication*, 107 Yale L.J. 273 (1997).

5. *See generally* Ian Shapiro, The Evolution of Rights in Liberal Theory (1986).

6. *See generally* Louis Henkin, The Age of Rights (1990) (discussing the relation of constitutionalism and the international human rights movement).

tended its founding.[7] Born at a time of unparalleled international cooperation, the human rights movement's normative projects would later appear to have fostered unrealistic expectations about the human rights system's potential.

These historical and political developments and contingencies engendered the postwar understanding of human rights. Genesis at Nuremberg and at Auschwitz expresses the paradigm shift's sad paradoxical story of catastrophe and failure in the international order, which somehow nevertheless ends on a hopeful note. Through the international human rights movement and its lead in responding to wartime atrocities, justice becames a liberal means to a redemptive resolution.

II. Rights Generation

The passage of time increased the distance from the engendering historical and political circumstances of the human rights movement. The distance led to questions about the continued viability of international human rights theory. Nevertheless, the international human rights movement is said to be in vital development and rights genesis considered an event capable of repetition. Consider rights "generation" in at least three senses. First, the language represents rights creation as a natural process. The rhetoric of "genesis" at once evokes the language of science and of nature. Scientific rhetoric imbues international human rights theory with legitimacy by implying that the theory follows the natural laws of the universe—as if human rights are just out there, existing as an autonomous and objective reality. Second, generation also conveys rights in a genetic sense.[8] Put this way, rights generation casts the human rights story in terms of the broader human condition—of scientific, historical, and political generations. Third, the rhetoric of genesis and generation propounds the international human rights movement's distinctive account of natural rights made positive.

The passage of time and the accompanying changes in circumstances put pressure on the prevailing rights narrative and the attempt to theorize in terms of a unitary international human rights apparatus. Every aspect of the Nuremberg legacy appeared vulnerable to normative incoherence.

The dominant paradigm, drawing largely from American constitutionalism, suggested that the proper response to human rights viola-

7. *See generally* Immanuel Kant, Perpetual Peace (Lewis White Beck ed., Liberal Arts Press 1957) (1795) (proposing interstate stability as minimal standard); John Rawls, Political Liberalism (1993) (affirming stability standard); *see also* Theodor Meron, Human Rights and Humanitarian Norms as Customary Law (1989) (discussing the changes in the law of war and humanitarian law).

8. *See* Louis Henkin, *A New Birth of Constitutionalism: Genetic Influences and Genetic Defects*, 14 Cardozo L. Rev. 533, 538-45 (1993).

tions was individual accountability. The postwar paradigm instantiated at Nuremberg represented a radical shift in the understanding of prevailing international legal norms. Absolute sovereignty had been violated, seemingly challenging the border between the international and the national, as well as the individual and the collective. While there have been occasional national trials, such as Argentina's military junta or those of unified Germany,[9] there has never been the same sort of adjudication of rights violations as at Nuremberg. The historical and political circumstances surrounding Nuremburg, including the predicates for international sovereignty, and the force of occupation law, were missing from the later trials.

Considering rights theory in concert with localized historical and political knowledge clarifies the postwar precedent and doctrine. The very understanding of human rights and justice is entwined in the postwar paradigm's engendering circumstances. International human rights' historical and political contexts elucidate the theory's putative incoherence. Acknowledging the extraordinary political circumstances of international human rights recognizes their parameters and their limits. As the postwar predicates of the international human rights model have not yet repeated themselves,[10] the question has become: What, if any, is the ongoing vitality of the reigning theory's generating structures and related norms?

This part has explored the human rights narrative that has long dominated our understanding. In addition, it contended that examining the reigning theory, in the light of its historical and political predicates, clarifies existing structures and perceived problems. The Article continues by explaining how a genealogically enriched perspective illuminates the problems said to pervade contemporary human rights theory.

III. Rights-Theoretical Divides

Consider the putative gap between human rights theory and practice: Prevailing human rights theory is generally conceded to lack full normative force because of a perceived gap between the theory and judicialized rights. These are commonly considered to signal incoherence in human rights theory. The absence of remedies is often considered fatal.[11] The juxtaposition of rights theory to rights enforcement

9. For a discussion of contemporary human rights trials relating to periods of political transition, see Ruti Teitel, *Transitional Jurisprudence: The Role of Law in Political Transformation*, 106 Yale L.J. 2009, 2035-51 (1997).

10. Even the ad hoc International Criminal Tribunal for the former Yugoslavia does not reflect the same judicialized human rights model. For a comparative discussion of the Yugoslavia Tribunal in the light of Nuremburg, see Ruti Teitel, *Judgment at The Hague*, E. Eur. Const. Rev., Fall 1996, at 80.

11. *See* Jack Donnelly, *International Human Rights: A Regime Analysis*, 40 Int'l Org. 599, 633-36 (1986) (characterizing the weakness of the human rights system in terms of enforcement).

or rights practices also comprehends other theoretical dichotomies: international and national, universalism and particularism, positivism and natural law.[12]

The postwar story of Nuremberg justice inspires the reigning paradigmatic conception of international human rights as judicial. The post-war model of justice is the all powerful Military Tribunal and judicial rights. This historical legacy generates a view of human rights norms backed by legal sanctions and judicial enforcement. This conception of rights also derived from a largely unspoken analogue of international human rights to constitutional rights on the domestic plane and to rights protection in an age of constitutional democracy. The view construed international human rights as traditional rights at law where meaningful rights were norms backed by sanctions. Indeed, one might think of these as "American" rights,[13] a conception nurtured by the Allied initiative in the postwar judicialized rights response.[14] The prevailing notion that there is a "gap" in rights enforcement is intimately connected to the insistence that as a normative matter human rights ought be protected within a judicial system.[15] In this account, the problem does not derive from the theoretical framework itself, but rather from its lack of actualization.

Despite the animating force of international human rights theory, the twentieth century has been characterized by genocidal massacres and impunity.[16] How can we explain this course of events within the international human rights narrative? Perhaps the most glaring example is the apparent disjunction between the enormous political support for the Genocide Convention and the failure of judicial enforcement.[17] Despite the existence of the World Court, the international community has not enacted an international criminal code or created a permanent international criminal court.[18] Indeed, the first tribunals

12. The attempt here to contribute a genealogical perspective to the prevailing human rights analysis should not be taken as an instance of further juxtaposition of theory and practice.

13. *See* Marbury v. Madison, 5 U.S. (1 Cranch) 137, 162-66 (1803); Martin Shapiro, Courts: A Comparative and Political Analysis (1981).

14. *See* Telford Taylor, The Anatomy of the Nuremberg Trials: A Personal Memoir (1992).

15. The view appears Hohfeldian in its understanding of rights as closely connected to duties. *See* Arthur J. Jacobson, *Hegel's Legal Plenum*, 10 Cardozo L. Rev. 877 (1989).

16. *See, e.g., Final Report of the United Nations Commission of Experts Established Pursuant to Security Council Resolution 780*, at 12-13, U.N. Doc. S/1994/674/Annex VI (1992).

17. *See* Convention on the Prevention and Punishment of the Crime of Genocide, Dec. 9, 1948, 78 U.N.T.S. 277, 282 (1951); *see generally* Beth Van Schaack, Note, *The Crime of Political Genocide: Repairing the Genocide Convention's Blind Spot*, 106 Yale L.J. 2259 (1997).

18. *See generally* James Crawford, *The ILC Adopts a Statute for an International Criminal Court*, 89 Am. J. Int'l L. 404 (1995) (discussing the International Law Commission's draft statute to create an international criminal court).

in the half century since Nuremberg are the ad hoc international tribunals convened to prosecute violations arising out of the Balkans conflict, and expanded to include the Rwandan genocide.[19]

The perceived gap between human rights theory and its normative enforcement is often explained in terms of political realism. The theoretical apparatus is commonly characterized as unresponsive to political circumstances. A disjunction arises between international human rights theory and its realization. International human rights norms are viewed as somehow existing as autonomous realities spiraling away from other political structures. The characterization is one of internal incoherence, of a theory at war with itself.

Politics is deemed to explain the absence of the reigning normative model's actualization. The lack of enforcement is said to relate to the absence of consent. Without political consent, there is a "race to the bottom." Here is a rare and limited concession to the role of politics within the international legal system. Understanding the role of politics implies commencment of the analysis of the human rights system before the extraordinary story of occupation justice. It entails returning to the Treaty of Westphalia and the view that the subjects of international law were sovereign states,[20] where external sovereignty was bound by international law and its related legal principle of nonintervention. In this regard, the postwar human rights paradigm challenged pre-existing principles of sovereignty,[21] nonintervention, and respect for borders. The conflict is evinced in slippage of the concepts of: international and national, war and peace, private and public, rights and remedies.

Reification of the postwar proceedings has utterly distorted our understanding and derailed contemporary human rights theory. From the postwar perspective of human rights as judicial rights, the normative response to rights abuses is deemed to be adjudicatory and drawing upon the historical legacy with associated punishment. Accordingly, for some time now, the emphasis has been upon expansion of enforcement. The critical human rights question is characterized as one of execution, the problem largely of political will.

Yet, the postwar narrative is itself a substantially idealized version of the historical experience. The precedent is overstated because the statement of the norm exceeded its instantiation—even at the time. Thus, the postwar paradigm is deemed inherently paradoxical, pro-

19. *See* Statute of the International Tribunal for the Former Yugoslavia, *Report of the Secretary-General Pursuant to Paragraph 2 of S.C. Res. 808*, U.N. SCOR, 48th Sess., Annex, U.N. Doc. S/2504 (1993), *reprinted in* 32 I.L.M. 1159 (1993) [hereinafter International Tribunal]; *see also* Statute of the International Tribunal for Rwanda, S.C. Res. 995, U.N. SCOR, 49th Sess., 3453d mtg., Annex, U.N. Doc. S/RES/955 (1994), *reprinted in* 33 I.L.M. 1598 (1994).

20. *See* Stanley Hoffman, *Sovereignty and the Ethics of Intervention*, *in* The Ethics and Politics of Humanitarian Intervention (Stanley Hoffman ed., 1996).

21. *See* Charles R. Beitz, Political Theory and International Relations (1979).

ducing an antinomian tension in its structuring categories. Indeed, a very different story could be told about Nuremberg.

Reconsider the dominant theory incorporating its historical and political circumstances. This reconsideration means another understanding of the core rights paradigm categories: of the relation of individual and collective, of positivism and natural law, of the universal and the particular, and of the law of peace and the law of war. Thus, for example, postwar international human rights are commonly represented as an instance of natural law norms made positive. Nevertheless, reconsideration of the postwar paradigm in a historical light implies something for the debate about authority for the sources of international human rights law,[22] and a move away from strict positivism to a recognition of customary international law.[23] Relatedly, despite postwar claims to the forging of new normative ground in humanitarian law, adjudication of the crime against humanity—a violation at the norm's apex—was, even as applied at Nuremberg restricted to its abiding nexus with war.[24]

The same is true of other normative claims where the postwar precedent is similarly antinomial. Thus, a closer look at the postwar circumstances offers a more nuanced understanding of the categories of sovereignty and jurisdiction.[25] Although the postwar rights paradigm is commonly characterized in terms of universal norms and the norms ratified in the postwar codifying instruments,[26] the postwar proceedings also related to offenses occurring, at least in part, in particular locations, instantiating an alternative positivist normative point. Ultimately, the postwar paradigm incorporates within it the antinomial tension between those opposing normative concepts. While this tension is somewhat mitigated in the extraordinary postwar circumstances, in subsequent periods, it has only grown. Thus, a broader inquiry into the historical and political context of international human rights clarifies, and even reconciles, the purported gap between theory and practice in the contemporary movement.

22. *See* Gerald L. Neuman, *Sense and Nonsense About Customary International Law: A Response to Professors Bradley and Goldsmith*, 66 Fordham L. Rev. 319 (1997).

23. *See* Quincy Wright, *Legal Positivism and the Nuremberg Judgment*, 42 Am. J. Int'l L. 405 (1948).

24. Justifying crimes against humanity in terms of this nexus is still true to date. *See* International Tribunal, *supra* note 19, art. 5, at 1193 (granting the International Tribunal the power to prosecute crimes against humanity that were committed in armed conflict, whether international or national); International Criminal Tribunal for the Former Yugoslavia, Excerpts from Prosecutor v. Dusko Tadic, 36 I.L.M. 908, ¶¶ 79-85 (1997) (App. Chamber decision) [hereinafter *Tadic Decision*]. However, in the most recent developments toward a permanent international criminal court, the emerging consensus is a predicate of international armed conflict.

25. *See* W. Michael Reisman, *Sovereignty and Human Rights in Contemporary International Law*, 84 Am. J. Int'l L. 866 (1990).

26. *See* Charter of the International Military Tribunal, Aug. 8, 1945, 59 Stat. 1544, 82 U.N.T.S. 279 (1945).

The international human rights founding story is one that is said to be *sua sponte*, a radical birthing, a discontinuous affair with only an ambivalent relation to preexisting rights theory. Nevertheless, consider the meaning of the idea of rights as being "born" in the mid-twentieth century, seemingly without preexisting rights forbears?[27] This representation as an immaculate conception preserves the natural law claims. Telling the story this way, as an extraordinary narrative that begins in the war's aftermath, represents international human rights in atomistic fashion, as somehow insulated from preexisting rights theory. The account also plays a role in distorting international human rights theory, generating tension and incoherence.

To some degree, the theoretical framework of international human rights rests awkwardly on preexisting theory. Historically, theories of consensus and the social contractarian tradition, predicated on assumptions about the relationship of the individual to the state, justified rights theory. Specifically, the political predicate of the state's role as protector and guarantor of individual rights provided justification for the theory. Indeed, this view drew from the social contract theory underlying the liberal state.[28]

Postwar revelations tragically challenged these theoretic bedrock assumptions, rendering them inappropriate for responding to the central Auschwitz problem of the twentieth century. The contractarian foundations of previous rights theory appeared inapt for comprehending the strange shift in recognition of the position of the modern state—from rights protector to rights violator. The shift could not help but have normative implications for understanding the political regime, as well as for related constitutional and other rights principles. With the move away from social contract as the source of rights authority, new questions arose regarding alternative sources of authority for international human rights and their constraints.

On these questions, the prevailing rights paradigm resolution is paradoxical. In the postwar "genesis" story, international human rights are represented in universal terms deemed of general applicability. Rights, however, are also cast as manifestly positivist creatures of convention. The paradigm is widely understood as having, at some level, moved from natural law ideas to those that are more positivist, for example, in the Nuremberg Charter and the many postwar conventions.[29] This shift raises a central tension that continues to be present

27. On this question, see Maurice Cranston, What are Human Rights? (1973); Louis Henkin, *International Human Rights as "Rights," in* Human Rights 257 (J. Roland Pennock & John W. Chapman eds., 1981); Rights (David Lyons ed., 1979).

28. *See* John Locke, *The Second Treatise of Government, in* Two Treatises of Government 283 (Peter Laslett ed., Cambridge Univ. Press 2d ed. 1967) (1714); Jean Jacques Rousseau, The Social Contract (Charles Frankel trans., Hafner Pub. Co. 1947) (1762).

29. *See, e.g.*, Convention on the Prevention and Punishment of the Crime of Genocide, *supra* note 17.

in contemporary rights debates.[30] Indeed, the question of what should "count" as a right raises a broader methodological question.[31]

The move out of classical rights theory leads to a rethinking of the nature of the sources of and authority for human rights. The postwar paradigm leads away from views of authority as inhering in democratic consensus to other sources. A broader array of sources are available for the construction of human rights, such as customary law.[32] This is nowhere more true than in the gravest abuses of customary law, the so-called "jus cogens" norms, which include conduct considered to be universally condemned.[33] The sources undergirding grave rights abuses mediate both international and national conventions and jurisdictions.[34] Human rights norms mediate international and national law. Indeed, one norm often guides the other and becomes incorporated within governing documents.[35]

Although, historically, international human rights theory generally eschews hierarchizing rights, such hierarchies are implied by the extent of the theory's nexus with its postwar circumstances. Thus, the dominant view of rights adheres closely to those impinged upon during the war—political rights relating to persecution. It is also undeniable that this view of human rights, represented largely as "civil" and "political" rights, bore a close semblance to rights conceptions in preexisting political theory. Human rights, as civil and political, related closely to the core associated with the modern state in working democracies: norms associated with principles of the rule of law and equal protection.

Further, there was a constructive effect on the postwar rights model of political circumstances relating to the conflict with the Soviet Union and later Cold War developments. This historical and political contingency illuminates putative theoretical rights differentiation: for

30. *See* Neuman, *supra* note 22; *see generally*, Human Rights on the Eve of the Next Century Symposium, Panel entitled U.N. Human Rights Standards and U.S. Law (Feb. 28, 1997) (transcript on file with the *Fordham Law Review*).

31. On human rights generally, see Henkin, *supra* note 27. Exploring some differences between rights in the international and domestic contexts, see Henkin, *supra* note 1.

32. Regarding *jus cogens*, see Restatement (Third) of the Foreign Relations Law of the United States § 702 (1986) (listing, for example, slavery and genocide). *See also* Change and Stability in International Law-Making (Antonio Cassese & Joseph H.H. Weiler eds., 1988).

33. *See* Oscar Schachter, International Law in Theory and in Practice 333-42 (1991); *see also* Meron, *supra* note 7.

34. Indeed, the so-called "Alien-Tort" litigation is illustrative. The leading case is *Filartiga v. Pena-Irala*, 630 F.2d 876 (2d Cir. 1980). For a clarifying article, see Anne-Marie Burley, *The Alien Tort Statute and the Judiciary Act of 1789: A Badge of Honor*, 83 Am. J. Int'l L. 461 (1989).

35. One place this is seen is in the comparison of the language of international agreements with that characterizing domestic constitutional rights. *See* Constitutionalism and Rights: The Influence of the United States Constitution Abroad (Louis Henkin & Albert J. Rosenthal eds., 1990).

example, the distinction between "political" and "economic" rights. Another manifestation was the so-called "big compromise," the bifurcation of the post World War II, Cold War era codification of international human rights into the Covenant on Civil and Political Rights and the Covenant on Economic, Social and Cultural Rights. This rights differentiation can only be understood as resulting from the construction of human rights that was set in the context of the postwar conflict with the communist bloc.

Given the massive political changes since the war and those that have taken place since the Soviet collapse, the constitutive distinction between civil/political and economic rights of international human rights theory has fallen under attack. Indeed, the subsequent wave of political and economic transitions in the region invite rethinking of the received wisdom. To what extent should economic rights be recognized as positive rights—whether under constitutional schemes, or within the international human rights system? This question has emerged as a central point of debate in the post communist transitions.[36] The contemporary debate reconsidering the purported distinctions of these rights—just as the political circumstances change—underscores the historical and political contingencies embedded in the prevailing human rights apparatus. Similarly, other differences have appeared over time, signaling the growing chasm that has emerged between the postwar rights model and its generating circumstances. This widening divide is best seen in the tension in the normative scheme that was thought to define human rights. Indeed, the relevant question is whether that old framework would be apt for normative development.

Still, other features of postwar human rights theory have been criticized for their inability to comprehend prevailing phenomena. Consider, for example, the elusive distinction between the public and private spheres in international human rights theory, as well as the theory's related emphasis on state action. The public/private state action distinction is, once again, best explained within its historical and political circumstances, namely, the postwar focus on states persecution. The public/private distinction also inhered in the constitutionalism of the time, emphasizing the view of state action derived from traditional liberal political theory. Nevertheless, massive historical, political, and social change have outstripped the postwar normative apparatus. This reconception implies reconsidering contemporary

36. On the debate over whether economic rights should be constitutionalized, see Cass R. Sunstein, *Against Positive Rights*, *in* Western Rights? Post-Communist Application 225 (András Sajó ed., 1996) [hereinafter Western Rights?]; Ruti Teitel, *Constitutional Costs to Free Market Transitions*, *in* Western Rights?, *supra*, at 361; Ruti Teitel, *Post-Communist Constitutionalism: A Transitional Perspective*, 26 Colum. Hum. Rts. L. Rev. 167 (1994); Richard Falk, *Comparative Protection of Human Rights in Capitalist and Socialist Third World Countries*, Universal Hum. Rts., Apr.-June 1979, at 3.

human rights violations beyond the public domain.[37] Here, the feminist critique is particularly compelling in its reconceptualization and proposed reconstruction of the private and public spheres.[38]

The so-called "third" generation of rights comprehends the rights of groups, collectivity rights, ethnicity rights, rights of "peoples," and rights to self-determination. This generation of rights incorporates the critique of prevailing human rights theory from the communitarian perspective,[39] as well as the critique from cultural relativism.[40] Although reigning normative human rights concepts emphasize the universal, recent rights developments suggest there is little that is essential in these normative distinctions.

Finally, there is the critique of the prevailing rights model—from the vantagepoint of its arch ontological dichotomy—of the claim that human rights inhere in sources in terms of objectivity and reason. Here, the challenge to human rights theorizing reflects broader concurrent epistemological challenges in theorizing of knowledge.[41]

Movement away from the prevailing conception can be seen in contemporary philosophical theorizing.[42] This theorizing offers fresh directions and new paths to human rights—not necessarily in the terms of the prevailing paradigm's rational, objective, and universalizing approach—but instead, through the pathways of friendship and solidarity. Indeed, these approaches indicate the prevailing arch antinomial differences paradigm, offering both normative rights principle and rights practice—a way to relate to the "other." The exhortation is a call for a return to the "human" in human rights and the repair of pervasive dehumanization.

After half a century, the foundational concepts of the reigning postwar model reveal growing slippage. The passage of time and change, both in the relevant political circumstances and in theories of knowledge generally, have put increasing pressure on the paradigmatic rights model. The mounting claim of incoherence in the received international human rights account has had profound consequences for the theory's positive and normative force. Nevertheless, the claim to

37. *See* Andrew Clapham, Human Rights in the Private Sphere (1993).

38. *See, e.g.*, Catherine MacKinnon, *On Torture: A Feminist Perspective on Human Rights*, *in* Human Rights in the Twenty-First Century 21 (Kathleen Mahoney & P. Mahoney eds., 1993), *reprinted in* International Human Rights in Context: Law, Politics, Morals 951 (Henry J. Steiner & Philip Alston eds., 1996).

39. *See* The Rights of Minority Cultures (Will Kymlicka ed., 1995).

40. *See* Michael J. Perry, *Are Human Rights Universal? The Relativist Challenge and Related Matters*, 19 Hum. Rts. Q. 461 (1997).

41. For a critique on the basis of multiplicity and indeterminacy, see Steven Connor, Postmodernist Culture: An Introduction to Theories of the Contemporary (2d ed. 1997); David Harvey, The Condition of Postmodernity: An Enquiry into the Origins of Cultural Change (1989).

42. *See* Annette C. Baier, Moral Prejudices: Essays on Ethics (1994); Richard Rorty, *Human Rights, Rationality, and Sentimentality*, *in* On Human Rights: The Oxford Amnesty Lectures 111 (Stephen Shute & Susan Hurley eds., 1993).

incoherence is best explained in terms of a growing chasm between a unitary human rights theory abstracted from its engendering circumstances, reified with perverse consequences.

IV. Constituting Contemporary Human Rights

What gives contemporary human rights law its force? I want to return to the question with which this Article began. Moving beyond the prevailing narrative enables the analysis of contemporary practices as the ongoing construction of human rights culture. Exploration of the practices, conventions, and discourses illuminates the contemporary meaning of human rights. These manifestations also invite a rethinking of the status and directions of contemporary human rights. Contemporary practices shed light on dynamic human rights norms, illuminating change in the postwar paradigm. Emergent practices lead us to recognize new human rights paradigms.

What is the significance of the contemporary human rights movement's discourse?[43] Practices here are an indication, not of theory gone awry, but rather as what comprises international human rights norms—as all there is.

The enormous expansion of the human rights domain is manifest. The attempt at normalization is seen in the generalizing and ambiguating of the postwar norms far beyond their animating circumstances. Whereas international human rights were previously characterized as largely discontinuous with other law practices, the notion of a bright line separation has disappeared. This melding can easily be seen in a number of areas where human rights law has merged with other established bodies of law, for example, human rights law and the humanitarian law of war, and human rights law and asylum law. Convergence of international human rights law and international humanitarian law can be seen in the normative slippage, whereby the laws of armed conflict have been extended to internal conflict and peacetime.[44] Such convergence in humanitarian and human rights law demarcates a broader domain for human rights. Further areas of convergence can be seen in the incorporation and protection of international and national rights protection in the various regional systems, for example, the European Court and the Inter-American systems.

The convergence in established areas of law relating to human rights challenges the theory's reigning conceptual oppositions. So it is, that in the slippage of the old dichotomies of war and peace, of inter-

43. On the human rights movement, see Jack Donnelly, Universal Human Rights in Theory and Practice (1989); Henkin, *supra* note 1, at 184-226; Henkin, *supra* note 6, at 16-41.

44. *See, e.g.*, Hague Convention IV Respecting the Laws and Customs of War on Land, Oct. 18, 1907, 36 Stat. 2277 (1907); Geneva Conventions for the Amelioration of the Condition of the Wounded and Sick in Armed Forces in the Field, August 12, 1949, 75 U.N.T.S. 31 (1950); *see also supra* note 24.

national and national, that the law of war leads back to the law of peace. Slippage exists in other directions, as international law and its rights protections help to define the rights of citizens under domestic constitutional law. The rights of the foreigner, of the alien, give us those of the citizen.

Human rights practices emphasize the relationship between the international legal system and other legal domains. Despite the postwar momentum within the new international legal system—reflected in instantiated Nuremberg-style justice, as well as the attendant wave of constitutionalism that emphasized individual rights—the international legal system alone could not protect deracinated individual rights. Transitional periods of political crisis revealed the extent to which meaningful rights protection presumes a working state. Responses to rights abuses in periods of national political transformation characterized as "transitional," while affirming individual rights norms are also limited, and as such illuminate the political predicates to a viable human rights system.[45] Thus, half a century later, the postwar primacy of individual rights ultimately leads back to the recognition of the state's role in protecting human rights in a rule of law system. Vindication of individual rights under international law presumes a strong and functioning state with liberal rule of law institutions that are responsive to individual rights.

In the face of ongoing political horror, what is the point of the new direction in human rights law? Of the value to human rights normalization? The focus is on practices, particularly the contemporary responses to the extreme human rights violations of the atrocities in the Balkans, which produce grave charges of crimes against humanity and genocide. In the radical political climate following the collapse of the Soviet Union and the transitions away from military rule, the practices of successor regimes throughout Eastern and Central Europe, Latin America, and Africa appear to instantiate liberalizing political change.

According to the prevailing human rights paradigm, the normative response is to subsume treatment of grave violations within the judicial system. Although there may appear to be some movement in that direction, with the contemporary Ad Hoc International Tribunal convened regarding Yugoslavia and Rwanda, the Tribunal at the Hague responds to a conflict that itself defies facile characterization.[46] Further, Tribunal practices underscore historical and political differences from the postwar Tribunal's prevailing circumstances, such as an absence of custody over the defendants and the evidence. These distinctions ultimately indicate that the leading form of international criminal justice in the contemporary moment is procedural. The role of the law here is largely procedural and hence, seemingly preserva-

45. *See* Teitel, *supra* note 9.
46. *See, e.g.*, *Tadic Decision*, *supra* note 24.

tive of other rights.[47] Procedural human rights emphasize the preparation and distillation of a record of rights abuses, whether through indictment or other processes, such as "truth commissions."[48]

This human rights function is part of a broader phenomenon: Human rights practices suggest that the most effective development of customary law could be characterized as procedural. Thus, for example, consider another area of emergent human rights practices: the response to the paradigmatic human rights violation of the late twentieth century—the disappearance. The responses to disappearances offer a way to understand contemporary human rights violations, their remedies, and ultimately the related conception of a human right. Rather than the reigning paradigmatic focus on criminal legal accountability rights violators, here emerges the move toward victim-centered remedies, for survivors, and the society at large. Hence, the newest human rights construction: the right "to truth" and the rights to an investigation, a record, and a hearing. The turn is toward an alternative understanding of human rights as threshold procedural rights. These understandings of human rights ultimately redefine the understanding of individual rights as well as the relationship of the individual and the state.

Responses to the worst human rights violations of this last half century—political executions and disappearances, totalitarian rule, apartheid, the national security state in Latin America, violations throughout Africa, and ethnic cleansing in the Balkans—reflect a broad phenomenology of international human rights responses that is a shift away from the paradigmatic judicial rights to more informal administrative sanctions and procedural rights.[49] To be sure, the law is highly normative and hortatory in nature.

There is a broader domain for human rights, one encompassing a culture that increasingly frames state behavior and decisionmaking in human rights terms. There is a movement away from an emphasis on the punishment of norm transgression to a broader representation of rights claims. Human rights practices of monitoring and reporting can tell us a lot about the changes in the conception of rights as well as the relation of states to their citizens regarding the protection of human rights. These new practices comprehend complex ideas of rights and ongoing obligations beyond the initial equal protection rights such as the duty to investigate. These ongoing rights obligations fall upon successor regimes temporizing the understanding of the relevant state action and inspiring rethinking of human rights and related obligations.

---

47. For a rights analogy, drawing from the domestic sphere, see John Hart Ely, Democracy and Distrust: A Theory of Judicial Review (1980) (proposing the view of constititutional rights as procedural).

48. For a catalog of such Truth Commissions, see Priscilla B. Hayner, *Fifteen Truth Commissions—1974 to 1994: A Comparative Study*, 16 Hum. Rts. Q. 597 (1994).

49. *See* Teitel, *supra* note 9.

Contemporary human rights come into the picture much earlier in the process. Whereas the prevailing paradigm conceives of human rights as ex post—of rights as "trumps"[50] or of rights that follow politics—contemporary practices suggest that human rights come into the picture much earlier. Human rights discourse occurs on an ongoing basis in the public sphere and the practices of documentation and reporting are normalized. Thus, reporting on the adherence to human rights takes place on two time lines—on an ordinary yearly basis, as well as on an extraordinary basis reactive to particular crises.[51]

What is also undeniable is that human rights practices are increasingly discursive. The significance given to deliberation in the international setting evidences this change. Such discursive practices are illustrated by the appeals to rights set forth in the Universal Declaration. The United Nations General Assembly is itself the site of regular and ongoing human rights deliberations. "Rights talk" is increasingly offered as performative, as remedy.[52] Rights themselves appear to be constructive in structuring political developments, in part because of the moral and social political force of the language of rights.

What is the point of these rights? Consider the purposes of human rights procedural discourse. These discursive practices are not mere signs of rights, not merely customary law. Adopting that view would be to persist in the received wisdom, in the prevailing insistence of measuring normative rights rhetoric against a putative autonomous rights reality. If the purpose is largely procedural—with an eye toward preserving other rights—one way to think about the value of these rights is as establishing a foundation for a prospective, more complete, international human rights justice. What kind of vision is this? Are these millennial rights? Is the point to ward off a repetition of the wartime events? Yet, a repetition of the Nuremberg circumstances is unlikely. Can we even imagine a similar international tribunal, divorced from its abiding historical and political circumstances?

Interestingly though, there is presently an attempt to reenact the Nuremberg trials with similar international tribunals. These transitional responses to contemporary human rights violations, however, fail to generate a comparable sense of the rule of law or security because they lack the background political conditions associated with the postwar judicialized rights model.[53] These transitional remedies exemplify the limits and ultimate temporizing of rights remedies in the

50. *See* Ronald Dworkin, *Rights as Trumps*, *in* Theories of Rights 153 (Jeremy Waldron ed., 1984).

51. Thus, for example, the U.S. State Department issues worldwide yearly reports and human rights organizations have emulated this. *See, e.g.*, Human Rights Watch, World Report 1997 (1996).

52. On increasing linguistification, see generally Judith Butler, Excitable Speech: A Politics of the Performative (1997).

53. For a broader elaboration of this point, see Teitel, *supra* note 9.

less than ideal circumstances presumed in the prevailing model. Although procedural rights may well comprise a virtue of justice, these ought not be mistaken for full justice. Record making in and of itself is not justice, although it enables preserving an idea of justice not presently realizable.

The above hints at clarifying the puzzle with which the Article commenced, regarding the elusive nature of international human rights' normative force. International human rights offer a widely shared language by which to represent abuses and violations of human dignity.[54] Demands cast in rights language become claims that cannot otherwise be rationalized away in the domestic scheme, such as in terms of war or national security. Indeed, just this role for rights discourse is evinced in the recent wave of liberalizing transformation. The language of international human rights not only captured the prior repression, but also offered a means to inspire and galvanize a liberal opposition as well as an image of hope. Here the language of rights shapes that of political discourse. The claim of right convergent with that of politic's demand promises mediating differences of culture,[55] and building such discourse promises solidarity among diverse peoples.[56] Ultimately, deliberations are thought to enable gradual consensus.[57] At the very least, the rights practices instantiate those of democracy.

Conclusion

This Article's goal has been to illuminate the genealogy, status, and directions of contemporary human rights theory. This alternative critical approach analyzes international human rights theory in terms of its relation to its abiding politics and from the perspective of its organizing language and structures. The approach advanced here seeks to contribute to a moving out of the problematic in present theorizing. Incorporating the genealogical should illuminate the received understanding of contemporary human rights theory. Incorporation of international human rights' engendering context illuminates a renewed coherence in contemporary human rights theory and appreciation of the sources of its normative force.

54. *See* Judith N. Shklar, The Faces of Injustice (1990) (describing the significance of representation in terms of injustice and rights violations as opposed to misfortune). For an example of the central role of rights construction in representations of "ethnic" as opposed to political conflict, see Human Rights Watch, Playing the "Communal Card:" Communal Violence and Human Rights (1995).

55. *See* Abdullahi Ahmed An-Na'im, *Human Rights in the Muslim World: Socio-Political Conditions and Scriptural Imperatives* A Preliminary Inquiry, 3 Harv. Hum. Rts. J. 13 (1990).

56. *See* Rorty, *supra* note 42.

57. *See* Rawls, *supra* note 7.

[3]

THE CONCEPT OF HUMAN RIGHTS: THE HISTORY AND MEANING OF ITS POLITICIZATION

*Joy Gordon**

Table of Contents

---

* Assistant Professor of Philosophy, Fairfield University; B.A., Brandeis University, 1980; J.D., Boston University School of Law, 1984; Ph.D, Yale University, 1993. I want to thank Morrie Lipson for his many helpful suggestions on several drafts of this article. I am also grateful to Lou Barsky, Rachel Bergeron, Renny Christopher, Ruth Emerson, Susan Neiman, Michael O'Hear, and Bruce Shapiro for their comments on earlier drafts and for many productive conversations on these issues. I also want to thank California State University-Stanislaus for providing the research support which made it possible to complete this project.

THE CONCEPT OF HUMAN RIGHTS: THE HISTORY AND MEANING OF ITS POLITICIZATION

Joy Gordon

INTRODUCTION

It is sometimes said that the concept of human rights is "the only political-moral idea that has received universal acceptance."[1] Some describe human rights as the central moral issue in international relations today—as the "currency of international moral discourse,"[2] or as the "modern tool of revolution" in "the struggle for . . . human dignity in our time."[3] The concept of human rights is also invoked with increasing frequency in the context of security issues and as justification of armed conflict.[4]

In one sense, the concept of human rights is as familiar to us as the nightly news. It would be hard to read a national newspaper on any given day without finding a reference to death squads, disappearances, torture, mutilation, mass rape, siege and starvation of civilian populations, or arrests of dissidents somewhere in the world.[5] Yet in another sense, it eludes discussion altogether: our ethical intuition is that human rights violations involve acts which are so patently monstrous that there could be no rational or moral justification for them; and that only someone who is depraved or irrational could seriously take issue with either the goodness or the urgency of human rights. At the same time, there is a further debate as to how broad the notion of human rights should be.[6]

---

1. LOUIS HENKIN, THE AGE OF RIGHTS ix (1990).

2. Martin Shupack, *The Churches and Human Rights: Catholic and Protestant Human Rights Views as Reflected in Church Statements*, 6 HARV. HUM. RTS. J. 127, 127 (1993).

3. Irwin Cotler, *Human Rights as the Modern Tool of Revolution*, *in* HUMAN RIGHTS IN THE TWENTY-FIRST CENTURY 7, 7 (Kathleen E. Mahoney & Paul Mahoney eds., 1993).

4. *See generally* Douglas Lee Donoho, *The Role of Human Rights in Global Security Issues: A Normative and Institutional Critique*, 14 MICH. J. INT'L L. 827 (1993). This is especially true for the United States.

5. A recent search of the NEXIS database revealed that during the last two years there were approximately 87,000 news articles in the United States which mentioned the term "human rights."

6. For many years now it has been suggested that the label of "human

Among contemporary commentators, the standard notion of human rights is sometimes framed in terms of "generations" of rights. "First-generation" rights are, as one scholar points out, "the traditional liberties and privileges of citizenship, covered by the first twenty articles of the [Universal Declaration of Human Rights]: free speech, religious liberty, the right not to be tortured, the right to a fair trial, the right to vote, and so forth."[7]

This notion is quite familiar to us. Less familiar are socio-economic "second-generation rights"—the right to work, the right to fair pay, the right to food, shelter and clothing, the right to education, etc.[8] In this Article, I will argue that the concept of human rights which is so familiar is in fact quite odd and inconsistent; and that underlying this oddness is a profoundly political structure and a history of political uses.

The claim that the concept of human rights has an under-

---

rights" is applied too broadly, with the result that the term is amorphous or overbroad. *See, e.g.*, Philip Alston, *Conjuring Up New Human Rights: A Proposal for Quality Control*, 78 AM. J. INT'L L. 607, 607 (1984) (observing that there has been an expansion of "new rights" achieved in a "haphazard, almost anarchic manner."); Anthony D'Amato, *The Concept of Human Rights in International Law*, 82 COLUM. L. REV. 1110, 1110 (1982) (noting that human rights "has been the subject of a burgeoning jurisprudential literature."); *see also generally* Theodor Meron, *On a Hierarchy of International Human Rights*, 80 AM. J. INT'L L. 1 (1986) (arguing for an enlarged core of non-derogable rights, rather than tiers of rights).

7. JEREMY WALDRON, LIBERAL RIGHTS 5 (1993).

8. *See id.* at 4-5. Third-generation rights, which I will not address here, concern collective and communal rights involving national self-determination, cultural practices, use of native languages and so on. *See, e.g.*, Berta Esperanza Hernández-Truyol, *Report of the Conference Rapporteur*, 44 AM. U. L. REV. 1389, 1407 (1995) (Final Report to the *Conference on the International Protection of Reproductive Rights*, referring to "first (civil and political rights), second (social and economic rights) and third (solidarity) generation human rights."); Kathleen Mahoney, *Theoretical Perspectives on Women's Human Rights and Strategies for their Implementation*, 21 BROOK. J. INT'L L. 799, 837-38 (1996) (noting that third generation "group or peoples' rights are of greatest interest to developing countries."); Stephen P. Marks, *Emerging Human Rights: A New Generation for the 1980s?*, 33 RUTGERS L. REV. 435, 441 (1981) (observing that Karel Vasak has distinguished the third generation of human rights as being "predicated on brotherhood (*fraternité*), in the sense of solidarity" as opposed to rights predicated on *liberté* (first generation rights) or *égalité* (second generation rights)); Feisal Hussain Naqvi, *People's Rights or Victim's Rights: Reexamining the Conceptualization of Indigenous Rights in International Law*, 71 IND. L.J. 673, 713 (1996) (understanding third generation rights, such as the right to "cultural integrity" and "the right to development" as "expand[ing] the economic entitlements of individuals."); Barbara Stark, *Conceptions of International Peace and Environmental Rights: "The Remains of the Day"*, 59 TENN. L. REV. 651, 654 (1992).

lying political agenda is not new. Feminist critics have made the claim in analyzing the consequences of the dominant concept for women.[9] In addition, both Western critics and non-Western nations have suggested that this concept, with its emphasis on political rather than economic rights, reflects a bias in favor of wealthy Western nations.[10] Many have suggest-

---

9. *See, e.g.*, Sarah Y. Lai & Regan E. Ralph, Recent Development, *Female Sexual Autonomy and Human Rights*, 8 HARV. HUM. RTS. J. 201, 203 (1995) (discussing the economic/political dichotomy as it impacts on protections of the rights of women); Shelley Wright, *Women and the Global Economic Order: A Feminist Perspective*, 10 AM. U. J. INT'L L. & POL'Y 861, 874 (1995) (observing the effect that the "division between political and civil rights versus economic, social and cultural rights" has had "on how economic rights and social justice are discussed."). Also relevant to this discussion are feminist arguments contending that effective political participation by women is undermined by the fact that the standard concept of human rights rests upon the public/private distinction. *See* Celina Romany, *Women as Aliens: A Feminist Critique of the Public/Private Distinction in International Human Rights Law*, 6 HARV. HUM. RTS. J. 87, 87 (1993); *see also* Pamela Goldberg & Nancy Kelly, *International Human Rights and Violence Against Women*, 6 HARV. HUM. RTS. J. 195, 195 (1993); Mahoney, *supra* note 8, at 800; Celina Romany, *Black Women and Gender Equality in a New South Africa: Human Rights Law and the Intersection of Race and Gender*, 21 BROOK. J. INT'L L. 857, 860 (1996); Barbara Stark, *International Human Rights Law, Feminist Jurisprudence, and Nietzsche's "Eternal Return": Turning the Wheel*, 19 HARV. WOMEN'S L.J. 169, 169-70 (1996).

10. *See* Sompong Sucharitkul, *A Multi-Dimensional Concept of Human Rights in International Law*, 62 NOTRE DAME L. REV. 305, 305 (1987) (observing that "the international instruments proclaiming the Rights of Man or the International Covenants of Human Rights merely incorporate the view and concepts advocated by the authors and draftsmen of those instruments, who have invariably been trained in Western or European legal traditions."). *See also* Ebow Bondzie-Simpson, *A Critique of the African Charter on Human and People's Rights*, 31 HOW. L.J. 643, 658 (1988) (discussing the primacy that economic development has for political leaders in Africa); Goler Teal Butcher, *The Immediacy of International Law for Howard University Students*, 31 HOW. L.J. 435, 445 (1988) (contending that the United States "stands out as the state which, while promoting the rights of individuals against the excesses of government, that is civil and political rights, is opposed to a concept of a human right not to be hungry, a right to have work, the right to education."). *But see* Mary Ann Glendon, *Rights in Twentieth-Century Constitutions*, 59 U. CHI. L. REV. 519, 523-24 (1992) (noting that welfare rights "have become a staple feature of post-war international declarations and have been accorded a place beside traditional political and civil liberties in the national constitutions of most liberal democracies."). This issue is sometimes addressed in the context of the debate over cultural relativism in human rights. *See, e.g.*, JACK DONNELLY, INTERNATIONAL HUMAN RIGHTS 35 (1993); Abdullahi Ahmed An-Na'im, *Toward a Cross-Cultural Approach to Defining International Standards of Human Rights*, *in* HUMAN RIGHTS AND CROSS-CULTURAL PERSPECTIVES 19, (Abdullahi Ahmed An-Na'im ed., 1992); Christina M. Cerna, *Universality of Human Rights and Cultural Diversity: Implementation of Human Rights in Different Socio-Cultural Contexts*, 16 HUM. RTS. Q. 740, 740 (1994); Jack Donnelly, *Cultural Relativism and Universal*

ed that human rights issues must be addressed in the context of the larger relations between First World and Third World, and in the context of development and modernization.[11]

During the Cold War, there was extensive debate about the political and economic interests underlying the notion of human rights. Western governments and non-governmental organizations (NGOs) (such as Amnesty International) routinely condemned the Eastern bloc countries for human rights violations, partly on the grounds that the judicial and electoral processes were inadequate or oppressive. The Soviets would respond that in *their* view, human rights entailed health care, education, employment and economic equity. They accused their Western critics of purporting to offer a "universal" standard which in fact reflected Western First World societies,

---

Human Rights, 6 HUM. RTS. Q. 400, 400-19 (1984) (examining the "competing claims of cultural relativism and universal human rights" and advocating an approach to reconciling them that "preserves the tension between and the insights of, both relativism and universalism."); Rhoda E. Howard, *Cultural Relativism and the Nostalgia for Community*, 15 HUM. RTS. Q. 315, 315 (1993) (analyzing the concept of cultural relativism, as that concept is employed by traditionalists and by communitarians, and concluding that it is in fact a form of cultural absolutism); Christopher C. Joyner & John C. Dettling, *Bridging the Cultural Chasm: Cultural Relativism and the Future of International Law*, 20 CAL. W. INT'L L.J. 275, 275 (1990); Nancy Kim, *Toward a Feminist Theory of Human Rights: Straddling the Fence Between Western Imperialism and Uncritical Absolutism*, 25 COLUM. HUM. RTS. L. REV. 49, 56-59 (1993); Fernando R. Tesón, *International Human Rights and Cultural Relativism*, 25 VA. J. INT'L L. 869 (1985).

11. *See, e.g.*, Arthur A. Baer, *Latino Human Rights and the Global Economic Order*, 18 CHICANO-LATINO L. REV. 80, 80-81 (1996); Susan M. Davis, *WEDO and the Public Advocacy Agenda in Creating Sustainable Human Development*, 69 ST. JOHN'S L. REV. 179, 187 n.14 (1995) (discussing the position of the Women's Environment and Development Organization); Robert F. Drinan, S.J. *Sovereignty and Human Rights*, 20 CAN.-U.S. L.J. 75, 84-85 (1994); J. Oloka-Onyango, *Beyond the Rhetoric: Reinvigorating the Struggle for Economic and Social Rights in Africa*, 26 CAL. W. INT'L L.J. 1, 1-2 (1995) (observing that economic, social and cultural rights have been neglected and emphasizing the need to devote more attention to those rights); Brian Z. Tamanaha, *The Lessons of Law-and-Development Studies*, 89 AM. J. INT'L L. 470 (1995) (reviewing LAW AND DEVELOPMENT (Anthony Carty ed., 1992) and LAW AND CRISIS IN THE THIRD WORLD (Sammy Adelman & Abdul Paliwala eds., 1993)). Davis, among others, contends that the extreme economic disparities between First World and Third World need to be recognized more explicitly as the context in which any discussion of human rights can take place. As Davis points out, Third World countries account for "three-fourths of the global population," while receiving "only 30% of the world's income." Davis, *supra*, at 187. She notes that "the North consumes 70% of the world[']s energy, 75% of its metal, 85% of its wood and 60% of its food." *Id.* at 188. Drinan notes that 40,000 children die each day from preventable diseases and that the United States, with 4% of the global population, consumes 40% of its food. *See* Drinan, *supra*, at 84-85.

which had highly developed political systems, but also great economic disparities. The Western governments and NGOs would reply that it was not *they* who were self-serving, but the Soviets, whose theory of human rights reflected the Communist view that political rights were insignificant compared to economic benefits.[12] Thus, each accused the other of claiming to set forth a universal and impartial standard of basic rights, which was in fact not impartial at all, but patently self-serving, and whose validity was therefore compromised.

I am not interested in resurrecting this particular exchange of accusations. However, what interests me about it is that in some sense both sides are right: it is impossible not to see how closely the two concepts correspond to the political and rhetorical agendas of the Cold War. If this is so, then we must

---

12. *See* Tracy E. Higgins, *Anti-Essentialism, Relativism, and Human Rights*, 19 HARV. WOMEN'S L.J. 89, 92 n.18 (1996) (commenting on Soviet and Western objections to the Universal Declaration of Human Rights and observing that "[t]he Soviets were opposed to the preponderance of Western civil liberties . . . . Western nations were persuaded to include economic, social and cultural rights in the document only after having been persuaded that it would not be legally binding" (citation omitted)). Another commentator, Aart Hendriks, notes that:

> For a long time, social rights were associated with communism, seen as the justification given by socialist governments to suppress the civil and political rights of their opponents. The degree of government interference that these rights seemed to necessitate were, in addition, often perceived to be "inherently incompatible" with the rules of a free market economy.

Aart Hendriks, *Promotion and Protection of Women's Right to Sexual and Reproductive Health Under International Law: The Economic Covenant and the Women's Convention*, 44 AM. U.L. REV. 1123, 1131 (1995). Henry Steiner, in reviewing Louis Henkin's THE AGE OF RIGHTS, noted that:

> Throughout the Cold War, it was notorious that many communist countries, particularly the Soviet Union, justified their political systems in terms of the priority given to and the asserted realizations of economic and social rights, while simultaneously mocking the significance of bourgeois civil and political rights in Western democracies.

Henry J. Steiner, *The Youth of Rights*, 104 HARV. L. REV. 917, 928 n.17 (1991) (review of HENKIN, *supra* note 1). Steiner additionally observed that, since the commencement of the Reagan Administration, the United States "has taken the position" that either "welfare claims cannot constitute rights or that the securing of civil and political rights is an essential condition to economic and social development and must be the focus of urgent attention." *Id.* (citations omitted). *See also* Philip Alston & Gerard Quinn, *The Nature and Scope of States Parties' Obligations Under the International Covenant on Economic, Social and Cultural Rights*, 9 HUM. RTS. Q. 156, 160 (1987); Barabara Stark, *Economic Rights in the United States and International Human Rights Law: Toward an "Entirely New Strategy"*, 44 HASTINGS L.J. 79, 84 (1992) (discussing our need to rethink "our Cold War aversion to 'economic rights.'").

ask ourselves: Is there a notion of human rights which has no agenda, which serves no political interests and which is truly universal? If there is not—if any concept of human rights is grounded in some political or economic interest—then is there nevertheless some principled, rational justification for adopting one concept of human rights rather than another?[13]

Part I of this Article traces the emergence of the standard notion of human rights in the second half of the twentieth century, in the context of international law and diplomacy. In the Nuremberg tribunal of 1946, we see a notion of human rights as atrocities, "crimes against humanity." In the United Nations' Universal Declaration of Human Rights[14] (Universal Declaration), the notion is broadened enormously such that it includes almost every dimension of life—social, economic, political, cultural and familial. In the 1960s, these rights were bifurcated into two treaties, one concerning atrocities and political and civil rights; and one concerning social and economic rights. The former contained requirements for immediate compliance by all states, as well as mechanisms for enforcement. The latter contained neither of these. The major NGOs (Amnesty International and Human Rights Watch) largely reiterate this distinction and define human rights violations in terms of atrocities and political rights; but not economic rights.

Part II considers the asymmetry of this bifurcated structure of the contemporary Western notion of human rights. The standard notion of human rights now consists roughly of two categories of acts: atrocities, such as torture, mass murder and summary executions; and deprivation of political rights, such

13. These questions, it seems to me, have to be resolved first in order to address issues related to the proliferation and conflicts among the purported rights advanced in the political, academic and legal literature—the right to life, the right to die, the right to employment, the right to subsistence in the absence of employment, the right to publish pornography, the right to live in a pornography-free society, individual rights, group rights, the right to use natural resources, the right of the environment to be protected from overuse, the right of non-discrimination, the right of free (and sometimes discriminatory) expression and so on. For general discussions of these matters see HUMAN RIGHTS IN THE TWENTY-FIRST CENTURY, *supra* note 3; PHILOSOPHICAL ISSUES IN HUMAN RIGHTS (Patricia H. Werhane et al. eds., 1986).

14. Universal Declaration of Human Rights, G.A. Res. 217A, U.N. GAOR, 3d Sess., pt. 1, 183d plen. mtg. at 71, U.N. Doc. A/810 (1948) [hereinafter Universal Declaration].

as rights of speech, press, multi-party elections and judicial process. It does not include economic rights, such as the right to employment, housing, food and medical care. Why is this so? I propose that we begin by adopting a reasonably uncontroversial definition of human rights (although I will consider other variations at a later point) and assume that "human rights" are those resources or conditions which constitute the minimal conditions for human existence. If by "human rights," we mean "those elements which constitute the minimal conditions for human existence," then freedom from torture or death would certainly be included; but food and shelter would be as well. At the same time, it is not clear that speech and press in fact occupy the same fundamental role in human survival (although they may be indirectly necessary as a means to ensuring the satisfaction of human needs which *are* direct and immediate). Thus, the standard notion on one hand classes together rights which are very different in nature (atrocities and political rights); while excluding other rights (economic rights) which seem as directly essential to human well-being (if not more so) than political rights.

Parts III and IV trace the particular content of the modern idea of human rights to two distinct sources: the doctrine of Just War starting with Augustine and the Enlightenment conception of rights. Just War theory concerns the duties owed in wartime to enemies—to those toward whom one has no legal or domestic ties at all. The Just War doctrine prohibits torture as well as the unnecessary killing of civilians, wounded soldiers and prisoners of war. Thus, it concerns the minimal level of decency owed to someone simply because he or she is a human being. The Enlightenment notion of rights, however, is very different. It envisions the assertion of the rights of liberty, equality, fraternity and happiness—in short, the conception of a good and full life—not the minimal conditions for survival and the minimal obligation of decency. The Enlightenment rights differ from Just War "rights" in nature as well as content. In the Enlightenment tradition, rights are abstract rather than concrete; political rather than personal; broadly rather than narrowly conceived; and counterfactual in form. Part V takes a brief look at the arguments of Dworkin and Gewirth regarding the "existence" of rights. It suggests that, although their arguments are quite sophisticated, the Enlightenment view of rights—which is not only problematic but paradoxical—is reiterated in their work as well.

Part VI revisits Bentham's and Marx's critiques of the Enlightenment notion of rights and their arguments that "a right to X" is not itself a thing that one can possess. The question is, "what is it that you *have*, exactly, when you have a 'right' to food, for example, but have no actual food?" If we hold to an idealist metaphysics, we would still consider that we have something of significance. If we hold to a materialist metaphysics, then the answer is "obviously nothing at all."

Finally, Part VII returns to the Nuremberg tribunals as a way of looking very concretely at the question of what has happened when "human rights" are invoked and looking also at the status of human rights as a "moral trump." Nuremberg is, after all, the first occasion on which the notion of human rights was treated as an actual law, on the basis of which trial and conviction took place. We are accustomed to thinking of the charges brought at Nuremberg as transcending political interests. We would generally think that if there are any "crimes against humanity" which would be universally recognized, they would be the acts of the Nazis in World War II. I review some of the many ways in which the trial served as a political project of the victors which explicitly rejected the rule of law at every turn, for the larger purpose of presenting a moral demonstration of the Nazis' absolute evil. We see this, for example, in the explicit exclusion of Allied war crimes; the fact that precisely the same parties served as legislators, prosecutors and judges; the tribunal's dubious claim to jurisdiction; and the tribunal's prohibition against raising the issue of jurisdiction in any forum. Because the denunciation of the Nazis in a sense consumed all the moral space, the victors could lay claim not only to relative goodness, but—implicitly and explicitly—absolute and universal goodness. The Nuremberg accusations, in the end, functioned not as an occasion for moral discourse, but as a moral diatribe which effectively excluded the possibility of moral discourse.

I suggest that we inherit these features in our current notion of human rights—both the implicit claim of absolute goodness and the suppression of moral discourse. This occurs insofar as a claim of human rights violations operates as a kind of "moral trump," alongside of which all other countervailing moral claims are dwarfed. Consequently, claims of human rights violations rhetorically work in a manner which is not unlike a holy war: as a claim of absolute righteousness which ironically can come to operate at the expense of simple decency. We can look at the asymmetry of the standard notion of human rights and see this easily. For example, someone who is homeless and begging on the streets, but has the right to hire a lawyer for $300 an hour or buy network television time, suffers no violation of his or her human rights. Or, for example, economic sanctions are sometimes imposed on a country in the name of the human rights of its citizens; despite the opposition of the citizens themselves and despite the fact that the sanctions cause direct hardship, hunger and sickness to the poorest and most fragile members of society.

Thus, I argue, the standard notion of human rights is in some degree actually dangerous in that it invokes ethical principles that it claims are not only universal, but absolute. At the same time, because it implicitly asserts the most extreme moral claim possible, it is not concerned merely with which acts are wrong, but rather with distinction between absolute righteousness and absolute evil. It can provide—and has on certain occasions provided—a justification for doing violence or inflicting suffering, if these take place on behalf of "human rights," much the way that claims of righteousness have justified the bloodiest acts of holy wars.

I conclude by suggesting alternative models for human rights which would address the problem of asymmetry and would offer an account of human rights which is more coherent philosophically and more consistent with our ethical intuitions. But my central concern in this essay is not simply to propose a more coherent model for the concept. Rather, I am deeply interested in examining the relation between the concept and the political interest; and in demonstrating that no purely abstract choice is possible, only a fundamentally interested one. I suggest that we might be well served by simply looking at the conceptual and rhetorical means used in international relations by which brutality is sometimes reconciled with claims of moral righteousness. I suggest that absolute ethical claims—of which the concept of human rights is an exemplar—are double-edged and that absolute righteousness is not possible in the face of political situations which are always and necessarily characterized by moral ambiguity.

I should mention that my interest in the concept of human rights derives from my experiences in 1991 and 1992, when I spent a good deal of time living and traveling in Guatemala, Nicaragua and Cuba. Although I had a strong academic background in both political philosophy and Latin America, I nevertheless found myself both deeply moved and deeply shaken. It was not so much that I learned new "facts"—I had always known, for example, that the infant mortality rate is a measure of development and that it is much higher in poor countries than wealthy countries. But I had never before been woken at 3:00 AM by a neighbor building a coffin for his baby who had died in the night for lack of $2 worth of medicine (which happened in Nicaragua). Nor had I ever been to a public garbage dump which contained an entire village made of garbage, as I saw in Guatemala City—an entire shanty town made of garbage, with women cutting their children's hair with broken scissors picked from the garbage, old men sitting on mounds of garbage and reading newspapers they had picked out of the heaps, and teenage boys playing soccer on a field of garbage with a torn soccer ball someone had thrown away.

I also got a bit of a sense of what it is like to live in a place marked by state terrorism, also in Guatemala, when a language teacher showed me the cigarette burns on his chest; and when I saw soldiers armed with Uzis and M-16s guarding not only the banks, but grocery stores, museums, bookstores and libraries; and when I visited an academic research institute surrounded by 12-foot-high cement walls, inset with broken glass, topped with barbed wire running horizontally and circled by razor wire.

As a result, at this point I have very strong views about what some people describe as "merely" economic harm. Likewise, I have very strong views about the nature and kinds of state violence and political intrusion, when it makes sense to equate them, and when it does not. It is because of my experiences and my views that I will now argue for a certain analysis of human rights, which I hope will stand up to the scrutiny of an academic community which does not necessarily share either my views or my memories.

I. The Standard Concept of Human Rights

The notion of human rights in general—as moral principles by which we can judge the legal acts of state—has its roots in the Greek notion that there is a transcendental standard of justice by which we measure the justness of particular laws and states.[15] This view is articulated in the distinction between universal law and particular laws; and the related distinction between natural or divine law (that which is inherently and absolutely just) and positive law (that which is articulated in the form of actual laws).

> Particular law is that which each community lays down and applies to its own members: this is partly written and partly unwritten. Universal law is the law of nature. For there really is, as every one to some extent divines, a natural justice and injustice that is binding on all men, even on those who have no association or covenant with each other.[16]

There are unwritten laws of justice which are not enforced, but exist permanently and without change.[17] Written laws change often; universal laws—"the law of nature"—do not. One may break a particular law and not act unjustly, if it is an unjust law which does not fulfill its true purpose, which is to do justice.[18] Aristotle refers to Sophocles' Antigone, who describes natural law as follows:

> Not of to-day or yesterday it is,
> But lives eternal: none can date its birth.[19]

The distinction between law (the acts of state) and justice (the ideal by which we judge the goodness of the state), or between particular laws and universal law, is the foundation of the notion of human rights. It is the basis for the moral claim by which we can justify passing judgment on a state's actions—given that the state is the source of law, the state by definition determines what is legal and what is not. The only moral justification by which those who are outside a state can pass judgment on the validity of its acts lies in the claim of a higher standard, or a universal law, or a conception of justice, against which the acts and laws of a particular state can be

---

15. *See, e.g.*, PLATO, REPUBLIC bk 1; Plato, *Gorgias*, *in* 1 PLATO, THE DIALOGUES OF PLATO 505 (Benjamin Jowett trans., 1937) (1892).

16. ARISTOTLE, RHETORIC bk 1, ch. 13 (W. Rhys Roberts trans., 1954).

17. *Id.*

18. *Id.*

19. *Id. See also* Sophocles *Antigone*, *in* I SOPHOCLES 187 (David Grene trans. & ed., 2d ed. 1991).

measured. Thus, "human rights" by definition are not concerned about ordinary crimes, which are offenses against the state. Rather, the conception of human rights necessarily concerns acts (or failures to act) of the state; and necessarily makes the claim that an act or policy which may be legal is nevertheless unjust. This moral claim in turn provides a standard by which to judge the acts of a sovereign government to be "criminal" in some sense and justifies the "punishment" of other states, as well as interference in their internal policies.

The concept of human rights which is currently the standard or dominant concept is one which has been articulated in approximately the same form in international law and diplomacy, by NGOs and in philosophical and theoretical literature. The dominant concept of human rights entails: (1) the right to be free from what are often called "atrocities," such as torture and genocide; and (2) political and civil rights, including elections and judicial process and freedom of thought, speech and press. The dominant concept of human rights does not include economic rights, such as the rights to food, shelter and employment.

If by "human rights" we refer to those elements which constitute the minimal conditions for human life, then we have a problem: not being tortured or killed is essential for human life, but running for political office is not. Thus, it is not clear that we can justify placing civil and political rights in the same category as the right not to be subject to atrocities. On the other hand, food and shelter *are* minimal conditions for life. So how did this dominant concept of human rights come to be formulated?

In the twentieth century, the Nuremberg trials at the end of World War II were perhaps the first significant attempt to articulate and enforce (or rather penalize violations of) principles of human rights.[20] At Nuremberg, from 1946 to 1949, the

20. There had, of course, been rules of war for many centuries. *See* discussion *infra* Part III. There had even been a thin attempt to try individuals for war crimes committed during World War I. The Hague Conventions of 1899 and 1907 articulated certain guidelines regarding "war crimes," including prohibitions on the use of poisonous gas, the sinking of hospital ships, etc. At the close of World War I, there was a pro forma attempt to bring the Kaiser to trial for initiating a war of aggression and there were a few isolated trials of German soldiers, who were acquitted or sentenced to short jail terms. *See* TELFORD TAYLOR, THE ANATOMY OF THE NUREMBERG TRIALS 12-20 (1992).

Nazis were prosecuted by the Allied tribunal for war crimes, crimes against peace and crimes against humanity. "War crimes" involved the violation of the rules of war, such as blanket bombing in civilian areas, gratuitous attacks on civilian populations of other nations and mistreatment of prisoners of war.[21] "Crimes against peace" consisted of waging a war of aggression, or waging war in violation of treaties.[22] Germany's "crime against peace" was its military aggression against sovereign nations. For both "crimes against peace" and "war crimes" there was some precedent, albeit tenuous, for the notion that a tribunal could legitimately claim jurisdiction over claims brought for these two types of crimes since they involved the violation of explicit conventions and treaties.[23] However, the extermination of German Jews, gypsies, communists and other groups constituted neither a war crime nor a crime against peace. It was only under the third category, "crimes against humanity," that a cognizable claim could be made against a state for violence done to its own citizens by its officials in accordance with its own laws. "Crimes against humanity" included genocide, enslavement, torture and racial or religious persecution.[24]

---

21. "War Crimes" were defined by the International Military Tribunal as

> violations of the laws or customs of war. Such violations shall include, but not be limited to, murder, ill-treatment or deportation to slave labor or for any other purpose of civilian population of or in occupied territory, murder or ill-treatment of prisoners of war or persons on the seas, killing of hostages, plunder of public or private property, wanton destruction of cities, towns, or villages, or devastation not justified by military necessity.

Charter of the International Military Tribunal, Aug. 8, 1945, art. 6(b), 59 Stat. 1546, 1547, 82 U.N.T.S. 284, 288 [hereinafter Nuremberg Charter], *reprinted in* 1 SECRETARIAT OF THE TRIBUNAL, INTERNATIONAL MILITARY TRIBUNAL, TRIAL OF THE MAJOR WAR CRIMINALS BEFORE THE INTERNATIONAL MILITARY TRIBUNAL 11 (1947) [hereinafter OFFICIAL DOCUMENTS OF THE TRIBUNAL].

22. "Crimes Against Peace" were defined as "planning, preparation, initiation or waging of a war of aggression, or a war in violation of international treaties, agreements or assurances, or participation in a Common Plan or Conspiracy for the accomplishment of any of the foregoing." *Id.* art. 6(a).

23. *See* TAYLOR, *supra* note 20, at 12-20.

24. "Crimes Against Humanity" were defined as:

> murder, extermination, enslavement, deportation and other inhumane acts committed against any civilian population, before or during the war; or persecutions on political, racial, or religious grounds in execution of or in connection with any crime within the jurisdiction of the Tribunal, whether or not in violation of domestic law of the country where perpetrated.

Nuremberg Charter, *supra* note 21, art. 6(c), 59 Stat. at 1547, 82 U.N.T.S. at 288.

Shortly after the Allied tribunal tried Nazi leaders on charges of crimes against humanity, the notion of human rights was incorporated in the charter of the newly-formed United Nations (UN). The UN Charter, which entered into force in 1945, provided that all signatory governments would promote "universal respect for, and observance of, human rights and fundamental freedoms."[25] The Universal Declaration, adopted in 1948,[26] enumerated these rights, giving them far broader meaning than the standards employed at Nuremberg. Insofar as the Nuremberg notion of "crimes against humanity" contains a conception of human rights, it is a minimalist one: it primarily describes those acts which are inconsistent with the minimum conditions for human life. By contrast, the Universal Declaration is extremely broad. It provides that "[e]veryone has the right to life, liberty, and security of person;"[27] that "[n]o one shall be held in slavery;"[28] that "[a]ll are equal before the law;"[29] that "[n]o one shall be subjected to torture or to cruel, inhuman or degrading treatment or punishment."[30] It states that "[e]veryone is entitled . . . to a fair and public hearing by an independent and impartial tribunal in the determination of his rights and obligations and of any criminal charge against him;"[31] that everyone has the "right to own property;"[32] that everyone has the "right to a nationality;"[33] and that men and women have the "right to marry and to found a family."[34] It provides that everyone has the right to work;[35] that everyone has the right "to free choice of employment,"[36] and to "just and favourable conditions of work;"[37] and that everyone has the right to "freedom of opin-

---

25. U.N. CHARTER art. 55(c).
26. *See* Universal Declaration, *supra* note 14.
27. *Id.* art. 3, at 72.
28. *Id.* art. 4, at 73.
29. *Id.* art. 7, at 73.
30. *Id.* art. 5, at 73.
31. *Id.* art. 10, at 73.
32. *Id.* art. 17(1), at 74.
33. *Id.* art. 15(1), at 74.
34. *Id.* art. 16(1), at 74.
35. *See id.* art. 23, at 75.
36. *Id.*
37. *Id.*

ion and expression,"[38] "freedom of thought,"[39] freedom of "conscience,"[40] and freedom of "religion."[41] Finally, it guarantees that everyone has the "right to a standard of living adequate for the health and well-being of himself and of his family, including food, clothing, housing and medical care;"[42] that everyone has the "right to rest and leisure, including reasonable limitation of working hours and periodic holidays with pay;"[43] that everyone has the right to education;[44] that everyone has the right to free elementary education[45] and to higher education accessible to all on the basis of merit;[46] and that everyone has the right "to enjoy the arts and to share in scientific advancement."[47]

The concept of human rights contained in the Universal Declaration stands in marked contrast to the notion of human rights contained in the Nuremberg notion of "crimes against humanity." The notion of "crimes against humanity" was very limited, in that it addressed one's right not to be subject to behavior which was in some sense beyond the pale of civilization. The concept of human rights in the Universal Declaration is not a minimal standard of civilized decency, but rather an extremely robust conception of the good. It seeks to identify every dimension of human life and every type of human need which must be met for an individual to have a rich and fulfilling life—socially, politically, economically and culturally.

The Universal Declaration does not contain an enforcement mechanism, or any specific binding obligations on the signatory governments. According to the Preamble, the Universal Declaration is "a common standard of achievement," which every individual and every organ of society shall "keep[] . . . constantly in mind."[48] Nations shall strive to achieve this standard, according to the Preamble, by "teaching and educa-

38. *Id.* art. 19, at 74.
39. *Id.* art. 18, at 74.
40. *Id.*
41. *Id.*
42. *Id.* art. 25(1), at 76.
43. *Id.* art. 24, at 75.
44. *See id.* art. 26(1), at 76.
45. *See id.*
46. *See id.*
47. *Id.* art. 27, at 76.
48. *Id.* preamble.

tion" to promote respect for these rights and freedoms and by "progressive measures" to secure their recognition.[49]

In the late 1940s and in the 1950s, other treaties were generated which specifically concerned matters such as torture and genocide.[50] In the 1960s, the UN set about producing legally binding documents and enforcement mechanisms addressing the rights enumerated in the Universal Declaration.[51] The elements of the Universal Declaration were reformulated in two separate covenants: the International Covenant on Economic, Social and Cultural Rights (ICESCR)[52] and the International Covenant on Civil and Political Rights (ICCPR).[53]

---

49. *Id.*

50. Other major human rights documents include the following: Convention on the Prevention and Punishment of the Crime of Genocide, *adopted* Dec. 9, 1948, 78 U.N.T.S. 277; International Convention on the Elimination of All Forms of Racial Discrimination, *opened for signature* Mar. 7, 1966, 660 U.N.T.S. 195; International Convention on the Suppression and Punishment of the Crime of Apartheid, *adopted* Nov. 30, 1973, 1015 U.N.T.S. 245; Convention on the Elimination of All Forms of Discrimination against Women, *opened for signature* Mar. 1, 1980, 1249 U.N.T.S. 13; Convention Against Torture and Other Cruel, Inhuman or Degrading Treatment or Punishment, *opened for signature* Feb. 4, 1985, S. TREATY DOC. NO. 100-20 (1988), 23 I.L.M. 1027. However, what is known as "the International Bill of Human Rights" consists of the Universal Declaration, *supra* note 14; International Covenant on Civil and Political Rights, *adopted* Dec. 19, 1966, SEN. EXEC. DOC. E, 95-2, at 23 (1978), 999 U.N.T.S. 171 [hereinafter ICCPR]; International Covenant on Economic, Social and Cultural Rights, *adopted* Dec. 16, 1966, 993 U.N.T.S. 3 [hereinafter ICESCR]; Optional Protocol to the International Covenant on Civil and Political Rights, *adopted* Dec. 16, 1966, 999 U.N.T.S. 302 [hereinafter Optional Protocol]; Second Optional Protocol to the International Covenant on Civil and Political Rights Aiming at the Abolition of the Death Penalty, *adopted* Dec. 15, 1989, G.A. Res. 44/128, U.N. GAOR Supp. No. 49 at 206, U.N. Doc A/44/824 (1989).

51. For a discussion of the formulation of these covenants see Asbjorn Eide, *Strategies for the Realization of the Right to Food*, *in* HUMAN RIGHTS IN THE TWENTY-FIRST CENTURY, *supra* note 3, at 460.

52. ICESCR, *supra* note 50.

53. ICCPR, *supra* note 50. Note that the European analogue has the same structure. The European System for the Protection of Human Rights, established by the Council of Europe, is based upon two treaties: the European Convention for the Protection of Human Rights and Fundamental Freedoms and the European Social Charter. *See* European Convention for the Protection of Human Rights and Fundamental Freedoms, Nov. 4, 1950, 213 U.N.T.S. 221 [hereinafter European Convention on Human Rights] (including the right to life, the right not to be subjected to torture, freedom of thought and expression and political and judicial rights); European Social Charter, Oct. 18, 1961, 529 U.N.T.S. 89 (including the right to work, the right to medical care, the right to safe and healthy working conditions and the right to social welfare). Thus, the European human rights system has the same bifurcated structure as the two United Nations (UN) covenants.

The mechanisms of enforcement for the European system likewise reiterate

The ICCPR basically concerns two types of rights: those pertaining to the physical integrity of the person, such as execution, torture and enslavement, and those pertaining to legal proceedings, to the legal status of persons and to "intellectual" rights, such as the right to hold and communicate one's ideas and beliefs.[54] The first category is concrete and substantive:

---

the same priorities as those contained in the UN covenants. Article 19 of the European Convention on Human Rights provides for enforcement by two institutions, the European Commission of Human Rights and the European Court of Human Rights. *See* European Convention on Human Rights, *supra*, art. 19. Under Article 25, complaints of human rights violations under the Convention can be brought by either individuals (where the state party recognizes the right of private petition) or other states. *See id.* art. 25. Under Article 54, the Committee of Ministers is then charged with enforcing the judgments of the European Court of Human Rights. *See id.* art. 54.

The European Social Charter, on the other hand, establishes a set of aspirations rather than explicit obligations. Part I of the Charter provides that the state parties "accept as the aim of their policy, to be pursued by appropriate means . . . the attainment of conditions in which [these] rights and principles may be effectively realised." European Social Charter, *supra*, preamble, 529 U.N.T.S. at 92. The Charter has no mechanisms of enforcement analogous to those contained in the Convention. The Charter only provides for a reporting system to monitor the parties' progress toward these goals. The reports are reviewed by a set of committees, which pass on their views to the Committee of Ministers, which in turn may make "recommendations" to the parties. *See id.* arts. 25-27, 29, 529 U.N.T.S. at 116, 118.

54. The ICCPR provides, among other things, that the states which are parties "undertake to ensure" the equal rights of men and women to the enjoyment of all civil and political rights set forth in the ICCPR. ICCPR, *supra* note 50, art. 3, 999 U.N.T.S. at 174. The ICCPR provides that "[e]very human being has the inherent right to life. This right shall be protected by law. No one shall be arbitrarily deprived of his life." *Id.* art. 6(1), 999 U.N.T.S. at 174. The ICCPR provides that the death penalty may be imposed only for the most serious crimes and only pursuant to a final judgment rendered by a competent court. *See id.* art. 6(2), 999 U.N.T.S. at 174. The ICCPR provides that no one shall be subjected to torture, or to cruel, inhuman, or degrading treatment or punishment. *See id.* art. 7, 999 U.N.T.S. at 175. The ICCPR provides that no one shall be held in slavery or in servitude and that "[e]veryone has the right to liberty and security of person. No one shall be subjected to arbitrary arrest or detention. No one shall be deprived of his liberty except on such grounds and in accordance with such procedures as are established by law." *Id.* arts. 8-9, 999 U.N.T.S. at 175.

The ICCPR further provides that anyone who is arrested shall be informed at the time of arrest of the reasons for his arrest and that anyone arrested or detained on a criminal charge shall be brought promptly before a judge. *See id.* The ICCPR provides that all persons shall be equal before the courts; and that all persons shall be entitled to be tried without undue delay. It provides that every person has the right to defend himself in person or through legal assistance; and to have legal assistance assigned to him without payment by him, when justice requires. *See id.* art. 14, 999 U.N.T.S. at 176-77. The ICCPR provides that everyone shall have the right to freedom of thought, conscience and religion; and to

when these rights are violated, individuals suffer concrete, physical harm; and there are no formal procedures which can legitimatize these acts. The second category is quite different. For those rights concerned with the form of judicial and political proceedings, as long as there is due process and free elections, the outcome by definition cannot constitute a violation of one's rights. Those rights concerning speech, press and religious expression involve abstract entities—ideas, beliefs, information and the exchange or dissemination of these.

There is also an Optional Protocol to the ICCPR (Optional Protocol), adopted at the same time as the two covenants,[55] which concerns enforcement. Under the Optional Protocol, individuals claiming a violation of rights under the ICCPR, who have exhausted all available domestic remedies, may submit a statement to the Human Rights Committee.[56] Under the Optional Protocol, the Human Rights Committee shall then bring such claims to the attention of the state party alleged to be violating the covenant and the state party must within six

---

manifest his religion and belief in practice and teaching. *See id.* art. 18, 999 U.N.T.S. at 178. The ICCPR provides that everyone shall have the right to hold opinions without interference; and that everyone shall have the right to freedom of expression. *See id.* art. 19, 999 U.N.T.S. at 178. It provides that the freedom of expression shall include "freedom to seek, receive and impart information . . . , either orally, in writing or in print, in the form of art, or through any other media of his choice." *Id.* The ICCPR provides that every citizen shall have the right to take part in the conduct of public affairs and to vote and to be elected at elections. *See id.* art. 25, 999 U.N.T.S. at 179. It provides that these elections shall be based on universal and equal suffrage; and shall be held by secret ballot, "guaranteeing the free expression of the will of the electors." *Id.* The ICCPR provides that all persons are entitled to the equal protection of the law, without discrimination; and that "the law shall prohibit any discrimination and guarantee to all persons equal and effective protection against discrimination on any ground such as race, colour, sex, language, religion, political or other opinion, national or social origin, property, birth or other status." *Id.* art. 26, 999 U.N.T.S. at 179.

Part IV of the ICCPR provides for the establishment of a Human Rights Committee, whose members are nominated and elected by the state parties. *See id.* arts. 28-30, 999 U.N.T.S. at 179-80. A state party may recognize the competence of the Human Rights Committee to hear claims of violations and may then present a claim that another state party is not fulfilling its obligations under the ICCPR. *See id.* art. 41, 999 U.N.T.S. at 182. The Human Rights Committee is then empowered to investigate and issue findings as to the claims made, if the matter cannot be amicably resolved to the satisfaction of the parties concerned. *See id.* arts. 41, 42, 999 U.N.T.S. at 182-83. The ICCPR states that the Secretary-General of the UN shall provide the necessary staff and facilities for the Committee to perform these functions. *See id.* art. 36, 999 U.N.T.S. at 181.

55. *See* Optional Protocol, *supra* note 50.

56. *See id.* art. 2, 999 U.N.T.S. at 302.

months provide a written explanation or statement regarding the remedial action taken by that state.[57]

The ICESCR, by contrast, addresses issues of food, shelter, employment, health care and education.[58] The degree of the obligation varies to some extent with the different rights. For example, the parties pledge to "undertake to ensure" the right to form and participate in trade unions;[59] whereas they merely "recognize that . . . [t]he widest possible protection and assistance should be accorded to the family."[60] Unlike the ICCPR, the ICESCR contains no mechanism to receive and investigate claimed violations, originating either from states or from individuals. The only form of enforcement consists of the agreement of the state parties to submit reports "on the measures which they have adopted and the progress made in achieving the observance of the rights recognized" by the covenant.[61] Unlike the ICCPR, the terms of the ICESCR contain

57. *See id.* art. 4, 999 U.N.T.S. at 303.

58. The ICESCR provides that the signatory states recognize the right to work, including the right of everyone to engage in work which he freely chooses or accepts and that the parties "will take appropriate steps to safeguard this right." ICESCR, *supra* note 50, art. 6(1), 993 U.N.T.S. at 6. The ICESCR provides that the parties "recognize the right of everyone" to fair wages, a decent living for themselves and their families, safe and healthy working conditions, rest, leisure and periodic holidays with pay. *Id.* art. 7, 993 U.N.T.S. at 6. The ICESCR provides that the parties "undertake to ensure" the right of everyone to form and join trade unions and the right to strike, in conformity with the laws of the state. *Id.* art. 8, 993 U.N.T.S. at 6. The ICESCR provides that the parties recognize the right of families to assistance for the care and education of children and paid maternity leave. *Id.* art. 10, 993 U.N.T.S. at 7. The ICESCR provides that the parties recognize the right of everyone to adequate food, clothing and housing and to the continuous improvement of living conditions. *Id.* art. 11, 993 U.N.T.S. at 7. Under the ICESCR, the parties "shall take . . . measures . . . which are needed" to improve methods of food production and distribution, including agrarian reform; and "to ensure an equitable distribution of world food supplies in relation to need." *Id.* The ICESCR provides that the states which are parties shall take those steps necessary for the reduction of infant mortality, improvement of the environment and creation of conditions which would assure medical service to all in the event of sickness. *Id.* art. 12, 993 U.N.T.S. at 8. The parties to the ICESCR "recognize the right of everyone" to take part in cultural life, to enjoy the benefits of scientific progress and to the protection of any benefits to be derived from their literary, scientific, or artistic production. *Id.* art. 15, 993 U.N.T.S. at 9.

59. *Id.* art. 8(1), 993 U.N.T.S. at 6.

60. *Id.* art. 10(1), 993 U.N.T.S. at 7.

61. *Id.* arts. 16(1), 17(1), 993 U.N.T.S. at 9. Parties may indicate in these reports the factors and difficulties affecting the fulfillment of the obligations of the covenant. *See id.* art. 17(2), 993 U.N.T.S. at 9. These reports are to be submitted to the Secretary-General of the UN, who then transmits them to the Economic

no agreement to immediately implement the rights identified in the covenant, but rather to work toward their "progressive implementation."[62]

Thus, the contents of the Universal Declaration were reformulated in 1966 in the form of two instruments, one concerned with overt state violence, civil and political rights, and rights of belief and expression; the other concerned with social, economic and cultural rights. The ICCPR contains a procedure for addressing complaints of violations, while the ICESCR has no comparable procedure. The ICCPR provides that the parties shall conform fully to its provisions immediately; the ICESCR provides that parties shall take steps to achieve these rights "to the maximum of its available resources, with a view to achieving *progressively* the full realization" of social and economic rights.[63] Thus, there is a significant difference between the two covenants as to the expectations of compliance and the mechanisms for enforcement. The ICCPR "has teeth" in ways that the ICESCR does not. The ICCPR has explicit requirements, explicit prohibitions and a procedure for responding to acts of a state party that violate these requirements and prohibitions. The ICESCR, on the other hand, may be immediately binding, but what is binding is an aspirational standard: the ICESCR provides an ideal goal which the parties must work toward, but not necessarily achieve. How hard they work toward this goal is a matter they determine for themselves, in accordance with their resources and their national priorities. Thus, under the ICESCR there is no standard, even in principle, by which another nation or outside organization can judge the validity of a nation's economic priorities. In short, under the ICCPR it is both possible and expected that parties shall comply; while the ICESCR anticipates that state parties will de facto determine for themselves what constitutes compliance and that noncompliance will not be challenged or penalized.[64]

---

and Social Council. The Economic and Social Council in turn may respond with comments or recommendations. *See id.* arts. 16-22, 993 U.N.T.S. at 9-10. The Economic and Social Council may transmit these reports to the Commission on Human Rights "for study and general recommendations" or "for information." *Id.* art. 19, 993 U.N.T.S. at 10.

62. *Id.* art. 22, 993 U.N.T.S. at 5.

63. *Id.* art. 2(1), 993 U.N.T.S. at 5 (emphasis added).

64. However, as Jack Donnelly notes, both sets of rights are essential and interrelated. Donnelly notes that "[a] long string of resolutions proclaim this [that

Why were the provisions of the Universal Declaration reformulated in this manner? Why is there such a dramatic difference between the enforcement provisions of the two covenants?

At the time the covenants were being drafted, several arguments were put forth justifying the disparity. First, it was maintained that political rights could be implemented immediately, while economic rights could be implemented only gradually. The argument was made that respecting political rights requires no substantial state expenditures, whereas meeting the economic needs of a population requires substantial economic outlays.[65] However, this argument is not persuasive. There are substantial costs involved in operating a judiciary system that protects the due process rights of defendants, particularly since under such a system they may be entitled to have counsel provided by the state. At the same time, there are social and economic rights the implementation of which does not require that the state provide subsidies out of pocket. This would include minimum wage standards, parental leave requirements, the right to form trade unions, child labor laws, agrarian reform, environmental protection and anti-trust regu-

---

is, that all human rights are interdependent and indivisible], most notably UN General Assembly [R]esolution 32/130, as well as an agenda item at the 41st General Assembly." JACK DONNELLY, UNIVERSAL HUMAN RIGHTS IN THEORY AND PRACTICE 28, n.1 (1989). Many commentators have held that the two sets of rights are both necessary—or are interdependent, or complementary—without resolving the conflicts that arise, or the relative priority that should be given particular rights or sets of rights. *See, e.g.*, HENKIN, *supra* note 1; Steiner, *supra* note 12, at 928; *see also generally* Melanie Beth Oliviero, *Human Needs and Human Rights: Which are More Fundamental?*, 40 EMORY L.J. 911, 915-16 (1991); Connie de la Vega, *Protecting Economic, Social and Cultural Rights*, 15 WHITTIER L. REV. 471, 471-72 (1994).

65. *See* Asbjorn Eide, *Strategies for the Realization of the Right to Food*, *in* HUMAN RIGHTS IN THE TWENTY-FIRST CENTURY, *supra* note 3, at 460.

For example, Hugo Bedau makes this argument in his discussion of Section 502B of the Foreign Assistance Act of 1961, 22 U.S.C. § 2304 (1994), which makes foreign assistance conditional upon the recipient country's human rights practices:

> A government may in fact be unable to do anything about the starvation of a good portion of its population; but a government is never unable to prohibit (and to that extent, end) the practice of torturing suspects . . . . The government's responsibility to undertake to feed its own people remains less central than its responsibility not to torture.

Hugo Adam Bedau, *Human Rights and Foreign Assistance Programs*, *in* HUMAN RIGHTS AND U.S. FOREIGN POLICY 37 (Peter G. Brown & Douglas MacLean eds., 1979).

lation.[66]

It was also argued that because civil and political rights only entail that the state abstain from action, it is reasonable to expect complete and immediate compliance; while such an expectation would not be reasonable regarding social and economic rights, which require the state to affirmatively undertake certain actions.[67] However, under the Nuremberg principles, state officials can be guilty of human rights violations for their acquiescence or failures to act.[68] A state which consents or acquiesces to acts of genocide or torture by paramilitary death squads, for example, may be deemed to be in violation of human rights for its failure to intervene. Thus, the human right of freedom from torture in fact requires not only that the state abstain from torturing individuals, but that it act affirmatively to prohibit and prevent non-state actors from engaging in these practices. Civil and political rights are neither self-generating nor free of costs; they "need legislation, promotion and protection and this requires resources."[69]

---

66. One scholar, Jeremy Waldron, notes that civil and political rights entail positive duties to act, as well as duties of omission. Waldron further points out that these duties stem from economic rights as well:

> The right not to be tortured generates a duty not to torture people, but it also generates a duty to investigate complaints of torture, a duty to pay one's share for the political and administrative setups that might be necessary to prevent torture and so on. As far as second-generation rights are concerned, they too may be correlated with duties that are positive or negative, depending on the context. If people are actually starving, their rights make a call on our active assistance, but if they are living satisfactorily in a traditional subsistence economy, the right may require we simply refrain from any action that could disturb that state of affairs. We talk sometimes as though it only happens by misfortune that people are starving and that the only issue rights raise in the matter is whether we should put ourselves out and come to their aid. But people often starve as a result of what we do as well as what we don't do.

WALDRON, *supra* note 7, at 25. Also relevant is Aart Hendriks discussion of negative and positive rights and the distinction between "obligation of conduct" and "obligation of result." Hendriks, *supra* note 12, at 1132-33 (1995). The distinction between positive and negative rights has been applied in numerous areas. *See, e.g.*, Dorothy Q. Thomas & Michele E. Beasley, *Domestic Violence as a Human Rights Issue*, 58 ALB. L. REV. 1119, 1143 (1995) (applying the negative and positive rights distinction to issues concerning domestic violence).

67. *See* discussion *infra* Part VII.

68. *See* discussion *infra* Part VII.

69. Dilys M. Hill, *Human Rights and Foreign Policy: Theoretical Foundations*, *in* HUMAN RIGHTS AND FOREIGN POLICY 6 (Dilys M. Hill ed., 1989). As one commentator points out:

The bifurcation of the rights articulated in the Universal Declaration was also justified by a pragmatic argument: that a covenant of civil and political rights, which only requires abstention from certain acts rather than the affirmative implementation of policies, would be more easily ratified than a document which required affirmative commitment of resources from state parties.[70] However, this has not proven to be the case.[71] As of January 1998, there were 137 parties to the

---

> [I]t was widely believed that compliance with civil and political rights was cost-free, whereas the realization of social rights posed an economic burden on the State. This argument also turned out to be unfounded. The organization of presidential or parliamentary elections, for example, may in fact be extremely expensive, while there are many preventive health measures that can be implemented at low or no cost.

Hendriks, *supra* note 12, at 1133.

70. These arguments continue to be made by commentators in the field of human rights. Marc Bossuyt, for instance, writes that:

> Civil rights require from the State essentially—but not exclusively—an abstention. Consequently, they must be observed immediately, totally and universally. On the contrary, social rights require an active intervention from the State. As a result, they may be implemented progressively, partially and selectively. It is precisely because observance of civil rights merely requires abstention that States have no excuse for not respecting human rights of everyone within its jurisdiction. On the other hand, because the implementation of social rights requires an active intervention by the State to the extent of its available resources—a State can be allowed to set priorities in the realization of social rights.

Marc Bossuyt, *International Human Rights Systems: Strengths and Weaknesses*, *in* HUMAN RIGHTS IN THE TWENTY-FIRST CENTURY, *supra* note 3, at 52. Bossuyt contends that this distinction—between a requisite state abstention necessary to secure civil rights and the need for active state intervention to implement social rights—is reflected in the allocation of responsibilities for rights among the judiciary on the one hand and the administrative and political departments on the other. As Bossuyt writes:

> This is also the reason why the control of the observance of civil rights can be entrusted to judicial bodies, while the control of the implementation of social rights is left to administrative or political bodies. Indeed, in spite of the often very general and vague formulations of civil rights, a judge—national or international—is able to decide whether or not civil rights have been observed in a specific case . . . . On the other hand, without further elaboration by national or regional legislation, no judge is in a position to rule whether in a specific case a State has fulfilled its obligations in the field of social rights, because—depending on the available resources—it is up to each State to decide which social rights should be implemented first and which citizens should be first entitled to the benefits of those rights.

Id.

71. According to one commentator, Asbjorn Eide:

> Following the adoption of the Universal Declaration in 1948, the United Nations set about adopting legally binding instruments, and decided in

ICESCR and 140 parties to the ICCPR.[72]

International banking institutions, such as the World Bank and the European Bank for Reconstruction and Development, adopt the same distinction.[73] The most prominent human rights NGOs structure their institutional priorities in the same way.[74] Amnesty International's mandate is to "contrib-

---

> the process to make a distinction between two sets of rights: the civil and political which were incorporated into [I]CCPR, and the economic, social and cultural rights which were incorporated into [I]CESCR . . . .
>
> Two major reasons were used in favour of their separation. One was the claim that the two sets of rights needed different kinds of implementation approaches at the national level. It has frequently been argued that the civil and political rights can be implemented immediately and without cost, whereas the economic and social rights can be implemented only gradually, and with cost . . . .
>
> The second claim, relating more to political considerations, was that many States might be willing to ratify the [I]CCPR but not the [I]CESCR. By separating them into two documents, States which had problems in implementing economic and social rights could nevertheless undertake binding obligations in regard to civil and political rights by ratifying the [I]CCPR. Empirical reality has shown this to be wrong. In practically all cases, States have ratified both Covenants. In those very few cases where States have ratified only one covenant, it has been the [I]CESCR, not the [I]CCPR. As of March 1990, there is no case in which a state has ratified the [I]CCPR but not the [I]CESCR.
>
> The only candidate likely to ratify the [I]CCPR but not the [I]CESCR would be the United States, which stands out as a very special case.

Eide, *supra* note 65, at 460-61 (referring to the AVOR and the ICESCR).

Indeed, as of 1997, only one country, the United States, has ratified only the VER. The United States did not ratify the CR until 1992 and has not yet ratified the ICESCR. *See* United Nations High Commissioner for Human Rights Website (visited Jan. 19, 1998) <http://www.unhchr.ch>.

72. *See* United Nations Treaty Collection (visited Jan. 19, 1998) <<http://www.un.org/depts/treaty>>.

73. *See* John Linarelli *The European Bank for Reconstruction and Development and the Post-Cold War Era*, 16 U. PA. J. INT'L BUS. L. 373, 400 (1995) (discussing the notion of "rights" and "the taxonomy of human rights" employed in international banking institutions).

74. *See* Makau wa Mutua, *The Politics of Human Rights: Beyond the Abolitionist Paradigm in Africa*, 17 MICH. J. INT'L L. 591, 605 (1996) (review of CLAUDE E. WELCH, PROTECTING HUMAN RIGHTS IN AFRICA: STRATEGIES AND ROLES OF NON-GOVERNMENTAL ORGANIZATIONS (1995)). Mutua discusses the civil liberties origins of the international non-governmental organizations (INGOs), as opposed to the domestic non-governmental organizations (NGOs) in Third World countries whose primary commitment is often economic rights or self-determination rather than civil rights.

> INGOs are based almost exclusively in the West even though the bulk of their work is directed at the South . . . INGOs are the ideological offspring of Western domestic NGOs such as the ACLU and the . . .

ute to the observance throughout the world of human rights as set out in the Universal Declaration of Human Rights," by seeking the release of those who are imprisoned because of their beliefs or because of their race, ethnicity, or gender; by opposing the detention of prisoners of conscience or political prisoners whose trial did not conform to certain norms for judicial procedure; and by opposing the death penalty, torture and other cruel and degrading punishments.[75] Thus, despite

---

> NAACP Legal Defense and Education fund . . . . Although the NAACP has also focused on questions of social and economic justice, both organizations rest their moral authority on a narrow range of civil and political rights. None challenge or question the fundamental character of economic and social structures and their underling philosophies and assumptions; they seek fair and equal treatment within the framework of the American liberal market economic arrangements. Leading INGOs, such as HRW, Amnesty International and ICJ promote similar ideals abroad.

Id. (citations omitted). Mutua notes that the individuals connected to the ACLU, including a former executive director, were prominent in the formation of American and British INGOs, including Human Rights Watch, International League for Human Rights and Amnesty International. *Id.* at 606. Furthermore, the Western-based INGOs have considerably more access to resources and public recognition than the domestic human rights NGOs in Third World countries. "INGOs," Mutua observes,

> derive financial, social, and moral support from [Western] philanthropists, foundations, and citizens; they enjoy access to "world" political centers, such as New York, London, Washington, Paris, and Geneva; they utilize the resources and ability of United Nations and regional human rights systems; they have access to the all-powerful Western media; and they have access to and, quite often, cooperation from the arms of government concerned with foreign affairs. In contrast, even the most visible human rights NGOs in the South operate at the bare margins of these structures.

Id. at 606. *See also* HENRY J. STEINER, DIVERSE PARTNERS: NON-GOVERNMENTAL ORGANIZATIONS IN THE HUMAN RIGHTS MOVEMENT 19 (1991) (observing that the term "First World NGOs" are "those committed to traditional Western liberal values associated with the origins of the human rights movement.").

75. Article 1 of the Statute of Amnesty International provides that the organization "adopts as its mandate:"

> To promote awareness of and adherence to the Universal Declaration of Human Rights and other internationally recognized human rights instruments, the values enshrined in them, and the indivisibility and interdependence of all human rights and freedoms;
>
> To oppose grave violations of the rights of every person freely to hold and to express his or her convictions and to be free from discrimination by reason of ethnic origin, sex, colour or language, and of the right of every person to physical and mental integrity, and, in particular, to oppose by all appropriate means irrespective of political considerations:
>
> a) the imprisonment, detention or other physical restrictions im-

Amnesty International's claimed commitment to "the observance of the provisions of the Universal Declaration of Human Rights," in fact its substantive commitment is to some of those provisions: those relating to the physical integrity of individuals (such as torture and execution); those relating to civil and political rights (such as judicial process, elections and freedom of belief and expression). While Amnesty International does not explicitly reject the notion of economic rights,[76] it does not identify, investigate, or address in any manner those actions or failures to act which would constitute violations of economic rights.

Amnesty International does not "take a stand on the legitimacy of military, economic, and cultural relations maintained with countries where human rights are violated, or on punitive measures such as sanctions or boycotts." Nor does it "address

---

> posed on any person by reason of his or her political, religious or other conscientiously held beliefs or by reason of his or her ethnic origin, sex, colour or language, provided that he or she has not used or advocated violence (hereinafter referred to as "prisoners of conscience"); Amnesty International shall work towards the release of and shall provide assistance to prisoners of conscience;
>
> b) the detention of any political prisoner without fair trial within a reasonable time or any trial procedures relating to such prisoners that do not conform to internationally recognized norms;
>
> c) the death penalty, and the torture or other cruel, inhuman or degrading treatment or punishment of prisoners or other detained or restricted persons, whether or not the persons affected have used or advocated violence;

Statute of Amnesty International, art. 1, *in* AMNESTY INTERNATIONAL REPORT 1995 327 (1995).

76. Thomas Hammarberg, a chairman of the International Executive Committee of Amnesty International, noted that Amnesty International is deeply committed to political prisoners and it is also

> deeply involved in combatting torture and the death penalty, and in working for fair trials and improved prison conditions. This focus certainly does not mean that Amnesty International downgrades other basic rights, such as the social and economic ones. These are often related to the political and civil rights. Neither would Amnesty International attempt to create a conflict between civil and political rights on the one hand and socio-economic rights on the other. That approach would be false. The *Universal Declaration* is quite clear in stating that both are needed. Often they complement one another: when those deprived of their socio-economic rights cannot make their voices heard, they are even less likely to have their needs met.

Thomas Hammarberg, *Preface to Chapter 5, Non-Governmental Organisations, in* 3 JAMES AVERY JOYCE, HUMAN RIGHTS: INTERNATIONAL DOCUMENTS 1559-60 (1978).

itself to the general economic or political system in any country, only to that country's observance of human rights within Amnesty International's mandate."[77]

Human Rights Watch and its offshoots[78] likewise have a mandate which addresses state violations of the physical integrity of individuals (torture, kidnapping and execution) and political and civil rights (judicial process, free elections, freedom of belief and expression). Human Rights Watch "defends freedom of thought and expression, due process of law and equal protection of the law; it documents and denounces murders, disappearances, torture, arbitrary imprisonment, exile, censorship and other abuses of internationally recognized human rights."[79]

The same two-tier notion of human rights has also been adopted by various individual governments, perhaps in its most extreme form by the United States. The United States has followed a curious path in its espousal of human rights principles. On one hand, Franklin Delano Roosevelt's "Four Freedoms" included "freedom from want" as well as political freedom.[80] The United States then had a leading role in both the Nuremberg tribunals[81] and the drafting of the Universal Declaration.[82] Since the Carter Administration, it has been commonplace to hear references to human rights in foreign policy discussions in the United States.[83] Since the end of the

---

77. THE AMNESTY INTERNATIONAL HANDBOOK 129 (Marie Staunton et al. eds., 1991).

78. Human Rights Watch began with the founding of Helsinki Watch in 1978 and now includes Africa Watch, Americas Watch, Asia Watch, Middle East Watch and other human rights projects. *See* HUMAN RIGHTS WATCH, THE LOST AGENDA: HUMAN RIGHTS AND UN FIELD OPERATIONS i (1993).

79. *Id.*

80. *See* Frank C. Newman, *United Nations Human Rights Covenants and the United States Government: Diluted Promises, Foreseeable Futures*, 42 DEPAUL L. REV. 1241, 1242 n.7 (1993).

81. *See* discussion *infra* Part VII.

82. *See* HENKIN, *supra* note 1, at 68 (discussing the U.S. role in the postwar formulation of international legal instruments and treaties).

83. Although the Carter Administration is most widely recognized for making human rights a centerpiece of foreign policy, human rights have at least formally been a foreign policy priority since the early 1960s. The U.S. concern with human rights was reflected in the passage of the Foreign Assistance Act of 1961, Pub. L. No. 87-195, 75 Stat. 424 (1961) (codified as amended in scattered sections of 7, 16, 22 and 42 U.S.C.). Section 502B of the Foreign Assistance Act, as amended, provides that the United States shall "promote and encourage increased respect for human rights and fundamental freedoms throughout the world without distinction

Cold War and the collapse of the Soviet Union, "human rights" has become one of the central principles invoked in the justification of U.S. foreign policy.[84] However, the United States has been one of the slowest nations in the world to ratify the major human rights instruments.[85] It has not yet ratified and does not abide by the ICESCR.[86]

as to race, sex, language, or religion. Accordingly, a principal goal of the foreign policy of the United States shall be to promote the increased observance of internationally recognized human rights by all countries." 22 U.S.C. § 2304(a)(1) (1994).

84. Since 1990, human rights have been invoked to justify U.S. interventions in Haiti and Somalia and U.S. support of United Nations intervention in Bosnia; human rights violations were one of the justifications given for the Persian Gulf War; human rights claims have justified the U.S. economic embargo of Cuba; and human rights violations have been raised to criticize U.S. military and financial support of Guatemala. *See, e.g.*, *The President's News Conference*, 27 WEEKLY COMP. PRES. DOC. 39 (Jan. 12, 1991) (press conference of President George H.W. Bush, contending that, throughout United States history, "we've been resolute in our support of justice, freedom, and human dignity. The current situation in the Persian Gulf demands no less of us and of the international community."); *Message to Congress on Haiti*, 31 WEEKLY COMP. PRES. DOC. 185 (Feb. 3, 1995) (message of President William J. Clinton, citing the expulsion of human rights observers as among the factors which precipitated the international intervention in Haiti); Luisette Gierbolini, *The Helms-Burton Act: Inconsistency with International Law and Irrationality at Their Maximum*, 6 J. TRANSNAT'L L. & POL'Y 289, 305 (1997).

85. *See* Glendon, *supra* note 10, at 521 (observing that the United States is notable for its "conspicuous unwillingness . . . to ratify several important international human rights instruments to which all other liberal democracies have acceded."). Similarly, Vega notes that the U.S. position "contradict[s] the vast authority in the international community which maintains that the enjoyment of both sets of rights is indivisible and interdependent." Vega, *supra* note 64, at 471-72.

86. *See* Stark, *supra* note 12, at 81-82. Stark identifies two justifications for the nonadherence of the United States to the ICESCR:

> First, it has been suggested that the rights set forth in the Covenant are "foreign" to our notion of rights. It has been argued that the Covenant represents aspirations, as distinguished from "real," enforceable, civil or political rights. During the Cold War, the U.S. Department of State viewed ICESCR as a socialist manifesto thinly veiled in the language of rights. It is settled that such rights are not protected under the U.S. Constitution.
>
> Second, political leaders have maintained that the concerns addressed by ICESCR are within the exclusive authority of the states, and national adoption would infringe on state sovereignty.

Id. See also Philip Alston, *U.S. Ratification of the Covenant on Economic, Social and Cultural Rights: The Need for an Entirely New Strategy*, 84 AM. J. INT'L L. 365, 366-67 (1990) (examining barriers to U.S. ratification of the ICESCR). Another commentator, Feisal Naqvi notes that the United States "partially justified its withdrawal from [UNESCO] on the basis [of] UNESCO's emphasis on economic rights." Feisal Hussain Naqvi, *People's Rights or Victim's Rights: Reexamining the Conceptualization of Indigenous Rights in International Law*, 71 IND. L.J. 673, 713 (1996).

Thus, the bifurcated notion of human rights—which treats both atrocities and political rights as essential, while treating economic rights as irrelevant or relatively trivial—is at present the only notion of human rights which is explicitly adopted and enforced in any fashion at all in the domains of international law, international diplomacy and NGOs. It is also a notion which has been widely maintained and defended among commentators on human rights as well, although there is considerably more diversity among the academic treatments of human rights than there is to be found in law, diplomacy and activist organizations.

Among political philosophers, one of the early defenders of the dominant notion of human rights is Maurice Cranston. In his influential critique of the Universal Declaration, Cranston argued that the criteria for determining what constitutes human rights are "practicability" and "paramount importance."[87] It is more practical to assert the existence of political rights than economic rights, he suggests: political rights "can be readily secured by legislation," whereas economic and social rights can rarely, if ever, be secured by legislation alone. Cranston points out that the legislation by which political rights are secured is more straightforward than that needed for economic rights. Often political rights can be achieved by restraining governmental conduct.[88]

Thus, Cranston argues, it is practical to articulate and enforce political rights and impractical to articulate and enforce socioeconomic rights. Cranston ridicules the notion of economic rights by focusing on one right included in the Universal Declaration which seems relatively frivolous: the right to holidays with pay.[89] "At present," Cranston writes, "it is utterly impossible, and will be for a long time yet, to provide 'holidays with pay' for everybody in the world. For millions of people who live in those parts of Asia, Africa, and South America, where industrialisation has hardly begun, such claims are vain and idle."[90]

---

87. MAURICE CRANSTON, WHAT ARE HUMAN RIGHTS? 66, 67 (1973).

88. *See id.* at 66.

89. *See* Universal Declaration, *supra* note 14, art. 24 (providing that "[e]veryone has the right to rest and leisure, including reasonable limitation of working hours and periodic holidays with pay.").

90. CRANSTON, *supra* note 87, at 66.

The second test "of a human right, or universal moral right," Cranston writes, "is the test of *paramount importance*." As Cranston explains, "[i]t is a paramount duty to relieve great distress, as it is not a paramount duty to give pleasure,"

> Common sense knows that fire engines and ambulances are essential services, whereas fun fairs and holiday camps are not. Liberality and kindness are reckoned moral virtues; but they are not moral duties in the sense that the obligation to rescue a drowning child is a moral duty.[91]

Although in recent years, some models have been proffered by philosophers and political theorists which do not fully reiterate this dichotomy,[92] this is still the most commonly held contemporary notion of human rights as it has emerged in the second half of the twentieth century.

Thus, the conception of human rights, as it has been formulated in the international and diplomatic arena in the twentieth century, has undergone a series of radical transformations. In the Nuremberg trials, the concept of "crimes against humanity" was defined in terms of the failure to meet minimal ethical obligations to human beings, by engaging in "murder, extermination, enslavement, deportation, and other inhumane acts committed against any civilian population, before or during war."[93] Three years later, the 1948 Universal Declaration defined human rights not only in terms of extermination and torture, but as an entitlement to all that which is necessary for a full and complete life in every dimension of human existence—economically, socially, politically and culturally. However, the Universal Declaration had no mechanism for enforcement. Twenty years later, the 1966 covenants then divided the "human rights" of the Universal Declaration into two categories, with a clear hierarchy. Civil and political rights consisted of entitlements to judicial and political processes, belief and

91. *Id.* at 67.

92. Donnelly discusses some of the other models which, to some extent, identify other sets of basic rights. Fouad Ajami's core rights would be survival, protection against torture and apartheid and food; Henry Shue's would be security, subsistence and liberty. *See* DONNELLY, *supra* note 64, at 38-41; *see also generally* WALDRON, *supra* note 7 (setting forth several essays reformulating the problem from a liberal perspective).

93. Nuremberg Charter, *supra* note 21, art. 6(c), 59 Stat. at 1547, 82 U.N.T.S. at 288.

expression, as well as freedom from torture, enslavement and execution—and the covenant regarding civil and political rights contained mechanisms for both investigation and enforcement. The covenant regarding social and economic rights to work, health care, food, shelter and education contained no comparable mechanism for investigation or enforcement. This two-tier formulation of human rights, which is now the dominant one in diplomacy and international law, was adopted in turn by the most prominent non-governmental organizations, including Human Rights Watch and Amnesty International, and has been defended by philosophers and political theorists.

II. The Oddness of the Concept

Let us look at four sets of implications of this formulation of the concept of human rights.

A. *Example One*

Imagine two scenarios. In the first, military personnel go to the home of a woodcutter. He is not home, but his mother, wife and four young children are. When the woodcutter returns, he finds the women and children decapitated. The torsos have been seated around the table, with the head of each placed on the table in front of the torso. The arms of each torso are extended forward, the hands resting on top of the head. The arms of the youngest child are too short to rest on top of his head; his hands are nailed to the head, to hold them in place. The executions committed by the soldiers constitute a human rights violation.

In the second scenario, a political activist lives in a country with a single political party, which is center-right. The activist is strongly committed to principles of economic equality and social justice and believes that capitalism is both morally wrong and historically doomed. The single political party and all of its candidates are committed to a free-market economic ideology, the privatization of education and health care, and the elimination of all government subsidies for the poor. In the upcoming election, there is only one presidential candidate. In local elections, there are multiple candidates, but all are from the same party. The activist is furious and frustrated at the lack of choice. Although he has the right to vote, he feels disenfranchised because there are no parties representing his views.

This is a violation of his human rights.

Under the dominant conception, one's rights as a citizen have the same standing as one's right not to be subject to cruel and extremely violent acts. Thus, under the dominant conception, the right not to have one's children hacked to death has the same status as the right to choose between Republicans and Democrats.

B. Example Two

Your human rights have been violated if:

- you can only vote for a candidate from the Republican Party;
- the law does not allow you an unlimited right to buy all the television time you can afford;
- the government requires you to wait your turn to go to Aruba for vacation.

No human rights have been violated if:

- your neighbor freezes to death for lack of heat;
- your infant daughter dies because you could not afford a doctor;
- your teenage children are illiterate;
- begging on the street is the most lucrative form of employment you can find.

The dominant conception of human rights ensures that individuals can express political views and pursue certain personal interests—activities which may be satisfying or important, but are not essential for human life. However, the dominant conception does not include any rights that are economic in nature, even if these concern actual physical survival, physical hunger, pain, helplessness and humiliation.[94]

---

94. This is a point that has been made by numerous commentators. *See, e.g.*, Butcher, *supra* note 10, at 445 (contending that "civil and political human rights, such as the right of free speech, only make sense to the person with basic economic rights."). Butcher observes that "[a] mother whose baby is dying of disease which he succumbed to because of debilitating diarrhea caused by massive malnutrition—and half the babies in AFRICA die before they are one for just this reason—would have little comprehension of our insistence on free speech as the

Thus, the dominant conception has a curious structure: it gives the same status to political and civil rights—including those which enhance one's life, but are not necessary for survival—as it does to the rights relating to extreme acts of physical brutality. At the same time, it excludes economic rights, even those which have implications for life and death, or the necessities required for basic health and physical safety.[95]

C. *Example Three*

Let us assume, with the dominant conception, that our human rights include the right to vote in free elections, the right to hold public office, the right to due process of law and the right to equal treatment and equal protection of the law.

Given this assumption, there are no violations of our human rights where:

- the law permits everyone—rich and poor alike—to spend the $12 million necessary to run for Congress;
- the law forbids everyone—rich and poor alike—to beg on the streets.[96]

---

fundamental right." *Id.* at 446. *See also* Bondzie-Simpson, *supra* note 10, at 658. Bondzie-Simpson refers to the following quote from an unnamed African political leader:

> Imperialists talk about human rights, drinking tea or sipping champagne. They can afford to—after all, they have made it. If we had slaves for two hundred (200) years to build our roads, build our homesteads, sow our fields; if we had multinationals for three hundred (300) years looting wealth from other people's lands; if we had literate, healthy, well-fed citizens—if we had a diversified economy and people had jobs—we too could talk human rights from our air conditioned offices and houses.

Id.

95. This issue can also be framed in terms of the dual nature of property rights. R. Andrew Painter offers the insight that:

> the right to property can be viewed from two perspectives: that of the landed and that of the landless. From the perspective of the landed, the right to property is a civil right, one intended to ensure protection against arbitrary State interference. From the perspective of the landless, the right to property is an economic and social right, a prerequisite to the fulfillment of other guaranteed human rights, such as the right to life and an adequate standard of living. Under the latter perspective, there is a positive State duty to ensure that sufficient lands are available to all.

R. Andrew Painter, *Property Rights of Returning Displaced Persons: The Guatemalan Experience*, 9 HARV. HUM. RTS. J. 145, 167 (1996).

96. I am of course appropriating the famous dictum of Anatole France, that

Under the dominant conception, political equality is a human right. Yet political equality is purely formal: the fact that all citizens of a certain age have the right to hold public office does not mean that substantively they have the means to do so. Political equality—the formal equality of all citizens in relation to government and to law—does not entail economic equality—substantively having the means to exercise one's political rights.

The dominant conception of human rights attributes great value to rights which are formal and abstract, or which are not self-standing, and for that reason are quite worthless to many. What is it that we have when we have the right to run for office, to start a newspaper, to buy television time—without the money necessary for each of these things? If I do not have $12 million and I do not receive $12 million in campaign contributions—what exactly is it that I have, then, if I have the right to run for Congress? What do I *have* when I have a right which is purely formal? What I have is either a promise of a very limited sort, or it is simply and entirely an abstraction.

If it is a promise, then it is the promise regarding the concrete and direct activities of the state. The promise is: if I have the inclination—and the funds—to run for public office, the state will not intervene to prevent me from doing so. If I want to buy television time—and can afford to—the state will not prevent me from doing so. If I am arrested, the state will not prevent me from hiring a competent and thorough lawyer—if I can afford to pay for her. If I and my organization contribute $100,000 to the Democratic National Committee and my Democratic senator is then willing to spend two hours meeting with me, the state will not prevent me from lobbying for laws that will serve my interests. If a political right is a promise, then it is a promise regarding the limitations on the state's intervention in how people make use of their resources. Thus, it is the *equal* right of all to make use of resources, where those resources are distributed *unequally*.

Yet if we want to consider political rights to be human rights, we must maintain that there is something which all persons have—not just the wealthy—when they have these

"The law, in its majestic equality, forbids the rich as well as the poor to sleep under bridges, to beg in the streets, and to steal bread." ANATOLE FRANCE, THE RED LILY 87 (1894).

rights. What is it that I have, exactly, when I have the right to start a newspaper but not the means? What is it that I have when I, who earn $5 an hour, have the right to lobby my senator who will not spend more than five minutes with someone who has not contributed $1000 to his campaign? When I cannot afford to buy television time, ad space, or the time and attention of my governmental representatives, what exactly does it mean to say that I have "the same" political rights as someone who contributes $50,000 to the Democratic Party, or a corporation which loans one of its jets to a presidential candidate to use during his campaign? In exactly what sense are my rights "equal" or "the same?"

What *exactly* does it mean to say that I "have" a right—which cannot be exercised? Let's say that I have a coupon for 10% off on any mink coat I buy for a retail price of $10,000 or more. But perhaps I earn only $5 per hour working at a fast food restaurant. What is the "right" that I "have" when I have an entitlement I cannot possibly actualize? What would I be missing if someone took away my coupon for the mink coat? Would my life be less rich? Would I live in more pain or fear? In fact, my life would be no different. I would not be any happier or less happy. I would not be in more pain or less pain. I would not be doing anything different in my life with possession of the coupon than I would without it. Is this so different from the right to buy television air time? Or to start a newspaper in competition with the New York Times? Or the right to travel to foreign countries? How can one have "essential rights" which are of no use to someone who does not have the necessary resources to exercise them? How can something be absolutely essential for every human being—and also quite worthless to those who are not wealthy?

D. *Example Four*

Since 1960, the United States has maintained an economic embargo against Cuba, actively interfering in Cuba's commercial relations with third-party nations. This embargo has prevented Cuban purchases of medicine, medical equipment, water purification chemicals, bicycles, soap, rice and milk. The justification that the United States gives for this policy is that the Cuban government violates the human rights of the Cuban people. The human rights of the Cuban people are violated, it is held, in that they do not have freedom of speech and press; that there is not a multi-party electoral system; that there has only been one candidate for president since the revolution; and that there are not certain rights of due process. Partly as a result of the economic embargo, malnutrition has increased; there have been severe shortages of electricity, public transportation and school supplies; the water is no longer consistently potable; and there has been a measurable increase in preventable deaths.

United States interference with Cuban trade has been justified as an ethical measure, intended to destabilize Fidel Castro's leadership and replace socialism with a "less repressive" government that will not violate the human rights of the Cuban people.[97] In this case, the purported human rights violations include no "atrocities"—death squads, torture, genocide, or enslavement. The claimed human rights violations involve press, speech, religious expression, electoral practices and judicial process.[98] Because civil and political rights are deemed to be "human rights," and economic rights are not, we see the ethically problematic situation in which "human rights" are invoked to justify the infliction of concrete, immediate physical suffering, by economic means, upon those members of society who are the most vulnerable and the least responsible for governmental policies—the elderly, the ill and the very young.

E. *Examples Analyzed*

I use these examples to raise four conceptual issues regarding human rights: (1) the inclusion of civil and political rights as human rights; (2) the exclusion of economic rights

---

97. *See, e.g.*, the Cuban Democracy Act of 1992, 22 U.S.C. § 6001 (1994) (finding, *inter alia*, that "[t]here is no sign that the Castro regime is prepared to make any significant concessions to democracy," and that "it is appropriate for" the United States and its allies "to cooperate . . . to promote a peaceful [political] transition in Cuba."); Cuban Liberty and Democratic Solidarity (LIBERTAD) Act of 1996, 22 U.S.C.A. § 6021 (West Supp. 1997) (finding, *inter alia*, that "the repression of the Cuban people . . . [has] isolated the Cuban regime as the only completely nondemocratic government in the Western Hemisphere," and that the "Cuban people deserve to be assisted in a decisive manner to end the tyranny that has oppressed them for 36 years, and the continued failure to do so constitutes ethically improper conduct by the international community.").

98. *See, e.g.*, 1996 AMNESTY INTERNATIONAL REPORT (1996).

from the conception of human rights; (3) the circumstances in which "human rights" are abstractions without concrete value; and (4) the consequences of this structure, whereby human suffering may actually be increased in the name of human rights.

If by the term "human rights" we want to somehow capture those elements essential to human life, then there is a problem; some are essential to human life, while others concern enrichment or happiness, but are by no means essential. Death squads and genocide, both of them human rights violations, deprive people of life. State control of television, on the other hand, which is a human rights violation under the dominant conception, does not. It is probably an understatement to say that to be physically tortured shatters the texture of one's daily life and replaces it with a single consuming focus of surviving extreme pain. State control of television does nothing of this sort. There is state control of television in dozens of countries, including, for example, the Netherlands. Would we really want to claim that the quality of human life in the Netherlands for a middle-class businessman is equivalent to being a victim of torture?

The question here is not whether state control of television is good or bad. The question is: is it comparable to torture? Is it indisputably wrong in the way that torture is? Is it devastating to human life in the way that torture is? Would we really say that it is "beyond the pale of civilization" and "inconsistent with the most basic precepts of human decency" in the way that we say torture is? Free access to the press may be a good thing; it may be a very good thing. It may be necessary for a full and happy life. It may be indirectly necessary as a tool to expose and address such things as torture and genocide. But is free access to the press, in itself, a prerequisite for human life or human well-being in the same way that not being tortured or enslaved is necessary for human well-being?

Recall also that, under the dominant conception, literacy is not a human right. Now, to what degree is a free press valuable (not to say essential) for the well-being of those who are illiterate? How is it that the dominant conception does not see any human rights violations if people are illiterate—but does see a human rights violation if an illiterate population does not have the right to publish and distribute newspapers? I suggest that our actual physical experiences in the world indicate that the genocide and torture—because they are physically concrete, direct, immediate experiences—are fundamentally dissimilar to formal political rights—which are indirect, less than essential and in some circumstances worthless.

Conversely, there are certain economic resources which *are* essential for human life, but are not included in the dominant conception: shelter, food, medical care, clothing. Without shelter and warm clothing, people who live in cold climates will simply, literally freeze to death. Without the safety that shelter provides, people who live on the streets are robbed, beaten and raped. Without medical care, people suffer literal, physical pain from illness and injury and may die or be crippled from lack of treatment. Without potable water, illness and an early death are more probable; the major cause of infant mortality in developing countries is amoebic dysentery from untreated drinking water.[99] Is the physical experience of starving to death from poverty different in any way from, say, being starved to death intentionally as a form of execution? Is the loss one feels for a child who has died for lack of a $2 medicine so different from the loss one feels for a child killed by the state?

Thus, if by "human rights" we refer to those things which are "essential for human life," then the dominant conception of human rights makes no sense: it includes things which may be highly desirable, but are not essential to life; and it excludes things which, in fact, *are* essential to human life. If by "human rights" we are concerned with acts or situations which "shock the conscience," which we "cannot imagine that human beings could endure," the dominant concept includes those; but it also includes acts or situations which are not only endurable, but quite ordinary. If by "human rights" we mean "those principles whose violation constitutes immediate and concrete harm," then the dominant conception includes some aspects of human experience, such as enslavement or torture, which are so concrete that they dominate and pervade every moment of one's conscious life. But it also includes formal and abstract rights which people may never exercise, may never want to exercise, may never have the means to exercise and whose absence would have no concrete consequences for their lives.

99. *See* Butcher, *supra* note 10, at 446.

Thus, I would argue, the dominant conception of human rights is not only disputable, but is indeed quite odd. It is an odd mixture of the very concrete and the purely abstract; of what is essential to everyone and what is worthless to many; of goods and protections which are immediately and directly effective and those which are only contingent, indirect, or hypothetical. Yet it is a concept which lays claim to being an absolute ethical standard, with universal validity. How is it that this came to be? In the first section, I gave a brief overview of the diplomatic and institutional processes in which this conception of human rights was formulated. Now I would like to look at the conceptual roots of the dominant conception, in order to explain its oddness and asymmetry, as well as its claim to absolute validity and universal applicability.

III. The Mixed Heritage of the Dominant Conception: The Just War Tradition

The dominant conception of human rights, I would maintain, has an asymmetrical structure because it derives from two very different sources: the Just War tradition, which dates back to Augustine; and the Enlightenment notion of rights, articulated in liberal political theory. The first essentially concerns the distinction between civilization and barbarity: what are the acts which are not only criminal or violent, but in some sense "go beyond the pale of civilized conduct?" What are the minimal ethical obligations owed to a person simply in virtue of his or her humanity? The second, in contrast, concerns a conception of the good: what is necessary for human beings to be happy? What is necessary for a good and full life? There is another fundamental distinction as well. The Just War tradition concerns acts and duties regarding those to whom one has no juridical or political relation—the obligations of a warrior toward those who are enemies of his nation, who are legally entitled to nothing from him; they are simply, merely, human beings. The Enlightenment tradition of rights, on the other hand, concerns the obligations of the state to its citizens and the limitations on the power of the state to intervene in the decisions and acts of its citizens.

There is a long tradition of reflection by both ethical thinkers and military theorists on the question of what constitutes a Just War. However, the prior question is: do ethics even apply to war in the first place? If an individual, acting on his own behalf, sets off a bomb in someone's home or workplace in his own country, he would be called a criminal (or terrorist or deviant). He would be tried and imprisoned or put to death for violation of the law. A soldier, acting on behalf of the state, against foreign nationals, is not bound by those laws. We do not consider that killing the enemy in battle is criminal or deviant; indeed, killing in these circumstances is rewarded and praised. The soldier is not restricted by the laws governing domestic order; but is he restricted by anything other than his obligation to his sovereign? Stated differently: once you are engaged in war—which is outside the lawful social order—are there any rules of civility by which you are bound, or are you simply outside the bounds of civilization altogether? Given that war takes place outside the rules of law, is war a rule-governed activity at all?[100]

In JUST AND UNJUST WARS,[101] Michael Walzer describes the cold-blooded realism of the Melian dialogue in Thucydides' HISTORY OF THE PELOPONNESIAN WAR;[102] in positions such as Sherman's "War is hell;" and in von Clausewitz' view that war in its pure form has no boundaries to its destruction. Walzer's concern is to reject that "realist" view that there is no distinction between war and atrocity. For realists, he says, "war strips away our civilized adornments and reveals our nakedness."[103] The realists would simply maintain: "yes, our soldiers committed atrocities in the course of the battle, but that's

100. *See* IAN CLARK, WAGING WAR 24-27 (1988) (discussing rules of military efficiency, rules of political instrumentality and proportionality, rules of utility, rules of positive law and rules of morality). Clearly war can be or is in fact "rule-governed" in some of these senses. Our concern in this discussion of Just War is the role of ethical rules. *See, e.g.*, James F. Childress, *Just-War Theories: The Bases, Interrelations, Priorities, and Functions of Their Criteria*, *in* WAR, MORALITY, AND THE MILITARY PROFESSION 256, 262-63 (Malham M. Wakin ed., 1986) (exploring the distinction between a model of war as a rule-governed activity and the model of "war as hell."). Although, as Terry Nardin writes, "it does not follow from the fact that in war the normal order of society is disrupted that the state of war is one without order. The alternative to life according to one set of rules is not necessarily life without any rules at all, but rather life according to different rules." TERRY NARDIN, LAW, MORALITY AND THE RELATIONS OF STATES 288 (1983).

101. MICHAEL WALZER, JUST AND UNJUST WARS 4 (1977).

102. *See* THUCYDIDES, HISTORY OF THE PELOPONNESIAN WAR 400-08 (Rex Warner trans., Penguin Books 1954).

103. WALZER, *supra* note 101, at 4.

what war does to people, that's what war is like."[104]

There is, however, an equally weighty tradition dating back to Augustine which specifically asserts the relevance of considerations of justice and articulates principles by which Just Wars are distinguished from unjust ones. The principle of *jus ad bellum* concerns the justice of the cause for which the war is fought; *jus in bello* concerns the means by which the war is conducted. In THE CITY OF GOD,[105] Augustine is using the principle of *jus ad bellum* when he suggests that the unity of the empire has been achieved only at the cost of just and necessary wars and that the very extent of the empire has also produced social and civil wars. However, the wise man is willing to wage Just Wars and is compelled to do so by the wrongdoing of the other party.[106]

Jus in bello concerns two general principles: proportionality and discrimination. The principle of proportionality requires that the harm done by the military action should be less than the harm it seeks to prevent or rectify.[107] The principle of discrimination concerns those who will be targeted or subject to attack in wartime and what types of weapons will be used. This principle involves making a moral distinction in wartime between combatants and noncombatants; wounded and nonwounded combatants; combatants who are fighting and combatants who have surrendered and handed over their arms. The principle of discrimination would prohibit blanket bombing in civilian areas; directly targeting civilian residential areas;

---

104. *Id.*

105. SAINT AUGUSTINE, THE CITY OF GOD (Marcus Dods trans., 1950).

106. *See id.* at 683. *See also* Paul Ramsey, *The Just War According to St Augustine*, *in* JEAN BETHKE ELSHTAIN, JUST WAR THEORY 8, 15-16 (Jean Bethke Elshtain ed., 1992). One commentator suggests that, in the twentieth century, the principle of *jus ad bellum* can principally be seen in the area of aggressive war and proscription (or condemnation) of wars of aggression in the Hague conferences, the Covenant of the League of Nations, the Kellogg-Briand Pact of 1928 and the Nuremberg tribunal. CLARK, *supra* note 100, at 78. But it is certainly the case that the notion of *jus ad bellum* can also be seen in the types of justifications given for military actions since World War II. The United States, for example, has variously invoked "making the world safe for democracy," human rights and "the drug war" as the moral justifications for military actions.

107. For a summary of this notion, see U.S. Catholic Bishops, *The Just War and Non-Violence Positions*, *in* WAR, MORALITY, AND THE MILITARY PROFESSION 239, 249-51 (Malham M. Wakin ed., 1986) (excerpting the pastoral letter of May 1983); CLARK, *supra* note 100, at 35; WALZER, *supra* note 101, at 129-30 (discussing the difficulty and the desirability of applying the proportionality principle).

intentionally and directly killing children, the elderly, hospital patients, farmers and workers not involved in war production, villagers not involved in combat, etc. The principle of discrimination would also prohibit the use of weapons which by their nature will kill or injure civilian populations, such as nuclear, biological, or chemical warfare.[108] The "laws of war" regarding such matters as the treatment of prisoners and civilians have changed as forms of war and their conventions have undergone transformation. In the twentieth century, they were codified in a series of treaties. The Fourth Hague Convention provided that enemy soldiers who surrendered should be taken prisoner rather than killed; captured cities could not be pillaged; civilian areas could not be bombed; poisoned weapons and arms "calculated to cause unnecessary suffering" could not be employed. The Geneva conventions required humane treatment of prisoners and protection of the sick and wounded.[109]

---

108. *See* U.S. Catholic Bishops, *supra* note 107, at 250-51; CLARK, *supra* note 100, at 35, 87-97. *See also* WALZER, *supra* note 101, at 138-59 (discussing the doctrine of necessity); JAMES TURNER JOHNSON, JUST WAR TRADITION AND THE RESTRAINT OF WAR xxiii (1981). *See also* Richard Wasserstrom, *The Laws of War*, *in* WAR, MORALITY, AND THE MILITARY PROFESSION 393 (summarizing *jus in bello* principles and observing that "[f]or the most part the laws of war deal with two sorts of things: how classes of persons are to be treated in war, e.g., prisoners of war, and what sorts of weapons and methods of attack are permissible, e.g., the use of poison gas.").

Johnson notes that this distinction can be traced in part to the Middle Ages. De Treuga et Pace ("Of Truces and Peace"), part of the canon law of the 13th century, "lists eight classes of persons who should have full security against the ravages of war: clerics, monks, friars, other religious, pilgrims, travelers, merchants, and peasants cultivating the soil." JOHNSON, *supra*, at 127. There were two other canonical limitations as well: the Truce of God prohibited combat on certain days; and, in 1139, the Second Lateran Council banned the use of certain weapons in combat among Christians (the crossbow, bows and arrows and siege engines). However, Johnson notes, "[n]o mention was made of the use of these weapons in warfare against infidels and heretics, and they remained acceptable there." *Id.* at 128. The second source of the distinction among classes of persons from the Middle Ages was the chivalric code, which excluded from combat both women and peasants. The code also established conventions of courtesy, by which it was deemed a virtue for a conquering knight to offer quarter to the vanquished knight. *Id.* at 133-39.

109. *See* Telford Taylor, *War Crimes*, *in* NUREMBERG AND VIETNAM: AN AMERICAN TRAGEDY 29-30 (1970). *See also generally* the Hague Conventions of 1907, the Geneva Conventions of 1949 and the 1977 protocols amplifying the Geneva conventions. Articles 48 and 51 of the 1977 Protocols provide that:

> In order to ensure respect for and protection of the civilian population and civilian objects, the Parties to the conflict shall at all times distinguish between the civilian population and combatants and between civil-

The conventions articulated in these "rules of war" underscore what an extraordinary situation war is; it is tempting to use the word "abnormal," or "deviant," or Durkheim's term "anomic." Within "normal" societal life, killing someone is murder, burning down their house is arson, taking their crops is theft and going into someone's home without permission is burglary. All of these are crimes and those who commit them are deemed to be deviant and anti-social in some sense, deserving of punishment, in need of rehabilitation and segregated from the trustworthy and law-abiding sector of society. Yet in wartime, these acts are normal and committed by one's own soldiers, who are in fact required to do these acts and lauded as heroes if they do them successfully. Given that all the obligations one would owe to other citizens under the laws of the nation are inapplicable—indeed, given that the instructions from one's own nation are to kill, maim, burn and destroy—what does it even mean to speak of "good" and "bad" acts? Within a society, obligations are owed to other members of the society, under the laws of the state; as members of this moral community, their lives and property have moral significance. War, however, involves interactions with those who are not members of one's own moral community; to whom one has no obligations under the laws of one's own state; to whom one has no relation except a relation of enmity. Under these circumstances, then, how are we obliged to act? The principle of discrimination explicitly creates a code of conduct and implicitly creates minimum moral obligations toward those who are not members of our moral community. Thus, it is ethical to kill an enemy soldier; but it is unethical to massacre unarmed women and children. It is ethical to kill a soldier in combat; but it is unethical to bomb an infirmary for the wounded. It is ethical to kill an enemy soldier who is armed; but it is unethical to shoot an enemy soldier in the back after he has surrendered and handed over his weapon. It is ethical to capture a soldier and hold him prisoner; but it is not ethical to torture him.[110]

> ian objects and military objectives and accordingly shall direct their operations only against military objectives . . . The civilian population as such, as well as individual citizens, shall not be the object of attack . . .

See also Jane Olson et al., *Bosnia, War Crimes and Humanitarian Intervention*, 15 WHITTIER L. REV. 445, 451 (1994).

110. I will not address here the issues of military necessity—that these acts

In the "rules of war," the appeal is not to explicit laws generated by a supra-national legislative body; there is no such body, although there are treaties among equal and sovereign state parties. The appeal (within the treaties and conventions, as well as in the face of actual war crimes) is rather to conscience and to an intuitive understanding of what acts, in themselves, "shock the conscience."[111] The appeal cannot be to the legal entitlements of, and obligations to, enemy soldiers and civilians, since they are not entitled to the protections claimed by citizens or residents of one's own country. Thus, rules of war constitute restrictions on the harm that may be done to persons—not because they are citizens, with formal legal entitlements, but simply and solely because they are human beings. Fundamentally, they speak to the question: what do I owe those with whom I have no social contract? What do I owe those to whom I have no explicit duties, no legal obligations? What do I owe those who are my enemies—who have tried to kill me, or who are the kin and protectors of those who are trying to kill me? What is the minimum standard of conduct that applies to a human being as such, even a human being who is my enemy?

The principles of proportionality and discrimination imply I am obliged to recognize, in some small degree, the humanity of my enemy. I am obliged to recognize that his death and pain are something of moral significance; that burning a village of people is not akin to burning a field of dry grass; that taking a human life, or causing human pain, is not akin to destroying or damaging an inanimate object. Thus, I am not entitled to indulge myself in conduct that is gratuitous and unboundaried bloodthirstiness, even when that conduct is directed at someone who wishes me dead. Thus, the rules of war implicitly draw a distinction between civilization and barbarism: the rules of war hold that even in the absence of law, even in the absence of contract, even in the absence of relationship, even in circumstances of enmity—there are still some acts whose brutality makes them indecent—inherently and directly inde-

---

are permitted when they are militarily necessary. I only wish to sketch out some of the general principles that have to do with the recognition of ethical duties owed outside of society and outside of law.

111. This is exemplified by the language used by the prosecutors at the Nuremberg tribunals. *See* discussion *infra* Part VII.

cent—simply because they are committed by human beings, against human beings.

This notion does not articulate an affirmative conception of happiness or goodness, but rather a minimum standard for ethical conduct and for ethical entitlements. To say that one has the right not to be tortured or executed only addresses the minimum conditions for human life. It says nothing about the larger possibilities for happiness. Note also that there is nothing abstract about the nature of the entitlements implied by the rules of war; death and extreme physical pain are the most concrete human experiences there are. If the rule against torture were violated and you were the object of torture, you would be very much aware that this violation had taken place. It would alter your life and well-being, directly, immediately and physically. You would require no further resources or intermediate steps in order to experience your right. To be the beneficiary of the rules of war does not mean that you have an entitlement to happiness; it means only that you will be protected against brutality that is direct, physical and gratuitous.

IV. The Mixed Heritage of the Dominant Conception: The Enlightenment Notion of Rights

As we have seen, the Just War tradition contains a notion of the minimum obligation owed to someone simply by virtue of their humanity. Furthermore, the Just War tradition consists first and foremost of a code of conduct; to the extent that there are "rights," they are inferred from the restraints on conduct, not articulated prior to it—or for that matter, not articulated at all by soldiers or military leaders, but only by historians and ethicists. The customs of war, for example, simply proscribe targeting civilians, but do not derive this proscription from an articulated underlying theory of universal rights (at least not prior to the twentieth century). However, the Enlightenment notion of rights is quite different. In one sense it is much broader, in that it entails a conception of the good—what is involved in a complete, fulfilled human life. Yet in a different sense it is narrower: it concerns only the political dimension—the relation of the individual to the state and the basis for the legitimacy of the state. And where the "rules of war" are an empirical description of customary conduct from which rights are only secondarily inferred, the revolutionary documents and political theory of the Enlightenment, which set forth claims about rights, do not necessarily describe or even claim to describe actual conduct. Finally, and crucially, the Enlightenment gives us one of the fundamental notions of modern political thought: that there are such things as rights and that they are universal,[112] inherent, self-evident and inalienable.[113]

In a sense it is presumptuous to speak at all of "an Enlightenment conception of rights," given the tremendous diversity among the thinkers of this era. The difference between the French and German Enlightenments, for example, is quite stark. However, my interest here is not in offering an extensive discussion of the political thought of the seventeenth and eighteenth centuries, but in tracing the influences on human rights theory of the mid and late twentieth century, by indicating some of the elements we have inherited and appropriated. I will do this by quickly reviewing some of the central themes which emerge again and again in Enlightenment political thought, looking specifically at social contract theory and the proclamations of rights in the French and American revolutions. The social contract theorists assert an original condition (whether historical or mythical) in which individuals have natural rights. The revolutionary proclamations assert the present existence and nature of rights.

A. *The Social Contract Theorists*

Hobbes' political writings set out the rational grounds for obedience to authority; while maintaining that those grounds consisted in the natural rights of individuals, prior to and

112. As has been pointed out on many occasions, the "universe" for the Enlightenment thinkers was in fact limited to white males of European descent. *See, e.g.*, CAROL PATEMAN, THE SEXUAL CONTRACT 221 (1988) (observing that "[t]hrough the mirror of the original contract, citizens can see themselves as members of a society constituted by free relations. The political fiction reflects our political selves back to us—but who are 'we'? Only men—who can create political life—can take part in the original pact."); *see also* DIANA H. COOLE, WOMEN IN POLITICAL THEORY 71-132 (1988) (discussing Hobbes, Locke and Rousseau). For a discussion of the implicit and explicit racism in the revolutionary thought of the Enlightenment, see RONALD T. TAKAKI, IRON CAGES: RACE AND CULTURE IN NINETEENTH-CENTURY AMERICA 1-15 (1979). My interest here lies in addressing the notion of universal rights as such.

113. *See* Louis Henkin, *Human Rights and State "Sovereignty"*, 25 GA. J. INT'L & COMP. L. 31, 40 n.34 (1995-96).

outside of the existence of the state. The state of nature was characterized by a fundamental equality: "Nature hath made men so equall, in the faculties of body, and mind . . . . For as to the strength of body, the weakest has strength enough to kill the strongest, either by secret machination, or by confederacy with others, that are in the same danger with himselfe."[114]

The result of this equality is an ongoing state of war, "where every man is Enemy to every man."[115] In this state, there is "continuall feare, and danger of violent death; And the life of man, solitary, poore, nasty, brutish, and short."[116] The "right of nature,"[117] consists in "the Liberty each man hath, to use his own power . . . for the preservation of his own Nature; that is to say, of his own Life" and to anything he conceives to be useful toward that end.[118] Hobbes defines liberty as the "absence of externall Impediments" which may "take away part of a mans power to do what he would."[119] Hobbes distinguishes "right" from "law," concluding that right consists in liberty to do or forebear from doing, while law determines and binds. Law, for Hobbes, is obligation, while right is liberty.[120] It follows, he says, that because everyone may make use of anything which is of use to him in preserving his life against his enemies, in such a condition, "every man has a Right to every thing."[121]

Consequently, the sovereign does not rule by divine right or a right of tradition; rather, sovereign power is conferred by consent of individuals living in the warlike state of nature. Hobbes writes that "[a] *Common-wealth* is said to be *Instituted*, when a *Multitude* of men do Agree, and *Covenant*, *every one*, *with every one*" and when they agree "to submit to some Man, or Assembly of men, voluntarily, on confidence to be protected by him against all others."[122] Thus, sovereignty is conferred by individuals; and it is conferred by individuals who

114. THOMAS HOBBES, LEVIATHAN 183 (Penguin Books, 1968) (1651).
115. *Id.* at 186.
116. *Id.*
117. Hobbes is here translating *jus Naturale*, or natural law. *Id.* at 189.
118. *Id.*
119. *Id.*
120. *See id.*
121. *Id.* at 190.
122. *Id.* at 228.

have a "right to everything."

Similarly, Locke, in replying to Filmer's defense of rule by divine right, rejects the position that "[m]en are not born free, and therefore could never have the liberty to choose either Governors, or Forms of Government."[123] In his *Second Treatise of Government*, Locke maintains that "[t]o understand Political Power right, and derive it from its Original, we must consider what State all Men are naturally in, and that is, a *State of Perfect Freedom* to order their Actions, and dispose of their Possessions, and Persons as they think fit . . . ."[124] Locke maintains that "[t]he *State of Nature* has a Law of Nature to govern it," which is reason; and that reason "teaches all Mankind . . . that . . . no one ought to harm another in his Life, Health, Liberty, or Possessions."[125] Reason, as law of nature, likewise indicates that everyone is bound to preserve himself and to preserve the rest of mankind as well.[126] Since the "Fundamental Law of Nature" dictates that man should be preserved, he has a right to destroy anyone who threatens him with destruction or enslavement.[127] The "*Natural Liberty* of Man is to be free from any Superior Power on Earth," Locke says, "but to have only the Law of Nature for his Rule."[128] Thus, legislative power over man within the commonwealth can be established only by consent.[129]

Unlike Hobbes, who spoke of equality in the state of nature as actual physical and mental equality, Locke asserts an "equal right" in the face of actual inequality:

> Though I have said above, Chap. II, *That all Men by Nature are equal*, I cannot be supposed to understand all sorts of *Equality*: *Age* or *Virtue* may give Men a just Precedency: *Excellency of Parts and Merit* may place others above the Common Level: *Birth* may subject some, and *Alliance* or *Benefits* others, to pay an Observance to those to whom Nature, Gratitude or other Respects may have made it due; and yet all this consists with the *Equality*, which all Men are in,

123. JOHN LOCKE, TWO TREATISES OF GOVERNMENT 143 (Peter Laslett ed., Student ed. 1988) (1690).

124. *Id.* at 269.

125. *Id.* at 271.

126. *See id.*

127. *See id.* at 278-79.

128. *Id.* at 283.

129. *See id.*

> in respect of Jurisdiction or Dominion one over another, which was the *Equality* I there spoke of, as proper to the Business in hand, being that *equal Right* that every Man hath, *to his Natural Freedom*, without being subjected to the Will or Authority of any other Man.[130]

Also unlike Hobbes, Locke distinguishes liberty from freedom. Liberty is freedom from restraint; but freedom is not the liberty for each person to do as he wishes, "[f]or who could be free, when every other Man's Humour might domineer over him?"[131] Freedom is rather the "*Liberty* to dispose, and order, as he lists, his Person, Actions, Possessions, and his whole Property, with the Allowance of those Laws under which he is . . . ."[132] With language that seems to anticipate Kant, Locke says that "[t]he Freedom then of Man and Liberty of acting according to his own Will, is *grounded on* his having *Reason*, which is able to instruct him in that Law he is to govern himself by . . . ."[133] Thus, he says, "we are *born Free*, as we are born Rational; not that we have actually the Exercise of either: Age that brings one [the age of majority], brings with it the other too."[134]

All of these discussions are from the chapters on the state of nature, the state of war, slavery, property and paternal power. Yet, in a rather different vein, in the chapter entitled *Of the Beginning of Political Societies*, Locke says that "[m]en being, as has been said, by Nature, all free, equal and independent, no one can be put out of this Estate, and subjected to the Political Power of another, without his own *Consent*."[135]

This contrasts markedly with Locke's earlier statements: that freedom is not the freedom for each to do as he wishes, but rather the freedom to act on one's will to the extent allowed by law; that there are inequalities of age, virtue, birth and so on; that one is dependent and subordinate to one's parents at birth; and that in the state of nature one has obligations both to and from mankind as a whole. Thus, it is as a citizen—that is, as an individual consenting to the formation of

130. *Id.* at 304.
131. *Id.* at 306.
132. *Id.*
133. *Id.* at 309.
134. *Id.* at 308.
135. *Id.* at 330.

government—that Locke describes man as "by Nature, all free, equal, and independent." Yet these qualities would not seem to apply to the individual in his family relations, his social relations, or his pursuit of his desires and interests.

Rousseau reiterates the conception of a state of nature as the origin of rights and consent as the basis for legitimate sovereignty. "Man is born free, and everywhere is in chains," he writes in the beginning of ON THE SOCIAL CONTRACT.[136] "Since no man has a natural authority over his fellow man," Rousseau writes, "and since force does not give rise to any right, conventions therefore remain the basis of all legitimate authority among men."[137]

The transition from the state of nature to the civil state takes place when each individual alienates his rights to the whole community, which is expressed in the general will.[138] For Rousseau, the state of nature was characterized by simplicity and an innocent goodness. Whereas individuals in civil society are competitive, deceitful and greedy, "savage man" has simple needs and is easily satisfied. "The only goods he knows in the universe," writes Rousseau, "are nourishment, a woman, and rest; the only evils he fears are pain and hunger."[139] In the state of nature, human beings are agile, robust and satisfied—"I see [the savage man] satisfying his hunger under an oak tree, quenching his thirst at the first stream, finding his bed at the foot of the same tree that supplied his meal; and thus his needs are satisfied."[140] The state of nature is characterized by savage man's "natural liberty and an unlimited right to everything that tempts him and that he can acquire."[141] "Every man by nature has a right," Rousseau writes, "to everything he needs."[142]

In civil society, according to Rousseau, the individual alienates his rights to the community as a whole: "*Each of us places his person and all his power in common under the su-*

136. JEAN-JACQUES ROUSSEAU, ON THE SOCIAL CONTRACT 17 (Donald A. Cress trans. & ed., 1983) (1762).

137. *Id.* at 20.

138. *See id.* at 26-27.

139. JEAN-JACQUES ROUSSEAU, DISCOURSE ON THE ORIGIN AND FOUNDATION OF INEQUALITY AMONG MEN 126 (Donald A. Cress trans. & ed., 1983) (1755).

140. *Id.* at 120.

141. ROUSSEAU, *supra* note 136, at 27.

142. *Id.* at 27.

preme direction of the general will; and as one we receive each member as an indivisible apart of the whole."[143] Sovereignty is then "merely the exercise of the general will," and the sovereign is the "collective being" that the general will represents.[144] The social contract, according to Rousseau, involves a transformation from inequality to equality. Rousseau writes that "the fundamental compact . . . substitutes a moral and legitimate equality [for] whatever physical inequality nature may have imposed upon men . . . however[] unequal in force or intelligence they may be, men all become equal by convention and by right."[145]

Thus, our status as equal or unequal is characterized by duality. We continue to be unequal in fact—in strength or intelligence—while being equal in some other sense, as "moral" equals in the face of the law. According to Rousseau, in the passage from the state of nature to civil society, the individual cedes all of his rights to the community as a whole.[146] The community as a whole is both the source of its own law and bound by that law. The sovereign consists of the community itself: "the social compact gives the body politic an absolute power over all its members, and it is the same power which . . . is directed by the general will and bears the name sovereignty."[147]

Since the citizen participates in the general will by virtue of his membership in the body politic, the citizen is—in some sense—the sovereign. However, the exercise of sovereign power concerns only public (civil) matters. While the sovereign power is "absolute, wholly sacred and inviolable," it does not dictate the private use and disposition of property, because when the matter becomes a private one, the sovereign's power is no longer competent.[148]

Within the social contract tradition, the claim that individuals possess rights prior to and apart from the state is the basis for determining both the legitimacy and the limitations of the acts of the state. At the same time, the state is the only

143. *Id.* at 24.
144. *Id.* at 29.
145. *Id.*
146. *Id.* at 24.
147. *Id.* at 32.
148. *Id.* at 34.

body which enforces and protects one's rights. For the social contract theorists, the individual in the state of nature had unlimited "rights." But this did not mean that he or she would be able to exercise or act on those rights. In the state of nature, everyone had the same natural rights, which were unlimited and mutually exclusive. But, of course, "having" natural rights to everything did not mean that an individual actually had everything, or even that an individual had anything at all, since anyone else who was able to take or monopolize resources might well have done exactly that.

Thus, in the social contract tradition, to have rights in the state of nature—for example, to have the right to kill for food—clearly did not mean that an individual would in fact have anything; a given individual might kill for food, or might himself be killed by someone or something stronger. On the other hand, to have rights after the formation of society means only that there are limits on the acts of the sovereign and the individual is entitled to take certain actions against the sovereign if these limits are violated.

The French and American revolutions at the end of the eighteenth century, I will argue, both invoked the concept of rights, in roughly the same sense as this notion was formulated by the social contract theorists: first, rights inhere in individuals and precede the formation of the state. They are the basis for the legitimacy of the *state*—not claims whose legitimacy is granted by the state. Second, the original rights held by individuals pertain to their self-interest—their sustenance, their self-preservation, their freedom to pursue their own ends and desires. This freedom is a negative freedom, that is, freedom from prohibitions. Finally, these rights speak to the relation between the individual and the state: the original rights are the basis on which the individual consents to be ruled; and they are the justification for rebellion in the event of tyranny by the sovereign.

This view of rights can also be seen in the documents which were promulgated as the justifications for the American and French revolutions. The American Declaration of Independence begins by proclaiming the people's dissolution of the existing political bands, "to assume among the powers of the earth the separate and equal station to which the Laws of

Nature and of Nature's God entitle them."[149] According to the Declaration of Independence, it is a "self-evident" truth that "all men are created equal, that they are endowed by their Creator with certain unalienable Rights," which include "Life, Liberty, and the pursuit of Happiness."[150] These rights are prior to government and legitimate government is a convention based upon consent: "to secure these rights, Governments are instituted among men, deriving their just powers from the consent of the governed."[151] The people retain the right to dissolve a government: "That whenever any Form of Government becomes destructive of these ends, it is the Right of the People to alter or to abolish it."[152]

The French Declaration of the Rights of Man and Citizen of 1789[153] (Declaration of the Rights of Man or French Declaration) echoes the language of Rousseau, the American Declaration of Independence and the social contract theorists. It holds that "ignorance, forgetfulness or contempt of the rights of man, are the sole causes of the public miseries and of the corruption of governments," and then sets forth the "natural, inalienable, and sacred rights of man," in order that "the acts of the legislative power and those of the executive power may be each moment compared with the aim of every political insti-

149. THE DECLARATION OF INDEPENDENCE para. 1 (U.S. 1776).

150. *Id.*

151. *Id.*

152. *Id.* The Virginia Declaration of Rights of June 12, 1776, is, interestingly, both more explicit and more concrete. It states:

> 1. That all men are by nature equally free and independent, and have certain inherent rights, of which, when they enter into a state of society, they cannot, by any compact, deprive or divest their posterity; namely, the enjoyment of life and liberty, with the means of acquiring and possessing property, and pursuing and obtaining happiness and safety.
>
> 2. That all power is vested in, and consequently derived from, the People; that magistrates are their trustees and servants, and at all times amenable to them.
>
> 3. That Government is, or ought to be, instituted for the common benefit, protection, and security of the people, nation, or community; . . . and that, whenever any Government shall be found inadequate or contrary to these purposes, a majority of the community hath an indubitable, inalienable, and indefeasible right to reform, alter or abolish it . . . .

VIRGINIA DECLARATION OF RIGHTS arts. 1-3, *reprinted in* 1 THE FOUNDERS' CONSTITUTION 6 (Philip B. Kurland & Ralph Lerner eds., 1987).

153. *See* DECLARATION OF THE RIGHTS OF MAN AND CITIZEN [hereinafter DECLARATION OF THE RIGHTS OF MAN], *reprinted in*, THE CONSTITUTION AND OTHER DOCUMENTS ILLUSTRATIVE OF THE HISTORY OF FRANCE 1789-1907 15 (2d ed. 1908).

tution," which is the preservation of the rights of man.[154] The Declaration of the Rights of Man then states that, accordingly:

> [T]he National Assembly recognizes and declares . . . the following rights of man and citizen.
>
> > 1. Men are born and remain free and equal in rights. Social distinctions can be based only upon public utility.
> >
> > 2. The aim of every political association is the preservation of the natural and imprescriptible rights of man. These rights are liberty, property, security, and resistance to oppression.
> >
> > . . .
> >
> > 4. Liberty consists in the power to do anything that does not injure others; accordingly, the exercise of the natural rights of each man has no limits except those that secure to the other members of society the enjoyment of these same rights. These limits can be determined only by law.
> >
> > . . .
> >
> > 6. Law is the expression of the general will; . . . . It must be the same for all, whether it protects or punishes. All citizens [are] equal in its eyes . . . .
> >
> > . . .
> >
> > 11. The free communication of ideas and opinions is one of the most precious of the rights of man; every citizen then can speak, write, and print, subject to responsibility for the abuse of this freedom in the cases determined by law.
> >
> > . . .
> >
> > 17. Property being a sacred and inviolable right, no one can be deprived of it, unless a legally established public necessity evidently demands it, under the condition of a

154. *Id.* preamble.

just and prior indemnity.[155]

These proclamations of rights are thoroughly familiar to us. Yet their very familiarity obscures something quite obvious: the literal meaning of the words. This is the basis of the empiricist critique of rights and it is worth reiterating the arguments of two of the leading empiricist critics of rights from the Enlightenment, Bentham and Hume, who assert that the declarations of rights are quite simply counterfactual.

B. *The Empiricist Critique*

In his essay, *On the Original Contract*, first published in 1748, Hume summarizes the basic claims of the social contract theorists:

> When we consider how nearly equal all men are in their bodily force, and even in their mental powers and faculties, till cultivated by education, we must necessarily allow, that nothing but their own consent could, at first, associate them together, and subject them to any authority. The people, if we trace government to its first origin in the woods and deserts, are the source of all power and jurisdiction . . . . Nothing but their own consent, and their sense of the advantages resulting from peace and order, could have had that influence.[156]

But, says Hume, look around us—there is no sign that there was, or is, consent by subjects or recognition by those who hold power that their legitimacy rests upon such consent.

> But would these reasoners look abroad into the world, they would meet with nothing that, in the least, corresponds to their ideas, or can warrant so refined and philosophical a system. On the contrary, we find every where princes who claim their subjects as their property and assert their independent right of sovereignty, from conquest of succession. We find also every where subjects who acknowledge this right in their prince and suppose themselves born under obligations of obedience to a certain sovereign . . . . Obedience or subjection becomes so familiar, that most men never make any inquiry about its origin or cause, more than about the gravi-

155. *Id.* arts. 1, 2, 4, 6, 11, 17.

156. David Hume, *On the Original Contract*, *in* SOCIAL CONTRACT: ESSAYS BY LOCKE, HUME AND ROUSSEAU 209, 211-12 (Ernest Barker ed., 1947).

ty, resistance, or the most universal laws of nature.[157]

Hume continues, observing that "[a]lmost all the governments which exist at present, or of which there remains any record in story, have been founded originally, either on usurpation or conquest, or both, without any pretence of a fair consent or voluntary subjection of the people."[158]

Hume asked where the social contract could be found in the world's shifting political fortunes:

> The face of the earth is continually changing, by the increase of small kingdoms into great empires, by the dissolution of great empires into smaller kingdoms, by the planting of colonies, by the migration of tribes. Is there anything discoverable in all these events but force and violence? Where is the mutual agreement or voluntary association so much talked of?[159]

Hume's point is quite obvious: in the social and political world around us, there is no sign of either the social contract or the natural rights on which it rests. If we look around us, or look at history, we see only the opposite: government based upon force or tradition and obedience based upon fear or habit.

Bentham's criticism concerns more the logical and linguistic issues: when we claim that we "have" a "right," what exactly is the referent? What is it exactly that we "have?" It is in this context that Bentham remarks: "*Natural rights* [are] simple nonsense: natural and imprescriptible rights, rhetorical nonsense,—nonsense upon stilts."[160]

The tone may be contemptuous, but his objection is a serious one. In *Anarchical Fallacies,* Bentham dissects the Declaration of the Rights of Man line by line and word by word. Bentham states that "[t]he criticism is verbal:—true, but what else can it be? Words—words without a meaning, or with a meaning too flatly false to be maintained by anybody, are the stuff it is made of. Look to the letter, you find nonsense—look

---

157. *Id.* at 213-14.
158. *Id.* at 215-16.
159. *Id.* at 216.
160. Jeremy Bentham, *Anarchical Fallacies; Being an Examination of the Declaration of Rights Issued During the French Revolution, in* NONSENSE UPON STILTS: BENTHAM, BURKE AND MARX ON THE RIGHTS OF MAN 53 (Jeremy Waldron ed., 1987).

beyond the letter, you find nothing."[161]

This is a serious and precise objection. On the one hand, the claims of the document, if taken literally, are flatly false. On the other, if one asserts that the words do not literally refer to reality—then to what do they refer? The answer can only be that they refer to a fiction, a fantasy, some sort of wishful thinking.

Bentham begins with the claims of freedom and equality. Article I of the Declaration of the Rights of Man provides that "*Men (all men) are born and remain free, and equal in respect of rights*."[162] Bentham responds:

> *All men are born free? All men remain free?* No, not a single man: not a single man that ever was, or is, or will be. All men, on the contrary, are born in subjection, and the most absolute subjection—the subjection of a helpless child to the parents on whom he depends every moment for his existence.[163]

As Bentham elaborates:

> *All men are born equal in rights*. The rights of the heir of the most indigent family equal to the rights of the heir of the most wealthy? In what case is this true? . . . The madman has as good a right to confine anybody else, as anybody else has to confine him. The idiot has as much right to govern everybody, as anybody can have to govern him. The physician and the nurse, when called in by the next friend of a sick man seized with a delirium, have no more right to prevent him throwing himself out of the window, than he has to throw them out of it. All this is plainly and incontestably included in this article of the Declaration of Rights: in the very words of it, and in the meaning—if it has any meaning.[164]

Bentham's intention is partly to point out that it is just factually incorrect to say that human beings are free and equal, and partly to suggest that we would not even want this

161. *Id.* at 49.

162. *Id.* (paraphrasing DECLARATION OF THE RIGHTS OF MAN, *supra* note 153, art. 1).

163. Bentham, *supra* note 160, at 49.

164. *Id.* at 50-51.

state of affairs to actually take place. We obviously don't want both the qualified and the unqualified to have equal rights to perform surgery;[165] and if we say that the former may perform surgery and the latter may not, then we have committed ourselves both to inequality and to restrictions on freedom. So what does it mean—in the face of actual inequality and restrictions on freedom, to insist on the "existence" of rights? In the end, Bentham argues, it makes no sense to speak of rights—literally, the word "right" has no referent. As much as we may wish for some natural entitlement to freedom or equality, prior to and independent of the acts of particular governments, there is no such thing; and insisting on its existence will not in fact bring it into existence.

> In proportion to the want of happiness resulting from the want of rights, a reason exists for wishing there were such things as rights. But reasons for wishing there were such things as rights, are not rights;—a reason for wishing that a certain right were established, is not that right—want is not supply—hunger is not bread.[166]

Bentham's and Hume's empiricist criticisms make starkly clear that the assertions about the existence and origin of rights, taken at face value, are not only counterfactual, but patently ridiculous. What does it mean to say that rights are "inherent?" This claim seems to suggest that they are natural and not artifacts; that they are discovered rather than invented. If they are inherent, why were they not known for thousands of years after the beginning of human society? When they are identified as "inherent" in a particular document, at a particular historical moment, are they not in fact being bestowed by virtue of their pronouncement? Which is to say: they are not inherent at all; they are invented, claimed, bestowed.

In what sense are these rights self-evident? Our experience in fact suggests the opposite—that if we look around us at human lives and human society, we in fact see very little evidence that all persons are happy, or are free, or are fraternal, or are prosperous. What is self-evident seems to be the oppo-

---

165. While the Declaration of the Rights of Man does say that social distinctions should be based on "common utility," Bentham points out that this does not resolve the problem, but only creates a contradiction.

166. *Id.* at 53.

site: that more often than not, human beings suffer; more often than not, that they are restricted and oppressed in innumerable ways; more often than not, they live their lives in hunger and poverty. And if these are the circumstances in which human beings generally live, then in what sense are rights to property, fraternity, liberty and equality "inalienable?" Of course these rights are "alienable"—it is possible to have a human life without them. In fact, most of us do.

Bentham and Hume are quite right: what is striking is how implausible the claims about rights are. The notion of rights is perhaps so familiar to us that the language and claims of rights seem obvious and plausible. But they are not. "Man is born free," writes Rousseau,[167] but in fact, human beings are born helpless and dependent. "[E]very man has a Right to every thing," writes Hobbes of the state of nature,[168] because everyone may make use of anything that will contribute to his self-preservation. But in fact, in a state of war of all against all, there is no "right" at all, only power: those who are stronger will take and use whatever they choose. The French and American Declarations of Rights would seem to be even more absurd. It is not self-evident that people are equal. What is evident is the opposite: that at all times in history and in all sectors of society, there are great inequalities in status, in power, in abilities, in property and in entitlements.

Thus, we seem to have a paradox on our hands. The rights which are held to be natural are, in fact, quite unnatural. The rights which are held to be inalienable are not only "alienable," but in fact quite rare. The rights which are held to be self-evident are in fact quite inconsistent with all of the evidence.

What, then, is a "right" exactly? What can we coherently argue that we actually "have" which is inherent, inalienable and self-evident? I suggest that it is at most either a moral imperative or a conception of the good: The claim that all people ought to be equal and all people ought to be free; or that it would be good if everyone were equal and it would be good if everyone were free. This means, however, that we are not talking about a "right" anymore, but a statement of universal desire—a description of the human ideal, not something which

167. ROUSSEAU, *supra* note 136, at 17.
168. HOBBES, *supra* note 114, at 190.

must in fact happen, or has ever happened, or will ever happen. At most, what is "inherent" or "self-evident" is a universal conception of the good.

V. Two Contemporary Philosophical Theories of Rights

We saw that the notion of rights that emerged in the political thought of the Enlightenment has four features.

First, rights are abstract. One can have a right to property, but at the same time have no actual property. The fact that one has no property presents no conflict or disproof of the existence of the right to property, since the right is neither an offer nor a promise of property.

Second, rights are political. These rights concern the relation of the individual to the state. The right to liberty means only that the state will not deprive an individual of liberty except under certain circumstances (although individuals may deprive other individuals of liberty in many circumstances, for example, by owning land and excluding others from its use).

Third, rights are very broadly conceived. The rights in the state of nature constitute an entitlement literally to everything; the rights under the social contract assert an entitlement to everything not prohibited by the state; and in the revolutionary proclamations, rights are stated as unconditional entitlements to such things as "freedom" and "equality."

Fourth, the notion of rights involves claims which are counterfactual. They have the curious feature of purporting to be natural, inalienable and eternal, even though, as a description of ordinary reality, they are quite false.

Fifth, rights are "reified" claims of entitlement. The notion of reification is used where a relationship, or process, or idea comes to be thought of as a thing or substance. Thus, the claim that one ought to be free is "reified" when it is said that one has a "right" which is implicitly treated as a thing insofar as it is seen as something which can be possessed.

Where the Enlightenment thinkers proclaimed the existence of rights, on the grounds that rights are inherent or natural, contemporary philosophers offer a more sophisticated structure for the justification of rights as ethical claims. One of the standard assumptions in this literature is that a right is some form of justified claim[169]—but also that a "right" is

169. For example, Joseph Raz writes, "'x has a right' means that, other things

something that is held, or enjoyed, or possessed, even when material reality is to the contrary. Consequently, I will argue, the contemporary philosophical discussion of the nature and justification of human rights reiterates the fundamental paradox of the Enlightenment notion of rights without resolving it. In this section, I will briefly review two of the attempts to address this issue in the contemporary philosophical literature.

Maurice Cranston maintains that a human right is a type of moral right. "[W]e justify the moral rights of an individual," he writes, "by arguing that those rights have been earned or that they have been acquired by gift, bequest, sale or some other contractual undertaking."[170] Human rights, while they "clearly belong to the category of moral rights," cannot be justified in this fashion, since they are not dependent upon a particular act of creation or contract. Cranston contends that these rights "belong to a man simply because he is a man."[171] Gewirth makes the same point: "Human rights are rights or entitlements that belong to every person; thus, they are universal moral rights."[172] Gewirth maintains that "[a]t bottom, the idea of human rights is a moral one. It becomes a legal and political idea only because of its supreme moral importance."[173]

---

being equal, an aspect of x's well-being (his interest) is a sufficient reason for holding some other person(s) to be under a duty." *See* Joseph Raz, *Right-Based Moralities*, *in* THEORIES OF RIGHTS 182, 183 (Jeremy Waldron ed., 1984). In A THEORY OF JUSTICE, John Rawls says that "[a] conception of right is a set of principles, general in form and universal in application, that is to be publicly recognized as a final court of appeal for ordering the conflicting claims of moral persons." JOHN RAWLS, A THEORY OF JUSTICE 135 (1971). Henry Shue says that "[a] moral right provides (1) the rational basis for a justified demand (2) that the actual enjoyment of a substance be (3) socially guaranteed against standard threats." HENRY SHUE, BASIC RIGHTS: SUBSISTENCE, AFFLUENCE, AND U.S. FOREIGN POLICY 13 (2d ed. 1996). Shue continues to contend that "[a] right provides the rational basis for a justified demand. If a person has a particular right, the demand that the enjoyment of the substance of the right be socially guaranteed is justified by good reasons and the guarantees ought, therefore, to be provided." *Id.* Sarat and Kearns state that "rights are assumed to be entitlements of persons whose status as persons is fixed and from which rights are said to issue." Austin Sarat & Thomas R. Kearns, *Introduction*, *in* IDENTITIES, POLITICS, AND RIGHTS 1 (Austin Sarat and Thomas R. Kearns eds., 1995).

170. CRANSTON, *supra* note 87, at 22.

171. *Id.* at 24.

172. ALAN GEWIRTH, HUMAN RIGHTS: ESSAYS ON JUSTIFICATION AND APPLICATIONS 42 (1982).

173. *Id.* at ix.

And what is a human right, exactly? In *The Epistemology of Human Rights*, Gewirth addresses the question of the "existence" of rights. "Human rights are rights which all persons equally have simply insofar as they are human. But are there any such rights? How, if at all, do we know that there are?"[174] It is with this question of knowledge and the related question of existence that I want to deal in this paper.

Gewirth argues that human rights are "personally oriented, normatively necessary, moral requirements."[175] Human rights are "personally oriented" in that they are "requirements that are owed to distinct Subjects or individuals for the good of those individuals."[176] Human rights are "normatively necessary" in that compliance with them is morally mandatory, rather than supererogatory. Human rights are "moral requirements" in that they are: (1) necessary needs; (2) justified entitlements; and (3) claims or demands addressed to other persons.[177] Thus, the justifying basis of human rights is "a normative moral principle that serves to prove or establish that every human morally ought, as a matter of normative necessity, to have the necessary goods as something to which he is personally entitled, which he can claim from others as his due."[178]

Gewirth observes that:

> In the phrase, "there are human rights", "there are" is ambiguous as between positive and normative meanings. In the sense of "existence" that is relevant here, the existence of human rights is independent of whether they are guaranteed or enforced by legal codes or are socially recognized.[179]

Thus, Gewirth resolves the ambiguity by essentially adopting the position that a human right is a type of "ought," and is binding as an "ought" insofar as a rational moral argument can be constructed in its support.[180] Human rights, then, share the features of all moral claims, morality being "a set of cate-

---

174. Alan Gewirth, *The Epistemology of Human Rights*, *in* HUMAN RIGHTS 1 (Ellen Frankel Paul et al. eds., 1984).
175. *Id.* at 2.
176. *Id.* at 2-3.
177. *See id.* at 2.
178. *Id.*
179. *Id.* at 3.
180. *See id.*

gorically obligatory requirements for action."[181] They also share the general features of rights: "a person's rights are what belong to him as his due, what he is entitled to, hence what he can rightly demand of others."[182] Gewirth justifies this position in terms of the nature of human action and the attribute of dignity: "By virtue of the voluntariness of his actions, the agent has a kind of autonomy or freedom . . . [the agent] can and does make his own decisions on the basis of his own reflective understanding . . . By virtue of these characteristics of his action, the agent has worth or dignity."[183] Consequently, he says "all humans are held to have rights to the necessary conditions of their action."[184]

Danto's criticism of Gewirth's claim could have been written by Bentham. He describes a situation in which he was on a committee charged with developing a disciplinary procedure for the university:

> We all wondered . . . what right we had to do what was asked of us, and a good bit of time went into expressing our insecurities. Finally, a man from the law-school said, with the tried patience of someone required to explain what should be as plain as day . . . : "This is the way it is with rights. You want 'em, so you say you got 'em, and if nobody says you don't then you do." In the end he was right. We worked a code out which nobody liked, but in debating it the community acknowledged the rights. Jefferson did not say that it was self-evident that there were human rights and which they were: he said we *hold* this . . . self-evident . . . . This is the way it is with rights. We *declare* we have them, and see if they are recognized. After that it is a matter of lobbying or something more extreme . . . .[185]

It is not clear that Gewirth is in a position to offer a satisfactory response to Danto's (or Bentham's) position. If his intention was to show that rights "exist," he has fundamentally shown only that there are certain justifications for saying that

181. GEWIRTH, *supra* note 172, at 45.
182. *Id.* at 48.
183. *Id.* at 22-23.
184. *Id.* at 24.
185. Arthur C. Danto, *Comment on Gewirth. Constructing an Epistemology of Human Rights: A Pseudo Problem?*, *in* HUMAN RIGHTS 25, 30 (Ellen Frankel Paul et al. eds., 1984).

people ought to act in a certain way. His argument in the end is an ethical rather than ontological one. Yet he wants to say that when we speak of how people ought to act, that this somehow translates into a thing that we possess. Gewirth claims that he rejects the reification of rights. Gewirth contends that "[a]lthough Thomas Jefferson wrote that all humans 'are endowed by their Creator with certain inalienable rights,' it is not the case that humans are born having rights in the sense in which they are born having legs."[186] Yet the language of reification continues to appear: rights are things that we "have;"[187] they are "normative property;"[188] "a person's rights are what belong to him as his due."[189]

Unlike Gewirth, Dworkin explicitly frames rights as in terms of their political context: "Individual rights are political trumps held by individuals. Individuals have rights when, for some reason, a collective goal is not a sufficient justification for denying them what they wish . . . ."[190] Thus, "rights" are the claims invoked by individuals against the collective or community interests. "If someone has a right to something, then it is wrong for the government to deny it to him even though it would be in the general interest to do so."[191] In TAKING RIGHTS SERIOUSLY, Dworkin explores the issue of whether "citizens have *some* moral rights against their Government."[192] The particular political rights for which Dworkin argues are derived, in turn, "from the abstract right to concern and respect taken to be fundamental and axiomatic."[193] Dworkin notes that he presumes "that we all accept the following postulates of political morality."[194] He further states:

> Government must treat those whom it governs with concern, that is, as human beings who are capable of suffering and frustration, and with respect, that is, as human beings who are capable of forming and acting on intelligent conceptions of how their lives should be lived. Government must not only

---

186. Gewirth, *supra* note 174, at 3.
187. GEWIRTH, *supra* note 172, at 19-20.
188. *Id.* at 10.
189. *Id.* at 48.
190. RONALD DWORKIN, TAKING RIGHTS SERIOUSLY xi (1977).
191. *Id.* at 269.
192. *Id.* at 184.
193. *Id.* at xv.
194. *Id.* at 272.

> treat people with concern and respect, but with equal concern and respect.[195]

Rejecting the positivist view, Dworkin argues for a theory of law that holds that political rights pre-exist legal rights, since they are to be invoked against the state. Yet these political rights are at the same time moral rights and they are justified in terms of the moral personality of the individual. Thus, Dworkin's position is ultimately that a right is a proposition about how government ought to act, as Gewirth's is fundamentally a position about how a person ought to act in the face of certain claims. Both fundamentally offer theories about which imperatives can be best justified. They are theories of how individuals and governments ought to act, based upon the assertions that individuals "have" dignity, or "are" equal. But no matter how much more sophisticated these contemporary theories of justified claims are than the earlier claims of the Enlightenment thinkers and political actors, they are no less problematic. Thus, the paradox remains: if we claim that a right is something we "have," then either the claim is often patently false, or what we "have" is just an empty abstraction. On the other hand, if a right is a statement of aspirations, of a goal toward which we are striving, then many of the descriptions of rights—that they are inalienable, universal and so on—simply make no sense.

Dworkin and Gewirth reject positivist arguments that rights are only those claims which are recognized and enforced and they offer arguments and a vision as to how human beings and governments ought to act. Yet, the vision is not purely normative; it is ontological as well. The arguments are not simply that "it would be good if governments treated individuals with equal respect and concern," but rather that individuals "have the right" to be treated with equal respect and concern; and that is why governments should do so. The thing that we have when we "have" a right would therefore be something more abstract than the (empirically observable) enforcement actions of the state; and more solid (indeed, reified) than an argument about how people and states should act. Gewirth and Dworkin, along with others, thus inherit the

195. *Id.*

Enlightenment's paradoxical project of devising a moral claim with an actual "existence."

VI. RESOLVING THE PARADOX: MARX AND THE METAPHYSICS OF RIGHTS

So let us re-ask Bentham's question of two hundred years ago: what is it you actually *have* when you have a right? What is it you actually are, when you are free or equal, in the sense used in proclamations of rights?

The problem is this: there are these claims—that we "have" something or that we "are" something—and that "something" is absolute, binding and eternal. Yet this eternally existing state is often or even always simply contrary to fact. "All men are free"—but of course they are not. Some are imprisoned, some are incapacitated. "All men are equal," yet some are stronger, richer, more powerful than others. "All persons have dignity," yet many are humiliated in their homes, in their workplaces, by the state, or in public discourse.

If claims about rights were simply and directly aspirational or normative statements—"All persons should be free and equal"—there would be no paradox. There might well be a very different sort of problem: we would disagree over what we should aspire to, or how people should act. But that is not how assertions about rights are framed. They are presented not as normative or aspirational, but as statements about our current (not to say eternal) condition; or as possessions we now (and since the beginning of time) have (and have had).

Under positive law theories, a "right" is just a description of how the state will act under certain circumstances.[196] In this view, "I have a right not to be assaulted" means that if I am assaulted, I can call the police and they will arrest the assailant, the district attorney will prosecute the assailant and so on. Legal positivism maintains that there is no such thing as a "right" independent of the institutional processes of the

196. *See* H.L.A. HART, THE CONCEPT OF LAW 203 (1961) (summarizing some of the basic ideas of the legal positivists). Hart asked what the underlying "concern of the great battle-cries of legal positivism" was, referring to Austin's "'[t]he existence of law is one thing; its merit or demerit another;' Gray's '[t]he law of a State is not an ideal but something which actually exists . . . it is not that which ought to be, but that which is;' and Kelson's '[l]egal norms may have any kind of content.'" *Id.*

state which define and explicate the rights that it will enforce. Under legal positivism, if we ask "what rights exist other than those which the state recognizes and enforces," the answer is "none." If the state changes its policy and its conduct, the right simply disappears. In this view, an individual has no entitlements prior to or outside of the acts of government. The "right" to inherit property or to collect a debt is a right created by the state, enforceable only on the terms dictated by the state and by means of procedures established by the state.

Alternatively, natural law asserts that there is some higher law which positive law aspires to, or approaches.[197] In this view, natural law is where justice resides; it operates as a regulative ideal, a standard toward which actual, particular laws aspire. If a "right" is something given by natural law, then we would speak of that toward which we strive—freedom, equality—but do not have. Natural law is the measure we use to gauge the justness of actual laws. But natural law is not concrete or enforceable in the way that the right to inherit is; natural law by definition transcends the state, which is the source of actual and particular laws, their articulation and their enforcement.

However, the thinkers of the Enlightenment, as well as contemporary philosophers of rights, maintain both that "rights" are that toward which we aspire; and that rights are nevertheless something we *have*, or describe what it is that we *are*.[198] The Enlightenment conception of rights does not fit cleanly within the framework of either natural law or positive law. It holds that, in contradistinction to positive legal entitlements, there exist legal rights inherent in the individual, prior to and outside of the state and society. Indeed, the relation between state and individual is a precise inversion of the one given in positive law: it is no longer the individual who looks to the state to determine his entitlements, but the state which looks to the contract among individuals to justify its very existence. And, in contrast to natural law, the Enlighten-

197. Hart notes that the notion of natural law includes the idea that "there are certain principles of human conduct, awaiting discovery by human reason, with which man-made law must conform if it is to be valid." *Id.* at 182.

198. The problem is made explicit in the grammar of statements about rights. They are statements made in the present tense, indicative mood; but which are in fact counterfactual imperatives in the subjunctive mood.

ment conception of rights very much anticipates enforcement in concrete ways: the Enlightenment rights were presented as things that we *have*, or the condition in which we *are*, and these possessions or factual states of affairs were presented as the grounds for revolutions and political institutions.

Thus, "rights" in the Enlightenment view had a curious ontological status from the beginning: they are neither positive laws, articulated by actual, particular governments; nor are they natural laws which guide positive law, but which in themselves transcend both explication and enforcement. Rather, the Enlightenment view holds that rights are in a sense justified by their other-worldly origin, though they equally lay claim to being present and active in this world. Marx argues that, for this reason, the Enlightenment conception of a right is thus, in a sense, simultaneously sacred and profane.

In his essay, *On the Jewish Question*, Karl Marx criticizes Bruno Bauer for addressing the question of political emancipation without examining the prior matter of human emancipation.[199] Marx explicitly rejects the entire Enlightenment treatment of rights for the same reason. This applies to the rights of equality, liberty, security and property from the Declaration of the Rights of Man, as well as the similar rights articulated in the American Declaration of Independence. Marx observes that these documents see the individual as a "self-sufficient monad," whose rights concern the pursuit of egoistic self-interest, with security serving as the guarantee of that egoism.[200]

If Marx's only response to the Enlightenment conception of rights was that such rights are bourgeois and self-serving, then his criticism would indeed be shallow and without much philosophical value. But, I would argue, the heart of his critique is not that "people should care about others and not be selfish and individualistic," or some comparable platitude. His critique, as I understand it, is that the notion of rights involves an idealist metaphysics;[201] that this idealism serves to not

199. *See* Karl Marx, *On the Jewish Question, in* KARL MARX, EARLY WRITINGS 211-16 (Rodney Livingstone & Gregor Benton trans., 1975).

200. *Id.* at 230. Note that these observations are generally the only part of Marx's critique of rights which are acknowledged or discussed by most commentators. *See, e.g.*, Asbjorn Eide, *National Sovereignty and Human Rights, in* HUMAN RIGHTS IN PERSPECTIVE: A GLOBAL ASSESSMENT 10-11 (Asbjorn Eide & Bernt Hagtvet eds., 1992).

201. By "idealist metaphysics" I refer to the position that concepts or abstrac-

only trivialize the concrete, but to literally deny the reality of the concrete; that, consequently, gratuitous human suffering is tolerated and justified; and that the delusion proffered by the idealism results in a crippling self-incapacitation, which prevents those who suffer unjustly from acting to alter the social structure.

In feudalism, Marx says, civil society had a directly political character. That is, "the elements of civil life such as property, family and the mode and manner of work were elevated in the form of seignory, estate and guild to the level of elements of political life."[202]

The political then becomes the realm of "the *universal* concern of the people, ideally independent of those *particular* elements of civil life."[203] Modern bourgeois society is characterized by a profound experience of bifurcation: we exist in two realms—the political and the civil, the universal and the particular, the ideal and the material, the abstract and the concrete. Politically, a democracy "regards man—not just one man but all men—as a *sovereign* and supreme being."[204] As citizen, each person in a democracy is literally deemed to be the sovereign. The leaders are chosen "by the people;" their election indicates "the will of the people;" their jobs are to "represent the people." A sovereign is the source of law and the enforcer of law; the sovereign ultimately holds all political power; a crime committed by an individual against another individual is an offense to the sovereign; the sovereign chooses to make war or not; property, freedom and security are all granted to individuals by the sovereign. As sovereign, then, the citizen is all-powerful, subject to the whims and laws of no one, has at his discretion the right to avail himself of all the wealth of the land and has an army to carry out his will abroad and a police force to enforce his will domestically. Yet, of course, the ordinary citizen—the one who is neither king nor president nor prime minister—does not have such a life, at least on the concrete level of day-to-day existence. The ordinary citizen will be careful to obey the law so as not to be jailed. He will hope he

---

tions are treated as entities that are quite real and in fact more real than material entities.

202. MARX, *supra* note 199, at 232.

203. *Id.* at 233.

204. *Id.* at 225-26.

has enough money to pay his rent and meet his needs. He will be at the mercy of a dozen different forces: the whim of his employer may send him out to the streets with no job; the market may drive the cost of fuel so high he cannot afford heat in the winter; he may be conscripted into the army and sent off to kill or to be killed. The concrete reality of his daily life will be characterized by fear, anxiety and helplessness in the face of these forces. The power and privileges held by a sovereign just do not characterize the texture of daily life for the individual. This is "man in his uncultivated, unsocial aspect, man in his contingent existence, man just as he is, man as he has been corrupted, lost to himself, sold, and exposed to the rule of inhuman conditions and elements by the entire organization of our society . . . ."[205]

Yet with the Enlightenment notion of rights, the ideal state we are in—insofar as we are citizens—is seen not as less real, nor is it seen as fantasy or aspiration, but rather as the higher reality. The language of rights posits a "true," original, human nature, which is characterized by liberty, equality, security, fraternity. It is in civil society that "the real man" has his "sensuous, individual and *immediate* existence."[206] The citizen or the political man "is simply abstract, artificial man, man as an *allegorical*, *moral* person. Actual man is acknowledged only in the form of the *egoistic* individual and *true* man only in the form of the *abstract citizen*."[207]

Where the political state is fully developed as something distinct from civil society, then, Marx says, man

> leads a double life, a life in heaven and a life on earth, not only in his mind, in his consciousness, but in *reality*. He lives in the *political community*, where he regards himself as a *communal being*, and in *civil society*, where he is active as a *private individual*, regards other men as means, debases himself to a means and becomes a plaything of alien powers . . . Man in his *immediate* reality, in civil society, is a profane being. Here, where he regards himself and is regarded by others as a real individual, he is an illusory phenomenon. In the state, on the other hand, where he is considered to be a species-being, he is the imaginary member of a ficti-

205. *Id.* at 226.
206. *Id.* at 234.
207. *Id.*

> tious sovereignty, he is divested of his real individual life and filled with an unreal universality.[208]

We need only look at the grammatical form in which the social contract theorists and the revolutionary documents of the Enlightenment declare the existence of rights to see what Marx is talking about: the declarations of rights are not in the future tense, the conditional tense, or the subjunctive mood. They are in the present tense and the indicative mood, as though they are descriptions of a present reality; and the descriptions of the state of nature in the social contract writings are in the past tense, as though they are descriptions of an historical reality. In the introduction to his *Discourse on the Origin of Inequality*, Rousseau actually says:

> O man, whatever country you may be from, whatever your opinions may be, listen: here is your history, as I have thought to read it, not in the books of your fellowmen, who are liars, but in nature, who never lies. Everything that comes from nature will be true . . . .[209]

Marx's description of the metaphysical dualism describes well the paradox of the Enlightenment conception of rights: they are abstractions which are reified and claim to be possessions; they are ideals which claim to be factual states of affairs.

Let us now look at the basic structure of the paradox. Why is it that a declaration of rights operates as a statement of a present condition or a present possession, even though such a claim is patently counterfactual? What are the underlying assumptions, such that these claims are not dismissed immediately as fiction, fantasy, or moral aspiration? The assumption must be that claims such as "All men are free and equal" refer to a present reality—but an ideal reality, not the material one. However, such a claim involves more than the notion of dual realities. The declarations of rights do not say: "In one sense we are free, in another, we are not. In an ideal sense we are free, though obviously on a material level we are not. On one level, all human beings are entitled to dignity and equality; yet, on another level, most human beings do not have that to

208. *Id.* at 220.

209. Jean-Jacques Rousseau, *Discourse on the Origin of Inequality, in,* ROUSSEAU, *supra* note 136, at 119, 119.

which they are entitled, since they are routinely reduced to desperation and humiliation, used and discarded by others, their poverty deepening alongside of the increasing wealth of others. In one realm we have many rights, in the other realm we have no rights at all, only good or bad luck."

Obviously, the political and philosophical claims about rights are *not* of this form. Rather, they operate *only* on the level of the ideal—for example, "everyone has the right to be treated with equal dignity and respect." This suggests a hierarchy within the dualism: it is the ideal reality which is the truer reality and the material world is in some sense less real. It seems to me that this is what Marx is speaking to when he distinguishes between "true reality" and "actual reality." In our "true" nature, we are free, equal and entitled to dignity, prosperity and security. In our actual lives, however, which are corrupt and distorted versions of our true selves, deformed and limited by the conditions of material reality, we have none of these qualities. The question demanded by the Enlightenment conception of rights is: "How is it that our actual human condition does not constitute an irrefutable disproof of the claims about the 'true nature' and 'inalienable entitlement' of human beings?" The answer must be that there is a hierarchy: the abstract and absolute claims are deemed real, while the historical and factual dimension of human existence are deemed to be merely an appearance—a transient, contingent state, subject to change and consequently subject to disregard or trivialization.

This also tells us something about what I referred to earlier as the "asymmetry" of the standard conception of human rights. Not only does the standard conception reflect a certain political and cultural perspective—that of Western First World countries with highly developed formal political rights and extreme economic disparities—but it also reiterates the paradoxical structure of the Enlightenment notion of rights. Thus, the standard notion treats political rights (which for most people will be purely abstract or flatly counterfactual) as essential and sees economic rights as vague, inessential, difficult to justify and difficult to implement.

VII. THE POLITICAL AGENDA OF HUMAN RIGHTS CLAIMS AND THE SUPPRESSION OF MORAL DISCOURSE: THE EXAMPLE OF NUREMBERG

At this point I would like to return to the Nuremberg tribunal to explore the relationship between what was at stake, on one hand, and the legitimacy of the concept and the suppression of moral discourse, on the other. In the contexts of both international law and ethical thought, the Nuremberg tribunals hold a central role: they established the legal precedent for all war crimes and human rights tribunals thereafter. They also served as the prototype in international relations for the moral denunciation of the acts of other nations as "crimes against humanity."[210] Yet, I will argue, even the Nuremberg tribunals—which purported to be the unequivocal triumph of justice and the rule of law over barbarity and evil[211]—are deeply intertwined with underlying political and rhetorical agendas. Furthermore, while the Nuremberg tribunals purported to explore the legal and moral issues raised by the conduct of the Nazi regime, in fact they controlled and severely restricted moral and legal discourse. Because our contemporary human rights discourse has all of these features, it may be valuable to look at Nuremberg as the occasion on which they first emerged.

I will look specifically at the legal structure of the Nuremberg trials and the tension between the political agenda and judicial legitimacy. The tribunal has been criticized as "victors' justice" on many occasions before, including by defense counsel at Nuremberg. It might be observed that the tribunal's structure would indeed offend our most basic sense of justice and law were it not for the nature of the accusations. But it seems to me compelling to go one step further as well and to

210. At the trial of Adolf Eichmann in Jerusalem in 1961, the Nuremberg Trials were cited as precedent for the Israeli court's claim of jurisdiction. *See* HANNAH ARENDT, EICHMANN IN JERUSALEM: A REPORT ON THE BANALITY OF EVIL 254 (1963).

211. The opening statement of Robert Jackson, the prosecutor for the United States, refers to the acts being condemned and punished as "calculated" and "malignant," and refers to the defendants as "evil" and "sinister." Opening Statement for the United States of America by Robert H. Jackson, Chief of Counsel for the United States at the Palace of Justice, Nürnberg, Germany, Nov. 21, 1945 [hereinafter Jackson, Opening Statement], *in* ROBERT H. JACKSON, THE NÜRNBERG CASE 30-31 (1947).

look at how it was that the question of the *legality* of the tribunal could be so completely subsumed and trivialized by the *urgency* of the tribunal. I will suggest that the political and moral urgency of the trial not only was used to justify the tribunal's patent illegality; but made it politically impossible and morally impermissible to even raise the question of its illegality.

The result, I would argue, is that our legacy from Nuremberg is twofold. We have a notion of human rights, which is commonly recognized in treaties, in international law and in international organization; and for which there are now established tribunals for the indictment, prosecution and punishment of those who commit human rights violations.[212] Yet at the same time, we inherit the view that "human rights violations" involve a moral claim which is not only sound and good, but is flatly unquestionable. We inherit the view that no rational member of the moral community could even question the validity of such claims. It is as if to say: "Of course the acts of the Nazis were unspeakable atrocities. How could any decent human being defend the Nazis, on any grounds whatsoever? Such a person would either have to be insane or devoid of moral sensibilities. And of course the Nazis should be punished. What moral or rational person could dispute that? And if there isn't exactly a law which was actually broken, the need for decrying the Nazis as criminals is far greater than the duty to abide by legal technicalities."

Indeed, this was the very language that appeared in the documents establishing the Nuremberg tribunal, as well as the documents generated by the tribunal. I will argue that the need to achieve the moral end of punishing awful acts and the need to achieve the political end of doing so publicly, not only outweighed, but precluded altogether the possibility of discussing the correctness of the concept or the law.

212. This was the case, for instance, with the recent war crimes tribunals held at the Hague concerning the Bosnian conflict. *See* Mark R. von Sternberg, *A Comparison of the Yugoslavian and Rwandan War Crimes Tribunals: Universal Jurisdiction and the "Elementary Dictates of Humanity"*, 22 BROOK. J. INT'L L. 111, 111 (1996); Anthony Goodman, *U.N. Council Sets Up Yugoslav War Crimes Tribunal*, *in* REUTER LIBR. REP., May 25, 1993, *available in* LEXIS, News Library, Curnws File.

A. The Establishment of the Tribunal

The basic notion of the rule of law is the distinction between the "rule of law" and the "rule of men"—that is, that the law is distinct from the will and desires of the king.

> [T]he doctrine of the rule of law means first "the absolute supremacy or predominance of regular law as opposed to the influence of arbitrary power, and excludes the influence of arbitrariness of prerogative, or even of wide discretionary authority on the part of government;" and secondly it means "equality before the law, or the equal subjection of all classes to the ordinary law of the land administered by the ordinary law courts."[213]

The "rule of law" involves the notions that the law exists outside of particular rulers and particular subjects; that a "crime" consists of violating the law, not simply displeasing the ruler; that the person judging a claim must be different from the person who claims to be injured; that an individual cannot be punished for breaking a law which did not exist at the time the individual acted; that law prohibits certain acts, rather than simply naming and punishing individuals. The rule of law "is contrasted with every system of government based on the exercise by persons in authority of wide, arbitrary, or discretionary powers of constraint."[214] "Arbitrariness," in this context, includes laws directed to particular individuals or particular acts (rather than general principles or classes of acts); laws which are retroactive and penalize acts which were not illegal at the time they were done; and laws whose meaning is uncertain or whose application is unpredictable.[215]

---

213. 10 WILLIAM HOLDSWORTH, A HISTORY OF ENGLISH LAW 649 (1938) (quoting ALBERT VENN DICEY, INTRODUCTION TO THE STUDY OF THE LAW OF THE CONSTITUTION 198 (7th ed. 1908)).

214. DICEY, *supra* note 213, at 188.

215. *See* Richard Flathman, *Liberalism and the Suspect Enterprise of Political Institutionalization: The Case of the Rule of Law*, *in* THE RULE OF LAW 297, 303 (Ian Shapiro ed., 1994). Friedrich Hayek suggests that the notion of the "rule of law" originates with Aristotle (although the phrase is often associated with Hobbes), who wrote in the *Politics* that "'it is more proper that the law should govern than any of the citizens.'" FRIEDRICH A. HAYEK, THE CONSTITUTION OF LIBERTY 164-65 (1960) (citations omitted). According to Hayek, one of the "achievements of the [English] Civil War was the abolition in 1641 of the prerogative courts and especially the Star Chamber which had become, in F.W. Maitland's often quoted words, 'a court of politicians enforcing a policy, not a court of judges

Some of the most basic precepts of the U.S. Constitution and American legal practice invoke this distinction. Criminal defendants are presumed to be innocent until proven guilty. The bill of attainder clause in the Constitution prohibits the legislature from passing a law which names individuals and imposes penalties on them, while the ex post facto clause prohibits the legislature from passing a law which punishes individuals retroactively for acts which did not violate any explicit law at the time they were committed.[216] Judges who are related to either of the parties, or have an interest in the outcome of a proceeding, must recuse themselves, or inform both parties of the judge's interest and give the parties the opportunity to request recusal. If a judge had a material interest in the outcome of a case and refused to recuse himself, the parties would be entitled to appeal that determination to a higher court.

The "rule of law" entails that the rules of procedure for court actions, such as rules of evidence, are generated by a legislative or administrative body. They are articulated and published prior to any court proceedings. If a judge issues a ruling which is not consistent with the rules of procedure, a party may appeal this error to a higher court. The court's jurisdiction is conferred prior to any case, before any particular claims are brought; not as a vehicle for imposing a predetermined punishment. Jurisdiction is granted by the constitution or legislature, not created by the members of the same tribunal upon which jurisdiction is conferred.[217] The parties are entitled to challenge a court's jurisdiction and the court may not

---

administering the law.'" *Id.* The debate for the next twenty years focused on the arbitrariness of law and government. The rule of law and the absence of arbitrariness meant "that there must be no punishment without a previously existing law providing for it, that all statutes should have only prospective and not retrospective operation, and that the discretion of all magistrates should be strictly circumscribed by law." *Id.* at 169 (citations omitted). Hayek notes that the rule of law was applied to legislatures by Locke in the SECOND TREATISE ON CIVIL GOVERNMENT—a legislature "cannot assume to itself a power to rule by extemporary arbitrary decrees, but is bound to dispense justice, and decide the rights of the subject by promulgated standing laws, and known authorized judges." *Id.* at 171 (citations omitted).

216. *See* U.S. CONST. art. I, § 9, cl. 3 ("No Bill of Attainder or ex post facto Law shall be passed.").

217. *See id.* art. III, § 1 (vesting the "judicial Power of the United States" in "one supreme Court, and in such inferior Courts as the Congress may from time to time ordain and establish.").

prohibit the parties from raising questions about the competence or appropriateness of the court to hear the case.

In a hearing in an American court in an ordinary matter, it is hard to imagine a scenario in which these precepts were violated without a reaction of shock or indignation. Imagine a judge who is the brother of the plaintiff, where the plaintiff and the judge discussed beforehand who the plaintiff could sue such that the judge could guarantee a favorable outcome for his brother. Would we not simply call that corruption? Imagine a group of individuals who signed an agreement in which they determined first that certain individuals should be punished; then, consequently, the acts of those individuals must be declared criminal; that the signatories themselves would be prosecutors and judges; and that the defendants would be prohibited from questioning the legitimacy of the judges, the procedure, or the tribunal itself. Would we not call that a "kangaroo court?" And finally, imagine a situation in which a group of persons declared themselves to be legislators and created a law to punish their enemies; and the same parties who had created the law then declared themselves empowered to prosecute their enemies, judge the defendants and execute their own judgments. Would we not consider this a gross violation of the principle of separation of powers upon which the Constitution is structured?

I use examples from American law in part because the design of the Nuremberg tribunal was primarily attributable to the Americans.[218] The problematic implications of the tribunal's legitimacy and jurisdiction were discussed at length by the architects of the tribunal, who included Francis Biddle (the U.S. Attorney General, who was later one of the judges at the tribunal) and Robert Jackson (the U.S. Supreme Court

---

218. As one scholar writes:

> [T]he Nuremberg trial system was created almost exclusively in Washington by a group of American government officials. The system was developed, altered, and redrafted during the last ten months of the European war and was then presented to the British, Soviet, and French governments for comment and concurrence at a four power conference held in June-July 1945. America's allies modified and shifted features in the United States plan, but its basic elements remained intact and were embodied in the London Charter and the indictments that became the legal ground rules for the main Nuremberg proceedings and for a series of subsequent trials of Nazi and Japanese leaders.

BRADLEY F. SMITH, THE ROAD TO NUREMBERG 4-5 (1981).

justice who was Chief Counsel for the U.S. prosecution team). There were in fact lengthy exchanges over the design of the tribunal, which involved the Departments of War, State, Treasury, Justice, Navy, Office of Strategic Services and the White House.[219] Yet what was unquestioned was the fundamental commitment to achieve a political aim by means of a judicial process; accompanied by indifference to or denial of the fundamental incompatibility of the political and judicial.[220] I do not suggest here that the architects of the tribunal publicly and explicitly acknowledged the political purpose of the trial, or that they conceded that the claims to judicial legitimacy were hollow. Indeed, it was the reverse. Robert Jackson's opening statement to the tribunal lauds the triumph of the rule of law: "That four great nations, flushed with victory and stung with injury stay the hand of vengeance and voluntarily submit their captive enemies to the judgment of law is one of the most significant tributes that Power has ever paid to Reason."[221] Jackson also pointed to the value the trial would hold for posterity: "To pass these defendants a poisoned chalice is to put it to our own lips as well. We must summon such detachment and intellectual integrity to our task that this trial will com-

219. TAYLOR, *supra* note 20, at 33. Note, however, that discussion of punishment for Axis and Japanese war crimes had in fact been going on for some time by the governments in exile and the UN War Crimes Commission (UNWCC). In January 1942, the governments-in-exile of Belgium, Czechoslovakia, France, Greece, Holland, Luxembourg, Norway, Poland and Yugoslavia met in London, where they drafted the St. James Declaration, calling for the "punishment, through the channel of organized justice, of those guilty of or responsible for these crimes . . . ." *Id.* at 25. In October 1943, the UNWCC was formed to document war crimes. Its members were Australia, Belgium, Britain, Canada, China, Czechoslovakia, France, Greece, Holland, India, Luxembourg, New Zealand, Poland, South Africa, the United States and Yugoslavia. In the end, however, the individual countries held trials for war crimes committed specifically in their territory; and the United States (rather than the UNWCC) was the dominant force in the design and operation of the Nuremberg tribunal for the prosecution of war crimes which were not limited to a specific country. *Id. See also* Jonathan A. Bush, *Nuremberg: The Modern Law of War and its Limitations*, 93 COLUM. L. REV. 2022, 2057 (reviewing TELFORD TAYLOR, NUREMBERG: THE MODERN LAW OF WAR AND ITS LIMITATIONS (1992)).

220. In a memorandum of June 1945, Telford Taylor, associate counsel for the U.S. prosecution team, wrote that "the thing we want to accomplish is not a legal thing but a political thing." Quoting the memorandum, he wrote later in his memoirs that the "ex post facto problem"—that the tribunal was prosecuting individuals for laws which did not exist at the time of their acts—was "not a bothersome question 'if we keep in mind that this is a *political* decision to declare and apply a principle of international law.'" TAYLOR, *supra* note 20, at 50, 51.

221. JACKSON, *supra* note 211, at 31.

mend itself to posterity as fulfilling humanity's aspirations to do justice."[222]

Yet the Nuremberg tribunal was indeed a political event and it was indeed devised to address a political problem. Jackson observed, in his June 1945 report to President Truman, that there are men whom we have cause to accuse of culpability in atrocities.[223] "We have many such men in our possession," he wrote, "What shall we do with them?"[224] He answered:

> We could, of course, set them at large without a hearing. But it has cost unmeasured thousands of American lives to beat and bind these men. To free them without a trial would mock the dead and make cynics of the living. On the other hand, we could execute or otherwise punish them without a hearing. But undiscriminating executions or punishments without definite findings of guilt, fairly arrived at, would violate pledges repeatedly given and would not set easily on the American conscience or be remembered by our children with pride. The only other course is to determine the innocence or guilt of the accused after a hearing as dispassionate as the times and horrors we deal with will permit, and upon a record that will leave our reasons and motives clear.[225]

Thus the most immediate political problem that the tribunal was to solve was simply: "now that we have all these Nazis in our possession—what exactly are we supposed to do with them?" It is worth noting that the idea of holding a trial was quite controversial among the Allied governments. This is not because there were questions of how to justify the legitimacy and jurisdiction of a judicial process used for political aims.[226]

---

222. *Id.* at 34.

223. Report to the President by Mr. Justice Jackson, June 6, 1945 [hereinafter Report to the President] *in* ROBERT H. JACKSON, REPORT OF ROBERT H. JACKSON: UNITED STATES REPRESENTATIVE TO THE INTERNATIONAL CONFERENCE ON MILITARY TRIALS 42, 46 (1945) [hereinafter LONDON CONFERENCE REPORT] (Dep't. of State Publication No. 3080, 1949) (providing a "documentary record of negotiations . . . culminating in . . . the International Military Tribunal.").

224. LONDON CONFERENCE REPORT, *supra* note 223, at 46.

225. *Id.*

226. I do not mean to suggest that no one was concerned about the judicial legitimacy of the tribunals. Within the U.S. government, during the period of internal debate over the nature and structure of the tribunal, there were some who did indeed question the legitimacy of certain aspects of the project. In December 1944, an attorney in the Judge Advocate General Corps, Lieutenant Alwyn Vernon

Rather, it was because a trial was seen as a cumbersome and uncertain way of dealing with the Nazis held by occupation forces. The more expeditious solution was simply to shoot them.

This was the policy proposed by Henry Morgenthau, the Secretary of the Treasury, which was initially adopted by Roosevelt. Morgenthau proposed that the names of the major war criminals should be distributed to the Allied Forces, with instructions to capture, identify and shoot anyone on the list. Morgenthau also proposed the "pastoralization" of Germany, which involved stripping Germany of its industrial capacity and reducing it to a nation of farmers.[227] Ironically mirroring Nazi policy, Morgenthau proposed putting all members of the SS in concentration camps, but then eventually relocating them outside of Germany, noting that they could not be interned in concentration camps forever.[228] Older children would be confined and banished as well. It was unclear what would happen to children under six.[229] In September 1944, Roosevelt met with Churchill in Quebec to discuss post-war policy. Morgenthau attended the meeting and presented his plan. Churchill and Roosevelt initialed a summary of the Morgenthau plan and Roosevelt came out in favor of summarily executing the Nazi leaders.[230]

This was also the position held by the British. A British

Freeman, wrote a detailed legal memorandum questioning the validity of the notion that launching a war was a "crime" which could be punished. According to one historian, this document represented the views of two of the generals at Judge Advocate General Corps (JAG). *See* SMITH, *supra* note 218, at 103. At the same time, Assistant Attorney General Herbert Wechsler addressed other issues of this sort in a memo to his superior Francis Biddle. Biddle would later be one of the judges at the tribunal. Wechsler objected to the idea of trying Nazi organizations as defendants, inasmuch as the idea of a trying an organization was without precedent. There was, of course, the notion of conspiracy, but conspiracy was peculiar to Anglo-American law; it did not exist in continental law. Wechsler also objected to bringing charges against German nationals that were based on ex post facto crimes. *See* ANN TUSA & JOHN TUSA, THE NUREMBERG TRIAL 57 (1984) (additionally observing that continental legal systems did have some concepts—the *association criminel* of France, Germany's Criminal associates, the "sweeping charges" Russia designed to "deal with banditry"—that bore a family resemblance to conspiracy but did not treat "the mere act of conspiracy . . . as a crime."). The objections of both Wechsler and Freeman were overridden.

227. *See* SMITH, *supra* note 218, at 36-37 (discussing the Morgenthau Plan).

228. *See id.* at 28.

229. *See id.*

230. *See id.* at 47.

memorandum from April 1945 stated:

> It being conceded that these leaders must suffer death, the question arises whether they should be tried by some form of tribunal claiming to exercise judicial functions, or whether the decision taken by the Allies should be reached and enforced without the machinery of a trial. But H.M.G. are also deeply impressed with the dangers and difficulties of this course and they wish to put before their principal Allies, in a connected form, the arguments which have led them to think that execution without trial is the preferable course.[231]

The British held this position consistently until late May 1945.[232]

The reason for this course of action was twofold: a trial would be "exceedingly long and elaborate," but also it might reveal the illegitimacy of the proceedings. Many of the Nazi transgressions "are not war crimes in the ordinary sense, nor is it at all clear that they can properly be described as crimes under international law."[233]

While the immediate purpose of the tribunals was to simply do something with the Nazi prisoners on hand, there were other objectives as well, which were somewhat grander in scope: to justify the casualties suffered in the war by the Allies, to preserve the truth for future historians, to teach a lesson to all humanity, to prove that—by virtue of the Allies'

---

231. Aide-Mémoire from the United Kingdom, April 23, 1945, *in* LONDON CONFERENCE REPORT, *supra* note 223, at 18, 18; *see also* RICHARD H. MINEAR, VICTOR'S JUSTICE: THE TOKYO WAR CRIMES TRIAL 9 (1971) (discussing the initial British preference for "executive action," as opposed to "judicial proceedings.").

232. In August 1942, Anthony Eden told the European leaders that it was "undesirable" to pursue "a policy of bringing [the Nazi leaders] to trial." TUSA & TUSA, *supra* note 226, at 61-62.

In May 1944 Eden proposed compiling a short list of Nazi war criminals (less than fifty) who were sufficiently notorious that their guilt could be assumed without resort to legal proceedings and without offending public opinion. *See id.* at 63.

In April 1945, Lord Simon, the Lord Chancellor, presented a memorandum to the Americans reiterating the British objections to a trial, objections the British maintained through the end of May 1945. A proper hearing would allow the defendants to put forth evidence that would be embarrassing to the Allies. The better route to take would be for the Allies to proceed by "joint executive action," which meant summary execution. *See id.* at 64.

233. *See* Aide-Mémoire from the United Kingdom, April 23, 1945, *in* LONDON CONFERENCE REPORT, *supra* note 223, at 19. *See also* MINEAR, *supra* note 231, at 9.

triumph—justice was vindicated in the end.[234] I would suggest that perhaps the singular and most compelling purpose was simply for the Allies to demonstrate the righteousness of their own cause and the evil of their enemies. Jackson was quite candid in his opening statement in saying that the trial did not have all that much to do with the actual defendants; it was rather their symbolism that was of value.

> In the prisoners' dock sit twenty-odd broken men. . . . Merely as individuals, their fate is of little consequence to the world.
>
> What makes this inquest significant is that these prisoners represent sinister influences that will lurk in the world long after their bodies have returned to dust. They are living symbols of racial hatreds, of terrorism and violence, and of the arrogance and cruelty of power. They are symbols of fierce nationalisms and of militarism, of intrigue and warmaking which have embroiled Europe generation after generation, crushing its manhood, destroying its homes, and impoverishing its life.[235]

For clearly the purpose of the Nuremberg tribunal was not to examine "the war crimes and crimes against humanity com-

234. In his memo of June 2, 1945 to the prosecution team, Taylor argued that the two most important things to be accomplished by the trials were "[t]o give meaning to the war against Germany[,] [t]o validate the casualties we have suffered" and "[t]o establish and maintain harmonious relations with the other United Nations in the presentation and successful prosecution of the case." TAYLOR, *supra* note 20, at 50.

In his closing address to the tribunal, made on behalf of the United Kingdom, Sir Hartley Shawcross said that the tribunal has conducted the proceedings "both that justice may be done to these individuals as to their countless victims, and also that the world may know that in the end the predominance of power will be driven out and law and justice shall govern the relations between States." Sir Hartley Shawcross, Closing Address for United Kingdom, Great Britain and Ireland, *in* OFFICE OF UNITED STATES CHIEF OF COUNSEL FOR PROSECUTION OF AXIS CRIMINALITY, NAZI CONSPIRACY AND AGGRESSION 61, 62 (Supp. A 1947) [hereinafter NAZI CONSPIRACY AND AGGRESSION].

M. Champetier de Ribes, France's chief prosecutor, believed that "the interesting point of these trials is above all that of historical truth. Thanks to them, the historian of the future, as well as the chronicler of today, will know the truth about the political, diplomatic and military events of the most tragic period in our history; he will know the crimes of Nazism as well as the hesitancies, the weaknesses, the omissions of the pacific democracies." M. Champetier de Ribes, Introduction to M. Dubost, Closing Argument for the Provisional Government of the French Republic, *in* NAZI CONSPIRACY AND AGGRESSION, *supra*, at 159, 159 (Supp. A).

235. Jackson, Opening Statement, *supra* note 211, at 31.

mitted during the course of the war." If this were the case, then all such acts would have been examined. All persons—of whatever nationality—who had committed them would have been potential defendants. But this was not the case. Rather, it would seem that the fundamental purpose of the Nuremberg proceedings was for the victors to display to the world the evil done by the vanquished. Thus, the victors created the tribunal, legislated the crime, appointed themselves prosecutors, appointed themselves justices and found the vanquished guilty.

B. *The Structure of the Tribunal*

Although both the prosecutors and the tribunal itself purported at various times to be acting on behalf of mankind in general,[236] all civilized nations,[237] civilization itself,[238] or "an overwhelming majority of all civilized people,"[239] in fact

---

236. In his closing argument for the Soviet Union, Lt. Gen. R.A. Rudenko stated that "[m]ankind calls the criminals to account; and on the behalf of mankind we, the prosecutors, accuse at this trial." R.A. Rudenko, Closing Argument for Union of Soviet Socialist Republics, *in* NAZI CONSPIRACY AND AGGRESSION, *supra* note 234, at 199, 199 (Supp. A).

237. The judgment of the tribunal states that the making of the Nuremberg Charter was the exercise of the four powers' "sovereign legislative power." "[T]he undoubted right of these countries to legislate for the occupied territories has been recognized by the civilized world." Judgment, *in* 1 OFFICIAL DOCUMENTS OF THE TRIBUNAL, *supra* note 21, at 171, 218.

238. "The wrongs which we seek to condemn and punish," said Jackson in his opening statement, "have been so calculated, so malignant and devastating, that civilization cannot tolerate their being ignored . . . . Civilization can afford no compromise with the social forces which would gain renewed strength if we deal ambiguously or indecisively with the men in whom those forces now precariously survive." Jackson, Opening Statement, *supra* note 211, at 30-31. The Allied response to the German threat is described in the following terms: "At length bestiality and bad faith reached such excess that they aroused the sleeping strength of imperiled Civilization. Its united efforts have ground the German war machine to fragments." *Id.* at 32.

239. In addressing the Nuremberg Tribunal, Jackson explained that their charter "does not express the views of the signatory nations alone. Other nations with diverse but highly respected systems of jurisprudence also have signified adherence to it. These are Belgium, The Netherlands, Denmark, Norway, Czechoslovakia, Luxembourg, Poland, Greece, Yugoslavia, Ethiopia, Australia, Haiti, Honduras, Panama, New Zealand, Venezuela and India. You judge, therefore, under an organic act which represents the wisdom, the sense of justice and the will of twenty-one governments, representing an overwhelming majority of all civilized people." Jackson, Opening Statement, *supra* note 211, at 80. It is interesting to note that this portion of Jackson's Opening statement allows for the inference that the many nations not participating—those making up most of Asia, Africa and Latin America—are outside the majority of civilized people and therefore are generally not

they were acting explicitly and solely on behalf of the victors in the European theater. This is explicit in the formal structure of the tribunal and in the documents of its establishment, including the very caption of the case.[240] The tribunal was established pursuant to the London Agreement of August 8, 1945.[241] The signatories on the London Agreement consisted of the four powers—the United States, France, the United Kingdom and the USSR. Nineteen other countries, all of them Allies, expressed their "adherence." The accompanying Charter of the International Military Tribunal (Nuremberg Charter) provided for the composition, jurisdiction and powers of the tribunal. Article 1 of the Nuremberg Charter provided that, "[i]n pursuance of the Agreement signed on the 8th day of August 1945 . . . there shall be established an International Military Tribunal . . . for the just and prompt trial and punishment of the major war criminals of the European Axis."[242] Thus, the document itself is a bill of attainder: it is an act of legislation passed for the purpose of punishing particular persons (only those in the Axis nations), rather than a law of general applicability, which names the acts to be punished, regardless of who commits them. The Nuremberg Charter, in framing the Tribunal's jurisdiction this way, literally precluded the tribunal from hearing claims of war crimes committed by the Allies (though that would have been unlikely in any event,

---

civilized.

240. The caption of the case reads:

> THE UNITED STATES OF AMERICA, THE FRENCH REPUBLIC, THE UNITED KINGDOM OF GREAT BRITAIN AND NORTHERN IRELAND, AND THE UNION OF SOVIET SOCIALIST REPUBLICS
>
> —against—
>
> HERMANN WILHELM GOERING, RUDOLF HESS, JOACHIM von RIBBENTROP, ROBERT LEY, [et al.]

NAZI CONSPIRACY AND AGGRESSION, *supra* note 234, at iii (Supp. A).

241. Agreement by the Government of the United States of America, the Provisional Government of the French Republic, the Government of the United Kingdom of Great Britain and Northern Ireland and the Government of the Union of Soviet Socialist Republics for the Prosecution and Punishment of the Major War Criminals of the European Axis, Aug. 8, 1945, 59 Stat. 1544, 82 U.N.T.S. 279 [hereinafter London Agreement].

242. Nuremberg Charter, *supra* note 21, art. 1, 59 Stat. at 1546, 82 U.N.T.S. at 284. This is reiterated in Article 6, which stated that "[t]he Tribunal . . . shall have the power to try and punish persons who, acting in the interests of the *European Axis countries*, whether as individuals or members of organisations, committed any of the following crimes." *Id.* art. 6, 59 Stat. at 1547, 82 U.N.T.S. at 286 (emphasis added).

since the prosecutors *were* the Allies).

This was quite intentional: the architects of the tribunal intended to ensure that claims of war crimes committed by the Allies, or a description of the pre-war condition of Germany, would not be heard. The fire-bombing of Dresden, the use of atomic weapons in Hiroshima and Nagasaki and the violation of rules of submarine warfare were all acts committed by the Allies which would have been well-suited for treatment as war crimes, if the tribunal had been concerned with war crimes as such, rather than the war crimes of the European Axis. The drafters of the Nuremberg Charter were concerned that the defendants would raise the issue of Allied war crimes and were careful to prevent such "propaganda." Robert Jackson voiced this concern at the conference in London that drafted the tribunal's charter:

> There is a very real danger of this trial being used, or of an attempt being made to use it, for propaganda purposes . . . , It seems to me that the chief way in which the Germans can use this forum as a means of disseminating propaganda is by accusing other countries of various acts which they will say led them to make war defensively. That would be ruled out of this case if we could find and adopt proper language which would define what we mean when we charge a war of aggression. Language has been used in a number of treaties which defines aggression and limits it in such a way that it would prevent their making these counter-accusations which would take lots of time and cause lots of trouble.[243]

That the tribunals were designed to punish persons—rather than to establish and enforce a law applicable to all—is also explicit in the discussions in 1944 and 1945 in which the idea of the tribunal was formulated. At the London conference where the Nuremberg Charter was drafted, for example, the chief British representative, Sir David Maxwell Fyfe, made it clear that he did not want certain individuals to escape prosecution:

> What is in my mind is getting a man like Ribbentrop or Ley. It would be a great pity if we failed to get Ribbentrop or Ley

243. Minutes of Conference Session, July 17, 1945, *in* LONDON CONFERENCE REPORT, *supra* note 223, at 262, 273. *See also* MINEAR, *supra* note 231, at 55-56.

or Streicher. Now I want words that will leave no doubt that men who have originated the plan or taken part in the early stages of the plan are going to be within the jurisdiction of the Tribunal. I do not want any argument that Ribbentrop did not direct the preparation because he merely was overborne by Hitler, or any nonsense of that kind.[244]

There was no presumption of innocence; indeed, the tribunal was designed specifically to ensure that trial would result in conviction. This conclusion was reached by one historian, Richard Minear, who wrote that

> [a]t least three of the four parties to the London Conference explicitly presupposed the conviction of the accused. The British Government began an early aide-memoire: "H.M.G. assume that it is beyond question that Hitler and a number of arch-criminals associated with him (including Mussolini) must, so far as they fall into Allied hands, suffer the penalty of death for their conduct leading up to the war and for the wickedness which they either themselves perpetrated or have authorized in the conduct of the war." The Soviet representative at the London Conference stated: "We are dealing here with the chief war criminals who have already been convicted and whose conviction has been already announced by both the Moscow and Crimea declarations . . . ." And Robert H. Jackson, while attacking the assumption behind the Soviet representative's statement, nevertheless felt "bound to concede" that "[t]here could be but one decision in this case."[245]

Perhaps the most striking feature which undermined the tribunal's claim to judicial legitimacy was simply that exactly the same parties—in some cases, the same individuals—were the legislators, prosecutors and judges. The "legislature" was not a neutral or broad-based international organization. The "legislature" consisted of the four powers, the victors, simply negotiating among themselves as to what should be done with the vanquished. Negotiating for the United States was Robert Jackson; for France, Robert Falco; for the United Kingdom, Jowitt; and for the U.S.S.R., Major General I.T. Nikitchenko and A. Trainin. These parties quite literally determined by

244. Minutes of Conference Session, July 19, 1945, *in* LONDON CONFERENCE REPORT, *supra* note 223, at 295, 301. *See also* MINEAR, *supra* note 231, at 37.

245. MINEAR, *supra* note 231, at 18.

agreement that the acts of the Nazis had been "crimes," and that there would be a court before which these crimes could be tried. Neither the prosecutors in this newly-created court nor the judges would be drawn from neutral countries, but rather would come from the victors-turned-legislators.[246] The legislative, judicial and prosecutorial functions were deeply intertwined; this was particularly obvious where exactly the same individuals simply changed hats and took on new roles. Jackson, who had negotiated the final charter on behalf of the United States, was the lead prosecutor for the United States. Francis Biddle, the U.S. Attorney General who had also been deeply involved in formulating the structure of the tribunal,[247] was the judge appointed by the United States. Sir David Maxwell-Fyfe, who was involved in negotiating the Nuremberg Charter for the United Kingdom, was deputy chief prosecutor for the U.K. at the trial. The Soviet Union appointed Nikitchenko, who had negotiated the Nuremberg Charter on behalf of the U.S.S.R., as judge. The French appointed Falco, who had negotiated the Nuremberg Charter on behalf of France, as judge.

The Allies justified this partly by maintaining that there were no neutral countries and that it would make no sense to let the Germans judge themselves. Thus, by process of elimination, the victors must take on the task. Jackson himself said:

> Unfortunately, the nature of these crimes is such that both prosecution and judgment must be by victor nations over vanquished foes. The world-wide scope of the aggressions carried out by these men has left but few real neutrals. Either the victors must judge the vanquished or we must leave the defeated to judge themselves.[248]

---

246. Article 2 of the Nuremberg Charter provides that "[t]he Tribunal shall consist of four members, each with an alternate. One member and one alternate shall be appointed by each of the Signatories." Nuremberg Charter, *supra* note 21, art. 2, 59 Stat. at 1546, 82 U.N.T.S. at 284. Article 14 provides that "[e]ach Signatory shall appoint a Chief Prosecutor for the investigation of the charges against and the prosecution of major war criminals." *Id.* art. 14, 59 Stat. at 1549, 82 U.N.T.S. at 292.

247. Biddle co-authored the "Memorandum to President Roosevelt from the Secretaries of State and War and the Attorney General, January 22, 1945," which concerned the structure and justification of the tribunals. *See Editorial Note* to *Memorandum to President Roosevelt from the Secretaries of State and War and the Attorney General*, *in* LONDON CONFERENCE REPORT, *supra* note 223, at 3.

248. Jackson, Opening Statement, *supra* note 211, at 33.

Yet this was not so. Within Europe, Switzerland, Sweden and Portugal were neutral; and outside of Europe, many countries in Latin America and Africa were neutral, or had very limited involvement in the war.[249]

The tribunal's jurisdiction and legitimacy were alternatively justified, by the Tribunal itself, as occupation law:

> The making of the Charter was the exercise of the sovereign legislative power by the countries to which the German Reich unconditionally surrendered; and the undoubted right of these countries to legislate for the occupied territories has been recognized by the civilized world. . . .
>
> The Signatory Powers created this Tribunal, defined the law it was to administer and made regulations for the proper conduct of the Trial. In doing so, they have done together what any one of them might have done singly; for it is not to be doubted that any nation has the right thus to set up special courts to administer law.[250]

Yet this flies in the face of the claim that it is not victory that gives the right of the victors to judge the vanquished, but rather law.

The procedural rules likewise reflected the Allies' concern to control the proceedings and determine their outcome. In American law, the rules of judicial procedure are promulgated either by the court or the legislature and are equally applicable to all parties. However, the Nuremberg Charter provided that the prosecutors were to draw up rules of procedure, which they were to submit to the tribunal for review, acceptance, or rejection.[251] The defense had no input into this process. The defense was not permitted to submit alternate rules, or in fact to

---

249. Article 5 of the London Agreement provided that "[a]ny Government of the United Nations may adhere to this Agreement by notice given through diplomatic channel to the Government of the United Kingdom, who shall inform the other signatory and adhering Governments of each such adherence." London Agreement, *supra* note 241, art. 5, 59 Stat. at 1545, 82 U.N.T.S. at 282. Only nineteen countries did so: Greece, Denmark, Yugoslavia, the Netherlands, Czechoslovakia, Poland, Belgium, Ethiopia, Australia, Honduras, Norway, Panama, Luxembourg, Haiti, New Zealand, India, Venezuela, Uruguay and Paraguay. *See* TUSA & TUSA, *supra* note 226, at 85, n.*.

250. Judgment, *in* 1 OFFICIAL DOCUMENTS OF THE TRIBUNAL, *supra* note 21, at 171, 218.

251. Nuremberg Charter, *supra* note 21, art. 14(e), 59 Stat. at 1549, 82 U.N.T.S. at 292.

comment or contribute in any way to the formulation of the rules of procedure.

Not surprisingly, the defense attempted to object to these features of the tribunal:

> [T]he Defense consider it their duty to point out at this juncture another peculiarity of this Trial which departs from the commonly recognized principles of modern jurisprudence. The Judges have been appointed exclusively by States which were the one party in this war. This one party to the proceeding is all in one: creator of the statute of the Tribunal and of the rules of law, prosecutor and judge. It used to be until now the common legal conception that this should not be so; just as the United States of America, as the champion for the institution of international arbitration and jurisdiction, always demanded that neutrals, or neutrals and representatives of all parties, should be called to the Bench. This principle has been realized in an exemplary manner in the case of the Permanent Court of International Justice at The Hague.[252]

The defense counsel did not ask that the tribunal be disbanded, but rather that the tribunal seek an opinion by "internationally recognized authorities on international law on the legal elements of this Trial under the Charter of the Tribunal."[253]

The question of jurisdiction is not trivial, since jurisdiction entails the basic right of the court to hear a case and render judgment. The proceedings of a court are not legitimate or binding if the court does not have jurisdiction. Given that the tribunal had not existed prior to 1945 and that jurisdiction was conferred by the victors upon themselves, the challenge to the tribunal's jurisdiction was predictable. The designers of the tribunal had anticipated such objections—and prohibited them. Article 3 of the Nuremberg Charter provided that "[n]either the Tribunal, its members nor their alternates can be challenged by the prosecution, or by the Defendants or their Counsel."[254] There were no additional grounds for conferring jurisdiction, other than the Nuremberg Charter and the London

252. Motion Adopted by All Defense Counsel, Nov. 19, 1945, *in* 1 OFFICIAL DOCUMENTS OF THE TRIBUNAL, *supra* note 21, at 168-70.

253. *Id.* at 170.

254. Nuremberg Charter, art. 3, 59 Stat. at 1546, 82 U.N.T.S. at 286.

agreement.[255] The jurisdiction question was "resolved" by simply prohibiting its introduction before the Tribunal or any other international body. The defendants' motion was rejected immediately.[256]

The Tokyo trials of the Japanese leaders had the same obvious and explicit features of a political show trial by the victors. The Tokyo tribunal was not even created by agreement

---

255. It must be mentioned that the nature and legitimacy of the tribunal's jurisdiction was thoroughly researched and hotly debated, particularly by the U.S. officials who were involved in devising the plans for the tribunal. *See generally* SMITH, *supra* note 218. In the end, the rationale for the tribunal relied heavily on two sources. The first involves the customary rules of war, which prohibit direct attacks on civilians and wounded combatants and also prohibit torture, the summary execution of prisoners of war, etc. However, there was no precedent for a foreign power to bring criminal charges against individuals who are not their own citizens, nor to try and punish them. The second source consisted mainly of treaties and declarations issued in the aftermath of World War I, denouncing war as a means of international dispute resolution. The tribunal and the Allies relied heavily on the Kellogg-Briand Treaty (the Pact of Paris) of 1928, which was binding on 63 nations, including Germany, Italy and Japan. Articles I and II of that treaty read:

> *Article I.* The High Contracting Parties solemnly declare in the names of their respective peoples that they condemn recourse to war for the solution of international controversies, and renounce it as an instrument of national policy in their relations to one another.
>
> *Article II.* The High Contracting Parties agree that the settlement or solution of all disputes or conflicts of whatever nature or whatever origin they may be, which may arise among them, shall never be sought except by pacific means.

General Treaty for Renunciation of War as an Instrument of National Policy, Aug. 27, 1928, arts. 1, 2, 46 Stat. 2343, 2345-46, 94 L.N.T.S. 57, 63.

However, the Pact did not provide for a mechanism of enforcement of these promises. Treaty violations had always been addressed diplomatically, or in the form of actions for breach of contract in international courts. The unilateral determination that the treaty constituted criminal law and that the Germans were "criminals" to be tried individually, by foreign powers, was not a concept that had been recognized or a procedure that had ever been employed prior to the Nuremberg Charter. The tribunal also relied heavily on a protocol of the League of Nations which stated that "a war of aggression . . . is an international crime." Protocol for the Pacific Settlement of International Disputes, Oct. 2, 1924, art. 2, L.N.O.J., Spec. Supp., No. 23, at 498. However, the protocol was never ratified; and at the time the Protocol was recommended, Germany was not a member of the League of Nations. *See* Judgment, *in* 1 OFFICIAL DOCUMENTS OF THE TRIBUNAL, *supra* note 21, at 216-24. The tribunal also relied on other resolutions after World War I which denounced wars of aggression as "international crimes." However, the concept and procedure of trying and punishing individual government officials, as criminals, for their government's war of aggression, was clearly novel.

256. The motion was rejected on November 21, 1945. *See* Motion Adopted by All Defense Counsel, Nov. 19, 1945, *in* 1 OFFICIAL DOCUMENTS OF THE TRIBUNAL, *supra* note 21, at 168, n.*.

of several countries; it was created by the "Proclamation by the Supreme Commander for the Allied Powers," which was General Douglas MacArthur.[257] The charter for that tribunal was written by Americans, primarily Joseph B. Keenan, who would also be the chief prosecutor.[258] Like the Nuremberg tribunal, the judges for the Tokyo trials were drawn from the victor nations.[259] Like the Nuremberg trials, the Tokyo tribunal did not consider possible war crimes committed by the Allies; evidence regarding the American use of atomic weapons was not admissible.[260] Like the Nuremberg trials, the Tokyo tribunal did not promulgate clear rules of evidence.[261] Despite the claim of the tribunals to be applying law in an impartial manner, the positions of the particular justices did indeed, to some extent, reflect their and their nations' losses. In the Nuremberg trial, the Soviet judge wrote a dissenting opinion in which he objected to the tribunal's leniency.[262] In the Tokyo

---

257. The proclamation read as follows:

> NOW, THEREFORE, I, Douglas MacArthur, as Supreme Commander for the Allied Powers, by virtue of the authority so conferred upon me, in order to implement the Terms of Surrender which requires the meting out of stern justice to war criminals, do order and provide as follows:
>
> *Article 1.* There shall be established an International Military Tribunal for the Far East . . .
>
> *Article 2.* The Constitution, jurisdiction and functions of this Tribunal are those set forth in the charter of the International Military Tribunal for the Far East, approved by me this day.

Douglas MacArthur, *Special Proclamation: Establishment of an International Military Tribunal for the Far East*, Jan. 19, 1946, *reprinted in*, 1 THE TOKYO WAR CRIMES TRIAL (1981).

258. *See* MINEAR, *supra* note 231, at 20.

259. There were eleven judges for the Tokyo trial, one each from Australia, Canada, China, France, Great Britain, India, the Netherlands, New Zealand, the Philippines, the Soviet Union and the United States. *See id.* at 23.

260. *See id.* at 100. It should be noted that the Charter does not explicitly name the Japanese as the objects of prosecution. Article 1 provides that the tribunal is established "for the just and prompt trial and punishment of the major war criminals in the Far East." Charter of the International Military Tribunal for the Far East, Jan. 19, 1946, art. 1, T.I.A.S. No. 1589, 4 Bevans 20, *reprinted in* MINEAR, *supra* note 231, at 185 (as amended Apr. 26, 1946). Although the tribunal in principle could have exercised jurisdiction over American war crimes, it obviously did not choose to do so.

261. The Charter provides that "The Tribunal shall not be bound by technical rules of evidence. It shall adopt and apply to the greatest possible extent expeditious and non-technical procedure, and shall admit any evidence which it deems to have probative value." Charter of the International Military Tribunal for the Far East, *supra* note 260, art. 13.

262. The Tribunal acquitted defendants Schacht, von Papen and Fritzsche; sen-

tribunal, two justices dissented: Justice Jaranilla of the Philippines, who was a survivor of the Bataan Death March, objected to the tribunal's leniency; and Justice Pal of India, a country which had suffered very little at the hands of Japan, acquitted all defendants, partly on the grounds that the tribunal was a political rather than judicial entity, which had no right or jurisdiction to try the defendants.[263]

C. *What We Inherit From Nuremberg*

How do we make sense of the architecture of the Nuremberg and Tokyo tribunals? How do we make sense of the multiple levels of protection against even the slimmest possibility that someone might mention the war crimes of the Allies or question the legitimacy of the tribunals? These layers of protection ensured not just that the monstrous acts of the Nazis and Japanese would be revealed to the world, but also that the relative goodness of the Allies would be demonstrated and that the Allied nations would feel vindicated and feel their sacrifices justified. Surely this would also have been accomplished with a genuinely judicial tribunal—where the justices were not also representatives of the plaintiff nations; where all those who committed war crimes would be prosecuted, not just the Axis nations. In a legitimate judicial structure, with neutral justices, explicit rules of evidence and so on—surely the result would have been nearly the same. The fire-bombing of Dresden—and even the atomic bombing of Hiroshima and Nagasaki—would still have paled alongside the German death

---

tenced Hess to life imprisonment and found that the Reichs-cabinet, the General Staff and high command of the armed forces were not criminal organizations. The Soviet dissent objected to all of these. *See* Dissenting Opinion of the Soviet Member of the International Military Tribunal, *in* 1 OFFICIAL DOCUMENTS OF THE TRIBUNAL, *supra* note 21, at 342.

263. In his dissent, Pal wrote:

> Whatever view of the legality or otherwise of a war may be taken, victory does not invest the victor with unlimited and undefined power now. International laws of war define and regulate the rights and duties of the victor over the individuals of the vanquished nationality. In my judgment, therefore, it is beyond the competence of any victor nation to go beyond the rules of international law as they exist, give new definitions of crimes, and then punish the prisoners for having committed offenses according to this new definition.

Remarks Concerning the Opinion of the Member for India (Pal), in 21 THE TOKYO WAR CRIMES TRIAL 32 (1981). *See also* MINEAR, *supra* note 231, at 63-64.

camps. But it seems that *nearly* the same wasn't good enough. This tells us a great deal about the project of the Nuremberg and Tokyo tribunals. The project was not at all about which of the various nations had done the worst things—given that war and aggression are inherently bloody and extreme, it is nothing new in human history when ethics and honor take a back seat in wartime to fear, vengeance, or desire for victory. The Nuremberg and Tokyo trials—in both their structure and their rhetoric—do not concern evil acts, but rather assert an essential distinction between evil human beings and righteous ones.

We can now make sense of the process by which the political is transformed and presented in the garb of the judicial; in which the interest of particular nations is transformed and presented as an interest that is universal (the interest of mankind, the interest of Civilization, the interest of all civilized nations); in which interest itself is transformed and presented as law. The Nuremberg project was never about *acts* which were indefensible, shocking, or evil; but rather about *persons* who were monstrous, beastly, not even human.

This is what lies at the heart of Hannah Arendt's EICHMANN IN JERUSALEM.[264] Recall Arendt's elaborate descriptions of Eichmann's ordinariness, his shallowness and self-absorption, his inability to speak without reliance on clichés and his inability to fully separate reality from a trite and hackneyed unreality. Although the work was received in some quarters as a justification of Nazism, a defense of Eichmann personally, or a trivialization of the Holocaust,[265] clearly it is none of these things. Rather, it suggests that there

264. Arendt's depiction of Eichmann suggests that it is almost as though he had spent his life in a B-rate movie and the line between fiction and non-fiction was blurred, or occasionally lost altogether. "Adolf Eichmann went to the gallows with great dignity," Arendt writes. She describes his last words:

> He began by stating emphatically that he was a *Gottgläubiger*, to express in common Nazi fashion that he was no Christian and did not believe in life after death. He then proceeded: "After a short while, gentlemen, *we shall all meet again*. Such is the fate of all men. Long live Germany, long live Argentina, long live Austria. *I shall not forget them*." In the face of death, he had found the cliche used in funeral oratory. Under the gallows, his memory played him the last trick; he was "elated" and he forgot that this was his own funeral.

ARENDT, *supra* note 210, at 252.

265. *See, e.g.*, Michael A. Musmanno, N.Y. TIMES BOOK REVIEW, May 19, 1963 (review of ARENDT, *supra* note 210).

is nothing intrinsically monstrous about Eichmann—if he had lived in different times, he might have been a vacuum cleaner salesman. If he was so ordinary and the situation gave him the possibility and motivation for behaving monstrously, then in a sense, none of us is "safe"—we all have within us the potential to commit monstrous acts. The acts are no less monstrous for this reason. Yet once we acknowledge Eichmann's ordinariness—once we acknowledge that his acts rather than his person were evil—then we can never in good conscience be certain that any of us is righteous. We can never be certain that we ourselves would not do monstrous things—not out of a conscious bloodthirstiness, but out of indifference, shallowness, or a kind of willing myopia.

Arendt's insight is echoed by the Costa Rican theologian Franz Hinkelammert, in an article on the Persian Gulf War. Hinkelammert describes some of the language used by George Bush, Norman Schwartzkopf, military officials and soldiers involving the notion of "work." They use expressions like: "We had a job to do, and we went in there and did it;" "We've been getting to our targets and getting the job done," and so on. Hinkelammert notes that such language treats destruction as a productive process; it is as though the factory that produced Baghdad's destruction were comparable to a factory that produces shoes. But, he says, only the executioner thinks his is a job like everyone else's.[266]

And that is the heart of the problem: there are many means by which executioners convince themselves that their jobs are like everyone else's. Executioners do not come into the world with the mark of Cain on their brows, any more than the righteous come with a saintly glow. If we deem acts, rather than persons, to be evil, then we acknowledge the possibility (at least in principle) that all of us, any of us, may do evil at some time. If we deem acts, rather than persons, to be evil, then we are compelled to acknowledge that the human condition requires us to struggle not only with temptation and weakness, but with the resolution of moral ambiguity as well. Like the executioners, we may convince ourselves that the particular acts we are doing are justified because we do them

266. *See* Franz J. Hinkelammert, *Subjectividad y Nuevo Orden Mundial: ¿Qué Queda Después de la Guerra de Irak?*, 1991 PASOS 18, 20.

in the name of the law, or that our acts bear the righteousness of our cause. Consequently, there may be a moment in history, or in our daily lives, in which we indeed *are* the executioners.

If we deem persons, rather than acts, to be evil, we create the illusion that we can somehow transcend the moral struggle. If *they* are evil and *we* are acting on behalf of the innocent, the good and mankind as a whole, then there is simply no ambiguity to resolve. There are only two issues we then need address: the list and decorum. Whose names shall we place on the list of those who are evil; and what should we do to them once we have them, that won't be too distasteful?

Far from resolving any ethical questions, the structure and rhetoric of the war crimes tribunals avoid the most pressing of the ethical issues raised by the Holocaust and the Nazi regime. How is it that human beings come to do evil acts? By equating the interests of the Allies with the interests of all humanity and by precluding even the possibility that war crimes by the Allies could even be mentioned, it seems to me that the architects of the tribunals were doing more than simply satisfying the post-war political interests of the Allies. The tribunals' fundamental assumption was that the accusers were righteous and the condemned were evil; this was both explicit and implicit in the structure and rhetoric of the tribunals. This assumption rested on a very basic distinction. *We* are fundamentally different kinds of creatures than *they* are; *we* are civilized, *they* are barbaric; *we* are human and *they* are something less than human—monstrous, animal, demonic. That is a dangerous view to hold. It is also part of the legacy we inherit from the tribunals where the concept of human rights first took on the character of law.

An equally important piece of the Nuremberg legacy is the advancement of a political and moral agenda by judicial means. While the atrocities committed in the Holocaust are bone-chilling, it is nonetheless shocking to see what a travesty the Nuremberg tribunal was from the perspective of judicial legitimacy. If the same method of legislation and procedure for trial had been followed in any domestic court of the Allied nations, it would have been denounced as patently illegitimate; if such a trial were held in American courts, it would have been patently unconstitutional on multiple grounds. We need only imagine such a court today, anywhere in the world, structured in the same manner: where the legislator, prosecutor and judge were all the same party; the legislation was explicitly created for the purpose of punishing certain individuals; the standards for evidence and procedure left to the discretion of the tribunal; and the tribunal's jurisdiction was created and conferred by the plaintiff, who then prohibited the defense from raising the issue of jurisdiction, before the tribunal itself or elsewhere. If such a court were to operate today in any domestic setting, we would consider it patently illegitimate and void of any judicial integrity. Ironically, we could expect to see Amnesty International denounce such a judicial process as a violation of human rights standards.

I am not suggesting here that it is wrong to document and publicize atrocities committed in wartime, or any other time. Nor am I disputing that such a project would be both morally and politically imperative. I am suggesting that it is important to note that in the Nuremberg tribunal, this moral and political imperative trumped, in an absolute fashion, the most fundamental mandates of law and judicial process. What Nuremberg tells us is that, measured against the moral and political imperative of denouncing atrocities, all competing moral or legal imperatives are completely without weight. It is not surprising that the Nuremberg trials have come to stand for the just and proper denunciation of atrocities; the genocidal project of the Nazis demanded denunciation. What is important to note is how this project of denunciation trumped all other moral issues and did so absolutely—not only the judicial illegitimacy of the tribunals themselves, but also the Allied war crimes, the use of atomic weapons and the callousness and anti-Semitism of the many countries which denied refuge to Jews fleeing the Holocaust.

We have inherited from Nuremberg not only the idea that genocide, torture and slave labor violate principles of human rights which transcend domestic positive law. We have equally inherited the notion that the denunciation of human rights violations is so compelling and consuming that, alongside of it, all else—all acts of other parties which are less than atrocious, which are merely brutal or shameful—not only pale in comparison, but disappear altogether. We inherit from Nuremberg the idea that when there are atrocities to denounce, we need not look at the acts of the denouncers themselves. Indeed, we may even be prohibited from doing so. It is as though the singular monstrousness of human rights violations consumes or inhabits the entirety of the moral space. When we are denouncing atrocities, evil acts are not only absolutely evil, but exclusively so; alongside them, acts that are merely wrong, or even awful, are relatively righteous.

Thus, bringing an accusation of atrocities and consequently invoking the notion of human rights, means positing a "bright line" distinction between evil and righteousness—both between evil persons and righteous persons and between evil acts and righteous acts. We inherit from Nuremberg a notion of human rights which posits a realm of evil acts and evil persons—absolutely and exclusively evil. We inherit from Nuremberg the notion that the moral denunciation of human rights violations does not itself have rules or limits, or ambivalence, or ambiguity.

CONCLUSION

In the introduction I suggested that I would explore the concept of human rights in terms of its rhetorical uses and its relation to political and economic agendas. Is it possible to disentangle this very powerful moral concept from its political uses? If not and if it is not universal or impartial but rather deeply political and politicized, then is its validity irredeemably compromised?

In a sense there is a relatively easy solution. If we take the ordinary philosophical standards that are applicable to a moral theory, such as consistency with our ethical intuitions and logical coherence, then we can easily construct three models that each have some reasonable grounds for justification:

1. If by "human rights" we mean that we want to articulate the most minimal and urgent conditions for human life, then a concept of human rights would entail protection from extreme physical violence. It would address "atrocities" of the sort articulated in Just War doctrine—torture, execution, genocide, enslavement.

2. If by "human rights" we mean that we want to articulate everything immediately necessary for human beings to live, then a concept of human rights would entail protection from extreme physical violence *and* economic security. It would include the things described in model one, and it

would also entail the provision of food, shelter, water, clothing, employment and medical care.

3. If by "human rights" we mean that we want to articulate everything necessary for a full and good life, *or* we are also concerned with everything *indirectly* necessary to protect essential economic and physical needs, then a concept of human rights would include models one and two and would also entail political and civil rights, including speech, press, association, travel and political participation.

The one arrangement that cannot be justified is the currently dominant concept, which holds that protection from atrocities are classed in the same category with political and intellectual activities; and that political and intellectual activities are deemed to be more essential and immediate than economic needs.

But I am not really interested in devising another model to throw into the ring of contemporary philosophical debate. My interest here lies more in exploring the relation between the concept of human rights and the stakes. If there are atrocities taking place and we do not intervene, then we are to some degree complicit. Conversely, if we claim that an atrocity is taking place and thereby justify, for example, military intervention or an economic blockade, then we have the blood of innocents on our hands if we are wrong, or if we are lying and only invoking human rights as rhetoric. My view is that the moral content of the conception of human rights is therefore inseparable from the agenda which is set once claims of human rights violations are invoked, because such claims both demand action and also justify any action short of further human rights violations.

My intention in writing this Article is not to propose and justify my preferred model of human rights. Rather, I am interested in making absolutely clear the relation between the concept and the political interest; and that no purely abstract choice is possible, only a fundamentally interested one. To the extent that I am successful, we will adopt both our concepts and our agendas with our eyes open. Neither states nor individuals will necessarily have more benevolent inclinations. If there is an exhortation, it is not for humanity to become better or for states to show some sort of moral progress. Has anyone since Comte really believed that this is a possibility? Rather, my ambition is more modest: to make a certain kind of hypocrisy unavailable as a device that may be used by individuals (or states) to delude themselves about their willingness to participate in brutality and to hide their capacity to engage in acts that are at the same time bloodthirsty and casual.

Because the concept of human rights is used to justify military actions (it was one of the justifications for the Persian Gulf War, in which an estimated 100,000 Iraqis were killed) while excluding economic policies (although 37,000 children die each day from "preventable causes" related to extreme poverty) I am deeply concerned with its content and its uses. I am concerned partly about the ways in which the concept of human rights takes on the character of the sacred. The concept of human rights purports to be an absolute and universal moral principle, yet it eludes and in fact prevents moral discourse. The moral position it asserts is seen as simply beyond question, such that no moral and rational person could seriously doubt its soundness. Furthermore, ideal and abstract entities ("rights") are deemed to have a reality and value wholly independent of concrete life activities. In the dominant conception, the danger of this ontological mistake, if you will, is that even those political rights which are purely formal and never actualized are treated as "things" of great substance and worth; and for that reason are placed in the same category as protection from torture, as though these two things have something in common. In this context, I would be inclined to take a materialist and utilitarian position, that one's profane life of eating, sleeping, working and existing on this earth is more real and valuable than one's abstract life, which includes the rights we have that are never actualized and the entitlements which have in fact given us nothing.

The dominant concept of human rights holds that political rights by their very nature cannot be trivial, just as protection from torture is never trivial. Yet we should hear how hollow this rings. I do not think that one has to be a communist to see how easily, for example, the right to vote, which is "sacred" in a democracy, can slip easily into the trivial. As a citizen in a democracy, my act of sovereignty truly lasts only a moment and happens quite rarely—once every two or four years. I vote for one of the candidates, neither of whom I have ever met, whose views and intentions I know only through carefully staged campaign events and television commercials produced by the same advertising agencies that market dishwashing liquid.

Conversely, the dominant conception of human rights holds that economic activity is less essential, less urgent—by its nature, it is always profane and trumps nothing. But we need to remember that economic activity includes not only going shopping at the mall. It refers also to the life of the body and all that entails—survival, pleasure, fear, struggle, respite, exhaustion, abundance; the daily concrete acts that occupy so very much of our lives—whether you get to work by car, or stand in the rain waiting for a bus, whether you have a doorman at the entrance of your apartment building or a cluster of junkies eyeing your purse and your body as you come home each night.

My concern about the dominant conception is also that, as with any absolute moral claim, it is possible for righteousness to justify acts that simple decency would not permit. Walzer reminds us that holy wars are longer and bloodier than others, because the righteousness of the cause demands nothing less than total conquest or total sacrifice. In the end I wonder if we aren't better off without any notion of absolute rights or moral trumps. I wonder if we aren't better off with adopting some garden-variety utilitarianism and reminding ourselves from time to time of how much of the human condition is characterized by moral ambiguity. I am reminded of Max Weber's discussion in his essay *Politics as a Vocation*.[267] Given that politics involves the legitimate use of violence, he suggests it is incumbent upon someone who has a calling to political leadership to understand that there are never clean decisions. The ethic of responsibility is incompatible with the ethic of ultimate ends, yet both are compelling. The political leader with a conscience will be obliged constantly to navigate this ethical paradox. There is nothing impressive, Weber says, about those who intoxicate themselves with the "sterile excitement" of pursuing an absolute end. What is immensely moving, however, is when an individual "is aware of a responsibility for the consequences

267. Max Weber, *Politics as a Vocation*, *in* MAX WEBER, FROM MAX WEBER 127 (Hans Gerth and C. Wright Mills eds. and trans., 1946).

of his conduct and really feels such responsibility with heart and soul . . . [But] somewhere he reaches the point where he says: 'Here I stand; I can do no other.'"[268] I wonder if, when we embrace a certain conception of human rights, we don't sometimes find ourselves intoxicated by the righteousness of the cause, at the cost of moral discourse, rather than by the service of it.

268. *Id.*

[4]

Voices of Suffering, Fragmented Universality, and the Future of Human Rights*

Upendra Baxi

I. Introduction

A. An Age of Human Rights?

Much of the Christian twentieth century, especially its later half, will be recalled as an "Age of Human Rights." No preceding century of human history[1] has been privileged to witness a profusion of human rights enunciations on a global scale. Never before have the languages of human rights sought to supplant all other ethical languages. No preceding century has witnessed the proliferation of human rights norms and standards as a core aspect of what may be called the politics of intergovernmental desire. Never before has there been a discourse so varied and diverse that it becomes necessary to publish and update regularly, through the unique discursive instrumentality of the United Nations system, in ever-exploding volumes of fine print, the various texts of instruments relating to human rights.[2] The Secretary-General of the United Nations was perhaps right to observe (in his inaugural remarks at the 1993 Vienna Conference on Human Rights) that human rights constitute a "common language of humanity."[3] Indeed, it would be true to say that, in some ways, a human rights "sociolect" has emerged, in this era of the end of

 This essay anticipates some themes and formulations from my work THE FUTURE OF HUMAN RIGHTS (forthcoming). A less refined version appears under a somewhat different title in 8 TRANSNAT'L L. & CONTEMP. PROBS. 125 (1998). Reprint permission granted.

1 I use the term "human" as an act of communicational courtesy. Human is marked by the presence of *man*; so is per*son*. My preferred non-sexist version is, therefore, a combination of the first letters of both words: *huper*. I await the day when the word "huper" will replace the word "human."

2 *See* THE UNITED NATIONS, HUMAN RIGHTS: A COMPILATION OF INTERNATIONAL INSTRUMENTS (1997).

3 Boutros Boutros-Ghali, *Human Rights: The Common Language of Humanity, in* UNITED NATIONS: WORLD CONFERENCE ON HUMAN RIGHTS, THE VIENNA DECLARATION AND PROGRAMME OF ACTION (1993).

ideology, as the only universal ideology in the making, enabling both the legitimation of power and the *praxis* of emancipatory politics.[4]

At the same time, the Christian twentieth century has been tormented by its own innovations in catastrophic politics. The echoes of Holocaust and Hiroshima-Nagasaki suffering vibrate in the Universal Declaration of Human Rights (UDHR)[5] as well as in the millennial dream of turning swords into ploughshares. But the politics of cruelty continue even as sonorous declarations on human rights proliferate. A distinctively European contribution to recent history, the politics of organized intolerance and ethnic cleansing, has been universalized in the "killing fields" of post-colonial experience. The early, middle, and late phases of the Cold War[6] orchestrated prodigious human suffering as well as an exponential growth of human rights enunciations. And if Cold War practices were deeply violative of basic human rights, post-Cold War practices—for example the "ethnic wars"—are no less so.[7]

Still, though not radically ameliorative of here-and-now suffering, international human rights standards and norms empower peoples' movements and conscientious policy-makers everywhere to question political practices. That, to my mind, is an inestimable potential of human rights languages, not readily available in previous centuries. Human rights languages are perhaps all that we have to interrogate the  barbarism of power, even when these remain inadequate to humanize fully the barbaric practices of politics.

---

4 For the notion of ideology as a set of languages characterized by reflexivity—or as "sociolect," see ALVIN GOULDNER, THE DIALECTIC OF IDEOLOGY AND TECHNOLOGY: THE ORIGINS, GRAMMAR AND FUTURE OF IDEOLOGY 61–65 (Oxford University Press 1982); J.B. THOMPSON, STUDIES IN THE THEORY OF IDEOLOGY (1984). A more recent variant is the use of the phrase "dialects of human rights." *See* MARY ANN GLENDON, RIGHTS TALK: THE IMPOVERISHMENT OF POLITICAL DISCOURSE (1991). *See also* DAVID JACOBSON, RIGHTS ACROSS BORDERS: IMMIGRATION AND THE DECLINE OF CITIZENSHIP 2–3 (1996) (the state, Jacobson rightly stresses, is becoming less constituted by sovereign agency and more by "a larger international and constitutional order based on human rights." Human rights provide a "vehicle and object of this revolution."); Upendra Baxi, *Human Rights Education: The Promise of the Twenty-first Century?, in* HUMAN RIGHTS EDUCATION 142 (George J. Andreopoulos & Richard Pierre Claude eds., 1997) (for a full version, *see* <http://www.pdhre.org> (visited Dec. 1, 1998)).

5 *See infra* Appendix I [hereinafter UDHR].

6 Periodization of "cold war" is crucial to any understanding of how the intergovernmental politics of desire pursued its own distinctive itineraries. The "cold war" condenses many a moment of practices of cruelty while simultaneously registering innovation in human rights enunciations. For an overall account of the politics of cruelty, see CLIVE PONTING, PROGRESS AND BARBARISM: THE WORLD IN THE TWENTIETH CENTURY (1998).

7 For an insightful analysis, see ANATOLY M. KAZANOV, AFTER THE USSR: ETHNICITY, NATIONALISM, AND POLITICS IN THE COMMONWEALTH OF INDEPENDENT STATES (1995).

In this essay, I ponder the future of human rights, a future that is periclated by a whole variety of developments in theory and practice. I do so by addressing seven critical themes:

- *first*, the genealogies of human rights, both "modern" and "contemporary," their logics of exclusion and inclusion, and the construction of ideas about "human";
- *second*, the realities of the overproduction of human rights norms and standards and their significance for human rights futures;
- *third*, the politics of difference and identity, which views human rights as having not just an emancipative potential but also a repressive one;
- *fourth*, the post-modernist suspicion of the power to tell large global stories (the "meta-narratives") which carries the potential of converting human rights languages into texts or tricks of governance;
- *fifth*, the resurfacing of arguments about ethical and cultural relativism interrogating the politics of universality of human rights, making possible, in good conscience, toleration of vast stretches of human suffering;
- *sixth*, the danger of conversion of human rights movements into human rights markets; and
- *seventh*, the emergence, with the forces and relations of "globalization" (attested to by such dominant ideologies as "economic rationalism," "good governance," and "structural adjustment"), of a trade-related, market-friendly paradigm of human rights seeking to supplant the paradigm of the UDHR.

In addressing these themes, I take it as axiomatic that the historic mission of "contemporary" human rights is *to give voice to human suffering*, to make it visible and to ameliorate it. The notion that human rights regimes may, or ought to, contribute to the "pursuit of happiness" remains the privilege of a miniscule segment of humanity. For hundreds of millions of the "wretched of the earth,"[8] human rights enunciations matter, if at all, only if they provide shields against torture and tyranny, deprivation and destitution, pauperization and powerlessness, desexualization and degradation.

Contrary to the range of expectations evoked by the title of this essay, I do not make explicit the actual voices of human suffering to assist our sense of the reality of human rights. But I try to do the next best thing: to relate the theory and practice of human rights to the endless varieties of preventible human suffering. Recovery of the sense and experience of human anguish provides the only hope that there is for the future of human rights.

---

8 *See* FRANTZ FANON, THE WRETCHED OF THE EARTH (1963).

B. Some De-Mystifications

At the outset, some approaches to keywords may be helpful. I shun the self-proclaimed post-modernist virtue that, even at its best moment, celebrates incomprehensibility as a unique form of intelligibility.

True, the worlds of power and resistance to power are rife with complexity and contradiction. True also, the production of human rights "truths" contesting those of power is marked by a surplus of meaning. For those who suffer violation, an appeal to public virtue, no matter how creatively ambiguous, remains a necessity. In contrast, brutal clarity characterizes regimes of political cruelty. All the same, I also believe that clarity of conviction and communication is a crucial resource for promoting and protecting human rights. Success in this performance is never assured, but the struggle to attain it is by itself a human rights task.

1. Human Rights

The very term "human rights" is deeply problematic.[9] It straddles several universes of discourse. Moral philosophers signify by it a set of ethical imperatives that contribute to making the basic structure of society and state to be and remain overall "just." International lawyers regard the term as a set of norms and standards produced juridically (as having some sort of binding effect on the behavior of states and regional and international organizations). Architects and administrators of regional governance (such as the European Union) regard "human rights" promotion and protection as symbolic of the syndrome of shared sovereignty. For national power-elites, "human rights" provides vocabularies of legitimation of governance. For those who regard practices and structures of governance as deeply unjust or morally flawed, "human rights" represent a rallying cry against oppression and sites for practices of "counter-power."

The abundance of its meanings may not be reduced to a false totality such as "basic human rights" inasmuch as all human rights are basic to those who are deprived, disadvantaged, and dispossessed. Nor may we succumb to an anthropomorphic illusion that the range of human rights is limited to human beings; the new rights to a clean and healthy environment (or what is somewhat inappropriately, even cruelly, called "sustainable development"[10]) take us far beyond such a narrow

---

9 The human rights discourse is not bloodless. Devout Nazis, or their lineal neo-Nazi descendants, are rarely affected by the afflictions of erudite discourse concerning properties of "human rights" (their universality, interdependence, indivisibility, and inalienability). They claim logics and paralogics of human rights as the weaponry that would destroy the very notion! The esoteric human rights discourse is at worst an ecological threat (forests have to be felled in order that human rights discourses thrive worldwide).

10 *See* ANDREW ROWELL, GREEN BACKLASH: GLOBAL SUBVERSION OF THE ENVIRONMENTAL MOVEMENT 4–41 (1996). For the extraordinary relation between Nazism and deep ecology, see LUC FERRY, THE NEW ECOLOGICAL ORDER 91–107 (Carol Volk trans., 1995).

notion. Nor should one reduce the forbiddingly diverse range of human rights enunciations or totality of sentiments that give rise to them to some uniform narrative that seeks family resemblance in such ideas as "dignity," "well-being," or human "flourishing." The expression "human rights" shelters an incredibly diverse range of *the politics of desire-in-dominance* and *the politics of desire-in-insurrection*. These forms of politics resist encapsulation in any formula. The best one may hope for is to let the contexts of domination and resistance articulate themselves as separate but equal perspectives on the meaning of "human rights."

2. Discursivity

By "discursivity" I refer to both erudite and ordinary practices of "rights-talk." Rights-talk (or discursive practice) occurs within traditions (discursive formations).[11] Traditions, themselves codes for power and hierarchy, allocate competences (who may speak), construct forms (how one may speak, what forms of discourse are proper), determine boundaries (what may not be named or conversed about), and structure exclusion (denial of voice). What I call "modern" human rights offers powerful examples of the power of the rights-talk tradition.

What I call "contemporary" human rights discursivity illustrates the power of the subaltern discourse. When that discourse acquires the intensity of a discursive insurrection, its management becomes a prime task of human rights diplomacy. Dominant or hegemonic rights-talk seeks but does not ever fully achieve the suppression of subaltern rights-talk. Human rights discursivity, to invoke a Filipino template, is marked by complexity and contradiction between the statist discourse of the educated (*illustrados*) and the subversive discourse of the indigenous (*indio*).[12]

Discourse theorists often maintain that discursive practice constitutes social reality; there are no violators, violated, and violations outside discourse. But all this ignores or obscures nondiscursive or material practices of power and resistance. The nondiscursive order of reality, the materiality of human violation, is just as important, if not more so, from the standpoint of the violated.[13]

---

11 For example, rights-talk (discursive practice) gives rise to distinct, even if related, regimes (discursive formations): the civil and political rights regime in international law is distinct from the social, cultural, and economic rights regime. The ways in which discursive formations occur determine what shall count as a violation of human rights. The prohibition against torture, cruel, inhuman, degrading punishment or treatment in the civil and political rights formation also prohibits rights-talk which equates starvation or domestic violence as a violation of human rights. The latter gets constituted as *violation* only when discursive boundaries are transgressed.

12 *See* ANTHONY WOODIWISS, GLOBALISATION, HUMAN RIGHTS AND LABOR LAW IN THE PACIFIC ASIA 104 (1998).

13 This point is cruelly established, for example, by the "productive" technologies entailed in the manufacture and distribution of landmines or weapons and instruments of mass

3. Logics and Paralogics of Human Rights

By the use of the notion of "paralogics," I conflate the notions of logic and rhetoric. Paradigmatic logic follows a "causal" chain of signification to a "conclusion" directed by major and minor premises. Rhetorical logic does not regard argument as "links in the chain," but rather, as legs to a chair.[14] What matters in rhetorical logic is the choice of *tópoi*, literary conventions that define sites from which the processes of suasion begin. These sites are rarely governed by any pre-given *tópoi*; rather, they dwell in that which one thinks one ought to argue about.[15] "Human rights" logic or paralogics are all about how one may or should construct "*techniques of persuasion [as] a means of creating awareness*."[16]

The human rights "we-ness" that enacts and enhances these techniques of suasion is multifarious, contingent, and continually fragmented. That "we-ness" is both an artifact of power as well as of resistance. Human rights discourse is intensely partisan; it cannot exist or endure outside the webs of impassioned commitment and networks of contingent solidarities, whether on behalf and at the behest of dominant or subaltern ideological practice. Both claim the ownership of a transformative vision of politics, of anticipation of possible human futures. The historic significance of human rights (no matter what we perform with this potter's clay) lies in the denial of administered regimes of disarticulation, even when this amounts only to the perforation of the escutcheon of dispersed sovereignty and state power.

---

destruction. It would be excessive to say that these are constituted by discursive practices and do not exist outside of these practices. The materiality of nondiscursive practices, arenas, and formations is relatively autonomous of discourse theories. It is another matter that human rights discursive practices are able, at times, to highlight victimage caused by the deployment of these technologies as violative of human rights.

14 *See* Julius Stone, Legal System and Lawyers' Reasonings 327 (1964).

15 This is expressed brilliantly by Umberto Eco:

> For example, I can argue as follows: "What others possess having taken it away from me is not their property; it is wrong to take from others what is their property; but it is not wrong to restore the original order of property, putting back into my hands what was originally in my hands." But I can also argue: "Rights of property are sanctioned by the actual possession of a thing; if I take from someone what is actually in their possession, I commit an act against the rights of property and therefore theft." Of course a third argument is possible, namely: "All property is *per se* theft; taking property from property-owners means restoring the equilibrium violated by original theft, and therefore taking from the propertied the fruits of their thefts is *not just right but a duty*."

Umberto Eco, Apocalypse Postponed 75–76 (Robert Lumley ed., 1994) (emphasis added).

16 *Id.* at 77. I borrow Eco's phrase explaining the task of rhetoric in general (emphasis added).

4. Future of Human Rights

A sense of unease haunts my heavy invocation of "the future of human rights." In a sense, this future is already the past of human rights time, manner, and circumstance. What may constitute the future history of human rights depends on how imaginatively one defines, both in theory and movement, the challenges posed by the processes of globalization. Already we are urged to appreciate the "need to relocate" human rights in the "current processes of change."[17] From this perspective, what is mandated is the mode of structural adjustment of human rights reflexivity itself. The prospects of recycling the moral languages of human rights appear rather bleak in our globalizing human condition in ways that they did not to the forerunners and founders of human rights, from a Grotius to a Gandhi.

A contrasting vision stresses "rooted Utopianism."[18] It conceives of human rights futures as entailing nontechnocratic ways of imaging futures. The technocratic imaging takes for granted "the persistence of political forms and structures, at least short of collapse through catastrophe."[19] In contrast, the nontechnocratic ways derive sustenance from exemplary lives of citizen-pilgrims "at work amidst us" who embody a "refusal to be bound by either deference or acquiescence to statism" and "relate fulfillment to joy in community, not materialist acquisition."[20]

This essay hovers uncertainly between the globalization (doomsday) anticipation of the human future and the vision of utopian transformation animated by exemplary lives of countless citizen-pilgrims.[21] Yet it must be acknowledged that "human rights" have not one but many futures.

5. Suffering

Save when expedient, statist human rights discourse does not relate to languages of pain and suffering in its enunciations. In contrast, peoples' struggles against

---

17 *The Realization of Economic, Social and Cultural Rights: Final Report on the Question of the Impunity of Perpetrators of Human Rights Violations (Economic, Social and Cultural Rights)* (El Hadji Guissé, Special Rapporteur) (on file with the author).

18 Richard Falk, Explorations at the Edge of Time: The Prospects for World Order 101–03 (1995).

19 *Id.*

20 *Id.*

21 Professor Falk mentions Mother Teresa, Bishop Desmond Tutu, Paulo Friere, Lech Walesa, Kim Dae Jung, and Petra Kelly. But alongside these charismatic figures exist "countless other women and men we will never know." Behind every legendary human rights life lie the lives of hundreds of human beings, no less exemplary. The task of historiography of human rights is to roll back the orders of anonymization. This task gets complicated in some troublesome ways by many a media-porous, U.N.-accredited, and self-certified NGO that obscures from view the unsurpassed moral heroism embodied in everyday exemplary lives. Falk, *supra* note 18.

regimes practicing the politics of cruelty are rooted in the direct experience of pain and suffering.

Even so, it remains necessary to problematize notions of suffering. Suffering is ubiquitous to the point of being natural, and is both creative and destructive of human potential. Religious traditions impart a cosmology to human suffering[22] towards which secular human rights traditions bear an ambivalent relationship. Additionally, recent social theory understanding of human suffering evinces many ways of enacting a boundary between "necessary" and "unnecessary" suffering,[23] sensitive to the problématique of the cultural/professional appropriation of human suffering.[24]

Crucial for present purposes is the fact that even human rights regimes enact an hierarchy of pain and suffering. Statist human rights regimes seek to legitimate capital punishment (despite normative trends signaling its progressive elimination); provide for the suspension of human rights in situations of "emergency" (howsoever nuanced); and promote an obstinate division between the exercise of civil and political rights, on the one hand, and social, economic, and cultural rights, on the other. Similarly, some global human rights regimes, policing via emergent post-Cold War sanctioning mechanisms, justify massive, flagrant, and ongoing human rights violations in the name of making human rights secure. Even non-statist human rights discursivity (at first sight "progressive") justifies the imposition of human suffering in the name of autonomy and identity movements. The processes of globalization envision a new dramaturgy of "justifiable" human suffering.

In sum, relating the future of human rights to human suffering is fateful for the futures of human rights.

II. Two Notions of Human Rights: "Modern" and "Contemporary"

The contrasting paradigms of "modern" and "contemporary" human rights mask forms of continuity within the framework of *raison d'état*. The basic contrasts seem to me to be four. First, in the "modern" paradigm of rights the logics of exclusion are pre-eminent, whereas in the "contemporary" paradigm, the logics of inclusion are paramount. Second, the relationship between human rights languages and governance differ markedly in the two paradigms. Third, the "modern" enunciation of human rights was almost ascetic; in contrast, "contemporary" enunciations present

---

22 *See, e.g.*, THOMAS AQUINAS, THE LITERAL EXPOSITION ON JOB: A SCRIPTURAL COMMENTARY CONCERNING PROVIDENCE (Anthony Damico trans., Martin D. Yaffe Interpretive Essay and Notes, Scholars Press 1989).

23 MAURICE GLASMAN, UNNECESSARY SUFFERING: MANAGING MARKET UTOPIA (1996).

24 *See, e.g.*, Arthur Kleinman & Joan Kleinman, *The Appeal of Experience; The Dismay of Images: Cultural Appropriation of Suffering in Our Times, in* SOCIAL SUFFERING 1 (Arthur Kleinman et al. eds., 1997).

a carnival. Finally, the "contemporary" paradigm inverts the inherent modernist relationship between human rights and human suffering.

The terms I use, *faute de mieux*, may mislead. What I call, "modern" also embraces a Hugo Grotius with his memorable emphasis on *temperamenta belli* (insistence on the minimization of suffering in war) and a Francisco Vittoria who valiantly proselytized, against the Church (to the point of heresy) and the Emperor (to the point of treason) the human rights of the New World. What I call the "contemporary" human rights paradigm is marked in some of its major moments by practices of *realpolitik*, above all the conscripting of human rights languages to brutal ends in former superpower Cold War rivalry and in emergent post-Cold War politics.

In any event, my description of the two paradigms is distinctly oriented to the European imagination about human rights. An adequate historiography will, of course, locate the originating languages of human rights far beyond European space and time. I focus on the "modern" precisely because of its destructive impact, in terms of both social consciousness and organization, on that which may be named—clumsily and with deep human violation—"pre-" or "non-" modern.

A. The Logics of Exclusion and Inclusion

The notion of human rights—historically the rights of *men*—is confronted with two perplexities. The first concerns the nature of human nature (the *is* question). The second concerns the question: who is to count as human or fully human (the *ought* question). While the first question continues to be debated in both theistic and secular terms,[25] the second—"Who should count as 'human'?"—occupies the center stage of the "modern" enunciation of human rights. The criteria of individuation in the European liberal traditions of thought[26] furnished some of the most powerful ideas in constructing a model of human rights. Only those beings were to be regarded as "human" who were possessed of the capacity for reason and autonomous moral will, although what counted as reason and will varied in the long development of the European liberal tradition. In its major phases of development, "slaves," "heathens," "barbarians," colonized peoples, indigenous populations, women, children, the impoverished, and the "insane" have been, at various times

---

25 The theistic responses trace the origins of human nature in the Divine Will; the secular in contingencies of evolution of life on earth. The theistic approaches, even when recognizing the holiness of all creation, insist on Man being created in God's image, and therefore capable of perfection in ways no other being in the world is. The secular/scientific approaches view human beings as complex psychosomatic systems co-determined by both genetic endowment and the environment and open to experimentation, like all other objects in "nature." These differences could be (and have been) described in more sophisticated ways, especially by various *ius naturalist* thinkers. *See, e.g.*, STONE, *supra* note 14.

26 *See* Bhikhu Parekh, *The Modern Conception of Rights and Its Marxist Critique*, *in* THE RIGHT TO BE HUMAN 1 (Upendra Baxi et al. eds., 1987). *See also* RAYMOND WILLIAMS, KEYWORDS 161–65 (1983).

and in various ways, thought unworthy of being bearers of human rights. In other words, these discursive devices of Enlightenment rationality were devices of exclusion. The "Rights of Man" were the human rights of all *men* capable of autonomous reason and *will*. While by no means the exclusive prerogative of "modernity,"[27] a large number of human beings were excluded by this peculiar ontological construction.[28]

Exclusionary criteria are central to the "modern" conception of human rights. The foremost historical role performed by them was to accomplish the justification of the unjustifiable, namely, colonialism and imperialism.[29] That justification was inherently racist; colonial powers claimed a collective human right of superior races to dominate the inferior ones ("the Other"). The Other in many cases ceased to exist before imperial law formulations such as the doctrine of *terra nullius*, following Blackstone's scandalous distinction between the inhabited and uninhabited colonies.[30] Since the Other of European imperialism was by definition not human or fully human, "it" was not worthy of human rights; at the very most, Christian compassion and charity fashioned some devices of legal or jural paternalism. That Other, not being human or fully human, also was liable to being merchandised in the slave market or to being the "raw material" of exploitative labor within and across the colonies. Not being entitled to a right to be and remain a human being, the Other was made a stranger and an exile to the language and logic of human rights being fashioned slowly but surely in (and for) the West. The classical liberal theory and practice of human rights, in its formative era, thus was innocent of the notion of universality of rights though certainly no stranger to its rhetoric.

The only *juristic* justification for colonialism/imperialism, if any is possible, is the claim that there is a *natural collective human right* of the superior races to rule the inferior ones, and the justification comes in many shapes and forms. One has but to read the "classic" texts of Locke or Mill to appreciate the range of talents that are devoted to the justification of colonialism.[31] The related but different logics combined to instill belief in the collective human right of the well-ordered

---

27 Religious traditions specialized, and still do, in ontological constructions that excluded, for example, Untouchables, rendering them beyond the pale of the *varna* system. *See* Upendra Baxi, *Justice as Emancipation: The Legacy of Babasaheb Ambedkar, in* CRISIS AND CHANGE IN CONTEMPORARY INDIA 122–49 (Upendra Baxi & Bhikhu Parekh eds., 1995).

28 *See* PETER FITZPATRICK, THE MYTHOLOGY OF MODERN LAW 92–145 (1992); MAHMOOD MAMDANI, CITIZEN AND SUBJECT: CONTEMPORARY AFRICA AND THE LEGACY OF LATE COLONIALISM 62–137 (1996).

29 Francisco de Vittoria, remarkably ahead of his times, made out a most cogent case for the human rights of the inhabitants of the "New World." *See* FRANCISCO DE VITTORIA, DE INDIS ET DE IVRE BELLI RELECTIONES (J. Bate trans., 1917) (1557).

30 *See* FITZPATRICK, *supra* note 28, at 72–91.

31 Bhikhu Parekh, *Liberalism and Colonialism: A Critique of Locke and Mill, in* THE DECOLONIZATION OF IMAGINATION: CULTURE, KNOWLEDGE AND POWER 81–88 (Jan Nederveen Pieterse & Bhikhu Parekh eds., 1995).

societies to govern the wild and "savage" races. All the well-known devices of the formative era of classical liberal thought were deployed: the logics of rights to property and progress; the state of nature and civil society; and social Darwinism, combining the infantalization and maturity of "races" and stages of civilization. The collective human right to colonize the less well-ordered peoples and societies for the collective "good" of both as well as of humankind was by definition indefeasible as well, and not in the least weakened in the curious logical reasoning and contradictions of evolving liberalism.

B. Human Rights Languages and the Power of Governance

The languages of human rights are integral to tasks and practices of governance, as exemplified by the constitutive elements of the "modern" paradigm of human rights—namely, the collective human right of the colonizer to subjugate "inferior" peoples and the absolutist right to property. The manifold though complex justifications offered for these "human rights" ensured that the "modern" European nation-state was able to marshal the right to property, as a right to world-wide *imperium* and *dominium*.

The construction of a collective human right to colonial/imperial governance is made sensible by the co-optation of languages of human rights into those of governance abroad and class and patriarchal domination at home. The hegemonic function of rights languages, in the service of governance at home and abroad, consisted in making whole groups of people socially and politically invisible. Their suffering was denied any authentic voice, since it was not constitutive of human suffering. "Modern" human rights, in their original narrative, entombed masses of human beings in shrouds of necrophilic silence.

In contrast, the "contemporary" human rights paradigm is based on the premise of radical self-determination. Self-determination insists that every person has a right to a voice, the right to bear witness to violation, and a right to immunity against "disarticulation" by concentrations of economic, social, and political formations. Rights languages, no longer exclusively at the service of the ends of governance, thus open up sites of resistance.

C. Ascetic versus Carnivalistic Rights Production

The "contemporary" production of human rights is exuberant.[32] This is a virtue compared with the lean and mean articulations of human rights in the "modern" period. In the "modern" era, the authorship of human rights was both state-centric

---

32 For an insightful overview, see Burns H. Weston, *Human Rights*, 20 ENCYCLOPEDIA BRITANNICA 714 (15th ed. 1998 prtg.), *revised and updated in* ENCYCLOPAEDIA BRITANNICA ONLINE (visited Dec. 1, 1998) <http://www.eb.com:180/cgi-bin/g?DocF=macro/5002/93. html>.

and Eurocentric; in contrast, the formulations of "contemporary" human rights are increasingly inclusive and often marked by intense negotiation between NGOs and governments. The authorship of contemporary human rights is multitudinous, and so are the auspices provided by the United Nations and regional human rights networks. As a result, human rights enunciations proliferate, becoming as specific as the networks from which they arise and, in turn, sustain. The "modern" notion of human rights forbade such dispersal, the only major movement having been in the incremental affirmation of the rights of labor and minority rights. The way collectivities are now constructed in human rights enunciations is radically different. They do not merely reach out to "discrete" and "insular" minorities;[33] they extend also to wholly new, hitherto unthought of, justice constituencies.[34]

D. Human Suffering and Human Rights

Even at the end of the Second Christian Millennium we lack a social theory about human rights. Such a theory must address a whole range of issues,[35] but for present purposes it is necessary only to highlight the linkage between human suffering and human rights.

---

33 This historic phrase comes from the famous footnote 4 in Carolene Products v. United States, 323 U.S. 18, 21 n. 4 (1944).

34 Contemporary enunciations thus embrace, to mention very different orders by way of example, the rights of the girl-child, migrant labor, indigenous peoples, gays and lesbians (the emerging human right to sexual orientation), prisoners and those in custodial institutional regimes, refugees and asylum-seekers, and children.

35 By the phrase "a social theory of human rights," a term frequently invoked in this essay, I wish to designate bodies of knowledge that address: (a) genealogies of human rights in "pre-modern," "modern" and "contemporary" human rights discursive formations; (b) contemporary dominant and subaltern images of human rights; (c) tasks confronting projects of engendering human rights; (d) exploration of human rights movements as social movements; (e) impacts of high science and "hi-tech" on the theory and practice of human rights; (f) the problematic of the marketization of human rights; (g) the economics and the political economy of human rights.

The listing is illustrative of bodies of reflexive knowledges. In select areas, these knowledges are becoming incrementally available but remain as yet in search of a new genre in social theory. Even as the era of "grand theory" in the imagination of social thought seems to begin to disappear, a return to it seems imperative if one is to make sensible a whole variety of human rights theory and practice. Daunting difficulties entailed in acts of totalization of human rights stand aggravated by this aspiration, but I continue to feel that the endeavor is worthy. Valuable beginnings in some of these directions have been made by FALK, *supra* note 18; WENDY BROWN, STATES OF INJURY: POWER AND FREEDOM IN LATE MODERNITY (1995); BOAVENTURA DE SOUSA SANTOS, TOWARDS A NEW COMMON SENSE: LAW, SCIENCE AND POLITICS IN THE PARADIGMATIC TRANSITION (1995); ROBERTO MANGABERIA UNGER, WHAT SHOULD LEGAL ANALYSTS BECOME? (1996). *See also* UPENDRA BAXI, THE FUTURE OF HUMAN RIGHTS (forthcoming).

The "modern" human rights cultures, tracing their pedigree to the Idea of Progress, Social Darwinism, racism, and patriarchy (central to the "Enlightenment" ideology), justified a global imposition of cruelty as "natural," "ethical," and "just." The "modern" liberal ideology that gave birth to the very notion of human rights, howsoever Euro-enclosed and no matter how riven with contradiction between liberalism and empire,[36] regarded the imposition of dire and extravagant suffering upon individual human beings as wholly justified. Practices of politics, barbaric even by the standards of the theological and secular thought of the Enlightenment, were somehow considered justified overall by ideologues, state managers, and the political unconscious that they generated (despite, most notably, the divergent struggles of the working classes). This "justification" boomeranged in the form of the politics of genocide of the Third Reich, often resulting in cruel complicity by "ordinary" citizens, unredeemed by even Schindler's list, in the worst foundational moments of present-day ethnic cleansing.[37]

In contrast, the post-Holocaust and post-Hiroshima angst registers a normative horror at human violation. The "contemporary" human rights movement is rooted in the illegitimacy of all forms of the politics of cruelty. No doubt what counts as cruelty varies enormously even from one human rights context/instrument to another.[38] Even so, there now are in place firm *jus cogens* norms of international human rights and humanitarian law, which de-legitimate and forbid barbaric practices of power in state as well as civil society. From the standpoint of those violated, this is no small gain; the community of perpetrators remains incrementally vulnerable to human rights cultures, howsoever variably, and this matters enormously for the violated. In a non-ideal world, human rights discursivity appears to offer an "ideal even if a second best" option.

36 *See* Uday Mehta, Liberalism and Empire: A Study in Nineteenth-Century Liberal Thought (1999).

37 Is this standpoint any more contestable in the wake of Daniel Jonah Goldhagen, Hitler's Willing Executioners: Ordinary Germans and the Holocaust (1996) and Richard Weisberg, Poethics: and Other Strategies of Law & Literature (1992)?

38 For example: Is capital punishment in any form and with whatever justification a practice of cruelty? When does discrimination, whether based on gender, class, or caste, assume the form of torture proscribed by international human rights standards and norms? When may forms of sexual harassment in the workplace be described as an aspect of cruel, inhuman, and degrading treatment forbidden under the current international human rights standards and norms? Do nonconsensual sex practices within marriage relationships amount to rape? Do all forms of child labor amount to cruel practice, on the ground that the confiscation of childhood is an unredressable human violation? Are mega-irrigation projects that create eco-exiles and environmental destruction/degradation acts of developmental cruelty? Are programs or measures of structural adjustment an aspect of the politics of imposed suffering? This range of questions is vast and undoubtedly more may be added. For an anthropological mode of interrogation of torture, see Talal Asad, *On Torture, or Cruel, Inhuman and Degrading Treatment, in* Social Suffering, *supra* note 24, at 285–308.

No matter how many contested fields are sustained by the rhetoric of the universality, indivisibility, interdependence, and inalienability of human rights, contemporary human rights cultures have constructed new criteria relative to the legitimation of power. These criteria increasingly discredit any attempt to base power and rule on the inherent violence institutionalized in imperialism, colonialism, racism, and patriarchy. "Contemporary" human rights make possible, in most remarkable ways, discourse on human suffering. No longer may practices of power, abetted by grand social theory, justify beliefs that sustain willful infliction of harm as an attribute of sovereignty or of a good society. Central to "contemporary" human rights discourse are visions and ways of constructing the ethic of power which prevent the imposition of repression and human suffering beyond the needs of regime-survival no matter how extravagantly determined. The illegitimacy of the languages of immiseration becomes the very grammar of international politics.

Thus, the distinction between "modern" and "contemporary" forms of human rights is focused on *taking suffering seriously*.[39] Outside the domain of the laws of war among and between the "civilized" nations, "modern" human rights regarded large-scale imposition of human suffering as just and right in pursuit of a Eurocentric notion of human progress. It silenced the discourses of human suffering. In contrast, "contemporary" human rights are animated by a politics of international desire to render problematic the very notion of the politics of cruelty.

III. Critiques of "Contemporary" Human Rights

Many critiques of human rights have gained wide currency. Unmitigated skepticism about the possibility and/or desirability of human rights is frequently promoted. Unsurprising when stemming from autocratic or dictatorial leaders or regimes who criticize human rights norms and standards on the grounds of their origin, scope, and relevance (almost always reeking of expediency and bad faith), such critiques, when they emanate from the foremost social thinkers, require response.

I sample here two overarching criticisms of the idea of human rights. Talking about "contemporary" human rights in the "normal U.N. practice," Alasdair MacIntyre, in his widely acclaimed *After Virtue*, says that it thrives on "not giving

---

[39] *See* Upendra Baxi, *Taking Suffering Seriously: Social Action Litigation Before the Supreme Court of India, in* Law and Poverty: Critical Essays 387 (Upendra Baxi ed., 1988). How may one explain this paradigm shift? At least six historic processes are entailed, which are both complex and contradictory. First, the many phases of the Cold War marked the birth and career of "contemporary" human rights, giving rise to fragmented "universality" of human rights. Second, the Cold War simultaneously "problematized" as well as naturalized human suffering. Third, within the fragmented universality emerged the outlawry of racism. Fourth, also within that fragmented universality emerged new forms of global solidarity for human rights. Fifth, the universalization of the Marxian critique of bourgeois human rights began to reshape these traditions. Sixth, all this created an endowment of practices of politics *of* and *for* human rights. I dwell on these features in Baxi, *supra* note 35, ch. 2.

good reasons for *any* assertion whatsoever;"[40] he even is moved to conclude that there are no natural or self-evident human rights and that belief in them is one with belief in witches and unicorns![41] Additionally Zygmunt Bauman asserts that human rights have "become a war-cry and blackmail weapon in the hands of aspiring 'community leaders' wishing to pick up powers that the state has dropped."[42] These eminent thinkers present their *ipse dixit*, however, as manifest truths. In contrast, responsible critiques of human rights are concerned with: (a) the modes of production of human rights; (b) the problems posed by the politics of universality of human rights and the politics of identity/difference; and (c) the arguments from relativism and multiculturalism. I examine each of these briefly.[43]

A. Too Many Rights or Too Few?

Is it the case that the late Christian twentieth century "suffers" from an overproduction of human rights standards and norms, entailing a policy and resource overload that no government or regime, however conscientious, can bear? Should every human need find an embodiment in a human rights norm? Does overproduction entail a belief that each and every major human/social problem is best defined and solved in terms of human rights, in terms of the talismanic property of human rights enunciations? Should concentrations of economic power be allowed to harness these talismanic properties?[44]

I address here only the issue of overproduction. The important question concerns, perhaps not the *quantity* but the *quality* of human rights norms and standards since the UDHR, with insistence on their universality and interdependence. Even more striking is the redefined scope of human rights, which now extends to material as well as nonmaterial needs. This conversion of needs into rights, however problematic, is the hallmark of "contemporary" human rights. It results in waves or "generations" of rights enunciations, at times characterized by a "blue," "red," and "green" rights color scheme.[45] Being color-blind, I do not know which color best signifies the emerging recognition of the collective rights of the foreign

---

40 ALASDAIR MACINTYRE, AFTER VIRTUE 69 (1984).

41 *Id.* at 66.

42 ZYGMUNT BAUMAN, POSTMODERN ETHICS 64 (1993).

43 For a fuller elaboration, see BAXI, *supra* note 35, ch. 3.

44 As is the case with the assorted interest groups of international airlines, hotels, and travel agents who assiduously lobby the U.N. to proclaim a universal human right of tourism? And when a group of predatory investment organizations produces a Draft Multilateral Agreement on Investment (MAI)? *See* the OECD web site (visited Oct. 24, 1998) <http://www.oecd.org/daf/cmis/mai/maitext.pdf>. Must the aggregations of capital and technology (the *proprietariat*) always be disabled from acting upon the capitalist belief that the protection of its rights as human rights is the best assurance there is for the amelioration of the life-condition of the proletariat?

45 *See* JOHAN GALTUNG, HUMAN RIGHTS IN ANOTHER KEY 151–56 (1994).

investor, global corporations, and international financial capital-in short, of global capitalism. But this much is compellingly clear: the emergent collective human rights of global capital presents a formidable challenge to the human rights paradigm inaugurated by the UDHR.

The astonishing quantity of human rights production generates various experiences of skepticism and faith.[46] Some complain of exhaustion (what I call "rights-weariness"). Some suspect sinister imperialism in diplomatic maneuvers animating each and every human rights enunciation (what I call "rights-wariness"). Some celebrate human rights as a new global civic religion which, given a community of faith, will address and solve all major human problems (what I call "human rights evangelism"). Their fervor is often matched by those NGOs that tirelessly pursue the removal of brackets in pre-final diplomatic negotiating texts of various United Nations' summits as triumphs in human solidarity (what I call "human rights romanticism"). Some other activists believe that viable human rights standards can best be produced by exploiting contingencies of international diplomacy (what I call "bureaucratization of human rights"). And still others insist that the real birthplaces of human rights are far removed from the ornate rooms of diplomatic conferences and are found, rather, in the actual sites (acts and feats) of resistance and struggle (what I call "critical human rights realism"[47]).

All these ways of "reading" the production of human rights are implicit discourse on "contemporary" human rights. I review, cursorily, five principal approaches.

First, an organizational way of reading this profusion, within the United Nations system, concerns hierarchical control over the normative contingency of rights production. Increasing autonomy by agencies within the system is seen as a hazard to be contained, as poignantly illustrated by the debate over the right to development.[48] Similarly, the manner in which treaty bodies formulate, through the distinctive device of the "General Comment," somewhat unanticipated treaty obligations upon state parties now begins to emerge as a contested process.

Second, some question the value and the utility of the inflation of human rights. Does this endless normativity perform any useful function in the "real world"? Is there an effective communication among (to invoke Galtung's trichotomy) the norm-senders (the U.N. system), norm-receivers (sovereign states), and the norm-objects

---

46 BAXI, *supra* note 35.

47 Also, some human rights activists believe in "aborting," as it were, global instruments favoring the rights of global capital as opposed to the human rights of human beings (what I call *free choice* politics *for* human rights).

48 *See* Philip Alston, *Revitalizing United Nations Work on Human Rights and Development*, 18 MELB. U.L. REV. 216 (1991); Jack Donnelly, *In Search of the Unicorn: The Jurisprudence and Politics of the Rights to Development*, 15 CAL. W. INT'L J. 473 (1985). *But see* Upendra Baxi, *The Development of the Right to Development*, *in* HUMAN RIGHTS (Janus Symonides ed., forthcoming from UNESCO in 1999). *See also* the essay by Stephen Marks, *infra* in this volume at pp. 291, 339–43.

(those for whose benefit the rights enunciations are said to have been made)?[49] Who stands to benefit the most by the overproduction of human rights norms and standards? Is it merely a symptom of a growing democratic deficit, sought to be redressed by "legitimation traffic" between norm-senders (the U.N. system) and norm-receivers (the member states)? 

A third reading, from the standpoint of high moral theory, warns us against the danger of assuming that the languages of human rights are the only, or the very best, moral languages we have. Rights languages, after all, are languages of claims and counter-claims that typically entail mediation through authoritative state instrumentalities, including contingent feats of adjudicatory activism. The overproduction of rights locates social movements on the grid of power, depriving human communities of their potential for reflexive ethical action. Being ultimately state-bound, even the best of all rights performances typically professionalize, atomize, and de-collectivize energies for social resistance, and do not always energize social policy, state responsiveness, civic empathy, or political mobilization. Not altogether denying the creativity of rights languages, this perspective minimizes its role, stressing instead the historic role of lived relations of sacrifice, support, and solidarity in the midst of suffering.

A fourth orientation views the production of human rights as perhaps the best hope there is for inclusive participation in the making of human futures. It assumes a world historic moment in which neither the institutions of governance nor the processes of the market, singly or in combination, is equipped to fashion just futures. It thrives on the potential of "peoples politics" (not as a system but as chaos) which may emerge only by a convergence of singular energies of dedication by (local, national, regional, and global NGOs). No other understanding of women's movements celebrating the motto "Women's Rights are Human Rights," for example, is possible except the one that regards as historically necessary and feasible the overthrow, by global praxis, of universal patriarchy in all its vested and invested sites. This viewpoint seeks to combat patriarchy, persistent even in the making of human rights, and to explore ways of overcoming the limits of human rights languages that constitute very often the *limits* of human rights action. 

A fifth perspective questions the very notion of the overproduction of human rights norms and standards. Not only does the global enunciation of rights entail a long, often elephantine, gestation period;[50] it also produces mainly "soft" human

49 *See* GALTUNG, *supra* note 45, at 56–70.

50 As is the case with the Declaration of the Rights of Indigenous Peoples, which emerges as a last frontier of contemporary human rights development. *See* Draft Declaration of the Rights of Indigenous Peoples, adopted by the U.N. Commission on Human Rights Sub-Commission on the Prevention of Discrimination and Protection of Minorities, Aug. 24, 1994, U.N. Doc. E/CN.4/1995/2; E/CN.4/Sub.2/1994/56 (Oct. 28, 1994), *reprinted in* 34 I.L.M. 541 (1995) *and* 3 INTERNATIONAL LAW AND WORLD ORDER: BASIC DOCUMENTS III.F.4 (Burns H. Weston ed., 5 vols., 1994–) [hereinafter 3 Weston]. M. Cherif Bassiouni offers a use-

rights law (exhortative resolutions, declarations, codes of conduct, etc.), that does not reach, or even at times aspire, to the status of operative norms of conduct. The "hard law" enunciations of human rights, which become enforceable norms, are very few and low in intensity of application. Contemporary human rights production remains both sub-optimal (whatever may be said in comparison with the "modern" period) and inadequate. The task is, from this perspective, to achieve an optimal production of internationally enforceable human rights.

These ways of reading the profusion of human rights norms and standards carry within them all kinds of impacts on the nature and future of human rights. A fuller understanding of these impacts is an important aspect of a social theory of human rights.

B. Politics of Identity/Difference

Informed by post-modernist mood, method, and message, critics of "contemporary" human rights, which champions the universality of human rights, remain anxious at the re-emergence of the idea of "universal reason," a legacy of the Age of Enlightenment that helped to perfect justifications for classical colonialism and racism and for universal patriarchy.[51] The notion of universality invokes not merely new versions of essentialism about human nature but also the notion of meta-narratives: global stories about power and struggles against power. In both of these tropes, do we return to "totalization" modes of thought and practice?

Critics of essentialism remind us that the notion "human" is not pre-given (if, indeed, anything is) but constructed, often with profound rights-denying impacts. Post-modernist critiques now lead us to consider that the idiom of the universality of human rights may have a similar impact. For example, the motto "Women's Rights are Human Rights" masks, often with grave costs, the heterogeneity of women in their civilizational and class positions.[52] So does the appellation "indigenous" in the search for a commonly agreed declaration of indigenous people's rights.[53] Similarly, the human

---

ful approach to the normative stages, which he classifies into the enunciative, declarative, prescriptive, enforcement, and criminalization stages. *See* M. Cherif Bassiouni, *Enforcing Human Rights through International Criminal Law, in* THROUGH AN INTERNATIONAL CRIMINAL COURT IN HUMAN RIGHTS: AN AGENDA FOR THE NEXT CENTURY 347 (Louis Henkin & John L. Hargrove eds., 1994). For a more extended analysis of these modes of reading, see BAXI, *supra* note 35.

51 Concerning patriarchy, see Sally Sedgwick, *Can Kant's Ethics Survive the Feminist Critique?, in* FEMINIST INTERPRETATIONS OF IMMANUEL KANT 77–110 (Robin May Schott ed., 1997). *See also* FEMINISTS READ HABERMAS: GENDERING THE SUBJECT OF DISCOURSE (Johanna Meehan ed., 1995).

52 *See* ELIZABETH V. SPELMAN, INESSENTIAL WOMAN: PROBLEMS OF EXCLUSION IN FEMINIST THOUGHT ix (1988) (maintaining that the endeavors of defining "women as women" or "sisterhood across boundaries" is the "trojan-horse of western feminist ethnocentrism").

53 *See* Russell Barsh, *Indigenous Peoples in the 1990s: From Object to Subject of International Law?*, 7 HARV. HUM. RTS. J. 33 (1994); Stephan Marquardt, *International Law and Indigenous Peoples*, 3 INT'L J. GROUP RTS. 47 (1995).

rights instruments on child rights ignore the diversity of children's circumstances. In many societies, the passage between the first and second childhood or the distinction between "child" and "adult" is brutally cut short, as with child labor, the girl child, or children conscripted into insurrectionist-armed warfare.

Are then identities, universalized all over again in positing a *universal* bearer of human rights, obscuring the fact that identities may themselves be vehicles of power, all too often inscribed or imposed? And do the benign intentions that underlie such performative acts of power advance the cause of human rights as well as they serve the ends of power?

Students of international law, knowingly or not, are familiar with post-modernisms. They know well the problematic of identity as vehicles of power, from the Kelsenite "constitutive" theory of recognition of states (under which states may be said not to exist unless "recognized" by others) to the travails of the right to self-determination. They know how that "self" is constructed, deconstructed, and reconstructed by the play of global power,[54] with attendant legitimations of enormous amounts of human misery. The evolution of the right to self-determination of states and people signifies no more than the power of hegemonic or dominant states to determine the "self" which then has the right to "self-determination." In sum, that right is only a right to access a "self" pre-determined by the play of hegemonic global powers.

Is it any longer true that, outside the contexts of self-determination, the shackles of state sovereignty no longer determine, even when they condition, the bounds of identity? Increasingly, the de-territoralization of identity is said to be a *global* social fact or human condition.[55] Identities are becoming fluid, multiple, contingent, perhaps even to the point where an individual (or the subject) is viewed, in Chantal Mouffe's words, as "the articulation of an ensemble of subject positions, constructed within specific discourses and always precariously sutured at the

---

54 *See* Hurst Hannum, *Rethinking Self-Determination*, 34 VA. J. INT'L L. 1 (1993). He contrasts effectively the reservation by India confining the right to self-determination in Article 1 of the International Covenant on Civil and Political Rights, *infra* Appendix III [hereinafter ICCPR], "only to peoples under foreign rule" with the German objection to it insisting on the availability of this right to "all peoples." The zeal with which the developed countries have sought to expand the range of self-determination rights arises from their unique capability for organizing the collective amnesia of their ruthless prowess in suppressing (not too long ago) even the softest voice urging freedom from the colonial yoke. This said, it also must be stated that the Indian reservation based on "national integrity" creatively mimes the very same order of enclosure of the politics of identity and difference, in vastly different postcolonial conditions, and the social imagery of colonial/imperial representation of European nation-states.

55 For a vivid account of the processes, see ARJUN APPADURAI, MODERNITY AT LARGE: CULTURAL DIMENSIONS OF GLOBALIZATION 27–65 (1996).

intersection of subject positions";[56] and the community appears as "a discursive surface of inscriptions."[57] There is a great appeal in Mouffe's notion of a "non-individualistic conception of the individual," a notion that rejects, relative to human rights, the idea of the individual in terms of "possessive individualism" and that, furthermore, conceives of the individual as "the intersection of a multiplicity of identifications and collective identities that constantly subvert each other."[58]

In any event, this kind of thinking raises several questions from the standpoint of those who are engaged in actual human rights struggles. Four are noted here.

First, are *all* the identities being made, by processes of globalization, "fluid," "multiple," and "contingent"? If we were to place ourselves in the (non-Rawlsian) position of a person belonging to an untouchable community (say, in a remote area of Bihar, India), would we agree that caste and patriarchal identity are fluid, multiple, and contingent? As an untouchable, no matter how you perceive your identity (as a mother, wife, or daughter), you still are liable to be raped; still will be denied access to water in the high caste village well; still will be subjected to all kinds of forced and obnoxious labor; still have your huts set ablaze; still have your adult franchise regularly confiscated at elections by caste Hindu militia.[59] Human rights logic and rhetoric, fashioned by historic struggles, simply and starkly assert that such imposition of primordial identities is morally wrong and legally prohibited. Discrimination on the grounds of birth, sex, domicile, ethnicity, disability, or sexual orientation, for example, counts as a violation of internationally proclaimed human rights. It is the mission of human rights logics and paralogics to dislodge primordial identities that legitimate the orders of imposed suffering, socially invisible at times even to the repressed. But it is a mission that is fraught with grave difficulties. When the imposition of primordial identities occurs in civil society, human rights logic and rhetoric require the state to combat it, raising liberal anxieties about augmenting the New Leviathan. In addition, the state and the law can oppose such imposition only by a reconstruction of that collective identity. The "untouchables" in India, constitutionally christened the "scheduled castes," will have to be burdened by this reconstitution because, in law and society, they necessarily will be either untouchables or ex-untouchables. Justifications of affirmative action programs worldwide, for example, depend on maintaining the integrity of their narratives of millennial histories of collective hurt. It is true that these narratives essentialize historic identities as new sites of injury. But is there a way out of embattled histories, shaped by the dialectics of human rights?

Second, what is there to subvert if identities are "fluid," "multiple," or "contingent"; if the individual or collective self no longer exists as a unified, discursive,

---

56 Chantal Mouffe, *Democratic Citizenship and the Political Community, in* DIMENSIONS OF RADICAL DEMOCRACY: PLURALISMS AND CITIZENSHIP 237 (Chantal Mouffe ed., 1992).

57 Chantal Mouffe, *Democratic Politics Today, in id.* at 14.

58 CHANTAL MOUFFE, THE RETURN OF THE POLITICAL 97, 100 (1993).

59 For a devastatingly accurate account, see ROHINTON MISTRY, A FINE BALANCE (1996).

or semiotic object that can be said to be a bearer of human rights? If the subject is no more, and only subject-positions exist, how are we to construct or pursue politics for human rights? Put another way, how may one theorize repression and violation? It would unduly burden this essay to sharpen these questions, attend to their genealogy, and salvage the possibility of conversation about human rights from the debris of post-identity discourse. I attempt it elsewhere.[60]

Third, how does this diaspora of identity narratives empower those who are haunted by practices of flagrant, massive, and ongoing violations of human rights? For the gurus of post-modern ethics, this is not a seriously engaged concern compared to the preoccupation of defining and contesting all that is wrong with liberalism and socialism.[61]

Fourth, is this human rights path (requiring us to internalize a primordial identity) counter-productive when, in particular, it casts the state and law "as neutral arbiters of injury rather than themselves invested with the power to injure?"[62] Emancipatory in origin, human rights, in the course of enunciation and administration, may become "a regulatory discourse, a means of obstructing or co-opting more radical political demands, or simply the most hollow of empty promises."[63] It is ironic that "rights sought by a politically defined *group* are conferred upon depoliticized *individuals*; at the moment a particular "we" succeeds in obtaining rights, it loses its 'we-ness' and dissolves into individuals."[64] Indeed, in certain moments, human rights development yields itself to tricks of governance; the

---

60 *See* BAXI, *supra* note 35.

61 Jacques Derrida properly assails the heady optimism of the liberalism of Fukuyama, asking, rightly, whether it is credible to think that "all these cataclysms (terror, oppression, repression, extermination, genocide *and so on*)" constitute "contingent or insignificant limitations" for the messianic and triumphant post-Cold War moment of liberalism." JACQUES DERRIDA, SPECTERS OF MARX: THE STATE OF THE DEBT, THE WORK OF MOURNING & THE NEW INTERNATIONAL 57 (Peggy Kamuf trans., 1994) (emphasis added). Note the gesture of exhaustion in the words italicized here! At the same time, Derrida asserts, "[o]ur aporia here stem from the fact that there is no longer any *name* or *technology* for determining the Marxist *coup* and its subject." *Id.* at 98. What follows? Derrida, after a fascinating detour on the work of mourning and narcissism, enjoins us thus: " [O]ne must constantly remember that the impossible . . . is, alas, possible. One must constantly remember that this absolute evil . . . can take place. One must constantly remember that it is even on the basis of the terrible possibility of the impossible that justice is desirable. . . ."; though beyond what Derrida calls "right and law." *Id.* at 175.

Who is this "one" addressed by Derrida? The avant-garde theorist or the being of those subjected continually to the absolute order of evil? No doubt, it is important to sensitize theoretical fellow travelers to the dangers of amnesia. But what does it or should it mean to the victims of orders of absolute evil?

62 BROWN, *supra* note 35, at 27.

63 *Id.*

64 *Id.* at 98.

pillar of emancipation turns out to be the pillar of regulation,[65] as seen in some striking detail in the next section. Were this the only moment of human rights, every triumphal attainment would also be its funerary oration. But does not often a regulatory discourse, at one moment, also become, at another moment, an arena of struggle?

If international human rights lawyers and movement people need to attend to the type of interrogation thus raised, post-modernist ethical thinkers need to wrestle with the recent history of the politics of cruelty, which has constructed, as it were, new primordial communities. These are the communities of the tortured and tormented, the prisoners of conscience across the world, represented with poignancy and unequaled moral heroism by Amnesty International. Would it be true to say that their identity as victims is random, contingent, rather than caused by the play of global politics? Until this question is seriously pursued, can it not be said that human rights enunciations and movements commit no mortal sin of essentialism or foundationalism in insisting upon a universal norm that de-legitimates this invention?

Nor does the post-essentialism that achieves many a rhetorical *tour de force* for a Derrida respond to the problematic posed by the archetypal Aung San Suu Kyi. She embodies human rights essentialism. So do the Afghan women who, under dire straits, protest the Taliban regime. So do UNICEF and Save the Children, which, thanks in part to the globalized media, seek at times to do the impossible, moving the atrophied conscience of the globalized middle classes to an occasional act of charity, even of genuine compassion, thanks to the unbearable CNN and equivalent depictions of cruelly starved children in Sudan midst a well-earned *aperitif* or first course of dinner.[66] No matter how flawed to the Parisian and neo-Parisian cognitive fashions, human rights discourse furnishes potential for struggle that the post-modernist discourse on the politics of identity as yet does not. These cognitive fashion parades must not be allowed to drain emergent solidarities in struggle unless the post-modernist, anti-essentialist critique demonstrates that human rights are *a mistake*.

Indeed, engaged human rights discourse makes possible a deeper understanding of the politics of difference insofar as it is an act of suffering rather than sanitized thought. It insists that the Other is *not* dispensable; it sensitizes us to the fact

---

[65] I adapt here Santos' analysis of dialectic of regulation and emancipation. *See* SANTOS, *supra* note 35, at 7–55.

[66] But perhaps suffering as a *spectacle* can do no more. For the very act of mass media producing the spectacle of suffering needs to divest it of any structural understanding of the production of suffering itself. In a way, the community of gaze can be only instantly constructed by the erasure of the slightest awareness of complicity. Thus, the mass media must obscure the fact that "all those weapons used to make far-away homelands into killing fields have been supplied by our own arms factories, jealous of their orderbooks and proud of their productivity and competitiveness—the life-blood of our own cherished prosperity." ZYGMUNT BAUMAN, GLOBALIZATION: THE HUMAN CONSEQUENCES 75 (1998).

that the politics of Otherhood is not ethically sensible outside the urgency of the maxim: "Ask not for whom the bell tolls; it tolls for thee." It insists, with Rabbi Israeli Salanter, that the *"the material needs of my neighbor are my spiritual needs."*[67] Critically engaged human rights discourse refuses to de-essentialize human suffering, even under the banner of dispersed identities.

C. The Summons for the Destruction of Narrative Monopolies

The post-modernist critique of human rights further maintains that the telling of large *global* stories ("meta-narratives") is less a function of emancipation than an aspect of the politics of intergovernmental desire that ingests the politics of resistance. Put another way, meta-narratives serve to co-opt into mechanisms and processes of governance the languages of human rights such that bills of rights may, with impunity, adorn many a military constitutionalism and that so-called human rights commissions may thrive upon state/regime sponsored violations. Not surprisingly, the more severe the human rights violation, the more the power elites declare their loyalty to the regime of human rights. The near-universality of ratification of the Convention on the Elimination of Discrimination Against Women (CEDAW), for example, betokens no human liberation of women. Rather, it endows the state with the power to tell more Nietschzean lies. "State is the name of the coldest of all cold monsters. Coldly, it tells lies, too; and this lie grows out of its mouth: 'I, the state, am the people'."[68]

All too often, human rights languages become stratagems of imperialistic foreign policy through military invasions as well as through global economic diplomacy. Superpower diplomacy at the United Nations is not averse to causing untold suffering through sanctions whose manifest aim is to serve the future of human rights.[69] The United States, the solitary superpower at the end of the millennium, has made sanctions for the promotion of human rights abroad a gourmet feast at the White House and on Capitol Hill.[70]

What is more, the post-modernist critique may rightly insist that the classic paradigm of universal human rights contains contradictory elements. The UDHR

---

67 *Cited in* EMMANUEL LEVINAS, NINE TALMUDIC READINGS 99 (Annette Aronwicz trans., 1991) (emphasis added).

68 WALTER KAUFMANN, THE PORTABLE NIETZSCHE 160–61 (1954).

69 *See* Noam Chomsky, *Great Powers and Human Rights: The Case of East Timor, in* NOAM CHOMSKY, POWERS AND PROSPECTS: REFLECTIONS ON HUMAN NATURE AND THE SOCIAL ORDER 169–221 (1996). *See also* CHANDRA MUZAFFAR, HUMAN RIGHTS AND THE NEW WORLD ORDER (1993); GUSTAVO ESTEVA & MADHU SURI PRAKASH, GRASSROOTS POSTMODERNISM: REMAKING THE SOIL OF CULTURE (1998); WININ PEREIRA, INHUMAN RIGHTS: THE WESTERN SYSTEM AND GLOBAL HUMAN RIGHTS ABUSE (1997).

70 American Association for World Health, *Denial of Food and Medicine, the Impact of the U.S Embargo on Health and Nutrition in Cuba* (visited Oct. 24, 1998) <http://www.usenagage.org./studies/cuba.html>.

provides for the protection of the right to property[71] and thereby makes possible its conversion, in these halcyon days of globalization, into a paradigm of trade-related, market-friendly human rights, (beginning its career with the World Trade Organization (WTO),[72] now maturing in obscene progression in the Multilateral Agreement on Investment (MAI) of the Organization for Economic Cooperation and Development (OECD).[73] Global trade relations now resonate with the moral rhetoric of human rights (witness, for example, the discourse on the "social clauses" of the WTO as well as many a bilateral/regional economic/trade arrangement). More to the point, many southern NGOs that merely critiqued globalization now look upon international financial institutions as instrumentalities of deliverance from the pathologies of the nation-state.

The range and depth of post-modernist critiques of human rights is not dissimilar to Karl Marx's critique *On the Jewish Question*,[74] though the unique idiom of post-modernism was not historically available to him. The summons for the destruction of "narrative monopolies"[75] in human rights theory and practice is of enormous importance, as it enables us to recognize that the authorship of human rights rests with communities in the struggle against illegitimate power formations and the politics of cruelty. The "local," not the "global," it needs to be emphasized, remains the crucial locus of struggle for the enunciation, implementation, and enjoyment of human rights. Almost every global institutionalization of human rights has been preceded by grassroots activism.[76]

---

71 UDHR, *infra* Appendix I, art. 17. Article 17 protects individual as well as associational rights to property, a provision which for all practical purposes negates the radical looking assurances in Articles 23–26. Not surprisingly, intellectual property rights are fully recognized in Article 27(2).

72 Agreement Establishing the World Trade Organization, Apr. 15, 1994, *reprinted in* 33 I.L.M. 1144 *and* 4 International Law and World Order: Basic Documents IV.C.2a (Burns H. Weston ed., 5 vols., 1994–) (hereinafter 4 Weston).

73 For the text of the MAI, see *supra* note 44.

74 For a post-modernist revisitation, see Brown, *supra* note 35, at 97–114.

75 Lyotard insists: "Destroy all narrative monopolies. . . . Take away the privileges the narrator has granted himself." Jean François Lyotard, The Lyotard Reader 153 (Andrew Benjamin ed., 1989).

76 To quote myself, immodestly:

> After all it was a man called Lokmanya Tilak who in the second decade of this century gave a call to India: *swaraj (independence) is my birthright and I shall have it*, long before international human rights proclaimed a right to self-determination. It was a man called Gandhi who challenged early this century racial discrimination in South Africa, which laid several decades later the foundations for international treaties and declarations on the elimination of all forms of racial discrimination and apartheid. Compared with these male figures, generations of legendary women martyred themselves in prolonged struggles against patriarchy and for gender equality. The current campaign based on the motto "Women's

From this perspective, claims of "Western" authorship of human rights are sensible only within a meta-narrative tradition that in the past served the domineering ends of colonial/imperial power formations and that now serve these ends for the Euro-Atlantic community or the "triadic states" (the U.S., the EC, and Japan). In this dominant discourse, both "modern" and "contemporary" notions of human rights emerge, though in different modes, as a "vision of a *novus ordo selcorum* in the world as a whole."[77] And this discourse prevents recognition of the fact that communities in struggle are the primary authors of human rights. As the golden dust of UDHR festivities settles, no task is more important than tracing the history of human rights from the standpoint of communities united in their struggle midst unconscionable human suffering.

Various feminists have rightly contested the destruction of meta-narratives as inimical to the politics of difference.[78] At the same time, they maintain that the telling of stories of everyday violation and resistance that recognize the role of women as authors of human rights is more empowering in terms of creating solidarity than weaving narratives of universal patriarchy or theorizing repression only as a discursive relation.[79] The feminization of human rights cultures begins only when one negotiates this conflict between meta- and micro-narratives of women in struggle. One may even call the task or mission as one of *humanizing human rights* —going beyond rarefied discourse on the variety of post-modernisms and post-structuralisms to histories of individual and collective hurt. Narratives of concrete ways in which women's bodies are held *in terroram*[80] do not pre-eminently feature or figure in human rights theory, and theorizing repression does not, to my mind,

---

Rights *Are* Human Rights" is inspired by a massive history of local struggles all around.

Upendra Baxi, *The Reason of Human Rights and the Unreason of Globalization*, Address at The First A.R. Desai Memorial Lecture, University of Bombay (1996), wherein I also note that "[t]he historic birthplaces of all human rights struggles are the hearth and the home, the church and the castle, the prison and the police precinct, the factory and the farm."

77 JACOBSON *supra* note 4, at 1.

78 *See* CHRISTINE DI STEFANO, DILEMMAS OF DIFFERENCE IN FEMINISM & POSTMODERNISM 76 (Linda Nicholson ed., 1990).

79 *See* ERNESTO LACLAU & CHANTAL MOUFFE, HEGEMONY AND SOCIALIST STRATEGY: TOWARDS A RADICAL DEMOCRATIC POLITICS 87–88, 115–16 (1985).

80 Mary Jo Frug, *A Postmodern Feminist Legal Manifesto, in* AFTER IDENTITY: A READER IN LAW AND CULTURE 7–23 (Dan Danielson & Karen Engle eds., 1995). The lived reality of sex-trafficking, sweat labor, agrestic serfdom, workplace discrimination, sexual harassment, dowry murders, rape in peacetime as well as in war as a means of doing "politics," torture of women and medicalization of their bodies—all these and related devices of state and society—present problems of routinization of terror. While feminist scholarship has demonstrated the power of story telling, social theory of human rights has yet to conceive of ways and means of investing individual biographies of the violated with the power of social texts.

best happen by contesting a Lacan, a Derrida, or a Foucault; it happens when the theorist shares both the nightmares and dreams of the oppressed. To give language to pain, to experience the pain of the Other inside you, remains the task, always, of human rights narrative and discourse. If the varieties of post-modernisms help us to accomplish this, there is a better future for human rights; if not, they constitute a dance of death for all human rights.

D. Arguments from Relativism

1. *The Universality Thesis*

The "historical forms in which the relationship between universality and particularity have been thought" are many and diverse.[81] It would take this work far afield to survey the discursive scene, even from the standpoint of Western metaphysics. Yet the thesis that "contemporary" human rights are "universal" remains firmly imbricated within this discursive field.

If human rights are said to be "universal" in the very same sense as a property or relation that may be "instantiated" by a whole variety of particular things, phenomena, or state of affairs, may one say that that to be "human" is to be possessed of certain kinds of rights? If "universality" is said to exist independently of things, phenomena, or states of affairs, is it conceivable that human rights exist independently of political things, phenomena, or states of affairs? Or does the universality of human rights exist in and through these things, phenomena, or states of affairs, that is rights "manifest" themselves through these? Or are universals nominal: just a matter of naming these under one linguistic practice? Or are these ultimately justifiable, capable of being grounded, in a comprehensive ethical feats of theorizing?[82] Or is the construction of universal human rights no more than an exercise in reification, the ideological praxis of converting the multitude of diversity under the totalizing banner of a unity? Or is the expression "human rights" merely an "empty signifier," a "signifier without a signified"?[83]

The questions are compounded by the different constructions of "human rights." Quite clearly, thinkers within the Enlightenment traditions of discourse were preoccupied with the problematic of "natural rights."[84] Leading contemporary ethical thinkers construct "human rights" either in social contractarian or communi-

---

81 Ernesto Laclau, Emancipations 22 (1996).

82 Of which Alan Gewirth is the foremost exemplar. *See* Alan Gewirth, The Community of Rights (1996).

83 *See* Laclau, *supra* note 81, at 36–46. I derive some of the questions here raised, though not their formulation in relation to human rights, from this work of Laclau as well as from Ernesto Laclau & Lilian Zac, *Minding the Gap: The Subject of Politics, in* The Making of Political Identities 11–39 (Ernesto Laclau ed., 1994).

84 For a recent exposition, see Steven B. Smith, Hegel's Critique of Liberalism: Rights in Context (1989) (hereinafter Smith).

tarian terms, terms that relate to ways of thinking about rights that make "just" the basic structure of a society.[85] The context of rights principles thus articulated is that of justice through rights within individual societies or cultures, even when the this notion is presented as universalizable. "Contemporary" human rights discursivity addresses, however, the problematic of a just international order, that is a world order based on the promotion and protection of "human rights" *within* and *across* human societies, traditions, and cultures. Respect for "human rights," or the right to be and remain human, entails a complex, interlocking network of meanings that have to be sustained (and renovated and replenished) at *all* levels; individuals, associations, markets, states, regional organizations of states, and international agencies and organizations constitute a new totality that now stands addressed by the logics and paralogics of human rights. This difference raises it own distinctive problems when we address the issue of "universality."

Indeed, it marks a break, a radical discontinuity with previous Enlightenment modes of thought.[86] The epistemological break is of the same order as that which occurred in the seventeenth century European tradition. If "prior to the seventeenth century, governments made no reference to rights as a standard of legitimacy,"[87] prior to the mid-twentieth century the world international order did not regard respect for human rights as a standard for legitimacy of international relations or affairs. This epistemological break complicates recourse to the Enlightenment discursivity on human rights as natural rights; for, as we have seen, the notion of being "human" was all along constructed on Eurocentric, or racist, lines.

The notion of "universality" of "human rights" raises heavy and complex questions that may seem distant from the real world of human rights praxis. But these erupt constantly in that "real" world where the lack of approaches to a response make the enterprise of promoting and protecting human rights even more difficult than, perhaps, it actually need be.

In a sense, these issues relate to how one may construct the "universal" in the proclaimed "universality" and which interpretive community, if any, may feel privileged to so do. The way the "universality" of human rights is constructed and contested, as we see later, matters a great deal. But Hegel states with finality (if such things can be!) the modes of construction when he distinguishes between three "moments": *abstract universality, abstract particularity*, and *concrete*

---

85 *See, e.g.*, MacIntyre, *supra* note 40; John Rawls, A Theory of Justice (1971); Michael Sandel, Liberalism and the Limits of Justice (1982); Michael Walzer, Spheres of Justice: A Defense of Pluralism and Equality (1983).

86 Thus, for example, when Hegel maintained that "the right to recognition," that is "respect for the person or 'free personality' as such," is the "core of the modern state," he was neither critiquing colonialism or imperialism, patriarchy or racism. *Quoted in* Smith, *supra* note 84, at 112.

87 Smith, *supra* note 84, at 61.

universality.[88] The first moment stands for "undifferentiated identity;" the second for "the differentiation of identity and difference;" and the third for "concrete universality, which is the full realization of individuality."[89]

The claim of universality of human rights may be constructed through these three moments. Its *abstract universality* addresses the undifferentiated identity of all bearers of human rights, regardless of history or future.[90] The second moment of *abstract particularity* occurs when the identity of the bearers of human rights cognizes that bearer by gender, indigeniety, vulnerability or persecution attributes. The third moment of *concrete universality* becomes possible of attainment when the first two moments prevail: the moment of identity of all beings as "fully" human and the moment of internal differentiation of that "human."

Should we chose to distinguish these three moments, many of the objections or difficulties with the "universality" of human rights recede or need to be recast. The UDHR proceeds on the basis of abstract universality through its enunciatory referents: "all human beings," "everyone," "all," and "no one." All these entities have human rights; the only occasion when the moment of abstract particularity stands comprehsively cognizant is in its very last article.[91] Subsequent rights-enunciations increasingly address abstract particularities: for example, women's rights as human rights, the rights of indigenous peoples, the rights of children and migrants, including migrant labor. These are particularities because they differentiate the *abstract human* in the UDHR. They are abstract because, as yet, the identities they constitute still do not address the specificity of subject-positions/locations of the constituencies of human rights/obligations constituencies. But this is what must be addressed in the third moment of concrete universality where rights come home, as it were, in lived and embodied circumstances of being human in time and place marked by finite individual existence. In the moment of the concrete universal, while structures of domination and power are cross-generational (though liable to disruption and collapse) individual life spans are not merely finite in the abstract but governed by the vagaries and whims of practices of politics of cruelty and of *catastrophic politics*.

The relation between the first two and the third form of universality of human rights remains deeply problematic. The moment of concrete universality appears, on one reading of human rights, contingent on the performative acts of the first two

---

88 *See* Mark C. Taylor, Altarity 16–17 (1987).

89 *Id.*

90 "[T]he mutual recognition of one another's rights," according to Hegel, "must take place at the expense of nature, by abstracting or denying all the individual differences between us until we arrive at a pure *I*, the free will or 'universal consciousness' which is at the root of these differences," Smith, *supra* note 84, at 124.

91 UDHR, *infra* Appendix I, art. 30: "Nothing in this Declaration may be interpreted as implying for any *State, group or person* any rights to engage in any activity or to perform any act aimed at the *destruction* of any of the rights and freedoms set forth herein" (emphasis added). I take the reference to *persons* as embracing *corporate persons* in addition to *natural persons*, that is, individual human beings.

moments. The concrete universality of human rights presupposes the movement of both abstract universality and abstract particularity. On the other hand, the moments are *reversible, entailing no logic of a hierarchy or progression of moments*, in the sense that often enough (as explained earlier) it is the here-and-now assertion of human rights that lack a *being in the world* that in turn creates the other two moments. The concrete universality of human rights often consists in the acts of prefigurative praxis. No theory of moments of human rights guided struggles for decolonization or Mohandas Gandhi's protests against the incipient but still vicious forms of an early regime of apartheid. Much the same may be truly said of the civil rights movements led by Martin Luther King, Jr., or of women's or environmental rights movements.

This suggests the possibility of two types of distinctions: first, between the *universality* of human rights and their *universalizability*; and second, between *globalization* and the *universality* of human rights as a mode of actualizing *preferred* conceptions. The first distinction concerns the dialectic among the three moments; the second concerns the power of the play of hegemons. The hegemon may *globalize* human rights without *universalizing* them. Globalization of human rights consists in those practices of governance by the dominant states that selectively target the enforcement of certain set of rights or sets of interpretation of rights upon the "subaltern" state actors in the world system. Such practices need no ethic of "universality" of human rights; these constitute an amoral exercise or enforcement of dominant, hegemonic power because the hegemon does not accept as a universal norm that its sovereign sphere, rife with human and human rights violations, ought to be equally liable to similarly based intrusion. Even when construed as ultimately designed to "serve," without their consent and against their will, the human rights of the peoples, the unilateral and ultimately unaccountable use of military force (as, yet again illustrated in the recent strikes against Iraq and the Federal Republic of Yugoslavia or the armed covert and overt operations by the United States in Chile and Nicaragua) remains an instance of globalization of human rights. Sometimes the globalization of human rights proceeds on moral maxims as yet not enunciated, because they are not acceptable to the hegemons themselves. The public discourse concerning the removal of President Saddam Hussain, for example, reiteratively explicit in statements by the U.S. President and the British Prime Minister in December 1998, seems based on the notion of justified tyrannicide, a notion as yet not articulated by "contemporary" human rights enunciations. The globalization of human rights is also marked by moral duplicity. People in struggle are denied the same order of impunity for committing tyrannicide as the incumbent heads of states "enjoy" in relation to the commission of genocide. The first constitutes "treason" at home and "terrorism" abroad; the second is thought essential to preserve structures of global power against themselves.

Much the same has to be said concerning aid conditionalities, whether under the auspices of the international financial institutions or of trade sanctions for violation of labor and associated human rights norms and standards. The hegemon insists that these standards may be enforced selectively against vulnerable and dependent states, denying that the same justification may extend to its promotion of the right of global capital to exploit workers at home and abroad. In contrast, the logics/paralogics of "universal" human rights are deeply ethical, *tormented by reflexivity all the way*.

These summary observations commend the distinction I make between two orders of discursivity: *globalization* and *universality* of human rights. The latter ought to "problematize" the former. In this sense, the discourse concerning "relativism" seems, from at least the standpoint of those violated, deeply diversionary. In any case, the inability to problematize this distinction, in theoretical and activist critique about the "universality" of human rights and their globalization casts a long shadow over their future.

2. Antifoundationalism

"Contemporary" human rights paradigms constantly invite interrogation when they stress the universality of human rights. It is maintained by many, and in various ways, that universal human rights are simply impossible because what counts as "human" and as "rights" belonging to humans are context-bound and tradition-dependent. There is no transcultural fact or being that may be called "human" to which universal human rights may be attached. Argentine jurist Eduardo Rabossi has recently urged that the "human rights phenomenon renders human rights foundationalism outmoded and irrelevant."[92] By human rights phenomenon, I believe that Rabossi means what I describe as the fact of the enunciative explosion of human rights. For him, that fact is all that matters; it is unnecessary to revisit the philosophical grounds on which human rights may be based.

Antifoundationalism is a close post-modernist cousin of relativism; each urges us to pay heed to contexts of culture and power. Both insist, though in somewhat different ways that matter, that whatever may be the agenda of human rights is best performed without the labors of grounding rights in any transcultural fact or "essence" named as "human being." The claim here is that such labors of theoretical practice are either futile or dangerous. They are futile because who or what counts as being "human" is always being socially deconstructed and reconstructed and cannot be legislated by any ethical imperative, no matter how hard and long one may try to so do. They are dangerous because under the banner of the universality of "human nature," regimes of human violation actually thrive and prosper. The danger for human rights is in the very construction of "human," which then allows the power of what Erick Erickson called "pseudospeciation," a process by which different regimes of psychopathic practices of the politics of cruelty may erect the dichotomy between "humans" and "nonhumans," "people" and "non-

---

92 *Quoted in* Richard Rorty, *Human Rights, Rationality, and Sentimentality, in* ON HUMAN RIGHTS: THE OXFORD AMNESTY LECTURES 1993, at 112, 116 (Stephen Shute & Susan Hurley eds., 1993).

people."[93] My own critique of what I call the "modern" human rights paradigm commits me to an acknowledgment of the power of this very danger.

The danger is compounded when we attend the mission of the Dead White Males, or what earlier was called the "White Man's Burden," drawing sustenance from the mission of universality of human rights. The American Anthropological Association, in its 1947 critique of the draft declaration of the UDHR, stated, memorably, that doctrines of "the white man's burden"

> have been employed to implement economic exploitation and to deny the right to control their own affairs to millions of peoples over the world, where the expansion of Europe and America has not meant . . . the literal extermination of the whole populations. Rationalized in terms of ascribing cultural inferiority to these peoples, or in conceptions of backwardness in development of their "primitive mentality," that justified their being held in the tutelage of their superiors, the history of the expansion of the western world has been marked by demoralization of human personality and the disintegration of human rights among the people over whom hegemony has been established.[94]

This was stated with elegant clarity in the pre-post-modern era! And even today critiques of the universality of human rights enact only variations on this theme.

The issues involved here relate to ways in which human rights logics and paralogics have been deployed for the ends of historic forms of domination and to ways through which practices of governance everywhere legitimate themselves through recourse to the languages of "human rights." The language game of human rights is also a power game, that phenomenon that I call "the politics *of* human rights."

3. *The "Histories" of Human Rights "Universality"*

It is at this juncture that one may raise the issue of how the histories of the "universality" of human rights may be narrated. I have endeavored to demonstrate through the distinction between "modern" and "contemporary" human rights paradigms the ways in which the "universality" notions get constructed in radically different ways. Apart from the unfolding of the politics *of* human rights, there arises also the need to trace the interaction between two forms of human rights politics: the politics *of* and *for* human rights.

From this perspective, whatever may have been the case with the UDHR, the argument concerning "relativism" is curious in terms of the actual history of author-

---

93 Tu Wei-Ming, *Maoism as a Source of Suffering in China, in* SOCIAL SUFFERING 149, 166–67 (Arthur Kleinman et al. eds., 1996).

94 The Executive Board, American Anthropological Association, *Statement on Human Rights*, 49 AM. ANTHROPOLOGIST 539 (1947).

ing contemporary international human rights standards and norms. If we were to accept the view that "contemporary" human rights authorship lies with the communities of states, no recourse to a grand theory or to a gourmet diet of a whole variety of "post-isms" or endologies[95] is required to maintain a just anxiety about the universality of human rights. Any international human rights lawyer worth her or his calling knows the riot of reservations, understandings, and declarations that parody the texts of universalistic declarations.[96] The "fine print" of reservations usually cancels the "capital font" of universality. In this sense, claims concerning the universality of human rights enunciations are diversionary, embodying the politics *of*, rather than *for*, human rights. What is "universal" about human rights is that they become binding on sovereign states when such states consent to treaty obligations or demonstrate by their belief and practice that certain enunciations are binding as the customary law of human rights. And in the making of these "universal" norms, states do articulate a measure of cultural and civilizational diversity. Even in respect of such "universal" human rights norms, the universality abides in the purported logic of aspiration, not always in the reality of attainment. Obviously, this petty detail concerning the making of internationally binding human rights gets wholly ignored in the high discourse of relativism, antifoundationalism, and "postmodernisms."

The dominant discourse wishes us to believe that the anticolonial struggles relied upon and wholly mimed the typical human rights discourse of the "West." This mode of thought relies upon catachresis, signifying the lack of an "adequate historical referent" in the cultures of the Other.[97]

If, on the other hand, we were to entertain a more "radical" view of authorship of human rights (which I have elaborated thus far) where peoples and communities are the primary authors of human rights, the argument from relativism falls. This is because, on this view, resistance to power has a creationist role in the making of "contemporary" human rights, which then, at a second-order level, get translated into standards and norms by the community of states. In the making of human rights, it is the "local" that translates into "global" languages the reality of its aspiration for a just world.

The context bears a moment's reflection, too, upon the world without rights. I refer to "modern" human rights enunciations that enacted—cruelly—many a vari-

---

95 Upendra Baxi, *The "Reason" of Human Rights and the "Unreason" of Globalization: The First Akshay Desai Memorial Lecture*, University of Bombay 1996 (forthcoming in 1999 in ECONOMIC AND POLITICAL WEEKLY).

96 Upendra Baxi, *"A Work in Progress?": Reflections on the United States Report to the United Nations Human Rights Committee*, 36 IND. J. INT'L L. 34 (1996); Ann Elizabeth Mayer, *Reflections on the Proposed United States Reservations to CEDAW*, 23 HASTINGS CONST. L.Q. 727–823 (1996).

97 Gayatri Chakravorty Spivak, *Constitutions and Culture Studies*, *in* LEGAL STUDIES AS CULTURAL STUDIES: A READER IN (POST) MODERN CRITICAL THEORY 155 (Jerry D. Leonard ed., 1995).

ety of exclusionary theory/practice. The "modern" epoch of human rights enunciation was unabashedly relativistic; it claimed individual and collective rights for some peoples and regimes and denied these wholesale to others. These latter were denied rights either because they were not fully human or the task of making them fully human required denial of rights to them. Do not the colonial practices of power provide a full repository for the practices of relativism?

Human rights universalism somehow begins to become problematic at the beginning of the end of colonialism, in association with the principle of self-determination proclaimed in the two covenants.[98] True, the UDHR also occurs at the onset of the Cold War. Also true, it embodies, in its Articles 17 and 27(2), exceptional regard for the right to property. But it contains also vital social rights (education, work, and health) that can, and have been used to impose an array of reasonable restrictions on the rights to property. The values repressed by empire, by the doctrines of the White Man's Burden, are no longer considered legitimate. Were not the anticolonial struggles partly about the realization of the right to a just "international and social order," respectful of the dignity and human rights of all people (art. 28)? Or about rights to freedom of opinion and expression (art.19)? Or about the right to peaceful assembly and association (art. 20) and a right to democracy (art. 21)?

And if these were typically "Western" values, how do we explain their resonance in the regional human rights instruments—for example, the 1948 American Declaration of the Rights and Duties of Man,[99] the 1969 American Convention on Human Rights,[100] and the 1988 Additional Protocol to the American Convention on Human Rights in the Area of Economic, Social and Cultural Rights[101] amplifying on the American Convention? Or the 1981 African Charter on Human and Peoples' Rights?[102] Or the Cairo Declaration on Human Rights in Islam?[103] Unquestionably, these instruments are innovative in their

---

98 The right to self-determination is expressly enunciated in Article 1 of the International Covenant on Economic, Social and Cultural Rights, *infra* Appendix II [hereinafter ICESCR]; also in Article 1 of the ICCPR, *infra* Appendix III.

99 Adopted May 30, 1948, OAS, Basic Documents Pertaining to Human Rights in the Inter-American System [hereinafter Basic Documents], OAS Res. OAS Off. Rec. OEA/Ser. L/V/I.4 Rev. (1965), OEA/Ser.L/VII.92, Doc. 31, Rev. 3 at 17 (1996), *reprinted in* 3 Weston III.B.23, *supra* note 50.

100 Concluded, Nov. 22, 1969, OASTS No. 36, OAS Off. Rec. OEA/Ser.L/V/IL.23, Doc. 21, Rev. 6 (1979), 1144 U.N.T.S. 123, *reprinted in* 9 I.L.M. 673 (1970) *and* 3 Weston III.B.24, *supra* note 50.

101 Concluded, Nov. 17, 1988 (not yet in force). OASTS No. 69, OAS Doc. OEA/Ser.A/42 (SEPF), *reprinted in* 28 I.L.M. 156 (1989) *and* 3 Weston III.B.25, *supra* note 50. The Protocol is not yet in force.

102 Concluded June 27, 1981 (entered into force Oct. 21, 1986). OAU Doc. CAB/LEG/67/3 Rev. 5, *reprinted in* 21 I.L.M. 58 (1982) *and* 3 Weston III.B.I, *supra* note 50.

103 For an English translation, see *World Conference on Human Rights*, U.N. GAOR, 4th

human rights enunciations (by their emphasis on the rights of peoples or on human duties). But a close comparison with the UDHR would also show that they converge on many a crucial human rights value as well.

Indeed, this historical evidence of *normative consensus* over the universality of some human rights norms and standards becomes all the more striking when discourse on relativism pauses to notice subsequent developments occurring, undoubtedly, under the auspices of Third World leadership during the 1960s and 1970s crystallizing its distinctive conceptions of global justice and human rights. Human rights norms and standards proliferate, extending to the collective rights of de-colonized states and peoples, from the 1962 Resolution on Permanent Sovereignty over Natural Resources[104] (to take a long leap!) to the 1986 Declaration on the Right to Development.[105] I suggest that the discourse on "relativism" remains afflicted by its very own political unconscious (to borrow Fredrick Jameson's fecund notion[106]).

That political unconscious, in relation to human rights discursivity, assumes many forms of historic, cultural, civilizational, and even epistemic racial arrogance toward the Other of Enlightenment and even post-Enlightenment thought and political action. That arrogance, which regards all human rights imagination as the estate of the West, which others can at best only mime, prevents recognition of authorship of human rights by states and peoples of the Third World. Must all the history of the latter be reduced to the thesis that the "universality" of human rights is the pervasive syndrome of Western hegemony? Does not, after all, this "cultural" or ethical" relativism talk, ostensibly directed to the recognition of diversity, perform, in reality, the labors of reinstalling the "Myth of Origins" about human rights in the West?

What is of interest here is the fact that the practices of the politics *of* human rights converge here with those of the politics *for* human rights. The very regimes and cliques that deny freedom and dignity and canons of political accountability by denouncing human rights "universality" as a sinister imperial conspiracy find support from intellectual and social activists critiquing the "universality" in the same prose. Undoubtedly, human rights rhetoric has been conspicuously consumed by the United States and its normative cohorts, most brutally in moves to "make the

---

Sess., Agenda Item 5, U.N. Doc. A/CONF. 157/PC/62/Add.18 (1993), *reprinted in* 11 HUMAN RIGHTS: A COMPILATION OF INTERNATIONAL INSTRUMENTS 478 (1997). *See also* Arab Charter on Human Rights, Sept. 15, 1994, Council of the League of Arab States, 102d Sess., Res. 5437. An unofficial translation of the Charter appears at 56 REV. INT'L COMM. JURISTS 57 (1996) and 4 INT'L HUM. RTS. REP. 850 (1997).

104 Adopted Dec. 14, 1962, G.A. Res. 1803, U.N. GAOR, 17th Sess., Supp. No. 17, at 15, U.N. Doc. A/5217 (1963), *reprinted in* 2 I.L.M. 223 (1963) *and* 4 Weston IV.F.1, *supra* note 72.

105 Adopted Dec. 4, 1986, G.A. Res. 41/128 (Annex), U.N. GAOR, 41st Sess., Supp. No. 53, at 186, U.N. Doc. A/41/53 (1987), *reprinted in* 3 Weston III.R.2, *supra* note 50.

106 *See* FREDERICK JAMESON, THE POLITICAL UNCONSCIOUS NARRATIVE AS A SOCIALLY SYMBOLIC ACT (1981).

world safe for democracy" (read global capital) during the Cold War and beyond. An exposé of this horrible practice of the politics *of* human rights is continually necessary and desirable. It is but natural that peoples and states that believe in "manifest destiny" to lead the world deploy all available normative resources, including the languages of human rights, to pursue it. But does that necessarily constitute the indictment of the very notion of universal human rights? Or, the notion of the universality of human rights? Should this ineluctable critique of the politics *of* human rights become also the *norm* of the politics *for* human rights?

Free-floating historians of ideas keep telling us that Asian, African, or other "non-Western" traditions had no analogue to the expression "human rights."[107] But neither had the "Western tradition" even the phrase "rights" until the mid-nineteenth century.[108] And the invention of the phrase "human rights" is very recent indeed. Apart from the socio-linguistic discovery of novelty, nothing much follows! No doubt, words and phrases carry burdens of histories. But histories also give rise to regimes of phrases that mold the future. Surely, the discourse on human struggles and movements that empower human beings in time, place, and circumstance to resist oppression (whether in East Timor or Myanmar) are also entitled to the same order of privilege that historians of ideas or cultural anthropologists claim for themselves!

This essay does not address the daunting tasks of tracing these scattered hegemonies of "relativist" desires, a task crucial for a social theory of human rights. But as a preliminary step towards it I undertake a critical overview of the agendum of relativism in relation to contemporary human rights discursive formation.

And in so doing I transgress simple logic. A logical way, exposing the fault line of relativism, is to present it as an axiom that maintains that there are no truths save the truth that all truths are relative! You may substitute for "truth" in this axiom "values," "human rights," notions of being "human" (or whatever the context requires) It is well known by now that logically such a position is simply incoherent.

4. *Multiculturalism*

In complete disregard of the fact that contemporary human rights norms and standards are not monologically but dialogically produced and enacted (and stand brokered and mediated by global diplomacy, including that of the NGOs), it still is maintained that human rights enunciations ignore cultural and civilizational diversity. This is bad, even wicked, sociology. The pro-choice women's groups at the U.N.

---

107 Interested readers may pursue the relevant literature via massive footnote 3 in Stephen P. Marks, *From the "Single Confused Page" to the "Declaration for Six Billion Persons": The Roots of the Universal Declaration of Human Rights in the French Revolution*, 20 HUM. RTS. Q. 459, 460 (1998) or equally massive note 16 in Burns Weston's essay *supra* in this volume at pp. 65, 69–70.

108 MACINTYRE, *supra* note 40, at 69.

Beijing Conference, for example, confronted by His Holiness the Pope's Open Letter to the Conference, or the participants at the U.N. Cairo summit on population planning, know this well.

The enactment of human rights into national social policies is even more heavily mediated by the multiplicity of cultural, religious, and even civilizational traditions. The American feminists on every anniversary of *Roe v Wade*[109] know this. So does the African sisterhood modulating public policy on female genital mutilation, and the Indian sisterhood in its moves to outlaw dowry murders. No engaged human rights theory or practice, to the best of my knowledge, enacts, in real life, pursuit of universal human rights without any regard for cultural or religious traditions. Nor does it completely succumb to the virtues and values of "theoretical" ethical relativism.

In ways that relativist arguments do not, the logic of the universality of rights is one that opens up for interrogation settled habits of representation of "culture" and "civilization." It makes problematic that which was regarded as self-evident, natural, and true and makes possible to friendly human rights reading of tradition or scripture[110] and, indeed, even the claim that some contemporary human rights were anticipated by these.

Of course, as is well known, conflicts over interpretation of tradition are conflicts not just over values but about power as well. In turn, both the "fundamentalists" and the human rights evangelists become prisoners of a new demonology. Both tend to be portrayed in the not always rhetorical warfare[111] that follows as *fiends*, not fully human and therefore unworthy of dignity of discourse. Practices of the politics of intolerance begin to thrive all around. Practices of solidarity among human rights activists, national and transnational, begin to be matched by powerful networks of power and influence at home and abroad. The politics of the universality of human rights becomes increasingly belligerent. And the martyrdom count of human rights activists registers an unconscionable increase.

At this point, the universality of human rights ceases to be an abstract idea with its history of doctrinal disputations, but, instead, a living practice, a form of struggle, a practice of transformative vision. Its truths of resistance, in constant collision with the truths of power, seek to universalize themselves. And its truths are formed not in the comfort of contemplative life but in and through the gulags.

---

109 410 U.S. 113 (1973).

110 Readings of scriptural traditions yield repressive as well as emancipative consequences. As is well known (or ought to be), long before feminism happened, the Koranic verse on polygamy generated a two century-old debate, before the doors of *ijehad* were declared to be closed in the 10th century A.D. on the verse on polygamy which was construed to *prohibit* the practice of polygamy which on established reading it permitted. Similarly, rights to sexual orientation-friendly readings have been discovered in major religious texts of the world by the hermeneutic labors of human rights praxis.

111 Those who proselytize "radical" readings of the scriptural traditions, though no longer burnt at the stake, are relentlessly subjected to territorial, and even extra-territorial, repression and punishment.

In this sense, the claim to the universality of human rights signifies an aspiration and movement to bring new civility to power among states and human societies. That civility consists in making power increasingly accountable. Does the dialogue over the relativity of values matter much *when so much* is at stake?

5. *"Westoxification"*

Although the complex history of the notion of "Westoxification" cannot be pursued here,[112] the critique insists that human rights enunciations and cultures represent secular versions of the Divine Right to rule the "Unenlightened." It demonstrates that the West seeks to impose standards of right and justice, which it has all along violated in its conduct towards Islamic societies and states.[113] It rejects the notion that the outpourings and actions of the U.S. Department of State and their normative cohorts are exhaustive of the totality of "contemporary" human rights discourse. It seeks to locate the politics of human rights within the tradition of the *shari'a*.[114] As Muhammad Shykh Fadalla has eloquently stated: "As Moslems, we consider politics to be part of our whole life, because the Koran emphasizes the establishment of justice as a divine mission. . . . *In this sense, the politics of the faithful is a kind of prayer*.[115] At the heart of the critique lies the epochal politics of difference, which of course does not regard Islam, in the image of "the recurrent Western myth," as a "monolithic" tradition.[116]

Responsible "Westoxification" notions seek to bring an element of piety within the logics and paralogics of the construction of human rights. If the politics *for* human rights is a kind of "prayer of the faithful" for pious Muslims, so it is also for the secular congregation of a civic religion called "human rights." The contribution that this kind of understanding brings for the future of human rights (of a very different order than that provided by post-modernisms or recrudescent forms of relativism) calls for inter-faith dialogue. A dialogue that will yield a sense of justice to the worlds of power provides invaluable resource to the universalization of human rights.

6. *The Types of Relativism*

Relativism, a coat of many colors,[117] indicts the logic of universality of human rights (as noted) on the ground that different cultural and civilizational traditions have

---

112 For a rich account of the history of origins, see JOHN L. ESPOSITO, THE ISLAMIC THREAT: MYTH OR REALITY? 188–253 (2d ed. 1995). Also see the provocative analysis by Booby Sayyid, *Sign O'Times: Kaffirs and Infidels Fighting the Ninth Crusade*, *in* THE MAKING OF POLITICAL IDENTITIES 233 (Ernesto Laclau ed., 1994).

113 *See* MUZAFFAR, *supra* note 69.

114 *See Cairo Declaration on Human Rights in Islam*, *supra* note 103.

115 *Quoted in* ESPOSITO, *supra* note 112, at 149 (emphasis added).

116 *Id.* at 201.

117 See the superb analysis in CHRISTOPHER NORRIS, RECLAIMING TRUTH: CONTRIBUTION TO A

diverse notions of what it means to be human and for humans to have rights. While this is true, it is also trivial[118] and simply does not make impossible cross- or inter- or trans-cultural understandings.

If, on the other hand, relativism is a claim that what people believe to be right or wrong determines what is wrong or right for them,[119] then universal standards of human rights (such as the prohibition of genocide, torture, racial discrimination, and violence against women) remain "universal" only for the groups of people who believe themselves to be so. The insistence on universality is also mistaken when it erects the notion that moral judgments apply not just to "a particular action but to a class of actions;"[120] that "these judgments apply to everybody,"[121] and that "others besides the speakers are assumed to share [them]."[122] That this form of relativism turns out to be logically or analytically flawed is, unfortunately, good news that does not travel fast! The fatal flaw lies in the fact that even when some people believe it to be good or moral to kill, torture, or rape, they may not claim a duty on the part of others (who believe otherwise) not to interfere with their practices of "virtue" (as seen, I must add, by them).[123] The bad news is that even so gifted a philosopher as Richard Rorty could base his entire Oxford-Amnesty Lectures meditation on human rights on the following initial statement:

> Serbian murderers and rapists do not think of themselves as violating human rights. For they are not doing these things to fellow human beings but to *Muslims*. They are not being inhuman, but rather are discriminating between the true humans and pseudo-humans. They are making the same sorts of distinction as the Crusaders made between humans and infidel

CRITIQUE OF CULTURAL RELATIVISM (1996). Of course, "relativism" is a vacuous word. We need to distinguish between several types relativism. See the useful effort by Fernando R. Tesón, *International Human Rights and Cultural Relativism*, 25 VA. J. INT'L L. 869 (1985). *See also* Adamantia Pollis, *Cultural Relativism Revisited: Through a State Prism*, 18 HUM. RTS. Q. 316 (1996). A more sustained analysis of relativism is offered by R. G. PEFFER, MARXISM, MORALITY AND SOCIAL JUSTICE 268–316 (1990) (hereinafter PEFFER) who distinguishes between four types of relativism.

118 Because what people may believe is an important social datum, nothing follows from this on the issue of what they *ought* to believe. *Cf.* PEFFER, *supra* note 117, at 272–73.

119 For the elaboration of the notion of "normative ethical relativism" as entailing two distinct positions, see PEFFER, *supra* note 117, at 273–74, and the literature cited there. Does the normative ethical relativistic position refer to an individual's criteria of moral rightness or does it refer to criteria accepted by a society or culture as a whole?

120 BERNARD R. MAYO, ETHICS AND MORAL LIFE 91–92 (1958), *quoted in* PEFFER, *supra* note 117, at 276.

121 *Id.*

122 *Id.*

123 See the logical demonstration of this in PEFFER, *supra* note 117, at 275.

> dogs, and Black Muslims make between humans and blue-eyed devils. The founder of my university was able both to own slaves and to think it self-evident that all men were created equal. . . . Like the Serbs, Mr. Jefferson did not think of himself as violating *human rights*.[124]

What follows? Does it follow that the "murderers and rapists" are justified? From the relativist position so far canvassed they could so maintain. But Professor Rorty suggests that the way out of all this lies in "making our own culture—the human rights culture—more self-conscious and powerful," not in "demonstrating its superiority to other cultures by an appeal to something transcultural."[125] By "our culture," "the culture of human rights," Rorty means primarily the United States culture (and more broadly the Euro-Atlantic culture). The Other has to be educated in human rights sensibility, not by any allegiance to the UDHR values (since these are transcultural). The acknowledgement about Jefferson and the Crusaders suggests heavily that there has been a progress in moral sentiments in the United States (and allied Northern cultures) which has yet to reach the benighted Serbs.[126] Probably what Rorty exemplifies is not so much a variety of normative ethical relativism but either, or even both, "meta-ethical" and "meta-evaluative" forms of relativism. Probably there are no "sure" or "objective" ways to prove to everyone's satisfaction that something is morally right or wrong or just that something is right or wrong. But who is that "everyone?" This is apparently a vexed question for ethical theorists[127] and may well remain so for the better part of the next millennium.

But both of these forms of relativism rely on, or at any rate invoke, the possibility of "intrasubjective consensus" on at least the *prima facie* validity of certain moral norms. Neither prevents us from claiming that "a certain moral principle (*e.g.*, slaughtering of defenseless infants) is *prima facie* wrong."[128] If so, "human rights" constitute at least the burden of ethical justification on those who engage in practices of "pseudospeciation" or indulge in catastrophic practices of the politics of cruelty. And if serious-minded relativism suggests that construction of such *onus probandi* is itself a complex moral affair, and accordingly requires great care in the enunciation of human rights norms and standards, this message is of considerable importance for those who would steer the future of human rights.

---

124 Rorty, *supra* note 92, at 112.

125 *Id.* at 117.

126 It is remarkable that Rorty collapses the "pre-modern" (Crusades), the "modern" (colonial/imperial), and "contemporary" (human rights era) into one master narrative! On the paradigm offered in this work, Jefferson was consistent with the logics and paralogics of "modern" human rights practices of exclusion. Rorty's Serbs are, however, located in a world that *invented human rights*, including perhaps the basic human right against (to invoke Eric Erickson's term again) "pesudospeciation." *See* Tu Wei-Ming, *supra* note 93.

127 *See* William K. Frankena, Ethics (1963); Kurt Bater, The Moral Point of View (1965); and the discussion in Peffer *supra* note 117, at 281–85, 305–13.

128 Peffer, *supra* note 117, at 273.

Anyone familiar with the Asian, Arab, African and Latin American charters or conventions on human rights (and at the spawning NGO re-articulation of the UDHR on its golden jubilee) surely knows that human rights enunciations are marked by such moral agonizing, though not always in languages that comfort moral philosophers. Arguments from relativism that remain willfully ignorant or dismissive of the histories of construction of the "universality" of human rights are altogether unhelpful. From the perspectives of sociology of knowledge, they may even appear to some as exercises in unconscious *realpolitik*, which it is the task of "contemporary" human rights to render problematic.

7. *What Is Living and Dead in Argument from Relativism?*

What, perhaps, is helpful in relativism regarding the "contemporary" human rights movement is the notion that human suffering is not wholly legible outside cultural scripts. Since suffering, whether defined as individual pain or as social suffering is egregious, different religions and cultural traditions enact divergent hierarchies of "justification" of experience and imposition of suffering, providing at times and denying at others, language to pain and suffering.

The universality of human rights, it has been argued recently by Talal Asad, extravagantly forfeits cultural understanding of social suffering[129] and alienates human rights discourse from the lived experience of culturally/civilizationally constituted humanness. Professor Asad highlights the fact that the Western colonial discourses on suffering valorized "[p]ain endured in the movement of becoming 'fully human'. . . [and] was seen as necessary because social or moral reasons justified why it must be suffered."[130] He shows the ways by which the very idea of cruelty and degradation becomes and remains "unstable, mainly because the aspirations and practices to which it is attached are themselves contradictory, ambiguous, or changing."[131] This instability, he argues, is scarcely remedied by neither the "attempt by the Euro-Americans to impose their standards by force on others nor the willing invocation of these standards by the weaker peoples in the Third World."[132] He alerts us to the fact that "cruelty can be experienced and addressed *in ways other than violation of rights*—for example, as a failure of specific virtues or as an expression of particular vices."[133]

This is, indeed, a responsible practice of cultural relativism, because, while maintaining skepticism concerning the "universalistic discourses" around the 1984 U.N. Convention Against Torture and Other Cruel Inhuman or Degrading Treatment

---

129 Asad, *supra* note 38, at 285.

130 *Id.* at 295.

131 *Id.* at 304.

132 *Id.*

133 *Id.* (emphasis added).

or Punishment,[134] it does not attack its norm on any ethical grounds. Rather, it shows us how ethnographies of cruelty may assist the progressive promotion and protection of human rights there enshrined, in ways that respect discursive traditions other than those of human rights.

Similarly, the ethnography of suffering summons us to focus on the difficult relationship between violence and rights. The promotion and protection of rights always has entailed regimes or practices of *justified* or legitimate violence, although rights-talk habituates us to the idea that violence is the very antithesis of rights. Moreover, human rights discursivity rarely concedes that violence of the oppressed often can be rights-generative. It can also be horrendously destructive.

Veena Das, in her pioneering exploration, expresses the latter. Her construction of violence brings to us the "unnamable" phenomenon (when the horrors of the partition of India inscribed on the bodies of women) led to the birth of citizen-monsters: "[I]f men emerged from colonial subjugation as autonomous citizens of an independent nation, they emerged simultaneously as monsters."[135] Her precious, anguished insights invite us to consider what Walter Benjamin called the *foundational violence of the law*[136] and, one may add, of historic practice of the human right to self-determination. The citizen-monster dialectic is reiterative as well, in the everyday life of modern Indian experience of women's suffering, despite law, policy, and administration, even when human rights-oriented.

The challenge that this genre of writing, which exposes writing as violence, poses for human rights logic and paralogics is simply enormous and cannot be captured by the unfeeling and dense prose of relativism. It directs attention to ways in which human rights languages lie at the surface (and not in any Foucaldian sense that treats *depth* as a mere fold on the surface) of lived and embodied human anguish and suffering. It interrogates distinctions between forms of suffering as an aspect of state-imposed and "people"/ "civil society" inflicted, or even self-chosen and imposed suffering, and hierarchies or "transactions in construction of suffering."

The practices of promotion and protection of universal human rights entail construction of moral or ethical hierarchies of suffering.[137] Such construction takes place when certain rights (such as civil and political rights) stand prioratized over other human rights (such as social, economic, and cultural rights). It occurs when even the former set of rights are subjected to the reason of the state (as when their

---

[134] Concluded, Dec. 10, 1984 (entered into force, June 26, 1987) G.A. Res. 39/46 (Annex), U.N. GAOR, 39th Sess., Supp. No. 51, at 197, U.N. Doc. A/RES/39/51 (1985), *reprinted in* 23 I.L.M. 1027 (1984) *and* 3 Weston III.K.2, *supra* note 50.

[135] Veena Das, *Language and Body: Transactions in Construction of Pain, in* SOCIAL SUFFERING 67, 86 (Arthur Kleinman et al. eds., 1996). *See also* Stanley Cavell, *Comments on Veena Das*, *id.* at 93.

[136] *See* Jacques Derrida, *The Force of Law: The Mystical Foundation of Authority, in* DECONSTRUCTION AND THE POSSIBILITY OF JUSTICE 3, 29–67 (Drucilla Cornell et al. eds., 1992).

[137] I derive this notion from Veena Das, *Moral Orientations to Suffering, in* HEALTH AND SOCIAL CHANGE 139 (L.C. Chen, et al. eds., 1994).

suspension is legitimated in "time of public emergency which threatens the life of the nation"[138]). It occurs when solemn treaties prohibiting genocide and torture, cruel, and degrading treatment or punishment allow scope for reservations and derogations that eat out the very heart of remedies otherwise declared available for the violated.

Not merely does the community of states construct such transactional hierarchies. Even human rights praxis does this.[139] This makes human rights praxis at best *global* but not *universal*, with deep implications for the future of human rights.

IV. Human Rights Movements and Human Rights Markets

A. Human Rights Movements as Social Movements

Human rights struggles are among the most defining characteristics of the second half of the Christian twentieth century; indeed, more often than not, we think of human rights praxis in terms of social movements. But the latter notion raises many perplexing issues concerning how one may define, classify, and evaluate them, and all remain apposite to a social theory of human rights yet in its infancy. Among the first necessary steps is understanding of how movements define their identity, their antagonists, and their teleology (visions of transformation).[140] Social theory about social movements stresses the importance of either the Weberian value-neutrality or the postmodern suspicion of "predetermined directionality." Thus writes Manuel Castells:

> Social movements may be socially conservative, socially revolutionary or both or none. After all, we now have concluded (and I hope for ever) that there is no predetermined directionality in social evolution, that the *only*

---

138 ICCPR, *infra* Appendix III, art. 4.

139 The way in which human rights mandates are fashioned or formed within the United Nations agencies and across the NGOs illustrates this problem rather strikingly. As concerns the former, it often is argued that specialized agencies claim a version of human rights for themselves rather than for the violated. Katarina Tomaševski has shown recently that much of the discourse of the U.N. High Commission for Refugees (UNHCR) has been focused on the *right of access* by intergovernmental agencies to victims of "wars of hunger" rather than on human rights of access by the violated to ameliorative agencies. *See* Katarina Tomaševski, *Human Rights and Wars of Starvation, in* WAR AND HUNGER: RETHINKING INTERNATIONAL RESPONSE TO COMPLEX EMERGENCIES 70–91 (Joanna Macrae & Anthony Zwi eds., 1994). As concerns the sculpting of human rights mandates, the activist grapevine all too often condemns Amnesty International for focusing too heavily on violations of civil and political rights at the expense of fully understanding the importance of the protection of economic, social, and cultural rights. Human rights NGOs who adopt a special mandate for themselves (*e.g.*, "sustainable development," "population planning") often are charged for neglecting other bodies of crucial human rights. It is pointless to multiply instances. In each such situation, the criticism is justified only from the standpoint of different constructions of hierarchy of suffering or evil, rarely made theoretically explicit.

140 *See* MANUEL CASTELLS, THE POWER OF IDENTITY 71 (1997).

sense of history is the history we sense. Therefore, from an analytical perspective, there are no "bad" and "good" social movements. They are all symptoms of our societies and all impact social structures, with variable intensities and outcomes that must be established by social research.[141]

Human rights movements as social movements demand such research.[142] But a social theory of human rights may have considerable difficulty with the demand that even the manifestly rights-denying social or human rights movements should escape moral evaluation pending social research. A willing suspension of ethical beliefs, deferring human rights action to sustained social science research, can have impacts on the power of human rights movements to name an evil and to create public concern and capacity to contain or eliminate it. For example, some social movements may defend as just traditions that confine women to home and hearth, or may find justifications for reinventing apartheid and genocide. Indeed, they may claim the protection of extant human rights regimes to do so. Hate speech missionaries seek to "justify" racism as an aspect of freedom of speech and expression. The protagonists of human life invoke the fetal human right to life even to justify aggression on abortion clinics and professionals. The recent Rawlsian notion valorizing the defense of "well-ordered societies" is eminently suitable to justify regimes of military intervention or superpower sanction against the less well-ordered societies.[143]

Such movements turn upside down the very power of human rights rhetoric to identify certain regimes of human rights! The power of human rights discourse to name an order of evil is used to name human rights as the very order of evil! Perhaps, to evoke Castells' phrase, this standpoint emerges as a "symptom" of our societies. No doubt, as he says, these symptoms "impact social structures, with variable intensities and outcomes,"[144] inviting a prolific growth of cognitive social science knowledge to empower us with some understanding. At the same time, human rights praxis (whether through movements or markets) may generate scientific knowledge rather than await it; the history of human rights praxis, from Mohandas Gandhi to Ken Saro-Wiwa, from Joan of Arc to Petra Kelly, is truly prefigurative of future knowledges about freedom and fulfillment.

A social theory of human rights must find bases for ethical judgment concerning "good" and "bad" social movements; howsoever contestable, human rights movements cannot take as axiomatic the notion that "the only sense of history is

---

141 *Id.* at 70 (emphasis added).

142 Upendra Baxi, *The State and Human Rights Movements in India, in* PEOPLE'S RIGHTS: SOCIAL MOVEMENTS AND THE STATE IN THE THIRD WORLD 335–52 (Manoranjan Mohanty et al. eds., 1998).

143 John Rawls, *The Law of Peoples, in* ON HUMAN RIGHTS: THE OXFORD AMNESTY LECTURES 1993, at 41 (Stephen Shute et al. eds., 1993).

144 CASTELLS, *supra* note 140.

the history we sense." It must seek to provide a "pre-determined directionality" in human social development by articulating an ethic of power, whether in state, civil society, or the market. It must contest the notion that certain human interactions and transactions constitute moral free-zones.[145]

B. From "Movements" to "Markets

Increasingly, human rights movements organize themselves in the image of markets. Of course, the use of terms like "market" and "commoditization" may be deeply offensive to human rights practitioners, and the analogy with markets may turn out, on closer analysis not to be too strong. Moreover, we should distinguish between the discourse of social movements and the "social processes with which they are associated: for example, globalization, informationalization, the crisis of representational democracy, and the dominance of symbolic politics in the space of media."[146] From this standpoint, and quite rightly so, "movements" are analytically distinguishable from "markets." A reductionist analysis, which disregards the relative autonomy of movements from markets, does not advance clarity or conviction. At the same time, the idiom of the "market" brings more sharply into view the complexity and contradiction of human rights movements.

Human rights markets consist of a network of transactions that serve the contingent and long-term interests of human rights investors, producers, and consumers. These transactions rely upon the availability, which they in turn seek to reinforce, of symbolic capital[147] in the form of international human rights norms, standards, doctrines, and organizational networks. Furthermore, since grids of power are globalized, human rights markets also create and reinforce global networks, each of which seek to influence the conduct of those actors who violate human rights norms and standards and the behavior of those who resist such violations. Human rights market rationality requires the production and re-production of human rights skills and competences, which enable negotiation of tolerably acceptable outcomes between and among the violators and the violated such that market failures do not erode the legitimacy of the network of overall transactions. Human rights markets thus share the salient features of service industries.

C. The Investor and Consumer Markets in Human Rights

Human rights movements at all levels (global, regional, national, and local) have tended to become "capital-intensive." That is, the praxis of promoting and protect-

[145] DAVID GAUTHIER, MORALS BY AGREEMENT 13, 83–112 (1986).

[146] *See* CASTELLS, *supra* note 140, at 70.

[147] *See generally* PIERRE BOURDIEU, THE FIELD OF CULTURAL PRODUCTION: ESSAYS ON ART AND LITERATURE 74–142 (1993); PIERRE BOURDIEU, OUTLINE OF A THEORY OF PRACTICE (Richard Nice trans., 1977).

ing human rights now entails entrepreneuership in raising material resources, including funding, from a whole variety of governmental, inter-governmental, and philanthropic sources. These sources are organized in terms of management imperatives, both of line-management and upward accountability. Any human rights NGO or NGI (nongovernmental individual) involved in programs for the celebration of the golden jubilee of the UDHR surely knows this! The promotion and protection of human rights is an enterprise that entails access to organized networks of support, consumer loyalty, efficient internal management, management of mass media and public relations, and careful crafting of mandates.

A full analysis of these variables would unconscionably burden this essay; but it needs to be acknowledged that both consumer NGOs and funding agencies compete *inter se* for scarce resources and that this scramble for support generates forms of investor rationality, which generally may be defined as seeking a tangible return on investment.[148] That rationality must negotiate the Scylla of mobilization of support of governmental, corporate, and community conscience-money contributions and the Charybidis of their "legitimation" in host societies and governments. This negotiation, in turn, requires the marshaling of high entrepreneurial talent suffused with a whole range of negotiating endowments. Understandably, investor rationality in human rights markets is constantly exposed to a crisis of "nervous rationality." Both the "inputs" and "outputs" in human rights portfolio investment protection remain indeterminate; nevertheless, these must be ledgered, packaged, sold, and purchased on the most productive terms.

The crisis of "nervous rationality" is replicated in consumer rationality. Human rights NGOs, especially in the Third World, must negotiate the dilemmas of legitimacy and autonomy. The ever so precarious legitimacy of human rights networks seems forever threatened by allegations of foreign funding orchestrated both by interested governments and by rival NGOs that want to do better than their "competitors." There exists, too, competition to capture the beneficiary groups who measure the legitimacy of human rights networks not in terms of any "cargo cult" or messianic rationality but according to what these networks bring to people in terms of here-and-now accomplishments or results.

At the same time, NGOs seek a free enterprise market relative to the agenda of their semi-autonomous human rights concerns. They seek to define their markets for human rights promotion and protection not merely in terms of what the markets of human rights investment will bear at any given moment but also in terms of how these markets may be re-orientated in terms of consumer power. This may partly explain the populous presence and participation of the best and the brightest of NGOs and NGIs in this decade and half of the United Nations summits in Vienna, Cairo, Copenhagen, Beijing, and Istanbul. By their determined participa-

148 *See* David Gillies, Between Principle and Practice: Human Rights in North-South Relations (1996); Katarina Tomaševski, Between Sanction and Elections: Aid Donors and Human Rights (1997).

tion at these summits (and the inevitably mandated "plus-5" meetings), they seek to re-orient the global investment markets in human rights. The interests of civil servants (national and international) intermesh, in this process, with those of the NGOs and the NGIs.

D. Techniques of Commodification of Human Suffering

The raw material for human rights investment and consumer markets is provided by here-and-now human misery and suffering. However morally deplorable, it is a social fact that the overall human capacity to develop a fellowship of human suffering is awesomely limited. It is a salient fact about the "contemporary" human scene that individual and associational life-projects are rarely disturbed, let alone displaced, by the spectacle of human suffering or human suffering as a spectacle. In such a milieu, human rights markets, no matter whether investor or consumer, are confronted with the problem of "compassion fatigue." This is a moral problem, to be sure, but it is also a material problem. Of necessity, markets for human rights concentrate on this aspect of the problem if only because when compassion fades, the resources for the alleviation of human suffering through human rights languages are depleted. This intersection registers the necessity for human rights entrepreneurs to commodify human suffering, to package and sell it in terms of what the markets will bear. Human rights violations must be constantly commoditized to be combated. Human suffering must be packaged in ways that the mass media markets find it profitable to bear overall.

But the mass media can commodify human suffering only on a dramatic and contingent basis. Injustice and human rights violations are headline news only as the "porn of power" and its voyeuristic potential lies in the reiterative packaging of violations that titillate and scandalize, for the moment at least, the dilettante sensibilities of the globalizing classes. The mass media plays also a creationist role in that they "in an important sense 'create' a disaster when they decide to recognize it. . . . [T]hey give institutional endorsement or attestation to bad events which otherwise will have a reality restricted to a local circle of victims."[149] Such institutional endorsement poses intractable issues for the marketization of human rights. Given the worldwide patterns of mass media ownership, and the assiduously cultivated consumer cultures of "info-entertainment," the key players in human rights markets need to manipulate the media into authentic representations of the suffering of the violated. They must marshal the power to mold the mass media, without having access to resources that the networks of economic/political power so constantly command, into exemplary communicators of human solidarity. So far, this endeavor has rested in the commodification of human suffering, exploiting the markets for instant news and views.

---

149 JONATHAN BENTHALL, DISASTERS, RELIEF AND THE MEDIA 3–4 (1993); *quoted in* STANLEY COHEN, DENIAL AND ACKNOWLEDGMENT: THE IMPACT OF INFORMATION ABOUT HUMAN RIGHTS VIOLATIONS 90 (1995). *See also* Kleinman et al., *supra* note 24.

In a germinal monograph, Stanley Cohen has brought home the daunting tasks entailed in the commodification of human suffering. The commodification of human suffering has as its task (according to Cohen, with whom I agree) the conversion of the "politics of denial" into that of the "politics of acknowledgment." Cohen brings to attention an entire catalogue of perpetrator-based techniques of denial of human violation and the variety of responses that go under the banner of "bystanderism," whether internal or external.[150]

The various techniques of marketing human suffering in the name of "human rights" succeed or fail according to the standpoint one chooses to privilege. Efficient market rationality perhaps dictates a logic of excess. The more human rights producers and consumers succeed in diffusing horror stories, the better it is, on the whole, for the sustenance of global human rights cultures. The more they succeed in establishing accountability institutions (truth commissions, commissions for human rights for women, indigenous peoples, children, and the urban and rural impoverished) the better commerce there is. Giving visibility and voice to human suffering is among the prime function of human rights service markets. But it is an enterprise that must overcome "compassion fatigue"[151] and an overall desensitization to human misery. When the markets are bullish, the logic of excess does seem to provide the most resources for the disadvantaged, dispossessed, and deprived human communities. But in situations of recession, serious issues arise concerning the ways in which human suffering is or should be merchandized; and when those who suffer begin to counter these ways, we witness crises in human rights market management.

Human rights markets are crowded with an assortment of actors, agencies, and agendas. But they seem united in their operational techniques. A standard technique is that of reportage: several leading organizations specialize in services providing human rights "watch" and "action alerts." A related market technique is that of lobbying, whereby official or popular opinion is sought to be mobilized around human rights situations, events, or catastrophes.

A third technique is that of cyberspace solidarity, spectacular uses of instant communication networks across the world. Manuel Castells has recently provided stunning examples of how cyber-technologies have made a dramatic difference in networking solidarities; but, as his analysis itself suggests, these solidarities may work for human rights advancement (as in the case of the Zapatistas) or, more

---

150 These consist of: (a) denial of injury; (b) denial of victims; (c) denial of responsibility; (d) condemnation of the condemners; and (e) appeal to higher loyalty. These "neutralization" techniques are firmly in place and violators only play variations on a theme. Professor Cohen also offers a typology of bystander passivity or effect, consisting of: (a) diffusion of responsibility; (b) inability to identify with the victim; and (c) inability of conceiving an effective intervention. *See* COHEN, *supra* note 149, at 32–35.

151 *Id.* at 89–116.

importantly, against the nascent human rights cultures (as in the case of the American militia or Japanese *Aum Shinrikyo* movements).[152] Apparently the days of the pre-cyberspace creation of mass movement solidarity are numbered or over, at least if one is to believe that the cyberspace markets for human rights provide the only or best creative spaces. In any case, once we recognize the danger of an historical cyberspace romanticism, it remains a fact that cyberspace offers a useful marketing technique. A fourth technique consists in converting the reportage of violation in the idiom and grammar of judicial activism. An exemplary arena is provided by the invention of social action litigation, pursuant to which Indian appellate courts, including the Supreme Court of India, have been converted from the ideological and repressive apparatuses of the state and global capital into an institutionalized movement for the promotion and protection of human rights.[153] The resonance of this movement extends to many a third world society.

A fifth technique is to sustain the more conventional networks of solidarity of which the facilitation of inter-NGO dialogue is a principal aspect. Usually done through conferences, colloquia, seminars, and the facilitation of individual visits by victims or their next of kin, this technique has in recent times extended to the holding of hearings/listenings of victim groups, a device that seeks to bring unmediated the voices and texts of suffering to empathetic observers across the world. The various U.N. summits have provided a spectacular illustration of this technique, but there are more institutionalized arrangements as well. All bring the raw material of human suffering for further processing and packaging in the media and related human rights markets.

A sixth technique is rather specialized, comprising various acts of lobbying of the treaty bodies of the United Nations. This form of human rights marketing specializes in providing legislative or policy inputs in the norm-creation process, with NGO entrepreneurs assuming the roles of quasi-international civil servants and quasi-diplomats for human rights, although it is the thinking and conduct of the *de jure* international diplomats and civil servants that they seek to influence. By this specialized intervention, this activity runs the risks of co-optation and alienation from the community of the violated, especially when the NGO activity becomes the mirror-image of inter-governmental politics. However, this sort of intervention does offer, when invested with integrity, substantial gains for the progressive creation of human rights norms.

A seventh, and here final, technique is that of global direct action against imminent or actual violations of human rights. Apart from the solitary though splendid example of Greenpeace, however, this technique is not considered sustainable by the leading global and regional NGOs. Of course, there are less spectacular and sustained examples furnished in the narratives of resistance to such global events, such

---

[152] *See* Castells, *supra* note 140, at 68–109.

[153] *See supra* note 39.

as the G-7 and Asia-Pacific Economic Cooperation (APEC) conferences where methods of "citizen arrest" of global leadership are enacted, or when celebrations of the golden jubilee of international financial institutions are sought to be converted into events of embarrassment. Not to be ignored in this context are recourses to direct action by the Argentine mothers against "disappearances" or of the British women's movements against the sites of civilian or military nuclear operations. At the end of the day, however, the dominant market cost-benefit rationality does not legitimate such recourse to direct action in the dramaturgy of human rights.

This sort of illustrative listing is to suggest the variety and complexity of human rights market initiatives, which entail high quotients of managerial and entrepreneurial talent and the ability to boost market or investor confidence in human rights ventures. It also is partly my intention to suggest that the "science" of risk-analysis and risk-management is as relevant to the markets of promotion and protection of human rights as it is to those that perpetrate violations.

It is true that as human suffering intensifies, markets for human rights grow. But to say this does not entail any ethical judgment concerning the commodification of human suffering, although the reader may feel justified in treating some anguished sub-texts in this paper as warranting a wholesale moral critique of human rights markets. The future of human rights praxis is linked with, as always, the success or failure of human rights missions and their latent or patent capability to scandalize the conscience of humankind. The modes of scandalization will, of course, remain contested among the communities of the violators and the violated. The task for those who find the commodification of human suffering unconscionable lies in the contested ways of its accomplishment, not in lamenting the global fact of the very existence of human rights markets.

E. The Problem of "Regulation" of Human Rights Markets

State regulation of human rights markets is fraught with complexities. When may it be said to be invasive of human rights? How far, if at all, should states regulate the very existence or modes of operation of the NGOs involved? Should the regime of accreditation of NGOs in the United Nations system be liberal or conservative? How and by whom is this process to be determined?

The problem of regulation of human rights markets is not just state-centric. Human rights investor as well as consumer communities are stakeholders, with investor-based regulation taking myriad forms of channeling and controlling human rights agendas and transactions, generating a product mix that is the very essence of an audit culture (of upward accountability and line management). But the investors in human rights themselves may be regulated and, in this regard, must establish their legitimacy with the host society and government in ways that are propitious for cross-border markets in human rights promotion and protection.

The operators of the local/global human rights markets, primarily NGOs, confront related but distinct problems in devising self-regulatory and other-oriented regulatory frameworks. Self-regulatory frameworks must address the crises of investor rationalities in a highly competitive scramble for resourcing. Other-directed regulatory approaches are no less complex. On the one hand, there is a need to maintain acceptable patterns of consumer solidarity in the global investor markets; on the other hand, there exists the historic need, from the standpoint of the ultimate beneficiaries, to keep a watch on sister NGOs that are exposed to corruption, co-optation, or subversion by the forces of global capitalism, a problem recently illustrated in the now happily aborted case of the Bangla Desh Grameen Bank, which initially proposed a "deal" with Monsanto for their terminator seed technology. If there is no peer group regulation of occasions of co-optation, human rights markets can undergo substantial downturns.

But forms of peer-group regulatory interventions raise difficult if not intractable issues. When are NGO communities entitled to sound the alarm? Which modes of alleviation of human suffering are more progressively "just" from the standpoint of human rights communities that otherwise do not contest the existence of human rights markets in the name of human suffering? What superogatory ethics are at play here? Put another way, what standards of critical morality are furnished by extant human rights instruments (addressed primarily to state morality) for NGO critiques of sister NGOs? Are human rights markets per se more sensibly moral than all other markets?

Just as surely as there is an ideology of human rights, abundantly illustrated by the discourse on human rights, so is there a materiality to it, ever present in cross-border transactions in the symbolic capital of human rights. The usefulness of the market metaphor therefore should be apparent.

V. The Emergence of an Alternate Paradigm of Human Rights

A. The Paradigm Shift

My thesis herein requires a brutally frank statement. I believe that the paradigm of the UDHR is being steadily supplanted by a trade-related, market-friendly, human rights paradigm. This new paradigm reverses the notion that universal human rights are designed for the dignity and well-being of human beings and insists, instead, upon the promotion and protection of the collective rights of global capital in ways that "justify" corporate well-being and dignity over that of human persons. The UDHR model assigned human rights responsibilities to states; it called upon the state to construct, progressively and within the community of states, a just social order, both national and global, that could meet at least the basic needs of human beings. The new model denies any significant redistributive role for the state. It calls upon the state (and world order) to free as many spaces for capital as possible, initially by fully pursuing the "Three-Ds" of contemporary globalization: de-regulation, de-nationalization, and disinvestment. Putting an end to national regulatory and redistributive potentials is the *leitmotif* of present-day economic globalization, as anyone who has read several drafts of the Multilateral Agreement on Investment (MAI) knows.[154] But the program of rolling back the state aims at the same time for vigorous state action when the interests of global capital are at stake. To this extent, de-regulation signifies not an end of the nation-state but an end to the redistributionist state.[155]

Recent history has shown that multinational capital needs at one and the same time a "soft" state and a "hard" one.[156] The production of soft states is a high priority for multinational capital and its normative cohorts, as exemplified by the continuing reports of Ms. Fatima-Zohra Ksentini, Special Rapporteur to the Commission on Human Rights, on the adverse effect of the illicit movement and dumping of toxic and dangerous wastes on the enjoyment of human rights.[157] The biggest waste exporters are, of course, the most "developed" countries, and wastes continue to be dispatched to regions lacking the political and economic power to refuse it.[158] This deficit is not innate, but caused, in the last instance, by the formations of the global economy.

All kinds of unfortunate business practices abound: use of falsified documents; bribing of officials in the "country of origin, the transit country, or . . . the country of final destination,"[159] and private contracts "between Western companies and African countries whereby the companies paid a pittance for the land on which to dump toxic products. . . ."[160] The latter scandal brought forth an anguished resolution from the Organization of African Unity a decade ago, declaring toxic dumping to be a "crime against Africa and African people."[161] The Special Rapporteur had no difficulty in cataloging a large number of violations that these practices knowingly—and criminally—entail.[162] Soft states and regimes need to be continually constituted for the benefit of global capital, benefiting a few communities of people. That this imposes the cost of incredible human suffering on the impoverished nations[163] is irrelevant to the ruling standards of global capital, which must

---

154 *See* Multilateral Agreement on Investment, *supra* note 73.

155 *See* JANE KELSEY, THE NEW ZEALAND EXPERIMENT: A WORLD MODEL FOR STRUCTURAL ADJUSTMENT? (1995).

156 *See* GUNNAR MYRDAL, ASIAN DRAMA: AN INQUIRY INTO THE POVERTY OF NATIONS (1968). Myrdal's concern was to portray South Asian states as lacking in social or institutional discipline and vulnerable to high levels of corruption.

157 *Adverse Effects of the Illicit Movement and Dumping of Toxic and Dangerous Products and Wastes on the Enjoyment of Human Rights*, U.N. GAOR, Hum. Rts. Comm, U.N. Doc. E/CN.4/1998/10 (1998) [hereinafter *Adverse Effects*].

158 *Id.* paras. 54 and 56.

159 *Id.*

160 *Id.*

161 *Id.* para. 57.

162 *Adverse Effects, supra* note 157, paras. 77–107.

163 If you find this too metaphorical, please recall children being exposed to radiation by

measure the excellence of economic entrepreneuership by standards other than those provided by seemingly endless human rights normativity.

The contextuality of this enterprise bids a moment of reflection. The multinational corporations may not perform toxic dumping projects, for example, without the active support of the international financial institutions, and such support causes some Third World countries, ridden by "over-indebtedness and collapse of raw material prices," to view the import of hazardous wastes as "attractive" as a last resort to improve their liquidity.[164] In this context, one is talking about no more bad business practice that international codes of conduct may prohibit but, rather, of genocidal corporate and international financial institutional regimes of governance. These are, to coin a neologism (a barbarism in language that is insufficient to cope with the savagery of the "free market"), *rightsicidal* practices of management of governance.

Hard-headed international business practices require also proliferation of "hard" states and regimes which must be market-efficient in suppressing and delegitimating human rights practices of resistance or the pursuit of alternate politics. Rule of law standards and values need to be enforced by the state on behalf and at the behest of formations of the global economy and global technology. When, to this end, it is necessary for the state to unleash a reign of terror, it must be empowered, locally and globally, to do so. The state must remain, at all times, sufficiently active to ensure maximal security to the global or foreign investor, who has corresponding duties to assist the state in managing or refurbishing any democratic deficit that might thus arise. The flagrant, massive, and ongoing violations of human rights thus entailed must be denied a voice by state-of-the-art management of public and political opinion, nationally and globally.

The new paradigm will succeed if it can render problematic the voices of suffering. This occurs primarily through "rationality reform"—that is, by the production of epistemologies that normalize risk (there is no escape from risk), ideologize it (some grave risks are justified for the sake of "progress," "development," and "security"); problematize causation (in ways that the catastrophic impacts may not be traced to the activity of global corporations); raise questions (so dear to law and economics specialists concerning the efficiency of legal regimes of liability); and interrogate even a modicum of judicial activism (compensating rights-violation and suffering, favoring unprincipled and arbitrary extra-judicial settlement when risk management and damage containment strategies fail). It is not surprising that some of the most important questions in globalization discourse relate to how we conceptualize "victim," who may authentically speak about victimage and what, indeed, may be said to constitute "suffering."

---

playing on irradiated nuclear waste dump sites in the Marshall Islands or the victims of Bhopal still suffering from the lethal impact of catastrophic exposure to 47 tons of MIC.

164 *See Adverse Effects, supra* note 157, para. 57.

The new paradigm asks us to shed the fetishism of human rights and to appreciate that, in the absence of economic development, human rights have no future at all. Some behavioral scientists urge us to believe in a quantitative methodology that "produces results," (certainly for them), that demonstrates a positive co-relation between foreign direct investment, multinational capital, and the observance of human rights. It is easier to combat dictatorial regimes that suspend human rights on the grounds of priority of economic development than to contest the gospel of economic rationalism, which is mystified by a new scholasticism with the assertion that, for example, "meso-development" is best promoted under conditions of authoritarianism. *Faute de mieux*, human rights communities must now work within the languages and imperatives of "economic rationalism"; they need to focus not on a conceptually elevated plateau of post-modern political theory, but, rather, on the new institutional economics, maintaining at the same time constant conversation with human suffering.

B. The Paradigms in Conflict

The paradigm of universal human rights has progressively sought normative consensus on the integrity of human rights, albeit expressed in different idioms. The diverse bodies of human rights found their highest summation with the Declaration on the Right to Development,[165] insisting that the individual is a subject of development, not its object.

The emergent paradigm reverses this trend. It seeks to make not just the individual human being but whole nations into the objects of development, as defined by global capital embodied in the "economic rationalism" of the supra-statal networks of the World Bank and the IMF, which are not democratically composed nor accountable to any constituency save investors. Their prescriptions for re-orientating the economic structures and polices of indebted and impoverished Third World societies, far from being designed to make the world order equitable, are addressed to the overall good of the world's hegemonic economies, in all their complexity and contradiction. Prescriptions of good governance are discriminatorily—and viciously —addressed only to states and communities outside the core Euro-Atlantic states. Even so, good governance is articulated as a set of arrangements, including institutional renovation, that primarily privileges and disproportionately benefits the global producers and consumers.

The paradigm of universal human rights enabled the emergence of the United Nations system as a congregation of faith. Regarded as no omnipotent deity but only as a frail, crisis-ridden arena, it became the privileged historic site for co-operative practices of reshaping the world through the idiom and grammar, as well as the vision, of human rights. This arena is being captured by the votaries of economic globalization who proselytize that free markets offer the best hope for human

165 *Supra* note 105.

redemption. But the residue of the past cultures of universal human rights remains nonetheless, as recently manifested in a U.N. document that dares to speak about perverse forms of globalization, namely, those that abandon any degree of respect for human rights standards and norms.[166] A moment's reflection on the WTO agreements and the proposed Multilateral Agreement on Investment (MAI)[167] should demonstrate the truth of this assertion. But, of course, no United Nations formulation would go this far, given its own diplomacy on resourcing the system and emerging global economic realities. The Vienna Conference on Human Rights summed it all up with its poignant preambulatory reference to "the spirit of our age" and the "realities of our time."[168] The "spirit" is human rights vision; the "realities" are furnished by the headlong and heedless processes of globalization that are creating in their wake cruel logics of social exclusion and enduring communities of misfortune.

Of course, the continuing appropriation by the forces of capital of hard-won human rights for its own ends is not a *sui generis* event. Long before slavery was abolished and before women won the right to contest and vote at elections, corporations had appropriated rights to personhood, claiming due process rights for regimes of property but denied to human beings. The unfolding of what I call "modern" human rights is the story of the near-absoluteness of the right to property, as a basic human right. So is the narrative of colonization/imperialism which began its career with the archetypal East India Company (which ruled India for a century) when corporate sovereignty was inaugurated. Politics was commerce and commerce became politics.

So, it may be said, is this the case now. Some would even maintain that it was the case even during the halcyon days of human rights enunciations (from the Declaration on Permanent Sovereignty over Resources[169] to the Declaration on the Right to Development[170]). Peel away the layers of human rights rhetoric, they would maintain, and you will find a core of historic continuity where heroic assertions of human rights remained, in fact and effect, the insignia of triumphant economic interests.

This continuity thesis deserves its moment. It directs attention to facts and feats of global diplomacy over human rights in ways that moderate or even cure the celebrationist approach to human rights (whether human rights romanticism, mysticism, triumphalism, or hedonism). It alerts us to the fact that within the modalities of human rights enunciation beats the regular heartbeats of hegemonic interests.

---

166 *See Adverse Effects, supra* note 157.

167 *See* proposed Multilateral Agreement on Investment, *supra* note 73.

168 *See* Upendra Baxi, *"The Spirit of Our Age, The Realities of Our Time": The Vienna Declaration on Human Rights, in* MAMBRINO'S HELMET? HUMAN RIGHTS FOR A CHANGING WORLD 1–18 (1994).

169 *Supra* note 104.

170 *Supra* note 105.

It directs us towards a mode of thought that relocates the authorship of human rights away from the politics of inter-governmental desire to the multitudinous struggles of people against human violation.

If all this be so, is there a paradigm shift or merely an extension of latent capitalism that always has moved (as the readers of *Das Kapital* surely know) in accordance with bourgeois human rights trajectories? This is an important and difficult question raised by Burns Weston in his indefatigable editorial labors. My short answer for the present is that, while the appropriation by the capital of human rights logic and rhetoric is not a distinctively contemporary phenomenon, it is the scale of reversal now manifest that marks a radical discontinuity. Global business practices cancel, for example, many normative gains of the "contemporary" human rights movement through techniques of dispersal of these evils. The exploitation of child and sweat labor through free economic zones, and accompanying sex-based discrimination even in subsistence wages, is the hallmark of contemporary economic globalization. So is the creation of a "global risk society"[171] through hazardous industry and the very legible scripts of "organized irresponsibility" and "organized impunity" for corporate offenders, of which the Bhopal catastrophe furnishes a mournful reminder.[172]

What distinguishes the paradigm shift is the "legitimation" of extraordinary imposition of human suffering in the cause and the course of the present contemporary march of global capital. In the "modern" epoch of human rights, such suffering was considered *per se* legitimate. "Contemporary" human rights logics and paralogics challenged, and at times denied, this self-evident axiom. The paradigm shift seeks to cancel the historic gains of the progressive universal human rights movement in seemingly irreversible ways. It seeks to mute the voices of suffering and, in the process, regress human rights futures.

VI. Toward a Conclusion?

History, especially current history, presents always confused pathways. It is difficult to foretell with any degree of assurance, despite advances in futurology, where the future of human rights or indeed any future may lie. In this situation, the only reflexive task open to human rights communities consists in "planning ahead." The CEOs of leading multinationals are preoccupied with planning the futures of global capital movements in 2025 A.D. even as, remarkably, they confine the energies of human rights activists to perfidious instances of the "local-in-the-global" causation of human suffering (as, for example, in Bhopal and Ogoniland). The *fin-de-siècle* need and ordeal for human rights communities, worldwide, is to develop an agenda of action to arrest the paradigm-shift, without them converting themselves into new

171 *See* ULRICH BECK, THE RISK SOCIETY: TOWARD A NEW MODERNITY (1992).

172 *See* Upendra Baxi, *Introduction, in* VALIANT VICTIMS AND LETHAL LITIGATION: THE BHOPAL CASE (Upendra Baxi & Amita Dhandha eds., 1990).

bureaucrats or technocrats of human suffering. To some, this may seem an insensible challenge, as nothing seems more ludicrous than sailing against the wind. What is necessary is to combat this kind of mind-set. Human rights futures, dependent as they are upon imparting an authentic voice to human suffering, must engage in a discourse of suffering that moves the world.

Over a century and half ago, Karl Marx put the notion of human futures presciently when he urged that they are best born when the following twin tasks occur: when suffering humanity reflects and when thinking humanity suffers. I know of no better way to unite the future of human rights to human suffering.

[5]

What Future for Economic and Social Rights?

DAVID BEETHAM

It is a commonplace of discussions about human rights that economic and social rights, like the poor themselves, occupy a distinctly second class status.[1] When human rights are mentioned, it is typically civil and political rights that spring to mind. When Western governments include the promotion of human rights in their foreign policy goals, it is the freedoms of expression and political association, the right to due process and the protection from state harassment that principally concern them rather than, say, access to the means of livelihood or to basic health care. And when the role of human rights NGOs is discussed, it is the work of organizations such as Amnesty International or civil liberties associations that we tend to think of. By the same token, our paradigm for a human rights violation is state-sponsored torture or 'disappearance' rather than, say, childhood death through malnutrition or preventable disease.

This disparity between the two sets of rights was acknowledged by the UN Committee on Economic, Social and Cultural Rights itself, in its statement to the Vienna World Conference of 1993:

> The shocking reality ... is that states and the international community as a whole continue to tolerate all too often breaches of economic, social and cultural rights which, if they occurred in relation to civil and political rights, would provoke expressions of horror and outrage and would lead to concerted calls for immediate remedial action. In effect, despite the rhetoric, violations of civil and political rights continue to be treated as though they were far more serious, and more patently intolerable, than massive and direct denials of economic, social and cultural rights.[2]

A number of reasons can be advanced as to why this disparity persists, despite the repeated assertions of human rights protagonists that the human rights agenda is 'indivisible'. One reason is intellectual. Ever since the Universal Declaration of 1948, the idea of social and economic rights has been subjected to sustained criticism. It is argued, typically, that the list of so-called 'rights' in the Declaration and in the subsequent International Covenant on Economic, Social and Cultural Rights (hereafter ICESCR) can at most be a statement of aspirations or goals rather than properly of *rights*. For an entitlement to be a human right it must satisfy a number of conditions: it must be fundamental

[1] This article will concentrate on economic and social, rather than cultural, rights for reasons of space. I am grateful to the other contributors, especially Susan Mendus, for comments on an earlier draft.

[2] UN Doc. E/C.12/1992/2, p. 83.

and universal; it must in principle be definable in justiciable form; it should be clear who has the duty to uphold or implement the right; and the responsible agency should possess the capacity to fulfil its obligation. The rights specified in the Covenant do not satisfy these conditions, it is argued.[3]

Indeed, they would seem to fail on every count. They confuse the fundamental with the merely desirable, or that which is specific to the advanced economies (holidays with pay, free higher education, the right of everyone to the continuous improvement of living conditions).[4] Even those that are fundamental cannot in principle be definable in justiciable form. At what level can the deprivation of nutrition, sanitation or health care be sufficient to trigger legal redress? And whose duty is it to see that these 'rights' are met – national governments, international institutions, the UN itself? If it is governments, can they be required to provide what they do not have the means or capacity to deliver? Since 'ought' entails 'can', since to have an assignable duty entails a realistic possibility of being able to fulfil it, can the positive requirements of the Covenant be reasonably expected of impoverished and less than fully autonomous regimes? While we may reasonably require them to *refrain* from torturing their citizens, it is not obvious that we can equally require them to guarantee them all a livelihood, adequate accommodation and a healthy environment. Moreover for them to do so, it is contended, would require a huge paternalist and bureaucratic apparatus and a corresponding extension of compulsory taxation, both of which would interfere with another basic right, the right to freedom.[5]

Such are the arguments that have been repeatedly advanced against the idea of economic and social rights. And it must be said that these arguments have had a certain echo within UN procedures themselves, with the initial division between the two separate human rights covenants, the weaker monitoring procedures of the ICESCR, its distinctive formula that states should 'take steps' towards the 'progressive achievement' of the rights according to available resources, and the distribution of responsibility for the ESCR agenda between different specialist agencies (FAO, WHO, UNICEF, UNESCO, ILO, UNDP), as well as a human rights committee.[6]

[3] See M. Cranston, 'Human rights, real and supposed', in D. D. Raphael (ed.), *Political Theory and the Rights of Man* (London, Macmillan, 1967), pp. 43–52; M. Cranston, *What Are Human Rights?* (London, Bodley Head, 1973). The most frequent objections are summarized in P. Alston and G. Quinn, 'The nature and scope of states parties' obligations under the ICESCR', *Human Rights Quarterly*, 9 (1987), 157–229, pp. 157–60; A. Eide, 'The realisation of social and economic rights and the minimum threshold approach', *Human Rights Law Journal*, 10 (1989), 35–51; G. J. H. van Hoof, 'The legal nature of economic, social and cultural rights: a rebuttal of some traditional views' in P. Alston and K. Tomasevski (eds), *The Right to Food* (Dordrecht, Martinus Nijhoff, 1990), pp. 97–110.

[4] These examples are from the ICESCR articles 7, 11 and 13 in I. Brownlie (ed.), *Basic Documents on Human Rights* (Oxford, Oxford University Press, 3rd ed., 1992), pp. 114–24.

[5] This last is a standard neo-liberal objection; see R. Nozick, *Anarchy, State and Utopia* (Oxford, Blackwell, 1974), pp. 30–3.

[6] For the establishment of the committee, see P. Alston, 'Out of the abyss: the challenges confronting the new UN Committee on Economic Social and Cultural Rights', *Human Rights Quarterly*, 9 (1987), 332–81. A repeated complaint of the Committee since its inception has been 'the continuing separation of human rights and social development issues' in UN development programmes. See the Statement by the Committee of May 1994 to the World Summit on Social Development (typescript), p. 1.

However, it would be mistaken to attribute the disparity of status between the two sets of rights to intellectual and institutional factors alone, and not also to political ones. There is a general agreement among commentators on economic and social rights that for them to be effectively realized would require a redistribution of power and resources, both within countries and between them. It is hardly surprising that many governments should be less than enthusiastic about such an agenda, and should resort to the alibi of 'circumstances beyond their control', and to the ready-made language of 'taking steps', 'available resources', etc., of the ICESCR itself. Indeed, this very language, and the procedural limitations of the Covenant, owe as much to political inspiration as to intellectual or institutional requirements.[7]

While the above could have been written at almost any time during the past thirty years, developments from the 1980s onwards have made the position of economic and social rights even more precarious. First are developments in the international economy itself. The normal processes of the international market, which tend to benefit the already advantaged, have been intensified by the effects of deregulation and the cutting of welfare provision, to the further disadvantage of the deprived in many societies. There has indeed been a politics of redistribution at work, but it has been a redistribution from the poor to the well-off, within and between countries: an upwards flood rather than a 'trickle down'.[8] In the process the capacity of governments to control their own economic destinies has been significantly eroded, as collective choice has been displaced by market forces, and economic policy has been conducted under the scrutiny of what 'average opinion' in financial circles 'believes average opinion to be'.[9]

A second development has been the demise of the USSR and the Communist model as a viable alternative to capitalism. Although in theory the end of the Cold War could have provided an opportunity for ending the sterile opposition between the two sets of human rights, in practice it has reinforced the priorities of the USA, the country which has been most consistently opposed to the idea of economic and social rights.[10] And the more general loss of credibility of socialism in any form has deprived the poor everywhere of an organizing ideology for political struggle and the politics of redistribution. This is not to mention the more specific effects that the end of Communism has had for the peoples of the former Soviet Union and other Communist states: the collapse of social security systems, and the extension of the zone of civil war to include the Balkans and central Asia.

In face of this depressing litany of developments, two alternative responses are possible. One is to conclude that the incorporation of economic and social rights in the human rights canon is simply spitting in the wind, when hundreds of millions suffer from malnutrition and vulnerability to disease and

[7] H. Shue, *Basic Rights* (Princeton, Princeton University Press, 1980), p. 158.

[8] For the widening global gap between rich and poor see United Nations Development Programme (UNDP), *Human Development Report 1992* (New York, Oxford University Press, 1992), ch. 3; for the UK see Rowntree Foundation, *Inquiry Into Income and Wealth*, 2 vols (York, Joseph Rowntree Foundation, 1995), vol. 2, ch. 3.

[9] J. Eatwell, 'A global world demands economic coordination', *New Economy*, 1 (1994), 146–150, p. 148.

[10] The USA has still not ratified the ICESCR.

starvation.[11] Worse, it is an insult to them to insist on their 'human rights' when there is no realistic prospect of these being upheld. It was precisely for confusing the promise with its actualization, the desire to have a right with having one, that Bentham denounced the fictional 'rights' of the French Declaration: 'want is not supply, hunger is not bread'.[12] It is one thing to describe the victim of an armed robbery as having been deprived of his or her rights, when these are normally upheld and legal recourse is available; quite another where such insecurity has become the norm. And this is the situation with food security in many parts of the world.

The opposite response is to insist that human rights most urgently need asserting and defending, both theoretically and practically, where they are most denied. Indeed the language of rights only makes sense at all in a context where basic requirements are vulnerable to standard threats (could we imagine a 'right' to clean air in a pre-industrial society?). The human rights agenda has therefore necessarily an aspirational or promotional dimension; but it is not mere rhetoric. The purpose of the two covenants and their monitoring apparatus is to cajole state signatories into undertaking the necessary domestic policy and legislation to ensure their citizens the protection of their rights in practice. This promotional aspect of the human rights agenda is not only addressed to those whose responsibility it is to secure the rights in question. It also serves as a legitimation for the deprived in their struggles to realize their rights on their own behalf, by providing a set of internationally validated standards to which they can appeal.

The purpose of this paper is to offer a defence of the second of these responses against the first. More particularly, it seeks to provide a defence of economic and social rights as human rights against the many different objections levelled against them. The first section deals with their definition and justification; the second outlines a theory of corresponding duties; the third assesses objections on the grounds of practicality; the final section evaluates the purpose of the economic and social rights agenda in an imperfect world.

Definition and Justification

The idea of economic and social rights as *human* rights expresses the moral intuition that, in a world rich in resources and the accumulation of human knowledge, everyone ought to be guaranteed the basic means for sustaining life, and that those denied these are victims of a fundamental injustice. Expressing this intuition in the form of human rights both gives the deprived the strongest possible claim to that of which they are deprived, and emphasizes the duty of responsible parties to uphold or help them meet their entitlement.

Those who do not share the intuition articulated above, or who believe that it conflicts with a more fundamental one they hold, are unlikely to be persuaded by anything written in this paper. Many who do share it, however,

[11] For a recent assessment of global poverty see World Bank, *World Development Report 1990* (New York, Oxford University Press for World Bank, 1990).

[12] J. Bentham, 'A critical examination of the Declaration of Rights' in B. Parekh (ed.), *Bentham's Political Thought* (London, Croom Helm, 1973), pp. 257–90, p. 269.

are unconvinced that the framework of human rights is the most appropriate vehicle for giving it expression. Here we might distinguish between strategic and specific objections. 'Strategic' objections are those which urge the superiority of an alternative moral framework for giving effect to the above intuition: the theory of justice,[13] say, or of Kantian obligation,[14] or of basic needs,[15] or human development.[16] There is not the space here to explore all these possible alternatives. Suffice to say, however, that the contrast between these other frameworks and a human rights perspective has been considerably overstated. Human rights theory itself embodies a theory of justice (albeit a partial or incomplete one);[17] it entails an account of obligation and of duties corresponding to the rights claimed;[18] and it presupposes a conception of human needs and human development.[19] Moreover, among strategic considerations for embracing a particular moral framework, it is not evident that philosophical claims should have *sole* place, to the exclusion of institutional or political considerations. This is a point I shall return to at the end of the paper.

Here I shall concentrate on what I call 'specific' objections to economic and social rights, which question whether they can meet the requirements of a human right, for the kinds of reason outlined earlier. If to have a right means to have a justifiable entitlement to x (the object of the right), by virtue of y (possession of the relevant attribute), against z (the agent with the corresponding obligation to meet the entitlement);[20] then this formula establishes both the criteria that have to be satisfied for a human right, and also an order of argument for the consideration of objections. Starting with questions of definition and justification, we can proceed to an examination of the corresponding duties, and of their practicability. Although these

[13] Although John Rawls' theory of justice (J. Rawls, *A Theory of Justice*, Oxford, Oxford University Press, 1972) is a rights based theory, there is doubt among human rights theorists whether his 'difference principle' of social distribution provides a sufficiently robust defence of basic economic and social rights, in the light of its lower lexical ordering, and the fact that it can be interpreted to justify 'trickle down' economics, or merely marginal improvements in a desperate situation. 'The Rawlsian difference principle can be fulfilled while people continue to drown, but with less and less water over their heads', Shue, *Basic Rights*, p. 128. For his part, however, Rawls agrees with Shue that 'subsistence rights are basic', since they are a condition of exercising liberty: J. Rawls, 'The law of peoples' in S. Shute and S. Hurley (eds), *On Human Rights* (New York, Basic, 1993), pp. 41–82, note 26.

[14] Onora O'Neill rejects the language of 'manifesto rights' and the 'rancorous rhetoric of rights' for its lack of underpinning by a theory of obligation. O. O'Neill, *Faces of Hunger* (London, Allen and Unwin, 1986), chs 6 and 7.

[15] Paul Streeten rejects giving basic needs the status of human rights on the grounds of scarcity of resources. See 'Appendix: basic needs and human rights', in Paul Streeten and associates, *First Things First: Meeting Basic Needs in Developing Countries* (New York, Oxford University Press for World Bank, 1981), pp. 184–192.

[16] UNDP distinguishes the material dimensions of human development from human rights, which it interprets exclusively as civil and political; see e.g. UNDP, *Human Development Report 1992*, p. 9.

[17] Its principle can be simply stated: securing basic economic and social rights takes priority over other distributional principles, whatever these happen to be.

[18] Shue, *Basic Rights*, ch. 2.

[19] Johan Galtung, *Human Rights in Another Key* (Cambridge, Polity, 1994), ch. 3; F. Stewart, 'Basic needs strategies, human rights and the right to development', *Human Rights Quarterly*, 11 (1989), 347–74.

[20] This is Gewirth's well-known formulation, A. Gewirth, *Human Rights* (Chicago, University of Chicago Press, 1982), p. 2.

elements are all interconnected, they can be treated separately for analytical purposes.

So I start with the definition of social and economic rights. Can they be defined in such a way that they meet the criteria for a human right of being fundamental, universal and clearly specifiable? That they should be *fundamental* conforms to the idea of the human rights agenda as being to protect the means to a minimally decent, rather than maximally comfortable, life; and to the perception that the seriousness of this purpose is compromised if the list of rights confuses the essential with the merely desirable.[21] The same conclusion can be reached from the standpoint of *universality*: human rights should be applicable to all, regardless of the level of development a country has reached. That they should be clearly *specifiable* follows from the fairly elementary requirement that we should be able to ascertain whether a right has been upheld or not, and when it has been infringed or violated.

From the standpoint of these criteria the text of the ICESCR suffers from its attempt to define the rights in a way that, on the one hand, serves to protect the social achievements of the advanced economies, and use them as a standard for best practice; and, on the other, to prescribe a necessary minimum that is within the capacity of all. This uneasy conjunction of a minimum and maximum agenda is apparent in many of the articles (e.g. Article 7 on conditions of work, Article 13 on education), and the language of 'progressive achievement as resources allow' stems partly from the attempt to bridge the two. With hindsight it might have been better if the original text had concentrated on establishing a minimum agenda, while leaving it to regional charters to develop their own formulation of rights which might be more ambitious than, yet consistent with, the universal one.

It should be said that the body charged with monitoring the Covenant (since 1987 the UN Committee on ESCR) is itself painfully aware of this problem, and has set itself the task of defining a minimum 'core' under each right, which should be guaranteed to all regardless of circumstances. As its current Chairman, Philip Alston wrote: 'The fact that there must exist such a "core" would seem to be a logical implication of the use of the terminology of rights ... Each right must therefore give rise to an absolute minimum entitlement, in the absence of which a state party is to be considered to be in violation of its obligations'.[22] This process of 'norm clarification' on the part of the Committee, and the monitoring procedures associated with it, constitute a serious attempt to deflect some of the recurrent objections to the ICESCR on the grounds of its lack of universalizability.

What, then, should be the minimum 'core' of economic and social rights? This question cannot be answered independently of the question of how human rights in general come to be *justified*. Such justification requires a number of different steps. Its starting point lies in identifying the grounds on which all humans deserve equal respect, or merit treating with equal dignity, whatever

[21] J. W. Nickel, *Making Sense of Human Rights* (Berkeley, University of California Press, 1987), ch. 3.

[22] Alston, 'Out of the abyss', pp. 352–3. Compare the pronouncement of the Committee itself in its 5th Session: 'A minimum core obligation to ensure the satisfaction of, at the very least, minimum essential levels of each right is incumbent upon every state party ... If the Covenant were to be read in such a way as not to establish such a core obligation, it would be largely deprived of its *raison d'être*.' UN Doc. E/C.12/1990/8, p. 86.

the differences between them. Although these grounds are contestable,[23] reference to some feature of distinctive human agency is unavoidable, such as: the capacity for reflective moral judgement, for determining the good for one's life, both individually and in association with others, for choosing goals or projects and seeking to realize them, and so on. These can be summed up in a concept such as 'reflective moral and purposive agency'.[24] A further step would then be to specify the most general preconditions for exercising human agency over a lifetime, whatever the particular goals, values or conceptions of the good that might be embraced. Such preconditions include physical integrity or security, the material means of existence, the development of capacities, and the enjoyment of basic liberties.[25] These necessary conditions of human agency constitute the basis of human rights.[26]

If on the one side, then, the specification of any list of human rights takes its justification from the general conditions for effective human agency, on the other side it is also grounded in a distinctively modern experience, both of the characteristic threats to the realization of these conditions, and of the means required to protect against such threats. It is the potentially (and historically experienced) absolute and arbitrary power of the modern state that has come to determine much of the content of the civil and political rights agenda. It is the insecurity generated by the unfettered market economy, and the threats to health produced by widespread urbanization and industrialization, that have likewise determined much of the economic and social rights agenda. At the same time, it is the historically acquired knowledge of the means to protect against these threats, that enables the human rights agenda to be defined as rights, rather than as utopia.

This conjunction of the universal with the historically specific helps explain some of the confusion about the universality of human rights. They are universal in that they rest on assumptions about needs and capacities common to all, and the rights apply to all humans alive now. Yet they are also distinctly historical in that any declaration of human rights has only been possible in the modern era. At a theoretical level, the idea of human rights could only be entertained once the status distinctions and privileges of traditional society had been eroded, and people could be defined as individuals independently of their birth-determined social statuses. From this viewpoint, an anti-discrimination clause can be seen as the most fundamental of human rights articles. At a practical level, it was precisely the same breakdown of traditional society, with its personalized guarantees and mutual responsibilities, that made the agenda of human rights *necessary*, in face of the depersonalizing forces of the modern state and market economy. Those who complain that their traditional societies managed perfectly well without any conception of human rights may be perfectly correct. It does not follow that they can continue without them, given the globalization of the forces that have made them both possible and necessary.

[23] M. Freeman, 'The philosophical foundations of human rights', *Human Rights Quarterly*, 16 (1994), 491–514.

[24] See A. Gewirth, 'The basis and content of human rights', in Gewirth, *Human Rights*, ch. 1.

[25] Gewirth summarizes these as 'freedom and well-being', Gewirth, *Human Rights*, p. 47.

[26] For a defence of this general structure of argument against both neo-liberals and communitarians, see R. Plant, *Modern Political Thought* (Oxford, Blackwell, 1991), chs 3 and 7; also L. Doyal and I. Gough, *A Theory of Human Need* (London, Macmillan, 1991), chs 1–5.

In the light of the above, a minimum agenda of economic and social rights will aim to secure those basic material conditions for human agency that modern experience has shown to be both necessary and effective. These are not that remarkable actually. Both the defenders of a 'basic needs' approach within development economics and human rights theorists would converge on a minimum core of rights such as the following: the right to food of an adequate nutritional value, to clothing, to shelter, to basic (or primary) health care, clean water and sanitation, and to education to at least primary level.[27] Although there may be other things to be added to this list (see below), it provides the foundation, together with the crucial principle of non-discriminatory access. All of those mentioned above concern the satisfaction of elementary physical needs, except for education; here the evidence suggests that the latter is a direct prerequisite for the others, since, in the absence of knowledge about what causes illness, or how to make the best use of available food, an otherwise adequate supply may prove insufficient to meet basic needs.[28]

If the rights in the above list can meet the criteria of being both fundamental and universally applicable, can they also meet the test of specificity, such that it is possible to specify a level below which a given right can be said to be denied? Even the level of necessary nutrition, which seems to be the most objectively definable, will vary according to person and circumstance. The level of clothing or shelter needed will vary according to the climate. And the need for health care and education, as is well known, is almost infinitely expandable as knowledge increases. Here there will inevitably be a *certain* arbitrariness about defining the required standard for a human right as that of primary health care and education, although that standard is based upon a general agreement that these constitute significant thresholds. That some minimum standards need to be established, however, is necessary to the idea of a 'core' of rights, and to the assumption of the UN Committee on ESCR that such rights can increasingly be justiciable, and amenable to individual petition and complaint.[29] In any case, the methods needed are perhaps not that complex for determining when girls are discriminated against in access to education, when children die through lack of food or clean water, or when people sleep rough because they have no access to housing; nor for deciding on the kind of comparative statistics – on infant mortality rates, life expectancy rates, literacy rates, school attendance rates, etc., – which can serve as evidence of rights denials.

On the supposition, then, that a minimum core of economic and social rights can be given appropriate specificity, they can also be defined in sufficiently general terms to allow differing approaches to their realization, whether through market or non-market mechanisms, or various mixtures of the two. The literature on basic needs from the outset emphasized its ideological neutrality as between politico-economic systems, and supported this with evidence that a profile of basic needs was being met by a number of developing

[27] Shue, *Basic Rights*, pp. 22–9; F. Stewart, *Planning to Meet Basic Needs* (London, Macmillan, 1985), chs 1 and 6; Streeten, *First Things First*, ch. 6; UNDP, *World Development Report 1992*, 'criteria of human deprivation', pp. 132–3. For a fuller list, which also includes the above, see Doyal and Gough, *A Theory of Human Need*, ch. 10.

[28] Streeten, *First Things First*, pp. 134–5. All these items are in fact interdependent requirements for health.

[29] For the Committee's proposal for an individual complaints procedure, see Annex IV of the 7th Session of the Committee, UN Doc. E/C. 12/1992/2, pp. 87–108.

countries with market-led, state-run and mixed economies, and at different levels of development.[30] What mattered, the argument ran, was that meeting basic needs should be targeted as a specific goal of policy, and not be assumed to follow as an automatic by-product of aggregate economic growth. In similar vein, the UN Committee on ESCR has insisted that 'in terms of political and economic systems the Covenant is neutral, and its principles cannot accurately be described as being predicated exclusively upon the need for, or desirability of, a socialist or capitalist system, or a mixed, centrally planned or laissez-faire economy, or upon any other particular approach'.[31] In legal terms, the duties undertaken by parties to the Covenant are duties of 'result' more than duties of 'conduct', of ends more than means.[32]

However, the ideological neutrality of the Covenant is more apparent than real, in two key respects. First, from a human rights perspective, it cannot be a matter of indifference if the institutions involved in the attainment of basic economic rights are also systematically engaged in the violation of civil and political liberties, as was typical of ruling Communist parties. The argument that one set of rights has to be sacrificed for the other is now thoroughly discredited; and historical experience shows that economic and social rights themselves cannot be guaranteed over time, if people are deprived of information about the effects of economic policies, and have no influence over their formulation or implementation.[33] It is in this sense that the two sets of rights are 'indivisible', and that democracy constitutes a necessary condition for the sustained realization of economic and social rights.[34] On the other hand, as the UN Committee insists, 'there is no basis whatsoever to assume that the realization of economic, social and cultural rights will necessarily result from the achievement of civil and political rights', or that democracy can be a *sufficient* condition for their realization, in the absence of specifically targeted policies.[35]

The insistence on the indivisibility of the two sets of rights should lay to rest the charge often levelled against the Covenant that it presents the bearers of economic and social rights as the passive recipients of paternalist state welfare, rather than as active providers for their own needs; and should discourage any simple division between 'welfare' and 'liberty' rights. Apart from any necessary provision of collective goods by public authority, most people prefer to have the opportunity to meet their own needs through their own efforts, whether through access to land for subsistence farming, through a fair price for the goods they produce, or through a sufficient wage for the labour they supply. It is only in the event of their inability to provide for themselves that 'welfare' in a narrow sense becomes necessary. By the same token, people also require the

[30] Stewart, *Planning to Meet Basic Needs*, pp. 70–3; Streeten, *First Things First*, ch. 5.

[31] UN Doc. E/C.12/1990/8, p. 85.

[32] For a discussion of this distinction see G. S. Goodwin-Gill, 'Obligations of conduct and result' in Alston and Tomasevski, *The Right to Food*, pp. 111–8.

[33] R. E. Goodin, 'The development-rights trade-off: some unwarranted economic and political assumptions', *Universal Human Rights*, 1 (1979), 31–42; R. Howard, 'The full-belly thesis: should economic rights take priority over civil and political rights?', *Human Rights Quarterly*, 5 (1987), 467–90.

[34] The UN Committee is thus somewhat disingenuous when it claims that the ICESCR 'neither requires nor precludes any particular form of government', since it immediately proceeds to add: 'provided only that it is democratic'! UN Doc. E/C.12/1990/8, p. 85.

[35] UN Doc. E/C.12/1992/2, pp. 82–3.

freedom to organize collectively to protect and improve the conditions for the provision of their needs, whether as groups of peasants, the landless, the self-employed, the unemployed, as well as wage workers. In this context, the more narrowly defined trade union rights of the ICESCR can be seen as a special case of the general right of association protected under the International Covenant on Civil and Political Rights; here more than anywhere there is an overlap between the two, and the case for their separation is most clearly indefensible.

If on one side, then, the achievement in practice of economic and social rights as *human* rights can now be seen to exclude the instrumentality of a command economy, on the other it is also incompatible with untrammelled private property rights and the unrestricted freedom of the market. Certainly the rights discussed above entail some property rights; and both private property and the market are useful instruments through which basic economic needs can be met. But the institution of private property, which depends upon a socially recognized principle of exclusion or limitation of freedom, cannot be defended as a 'natural' right, any more than the market can be construed as a 'natural' rather than a socially constructed and validated institution.[36] If their primary justification as social institutions lies in their effectiveness in securing people's means of livelihood, then their justifiable limitation (of accumulation and use in the one, of freedom to exchange in the other) must lie at the point of their failure to do so. To this extent the agenda of economic and social rights is necessarily at odds with a neo-liberal approach to the market and private property.[37]

In this section I have sought to defend a minimum agenda of economic and social rights which will meet the criteria of being fundamental, universal and specifiable. The agenda comprises a list of rights necessary to meet basic human needs (rights to food, clothing, shelter, primary health care, clean water and sanitation, and primary education), combined with the right of association necessary to the collective protection and promotion of these rights by the bearers themselves. I have also argued that, though much of the literature presents the achievement of these rights as ideologically neutral, or non institution-specific, their realization is in practice incompatible with both ends of the ideological spectrum.[38]

Corresponding Duties

Among the most substantial objections which the theory of human rights has to face is that it is impossible to specify the duties which correspond to the rights claimed, to show who should fulfil them or to demonstrate that they can

[36] For the argument that private property constitutes a major restriction on freedom see G. Cohen, 'Freedom, justice and capitalism', in Cohen, *History, Labour and Freedom* (Oxford, Oxford University Press, 1988), pp. 286–304.

[37] In effect the principle of basic economic and social rights, together with whatever compulsory transfers are necessary to secure them, constitutes a modern version of the original Lockean limitation on the duty to respect private property in land: that its enclosure did not prejudice the livelihood of others, because 'enough and as good' was left for them. J. Locke, *Two Treatises on Government*, P. Laslett (ed.), (Cambridge, Cambridge University Press, 1988), p. 291.

[38] This conclusion is similar to that reached by Doyal and Gough, *A Theory of Human Need*, ch. 13; see also M. Ramsay, *Human Needs and the Market* (Aldershot, Avebury, 1992).

realistically be fulfilled. In the absence of a satisfactory theory of obligation, it is urged, human rights must remain merely 'manifesto' claims, not properly rights. This objection is held to be particularly damaging to economic and social rights, which require from individuals and governments, not merely that they refrain from harming others or undermining their security, but that they act positively to promote their well-being.[39] This requirement not only presupposes resources which they may not possess. It also contradicts a widely held moral conviction to the effect that, while we may have a general negative duty not to harm others, the only positive duties we have are *special* duties to aid those to whom we stand in a particular personal, professional or contractual relationship. There can be no general duty to aid unspecified others; and, insofar as it presupposes such a duty, the inclusion of economic and social rights in the human rights agenda is basically flawed.

This formidable charge-sheet rests, I hope to show, on a number of fallacies. Easiest to refute is the assumption of a principled difference between the two sets of rights in the character of the obligations each entails, negative and positive respectively. As many commentators have shown, this difference will not hold up.[40] Certainly the so-called 'liberty' rights require the state to refrain from invading the freedom and security of its citizens. However, since governments were established, according to classical liberal theory itself, to protect people from the violation of their liberty and security at the hands of one another, it requires considerable government expenditure to meet this elementary purpose. Establishing 'the police forces, judicial systems and prisons that are necessary to maintain the highest achievable degree of security of these (sc. civil and political) rights ... is enormously expensive and involves the maintenance of complex bureaucratic systems'.[41]

Henry Shue has developed this argument furthest in his distinction between three different kinds of duty that are required to make a human right effective. There is, first, the duty to *avoid* depriving a person of some necessity; the duty to *protect* them from deprivation; and the duty to *aid* them when deprived. All three types of duty, he argues, are required to secure human rights, whether these be civil and political, or social and economic. Personal security, for example, requires that states refrain from torturing or otherwise injuring their citizens; that they protect them from injury at the hands of others; and that they provide a system of justice for the injured, to which all equally have access. Similarly, subsistence rights require that states do not deprive citizens of their means of livelihood; that they protect them against deprivation at the hands of others; and that they provide a system of basic social security for the deprived. The examples are entirely parallel. The difference is not between

[39] For the distinction between positive and negative rights see C. Fried, *Right and Wrong* (Cambridge MA, Harvard University Press, 1978), pp. 108–13; H. A. Bedau, 'Human rights and foreign assistance programs' in P. G. Brown and D. MacLean (eds), *Human Rights and US Foreign Policy* (Lexington, Lexington Books, 1979), pp. 29–44; Cranston, 'Human rights, real and supposed'.

[40] S. M. Okin, 'Liberty and welfare: some issues in human rights theory' in J. R. Pennock and J. W. Chapman (eds), *Human Rights: Nomos XXIII* (New York, New York University Press, 1981), pp. 230–56; R. Plant, 'A defence of welfare rights', in R. Beddard and D. M. Hill (eds), *Economic, Social and Cultural Rights* (Basingstoke, Macmillan, 1992), pp. 22–46; Plant, *Modern Political Thought*, pp. 267–86; Shue, *Basic Rights*, ch. 2.

[41] Okin, 'Liberty and welfare', p. 240.

different categories of *right*, but between different types of *duty* necessary to their protection, Shue concludes. 'The attempted division of rights, rather than duties, into forbearance and aid ... can only breed confusion. It is impossible for any basic right – however "negative" it has come to seem – to be fully guaranteed unless all three types of duties are fulfilled.'[42]

Shue's argument is persuasive. However, two opposite conclusions can be drawn from it. One (the conclusion which Shue, and others who argue similarly, invite us to draw) is that economic and social rights have to be considered as equally solid as civil and political rights, since there is no difference of principle between the state's provision of security for the vulnerable and of social security for the deprived. Those who are prepared to defend the one have to treat the other with equal seriousness. The opposite response, however, is to conclude that Shue's argument makes civil and political rights every bit as precarious as economic and social ones. If the most that can realistically be required from governments with limited resources, as from individuals with limited moral capacities, is duties of restraint or avoidance of harm to others; and if these negative duties are on their own insufficient to guarantee any human rights, as Shue has ably demonstrated: then no human right can be regarded as secure, since they all remain unanchored by the full range of corresponding duties. In other words, to make the case for human rights it is not enough simply to show what range of duties *would be* required to make the rights effective; it has also to be shown that these are duties which appropriate agents can reasonably be expected to fulfil.

The argument has therefore to be engaged at a deeper level, and a second assumption – that we have no general duty to aid others – needs examination. This is particularly important to economic and social rights, because the suspicion remains, despite all Shue's endeavours, that the two sets of rights are not after all symmetrical. More seems able to be achieved comparatively in the civil and political field by government abstention; and more seems required comparatively in the economic and social sphere by way of positive aid and provision. Moreover, while the provision of defence and law and order can readily be presented as a public good, from which all benefit, key elements of a basic economic and social agenda more readily assume the aspect of a particular good, which benefits definable sections of the population through transfer from the rest. Examining the logic of duties, therefore, is particularly necessary in respect of economic and social rights.

The argument that the only general duties we owe to unspecified others are negative ones, to refrain from harming them, not positively to give aid, is rooted not merely in liberal categories of politics, which prioritize non-interference, but also in a basic moral intuition about what we can reasonably be held responsible for. The objections to holding people responsible (and therefore morally reprehensible) for all the good that they could do, but do not, as well as for the harm they actually do, are twofold. Whereas the latter, sins of commission, are clearly assignable (to *our* actions), and to avoid them entails a clearly delimited responsibility (we can reasonably be required to take care not to harm others, and it is usually evident what this involves), a general duty to aid others is both potentially *limitless*, and also *non-assignable* (why us rather

[42] Shue, *Basic Rights*, p. 53.

than millions of others?). By contrast, special duties to give aid – to family, friends, clients, etc. – derive their moral weight precisely from the fact that they are both clearly assignable and delimited, and in this they share with the general negative duty to avoid harming others the necessary characteristics of *circumscription* for a duty which a person can reasonably be required to fulfil.[43]

There is much force in these considerations. Most of us remain unconvinced by philosophical arguments which show that inaction is simply another form of action, and omissions therefore as culpable as commissions. A morality which requires us to go on giving up to the point where our condition is equal to that of the poorest of those we are aiding is a morality for saints and heroes, perhaps, but not for ordinary mortals; and not one, therefore, on which the delivery of basic rights can rely. However, it does not follow from these arguments that there can be *no* general duty to aid the needy, or that such a duty cannot be specified in a form sufficiently circumscribed to meet the criteria outlined above.

Consider an elementary example. All would surely agree that children have a variety of needs which they are unable to meet by themselves, and that a duty therefore falls on adults to aid and protect them. In most cases this responsibility is fulfilled by their parents or other close relatives as a 'special' duty by virtue of their relationship. However, where there is no one alive to perform this duty, or those who have the responsibility are incapable of meeting it, then it falls as a general duty on the community as a whole. Here is an example of a general duty to aid the needy, whose ground lies in the manifest needs of the child.[44] Yet it is neither limitless nor unassignable. It is not a duty to aid all children, but only those for whom no one is able to care as their 'special' duty; they are, so to say, a residual rather than a bottomless category. And the duty falls upon members of the society in which they live as those most appropriately placed to help, just as when someone is in danger of drowning those most appropriately placed to help, and therefore with the duty to do so, are those present at the incident. In the case of children, however, those responsible will typically fulfil their duty, not as individuals in an *ad hoc* manner, but collectively, by establishing arrangements whereby the children are placed in the care of professionals or foster parents, and paid for by a levy on all members capable of contributing. A publicly acknowledged duty so to aid those in need, with whom we stand in no special relationship, forms one of the principles of the modern welfare state.[45]

It is mistaken therefore to assume that, if there is a general duty to aid those in need, it can only be unlimited and unassignable, and so must be either unrealistically burdensome or inadequate to guarantee any universal rights. We incur general duties to aid the needy in a social world already structured with special relationships and special duties, and in which most people meet their

[43] See P. Foot, *Virtues and Vices* (Oxford, Blackwell, 1978); H. L. A. Hart, 'Are there any natural rights?', *Philosophical Review*, 84 (1955), 3–22.

[44] For a thoroughgoing defence of the principle that duties to aid derive from the vulnerability of those aided, not from self-assumed obligations, see R. E. Goodin, *Protecting the Vulnerable* (Chicago, University of Chicago Press, 1985).

[45] Goodin, *Protecting the Vulnerable*, pp. 134–44; see also Plant, *Modern Political Thought*, pp. 284–5.

basic needs for themselves either individually or collectively. As Henry Shue argues in a more recent article:

> One should not leap from universal rights to universal duties ... On the side of duties there can be a division of labour ... For every person with a right, and for every duty corresponding to that right, there must be some agents who have been assigned that duty and who have the capacity to fulfil it. We have no reason to believe, however, that everyone has burdensome duties toward everyone else even if everyone else has meaningful rights.[46]

As the ICESCR recognizes, it is governments that have the overarching duty to ensure a division of labour in the matter of positive duties, and one that is both appropriate to their own societies and sufficient to ensure that the rights are effectively secured. This is an obligation on all states, but one with quasi-legal or contractual status for the 130 (as of 1994) that have ratified the Covenant. As the so-called Limburg principles of interpretation of the Covenant insist, states are 'accountable both to the international community and to their own people for their compliance with the obligations under the Covenant'.[47] In other words, the obligations corresponding to the rights are not merely derivable from a general moral duty, on the part of both individuals and governments, to aid those in need; they are also publicly acknowledged by international agreement.

But what if states are unable to meet their obligation to realize a minimum agenda of basic rights? Whose duty does it then become to assist them, and to aid the deprived to realize their rights? By a logical extension of the general duty to aid those in need, and the principle of a division of labour in fulfilling that duty, it clearly falls to other governments with the resources to do so, coordinated by an international body such as the UN and its agencies. A prior duty to aid those within our own country – whether we argue this on the 'kith and kin' principle, or, more plausibly, from the logic of a world organized into territorial citizenships[48] – does not absolve us of any wider duty. This is indeed publicly acknowledged in internationally agreed aid targets for the developed countries, in their contributions to UN agencies, in the continuous public support for the work of NGOs, in the massive (if spasmodic) public response to emergency appeals, and so on. These may be all insufficient, but the duty is at least generally acknowledged.

A clear answer can thus be given to the objection that economic and social rights remain unanchored by any corresponding duties. The ground of the duty is the same as for the rights themselves: in human needs. The general duty to aid those in need is, however, neither unlimited nor unassignable. It falls in the first instance upon governments, from societal resources, to ensure that basic rights are realized where individuals, families or groups prove insufficient by themselves; and to the international organizations in turn, from the resources of the developed world, to support this effort where national resources prove insufficient. Such duties are widely acknowledged. But are they realizable in practice?

[46] H. Shue, 'Mediating duties', *Ethics*, 98 (1988), 687–704, p. 689.

[47] UN Doc. E/C.4/1987/17, Annex, principle 10.

[48] R. E. Goodin, 'What is so special about our fellow countrymen?', *Ethics*, 98 (1988), 663–86.

Practicalities

The question of the practicability of the corresponding duties is for many the chief stumbling block to a theory of economic and social rights. If the requisite duties cannot be fulfilled, either because the size of the task continually outstrips the resources, or because of constraints on the way existing institutions operate, or both, then the claim that the rights are, or could effectively be made, universal must fail. We may still acknowledge the duties, but only be able to fulfil them in a partial or unpredictable manner, and one that is insufficient to guarantee the relevant claims as *rights*. Moreover, the incommensurability between duty and possible fulfilment may simply erode the will to action or the sense of responsibility altogether.

In addressing this question of practicability, it is difficult not to become schizophrenic. From one point of view – the technical-economic – a joint programme on the part of the international community and national governments to ensure that everyone's basic rights are met, and on a continuing basis, appears eminently practicable. From another point of view – the politico-economic – the difficulties seem equally insuperable. It is this conjunction of the eminently practicable with the seemingly impossible that renders judgements about the feasibility of guaranteeing basic economic and social rights so contradictory, depending upon the standpoint taken.

Let me take each of them in turn. From the technical-economic standpoint, there are now many studies which show that sufficient resources and economic and technical knowledge exist to ensure that the basic rights of practically everyone in the world could be guaranteed within a decade or so, and without huge cost to taxpayers in the developed world. A comparison of the World Bank study of basic needs published in 1981 with the UNDP Human Development Reports from 1990 onwards reveals important continuities over the past decade, as well as changes of emphasis in terminology, proposed methods of resourcing and administrative reforms required.[49]

As far as technical knowledge is concerned, the conclusions of the World Bank's systematic study of experience from different countries about how the basic needs (for food, shelter, primary health care, etc.) of the world's poorest could be met were summarized in its 1981 volume. Meeting these basic needs, it concluded, has to be the subject of specific policy initiatives; each is more effectively addressed in combination with the others than on its own; appropriate technologies have to be selected; policies must be formulated in consultation with the potential beneficiaries; a decentralized administrative structure with effective central support works best. Of the individual 'sectors', shelter, clean water, sanitation and primary health care are the cheapest to guarantee, given the use of appropriate technologies. Food is the most complex, since it involves interactions between agrarian policy, the structure of prices and wages, the form in which the residual guarantee of food security is assured, and other factors. Education is the most expensive, but at the same time the most important for ensuring the effectiveness of the others, and is especially effective when directed at women. In sum, enough experience has been accumulated in many countries and contexts, including problems of

[49] Streeten, *First Things First* for the 1981 World Bank study; UNDP, *Human Development Report, 1990, 1991, 1992, 1993, 1994* (New York, Oxford University Press). Of these the 1992 Report deals with the international context of development.

transition and 'reflexivity', for a programme not to be unattainable through lack of knowledge.[50]

As far as *resources* are concerned, although the funds required to finance such a programme are huge in absolute terms, they are also minuscule when expressed as a percentage of the GNP of the developed economies. The World Bank study put the figure required, if the OECD countries were to fund 50% of the cost, as requiring only an increase in aid from 0.35 to 0.45% per annum of their GNP (i.e. well below the already agreed aid 'target' of 0.7%), if existing aid were progressively redirected towards a basic needs programme.[51] The UNDP report of 1992, while regarding any new resources from OECD taxation as unrealistic, also concludes that a basic programme to meet 'essential human development targets' could be financed from a redirection of existing aid towards the poorest countries and poorest groups, if combined with a progressive conversion of military to development aid, the opening up of OECD markets to Third World goods, and a write-down of international debt.[52]

Sufficient evidence also exists to refute two common misconceptions about a programme to meet basic needs or 'essential human goals'. One is that it would undermine economic growth in the LDCs by redirecting resources to current consumption. Some developing countries are themselves sceptical about setting minimum economic rights standards on the ground that development is a progressive concept, and that the acknowledged 'right to development' cannot imply static levels of attainment.[53] However, the evidence suggests that securing a minimum platform and aiming for progressive levels of development are more likely to be mutually reinforcing than contradictory, in view of the contribution to growth made by investment in human capital. What a basic rights programme does is to alter the pattern of growth and the distribution of its benefits, rather than to undermine it.[54]

A second common misconception is that a strategy to meet basic rights could never keep up with population growth. Again, the evidence suggests that the most effective combination of policies to control population involves the ready availability of contraceptive facilities within a primary health care programme, improved education opportunities for girls, and greater confidence on the part of parents in their children's survival and their own economic security. These are precisely what a basic rights programme would be designed to secure.[55]

From one point of view, then, a programme to guarantee basic economic and social rights looks eminently feasible. From a politico-economic standpoint, however, it looks equally impossible. The structures of power and interest and the forces at work in the international economy and within developing countries themselves pull remorselessly in the opposite direction to

[50] Streeten, *First Things First*, chs 6 and 7.

[51] Streeten, *First Things First*, pp. 174–5.

[52] UNDP, *Human Development Report 1992*, pp. 9 and 89–90; cp. UNDP, *Human Development Report 1994*, pp. 77ff.

[53] R. L. Barsh, 'The right to development as a human right: results of the global consultation', *Human Rights Quarterly*, 13 (1991), 322–38.

[54] Goodin, 'The development-rights trade-off', pp. 33–5; N. Hicks, 'Growth vs. basic needs: is there a trade-off?', *World Development*, 7 (1979), 985–94; Streeten, *First Things First*, ch. 4.

[55] Shue, *Basic Rights*, ch. 4, esp. pp. 101–4.

a basic rights agenda.[56] The relevant features have been frequently rehearsed, and can merely be enumerated here.

1. *International.* The structure and terms of international finance and trade systematically favour the North at the expense of the South, especially of those countries which are heavily dependent on the export of a few primary commodities.[57] The institutions which regulate the international economy (IMF, World Bank, GATT) are controlled by the North, and work to protect the interests of their banks, investment funds and multinational companies. Although the effects of the structural adjustment programmes of the 1980s are hotly contested, the least that can be said of them is that they have failed to protect the poorest from the harmful side-effects of adjustment; the worst, that they have served to intensify the flow of resources from South to North, and to further the erosion of the economic and social rights of the poorest.[58]
2. *Domestic.* The capacity of states in many developing countries to effect basic needs programmes is further constrained by internal factors. Huge inequalities of wealth, especially of landownership, and of access to the state skew policies towards the already advantaged.[59] In many countries a weakly developed sense of public interest renders the state vulnerable to those seeking to use it for merely private benefit. The interests of state personnel themselves bias public expenditure towards prestige projects and military hardware at the expense of basic services. As a consequence the poor often regard the state not merely as indifferent, but actively hostile, to their needs, even under a nominally democratic regime.

From the second standpoint, then, what from the first standpoint seems eminently practicable, appears simply impossible, because none of the responsible agents is sufficiently in control of the factors which would need to be changed for a basic rights programme to be agreed, let alone effectively implemented. Instead these factors provide a cast-iron alibi for each party's inability to meet its obligations. 'The North blames corrupt regimes and poor planning for economic disvelopment, the South blames the World Economic Order.'[60]

In the face of such an impasse, the strategy adopted by the UN Committee on ESCR is to occupy the moral high ground, and expose beneath the evidence

[56] 'Resources are quite adequate to end destitution immediately ... if those in power were determined to do so.' D. Seers, 'North-South: muddling morality and mutuality', *Third World Quarterly*, 2 (1980), 681–93, p. 684.

[57] Even a relatively market-friendly document such as the UNDP *Human Development Report 1994* acknowledges that 'where world trade is completely free and open – as in financial markets – it generally works to the benefit of the strongest. Developing countries enter the market as unequal partners, and leave with unequal rewards' (p. 1). At the same time it points out the market *restrictions* which work to the disadvantage of developing countries (p. 67).

[58] The issue is partly how to assess claims that countries would have been even worse off without structural adjustment. For World Bank studies see L. Squire, 'Poverty and adjustment in the 1980s', *World Bank Policy Research Bulletin*, 2.2 (March–April 1991), 1–5. For a more critical assessment see the Oxfam reports on Africa and Latin America: *Africa: Make Or Break* (Oxford, Oxfam, 1993); *Structural Adjustment and Inequality in Latin America* (Oxford, Oxfam, 1994). For a range of assessments of structural adjustment in Africa see W. van der Geest (ed.), *Negotiating Structural Adjustment in Africa* (London, James Currey for UNDP, 1994).

[59] For comparative figures on inequality of landownership see UNDP, *Human Development Report 1993*, pp. 28–9.

[60] Barsh, 'The right to development as a human right', p. 324.

of inability a deficiency of will. Its many pronouncements recall the signatories of the Covenant to their duty to uphold a minimum agenda of rights regardless of circumstances. 'States parties are obligated, regardless of the level of economic development, to ensure respect for the minimum subsistence rights for all.'[61] The Committee 'draws attention to the obligations devolving upon States parties under the Covenant, whatever their level of development'. 'A State party in which any significant number of individuals is deprived of essential foodstuffs, of essential primary health care, of basic shelter or housing, or of the most basic forms of education is, prima facie, failing to discharge its obligations under the Covenant.'[62] In the absence of the IFIs from the dock, however, since they are not signatories to the Covenant, the Committee is unable to be completely evenhanded in its strictures.

The task of the political theorist at this point is perhaps to exchange the hortatory for the analytical mode, and to explore what might be termed the moral low ground: how people in practice come to acknowledge a responsibility to others through the convergence of duty with self-interest. Behind institutions stand people. If institutions, whether Northern or Southern states or IFIs, are unable to fulfil their responsibilities it is partly because not enough of the people to whom they are accountable are sufficiently convinced of any obligation to aid those in need. How they might become convinced is a complex question; but the history of the development of the welfare state suggests it is a matter of incentives as much as of exhortation or moral leadership.[63]

Two different processes of convergence between duty and self-interest suggest themselves. One, the 'insurance principle', occurs when the same insecurity that afflicts the poor penetrates sufficiently deeply into the ranks of the contented for the latter to discover that they share a common interest in developing or sustaining a system of collective insurance against misfortune or destitution.[64] It may be that a process of rediscovery is now taking place in the advanced economies, as the insecurity generated by the latest phase of capitalism spreads more widely.

If the first process involves an extension of sympathy through the prospect of shared experience, the second is based more on fear. This is the 'boomerang effect', whereby neglect of the deprived returns, through direct or indirect effects, to threaten the interests of the rest. The classic example is the fear of contagion in early Victorian Britain, which fuelled the public health movement, as the wealthy discovered that disease was no respecter of housing zones.[65] Other examples are the discovery that widespread unemployment among young males produces a chronic surge in crime against property and the

[61] UN Doc. E/C.4/1987/17, principle 25.

[62] UN Doc. E/C.12/1990/8, pp. 41, 86.

[63] See R. E. Goodin, *Motivating Political Morality* (Oxford, Blackwell, 1992). For Richard Rorty, posing the motivational issue as one of tension between duty and interest (even group interest) is wholly mistaken. His solution lies in a combination of 'sentimental story-telling' and avoiding 'having children who would be like Thrasymachus and Callicles'. R. Rorty, 'Human rights, rationality, and sentimentality' in Shute and Hurley, *On Human Rights*, pp. 111–34.

[64] Goodin, *Motivating Political Morality*, ch. 3.

[65] E. C. Midwinter, *Victorian Social Reform* (London, Longman, 1968), p. 24. Cf. Carlyle's account of the Irish woman in Edinburgh who was refused help from all charitable institutions, but went on to infect a whole street with typhus. 'She proves her sisterhood: her typhus-fever kills *them*.' T. Carlyle, *Past and Present* (London, Chapman and Hall, 1893), p. 128.

person, which no expansion of the police or the prisons can contain; or that neglect of education retards economic development in a way that affects even the educated to their detriment.[66]

Then there is the 'heavy boomerang', the prospect of social revolution, which did much throughout the past century to reconcile the advantaged to social reform, through fear of something worse. With the collapse of Communism that fear has now subsided, much to the disadvantage of social democracy, for all that the practice of 'actually existing socialism' appeared to discredit it also. Whether new forms of revolutionary movement or social uprising will take place in the future, to provide the spur to reform, is an open question. Equally unpredictable is the point at which the more ruthless strategies of the rich to seal themselves off from the effects of destitution on their own doorstep become politically unsustainable.[67]

Both the processes discussed above, whether operating through fear or the extension of shared experience, have been effective in the past in producing a convergence of principle and self-interest *within* countries. Can they also operate *between* them, across frontiers and at long distances? At present the spillover effects of war, of environmental degradation or pollution, of population increase and migration, may seem too remote and uncertain to convince people of their interdependency at the international level. Yet the fact that these global interdependencies are increasing suggests that the pressures to develop a new global compact and a corresponding reform of international economic institutions to meet the demands of basic economic and social rights will themselves increase rather than diminish in the future, for all their apparent impracticality in the present.

Conclusion

In this paper I have sought to provide a defence of the idea of economic and social rights against its critics, by defining and justifying a minimum agenda of basic rights, and by showing that the corresponding duties are assignable, delimited and, from one point of view at least, practicable. There remains the huge gulf between the promise and its fulfilment. It is here that philosophical critics from Bentham onwards have tended to lose patience with the protagonists of human rights, for trading on an inherent ambiguity in the language of a 'right': between having a morally justifiable entitlement, and having that entitlement legally recognized and enforced. The human rights agenda is not based on sloppy thinking, however, but constitutes a self-conscious project for moving the rights in question from the first status to the second. A final issue to consider is whether the language of human rights itself can be effective as a *persuasive political discourse* in this process.

Compared with other approaches, couching the basic economic and social requirements for human agency, human self-realization, or human development, in the language of *rights* not only has the advantage that such rights enjoy the authority of international recognition and agreement. They also correspond to conceptions widely held among the poor themselves. As Pierre Spitz shows in his historical survey of laws regulating food supply, the concept

[66] For the UK see W. Hutton, *The State We're In* (London, Cape, 1995), ch. 7.

[67] J. K. Galbraith, *The Culture of Contentment* (London, Sinclair-Stevenson, 1992), ch. 14.

of a basic entitlement to food has been widespread in many historical cultures.[68] Similarly, James Scott has shown in his comparative studies of peasant attitudes to exploitation that the guarantee of basic subsistence is much more central to peasant conceptions of justice than the precise percentage of crop appropriated by landlords.[69] Framing such intuitions in terms of human rights provides a language that is both more urgent and more authoritative than alternative discourses of 'human security' or 'basic welfare goals'. It also identifies the deprived as themselves the potential agents of social change, as the active claimants of rights, and thus offers an 'empowering potential which is far greater than any of the "new" terms that seem (temporarily) so compelling to many development specialists ... but which are devoid of any power of mobilization or transformation'.[70]

Expressing basic economic and social requirements in the language of human rights, then, does more than emphasize the obligations of governments or international agencies and their respective publics, or provide a challenge to legal experts to develop justiciable norms to assist their effective implementation; it also offers an internationally authorized discourse to the deprived, to legitimate their own struggles for their realization.

[68] P. Spitz, 'Right to food for peoples and for the people: a historical perspective', in Alston and Tomasevski, *The Right to Food*, pp. 169–86. Spitz points out that in the rarely quoted French Declaration of Rights of 1793, article 21 contained a specific economic right that was absent from the 1789 version: 'society has the duty to ensure the sustenance of the poor either by providing them with work or by giving the means of livelihood to those who are unable to work' (p. 174).

[69] J. C. Scott, *The Moral Economy of the Peasant* (New Haven, Yale University Press, 1976).

[70] Statement by the UN Committee on ESCR, May 1994, to the World Summit on Social Development (typescript), p. 3.

[6]

The Banjul Charter and the African Cultural Fingerprint: An Evaluation of the Language of Duties

MAKAU WA MUTUA*

I. INTRODUCTION

The African Charter on Human and Peoples' Rights (the African Charter),[1] the basis of Africa's continental human rights system, entered into force on October 21, 1986, upon ratification by a simple majority of member states of the Organization of African Unity (OAU).[2] The African Charter has attracted criticism because it departs from the narrow formulations of other regional and international human rights instruments.[3] In particular, it codi-

* Projects Director, Human Rights Program, Harvard Law School. University of Dar-es-Salaam, L.L.B. 1983, L.L.M. 1984; Harvard Law School, L.L.M. 1985, S.J.D. 1987. The author wishes to thank Athena Mutua, Hope Lewis, John Witte, Jr., Henry J. Steiner, David Kennedy, Henry Richardson, and Joe Oloka-Onyango for their insightful comments and suggestions. The author wishes to devote this Article to his three sons: Lumumba, Amani, and Mwalimu, whose duty it is to continue the search for a coherent, just, and defensible African cultural identity.

1. The African Charter on Human and Peoples' Rights, June 27, 1981, OAU Doc. CAB/LEG/67/3/Rev.5 (1981), reprinted in 21 I.L.M. 59 (1982) [hereinafter African Charter].

2. The African Charter, also referred to as the Banjul Charter, was adopted in 1981 by the 18th Assembly of Heads of State and Government of the Organization of African Unity (OAU), the official body of African states. It is known as the Banjul Charter because the final draft was produced in Banjul, the capital of the Gambia. The Charter's sole implementing organ, the African Commission on Human and Peoples' Rights (the African Commission), was established in 1987. The African Commission's eleven members, known as commissioners, are elected by the OAU by secret ballot for a six-year term and serve in their own personal capacities. See African Charter, supra note 1, arts. 31, 33, 36, 45, 21 I.L.M. at 64-65.

3. The major human rights instruments include the trilogy of documents commonly referred to as the International Bill of Rights: (i) the 1948 Universal Declaration of Human Rights, G.A. Res. 217 A(III), U.N. Doc. A/810, at 71 (1948) [hereinafter UDHR]; (ii) the 1966 International Covenant on Civil and Political Rights, G.A. Res. 2200 A(XXI), U.N. GAOR, 21st Sess., Supp. No. 16, at 52, U.N. Doc. A/6316 (1966) [hereinafter ICCPR],

fies the three generations of rights, including the controversial concept of peoples' rights, and imposes duties on individual members of African societies.[4] While a number of scholars have focused attention on apparent tensions between human and peoples' rights, there has been little discussion of the notion of individual duties in the context of the African Charter.[5] Yet a thorough understanding of the meaning of human rights, and the complicated processes through which they are protected and realized, would seem to link inextricably the concepts of human rights, peoples' rights, and duties of individuals. Individual rights cannot make sense in a social and political vacuum, devoid of the duties assumed by indi-

---

what many call the Bible of the human rights movement; and (iii) the 1966 International Covenant on Economic, Social and Cultural Rights, G.A. Res. 2200 A(XXI), U.N. GAOR, 21st Sess., Supp. No. 16, at 49, U.N. Doc. A/6316 (1966) [hereinafter ICESCR]. The last two instruments entered into force in 1976.

Apart from the African Charter, the other major regional human rights instruments include (i) the American Convention on Human Rights, Nov. 22, 1969, 36 O.A.S.T.S. No. 36, at 1, O.A.S. Off. Rec. OEA/Ser. L/V/II.23 Rev.2, reprinted in 9 I.L.M. 673 (1970), the document that anchors the inter-American human rights system; (ii) the [European] Convention for the Protection of Human Rights and Fundamental Freedoms, Nov. 4, 1950, 213 U.N.T.S. 221 (1955); and (iii) the European Social Charter, Oct. 18, 1961, 529 U.N.T.S. 89 (1965), which forms the basis for the European human rights system. See generally Thomas Buergenthal, International Human Rights (1988); Guide to International Human Rights Practice (Hurst Hannum ed., 1992) [hereinafter Human Rights Practice Guide]; United Nations, 1 Human Rights: A Compilation of International Instruments, U.N. Doc. ST/HR/1/Rev.4 (1993).

4. Civil and political rights, the staple of the human rights movement, have been commonly referred to as "first generation" rights, while economic, cultural, and social rights, are called "second generation" rights. In addition to these, the African Charter provides for "peoples' rights," known also as collective or group rights, which include the right of peoples to self-determination, political sovereignty over their natural resources, and the right to development. Buergenthal, supra note 3, at 176-77. One group right, the right to self-determination, is widely recognized and enshrined in article 1 common to both the ICCPR and the ICESCR. ICCPR, supra note 3, art. 1, para. 1; ICESCR, supra note 3, art. 1, para. 1. Chapter II of the African Charter, which imposes various duties on individuals, is that document's most radical contribution to human rights law. See African Charter, supra note 1, arts. 27-29, 21 I.L.M. at 63.

5. For detailed discussions and analyses of the relationships between peoples and human rights in the African Charter, see generally Richard Gittleman, The African Charter on Human and Peoples' Rights: A Legal Analysis, 22 Va. J. Int'l L. 667 (1982); U. Oji Umozurike, The African Charter on Human and Peoples' Rights, 77 Am. J. Int'l L. 902 (1983); Theo van Boven, The Relations Between Peoples' Rights and Human Rights in the African Charter, 7 Hum. Rts. L.J. 183 (1986); Jean-Bernard Marie, Relations Between Peoples' Rights and Human Rights: Semantic and Methodological Distinctions, 7 Hum. Rts. L.J. 195 (1986); Burns H. Weston et al., Regional Human Rights Regimes: A Comparison and Appraisal, 20 Vand. J. Transnat'l L. 585 (1987); Richard Kiwanuka, The Meaning of 'People' in the African Charter on Human and Peoples' Rights, 82 Am. J. Int'l L. 80 (1988).

viduals.[6] This appears to be more true of Africa than any other place. The individualist, narrow formulation of human rights is not sufficient to pull the African continent back from the abyss.[7]

The argument by current reformers that Africa merely needs a liberal democratic, rule-of-law state to be freed from despotism is mistaken. The transplantation of the narrow formulation of Western liberalism cannot adequately respond to the historical reality and the political and social needs of Africa. The sacralization of the individual and the supremacy of the jurisprudence of individual rights in organized political and social society is not a natural, "transhistorical," or universal phenomenon, applicable to all societies, without regard to time and place. The ascendancy of the lan-

6. There seems little doubt that private duties, implied and direct, are contemplated by most human rights instruments. Examples abound. Article 5 of the ICCPR provides, in part, that nothing contained therein can imply "for any state, group or person" any right to limit the rights of others. ICCPR, supra note 3, art. 5. Moreover, individuals can be punished for violations of human rights, as was the case in Nuremburg, given that the Geneva Conventions impose duties on private individuals. See generally Jordan Paust, The Other Side of Right: Private Duties Under Human Rights Law, 5 Harv. Hum. Rts. J. 51-63 (1992).

7. The human rights movement is based on the Western liberal tradition which conceives of the individual as atomistic and alienated from society and the state. Although Jack Donnelly makes a case for other trajectories within the liberal tradition, he concedes that "[t]he 'Western' or 'liberal' conception of human rights is conventionally characterized as resting on a social vision of largely isolated individuals holding (only) property rights and 'negative' civil and political liberties." Jack Donnelly, Human Rights and Western Liberalism [hereinafter Donnelly, Human Rights and Western Liberalism], in Human Rights in Africa: Cross-Cultural Perspectives 31, 31 (Abdullahi A. An-Na'im & Francis M. Deng eds., 1990) [hereinafter Cross-Cultural Perspectives]. This formulation, which this author terms Eurocentric because it grows out of European history and philosophy, sees the human rights corpus merely as an instrument for individual claims against the state. Donnelly argues that this "conventional, or minimalist, conception of liberalism. . . . is only one strand of the liberal tradition of political theory and practice." Id. at 32. In fact, Donnelly posits that there is an "alternative strand that rests on a broader, more subtle—and . . . more coherent and defensible—social vision." Id. In this more radical liberal tradition, Donnelly argues, "individualism is moderated by social values, private property rights are limited rather than absolute, and civil and political rights are coupled with economic and social rights." Id. at 33. It is this strand of liberalism that is the source of the social democratic regimes and the welfare states of the Western industrial democracies.

Notwithstanding Donnelly's alternative insight, it is primarily the conventional strand of liberalism that has dominated the theory and practice of the human rights movement. Scholars and activists in the West, the main authors of the discourse, have articulated a vision that places civil and political rights above other categories of rights. In effect, the human rights movement has become an anti-catastrophe crusade, under the captive leadership of Amnesty International and Human Rights Watch, to contain and control state action against the individual. The practice of human rights by inter-governmental organizations (IGOs), non-governmental organizations (NGOs), and national human rights institutions has been primarily focused on civil and political rights. Economic, social, and cultural rights, while part of the rhetoric of rights, remain severely underdeveloped.

guage of individual rights has a specific historical context in the Western world. The rise of the modern nation state in Europe and its monopoly of violence and instruments of coercion gave birth to a culture of rights to counterbalance the invasive and abusive state.[8] John Locke reduced this thinking to a philosophy in his *Two Treatises of Government.*[9] He argued that each individual, together with his compatriots, contractually transfers to a public authority his individual right to implement the law of nature.[10] But this power is conditional and limited to the state's duty to "protect individual rights and freedoms from invasion and to secure their more effective guarantee."[11] According to Locke, a government that systematically breaches these duties becomes illegitimate. While Locke's conception is the floor—the modern state is more intrusive and pervasive than he imagined—it remains the basic justification for the existence of the state in the West.

The development of the state in Africa is so radically different from its European equivalent that the traditional liberal conception of the relationship between the state and the individual is of limited utility in imagining a viable regime of human rights. The modern African state was imposed on ethno-political communities by European imperialists and did not result from the natural progression or evolution of those societies.[12] Only a handful of modern African states bear any territorial resemblance to the political formations which existed prior to penetration and subjugation by European states.[13] The majority of states were contrived overnight, often dismantling existing ethno-political communities and

---

8. See generally Robert M. Cover, Obligation: A Jewish Jurisprudence of the Social Order, 5 J. L. & Religion 65 (1987). Cover argues that the myth, the jurisprudence of rights, is essential to counterbalance the omnipotent state. This myth "a) establishes the State as legitimate only in so far as it can be derived from the autonomous creatures who trade in their rights for security—i.e., one must tell a story about the States's utility or service to us, and b) potentially justifies individual and communal resistance to the Behemoth." Id. at 69. It is not surprising that Western individuals and movements employ the language of rights in their claims against society or the state. Examples range from civil rights groups to women's organizations and gay and lesbian individuals and groups.

9. John Locke, Two Treatises of Government (Peter Laslett ed., 1988).

10. Id.

11. Donnelly, Human Rights and Western Liberalism, supra note 7, at 34.

12. In 1885 at the Berlin Conference, European powers carved up the map of Africa and created dozens of entirely new countries without regard to existing political entities, ethnic boundaries, economic considerations, historical alliances, or geographic and demographic variables. See Crawford Young, The Heritage of Colonialism, in Africa in World Politics 19, 19 (John W. Harbeson & Donald Rothchild eds., 1991).

13. Only Morocco, Tunisia, Ethiopia, Burundi, Rwanda, Madagascar, Swaziland, Lesotho, and Botswana have any meaningful pre-colonial territorial identities. Id.

their organizational structures. Communities that lived independently of each other were coerced to live together under the newly-created colonial state. Most of these new citizens lacked any instinctual or nationalistic bond to the colonial state. The failure of the successor post-colonial state points to the continued inability of the "unnatural" and forced state to inspire loyalty and distinct national identities.[14] This disconnection, between the people and the modern African state, is not merely a function of the loss of independence or self-governance over pre-colonial political and social structures and the radical imposition of new territorial bounds with unfamiliar citizenry. It is above all a crisis of cultural and philosophical identity: the delegitimation of values, notions, and philosophies about the individual, society, politics, and nature developed over centuries. Severe as these problems are, the crisis of the African state is not insoluble. The purpose of this Article is to imagine and reconfigure a rights regime that could achieve legitimacy in Africa, especially among the majority rural populace, and become the basis for social and political reconstruction. The reconstruction proposed here is not merely that of human rights norms. In order for the proposal to make sense, a reconfiguration of the African state must also be simultaneously attempted. The imposed colonial state, and its successor, the post-colonial state, stand as moral and legal nullities, entities whose salvation partially lies in new map-making in the context of self-determination for Africa's many nationalities, democratization, and, most importantly, historical reconnection with certain pre-colonial ideals. However, the purpose of this Article is not to explore the creation of a new polit-

14. This author has argued elsewhere that "[s]ince citizens lack an instinctual and nationalistic bond to the state, those who become rulers pillage it." Makau wa Mutua, Redrawing the Map along African Lines, Boston Globe, Sept. 22, 1994, at 17 [hereinafter Redrawing the Map]. Furthermore,

> [f]ew Africans owe their allegiance to the emergent state; many identify with an ethnic group—a loyalty that predates colonialism—or the pan-Africanist idea of Africa as home. The colonial state and its successor have been so alienated from the people that the development of national consciousness was not possible.

Id. Other writers have characterized the transformation of the African political and cultural landscape in more modest terms. According to Crawford Young, "the depth and intensity of alien penetration of subordinated societies continues to cast its shadow." Young, supra note 12, at 19-20. He notes further that the

> cultural and linguistic impact [of colonialism] was pervasive, especially in sub-Saharan Africa. Embedded in the institutions of the new states was the deep imprint of the mentalities and routines of their colonial predecessors. Overall, colonial legacy cast its shadow over the emergent African state system to a degree unique among the major world regions.

Id. at 19-20.

ical map, but to reconstruct the human rights corpus. This choice does not imply a hierarchy or ranking. In practice, both paradigms must be simultaneously addressed for the formulation to bear fruit.

For the present purposes, the current human rights movement must be understood as only a piece of the whole. Its roots in the Western liberal tradition necessarily deny it completeness, though not the universality of many of its ideals and norms. To paraphrase the famous metaphor, the gourd is only partially filled by the Western tradition: it falls on other traditions to fill it. On this premise, this Article makes several interrelated arguments. Part II stresses the African notions of human rights which existed prior to colonization and how those notions differed from the contemporary Eurocentric articulation of human rights. In particular, these notions saw the individual social being as the bearer of both rights and duties. Accordingly, Part III asserts that the pre-colonial concept of duty remains a valid means of conceptualizing human rights and, thus, should be the basis for the construction of a regime of unitary, integrated rights regime capable of achieving legitimacy in Africa. Finally, Part IV of this Article presents a vision that strikes a balance between duties and rights. Not only does this vision restrain the runaway individualism of the West, but its also has strong roots in the continent and indeed may be Africa's last hope for reversing societal collapse. The present attempt is not meant to deny the validity of the Western liberal tradition to the human rights corpus, but only to inform it with an African contribution that entwines duties and rights in a society consumed by the socialization of the individual, a concept articulated by the African Charter.

The purpose of this Article is not to find parallel rights in African conceptions of human rights in order to show the equality of African cultures to European ones. Although that is one incidental by-product, this Article did not set out to clothe these parallel rights in the language of rights. In fact, the vindication of rights in Africa had a very different dimension. In the West, the language of rights primarily developed along the trajectory of claims against the state; entitlements which imply the right to seek an individual remedy for a wrong. The African language of duty, however, offers a different meaning for individual/state-society relations: while people had rights, they also bore duties. The resolution of a claim was not necessarily directed at satisfying or remedying an individual wrong. It was an opportunity for society to contemplate the complex web of individual and community duties and rights to seek a balance between the competing claims of the individual and society.

This view is not relativist. It does not advance or advocate the concept of apartheid in human rights or the notion that each cultural tradition has generated its own distinctive and irreconcilable concept of human rights.[15] It proceeds from the position that, although cultural relativism in human rights as an anti-imperial device is admirable, it is a misunderstanding inspired by cultural nationalism. What its proponents see as radically distinctive, irreconcilable traditions also possess ideals which are universal. Most critiques of cultural relativism, on the other hand, are ethnocentric and symptomatic of the moral imperialism of the West.[16] Both extremes only serve to detain the development of a universal jurisprudence of human rights.[17]

In reality, the construction and definition of human rights norms are dynamic and continuous processes. Human rights are not the monopoly or the sole prerogative of any one culture or people, although claims to that end are not in short supply.[18] In one cul-

15. For more detailed views of the concept of cultural relativism in human rights, see generally Jack Donnelly, Universal Human Rights in Theory and Practice (1989) [hereinafter Donnelly, Universal Human Rights]; Raimundo Panikkar, Is the Notion of Human Rights a Western Concept? 120 Diogenes 75 (1982); Adamantia Pollis & Peter Schwab, Human Rights: A Western Construct with Limited Applicability, in Human Rights: Cultural and Ideological Perspectives, (Adamantia Pollis & Peter Schwab eds., 1979) [hereinafter Human Rights Perspectives].

16. Rhoda Howard, a well known Canadian Africanist, refuses to acknowledge that precolonial African societies knew human rights as a concept. She emphasizes that "traditional Africa protected a system of obligations and privileges based on ascribed statuses, not a system of human rights to which one was entitled merely by virtue of being human." Rhoda Howard, Group Versus Individual Identity in the African Debate on Human Rights [hereinafter Howard, Group Versus Individual], in Cross-Cultural Perspectives, supra note 7, at 159, 167. Howard is so fixated with the Western notion of rights attaching only to the atomized individual that she summarily dismisses arguments by African scholars, some of whom could be classified as cultural relativists, that individual rights were held in a social, collective context.

17. Francis Deng disagrees with the view "widely held in the West and accepted or exploited in developing countries, that the concept of human rights is peculiarly Western." Francis M. Deng, A Cultural Approach to Human Rights Among the Dinka, in Cross-Cultural Perspectives, supra note 7, at 261, 261. "[T]o arrogate the concept," writes Deng, "to only certain groups, cultures, or civilizations is to aggravate divisiveness on the issue, to encourage defensiveness or unwarranted self-justification on the part of the excluded, and to impede progress toward a universal consensus on human rights." Id.

18. Donnelly, for example, dismisses cultural relativists and then declares, rather hastily, that "human rights are foreign to such communities [African, Native American, traditional Islamic social systems], which employed other mechanisms to protect and realize human dignity." Donnelly, Universal Human Rights, supra note 15, at 118. Unless the contrary is established, this author assumes that all cultures have evolved moral and ethical standards

ture, the individual may be venerated as the primary bearer of rights; while, in another, individual rights may be more harmonized with the corporate body. Rather than assert the primacy of one over the other, or argue that only one cultural expression and historical experience constitutes human rights, this author views each experience as a contributor to the whole. The process of the construction of universal human rights is analogous to the proverbial description of the elephant by blind men: each, based on his sense of feeling, offers a differing account. However, all the accounts paint a complete picture when put together. As a dynamic process, the creation of a valid conception of human rights must be universal. That is, the cultures and traditions of the world must, in effect, compare notes, negotiate positions, and come to agreement over what constitutes human rights. Even after agreement, the doors must remain open for further inquiry, reformulation, or revision.

II. Human Rights in Pre-colonial Africa: Content and Context

This segment of the Article will explore the validity of both the argument made often by Africans, and the controversy it engenders, that the concept of human rights was not alien to pre-colonial societies and that such notions were the foundation of social and political society. Recent debates, which are primarily interpretive, have focused attention on this divisive theme. They agree on basic behavioral, political, and social characteristics but disagree as to their meaning.[19] There are no easy answers for a number of reasons. In particular, methodological pitfalls exist for any analysis that attempts to address the length and width of sub-Saharan Africa. The sheer size of the continent, and the diversity of African peoples and their societies, defy easy categorization or generalization. Secondly, with regard to human rights, there are very few extant sources of pre-colonial societies. The oral tradition common

as well as norms and processes that protect the dignity and worth of human beings in both their individual and collective personalities. It is these norms and processes—which manifest themselves in all cultures of the world—that germinate the concept of human rights.

19. Timothy Fernyhough, Human Rights and Precolonial Africa, in Human Rights and Governance in Africa 39, 39 (Ronald Cohen et al. eds., 1993) [hereinafter Human Rights and Governance]. Fernyhough notes that this division is ironic because "both groups take as their starting point a precolonial Africa that they agree was precapitalist and predominantly agrarian, relatively decentralized politically, and characterized by communal social relations." Id.

to most of Africa had its own imprecision even before its interruption by the forces of colonialism.

Nevertheless, several broad themes are discernable from the past. It is now generally accepted that the African pre-colonial past was neither idyllic nor free of the abuses of power and authority common to all human societies. However, the despotic and far-reaching control of the individual by the omnipotent state, first perfected in Europe, was unknown.[20] Instead, pre-colonial Africa consisted of two categories of societies: those with centralized authority, administrative machinery, and standing judicial institutions, such as the Zulu and the Ashanti, and those with more communal and less intrusive governmental paraphernalia, such as the Akamba and Kikuyu of Kenya.[21] But a feature common to almost all pre-colonial African societies was their ethnic, cultural, and linguistic homogeneity—a trait that gave them fundamental cohesion.[22]

Had these political societies developed the concept of human rights? Proponents of the concept of human rights in pre-colonial African societies are accused by their opponents of confusing human dignity with human rights.[23] This view holds that the "Afri-

---

20. Although the majority of pre-colonial authorities in Africa were not rigidly stratified, a number of highly centralized states such Buganda and the Nigerian emirates divided society into the repressive categories of nobles, freemen, and slaves. See Rhoda Howard, Evaluating Human Rights in Africa: Some Problems of Implicit Comparisons, 6 Hum. Rts. Q. 160, 175-76 (1984) [hereinafter Howard, Evaluating Human Rights]. Howard errs, however, when she asserts that the "picture of precolonial African social relations on which the communal model is based is inaccurate even regarding the past." Id. at 175. She deliberately fails to admit that highly centralized societies were the exception, not the norm; most were governed by ideals of communitarianism.

21. An examination of pre-colonial societies yields two basic models. A majority of societies, many of which were agricultural, pastoralist or both, were relatively free of rigid social stratification, although age and gender played significant roles in determining both social and political status. A number of others had developed coercive state structures. See generally Eric O. Ayisi, An Introduction to the Study of African Culture (1979); Myer Fortes & Edward Evans-Pritchard, African Political Systems (1940).

22. A basic contradiction between the European nation-state and pre-colonial Africa societies lies in the constitution of political society. In distinguishing what he calls "African cultural-nations" from the modern state, Mojekwu argues that

> [w]hile the European impersonal governments were able to accommodate and control peoples from several ethnic, racial, and cultural origins within the nation-state, African cultural-nations controlled kinship groups within their cultural boundaries. A cultural-nation governed through familial chiefs and elders who shared authority with the community at large.

Chris Mojekwu, International Human Rights: An African Perspective, in International Human Rights: Contemporary Issues 85, 87 (Jack L. Nelson & Vera M. Green eds., 1980). Few pre-colonial African societies were multi-ethnic.

23. Howard, Group Versus Individual, supra note 16, at 165.

can concept of justice," unlike human rights, "is rooted not in individual claims against the state, but in the physical and psychic security of group membership."[24] While it is probably correct to argue that African societies did not emphasize individual rights in the same way that European societies did, it is not a correct presumption to claim that they did not know the conception of individual rights at all.

According to Ronald Cohen, a right is an entitlement:

> At its most basic level, a human right is a safeguarded prerogative granted because a person is alive. This means that any human being granted personhood has rights by virtue of species membership. And a right is a claim to something (by the right-holder) that can be exercised and enforced under a set of grounds or justifications without interference from others. The subject of the right can be an individual or a group and the object is that which is being laid claim to as a right.[25]

Moreover, a brief examination of the norms governing legal, political, and social structures in pre-colonial societies demonstrates that the concept of rights, like that articulated by Cohen, informed the notion of justice and supported a measure of individualism. Two societies which are representative of the two basic organizational paradigms prevalent in pre-colonial Africa illustrate the point. The Akamba of east Africa were symptomatic of the less rigidly organized societies, whereas the Akans of west Africa were characteristic of the more centralized state systems. In Akan thought, the individual had both descriptive and normative characteristics.[26] Both endowed the person with individual rights as well

24. Id. at 166. Howard sees no middle ground between individual and group consciousness. She writes, incredibly, that for Africans to "assert their human rights as individuals would be unthinkable and would undercut their dignity as group members." Id.

25. Ronald Cohen, Endless Teardrops: Prolegomena to the Study of Human Rights in Africa, in Human Rights and Governance, supra note 19, at 3, 4. Wiredu defines a right as a "claim that people are entitled to make on others or on society at large by virtue of their status." Kwasi Wiredu, An Akan Perspective on Human Rights, in Cross-Cultural Perspectives, supra note 7, at 243, 243.

26. Wiredu, supra note 25, at 243. Akans believed that each individual had intrinsic value and was entitled to a measure of basic respect. But individuals were also members of matrilineal kinship lineages which generated duties and obligations. A person could enhance his or her "individuality" or "personhood" by executing duties such as participating in public works and sustaining a prosperous household. Conversely, if one failed to make these contributions, their personhood diminished. This "normative layer" in the conception of an individual bears obligations, but it is also "matched by a whole

as obligations. Similarly, the Akamba believed that "all members were born equal and were supposed to be treated as such beyond sex and age."[27] The belief prevailed in both societies that, as an inherently valuable being, the individual was naturally endowed with certain basic rights.

Akan political society was organized according to the principle of kinships. A lineage of those who were descended from the same ancestress formed the basic political unit. Adults in each lineage elected an elder. All lineage heads, in turn, formed the town council which was chaired by a chief who, though chosen according to descent, was in part elected.[28] The chief, however, could not rule by fiat, because decisions of the council were taken by consensus. Moreover, council decisions could be criticized publicly by constituents who found them unacceptable. As Wiredu explains, there was no "doubt about the right of the people, including the elders, to dismiss a chief who tried to be oppressive."[29]

Among the Akamba, individuals joined the elders council, the most senior rank in Akamba society, after demonstrating commitment to the community and responsibility in personal matters. Maintaining a stable household, which included a spouse or spouses and children, was a necessary precondition. The council was a public forum which made decisions by consensus. Although

---

series of rights that accrue to the individual simply because he lives in a society in which everyone has those obligations." Id. at 247.

27. Joseph Muthiani, Akamba From Within 84 (1973). While all "people were considered equal in status as human beings" everyone was expected to show strangers "special generosity." Id. at 18. The age-gradation on which the Akamba were organized was a functional structure based on the level of physical maturity. Equality and democracy were required within each age grade. Women had their own comparable but separate prestige structure which, however, was rarely consulted by the council of elders in matters of public concern. Id. at 80-82.

28. Wiredu, supra note 25, at 248-49. On occasion, an election was necessary to determine who in the royal lineage was the rightful heir. The town was the basic unit of government among the Akans. Several Akan towns could group together to form larger governmental units.

29. Id. at 251 ("The stool was the symbol of chiefly status, and so the installation of a chief was called enstoolment and his dismissal destoolment."). The "destooling" of a chief was governed by certain processes and rules. Charges would be filed and investigations conducted before a decision could be reached. Id. On rules governing a chieftainship, see Ayisi, supra note 21, at 48. Further evidence of democratic governance in traditional African society is offered by Kobia's description of the political organization among the Meru of Kenya. Members of the *njuri ncheke*, the supreme council of elders, were "very carefully elected and had to be individuals of unquestionable integrity and in good standing with the society." Samuel Kobia, The Quest for Democracy in Africa 12 (1993). The chair of the *njuri ncheke*, which held legislative and judicial powers, "rotated among the *agwe*," leaders of the six sub-groups of the Meru nation. Id.

the Akamba resented any social organization with a central authority, the council's services included the legislation of public norms and customs.[30] These two examples demonstrate that individuals in pre-colonial society had a right to political participation in determining by whom and through what policies to be ruled.

Much of the discussion about whether pre-colonial societies knew of and enforced individual human rights has taken place in the absence of considered studies of, and reference to, judicial processes in those societies. A preliminary examination of both the Akan and Akamba societies strongly indicates individual-conscious systems of justice. With respect to the Akamba, a party to a complaint appeared before the council of elders in the company of his jury, a selection of individuals who enjoyed the party's confidence. Unlike Western-style jurors, the Akamba did not hand down a verdict, but advised the party on how to plead and what arguments to put forth to win the case. They had to be steeped in Kamba law, customs, and traditions. The threat of the administration of *kithitu*, the Kamba oath, which was believed to bring harm to those who lied, encouraged truthfulness.[31] After presentations by parties, the elders would render judgement or give counsel on the appropriate settlement. Each offense carried a punishment: murder was compensated by the payment of over ten head of cattle; rapists were charged goats; assaults, depending on their seriousness, could cost over ten head of cattle; adultery was punishable by the payment of at least a goat and bull; and an arsonist was required to build his victim a new house or replace the lost property. Individual rights to cultivated land were also recognized and protected.[32] These elaborate punishments present just one indication of the seriousness with which Kamba society took individual rights to personal security, property, marriage, and the dignity and integrity of the family.

In Akan society, the principle of innocent-until-proven-guilty was deeply embedded in social consciousness. According to Wiredu, "it was an absolute principle of Akan justice that no

30. Muthiani, supra note 27, at 83.

31. Id. at 85; see also Charles W. Hobley, Ethnology of the A-Kamba and Other East African Tribes 78 (1971).

32. Hobley, supra note 31, at 78-79. Cattle were highly valued as a measurement of wealth. Among the Maasai, another east African people, the murder of a man was compensated by the fixed fine of forty-nine head of cattle. It is interesting to note that no fine was set for the murder of women because the Maasai almost never murdered women, due to the belief that ill-luck would strike the murderer. See S.S. Ole Sankan, The Maasai 14 (1971).

human being could be punished without trial."[33] The Akans, like the Akamba, also recognized a wide range of individual rights: murder, assault, and theft were punished as violations of the person.[34]

For those who deny the recognition of human rights in pre-colonial societies, it must come as a strange irony that the human rights corpus shares with pre-colonial Africa the importance of personal security rights. The right to life, for example, was so valued that the power over life and death was reserved for a few elders and was exercised "only after elaborate judicial procedure, with appeals from one court to another, and often only in cases of murder and manslaughter."[35] This respect for human life was not an aberration. Fernyhough notes that much of Africa is characterized by a "preoccupation with law, customary and written, and with legal procedure."[36] He adds that the Amhara of Ethiopia, for example, have historically relished litigation and the lengthy cross-examination of witnesses. Whether a society was highly centralized or not, "there existed elaborate rules of procedure intended to protect the accused and provide fair trials."[37] The protection of individual rights was of preeminent importance to pre-colonial societies.

Many of the Akamba and Akan socio-political norms and structures were common to other pre-colonial ethno-political entities or cultural-nations. This Article refers to these shared basic values as the index of the African cultural fingerprint, that is, a set of institutional and normative values governing the relationship between individuals, the society, and nature. To be sure, the fingerprint belongs to Africa although it is also human and, thus, aspects of it reveal universal characteristics. In the search for the definition of the continent, for what sets it apart from Asia and Europe or the

---

33. Wiredu, supra note 25, at 252 (emphasis added). He notes, further, that neither at the "lineage level nor at any other level of Akan society could a citizen be subjected to any sort of sanctions without proof of wrongdoing." Id. Even dead bodies were tried posthumously before a symbolic sentence could be imposed.

34. See generally Ayisi, supra note 21, at 64-70.

35. Fernyhough, supra note 19, at 56.

36. Id. at 61. See generally Ideas and Procedures in African Customary Law (Max Gluckman ed., 1969).

37. Fernyhough, supra note 19, at 62. For example, in the Tio kingdom in present-day Brazzaville, the Congo, "as elsewhere in Africa, a strong tradition of jurisprudence existed, with specific rulings for penalties cited as precedents, such as levels of fines for adultery". Id. Among the Akamba, for instance, the offense of assault carried numerous fines, which varied depending on the degree of assault and whether it resulted in the loss of a limb or limbs. See Hobley, supra note 31, at 79.

Americas, some writers have labelled the cultural and social patterns distinctive to the continent as the "African personality."[38] Léopold Sédar Senghor, for one, called it negritude or "the manner of self-expression of the black character, the black world, black civilization," while Aimé Césaire described it simply as "recognition of the fact of being black, and the acceptance of that fact, of our destiny of black, of our history and our culture."[39] Julius Nyerere named it *ujamaa*, the Kiswahili term for African socialism.[40] The principles and ideals common to all these conceptions are, according to the author's own observations of various African societies, *respect* for, and *protection* of, the individual and individuality within the family and the greater socio-political unit; *deference* to age because a long life is generally wise and knowledgeable; *commitment* and *responsibility* to other individuals, family, and community; *solidarity* with fellow human beings, especially in times of need; *tolerance* for difference in political views and personal ability; *reciprocity* in labor issues and for *generosity*; and *consultation* in matters of governance.[41] As aptly put by Cohen,

---

38. See generally Joseph Ki-Zerbo, African Personality and the New African Society, in Independent Black Africa: the Politics of Freedom 46-59 (William J. Hanna ed., 1964).

39. Léopold S. Senghor, *Problématique de la négritude*, in *Liberté 3: Négritude et civilisation de l'universel* 269-70 (1977), quoted in Janet G. Vaillant, Black, French, and African: A Life of Léopold Sédar Senghor 244 (1990). The concept of "negritude" was initially coined by Aimé Césaire and Léopold Sédar Senghor as a reaction to white racism of the French variety. Under the philosophy of negritude, "collective organizations enfold the individual in Africa. Yet he is not crushed. What the African knows, Senghor points out, is that the realization of the human personality lies less in the search for singularity than in the development of his potential through participation in a community." Id. at 257. It emphasizes the importance of the family, nuclear and extended, the role of democratic, consensual decision-making with the community through the council of elders, and respect for nature.

40. The concept of *ujamaa*, the Kiswahili concept for kinship, was based on three prongs: (i) respect, where each family member recognized the place and rights of others within the family; (ii) common ownership of property, that all must have the same basic necessities; and (iii) obligation to work, that every family member has the right to eat and to shelter but also the obligation to work. See Goran Hyden, Beyond Ujamaa in Tanzania: Underdevelopment and an Uncaptured Peasantry 98 (1980).

41. Ki-Zerbo, supra note 38. In her work on family structures, Sudarkasa groups the cultural factors that account for the cohesion of the African family into four principles: respect, restraint, responsibility, and reciprocity. These principles create a complex balance of rights and duties within the family structure. See Niara Sudarkasa, African and Afro-American Family Structure: A Comparison, 11 Black Scholar 37, 50 (Nov./Dec. 1980); see also Josiah Cobbah, African Values and the Human Rights Debate: An African Perspective, 9 Hum. Rts. Q. 309-31 (1987). Special mention must be made of the importance of generosity in traditional society. As noted by Kobia, there was a "mutual caring for one another, especially strangers and travellers." Kobia, supra note 29, at 13. It was, for example, a "cardinal custom" in every household to prepare enough food for the

> [m]any African cultures value the group—one should never die alone, live alone, remain outside social networks unless one is a pariah, insane, or the carrier of a feared contagious disease. Corporate kinship in which individuals are responsible for the behavior of their group members is a widespread tradition. *But in addition, the individual person and his or her dignity and autonomy are carefully protected in African traditions, as are individual rights to land, individual competition for public office, and personal success.*[42]

Both Nyerere and Wai have argued, separately, that pre-colonial societies supported individual welfare and dignity and did not allow gross inequalities between members.[43] To buttress his claim that African societies "supported and practiced human rights," Wai argues that the rulers were bound by traditional checks and balances to limit their power and guarantee a "modicum of social justice and values concerned with individual and collective rights."[44] Legesse emphasizes the importance of distributive justice in "formally egalitarian," as well as hierarchical, societies to ensure that "individuals do not deviate so far from the norm that they overwhelm society".[45] Wiredu likewise tabulates a list of rights and responsibilities borne by the Akans in the pre-colonial era. These included rights to political participation, land, and religion, as well as the duty to defend the nation.[46] Fernyhough though not sub-

---

unexpected stranger. Id. Even in today's economic difficulties, Africans—rural and urban—generally offer food to strangers and visitors.

42. Cohen, supra note 25, at 14 (emphasis added). For pre-colonial human rights conceptions in Africa, see also Tunji Abayomi, Continuities and Changes in the Development of Civil Liberties Litigation in Nigeria, 22 U. Tol. L. Rev. 1035, 1037-41 (1991); Fasil Nahum, African Contribution to Human Rights, Paper presented at the Seminar on Law and Human Rights in Development, Gaborone, Botswana, May 24-28, 1982 (on file with author); Nana Kusi Appea Busia, Jr., The Status of Human Rights in Pre-colonial Africa: Implications for Contemporary Practices, in Africa, Human Rights, and the Global System: The Political Economy of Human Rights in a Changing World 225-50 (Eileen McCarthy-Arnolds et al., 1994) [hereinafter Political Economy].

43. See generally Dunstan M. Wai, Human Rights in Sub-Saharan Africa, in Human Rights Perspectives, supra note 15, at 115-44; Julius Nyerere, Essays on Socialism (1968).

44. Wai, supra note 43, at 116. He notes, further, that channels for political participation existed in which "[d]iscussion was open and those who dissented from the majority opinion were not punished . . . . There was a clear conception of freedom of expression and association." Id. at 117.

45. Asmaron Legesse, Human Rights in African Political Culture, in The Moral Imperatives of Human Rights: A World Survey 123, 125 (Kenneth W. Thompson ed., 1980).

46. See generally Wiredu, supra note 25.

scribing to a unique African concept of human rights, has outlined many of the rights protected in pre-colonial societies, including the rights to life, personal freedom, welfare, limited government, free speech, conscience, and association.[47] Many of these rights were protected in complex processes of interaction between the individual and the community.

Thus far, this Article has identified and elaborated human rights ideals which existed in pre-colonial societies. However, as in other cultures, notions or practices that contradict concepts of human dignity and human rights also existed, some particularly severe. Among the Akamba, for example, a suspect in a serious crime could be tried by a fire or water ordeal if he did not admit guilt.[48] When a chief died in Akan society, a common citizen's life would be taken so that he could "accompany" the chief and "attend" to him on his "journey to the land of the dead."[49] This practice of human sacrifice was a clear abrogation of the right to life, even by Akan norms which attached an intrinsic value to every individual. Speech and dissent rights of non-adults or minors were also severely restricted.[50] The discriminatory treatment of women—by exclusion from decision-making processes and the imposition of certain forms of labor based on gender—in the home and outside of it flew in the face of the concept of gender equality.[51] However, these practices which were inimical to human rights are not peculiar to Africa; all cultures suffer from this duality of the good and the bad.

A number of Western academics have attacked the index of the African cultural fingerprint and the concept it represents—the African contribution to the human rights corpus—as false and erroneous. In an impassioned critique of scholars she regards as African cultural relativists, Howard notes that although "relatively homogeneous, undifferentiated simple societies of pre-colonial Africa" had "effective means for guaranteeing what is now known

47. See generally Fernyhough, supra note 19; Lakshman Marasinghe, Traditional Conceptions of Human Rights in Africa, in Human Rights and Development in Africa 32 (Claude Welch & Ronald Meltzer eds., 1984).

48. In the fire ordeal, the suspect would be asked to lick a red hot sword to prove his innocence. Hobley, supra note 31, at 81.

49. Wiredu, supra note 25, at 258.

50. Id. at 259.

51. In pre-colonial Africa, women were primarily responsible for housework including child care. Men generally handled "public" affairs such as security and governance of the community.

as human rights,"[52] there was nothing specifically African about them. Such a model, which she calls the communitarian ideal, "represents typical agrarian, precapitalist social relations in non-state societies."[53] Elsewhere, Howard argues that industrialization has dismantled what she refers to as the peasant worldview, or communitarian ideal, and replaced it with "values of secularism, personal privacy, and individualism."[54]

Donnelly, in many respects Howard's ideological counterpart, concedes that while societies based on the communitarian ideal existed at one point in Africa, they are now the exception. He dismisses the notion that pre-colonial societies knew the concept of human rights; an argument he thinks moot because the communitarian ideal has been destroyed and corrupted by the "teeming slums" of non-Western states, the money economy, and "Western" values, products, and practices.[55] In effect, both Donnelly and Howard believe that human rights are only possible in a post-feudal state, and that the concept was alien to specific pre-capitalist traditions and ideals such as Buddhism, Islam, or pre-colonial African societies. In other words, these traditions can make no normative contribution to the human rights corpus. But the other implausible suggestion derived from these positions is that societies—governed under a centralized modern state—necessarily Westernize through industrialization and urbanization. Moreover,

52. Howard, Evaluating Human Rights, supra note 20, at 176.

53. Id. at 176. Howard attempts to explain away the index or the African notions of rights and duties by analogizing the simplicity of feudal Europe to pre-colonial Africa. In "closed-village societies of premodern Europe, we would also discover that people thought of themselves more as members of their own local groups than as individuals, finding a sense of identity by fulfilling their assigned roles rather than by fulfilling 'themselves.' " Id. To her, what some writers "view as essentially different African and Western social structures and ways of thinking are actually differences between relatively simple and relatively complex societies." Id. In other words, Howard believes that pre-industrial African societies could not generate the complex concept of human rights.

54. Howard, Group Versus Individual, supra note 16, at 170. Howard believes that the "African" worldview, which is "peasant" and "traditional," must give way to the "Western" worldview, which is "urban" and "modern" and anchored around the individual. She cites Kenya and Nigeria, the "more developed economies of contemporary Africa" as examples of societies where the "traditional concept of solidarity is giving way to individualism." Id.

55. Donnelly, Universal Human Rights, supra note 15, at 119. He writes, further, that "[i]n the Third World today we see most often not the persistence of traditional culture in the face of modern intrusions, or even the development of syncretic cultures and values, but rather a disruptive 'Westernization', cultural confusion, or the enthusiastic embrace of 'modern' practices and values." Id.

such societies become fertile ground for the germination of human rights.

Donnelly and Howard dismiss with too much haste the argument that many Africans are still influenced by pre-colonial norms and notions. They assume, apparently without adequate research, that the old ways have been eroded by modernization. The examples that Howard gives, those of Kenya and Nigeria, two of the "more developed" economies on the continent, in fact point in the opposite direction: that in spite of the ubiquity of the centralized modernizing state, kinship ties and group-centered forms of consciousness still influence growing urban populations. Matters concerning marriage, birth, and death are still supported by extensive family and kinship networks. This is evident even among the peoples of South Africa and Zambia, Africa's most urbanized countries. Fernyhough, correctly finds "Howard's assessment of the new culture of modernity, like her new 'modern' African, strangely unsophisticated and lacking in sensitivity."[56] It is difficult, if not impossible, he adds, to "measure individuation or judge changing worldviews by counting radios and cinemas."[57] Without a doubt, pre-colonial values have been undermined and deeply affected by the forces of change. But it is difficult to believe that this process will completely invalidate them, just as it is unlikely that the modernization of Japan, China, and Saudi Arabia will completely destroy the cultural norms and forms of consciousness evolved through Buddhism and Islam.

Donnelly and Howard face other problems as well. The first difficulty, and perhaps the most troublesome, is the implication in their works that only European liberalism—a philosophy they seem to think inevitable under modernization—can be the foundation for the concept of human rights. Although Donnelly and Howard would deny it, this argument in effect destroys any claim of universality because it places the concept of human rights exclusively within a specific culture. Unless they believe that the ideals of liberalism are inherently universal, it is impossible to reconcile their assertion that the concept of human rights is universal, while at the same time assigning to it uniqueness and cultural specificity.

The second difficulty, which is an extension of the first, is the implied duty on Westerners to impose the concept of human rights on non-European cultures and societies because it is a universal

56. Fernyhough, supra note 19, at 49.
57. Id.

concept that all societies must accept for their own good. Seen from other cultural perspectives, such a view barely masks the historical pattern by the West—first realized through colonialism—to dominate the world by remaking it for the benefit and in the image of Europe.

This conflict between Howard and Donnelly, on the one hand, and their opponents, on the other, is summed up beautifully by Fernyhough who illustrates how politicized the debate about the origin of the concept and content of human rights has become:

> From one perspective the human rights tradition was quite foreign to Africa until Western, "modernizing" intrusions dislocated community and denied newly isolated individuals access to customary ways of protecting their lives and human dignity. Human rights were alien to Africa precisely because it was precapitalist, preindustrial, decentralized, and characterized by communal forms of social organization. From the opposing viewpoint there is a fundamental rejection of this as a new, if rather subtle, imperialism, an explicit denial that human rights evolved only in Western political theory and practice, especially during the American and French revolutions, and not in Africa.[58]

Fernyhough adds, and this author agrees, that the protest of those who reject the chauvinistic view of the West articulate the "very plausible claim that human rights are not founded in Western values alone but may also have emerged from very different and distinctive African cultural milieus."[59] It is impossible to sustain the argument made by Donnelly and Howard because of its internal inconsistency and ethnocentric, moral arrogance. Conversely, African writers who claim a distinctively African concept of human rights exaggerate its uniqueness. By implication they make the point that such a concept could not have any universal application, a position which fails to recognize that concepts of human dignity—the basis of a concept of human rights—are inherent in all *human* societies. As Fernyhough notes:

58. Id. at 40 (citations omitted).

59. Id. at 40-41. To argue, as Donnelly and Howard do, that the individual in precolonial African societies was not entitled, in certain circumstances, to be left alone—for that is what the concept of human rights is partially about—betrays gross and surprising ignorance about African societies.

> Thus Donnelly and Howard contend that in pre-colonial Africa, as in most non-Western and preindustrial societies, forms of social and political organization rendered the means to attain human dignity primarily through duties and obligations, often expressed in a communally oriented social idiom and realized within a redistributive economy. Yet both reject with unwarranted emphasis the notion that in the search for guarantees to uphold human life and dignity precolonial Africans formulated or correlated such claims to protection in terms of human rights.[60]

It is indeed the notion, common to all societies, that human beings are special and worthy of protection that distinguishes humans from animals. The dogged insistence, even in the face of evidence to the contrary, on the exclusive or distinctive "possession" of human rights has no real place in serious scholarship; the only purpose of such a claim could only lie either in the desire to assert cultural superiority or to deny it. It would be more fruitful to vigorously study other cultures and seek to understand how they protect—and also abuse—human rights.

Above all else, the view of the ethnocentric universalist is at best counterproductive. It serves only to alienate state authorities who would purposefully manipulate concepts in order to continue their repressive practices. How are human rights to be realized universally if cultural chauvinists insist that only their version is valid? Through coercion of other societies or modern civilizing crusades? The only hope for those who care about the adherence by all communities to human rights is the painstaking study of each culture to identify norms and ideals that are in consonance with universal standards. Only by locating the basis for the cultural legitimacy of certain human rights and mobilizing social forces on that score can respect for universal standards be forged. It would be ridiculous, for example, for an African state to claim that, on the basis of African culture, it could detain its own citizens without trial. As An-Na'im succinctly explains:

> Enhancing the cultural legitimacy for a given human right should mobilize political forces within a community, inducing those in power to accept accountability for the implementation or enforcement of that right. With internal cultural legitimacy, those in power could no longer

60. Id. at 39.

> argue that national sovereignty is demeaned through compliance with standards set for the particular human right as an external value. Compliance with human rights standards would be seen as a legitimate exercise of national sovereignty and not as an external limitation.[61]

III. NO RIGHTS WITHOUT DUTIES: AN AFRICAN DIALECTIC

Except for the African Charter's clawback clauses[62] and provisions concerning peoples' rights, much of the criticism of the Charter has been directed at its inclusion of duties on individuals.[63] This criticism, which this author shared at one point, appears to be driven primarily by the gross and persistent violations of human rights in post-colonial African states and the fear that vesting more power in the states can only result in more abuses.[64] This fear aside, this Article will examine the concept of duty in pre-colonial African societies and demonstrate its validity in conceptualizing a unitary, integrated conception of human rights in which the extreme individualism of current human rights norms is tempered by the individual's obligation to the society.

Capturing the view of many Africans, Okere has written that the "African conception of man is not that of an isolated and abstract individual, but an integral member of a group animated by a spirit

61. Abdullahi A. An-Na'im, Problems of Universal Cultural Legitimacy for Human Rights, in Cross-Cultural Perspectives, supra note 7, 331, 332.

62. Clawback clauses qualify rights and permit a state to restrict them to the extent permitted by domestic law. Their purpose, apparently, is to place vague constraints on government action against the individual. For an example, article 6 of the African Charter provides, in part, that "[e]very individual shall have the right to liberty and to the security of his person. No one may be deprived of his freedom *except for reasons and conditions previously laid down by law*." African Charter, supra note 1, art. 6, 21 I.L.M. at 60 (emphasis added). The Charter has also been criticized for the weaknesses inherent in its enforcement mechanisms. See Cees Flinterman & Evelyn Ankumah, The African Charter on Human and Peoples' Rights, in Human Rights Practice Guide, supra note 3, at 159, 167-69. See generally N.R.L. Haysom, The African Charter: Inspirational Document or False Start, paper presented at the Bill of Rights Conference, Victoria Falls, Zimbabwe, Dec. 10-14, 1994; Olosula Ojo & Amadu Sessay, The OAU and Human Rights: Prospects for the 1980s and Beyond, 8 Human Rights Quarterly, 89 (No. 1 1994).

63. See, e.g., Flinterman & Ankumah, supra note 62, at 166-67; Makau wa Mutua, The African Human Rights System in a Comparative Perspective: The Need for Urgent Reformulation, 5 Legal F. 31, 33 (1993) [hereinafter African Human Rights System]; Amnesty International, Amnesty International's Observations on Possible Reform of the African Charter on Human and Peoples' Rights (1993).

64. Mutua, African Human Rights System, supra note 63, at 32. For duties imposed on individuals, see African Charter, supra note 1, arts. 27-29, 21 I.L.M. at 63.

of solidarity."[65] Keba Mbaye, the renown African jurist, has stated that in Africa "laws and duties are regarded as being two facets of the same reality: two inseparable realities."[66] This philosophy has been summed up by Mbiti as well: "I am because we are, and because we are therefore I am."[67] According to this view, individuals are not atomistic units "locked in a constant struggle against society for the redemption of their rights."[68] The Dinka concept of *cieng*, for example, "places emphasis on such human values as dignity, integrity, honor, and respect for self and others, loyalty and piety, compassion and generosity, and unity and harmony."[69] But *cieng* not only attunes "individual interests to the interests of others; it requires positive assistance to one's fellow human beings."[70] Among the Bantu peoples of east and southern Africa, the concept of a person, *mundu* in Kikamba or *mtu* in Kiswahili, is not merely descriptive; it is also normative and refers to an individual who lives in peace and is helpful to his community.[71] Léopold Senghor, then president of Senegal, captured this view at a meeting of African legal experts in 1979:

> Room should be made for this African tradition in our Charter on Human and Peoples' Rights, while bathing in our philosophy, which consists in not alienating the subordination of the individual to the community, in co-existence, in giving everyone a certain number of rights and duties.[72]

65. B. Obinna Okere, The Protection of Human Rights in Africa and the African Charter on Human Rights and Peoples' Rights: A Comparative Analysis with the European and American Systems, 6 Hum. Rts. Q. 141, 148 (1984).

66. International Commission of Jurists, Human and Peoples' Rights in Africa and the African Charter 27 (1986).

67. The individual's needs, rights, joys, and sorrows are woven into a social tapestry that denies singular individuality. John Mbiti, African Religions and Philosophy 141 (1970).

68. Kiwanuka, supra note 5, at 82.

69. Deng, supra note 17, at 266.

70. Id.

71. The word Bantu consists of *ntu*, a root, which means *human-ness*. Quite often, speakers of Kikamba or Kiswahili will rhetorically ask of an abusive person if he is or has become an animal. An individual is not a *mundu* or a *mtu*, and loses his human-ness if he abuses or mistreats fellow community members.

72. Address of President Léopold Sédar Senghor of Senegal to the Meeting of Experts for the Preparation of the Draft African Charter on Human and Peoples' Rights, Dakar, Senegal (Nov. 28-Dec. 8, 1979), OAU Doc. CAB/LEG/67/3/Rev.1, at 6; also reprinted in Philip Kunig et al., Regional Protection of Human Rights by International Law: The Emerging African System 123 (1985) [hereinafter Emerging African System].

In practical terms, this philosophy of the group-centered individual evolves through a series of carefully taught rights and responsibilities. At the root were structures of social and political organization, informed by gender and age, which served to enhance solidarity and ensure the existence of the community into perpetuity. The Kikuyu of Kenya, for example, achieved a two-tiered form of community organization: at the base was the family group composed of blood relatives, namely a man and his wife or wives, their children, and grand-children, and often great grand-children; the second tier consisted of the clan, a combination of several family groups bearing the same name and believed to have descended from one ancestor.[73] Social status and prestige were based on the execution of duties within a third tier: the age-group. Marriage conferred eligibility for the elders council, the governing body.[74] Like the Kikuyu, the Akamba were organized in similar lineages and age-groups, culminating in the elders council, the supreme community organ.[75] The Akan organizational chart also was similar.[76]

Relationships, rights, and obligations flowed from these organizational structures, giving the community cohesion and viability. Certain obligations, such as the duty to defend the community and its territory, attached by virtue of birth and group membership. In the age-grading system of the Akamba, for example, each able-bodied male had to join the *anake* grade which defended the community and made war.[77] In return for their services, the warriors were allowed to graduate into a more prestigious bracket, whereby others would defend them and their property thereafter. The expectations were similar among the Akans:

> But if every Akan was thus obligated by birth to contribute to defense in one way or another, there was also the complementary fact that he had a right to the protection of his person, property, and dignity, not only in his own state but also outside it. And states were known to go to war to secure the freedom of their citizens abroad or avenge their mistreatment.[78]

---

73. Jomo Kenyatta, Facing Mount Kenya 1-2 (1953); see also H.E. Lambert, Kikuyu Social and Political Institutions (1965).
74. Kenyatta, supra note 73, at 200.
75. Muthiani, supra note 27, at 80-85.
76. See generally Wiredu, supra note 25.
77. Muthiani, supra note 27, at 82.
78. Wiredu, supra note 25, at 249.

Defense of the community, a state-type right exacted on those who came under its protection, was probably the most serious positive public obligation borne by young men. The commission of certain offenses, such as murder, treason, and cowardice, were also regarded as public offenses or crimes against the public dimension of the community or state, imposing negative public duties on the individual. But most individual duties attached at the family and kinship levels and were usually identifiable through naming: an aunt was expected to act like a mother, an uncle like a father.[79] This is the basis of the saying, found in many African cultures, that it takes a whole village to raise a child.[80] As Cobbah correctly explains, the naming of individuals within the kinship structure "defines and institutionalizes" the family member's required social role. These roles, which to the Western outsider may appear to be only of morally persuasive value, are "essentially rights which each kinship member customarily possesses, and duties which each kinship member has toward his kin."[81] Expressed differently, "the right of one kinship member is the duty of the other and the duty of the other kinship member is the right of another.[82] Sudarkasa and Cobbah thematically group the principles tying the kinship system together around respect, restraint, responsibility, and reciprocity.[83] In a very real sense, "entitlements and obligations form the very basis of the kinship system."[84]

The consciousness of rights and correlative duties is ingrained in community members from birth. Through every age-grade, the harmonization of individual interests with those of the grade is instilled unremittingly. As Kenyatta remarked, the age-group is a

79. In Africa, "the extended family unit, like family units in nearly all societies, assigns each member a social role that permits the family to operate as a reproductive, economic and socialization unit." Cobbah, supra note 41, at 320. But unlike the West, kinship terminologies in Africa relate to actual duties and obligations borne by members. Furthermore, the terminologies are more encompassing: aunts and mothers, for example, have similar roles within the kinship unit, regardless of biological parentage. The same is true of uncles and older cousins. Id.

80. Most pre-colonial African villages were be inhabited by people related through blood or marriage.

81. Cobbah, supra note 41, at 321.

82. Id.

83. This matrix of group solidarity revolves around respect, based on seniority in age; restraint or the balancing of individual rights with the requirements of the group; responsibility, which requires commitment to work with and help others in return for security; and reciprocity through which generous acts are returned. Id. at 322; see also Sudarkasa, supra note 41, at 50.

84. Cobbah, supra note 41, at 322.

"powerful instrument for securing conformity" with the community's values; the "selfish or reckless youth is taught by the opinion of his gang that it does not pay to incur displeasure."[85] Through age-groups and the "strength and numbers of the social ties,"[86] community solidarity is easily transmitted and becomes the basis for cohesion and stability. Furthermore, initiation ceremonies—for both girls and boys—taught gender roles and sexual morality.[87] Among the Kikuyu, a series of ceremonies culminating in clitoridectomy for girls and circumcision for boys, marked passage into adulthood. Clitoridectomy, which was brought under sharp attack first by Christian missionaries and now by Western or Western-inspired human rights advocates, was a critical departure point in socialization.

This conception, that of the individual as a moral being endowed with rights but also bounded by duties, proactively uniting his needs with the needs of others, was the quintessence of the formulation of rights in pre-colonial societies. It radically differs from the liberal conception of the individual as the state's primary antagonist. Moreover, it provides those concerned with the universal conception of human rights with a basis for imagining another dialectic: the harmonization of duties and rights. Many of those who dismiss the relevance of the African conception of man by pejoratively referring to it as a "peasant" and "pre-industrial" notion fail to recognize that all major cultures and traditions—the Chinese, European, African, and the Arab, to mention a few—have a basic character distinctive to them. While it is true that no culture is static, and that normative cultural values are forever evolving, it is naive to think that a worldview can be eroded in a matter of decades, even centuries. Why should the concession be made that the individualist rights perspective is "superior" to more community-oriented notion? As Cobbah has noted, "in the same way that people in other cultures are brought up to assert their independence from their community, the average African's worldview is one that places the individual within his community."[88] This African worldview, he writes, "is for all intents and

85. Kenyatta, supra note 73, at 115. Kenyatta writes that "early and late, by rules of conduct in individual instances, by the sentiment of the group in which he lives, by rewards and punishments and fears of ceremonial uncleanness, the younger generation learns the respect and obedience due to parents. The older generation do likewise." Id.

86. Id. at 116-17.

87. See id. at 130-54.

88. Cobbah, supra note 41, at 323.

purposes as valid as the European theories of individualism and the social contract."[89] Any concept of human rights with pretensions of universality cannot avoid mediating between these two seemingly contradictory notions.

IV. PROSPECTS AND PROBLEMS FOR THE DUTY/RIGHTS CONCEPTION

The idea of combining individual rights and duties in a human rights document is not completely without precedent. No less a document than the Universal Declaration of Human Rights (UDHR) blazed the trail in this regard when it provided, in a rare departure from its individualist focus, that "[e]veryone has the duties to the community in which alone the free and full development of his personality is possible."[90] However, the African Charter is the first human rights document to articulate the concept in any meaningful way. It is assumed, with undue haste, by human rights advocates and scholars that the inclusion of duties in the African Charter is nothing but "an invitation to the imposition of unlimited restrictions on the enjoyment of rights."[91] This view is simplistic because it is not based on a careful assessment of the difficulties experienced by African countries in their miserable attempts to mimic wholesale Western notions of government and the role of the state. Such critics are transfixed by the allure of models of democracy prevalent in the industrial democracies of the West, models which promise an opportunity for the redemption of a troubled continent.

Unfortunately, such a view is shortsighted. Perhaps at no other time in the history of the continent have Africans needed each other more than they do today. Although there is halting progress towards democratization in some African countries, the continent is generally on a fast track to political and economic collapse. Now in the fourth decade of post-colonialism, African states have

89. Id.

90. UDHR, supra note 3, art. 29. The American Declaration of the Rights and Duties of Man, O.A.S. Res. XXX, International Conference of American States, 9th Conf. (1948), O.A.S. Doc. OEA/Ser. L/V/1.4 Rev. XX (1965), also proclaimed a list of 27 human rights and ten duties. Buergenthal, supra note 3, at 128. The American Convention on Human Rights, supra note 3, did not follow the same course.

91. Buergenthal, supra note 3, at 178. Others, such as Haysom, have made blanket condemnations of the concept of duties. Fearing that the concept of duties could be used to suppress rights guaranteed by the African Charter, Haysom has written that the "interpretation of a duty towards the community as to mean duty towards the state, lends itself to an autocratic style of Government." Haysom, supra note 62, at 6.

largely failed to forge viable, free, and prosperous countries. The persistence of this problem highlights the dismal failures of the post-colonial states on several accounts. The new African states have failed to inspire loyalty in the citizenry; to produce a political class with integrity and a national interest; to inculcate in the military, the police, and the security forces their proper roles in society; to build a nation from different linguistic and cultural groups; and to fashion economically viable policies. These realities are driving a dagger into the heart of the continent. There are many causes of the problem, and, while it is beyond the scope of this Article to address them all, it will discuss one: namely, the human rights dimensions of the relationship between the individual, the community, and the state.

Colonialism profoundly transformed and mangled the political landscape of the continent through the imposition of the modern state.[92] Each pre-colonial African "nation," and there were thousands of them to be sure, had several characteristics: one ethnic community inhabited a "common territory; its members shared a tradition, real or fictitious, of common descent; and they were held together by a common language and a common culture."[93] Few African nations were also states in the modern or European sense, although they were certainly political societies. In contrast, the states created by European imperialists, comprising the overwhelming majority of the continent, ordinarily contained more than one nation:

> Each one of the new states contains more than one nation. In their border areas, many new states contain parts of nations because of the European-inspired borders cut across existing national territories.[94]

The new state contained a population from many cultural groups coerced to live together. It did not reflect a "nation," a people with the consciousness of a common destiny and shared history and culture.[95] The colonialists were concerned with the exploitation of

---

92. For a commanding history of the continent, spanning the pre-colonial era to the present, see Basil Davidson, Africa in History (1991); see also Ali A. Mazrui, The Africans: A Triple Heritage (1986).

93. K. A. Busia, Africa in Search of Democracy 31 (1967). Hansen defines a nation as "a group that shares a common history and identity and is aware of that; they are a people, not just a population." Art Hansen, African Refugees: Defining and Defending Their Human Rights, in Human Rights and Governance, supra note 19, at 139, 161.

94. Hansen, supra note 93, at 161.

95. According to Busia, the

Africa's human and natural resources, and not with the maintenance of the integrity of African societies. For purposes of this expediency, grouping many nations in one territory was the only feasible administrative option. To compound the problem, the new rulers employed divide-and-conquer strategies, pitting nations against each other, further polarizing inter-ethnic tensions and creating a climate of mutual fear, suspicion, and hatred. In many cases, the Europeans would openly favor one group or cluster of nations over others, a practice that only served to intensify tensions. For example, in Rwanda, a country rife with some of the worst inter-communal violence since decolonization, the Belgians heightened Hutu-Tutsi rivalry through preferential treatment toward the Tutsi.[96]

Ironically, colonialism, though a divisive factor, created a sense of brotherhood or unity among different African nations within the same colonial state, because they saw themselves as common victims of an alien, racist, and oppressive structure.[97] Nevertheless, as the fissures of the modern African state amply demonstrate, the unity born out of anti-colonialism has not sufficed to create an enduring identity of nationhood in the context of the post-colonial state. Since in the pre-colonial era the primary allegiances were centered on lineage and the community,[98] one of the most difficult challenges facing the post-colonial political class was the creation of new nations. This challenge, referred to as "creating a national consciousness . . . was misleading," as there was "no nation to

---

> new African States are composed of many different tribes. A state can claim to be a common territory for all the tribes within it, but common descent, real or fictitious, cannot be maintained among tribes, some of which have a history of different origins and migrations, such as the Buale, Senufo, Guro of the Ivory Coast; the Yoruba, Hausa, Ibo of Nigeria; Ewe, Fanti, Dagomba of Ghana . . . . Instead of the bond of a common culture and language, there are language and cultural differences which tend to divide rather unite.

Busia, supra note 93, at 33; see also Mutua, Redrawing the Map, supra note 14.

96. Although, before the arrival of the Belgians, the Tutsi minority ruled over the Hutu majority and the Twa in a feudal-client relationship, the colonial state "transformed communal relations and sharpened ethnic tensions by ruling through a narrow Tutsi royalty. The access to resources and power that the Tutsi collaborators enjoyed under the colonial state irreversibly polarized Hutu-Tutsi relations." Makau wa Mutua, U.N. Must Make Rwanda a Priority, Oakland Tribune, May 25, 1994, at A13.

97. "One need not go into the history of colonisation of Africa, but that colonisation had one significant result. A sentiment was created on the African continent—a sentiment of oneness." Mazrui, supra note 92, at 108, quoting Julius Nyerere, Africa's Place in the World, Wellesley College Symposium at 149 (1960).

98. Busia, supra note 93, at 30.

become conscious of; the nation had to be created concurrently with a consciousness."[99]

This difficult social and political transformation from self-governing ethno-cultural units to the multi-lingual, multi-cultural modern state—the disconnection between the two Africas: one pre-colonial, the other post-colonial—lies at the root of the current crisis. The post-colonial state has not altered the imposed European forms of social and political organization even though there is mounting evidence that they have failed to work in Africa.[100] Part of the problem lies in the domination of the continent's political and social processes by Eurocentric norms and values. As correctly put by Hansen:

> African leaders have adopted and continued to use political forms and precedents that grew from, and were organically related to, the European experience. Formal declarations of independence from direct European rule do not mean actual independence from European conceptual dominance. African leaders and peoples have gone through tremendous political changes in the past hundred years. These profound changes have included the transformation of African societies and polities. *They are still composed of indigenous African units, such as the lineage, village, tribe, and chieftainship, but they have been transformed around European units, such as the colony, district, political party, and state.*[101]

This serious and uniquely African crisis lacks the benefit of any historical guide or formula for its resolution. While acknowledging that it is impossible to recapture and re-institute pre-colonial forms of social and political organization, this Article nonetheless asserts that Africa must partially look inward, to its pre-colonial past, for possible solutions. Certain ideals in pre-colonial African philosophy, particularly the conception of humanity, and the interface of rights and duties in a communal context as provided for in the African Charter, should form part of that process of reconstruction. The European domination of Africa has wrought social

99. Hansen, supra note 93, at 161-62.

100. Id. at 161. Hansen notes that the "most obvious and powerful expressions of the continued African conceptual reliance on European political forms are the African states themselves. *The states are direct and uncritical successors of the colonies.*" Id. (emphasis added).

101. Id. (emphasis added).

changes which have disabled old institutions by complicating social and political processes. Pre-colonial and post-colonial societies now differ fundamentally. In particular, there are differences of scale; states now have large and varied populations. Moreover, states possess enormous instruments of control and coercion, and their tasks are now without number. While this is true, Africa cannot move forward by completely abandoning its past.

The duty/rights conception of the African Charter could provide a new basis for individual identification with compatriots, the community, and the state. It could forge and instill a national consciousness and act as the glue to reunite individuals and different nations within the modern state, and at the same time set the proper limits of conduct by state officials. The motivation and purpose behind the concept of duty in pre-colonial societies was to strengthen community ties and social cohesiveness, creating a shared fate and common destiny. This is the consciousness that the impersonal modern state has been unable to foster.[102] It has failed to shift loyalties from the lineage and the community to the modern state, with its mixture of different nations.

The series of explicit duties spelled out in articles 27 through 29 of the African Charter could be read as intended to recreate the bonds of the pre-colonial era among individuals and between individuals and the state.[103] They represent a rejection of the individual "who is utterly free and utterly irresponsible and opposed to society".[104] In a proper reflection of the nuanced nature of societal obligations in the pre-colonial era, the African Charter explicitly provides for two types of duties: direct and indirect. A direct duty is contained, for example, in article 29(4) of the Charter which requires the individual to "preserve and strengthen social and national solidarity, particularly when the latter is threatened."[105] There is nothing inherently sinister about this provision; it merely repeats a duty formerly imposed on members of pre-colonial communities. If anything, there exists a heightened need today, more

102. In his discussion of the absence of the requirements of empirical statehood in post-colonial Africa, Jackson has written that, in these "ramshackle" regimes, "[c]itizenship means little and carries few substantial rights or duties compared with membership in a family, clan, religious sect or ethnic community. Often the 'government' cannot govern itself, and its officials may in fact be freelancers, charging what amounts to a private fee for their services." Robert H. Jackson, Juridical Statehood in Sub-Saharan Africa 46 J. Int'l Aff. 1 (1992).

103. See African Charter, supra note 1, art. 45, 21 I.L.M. at 65.

104. See OAU Doc. CAB/LEG/67/3/Rev.1, supra note 72, at 2.

105. African Charter, supra note 1, art. 29, para. 4, 21 I.L.M. at 63.

than at any other time in recent history, to fortify communal relations and defend national solidarity. The threat of the collapse of the post-colonial state, as has been the case in Liberia, Somalia, and Rwanda, is only too real. Political elites as well as the common citizenry, each in equal measure, bear the primary responsibility for avoiding societal collapse and its devastating consequences.

The African Charter provides an example of an indirect duty in article 27(2), which states that "[t]he rights and freedoms of each individual shall be exercised with due regard to the rights of others, collective security, morality and common interest."[106] This duty is in fact a limitation on the enjoyment of certain individual rights. It merely recognizes the practical reality that in African societies, as elsewhere in the world, individual rights are not absolute. Individuals are asked to reflect on how the *exercise of their rights in certain circumstances* might adversely affect other individuals or the community. The duty is based on the presumption that the full development of the individual is only possible where individuals care about how their actions would impact on others. By rejecting the egotistical individual whose only concern is fulfilling self, article 27(2) raises the level of care owed to neighbors and the community.

Duties are also grouped according to whether they are owed to individuals or to larger units such as the family, society, or the state. Parents, for example, are owed a duty of respect and maintenance by their children.[107] Crippling economic problems do not allow African states to contemplate some of the programs of the welfare state. The care of the aged and needy falls squarely on family and community members. This requirement—a necessity today—has its roots in the past: it was unthinkable to abandon a parent or relative in need.[108] The family guilty of such an omission

106. Id. art. 27, para. 2, 21 I.L.M. at 63.

107. Article 29 of the African Charter provides that the individual shall have the duty to "preserve the harmonious development of the family and to work for the cohesion and respect of the family; to respect his parents at all times, to maintain them in case of need." Id. art. 29, para. 1, 21 I.L.M. at 63. The state, however, does not shirk responsibility for the aged and disabled. The Charter gives them "the right to special measures of protection in keeping with their physical or moral needs." Id. art. 18, para. 4, 21 I.L.M. at 62.

108. In defense of the duty of the individual to parents, the aged, and the needy, Isaac Nguema, the first chair of the African Commission, has rhetorically asked: "[h]ow can society be so ungrateful to people who once helped to build it, on the grounds that they have become a burden, maybe no more than waste?" Isaac Nguema, Universality and Specificity in Human Rights in Africa, The Courier, Nov./Dec. 1989, at 16, 17. He pleads for Africa to "foster the cult and the veneration of the aged." Id.

would be held in disgrace and contempt pending the intervention of lineage or clan members. Such problems explain why the family is considered sacred and why it would be simply impracticable and suicidal for Africans to adopt wholesale the individualist conception of rights. Duty to the family is emphasized elsewhere in the Charter because of its crucial and indispensable economic utility.[109] Economic difficulties and the dislocations created by the transformation of rural life by the cash economy make the homestead a place of refuge.

Some duties are owed by the individual to the state. These are not distinctive to African states; many of them are standard obligations that any modern state places on its citizens. In the African context, however, these obligations have a basis in the past, and many seem relevant because of the fragility and the domination of Africa by external agents. Such duties are rights that the community or the state, defined as all persons within it, holds against the individual. They include the duties to "preserve and strengthen social and national solidarity;"[110] not to "compromise the security of the State;"[111] to serve the "national community by placing his physical and intellectual abilities at its service;"[112] to "pay taxes imposed by law in the interest of the society;"[113] and to "preserve and strengthen the national independence and the territorial integrity of his country and to contribute to its defence in accordance with the law."[114]

The duties that require the individual to strengthen and defend national independence, security, and the territorial integrity of the state are inspired by the continent's history of domination and occupation by outside powers over the centuries.[115] The duties represent an extension of the principle of self-determination, used

109. Article 27(1) of the African Charter provides, inter alia, that "[e]very individual shall have duties towards his family." African Charter, supra note 1, art. 27, para. 1, 21 I.L.M. at 63.

110. Id. art. 29, para. 4, 21 I.L.M. at 63.

111. Id. art. 29, para. 3, 21 I.L.M. at 63.

112. Id. art. 29, para. 2, 21 I.L.M. at 63.

113. Id. art. 29, para. 6, 21 I.L.M. at 63.

114. Id. art. 29, para. 5, 21 I.L.M. at 63.

115. It would be surprising if the first Africa-wide human rights document did not show sensitivity to the subjugation of African peoples, a condition that has largely defined what the continent is today. Beginning with the invasion, enslavement, and colonization by Arabs and later the Europeans, Africans have been keenly aware of the traumatic consequences of the loss of sovereignty over their political and social life. As a general rule, they have not exercised domination over others; that ledger is heavily weighted against them.

in the external sense, as a shield against foreign occupation. Even in countries where this history is lacking, the right of the state to be defended by its citizens can trump certain individual rights, such as the draft of younger people for a war effort. Likewise, the duty to place one's intellectual abilities at the service of the state is a legitimate state interest, for the "brain drain" has robbed Africa of massive intellect.[116] In recognition of the need for the strength of diversity, rather than its power to divide, the Charter asks individuals to promote African unity, an especially critical role given arbitrary balkanization by the colonial powers and the ethnic animosities fostered within and between the imposed states.[117]

In addition to the duties placed on the state to secure for the people within its borders economic, social, and cultural rights, the Charter also requires the state to protect the family, which it terms "the natural unit and basis of society"[118] and the "custodian of morals and traditional values."[119] There is an enormous potential for advocates of equality rights to be concerned that these provisions could be used to support the patriarchy and other repressive practices of pre-colonial social ordering. It is now generally accepted that one of the strikes against the pre-colonial regime was its strict separation of gender roles and, in many cases, the limitation on, or exclusion of, women from political participation. The discriminatory treatment of women on the basis of gender in marriage, property ownership, and inheritance, and the disproportionately heavy labor and reproduction burdens were violations of their rights.

However, these are not the practices that the Charter condones when it requires states to assist families as the "custodians of morals and traditional values." Such an interpretation would be a cynical misreading of the Charter.[120] The reference is to those

116. Although the "brain drain" is partially a result of the abusive state, the cost of education is so high that a state is entitled to ask its educated elites to contribute to national welfare.

117. Every African is required to "contribute to the best of his abilities, at all times and at all levels, to the promotion and achievement of African unity." African Charter, supra note 1, art. 29, para. 8, 21 I.L.M. at 63. "[A]ll levels" here implies, inter alia, unity between different ethnic groups within the same state. This provision reflects a recognition by the Charter of the destructive power of ethnic hatred or tribalism, the term Westerners prefer when referring to ethnic tensions in Africa.

118. African Charter, supra note 1, art. 18, para. 1, 21 I.L.M. at 61.

119. Id. art. 18, para. 2, 21 I.L.M. at 61.

120. The Charter's reference to "traditional values" cannot in good faith be interpreted as a call for the continued oppression of women. The Charter requires the individual to "preserve and strengthen *positive African cultural values in his relations with other*

traditional values which enhanced the dignity of the individual and emphasized the dignity of motherhood and the importance of the female as the central link in the reproductive chain; women were highly valued as equals in the process of the regeneration of life. The Charter guarantees, unambiguously and without equivocation, the equal rights of women in its gender equality provision by requiring states to "eliminate every discrimination against women" and to protect women's rights in international human rights instruments.[121] Read in conjunction with other provisions, the Charter leaves no room for discriminatory treatment against women.

The articulation of the duty conception in the Charter has been subjected to severe criticism. Some of the criticism, however, has confused the African conception of duty with the socialist or Marxist understanding.[122] Such confusion is unfortunate. In socialist ideology, states—not individuals—are subjects of international law.[123] Thus the state assumes obligations under international law, through the International Covenant on Civil and Political Rights (ICCPR) for example, to provide human rights.[124] Under socialism, the state secures economic, cultural, and social benefits for the individual. Hence, the state, as the guardian of public interest, retains primacy in the event of conflict with the individual.[125] Human rights, therefore, are conditioned on the interest of the state and the goals of communist development.[126] There is an organic unity between rights and duties to the state.[127] In this col-

members of the society, in the spirit of tolerance, dialogue and consultation and, in general, to contribute to the promotion of the moral well-being of society." African Charter, supra note 1, art. 29, para. 7, 21 I.L.M. at 63 (emphasis added).

121. "The state shall ensure the elimination of every discrimination against women and also ensure the protection of the rights of the woman and the child as stipulated in international declarations and conventions." Id. art. 18, para. 3, 21 I.L.M. at 62. Note, however, that the pairing of women and children in this instance is not merely a function of sloppy draftsmanship; it most probably betrays the sexist perception of the drafters.

122. Donnelly, for example, thinks that the Soviet or socialist conception of human rights, reflected in practice and official doctrine, is "strikingly similar" to African and Chinese conceptions. Donnelly, Universal Human Rights, supra note 15, at 55.

123. See Vladimir Kartashkin, The Socialist Countries and Human rights, in The International Dimensions of Human Rights 631, 645 (Karel Vasak & Philip Alston eds., 1982).

124. Id. at 644-45.

125. Roman Wieruszewski, National Implementation of Human Rights, in Human Rights in a Changing East-West Perspective 264, 270 (Allan Rosas et al. eds., 1990).

126. Articles 39, 50, 51, and 59 of the 1977 Constitution of the Union of Soviet Socialist Republics link individual duties to the state with the enjoyment of individual rights. Konst. SSSR, arts. 39, 50, 51, 59 (1977).

127. V. Chkhidvadze, Constitution of True Human Rights and Freedoms, 1980 Int'l Aff. 18, cited in Donnelly, Universal Human Rights, supra note 15, at 55.

lectivist conception, duties are only owed to the state. In contrast, in the pre-colonial era, and in the African Charter, duties are primarily owed to the family—nuclear and extended—and to the community, not to the state.[128] In effect, the primacy attached to the family in the Charter places the family above the state, which is not the case under communism.[129] In pre-colonial Africa, unlike the former Soviet Union or Eastern Europe, duties owed to the family or community were rarely misused or manipulated to derogate from human rights obligations.[130]

The most damaging criticism of the language of duties in Africa sees them as "little more than the formulation, entrenchment, and legitimation of state rights and privileges against individuals and peoples."[131] However, critics who question the value of including duties in the Charter point only to the theoretical danger that states might capitalize on the duty concept to violate other guaranteed rights.[132] The fear is frequently expressed that emphasis on duties may lead to the "trumping" of individual rights if the two are in opposition.[133] It is argued that:

> If the state has a collective right and obligation to develop the society, economy, and polity (Article 29), then as an instrument it can be used to defend coercive state actions against both individuals and constituent groups to achieve

---

128. Individual duties owed to intermediate groups—groups falling between the family and the state such as ethnic, professional, and other associational entities—would seem to be implied by article 27 which refers to "society" and "other legally recognized communities." African Charter, supra note 1, art. 27, para. 1, 21 I.L.M. at 63. Such a reading could also be attached to article 10 which refers to the "obligation of solidarity" in associational life. Id. art. 10, para. 2, 21 I.L.M. at 61. "Solidarity" is both "social" and "national." Id. art. 29, 21 I.L.M. at 63.

129. Article 18(1) compels the state to protect the family, the "natural unit" of society. Id. art. 18, para. 1, 21 I.L.M. at 61.

130. According to Benedek, "[t]he human rights approach to be found in traditional African societies is characterized by a permanent dialectical relationship between the individual and the group, which fits neither into the individualistic nor the collectivistic concept of human rights." Wolfgang Benedek, Peoples' Rights and Individuals' Duties as Special Features of the African Charter on Human and Peoples' Rights, in Emerging African System, supra note 72, at 59, 63.

131. H.W.O. Okoth-Ogendo, Human and Peoples' Rights: What Point is Africa Trying to Make?, in Human Rights and Governance, supra note 19, at 74, 78-79; see Okere, supra note 65, at 148-49; Amnesty International, Protecting Human Rights: International Procedures and How to Use Them 15 (1991). See generally Issa J. Shivji, The Concept of Human Rights in Africa (1989).

132. See supra note 62 and accompanying text; Okoth-Ogendo, supra note 131, at 79.

133. See Cohen, supra note 25, at 15.

state policies rationalized as social and economic improvement.[134]

While the human rights records of African states are distressingly appalling, facts do not indicate that the zeal to promote certain economic and political programs is the root cause of human rights abuses. The regime of Daniel arap Moi in Kenya, for example, has not engaged in the widespread suppression of civil and political rights because of adherence to policies it deems in the national interest; instead, abuses have been triggered by an insecure and narrow political class which will stop at nothing, including political murder, to retain power.[135] Similarly, Mobutu Sese Seko of Zaire has run the country into the ground because he cannot contemplate relinquishing power.[136] Alienated and corrupt elites, quite often devoid of a national consciousness, plunder the state and brutalize society to maintain their personal privileges and retain power.[137] The use of the state to implement particular state

134. Id. Cohen adds that "[m]ore importantly, the dangers of supporting state power as a fundamental 'right' are obvious. Indeed, the African record to date on that score provides serious grounds for concern." Id. Donnelly points to the perversion of the ordinary correlation between duties and rights in the former Soviet Union where a totalitarian, undemocratic state manipulated the concept to abrogate individual rights. Donnelly, Universal Human Rights, supra note 15, at 55-57. However, this author disagrees with Donnelly when he states that rights are completely independent of duties. The link between rights and duties is a social dialectic; one implies the other.

135. For exhaustive catalogues of human rights abuses by the Kenyan government, see Africa Watch, Kenya: Taking Liberties (1991); Robert F. Kennedy Memorial Center for Human Rights, Failing the Democratic Challenge: Freedom of Expression in Multi-Party Kenya (1993); Kenya Human Rights Commission, Independence Without Freedom: The Legitimization of Repressive Laws and Practices in Kenya (1994). For a more conceptual discussion about the difficulties of creating rights-respecting governments, see generally Akwasi Aidoo, Africa: Democracy Without Human Rights 15 Hum. Rts. Q. 703 (1993); Emerging Human Rights: The African Political Economy Context (George W. Shepherd, Jr. & Mark O.C. Anikpo eds., 1990) (presenting theoretical considerations about emerging rights from the standpoint of political economy); Political Economy, supra note 42; Sakah S. Mahmud, The State and Human Rights in Africa in the 1990s: Perspectives and Prospects, 15 Hum. Rts. Q. 485 (1993) (attributing human rights violations in Africa to the African interpretation of human rights and to structural inadequacies).

136. For a comprehensive report on human rights abuses in Zaire, see Lawyers Committee for Human Rights, Zaire: Repression As Policy (1990); Africa Watch, Zaire: Two Years Without Transition (1992).

137. During its first two decades after achieving independence in 1961, Tanzania, under the leadership of Julius Nyerere and the Tanzania African National Union (TANU) and later Chama Cha Mapinduzi (CCM), the ruling party, appeared to be an exception to the kleptocratic oligarchies then prevalent in Africa. The state seemed genuinely committed to the realization of *ujamaa*, the policy of socialism and self-reliance. See generally Makau wa Mutua, Tanzania's Recent Economic Reform: An Analysis, 1988 Transafrica Forum 69 (discussing Tanzania's progression towards self-reliance and socialism under Nyerere); Hyden, supra note 40 (discussing the implementation of *ujamma* policies and politics in

policies is almost never the reason, although such a rationale is frequently used as the pretext. Okoth-Ogendo persuasively argues that the attack on the duty conception is not meritorious because the "state is the villain against which human rights law is the effective weapon" and towards which "individuals should not be called upon to discharge any duties."[138] Valid criticism would question the "precise boundaries, content, and conditions of compliance" contemplated by the Charter.[139] It should be the duty of the African Commission in its jurisprudence to clarify which, if any, of these duties are moral or legal obligations, and what the scope of their application ought to be.[140] The Commission could lead the way in suggesting how some of the duties—on the individual as well as the state—might be implemented. The concept of national service,[141] for example, could utilize traditional notions in addressing famine, public works, and community self-help projects. The care of parents and the needy[142] could be formalized in family/state burden-sharing. The Commission should also indicate how, and in what forum, the state would respond to the breach of individual duties. It might suggest the establishment of community arbitration centers to work out certain types of disputes. As suggested by Umozurike, a former chairman to the Commission, state responsibility for these duties implies a "minimum obligation to inculcate the underlying principles and ideals in their subjects."[143]

Tanzania from a political economy perspective with particular focus on the role of the peasants).

138. Okoth-Ogendo, supra note 131, at 79. The misappropriation of tradition by some of Africa's despots and political charlatans to justify coercive measures against individuals should not be reason for the emotional denunciation of the duty/rights conception. Hastings Kamuzu Banda, the former president of Malawi, used "traditional courts" to silence his critics, and Mobutu Sese Seko, the long term Zairian ruler, at one point instituted *salongo*, a thinly disguised colonial practice of forced labor. Both practices, which had nothing to do with pre-colonial values, were cynically designed to increase the state's power over the people. See Robert F. Kennedy Memorial Center for Human Rights, Confronting the Past: Accountability for Human Rights Violations in Malawi (1994); Donnelly, Universal Human Rights, supra note 15, at 120.

139. Okoth-Ogendo, supra note 131, at 79.

140. Article 45 of the African Charter outlines the mandate of the African Commission, which includes the interpretation of the Charter and the formulation of principles and rules relating to human rights. African Charter, supra note 1, art. 45, 21 I.L.M. at 65.

141. Id. art. 29, 21 I.L.M. at 63.

142. Id.

143. Umozurike, supra note 5, at 907. The African Charter also imposes similar obligations on states:

> States parties to the present Charter shall have the duty to promote and ensure through teaching, education and publication, the respect of the rights and

The duty/rights formulation is also inextricably tied to the concept, articulated in the African Charter, of peoples' rights. Although a long discussion about the concept itself and the controversy it has attracted will not be made here, this Article will outline its necessity to the duty conception. Like the duty concept, the idea of peoples' rights is embodied in the African philosophy which sees men and women primarily as social beings embraced in the body of the community.[144] It was pointed out during the drafting of the African Charter that individual rights could only be justified in the context of the rights of the community; consequently the drafters made room in the Charter for peoples' rights.[145]

The concept was not new in a human rights document. For example, Common Article 1 of the two basic international human rights covenants makes peoples the subject of rights, a departure from Western notions that human rights only attach to individuals.[146] There is recognition of the fact that individual rights cannot be realized unless groups hold collective rights. As clearly noted by Sohn:

> One of the main characteristics of humanity is that human beings are social creatures. Consequently, most individuals belong to various units, groups, and communities; they are simultaneously members of such units as a family, religious community, social club, trade union, professional association, racial group, people, nation, and state. It is not surprising, therefore, that international law not only recognizes inalienable rights of individuals, but also recognizes certain collective rights that are exercised jointly

---

> freedoms contained in the present Charter and to see to it that these freedoms and rights as well as corresponding obligations and duties are understood.

African Charter, supra note 1, art. 25, 21 I.L.M. at 63.

144. Benedek observes further, that in traditional African societies "the human being could not survive apart from his people, the community, who in turn was dependent on the participation of all its constituent parts." Benedek, supra note 130, at 63. This relationship was one of duality, "not one of subordination but of complementary, participation, and dialogue." Id. The "support and allegiance" of these relationships "are still a predominant factor of the life of most Africans." Id.

145. Rapporteur's Report, OAU Doc. CM/1149 (XXXVII), Ann. 1, at 3, para. 10, quoted in Kiwanuka, supra note 5, at 82.

146. Article 1 of both the ICESCR and ICCPR provides: "All peoples have the right of self-determination. By virtue of that right they freely determine their political status and freely pursue their economic, social and cultural development." ICESCR, supra note 3, art. 1; ICCPR, supra note 3, art. 1 [hereinafter Common Article 1]. During the drafting of the ICESCR and the ICCPR, Western governments stiffly opposed Common Article 1 because it put at risk the continued domination of the colonies.

> by individuals grouped into larger communities, including peoples and nations. *These rights are still human rights; the effective exercise of collective rights is a precondition to the exercise of other rights, political or economic or both. If a community is not free, most of its members are also deprived of many important rights.*[147]

The African Charter distinguishes human rights from peoples' or collective rights, but sees them in cooperation, not competition or conflict. The Charter's preambular paragraph notes this relationship and recognizes "on the one hand, that fundamental human rights stem from the attributes of human beings, which justifies their national and international protection and on the other hand, that the reality and respect for peoples rights should necessarily guarantee human rights."[148] This unambiguous statement, notes van Boven, is conclusive proof of the Charter's view: human rights are inalienable and intrinsic to man individuals and are not in conflict with peoples' rights, which they complement.[149] The exercise of sovereignty rights by a "people" or "peoples" as contemplated by the Charter is a necessary precondition for the enjoyment of individual rights.[150] This dialectic between individual and peoples' rights is one of the bases for the Charter's imposition of duties on individuals. Solidarity between the individual and the greater soci-

147. Louis B. Sohn, The New International Law: Protection of the Rights of Individuals Rather Than States, 32 Am. U. L. Rev. 1, 48 (1982) (emphasis added). See generally, Kiwanuka, supra note 5.

148. African Charter, supra note 1, pmbl., 21 I.L.M. at 59.

149. van Boven, supra note 5, at 188-89. In its usage of "peoples," the African Charter neither contemplates internal self-determination, the right of a people to overthrow an oppressive, undemocratic, and illegitimate regime, nor the claims of a minority or group within an independent state to its own self-determination or secession. Self-determination in the context of the OAU without a doubt refers to situations of foreign, colonial-type domination (previously the case in Namibia), or to minority-ruled regimes (formerly the case in South Africa). Ethnic groups or communities within an independent state, such as the Luo or Luhyia of Kenya, are not envisaged by the Charter in this regard. The individual rights guaranteed in the Charter, particularly the rights to political participation, speech, association, and assembly, imply the right of citizens to a rule of law, democratic state.

150. Kiwanuka has identified at least four interpretations or usages of a "people" or "peoples" in the Charter. They are: (i) all persons within the territorial limits of a colonial state or minority-ruled regime; (ii) all groups of people with certain common characteristics who live within a colonial territory or a minority-ruled state, or minorities within an independent state (external self-determination would not be permitted under the OAU in this case); (iii) the people and the state as interchangeable; and (iv) all persons within the state. See generally Kiwanuka, supra note 5. These are the bearers of collective rights against the state which it has the duty to realize.

ety safeguards collective rights, without which individual rights would be unattainable.

V. CONCLUSIONS

Today Africa is at a cross-roads. Since colonization, when Europe restructured its political map, Africa has lunged from one crisis to another. Whether it was famine consuming millions, Idi Amin dispatching political opponents and innocents with impunity, senseless coups by soldiers who could barely read, the recent Rwandese carnage or ethnic tensions turned deadly, or corrupt political elites, the list of abominations is simply unbearable. The failure of the post-colonial state is so pervasive that it has become the rule, not the exception. Needless to say, there are numerous causes for this crisis, perhaps the most important of which is the disfiguration of the continent's political identity by the imposition of European forms and values of government and society. Narrow political elites who barely comprehend the Western notions they eagerly mimic—and who have lost the anchor in their past—remain in power, but without a rudder.[151] This crisis of cultural identity is Africa's most serious enemy. But with the end of colonization and the cold war—the two driving reasons for past European and American interest in Africa—Africans should reexamine the assumptions underlying the role and purpose of the state and its organization.

This Article is not intended to dismiss concerns about the potential for the misuse of the duty/rights conception by political elites to achieve narrow, personal ends. However, any notions are subject to abuse by power-hungry elites. There is no basis for concluding that the duty/rights conception is unique in this respect. While it is true that the pre-colonial context in which the conception originally worked was small in scale and relatively uncomplicated, the argument made here is not about magnitudes. Instead, the ideals that can be distilled from the past are the central thrust of this argument. Is it possible to introduce in the modern African state grassroots democracy, deepening it in neighborhood communities and villages in the tradition of the pre-colonial council of elders? Can the family reclaim its status as the basic organizational polit-

151. See Michael Chege, Between Africa's Extremes, 6 J. Democracy 44, 45 (1995). Chege notes the minimum conditions for the institutionalization of free and popular government which include shared democratic principles, an engaged middles class, and democratic leadership in a reasonably viable state. Id.

ical unit in this re-democratization process? Is it possible to create a state of laws—where elected officials are bound by checks and balances—as in the days of the old where chiefs were held accountable, at times through destooling? Can the state and the family devise a "social security" system in which the burden of caring for the aged and the needy can be shared? Is it possible to require individuals to take responsibility for their actions in matters relating to sexuality, community security, and self-help projects in the construction of community schools and health centers, utilizing concepts such as *harambee*,[152] the Kenyan slogan for pulling together? Child care and rearing, including lighter forms of discipline such as a reprimand, for example, have always been community affairs in Africa.[153] Could community-based programs be devised and encouraged to promote the "village-raising" of children? These are the typical questions that the new formulation of human rights must ask in the context of recreating the African state to legitimize human rights on the continent.

This Article represents a preliminary attempt to begin rethinking Africa's pre-colonial articulation of human rights and propose how some of the ideals imbedded in the past could be woven into conceptions of man, society, and the state in a way that would make the human rights corpus more relevant to Africa today. Senghor stressed the need for an Afro-centric document which would "assimilate without being assimilated," but also cautioned against a charter for the "African Man" only: he emphasized that "[m]ankind is one and indivisible and the basic needs of man are

152. *Harambee* has been used in contemporary Kenya as a philosophy to drive domestic development groups. For an example, *harambee* self-help projects in rural communities account for the construction of 70% of Kenya's secondary schools. David Gillies & Makau wa Mutua, A Long Road to Uhuru: Human Rights and Political Participation in Kenya (Report of the International Centre for Human Rights and Democratic Development, Montreal, Canada), at 2 (1993). *Harambee* projects have been undertaken with little or no state assistance. Conceived originally as "the social glue binding the state to society," it forced the state to be "accountable in the realm of social services" because under Kenyatta, the country's first president, it worked as "an extra-parliamentary bargaining system" for elected politicians to negotiate alliances and attract additional private resources to their constituencies. Id. It acted, in effect, as a redistributive mechanism where the influential politician would assemble prosperous friends to make personal monetary contributions or material to self-help projects. Id. However, as the state became more repressive and the political elites more cynical, *harambee* was turned into a "forced tax and an instrument of patronage" through which senior politicians would extort funds from businesses or frighten away contributors for particular causes or institutions. Id. at 3; see also Jennifer A. Widner, The Rise of a Party State in Kenya: From "Harambee!" to "Nyayo!" (1992).

153. See Cobbah, supra note 41, at 322.

similar everywhere."[154] Part of the reason for the failure of the post-colonial state to respect human rights lies in the seemingly alien character of that corpus. The African Charter's duty/rights conception is an excellent point of departure in the reconstruction of a new ethos and the restoration of confidence in the continent's cultural identity. It reintroduces values that Africa needs most at this time: commitment, solidarity, respect, and responsibility. Moreover, it also represents a recognition of another reality. Individual rights are collective in their dimension. "[T]heir recognition, their mode of exercise and their means of protection" is a collective process requiring the intervention of other individuals, groups, and communities.[155] The past, as the Africans of the old used to say, is part of the living. It ought to be used to construct a better tomorrow.

154. See Kunig, supra note 72, at 122, 124 (quoting Senghor's speech) (emphasis omitted).

155. Marie, supra note 5, at 199. This was the vision of pre-colonial societies.

[7]

Human Rights, Group Rights, and Peoples' Rights

*Peter Jones**

Can a right borne by a group be a human right? For some analysts, the answer is obviously, "No."[1] They argue that human rights are the rights of human beings and, self-evidently, each human being is an individual being. Groups may have rights of some sort, but, whatever those rights might be, they cannot be human rights. Human rights must be rights borne by human individuals.

Other analysts, unimpressed by that simple logic, insist that human rights can take collective as well as individual forms.[2] They argue that much

---

* *Peter Jones* is Professor of Political Philosophy at the University of Newcastle, United Kingdom. He has written on a variety of issues in contemporary political philosophy, including the nature of liberalism, the foundations of democracy, welfare rights, freedom of belief and expression, the Rushdie Affair, and multiculturalism. He is the author of *Rights* (1994) and is currently working on strategies for dealing with diversities of belief and value, both nationally and globally. Part of the work for this article was conducted during the author's tenure of a Nuffield Foundation Social Sciences Research Fellowship; he wishes to record his gratitude to the Foundation for its support.

1. *See, e.g.*, JACK DONNELLY, UNIVERSAL HUMAN RIGHTS IN THEORY AND PRACTICE (1988); Jack Donnelly, *Human Rights, Individual Rights and Collective Rights, in* HUMAN RIGHTS IN A PLURALIST WORLD: INDIVIDUALS AND COLLECTIVITIES 39 (Jan Berting et al. eds., 1990); James A. Graff, *Human Rights, Peoples, and the Right to Self-Determination, in* GROUP RIGHTS 186 (Judith Baker ed., 1994); MARLIES GALENKAMP, INDIVIDUALISM VERSUS COLLECTIVISM: THE CONCEPT OF COLLECTIVE RIGHTS (1993); Jean-Bernard Marie, *Relations Between Peoples' Rights and Human Rights: Semantic and Methodological Distinctions,* 7 HUM. RTS. L.J. 195 (1986); Johan Nordenfelt, *Human Rights—What They Are and What They Are Not,* 56 NORDIC J. INT'L L. 3(1987); PAUL SIEGHART, THE LAWFUL RIGHTS OF MANKIND: AN INTRODUCTION TO THE INTERNATIONAL LEGAL CODE OF HUMAN RIGHTS (1985).
2. *See, e.g.*, J. Herman Burgers, *The Function of Human Rights as Individual and Collective Rights, in* HUMAN RIGHTS IN A PLURALIST WORLD: INDIVIDUALS AND COLLECTIVITIES, *supra* note 1, at 63; James Crawford, *The Rights of Peoples: Some Conclusions, in* THE RIGHTS OF PEOPLES 159 (James Crawford ed., 1988); Yoram Dinstein, *Collective Human Rights of Peoples and Minorities,* 25 INT'L & COMP. L.Q. 102 (1976); William F. Felice, *The Case for Collective Human Rights: The Reality of Group Suffering,* 10 ETHICS & INT'L AFF. 47 (1996); Michael Freeman, *Are There Collective Human Rights?,* 43 POL. STUD. 25 (1995); Koo

of what is fundamentally important to human beings relates to "goods" and "bads" that people experience collectively rather than individually: if we insist that human rights must be rights that people can hold only as independent individuals, our conception of human rights will not match the social reality of the human condition.

Among those who distinguish between group rights and human rights, a further division is discernible. For some, the reality of the conceptual difference between human rights and group rights does not betoken any antagonism between the two forms of rights.[3] Rather, they regard some group rights, such as the rights of peoples or the rights of cultural minorities, as close complements of human rights. They believe that the reasons that lead us to ascribe rights to individuals are also reasons why we should recognize certain forms of group rights: human rights may be conceptually distinct from group rights, but the two sorts of rights are united by the same underlying values and concerns.

For others, however, the distinction between group rights and human rights is of more than merely analytical significance.[4] They conceive group rights as potential threats to individual rights: group rights are often rights claimed against, or over, individuals. Traditionally, a major purpose of the

---

VanderWal, *Collective Human Rights: A Western View, in* HUMAN RIGHTS IN A PLURALIST WORLD: INDIVIDUALS AND COLLECTIVITIES, *supra* note 1, at 83; VERNON VAN DYKE, HUMAN RIGHTS, ETHNICITY, AND DISCRIMINATION (1985). The issue of whether human rights might assume a collective form also figured in UN debates leading up to the adoption of common Article 1 of the International Covenant on Civil and Political Rights, *adopted* 16 Dec. 1966, G.A. Res. 2200 (XXI), U.N. GAOR, 21st Sess., Supp. No. 16, art. 1, U.N. Doc. A/6316 (1966), 999 U.N.T.S. 171 (*entered into force* 23 Mar. 1976) [hereinafter ICCPR] and the International Covenant on Economic, Social and Cultural Rights, *adopted* 16 Dec. 1966, G.A. Res. 2200 (XXI), U.N. GAOR, 21st Sess., Supp. No. 16, art. 1, U.N. Doc. A/6316 (1966), 993 U.N.T.S. 3 (*entered into force* 3 Jan. 1976) [hereinafter ICESCR], which are sometimes referred to together as the Human Rights Covenants. *See* ANTONIO CASSESE, SELF-DETERMINATION OF PEOPLES: A LEGAL REAPPRAISAL 51–52 (1995); Sally Morphet, *Article 1 of the Human Rights Covenants: Its Development and Current Significance, in* HUMAN RIGHTS AND FOREIGN POLICY: PRINCIPLES AND PRACTICE 67, 75–76 (Dilys M. Hill ed., 1989).

3. *Cf., e.g.*, Marie, *supra* note 1. Theo van Boven argues that the African Charter on Human and Peoples' Rights, *adopted* 26 June 1981, O.A.U. Doc. CAB/LEG/67/3 Rev. 5 (*entered into force* 21 Oct. 1986), *reprinted in* 21 I.L.M. 58 (1982) reflects the belief that peoples' rights and human rights are distinct but complementary. Theo van Boven, *The Relation Between Peoples' Rights and Human Rights in the African Charter*, 7 HUM. RTS. L.J. 183 (1986). François Rigaux argues the same regarding the Universal Declaration of the Rights of Peoples (Algiers Declaration), *adopted* 4 July 1976, International Commission of Jurists, *reprinted in* UN LAW/FUNDAMENTAL RIGHTS: TWO TOPICS IN INTERNATIONAL LAW 219 (Antonio Cassese ed., 1979). François Rigaux, *The Algiers Declaration of the Rights of Peoples, in* UN LAW/FUNDAMENTAL RIGHTS: TWO TOPICS IN INTERNATIONAL LAW, *supra*, at 211.
4. *See, e.g.*, DONNELLY, *supra* note 1; Donnelly, *supra* note 1; GRAFF, *supra* note 1; Nordenfelt, *supra* note 1. Galenkamp also emphasizes the tension between human rights and group rights but mounts a communitarian case for group rights and defends them as correctives to the liberal individualism of human rights. GALENKAMP, *supra* note 1, at 20–25, 64–73, 77–100.

doctrine of human rights has been to protect individuals from the power of groups, whether or not that power is institutionalized. These theorists contend that revising the doctrine of human rights so that it incorporates group rights entails the risk of defeating that very purpose. Instead of safeguarding individuals against the predations of groups, they argue, a doctrine that legitimates those predations would result.

This article will attempt to clarify these issues by distinguishing between two conceptions of group rights. It will argue that, if one of these conceptions were to be adopted, there is no case for absorbing group rights within, or assimilating them to, human rights. If, however, the other conception were adopted, some group rights could be conceived as human rights or, at least, as closely akin to human rights. Before embarking on that argument, the general notions of a group right and a human right, as they will be used in this article, need clarification.

I. GROUP RIGHTS AND HUMAN RIGHTS

A right is a group right only if it is borne by the group *qua* group. If the individuals who form a group hold rights as separate individuals, their several individual rights do not add up to a group right. For example, scientologists constitute a group whose members might be said to have a right to conduct their lives according to their beliefs (provided that, in doing so, they do not violate the rights of others). In saying that, however, we need not be ascribing a group right to scientologists. Rather, we may be saying only that individuals, including scientologists, have the right to conduct their lives as they choose. Thus, the relevant right is one held by each individual scientologist rather than by scientologists as a collectivity.

In the same way, a right may have a content that relates to a collectivity without its being a group right. An individual can have a right to join a group, such as a trade union, only if there is a group for him to join. Having joined the group, that individual may have rights that he possesses only as a member of the group. In both instances, however, these typically will be rights held in an individual capacity rather than rights that belong to the group. If someone prevents another person from joining the group or prevents an individual from exercising his rights as a member of the group, the rights he violates are typically the individual's rights rather than the group's rights. We might, of course, hold that if someone prevents individuals from joining a group such as a trade union, such action violates not only rights held by the would-be joiners, but also a right held by the trade union as a group. In that case a genuine group right would be at stake. Simply put, not every right that is associated with group membership or group activity need be a group right. What distinguishes a right as a group right is its subject rather than its object—who it is that holds the right rather than what the right is a right to.

If we go on to ask whether a group right, so understood, might be a human right, we could respond to that inquiry in a purely positivist spirit. That is, we might assert that human rights are whatever the relevant international authority says they are. Thus, we might examine the declarations of some standard-setting body, such as the United Nations or the Organization of African Unity, and accept that if that body designates certain group rights as human rights, then that settles the matter. Disposing of the issue in that way, however, trivializes the idea of human rights, and most people would find this response unsatisfactory for that reason.

Serious commitment to human rights is commitment to the idea that there are certain rights that human beings possess, or should possess, simply as human beings. If a right is to have a serious claim to be a human right, it must be a right that we can plausibly ascribe to human beings as such and one that we can plausibly ground in their humanity. The adjective "human" indicates both the range of beings that have the right and the status in virtue of which they have it. Thus, when this article asks whether a group right can be a human right, the question is whether it can be a human right so understood. The inquiry is not whether international instruments categorize group rights as human rights in fact, but, if they do, whether that categorization is defensible.

II. GROUP RIGHTS: THE COLLECTIVE CONCEPTION

The first conception of group rights is the "collective" conception. Joseph Raz sets it out most clearly.[5] Raz subscribes to an interest theory of rights, and he defines what it is to possess a right as follows: "'X has a right' if and only if X can have rights, and, other things being equal, an aspect of X's well-being (his interest) is a sufficient reason for holding some other person(s) to be under a duty."[6]

Thus, according to Raz, to have a right to something is to have an interest in that something. Merely having an interest, though, is not by itself enough to create a right. An interest translates into a right only if it is an interest of sufficient moment, all things considered, to justify imposing a duty upon another. Therefore a right, for Raz, is conceptually tied to a duty. That relation, however, is more than one of mere correlation: a right grounds a duty in that the right provides the reason for the duty.

5. Joseph Raz, The Morality of Freedom (1986). For Raz' general analysis of rights, see *id.* at 165–216, 245–63. For his understanding of group rights, see *id.* at 207–09.

6. *Id.* at 166.

Individuals can have rights as individuals. That is, their individual interests are sometimes such as to satisfy the conditions Raz lays down for a right. Yet, they also may hold rights as groups. These group rights arise when the joint interest of a number of individuals provides sufficient justification for imposing duties upon others even though, if we were to consider the interest of only one of those individuals, that single interest would not provide the necessary justification. The formal conditions Raz lays down for a group right are as follows:

> First, it exists because an aspect of the interest of human beings justifies holding some person(s) to be subject to a duty. Second, the interests in question are the interests of individuals as members of a group in a public good and the right is a right to that public good because it serves their interest as members of the group. Thirdly, the interest of no single member of that group in that public good is sufficient by itself to justify holding another person to be subject to a duty.[7]

Thus, imagine that a factory gives off polluting fumes that adversely affect the lives of people who live in its vicinity. Do those people have a right to stop the factory from engaging in the polluting activity? In answering that question, we would have to consider not only the adverse effects of the pollution, but also the costs of putting a stop to them. Suppose that the pollution is serious in that it has a significantly adverse impact upon the quality of people's lives, but is not so serious that it constitutes a significant threat to any individual's health. Suppose also that the costs of stopping the pollution are serious: the process will be financially expensive and will result in some of the factory's workers losing their jobs. In that case, we may conclude that the interest of any single individual in not suffering the pollution is not enough, on its own, to justify imposing a duty upon the factory's owner to stop the pollution. However, if we consider the interests of all of the individuals adversely affected by the pollution, their aggregate interest may well suffice to ground the duty. If it does, then those living in the vicinity of the factory have a right, as a group, to stop the factory's polluting activity. As a group, they jointly possess a right that none of them possesses individually. Thus, in this case, we have a right that is properly described as a group right.

---

7. *Id.* at 208. For other theorists who have followed Raz in using this collective conception of group rights, though sometimes with significant qualification, see Freeman, *supra* note 2; Leslie Green, *Two Views of Collective Rights,* 4 Can. J.L. & Juris. 315 (1991); Leslie Green, *Internal Minorities and Their Rights, in* Group Rights, *supra* note 1, at 101; Avishai Margalit & Moshe Halbertal, *Liberalism and the Right to Culture,* 61 Soc. Res. 491 (1994). For an interpretation of group rights that is critical of Raz, but retains features of the collective conception, see Denise Réaume, *Individuals, Groups, and Rights to Public Goods,* 38 U. Toronto L.J. 1 (1988); Denise G. Réaume, *The Group Right to Linguistic Security: Whose Right, What Duties?, in* Group Rights, *supra,* note 1, at 118.

In this collective conception, a group right is a right held jointly by those who make up the group. The group has no existence or interest that cannot be explicated as that of its members. In particular, the collective conception does not require us to give a moral standing to the group that is separate from the moral standing of each of its individual members. Certainly, the right is held only by the group, but the interests that make the case for the right are the separate, yet identical, interests of the group's members. The moral standing necessary for any claim of right is provided by the moral standing of the several individuals who make up the group. In the collective conception, the group *qua* group has no standing that is not reducible to the moral standing of its members.

In the previous example, the individuals who formed the right-holding group were related by a common but contingent interest. But we can also apply the collective conception to groups that have strong sociological identities. Suppose, for example, that a society contains a cultural minority and that the culture of that minority is central to the lives of its members. In that case, we might claim that the minority has a right, as a group, that the majority society shall take steps to accommodate and protect the minority's culture. The costs and inconvenience of safeguarding the minority's culture could not be justified by the interests of any single member of the minority. Yet the combined interests of all of the members of the minority may provide that justification. In that case, as before, we have a set of individuals that, as a group, holds a right that no one individual holds independently.

A cultural minority is a body of people with a strong common identity as a group. By contrast, the people living in the vicinity of the factory in the earlier example may exhibit no such identity—they may share nothing with one another beyond their experience of the factory's pollution. Yet, the moral structure of the group right, understood as a collective right, is the same in both cases. The right is grounded in the interests of those who jointly hold the right. Of course, groups with strong sociological identities may be more likely to possess shared interests of a sort that will ground collective rights. Also, the interests of those who belong to a group that, like a cultural minority, has a strong identity may not be of a sort that could exist as the interests of isolated individuals. Compare only one individual living near a polluting factory: that single individual could still have an interest in not suffering the factory's pollution.

The collective conception of group rights does not suppose that the interests that individuals have as members of a group can always be represented as interests that they might have as independent and unrelated individuals. Morally, however, the case for a group right rests upon the interests of the individuals who form the group, regardless of the strength of their shared identity and the interdependence of their shared interests. As Raz himself observes: "Cultural, and other, groups have a life of their own.

But their moral claim to respect and to prosperity rests entirely on their vital importance to the prosperity of individual human beings."[8]

III. GROUP RIGHTS: THE CORPORATE CONCEPTION

The collective conception can be contrasted with the "corporate" conception of group rights. The principal difference between these conceptions is that, while the collective conception ascribes moral standing only to the individuals who jointly hold the group right, the corporate conception ascribes moral standing to the group as such.[9] Thus, under the corporate conception, the holder of the right is the group conceived as a single, integral entity. Morally, the group might be said to constitute a right-bearing "individual." The right is held not jointly by the several individuals who make up the group, but by the group as a unitary entity: the right is "its" right rather than "their" right.

Typically, when people ask whether a group can bear rights, they are envisioning this corporate conception of group rights.[10] They ask that question of groups in the same way that they might ask it of fetuses, animals, or future generations: is a group the sort of entity that is capable of bearing rights? To ask that question is to ask whether we should ascribe moral standing to groups in the way that we ascribe moral standing to individual persons. If the answer is yes, then we can conceive a group, as we can conceive an individual, as an irreducible right-bearing entity. Similarly, when people deny that groups can have rights, they usually mean to reject group rights corporately conceived. They deny that groups can bear rights precisely because they deny that we can properly ascribe to groups the sort of irreducible moral standing that we ascribe to individuals.[11]

---

8. Joseph Raz, *Multiculturalism: A Liberal Perspective, in* Ethics in the Public Domain: Essays in the Morality of Law and Politics 155, 163 (1994).
9. For analyses of group rights that suppose, more or less explicitly, that group rights must be corporate in form (even though the authors may use the term "collective right"), see Galenkamp, *supra* note 1; Larry May, The Morality of Groups: Collective Responsibility, Group-Based Harm, and Corporate Rights (1987); Michael McDonald, *Should Communities Have Rights?: Reflections on Liberal Individualism,* 4 Can. J.L. & Juris. 217 (1991); Vernon Van Dyke, *The Individual, the State, and Ethnic Communities in Political Theory,* 29 World Pol. 343 (1977); Van Dyke, *supra* note 2; John Neville Figgis, Churches in the Modern State (1913); Adeno Addis, *Individualism, Communitarianism, and the Rights of Ethnic Minorities,* 67 Notre Dame L. Rev. 615 (1992); Roger Scruton, *Corporate Persons,* 63 Proceedings of the Aristotelian Society 239 (Supp. 1989).
10. Compare the approaches to this issue in Peter A. French, Collective and Corporate Responsibility (1984); May, *supra* note 9; and Galenkamp, *supra* note 1.
11. For this sort of skeptical view of group rights, see Michael Hartney, *Some Confusions Concerning Collective Rights,* 4 Can. J.L. & Juris. 293 (1991); and Jan Narveson, *Collective Rights?,* 4 Can. J.L. & Juris. 329 (1991).

This sort of right is familiar enough from the case of legal corporations and from the form in which corporations hold their rights. However, the primary concerns of this article are with moral, rather than legal, rights and with groups whose legal rights, if they possess any, might be conceived as legal acknowledgments of their moral rights. The adjective "corporate" is used to indicate that only the right-holding group is ascribed a standing *qua* group such that it bears its rights as a corporate entity. This argument does not imply that only groups that possess all of the features that we normally associate with legal corporations can possess "corporate rights." The only element of analogy between the two cases is that corporate rights, like the rights of a legal corporation, are held by a single corporate entity rather than, as in the case of collective rights, jointly by a set of separately identifiable individuals.

What features a group must exhibit to be the sort of group to which we might properly ascribe moral standing and corporate rights will remain unanswered for now. Clearly, it is a question that people might answer in significantly different ways.[12] The purpose of this article is to distinguish group rights conceived corporately from group rights conceived collectively, and, for that purpose, the critical matter is the locus of moral standing. The corporate conception locates standing in the group rather than in the group's members severally. By contrast, the collective conception locates standing in the individuals who jointly hold the right rather than in the group as such.

Whatever view we take of the criteria that a group must satisfy if it is to possess moral standing *qua* group, the groups that can bear corporate rights are likely to form a more limited set than the groups that can bear collective rights. A group that holds collective rights might be a tightly knit community with a common culture and a distinct form of life. Yet, it might also be a set of individuals who share nothing in common but a single interest, as in the example of the individuals affected by factory pollution. For the collective conception, all that identifies a group as a group for right-holding purposes is that its members share an interest of sufficient moment to justify the imposition of duties in respect of that interest. Aside from that single interest, there need be nothing that identifies the group as a group.

On the corporate conception, by contrast, a group must possess a morally significant identity as a group independently, and in advance, of

12. For some different answers, see French, *supra* note 10; Galenkamp, *supra* note 1; and May, *supra* note 9. This article's line of argument implies that the issue of which groups, if any, can possess corporate (moral) rights can be settled only after the more general issue of which sorts of entities possess moral standing has been settled.

whatever interests and rights it may possess. Just as an individual has an identity and a standing as a person independently and in advance of the rights that he possesses, so a group, if it is to be conceived as a corporate entity, must possess a morally significant identity and status independently and in advance of whatever rights it may hold. Its interests and rights follow upon its identity as a group; they are not what identifies the group as a group.

Thus, a group of individuals who distinguish themselves as a set only by their shared interest in clean air, coastal defenses, or community health measures might possess collective rights to those goods, but they do not constitute the sort of group that will possess corporate rights. They do not possess a morally significant identity *qua* group such that we might ascribe moral standing to the group separately from its individual members. If, however, we recognize a group as a "nation" or a "people," that could be the sort of group to which we attribute standing *qua* group and whose rights we might think of in corporate terms.

IV. CORPORATE RIGHTS, COLLECTIVE RIGHTS, AND HUMAN RIGHTS

A. Fundamental Considerations

The principle claim of this article is that, if we conceive group rights as corporate rights, then we cannot represent them as human rights; but if we conceive them as collective rights, then we can represent some group rights either as human rights or as closely akin to human rights. Corporate rights cannot be human rights because they are rights held by corporate entities rather than by human beings. They are also rights grounded in whatever gives those corporate entities their special moral status rather than rights grounded in the status of humanity or personhood. Collective rights, on the other hand, might be represented as human rights in that they are rights held by individuals, albeit by individuals jointly rather than severally. They might also be rights grounded in considerations that relate to human beings and human interests in general.

Of course, there can be collective rights that are not human rights, just as there are individual rights that are not human rights.[13] A collective right

13. Relatively straightforward examples of rights that are not, morally, human rights are rights that are special to particular individuals or groups because those rights arise from special arrangements to which those individuals or groups are party. So, for example, if a particular person has a right to something, but only because some other person has promised to provide him with it, that individually-held right will not be a human right. Similarly, if a particular group has a collective right only because the group is party to a treaty or some other form of agreement, then its collective right will not be a human right.

will be eligible for consideration as a human right, or for membership in the same moral family as human rights, only if it is a right that we can ascribe universally to human beings and that rests upon their moral status as human beings. If a collective right satisfies those conditions, there is reason to characterize it as a "collective human right."

Consider the right of a nation or a people to be self-determining.[14] (For the moment, this article will leave open the question of whether the terms "nation" and "people" describe a group distinguished by an ethnocultural identity or merely by membership in the same political community.) Suppose that we accept that there is such a right and that we conceive it as a corporate right. In that case, the right will be held not by human beings, but by nations or peoples conceived as corporate entities. Because we would be ascribing moral standing to nations or peoples as such, we would not be able to represent the ultimate holders of the right as the individuals who make up the nation or people. Moreover, the status that grounds the right will be the status of "nationhood" or "peoplehood" rather than humanity or personhood. Thus, neither the holder of the right nor the status upon which it depends provides any justification for characterizing the right as a human right.

A corporate right can, of course, be a universal right: it can be held by all tokens of the corporate type. The right of national self-determination can be, and typically is, asserted in a way that makes it universal to all nations. The right might also range comprehensively over humanity: if we assign each and every human being to a nation and claim that all nations have a right of self-determination, that right of national self-determination will encompass all humanity. However, this combination of universality and comprehensiveness is no reason to identify the right as a human right: the right will be simply a universal and comprehensive corporate right.

Consider now how a nation's or people's right of self-determination appears if we reinterpret it as a collective right. It will now be a right held by the individuals who make up each nation or people, even though each individual right holder will hold the right jointly with, rather than independently of, his fellow nationals. In addition, the right will be grounded in the interest that those individuals share in living in a self-determining nation. We can characterize that interest as one universal to all human beings. For any particular individual, the interest will relate immediately to the particular nation to which he belongs. Even so, that is not the sort of

14. This analysis assumes without argument that one is to understand a nation's or a people's right of self-determination as a group right of some form. Others have attempted to understand these rights as individual rights. *See* Donnelly, *supra* note 1, at 147; Yael Tamir, Liberal Nationalism 35 (1993); Carl Wellman, Real Rights 173 (1995).

particularity that prevents the right, and the ultimate interest upon which it depends, from being universal to all human beings. Similarly, rights of political participation are, for any particular individual, rights held in relation to a particular state. Yet, they can still be represented as rights possessed universally by human beings. Therefore, if we interpret a nation's or people's right of self-determination as a collective right, we can interpret it as a right grounded in interests general to humanity and in the moral standing of human beings rather than in any independent moral standing that allegedly stems from nationhood or peoplehood. Thus, we now have an understanding of the right in which it remains a group right but becomes a right that we can place either within, or in close proximity to, the doctrine of human rights.

Those who are wary of mixing group rights with human rights may still resist the claim that there can be collective as well as individual human rights. They may insist that a right can be a human right only if it is tenable by a human being as an independent individual, and that a jointly held right cannot be the genuine article. At this level, it is not easy to know how to determine correct usage, nor, perhaps, does that matter very much. This article's principle claim is that, if group rights are understood as corporate rights, they will be rights that are categorically different from human rights. If, however, group rights are understood as collective rights, thinking about group rights can approximate thinking about human rights.

B. Conflicting or Complementary Rights?

There are many other ways in which human rights sit more comfortably with group rights conceived collectively than with group rights conceived corporately. For example, the idea of collective rights functions with the same fundamental moral units as the idea of human rights: individual persons. An argument for a collective right must appeal to the good of the individuals who make up the collectivity, and individuals will figure in a right-holding collectivity only if they share in the interest that grounds its right. There is, therefore, a continuity and complementarity between individual and collective rights: respect and concern for the individual drive both. The difference between the two sorts of rights simply reflects the fact that, sometimes, our respect and concern relates to features of people's lives that they share with others and in relation to which they hold shared, rather than independent, claims.

For example, the respect and concern that leads us to ascribe to people individually held rights to freedom of worship and individually held rights against religious discrimination should also lead us to ascribe to people rights that their religious sites not be desecrated.[15] Yet, the right of the members of a religious faith that their sacred sites be respected really makes sense only as a right that those individuals hold collectively. Similarly, recognition of the evils of racism and racial discrimination leads us to oppose racist conduct targeted both at particular individuals and at racial groups generally. If, in a particular case, a racial group, but not specific individuals within that group, is the target of incitement to racial hatred, and if that incitement violates a right, then the right it violates is more intelligible as a right held by the group collectively than by its members severally.[16] Many of the rights that relate to people's enjoyment of their culture and use of their language are rights that they can hold and exercise as individuals. Sometimes, however, governments embark on policies designed to erode gradually the identity of a cultural or linguistic minority. Those policies can adversely affect the minority in general without visiting more specific harms on individuals within the minority. Again, if those policies violate a right, the violated right makes more sense as a right held by the members of the minority collectively than by each of them separately.[17]

Thus, the respect and concern that generate a claim of individual right can generate a cognate claim of collective right. That commonality of concern applies to the burdens imposed, as well as to the benefits conferred, by collective rights. A group of individuals may share an interest that gives them a *prima facie* claim to a collective right. If, however, the duties entailed by that putative right would prove unduly burdensome for

15. *See, e.g.,* Vienna Declaration and Programme of Action, U.N. GAOR, World Conf. on Hum. Rts., 48th Sess., 22d plen. mtg., pt. II, ¶ 22, U.N. Doc. A/CONF.157/4 (1993), *reprinted in* 32 I.L.M. 1661 (1993).

16. *Cf.* International Convention on the Elimination of All Forms of Racial Discrimination, *adopted* 21 Dec. 1965, art. 4, 660 U.N.T.S. 195 (*entered into force* 4 Jan. 1969), *reprinted in* 5 I.L.M. 352, 355 (1966).

17. *Cf.* Declaration on the Rights of Persons Belonging to National or Ethnic, Religious and Linguistic Minorities, *adopted* 18 Dec. 1992, G.A. Res. 47/135, U.N. GAOR, 47th Sess., Annex, arts. 1, 4(2), U.N. Doc. A/Res/47/135/Annex (1992), *reprinted in* 32 I.L.M. 911, 914, 915; Draft Declaration on the Rights of Indigenous Peoples, U.N. ESCOR, Comm'n on Hum. Rts., 45th Sess., Annex Agenda Item 14, arts. 6–39, U.N. Doc. E/CN.4/Sub.2/1993/29/Annex I (1993). Article 27 of the ICCPR reads: "In those States in which ethnic, religious or linguistic minorities exist, persons belonging to such minorities shall not be denied the right, in community with the other members of their group, to enjoy their own culture, to profess and practice their own religion, or to use their own language." ICCPR, *supra* note 2, art. 27. In examining Article 27, commentators have frequently fastened on the phrase "persons belonging to such minorities" and inferred that it indicates that the Article invests rights in individuals rather than groups. *See, e.g.,* Patrick Thornberry, International Law and the Rights of Minorities 173 (1991). However, once the distinction between collective rights and corporate rights is appreciated, it can be seen that the wording of the Article is entirely consistent with its providing a foundation for collective as well as individual rights.

the individuals upon whom they would fall, then the case for the collective right will fail. Provided we use only a collective conception of group rights, a moral contest between the claims of groups and the claims of individuals must reduce, ultimately, to a contest between the claims of individuals.

In contrast, by giving moral standing to a group as such, the corporate conception does not allow the claims of groups to be analyzed as those of individuals. The corporate conception accords groups a status that is ultimate rather than derivative. Consequently, a potential for rivalry between groups and individuals arises that is both fundamental and ineliminable. In turn, that potential gives rise to the reasonable fear that individuals and their claims of right will be crushed beneath the greater weight of groups and their claims of right.

One way in which a corporate conception of group rights threatens individuals is by making it possible for the moral standing of the group to displace that of individuals within the group. Suppose, for example, that within a well-established and well-defined cultural group some individuals develop a wish to live in ways that depart from, and are at odds with, the group's traditions. Should they be free to break from the group's traditional pattern of life? If we ascribe ultimate moral standing on the issue of how people should live to the group's members individually, it will be for each individual to decide how he shall live. However, if we ascribe ultimate standing on this matter to the group *qua* group, the group's voice will be authoritative. Of course, where there is dissension within a group, a corporate conception has to find some way of determining which voice is the authoritative or authentic voice of the group. Once that voice has been detected, however, that voice, not the voices of the dissenting individuals, should be heard. In particular, this question of who has standing on a matter—the group or its members severally—will determine to which of these voices the outside world should listen and to which it should defer. That is one of the issues that faces the outside world when it agonizes over whether it should intervene to "save" individuals from practices, such as female circumcision, that are sanctioned by the cultural group to which those individuals belong.

Corporate rights can also compete with the claims of individuals outside the right-holding group, although we need not suppose that they will in every case. If we conceive groups, such as nations or cultural groups, as corporate entities, then we are also likely, in some measure, to conceive their rights as entitlements directed against other corporate entities—other nations or other cultures—rather than at individuals. Nevertheless, individuals can also bear the costs of a group's corporate right. Where, for example, a nation asserts its corporate right to a territory, it may embark on a policy of ethnic cleansing that aims to purge from its territory individuals whom it deems not to be part of itself and who, therefore, have no right to reside in its territory.

Corporate rights need not always exist at the expense of human rights. Indeed, human rights can be used to limit the range of corporate rights. In particular, we can insist that human rights must always take priority over corporate claims. The point is only that the corporate conception, in giving moral standing to groups as such, creates a world in which the claims of groups are not analyzable morally as the claims of individuals. Accordingly, in the corporate conception, it becomes morally possible for the claims of groups to challenge and override the claims of individuals.

This article does not claim that proponents of individual rights have nothing to fear from group rights collectively conceived. In particular, the aggregative nature of Raz' version of the collective theory—that interests accumulate across individuals to make the case for a collective right[18]—may provide reason to worry about how the claims of individuals taken singly will fare when set against those of individuals taken collectively. The same aggregative feature of collective rights may create reason to worry about how the claims of small groups will fare when they compete with those of large groups. However, that is ultimately a matter of how we regard the various interests at stake, and there remains a critical difference between the two theories.

The corporate theory can characterize a matter as one on which a group alone has standing and, therefore, on which the competing or dissenting claims of individuals should simply be ignored. The collective theory provides no similar warrant for writing individuals out of the moral calculation. If we adopt the collective theory, the claims of the few may have to yield to those of the many, but at least the claims of the few will be heard and counted.

This is one context in which it matters whether a collective right is a human right. If it is, it must be a right possessed by everyone, so that one set of individuals cannot prevail over another because the former has collective human rights while the latter does not. Collective human rights also must be consistent with whatever other rights we ascribe to human beings. In particular, the assessment of what should be the form and content of the entire set of human rights requires an intra-personal, rather than an interpersonal, calculation. It is a matter of weighing different interests possessed by each and every human individual: it is not a matter of pitting the interests of some against those of others. If there is a tension between a putative collective human right and a putative individual human right, it must reflect a tension within the interests of each human being. Such tension cannot reflect a conflict between two rival moral claimants, group and individual. For example, if we conceive both the right of collective

18. Raz, *supra* note 5, at 187, 209.

self-determination and the right to individual liberty as human rights, we must think of the balance between those rights as a balance to be struck within the interests of each person. We should not think of ourselves as balancing the collective interests of some against the individual interests of others.

There is a further contrast between corporate and collective rights that is significant for human rights theorists troubled by the idea of group rights. One of the most common fears is that the rights of a group will be held against or over its own members so that, in ascribing rights to a group, we are simultaneously placing its individual members at the mercy of the group.[19] Group rights may then seem to license group oppression. Such a fear is properly directed at corporate rights but not at collective rights.

It is generally accepted that one cannot hold rights against oneself. The duties entailed by one's rights must be duties borne by others. In other words, a right-duty or a power-liability relation must involve two separately identifiable parties: a party that has the right or power, and another that incurs the corresponding duty or liability. The corporate conception of group rights makes it possible for a group to hold rights against its own members because it accords moral standing to the group independently of its members. Existentially, there may be no group that can be separated from its members, but, morally, the group has a being that is separate from that of each of its members taken severally. Therefore, on the corporate theory, a group can hold rights against, or powers over, individuals within its own ranks.

By contrast, the collective conception of group rights provides no warrant for the claim that a group can hold rights against its own members. In the collective conception, the right is held jointly by the individuals who make up the group, and the group has no standing that is separate from the standing of its individual members. Thus, morally, there is no group that has an existence independently of, and that can hold rights against, its own members. There are only individuals who hold rights jointly, and, by common consent, right holders cannot hold rights against themselves. Rights held by individuals jointly, like those held individually, must be rights directed "outward" at other individuals or groups of individuals rather than

19. *See* Donnelly, *supra* note 1, at 145; Graff, *supra* note 1; Nordenfelt, *supra* note 1, at 7; Peter R. Baehr & Koo VanderWal, *Introduction Item: Human Rights as Individual and as Collective Rights, in* Human Rights in a Pluralist World: Individuals and Collectivities, *supra* note 1, at 33, 36; Green, *supra* note 7; Eugene Kamenka, *Human Rights, Peoples' Rights, in* The Rights of Peoples, *supra* note 2, at 127, 131–34. For discussions of this fear of group rights, see Gillian Triggs, *The Rights of Peoples and Individual Rights: Conflict or Harmony?, in* The Rights of Peoples, *supra* note 2, at 141; Maleiha Malik, *Communal Goods as Human Rights, in* Understanding Human Rights 138 (Conor Gearty & Adam Tomkins eds., 1996).

"inward" to the right holders themselves. Thus, if we ascribe collective rights to ethnic, cultural, religious, or linguistic groups, such groups hold those rights against the outside world. Such rights will not entitle the group to tyrannize its own members.[20]

V. PEOPLES AND THE RIGHT TO SELF-DETERMINATION

A number of group rights have been claimed as, or associated with, human rights.[21] Foremost among these have been rights claimed for peoples, indigenous minorities, and cultural groups that, in various ways, entitle them to shape their own destinies.[22] Those who embrace so-called "third-generation" or "solidarity" human rights—rights to peace, development, a healthy environment, communication, humanitarian assistance, or a share in the common heritage of mankind—often characterize these as group rights.[23] That characterization, however, has proven controversial.[24] That the

---

20. The author investigates the implications of group rights for the rights and standing of individuals at greater length in Peter Jones, *Group Rights and Group Oppression*, 7 J. Pol. Phil. (forthcoming 1999).
21. Examples of UN human rights documents that (clearly or arguably) ascribe rights to groups, frequently but not always in the form of peoples' rights, include: Convention on the Prevention and Punishment of the Crime of Genocide, *adopted* 9 Dec. 1948, art. 2, 78 U.N.T.S. 277 (*entered into force* 12 Jan. 1951); ICCPR, *supra* note 2, art. 1; ICESCR, *supra* note 2, art. 1; Vienna Declaration and Programme of Action, *supra* note 15, pt. I, art. 2; Draft Declaration on the Rights of Indigenous Peoples, *supra* note 17. Compare with these, however, the Vienna Declaration and Programme of Action, *supra* note 15, pt. I, art. 20 and pt. II, arts. 28–32 (recognizing the rights of "indigenous people," rather than "indigenous peoples"). The African Charter on Human and Peoples' Rights, *supra* note 3, catalogues several rights of peoples but, as explained in note 3, *supra,* it presents them as rights that are distinct from, rather than encompassed by, human rights.
22. For discussions of the rights of cultural and indigenous groups, see generally Addis, *supra* note 9; Robert N. Clinton, *The Rights of Indigenous Peoples as Collective Group Rights,* 32 Ariz. L. Rev. 739 (1990); Allen Buchanan, *The Role of Collective Rights in the Theory of Indigenous Peoples' Rights,* 3 Transnat'l L. & Contemp. Probs. 89 (1993); Vernon Van Dyke, *The Cultural Rights of Peoples,* 2 Universal Human Rights, Apr.–June 1980, at 1; Lyndel V. Prott, *Cultural Rights as Peoples' Rights in International Law, in* The Rights of Peoples, *supra* note 2, at 93; Garth Nettheim, *'Peoples' and 'Populations'—Indigenous Peoples and the Rights of Peoples, in* The Rights of Peoples, *supra* note 2, at 107; Erica-Irene A. Daes, *The Right of Indigenous Peoples to "Self-Determination" in the Contemporary World Order, in* Self-Determination: International Perspectives 47 (Donald Clark & Robert Williamson eds., 1996); Gudmundur Alfredsson, *Different Forms of and Claims to the Right of Self-Determination, in* Self-Determination: International Perspectives, *supra,* at 58; Will Kymlicka, Liberalism, Community, and Culture (1989); Will Kymlicka, Multicultural Citizenship: A Liberal Theory of Minority Rights (1995); The Rights of Minority Cultures (Will Kymlicka ed., 1995).
23. *See, e.g.,* Stephen P. Marks, *Emerging Human Rights: A New Generation for the 1980s?,* 33 Rutgers L. Rev. 435 (1981); Roland Y. Rich, *The Right to Development as an Emerging Human Right,* 23 Va. J. Int'l L. 287 (1983); Roland Rich, *The Right to Development: A Right of Peoples?, in* The Rights of Peoples, *supra* note 2, at 39; George W. Shepherd, Jr., *African People's Rights: The Third Generation in a Global Perspective, in* Emerging Human

bearers of these rights must be distinct groups of human beings, rather than individuals or mankind at large, is not readily obvious from the content of these rights. Insofar as solidarity rights are conceived as rights that are collective to mankind as a whole, they might be better characterized as common objectives for humanity rather than as rights that are particular to individuals or groups. This article will not, however, pursue the much discussed issue of whether these third-generation rights are properly characterized as group rights or human rights, or as rights of any kind.[25] Rather, the remainder of this article limits itself to examining more closely how the collective and corporate conceptions of group rights bear upon our understanding of peoples and the rights of political self-determination claimed for them.

A. The Identity of "Peoples"

What is it that distinguishes a population as a "people" entitled to self-determination? That question has proven difficult to answer with any theoretical precision.[26] It has also proven to be a potent source of political conflict.[27] This article strives here to indicate only how the corporate and

---

Rights: The African Political Economy Context 39 (George W. Shepherd, Jr. & Mark O.C. Anikpo eds., 1990); Anthony Carty, *The Third World Claim to Economic Self-Determination: Economic Rights of Peoples: Theoretical Aspects, in* The Right to Development in International Law 43 (S.R. Chowdhury et al. eds., 1992).

24. *See* Donnelly, *supra* note 1, at 143; Galenkamp, *supra* note 1, at 31, 114.

25. On these issues, see Philip Alston, *A Third Generation of Solidarity Rights: Progressive Development or Obfuscation of International Human Rights Law?*, 29 Neth. Int'l L. Rev. 307 (1982); Philip Alston, *Conjuring Up New Human Rights: A Proposal for Quality Control*, 78 Am. J. Int'l L. 607 (1984); Cees Flinterman, *Three Generations of Human Rights, in* Human Rights in a Pluralist World: Individuals and Collectivities, *supra* note 1, at 75; Jeremy Waldron, *Can Communal Goods Be Human Rights?, in* Liberal Rights: Collected Papers, 1981–1991, at 339 (1993); P.H. Kooijmans, *Human Rights—Universal Panacea?: Some Reflections on the So-Called Human Rights of the Third Generation*, 37 Neth. Int'l L. Rev. 315 (1990); and Ian Brownlie, *The Rights of Peoples in Modern International Law, in* The Rights of Peoples, *supra* note 2, at 1.

26. *Cf.* Michla Pomerance, Self-Determination in Law and Practice: The New Doctrine in the United Nations 14 (1982); David Makinson, *On Attributing Rights to All Peoples: Some Logical Questions*, 8 Law & Phil. 53 (1989); Peter R. Baehr, *Human Rights and Peoples' Rights, in* Human Rights in a Pluralist World: Individuals and Collectivities, *supra* note 1, at 99; Michael Freeman, *Democracy and Dynamite: The Peoples' Right to Self-Determination*, 44 Pol. Stud. 746 (1996); Richard N. Kiwanuka, *The Meaning of "People" in the African Charter on Human and Peoples' Rights*, 82 Am. J. Int'l L. 80 (1988); Cassese, *supra* note 2, at 141.

27. The breakups of the former Yugoslavia and of the Soviet Union have provided graphic illustrations of the conflict that can be generated by the issue of who is to count as a 'people' for purposes of self-determination. A list of conflicts over that issue elsewhere in the world would be a long one and would include, for example, conflicts concerning Sri Lanka, Eritrea, Somalia, Kashmir, Khalistan, Quebec, the Basques, the Kurds, the

the collective conceptions of group rights can embody different understandings of what it is that makes a population a right-holding people.[28]

1. Conceptual Distinctions

If we conceive a people's right of self-determination as a corporate right, a people must be identifiable as a corporate entity. It makes sense to attribute moral standing to a group *qua* group only if that group has a clear identity to which we can ascribe moral significance. If we confront a set of disparate individuals bereft of any unifying identity, we have reason to ascribe to them moral standing as so many individuals, but no reason to accord them any independent moral standing as a group. Therefore, if a population is to constitute a group that can bear a corporate right, then it must be distinguished by an identity that marks it off as a people such that the group can be regarded as a moral being in its own right.[29] What sort of identity that must be is open to argument. Nevertheless, the most obvious candidate is the sort of identity that is commonly thought to mark off a population as a "nation," where nationhood is understood to mean something more than, or other than, mere statehood. Thus, a population may be distinguished as a people by virtue of its ethnicity, culture, history, or some other feature or combination of features that separates it from the rest of humanity. Identifying populations as peoples in this sense is fraught with difficulties that are too well-known to merit rehearsal here.[30] Yet, escaping those

---

Palestinians, Northern Ireland, East Timor, Tibet, and Taiwan. For studies of a range of cases of conflict over the 'self' that is to be self-determining, see CASSESE, *supra* note 2, at 205–73; HURST HANNUM, AUTONOMY, SOVEREIGNTY AND SELF-DETERMINATION: THE ACCOMMODATION OF CONFLICTING RIGHTS (1990); SELF-DETERMINATION: INTERNATIONAL PERSPECTIVES, *supra* note 22; Donald L. Horowitz, *Self-Determination: Politics, Philosophy, and Law, in* ETHNICITY AND GROUP RIGHTS 421 (Ian Shapiro & Will Kymlicka eds., 1997).

28. This analysis takes for granted that peoples' rights are not to be understood as the rights of states, although the state may serve as an instrument through which a people secures and exercises its rights.

29. John Rawls adopts a corporate rather than a collective conception of peoples and their rights. John Rawls, *The Law of Peoples, in* ON HUMAN RIGHTS: THE OXFORD AMNESTY LECTURES 1993, at 41 (Stephen Shute & Susan Hurley eds., 1993). He treats peoples rather than persons as the fundamental moral units of international society, *see generally id.*, and his insistence that one must not transpose the liberal conception of the person from liberal to nonliberal societies seems to rule out a collective conception of the rights of peoples. *Id.* at 65–66. Rawls' adoption of peoples rather than persons as the fundamental moral units of international life creates difficulties for his attempt to find a place for human rights in his account of international justice. *See* Peter Jones, *International Human Rights: Philosophical or Political?, in* NATIONAL RIGHTS, INTERNATIONAL OBLIGATIONS 183 (Simon Caney et al. eds., 1996).

30. Nationhood is the quality most commonly invoked to identify peoples pre-politically, where nationhood is supposed to identify a people independently of statehood. However, the claim that humanity divides into 'nations' in this sense frequently attracts skepticism. *See, e.g.*, Graff, *supra* note 1; ELIE KEDOURIE, NATIONALISM (4th ed. 1993); David

difficulties is not possible if we wish to conceive a population as a pre-legal entity distinguished by a common identity and possessing, in virtue of its identity as a people, a corporate right of self-determination.

If, however, we understand the right to self-determination as a collective right, the people that bears the right can be understood in a much less demanding way. Indeed, the group that bears the collective right may be defined merely in political terms. To share in a collective right, a group of individuals need share only in the interest that grounds the right. A set of individuals may be members of the same state but, apart from falling within a common political jurisdiction, may share nothing that distinguishes them as a group. Even so, the mere fact that they belong to the same political community is enough, we might argue, to give them a shared interest in that community being self-determining. Individuals who fall within the same political jurisdiction share an interest in being able to determine their common political future and in not being subject to external rule. That shared interest is, we may hold, of sufficient moment to give such a population a jointly held right of collective self-determination.

A collective right of self-determination is, then, consistent with a purely political conception of the people that holds the right. In this form, the right of self-determination is neutral with respect to the issue of where political boundaries should fall.[31] The "self" that is to be self-determining is something that is defined by, rather than something that itself defines, the unit of political rule. The claim is simply that, however political boundaries are drawn, individuals encompassed within the same political unit have a shared interest in that unit being self-determining. It is this shared interest that makes the case for the existence of their collective right of self-determination.

This purely political conception of a people is one that matches some

---

George, *National Identity and National Self-Determination, in* National Rights, International Obligations, *supra* note 29, at 13; John Charvet, *What is Nationality, and Is There a Moral Right to National Self-Determination?, in* National Rights, International Obligations, *supra* note 29, at 53; Martti Koskenniemi, *National Self-Determination Today: Problems of Legal Theory and Practice,* 43 Int'l & Comp. L.Q. 241 (1994). For more sympathetic appraisals of the claims of national identity, see Neil MacCormick, *Nation and Nationalism, in* Legal Right and Social Democracy: Essays in Legal and Political Philosophy 247 (1982); Avishai Margalit & Joseph Raz, *National Self-Determination,* 87 J. Phil. 439 (1990); David Miller, On Nationality (1995); Tamir, *supra* note 14.

31. This statement includes the supposition, which this article accepts as correct, that democracy cannot tell us which sets of individuals should form self-determining peoples: all that it can tell us is that a people, once defined, ought to be self-governing. For an argument that reverses that order of reasoning and endeavors to use democracy to explain why a people with a common identity should form a self-determining unit, see Daniel Philpott, *In Defense of Self-Determination,* 105 Ethics 352 (1995).

appeals to the popular right of self-determination better than the corporate conception. For example, much of the drive that led to the inclusion of peoples' rights of self-determination in UN declarations and covenants came from anticolonialism.[32] Yet, many of the colonial units for which self-determination was demanded had populations that were far too diverse to have any convincing claim to be peoples in the corporate sense.[33] This demand for self-determination made more sense as a claim that, whatever the demographics of a population that formed a political unit, that population was entitled to be governed internally rather than externally.

Why cannot we identify a people as a corporate entity in a similarly political fashion? We can, but its right of self-determination will then be legal, rather than moral, in origin. Any population can be legally incorporated as a people and invested with rights of a corporate form, but those rights will then be merely legal rights, rather than moral rights that indicate what legal rights there ought to be. In the collective right of self-determination, the people is certainly an artifact of legal definition, but its right of self-determination is not. The right is not a legal creation but a moral entitlement arising from the interests that individuals have in living in a self-determining community.

In arguing that a collective right of self-determination can be borne by a people defined merely politically, this article does not mean to suggest that it can be associated only with that conception of a people. On the contrary, we might point to common cultural and sociological features exhibited by a group, then argue that the individuals who share those features have a joint interest in forming a self-determining unit. Joseph Raz and Avishai Margalit argue for a collective right of national self-determination in just that way.[34] They identify a number of features—such as a common culture, a shared history, and significance for individuals' self-identity—that distinguish groups that are commonly labeled "nations" or "peoples," and argue that a group of individuals who share those features also share an interest in forming a distinct political community.[35] Thus, we might appeal to the idea of a collective right not only to argue that a politically defined people has a right to be self-determining, but also to establish which sets of individuals have a right to form self-determining peoples. In making the case for that sort of collective right, we are likely to appeal to the same kinds

---

32. *See* Cassese, *supra* note 2, at 44; Hurst Hannum, *Self-Determination in the Post-Colonial Era, in* Self-Determination: International Perspectives, *supra* note 22, at 16; Morphet, *supra* note 2.
33. This is true of most of the post-colonial states of sub-Saharan Africa. *See* William Tordoff, Government and Politics in Africa 28 (3d ed. 1997); Naomi Chazan et al., Politics and Society in Contemporary Africa 73 (2d ed. 1992).
34. Margalit & Raz, *supra* note 30.
35. *Id.* at 442–447.

of distinguishing features as figure in a conception of peoples as corporate entities.

So is there any significant difference between the collective and the corporate approaches to the issue of which populations should form self-determining peoples? Perhaps the major difference is that a collective approach can be more "relaxed" and flexible than a corporate approach in its handling of that issue. A theory that regards peoples as right-bearing corporate entities is one that will have to use fairly strict criteria of what distinguishes a group as a people. The critical matter for that theory is whether a group possesses moral standing *qua* group, and moral standing cannot be a matter of more or less: a group either has it or it does not. Thus, a population will either meet the criteria, in which case it will be deemed a people with full rights of self-determination, or it will not, in which case it will have no equivalent status or entitlement.

For a theory that adopts the collective approach, the critical test is rather different. It is not a matter of which groups have standing and which do not; rather it is a matter of which sets of individuals share features of a kind that give them an interest in forming a self-determining community. In one case, the shared feature that gives them that interest may be a common language. In another case, it may be their shared religious beliefs. In a further case, it may be simply a shared sense of identity. Thus, the feature or features that relate to the right of self-determination might be quite different from one population to another, and those features need not form part of a single conception of nationhood or peoplehood. The considerations that argue for independence for Tibet may be quite different from those that argue for independence for Taiwan, yet, provided that each set of considerations is of sufficient moment, each can ground a collective right of self-determination. Where interest rather than status is the test, larger considerations, such as beneficial or adverse consequences for the outside world, may enter the calculus of whether a population should become a self-determining people.

The form that self-determination should take might also vary more readily if it is a matter of collective rather than corporate right. An identical status implies an identical right. For a corporate theory, then, all peoples will be entitled to the same form of self-determination: typically, fully independent statehood. However, an approach that turns on a calculus of interests can argue for different rights in different circumstances. An all-things-considered judgment might yield a right to full political independence for one population but a right to a more limited degree of autonomy, such as a federal or devolutionary arrangement, for another. Thus, although the corporate and collective approaches may overlap at certain points in their response to the question of who should form a self-determining people, they can also deliver significantly different answers to that question.

2. Distinctions in Application

How do these different ways of conceiving peoples bear upon the question of whether peoples' rights of self-determination can be interpreted as human rights? It should be clear that, if we conceive the right as a corporate right, then there is no case for characterizing it as a human right. If, on the other hand, we conceive it as a collective right, then the answer depends upon what sort of collective right we claim. If we claim that the right is held by a people understood only as a politically defined unit of population, the right has as good a claim as any to be a collective human right. All individuals live in, and are subject to the authority of, political communities. The individuals forming any particular political community have a shared interest in determining, and arguably, therefore, a jointly held right to determine, the future of their political community. Understood in this way, peoples' rights of self-determination are universal to humanity and are held jointly by individuals in politically defined groups.

What about the other sort of collective right identified above: the pre-political collective right of a group to form a self-determining people in virtue of the shared identity of its members and their shared interest in forming a self-determining unit? Characterizing this right as a human right is altogether more problematic. Some segments of humanity may have sharply defined sociological or cultural identities that mark them out as groups that have an interest in forming separate political communities, but others may not. In addition, movements in the world's population and the polyethnic and multicultural character of most contemporary societies belie the feasibility of suggesting that each and every individual has a jointly held right to live in a political community (whether sovereign or less than sovereign) distinguished by that particular individual's culture, religion, language, or whatever else contributes significantly to his identity. That is not to say that there are no cases in which a group can reasonably claim a collective right to form a politically self-determining community by virtue of its shared identity. It is to observe only that, in our world, it is hard to see how that right could be realized such that it ranges over, and provides for, each and every human being. It is difficult, then, to see how this particular version of the collective right to self-determination can be represented as a form of human right—not because it is a group right, but simply because it lacks the universality that is an essential property of a human right.

B. Self-Determination: External and Internal

In the arena of international relations, a people's right of self-determination is asserted, first and foremost, as a right against "outsiders": *ceteris paribus,* it vetoes any form of external government, such as imperial rule, and any form of unsolicited external intervention.[36] Understood as a corporate right, the right is an essential concomitant of the moral status enjoyed by a people. Depriving a people of self-determination is the international equivalent of depriving a person of self-determination. In both cases, the act of deprivation fails to accord the "self" the recognition and respect to which it is entitled. Understood as a collective right, the right is one jointly held by those individuals who form a people and is grounded in their shared interest in not being subject to external rule or interference.

Scholars and commentators frequently hold that self-determination has an internal as well as an external dimension.[37] This may be no more than the flip side of the same coin: if a people's affairs are not determined externally, they must be determined internally. Yet, self-determination is often taken to imply rather more than that. If a people is said to be self-determining, that may mean that its members themselves choose, control, and participate in the government of their society. An internal military coup that displaces a popularly elected government would not violate the people's right of self-determination understood as a right against the outside world, but would violate its right of self-determination understood as its right to conduct or control its own affairs.

We may then inquire, how do the corporate and collective conceptions of group rights compare when they are applied to self-determination internally? More particularly, how does each relate to the right to democratic government? If we start from the right of self-determination as a right against the external world, and work back from that right, neither conception of group rights need deliver a right to a popular form of government.

Conceiving a people as a corporate entity with rights against the outside world need entail no view of how the internal life of that corporate entity should be structured. That is what makes it possible for a dictatorial and undemocratic regime to feel no compunction about the lack of internal self-determination that it extends to those it governs, even though it insists that the outside world must recognize and respect its people's (corporate) right of self-determination.

For the collective conception, the issue turns upon how we construe the interest that grounds the right that people hold against the outside world. The interest could be linked to democratic government, but it need not be. We might claim, for example, that external rulers are likely to be less well-informed about the society and less committed to promoting its good than internal rulers, and that is why people have an interest in being governed

36. *See* Cassese, *supra* note 2, at 55, 67; Pomerance, *supra* note 26, at 24.
37. *See* Cassese, *supra* note 2, at 52, 101; Pomerance, *supra* note 26, at 37.

internally rather than externally. Or we might claim merely that it is humiliating for a people to be subject to external government, and that is why they have a right not to be so governed. In either case, the interest that grounds a people's external right of self-determination does not, of itself, imply that a people must be governed democratically.

We might, however, interpret the right of self-determination the other way around. Rather than treating the externally directed right as primary and searching for its internal implications, we might give primacy to self-determination as an internally directed right. That is, we might give primacy to the right of a people to order its own affairs and regard its right to be free from external interference as merely a secondary and consequential requirement of that internally focused right. Clearly, while a right to be free from external interference need not entail a popular form of government, a right of popular self-government will preclude the legitimacy of externally imposed rule.

Even if we shift the focus of self-determination in this way, the right of self-determination can be interpreted in a form that does not require democratic government. It might be understood as the right of popular sovereignty—the right of a people to determine how it shall be governed, which, of course, will include its right to opt for an undemocratic government. An unconstrained right of popular sovereignty also allows a people to forsake its independence and make itself part of a larger political entity, and perhaps even to opt to be governed externally.[38]

Notwithstanding that possibility, suppose that self-determination requires democracy.[39] In one respect, the right to democratic government makes more sense as a group right than as an individual right. There is something oddly disproportionate and implausible in the claim that a single individual, solely as an individual, has a right that an entire society should be governed democratically. How could a single individual, all on his own,

---

38. The doctrine of popular sovereignty does not entail a commitment to democracy. To be committed to democracy is to be committed to the rightness of a particular form of government. To be committed to the doctrine of popular sovereignty is to be committed to the rightness of whatever form of government a people chooses for itself. Article 1(1) of the ICCPR states that all peoples, by virtue of their right of self-determination, "freely determine their political status." ICCPR, *supra* note 2, art. 1(1). That phrasing, which also occurs in several other UN documents, suggests the doctrine of popular sovereignty rather than the unique legitimacy of democracy. The ICCPR does go on, however, to lay down rights of a specifically democratic character. *Id.* art. 25.

39. Whether the self-determination of peoples endorsed in various UN documents requires democracy and, if so, in what form, has proved controversial. *See* POMERANCE, *supra* note 26, at 37. For an argument that international law now requires democratic government, see Thomas M. Franck, *The Emerging Right to Democratic Governance*, 86 AM. J. INT'L L. 46 (1992). For a sharp differentiation between the concepts of self-rule and national self-determination, see TAMIR, *supra* note 14, at 69–72.

have a right that not just he but that everyone else should be governed in a particular way? If there is a right that a people should be governed democratically, *prima facie*, that right seems more credible as one possessed by a people as a whole rather than by any single member of its population.

There is, however, a plausible way of arriving at democracy through individual rights. Rather than formulate the right as simply a right to democracy, we might formulate it in more modest terms: if an individual is to be subject to political authority, that individual has a right to participate in the exercise of that authority on terms equal with others. This formulation is more modest in that the individual's right registers a claim only for the way in which that individual is to be governed rather than for the way in which everyone else is to be governed. However, the consequence of every individual having that right is, of course, a democratic form of government.

That we might arrive at democracy via rights possessed by individuals does not preclude the possibility that democracy might also be the object of a group right, particularly because we may have many reasons for considering democracy the best, or the uniquely right, form of rule. It may then be that the case for democracy is morally "overdetermined," but there is nothing wrong with that. Once again, however, a group right to democracy will assume a significantly different form depending upon whether one conceives it as a collective or a corporate right. This article can do no more than give the briefest indication of the difference between these two forms of democratic right, including the different traditions of democratic thinking associated with each, and the way in which each relates to human rights.

1. Democracy and the Collective Conception

Consider first the proposition that a people has a collective right to democratic government. There are many ways in which democracy may be characterized as a public good—a good public to the individuals who make up a *demos*. For example, people may have a shared interest in having their political system assume a form that will be most consonant with the ideal of individual self-determination,[40] will minimize the risk of abuses of power, or will ensure that governmental decisions remain reasonably close to the

40. The phrase "most consonant" is apt because, in the absence of enduring unanimity within a population, one cannot claim a simple equivalence between individual self-determination and collective self-determination. Rousseau, though, famously did try to show that one might. Jean-Jacques Rousseau, The Social Contract (1762). That does not mean, however, that the ideal of individual self-determination has no implications for the form that collective decision making should take. *See* Peter Jones, Rights 177 (1994); Keith Graham, The Battle of Democracy: Conflict, Consensus and the Individual 75 (1986).

wishes of the general population. These are the sort of grounds upon which we might claim that the individuals who form a political community have a collective right to a democratic political system.

There seems to be no difficulty in finding a place for this sort of group right within the tradition of liberal-democratic thinking. Holding that democracy is, in some respects, the object of a collective right is consistent with holding that it is, in other respects, the object of an individual right. In particular, the ultimate bearers of these two sorts of democratic rights are the same persons even though they bear their rights jointly in one case and singly in the other.

This sort of group right does not hold out the prospect of a collective *demos* tyrannizing its individual members. A collective right is a right held jointly by individuals, and it makes no sense to suppose that those individuals hold their right against themselves such that they incur the duties and liabilities consequent upon their own right. The right to democracy as a collective right is not about subordinating individuals to the group. It is simply the right of a people, grounded in the shared interests of its members, to be able to conduct its public affairs in a particular way. A people holds that right against anyone who might seek to impose upon it any other form of government.

The interests that might ground a collective right to democracy are general to humanity and are, therefore, consistent with the claim that democratic government is the object of a collective human right. That collective right is also entirely consistent with the claim that individuals have human rights that limit the extent to which their lives remain at the mercy of political power. We can hold that human beings have rights that limit the proper domain of political power, for example, rights to freedom of religion, freedom of expression, or to be tried fairly. We can also hold that they have rights, individual or collective, or both, that dictate the form that political power should take within its proper domain.

2. Democracy and the Corporate Conception

If we conceive the group right to democracy as a corporate right, things become very different. The right is no longer one held jointly by individual citizens: it is a right borne by a people conceived as a single corporate entity. It arises not from the confluence of interests of the several individuals who make up a body politic, but from the moral status claimed for a people as a corporate entity. Democracy, then, describes a political order that enables a people to realize its will to be, as a unified "self," self-determining.

Whereas the notion of a collective right to democracy can find a place in an individualist or liberal conception of democracy, the corporate democratic right belongs to a very different mode of democratic thinking.

The latter can be located within that tradition of democratic thinking that has its origins in Rousseau's conception of the general will, that was developed by the Jacobins during the French Revolution, and that found expression in the Communist idea of people's democracy.[41]

There are two ways in which human rights thinking must find it more difficult to accommodate a corporate than a collective right to democracy. First, claiming that democracy can be simultaneously the object of an individual and a corporate right seems incongruous. Collective and individual claims relating to democracy marry easily because both appeal, ultimately, to the moral standing and the interests of the same set of individuals. By contrast, a people, as the bearer of a corporate right, has an identity, a standing, and a will that is not reducible to those of individuals. The implication of a people having a corporate right to democracy is that the entitlement to democracy belongs to it rather than to individuals. Moreover, the sort of democracy that aspires to realize (what is reckoned to be) a people's corporate will is likely to be very different in character from one grounded in the moral claims of individuals.

Second, the corporate conception sets up a fundamental tension between democracy and individual rights, the latter of which aim, implicitly or explicitly, to limit democracy's scope. Of course, even if we give moral standing only to individuals, we still must confront the issue of where democratic political power should end and where the immunity of individuals from that power should begin. As long as we recognize only the single and joint claims of individuals, however, that issue will be an intra-personal rather than an interpersonal issue: the competition will be between competing interests possessed by each and every person rather than between different persons. The issue becomes very different if we introduce a corporate right to democracy. The competition is then between two rival moral claimants: the people with its right of self-determination, and individuals with claims that compete with that right. There is nothing in the idea of a corporate right of self-determination that implies that, at some point, it should defer to claims of individual rights. This does not mean that a corporate conception of democracy must exist at the expense of individual human rights. Logically, it is possible to recognize a corporate right to democracy while insisting that the scope of that right is circumscribed by a number of individual human rights. Nevertheless, it is easy to see why corporate conceptions of democracy might not be ready to defer to individual claims of right that frustrate the people's will.

---

41. *See* J.L. Talmon, The Origins of Totalitarian Democracy (1960); Barry Holden, The Nature of Democracy 41–51 (1974).

VI. CONCLUSION

A people's right of political self-determination is only one of a number of group rights that are commonly placed within, or alongside, the doctrine of human rights. For example, the UN 1966 Covenants also credit each people with closely associated rights "freely [to] pursue their economic, social and cultural development"[42] and "freely [to] dispose of their natural wealth and resources."[43] Rights of a similar, if more qualified, sort are frequently ascribed to indigenous peoples and cultural minorities.

The central thrust of this article has been that these group rights take on an essentially different character depending upon whether we interpret them as collective rights or corporate rights. The two sorts of group rights are differently grounded and carry significantly different implications, and that makes their differentiation a matter of practical importance rather than mere conceptual nicety. In particular, the distinction between the two forms of rights is crucial to the issue of whether group rights are in sympathy with, and perhaps form part of, the morality of human rights, or whether they belong to a quite different and potentially conflicting morality. We cannot, therefore, profitably debate whether we should find a place for group rights within the doctrine of human rights without first deciding whether the group rights at issue are collective rights or corporate rights.

42. ICCPR, *supra* note 2, art. 1(1); ICESCR, *supra* note 2, art. 1(1).
43. ICCPR, *supra* note 2, art. 1(2); ICESCR, *supra* note 2, art. 1(2).

[8]

Rethinking Universals: Opening Transformative Possibilities in International Human Rights Law

*Dianne Otto**

The Charter of the United Nations (UN Charter) marked the first formal global agreement by States that a core of human rights and fundamental freedoms applied universally.[1] An earlier attempt to include a more limited reference to human rights in the 1919 Covenant of the League of Nations had failed.[2] However, there were important customary and treaty-based antecedents including humanitarian law, humanitarian intervention, guarantees of natural justice for foreign nationals, the outlawing of piracy and slavery, and European treaties following the First World War which protected the rights of minorities.[3] In Professor Louis Henkin's view, the motivation for these early developments was "largely political" while the 1945 approach was expressed differently, in terms of "humanitarian" goals.[4] In making an assessment of the post Second World War commitment to universal human rights, I will argue that the humanitarianism of 1945 was not the expression of a "pure" ideal, but was also allied with political and economic power — that of the post-war global

---

* Senior Lecturer in Law, The University of Melbourne. I would like to thank Rosemary Hunter, Wayne Morgan and Sarah Pritchard for their thoughtful support for this project. This article is the second in a series of three interrelated articles. The other two articles are as follows: "Everything Is Dangerous: Some Poststructural Tools for Rethinking the Universal Knowledge Claims of Human Rights Law" (1998) *Australian Journal of Human Rights* (forthcoming); "Rethinking the 'Universality' of Human Rights Law" (1997) 29 *Columbia Human Rights Law Review* 1.

1 Charter of the United Nations (UN Charter) adopted 26 June 1945, entered into force 24 October 1945. A total of 8 references to human rights appear. See preamble 2nd para, Articles 1(3), 13(1)(b), 55(c), 56, 62(2), 68, 76.

2 Leary VA, "The Effect of Western Perspectives on International Human Rights" in An-Na'im AA and Deng FM eds, *Human Rights In Africa: Cross-Cultural Perspectives* (1990) p 15 at 18–19. In Leary's assessment, the proposal by the US to include a reference to freedom of religion was abandoned when Japan suggested that guarantees of the equal treatment of all races, including non-discriminatory treatment of aliens, should also be included. However, the Versailles Treaty of Peace 1919 did establish by Part I the Covenant of the League of Nations which included the Mandate system (Article 22) and by Part XIII of the International Labour Organisation (ILO) which were important antecedents to an international human rights regime.

3 Henkin L, *International Law: Politics and Values* (1995) pp 169–173; Buergenthal T, *International Human Rights in a Nutshell* (1995) pp 2–18.

4 Henkin L, "Introduction" in Henkin L ed, *The International Bill of Rights: The Covenant on Civil and Political Rights* (1981) p 1 at 4.

configuration dominated by the Great Powers,[5] particularly the United States of America (US).

In assessing the UN Charter approach, it is instructive to consider President Roosevelt's 1941 speech to Congress in which he described the aim of the War as achieving a global world order based on "four essential freedoms":

> The first is freedom of speech and expression everywhere in the world. The second is freedom of every person to worship God in his [or her] own way everywhere in the world. The third is freedom from want, which, translated into world terms, means economic understandings which will secure to every nation a healthy peacetime life for its inhabitants — everywhere in the world. The fourth is freedom from fear, which, translated into world terms, means a world-wide reduction of armaments ... [and] that no nation will be in a position to commit an act of physical aggression against any neighbour — anywhere in the world.[6]

The UN Charter clearly reflects Roosevelt's vision and marks an extraordinary shift in the boundaries of the international legal arena to encompass, for the first time, the peace-time regulation of social and economic development. The new boundaries included the recognition, albeit limited, of individuals as subjects of international law to whom international legal obligations are owed directly. This shift opened vast new possibilities for both dominating and transformative[7] outcomes by way of the articulation of universal human values, applicable to daily lives — "everywhere in the world".

The liberal-humanitarian categories of modernity[8] in the context of 1945, and again in the wake of the Cold War, have continued to promise the egalitarian goals of modern Europe: liberty, equality, democracy, self-determination and fraternity. However, I will argue that these modern ideals, despite claiming universal applicability, carry with them certain political baggage and allegiances which legitimate notions of European, masculinist,

---

5 The United States of America, France, the United Kingdom, the Union of Soviet Socialist Republics and China.

6 "Address of the President of the United States", 6 January 1941, *Congressional Record* (1941) vol 87, pp 46–47, cited in Leary, "The Effect of Western Perspectives on International Human Rights", n 2 above, p 19.

7 By "transformative" I mean something more fundamental than reform of the current system. Poststructural feminist Drucilla Cornell, *Transformations: Collective Imagination and Sexual Difference* (1993) p 1, describes transformative change as:

> radical enough to so dramatically restructure any system — political, legal or social — that the "identity" of the system is itself altered. The second meaning, defined as broadly as possible, turns us to the question of what kind of individuals we would have to become in order to open ourselves to new worlds.

8 Modernity has its origins in eighteenth century Enlightenment thinking and is the dominant philosophical production of present day "Europe" which extends beyond the West to include post-colonial elites who have embraced European knowledges and institutions as their own. Modernity is described by Margaret Davies, *Asking the Law Question* (1994) p 221, as "the attempt to find absolute grounds for knowledge, to discover abstract, transcendent principles which would be the foundation for all philosophical questioning".

heterosexual supremacy. At the same time, modern ideals also have the potential to open the transformative possibility of a world without domination. Understanding this paradox in international human rights law, with a view to strengthening its transformative potential, requires a reexamination of its foundational knowledges in order to reveal their loyalties to Europe and to problematise the relations of power that they support.

With the goal of rethinking modern ideals and their claim to universal Truth in mind, I engage poststructural[9] theoretical tools to trace the "genealogy"[10] of the UN discourse of human rights in order to uncover its specific allegiances to economic and political power. Drawing on the work of French philosopher Michel Foucault, and on theoretical perspectives from the margins of modernity developed by feminists, post-colonial scholars, indigenous peoples, queer and critical race theorists, I examine the local and global productivity of human rights discourse. I look for its dominating effects as well as its transformative potential, rather than for its intrinsic Truth or its authority as law. I argue that international human rights are not a timeless universal ideal, but a discursive production that can be both "dangerous"[11] and liberating.

I begin, in Part I, with an examination of the foundational universal Truth claims of human rights law which rest on the ontological notion of human "dignity". By examining the specificities of the dignity produced by human rights discourse, and the relationship it posits between the individual and society, I suggest that its apparent coherence is produced by modern European, masculinist knowledges. I argue that far from being "universal", the dominant paradigm of human rights erases or compromises human traditions and experience that are not commensurate with Europe's androcentric standards of human dignity. In Part II, I examine how the modern techniques of dualising and hierarchising non-standard "difference" have produced and legitimated the generational development of human rights law and the exclusionary application

---

9 The terms "poststructuralism" and "postmodernism" are often used interchangeably and there is considerable overlap between the two projects in their fundamental challenge of the certainties of modern knowledges. Carol Smart, *Law, Crime and Sexuality: Essays in Feminism* (1995) pp 7–9, distinguishes poststructuralism as being more concerned with the local, embodied, situated construction of knowledge while postmodernism is a critique of the epistemological foundations of modernity. Like Smart, I use the term poststructuralism to indicate my interest in the local mechanisms of power, how concrete bodies are invested with particular meanings and subjectivities, and how these effects of power can be resisted.

10 Foucault M, "Two Lectures" in Gordon C ed, *Power/Knowledge* (1980) p 78 at 81. Foucault describes genealogical investigations as "anti-sciences" rather than empirical investigations which

> entertain the claims to attention of local, discontinuous, disqualified, illegitimate knowledges against the claims of a unitary body of theory which would filter, hierarchise and order them in the name of some true knowledge and some arbitrary idea of what constitutes a science and its objects.

11 Gordon C, "Governmental Rationality: An Introduction" in Burchell G, Gordon C and Miller P eds, *The Foucault Effect: Studies in Governmentality* (1991) p 1 at 46. Gordon explains that Foucault considers nothing to be intrinsically "evil" but that everything has the potential for evil within it and is therefore "dangerous".

of the notion of equality. Finally, in Part III, I draw on Foucault's notion of "governmentality" to examine the role of the Nation-State in universalising modernity and show how modernity's amalgam of discipline and law operates in international human rights discourse. I suggest that the possibility of transformative human rights strategies depends on rejecting the hierarchies and discipline of the dominant discourse and learning how to converse across difference, and understand human dignity, without domination. Such a rethinking of the human rights paradigm relies on a deeper analysis of the relationship between dispersed local knowledges and global regimes of power.

I. Foundational Power/Knowledge

The preamble and Article 1 of the Universal Declaration of Human Rights (UDHR)[12] follow the lead of the UN Charter and use the language of dignity to express human value.[13] Since then, human rights instruments have repeatedly asserted a link between dignity and human rights.[14] The preambles of both the

12 Universal Declaration of Human Rights (UDHR) adopted 10 December 1948, GA Res 217 A (III) UN Doc A/810 at 71 (1948). It was adopted by 48 votes, with eight abstentions and none against. The abstaining States were Saudi Arabia, South Africa, and 6 members of the Eastern European bloc: Belarus, Czechoslovakia, Poland, Ukraine, Union of Soviet Socialist Republics (USSR) and Yugoslavia.

13 UN Charter, n 1 above, preamble, reaffirms faith "in fundamental human rights [and] in the dignity and worth of the human person".

14 International Convention on the Elimination of All Forms of Racial Discrimination (CERD) adopted 21 December 1965, entered into force 4 January 1969, (GA Res 20/2106A (xx)) 660 UNTS 195, preamble, "affirms the necessity of speedily eliminating racial discrimination ... and of securing understanding of and respect for the dignity of the human person"; Convention on the Elimination of All Forms of Discrimination Against Women (CEDAW) adopted 18 December 1979, entered into force 3 September 1981, GA Res 34/180, UN Doc A/34/46 at 193, preamble, "discrimination against women violates the principles of equality of rights and respect for human dignity"; text also available (1980) 19 ILM 33; Convention on the Rights of the Child (CRC) adopted 20 November 1989, entered into force 2 September 1990, GA Res 44/25, UN Doc A/44/49 at 166, preamble, "recognition of the inherent dignity ... of all members of the human family is the foundation of freedom, justice and peace in the world"; text also available (1989) 28 ILM 1448; African Charter on Human and Peoples' Rights, adopted 27 June 1981, entered into force 21 October 1986, OAU Doc CAB/LEG/67/3 Rev 5, preamble, "freedom, equality, justice and dignity are essential objectives" and Article 5, "Every individual shall have the right to the respect of the dignity inherent in a human being"; text also available (1982) 21 ILM 58; American Convention on Human Rights, signed 22 November 1969, entered into force 18 July 1978, OASTS 36, OAS Off Rec OEA/Ser.L/V/II.23, doc 21, Rev 2, Article 5, "All persons ... treated with respect for the inherent dignity of the human person"; text also available (1970) 9 ILM 673; Declaration of the Basic Duties of ASEAN Peoples and Governments (1982 Asian NGO declaration) "inspired by Asian reverence for human life and dignity which recognizes in all persons basic individual and collective rights", cited in Leary VA, "The Asian Region and the International Human Rights Movement" in Welch CE and Leary VA eds, *Asian Perspectives on Human Rights* (1990) p 13 at 23.

International Covenant on Civil and Political Rights (ICCPR)[15] and the International Covenant on Economic, Social and Cultural Rights (ICESCR)[16] declare that human rights derive from "the inherent dignity of the human person". The value of human dignity is presented as the self-evident foundation of "freedom, justice and peace in the world".[17] Implicit in this approach is the assumption that dignity has content as a universal Truth that precedes cultural diversity and transcends the contingency and allegiances of politics and economics. This assumption reflects what feminist theorist Jane Flax fittingly calls the "innocent knowledge" foundations of Western philosophy, by which she means the belief that it is possible to discover "some sort of truth which can tell us how to act in the world in ways that benefit or are for the (at least ultimate) good of all".[18] While this is a critically important aspiration, my concern is to expose the dominating dimensions of its application in order to further open its transformative possibilities.

In this Chapter I will explore the effects of the innocent ideal of universal human dignity as it is presently constituted by the economy of Truth of human rights discourse and argue that the coherence and determinacy attributed to dignity is distinctly modern. To illustrate this point I contrast modernity's construction of dignity with the understanding of dignity in some non-European traditions. I then highlight the relationship between the individual and her/his society that is assumed by the human rights paradigm and argue that it erases many women's experiences and is anathema to non-European communitarian traditions. I conclude that the claim of human rights law to innocent universal foundations must be rejected.

(a) The foundation of dignity

Neither the UN Charter, nor the human rights instruments that have followed it, formally invoke a philosophical basis for human rights beyond their references to the "dignity", "dignity and worth" or "inherent dignity" of the human person. At face value, the terms are merely suggestive of an ethical or natural law foundation. According to international human rights lawyer Oscar Schachter, the meaning of dignity "has been left to intuitive understanding, conditioned in large measure by cultural factors".[19] Mainstream commentators generally agree that the reason for the absence of an articulated definition is that consensus between diverse cultural, political and economic traditions would never have

15 International Covenant on Civil and Political Rights (ICCPR) adopted 16 December 1966, entered into force 23 March 1976, GA Res 2200 A (XXI) UN Doc A/6316 (1966); 999 UNTS 171.

16 International Covenant on Economic, Social and Cultural Rights (ICESCR) adopted 16 December 1966, entered into force 3 January 1976, GA Res 2200 A (XXI) UN Doc A/6316 (1966); 993 UNTS 3.

17 UDHR, n 12 above, preamble.

18 Flax J, "The End of Innocence" in Butler J and Scott JW eds, *Feminists Theorize The Political* (1992) p 445 at 447.

19 Schachter O, "Human Dignity As A Normative Concept" (1983) 77 *American Journal of International Law* 848 at 849.

been reached.[20] This open-endedness is a promising starting point for the acknowledgment of human diversities in human rights law. But the critical issue is how a global discourse of human rights can be constructed which remains true to these beginnings. Many human rights theorists have attempted to address this question.

Henkin, whose work I use as a mainstream liberal-humanitarian reference point in this discussion, takes a positive view of the lack of philosophical exposition of human dignity as the foundation of human rights law. In his assessment it is a means of avoiding the endorsement of any particular account of the relationship between the individual and society.[21] Henkin's argument is that this approach has enabled a combination of liberal and socialist ideas to shape international human rights which has resulted in a core of fundamental rights that are applicable across a range of different systems of government and economics.[22] As evidence, he points to the wide acceptance of the concept of human rights in agreements between States and suggests this indicates its "contemporary philosophical respectability".[23] The existence of inherent universal human rights is, in Henkin's view, an article of faith[24] and from this belief flows his innocent contention that human rights law, unlike other international law, serves no apparent national or political interest. Rather "its true and deep purpose is to improve the lot of individual men and women everywhere".[25]

In contrast, Schachter takes the view that the lack of definition of dignity is not entirely satisfactory because, as he asks, how then are implications to be drawn from it?[26] He suggests that cross-cultural ontological commonality does exist and it is this which provides the justification for universal human rights. He proposes that a general definition is supplied by Immanuel Kant's moral imperative that we consider ourselves and others as ends and never merely as means.[27] Schachter goes on to suggest that certain implications flow from this injunction which determine the substantive content of human rights law. These implications include according individual choice a high priority, guaranteeing protections from demeaning treatment, ensuring respect for individual responsibility, acknowledging that the dignity of groups must also be protected

---

20 Donnelly J, "Human Rights and Human Dignity: An Analytic Critique of Non-Western Conceptions of Human Rights" (1982) 76 *American Political Science Review* 303 at 314; Leary, "The Effect of Western Perspectives on International Human Rights", n 2 above, p 21.

21 Henkin, *The International Bill of Rights*, n 4 above, p 12. Although Henkin does concede that the concept of "rights" implies a particular relationship between the individual and society.

22 *Ibid*, p 28.

23 *Ibid*, pp 1–2.

24 *Ibid*, p 12. In a similar vein, Rosalyn Higgins states: "I believe, profoundly, in the universality of the human spirit", Higgins R, *Problems and Process: International Law and How We Use It* (1994) p 96.

25 Henkin, *The International Bill of Rights*, n 4 above, p 7.

26 Schachter, n 19 above, at 849.

27 *Ibid*.

and, more tentatively, instituting a minimum concept of distributive justice and securing some idea of substantive equality.[28]

Ultimately, both Henkin and Schachter rely on the innocent knowledge claims of modern philosophy: that the post Second World War formulation of fundamental human rights based on human dignity expresses no allegiance to any particular tradition and therefore has legitimate, neutral and universal applicability. In Henkin's paradigm universality lies within limits set by liberalism and socialism and emerges in the practical negotiation of the content of human rights instruments, while Schachter posits a Kantian philosophical agreement that precedes the determination of normative content. Either way, both theorists thwart the realisation of a global human rights discourse that is attentive to the differences of disparate cultural and economic traditions, and to the diversity of human experience that results from hierarchies of gender, race, sexuality and class. Both theorists uncritically embrace the modern philosophical assumption that a coherent universal essence to human dignity can be identified which constitutes the foundation for human rights law.

The content of human dignity, as understood in the paradigm of modernity, is determinable through "scientific", "objective" reasoning processes. Kant's work illustrates this well. He arrives at his universal moral imperatives, through "practical reasoning".[29] Universal respect for human dignity becomes self-evident in Kant's second formulation of the categorical imperative, as contemporary Kantian Ferdinand Tesón explains:

> because rationality defines the moral agent and because the categorical imperative requires universalization, we must presuppose rationality in all the persons on whom the agent's behaviour impinges ... this rationality makes persons objects that are worthy of respect, ends in themselves.[30]

The Kantian legacy is readily apparent in human rights texts.[31] Without wanting to suggest that individuals are anything other than ends in themselves, my point is that the belief that dignity and human rights are inherent and self-evident by way of reason, which is able to transcend the multiplicity of human traditions and cultures, is a distinctly European philosophical production. The dangers of this approach lie in its vast potential to enforce a hegemonic world view, obscured by its immense abstractions and reliance on a particularised form of reason that nevertheless claims universality.

As queer theorist Judith Butler warns,

> to assume from the start a procedural or substantive notion of the universal is of necessity to impose a culturally hegemonic notion on the social field. To herald that notion then as the philosophical instrument that will negotiate between conflicts of power is precisely to safeguard and reproduce a position of

---

28 *Ibid*, at 849–851.

29 Kant I, *Critique of Practical Reason* (LW Beck translation 1956) pp 42–50.

30 Tesón F, "The Kantian Theory of International Law" (1992) 92 *Columbia Law Review* 53 at 64.

31 UDHR, n 12 above, Article 1 states "All human beings ... are endowed with reason and conscience and should act towards one another in the spirit of brotherhood [sic]".

hegemonic power by installing it in the metapolitical site of ultimate normativity.[32]

From a poststructural perspective, the question is not how to determine an overarching universal unity but, rather, how the formulation and practice of human rights law could recognise that human dignity has different and contested meanings in diverse social and political contexts. The poststructural question is not designed to serve the ends of torturers, authoritarian governments and rapists, although it is often dangerously misunderstood in this way. Rather, the question arises from the imperative to give voice to those non-elite groups who are marginalised, even erased, by the European and masculinist knowledge base of human rights discourse in its present form.

It is possible to mount a realist defence of the modern foundations of human rights law as, for example, do legal theorists Rhoda Howard and Robert Cover. Howard argues that human rights are universally relevant because of the now globally instituted form of the centralised Nation-State,[33] and Cover argues in a similar vein that human rights provide a critical defence against the appalling levels of violence that the modern State has proved capable of.[34] But these arguments merely relocate the universality debate in the question of the universal applicability of the modern Nation-State rather than of human rights,[35] which is a question I will return to later in this article.[36] Nevertheless, the arguments of Cover and Howard are different from those which elevate modernity to the position of expressing some underlying universal Truth about dignity and social relationships.

The failure of both Henkin and Schachter to acknowledge the European specificity of their constructions of dignity positions them among those "empowered to know" by modernity's rational discourses.[37] As postcolonial theorist Raimundo Pannikar observes, "human rights are universal from the vantage point of modern Western culture, but not universal from the outside looking in".[38] Further, feminists from around the world have revealed the

---

32 Butler J, "Contingent Foundations: Feminism and the Question of Postmodernism" in Butler J and Scott JW eds, *Feminists Theorize The Political* (1992) p 3 at 7–8.

33 Howard R, "Dignity, Community and Human Rights" in An-Na`im AA ed, *Human Rights in Cross-Cultural Perspectives* (1992) p 81 at 81.

34 Cover RM, "Obligation: A Jewish Jurisprudence of the Social Order" (1988) 5 *Journal of Law and Religion* 65 at 69. See also Donnelly, "Human Rights and Human Dignity", n 20 above, at 310 who argues that the universality of human rights law is justified by the severing of earlier communal ties because of westernisation which has destroyed traditional means of realising human dignity.

35 Otto D, "Subalternity and International Law: The Problems of Global Community and the Incommensurability of Difference" (1996) 5 *Social and Legal Studies* 337 at 341.

36 See below, part 3(a) Universalising the Nation-State and governmentality", p 28.

37 Davies, n 8 above, p 177. "'Neutrality' is only the position which is culturally enabled to deny its positionality — it is the position which is empowered to know".

38 Pannikar R, "Is The Notion of Human Rights a Western Concept?" (1982) 120 *Diogenes* 76 at 94.

masculinist specificity of human rights law.[39] The uncritical assertion of modernity's neutrality and transcendence universalises the Truth and power of the elites of Europe rather than, as many human rights lawyers and activists believe, advancing the interests of all individuals without favour or exception.

One way in which the European specificities of human rights discourse can be illustrated is by contrasting the conception of dignity in Islamic traditions,[40] where it derives from humanity's privileged status of fulfilling God's purpose on earth.[41] According to postcolonial feminist Marnia Lazreg, Saudi Arabia's abstinence from voting for the adoption of the UDHR in 1948 was because the document lacked the unifying framework of a belief in God.[42] Islam does not conceive of human rights as inherent in being human.[43] Rather divine commands, expressed in the holy writings of the *Qur`an* and *Sunna*[44] and interpreted by religious and legal scholars in the *Shari`a*, set out the duties of rulers and individuals. Although social classifications built around religion and gender are central to the tradition,[45] human rights advocate Abdullahi An-Na`im argues that the *Qur`an* as the word of God emphasises the honour and dignity of all, without distinction.[46] In a similar vein, human rights activists Mahnaz Afkhami and Haleh Vaziri argue that the *Qur`an* expresses the moral imperative to achieve equality for all, and that interpretations indicating otherwise reflect the social realities of a particular age, not the word of God.[47]

---

39 Bunch C, "Women's Rights As Human Rights: Toward a Re-Vision of Human Rights" (1990) 12 *Human Rights Quarterly* 486; Peterson VS, "Whose Rights? A Critique of the 'Givens' in Human Rights Discourse" (1990) 15 *Alternatives* 303; Charlesworth H, "What Are 'Women's International Human Rights'?" in Cook RJ ed, *Human Rights of Women* (1994) p 58; Cook RJ, "Women's International Human Rights Law: The Way Forward" (1993) 15 *Human Rights Quarterly* 230; Romany C, "State Responsibility Goes Private: A Feminist Critique of the Public/Private Distinction in International Human Rights Law" in Cook RJ ed, *Human Rights of Women* (1994) p 85; Bunting A, *Theorising Women's Cultural Diversity in Feminist International Human Rights Strategies* (1993).

40 This brief discussion involves a level of generality by which I do not mean to suggest that either tradition is monolithic or without diverse local variations and resistances. See Hom S, "Commentary: Re-Positioning Human Rights Discourse on 'Asian' Perspectives" (1996) 3 *Buffalo Journal of International Law* 209 at 211.

41 Lazreg M, "Human Rights, State and Ideology: An Historical Perspective" in Pollis A and Schwab P eds, *Human Rights: Cultural and Ideological Perspectives* (1979) p 32 at 34.

42 *Ibid*, p 35.

43 An-Na`im AA, "Human Rights in the Muslim World: Socio-Political Conditions and Scriptural Imperatives" (1990) 3 *Harvard Human Rights Journal* 13 at 22.

44 The *Qur`an* is the word of God as revealed to the final Prophet Muhammad between 610 and 632 AD. The *Sunna* are records of the Prophet's interpretations and applications of Islam.

45 An-Na`im AA, "The Rights of Women and International Law in the Muslim Context" (1987) 9 *Whittier Law Review* 491 at 495–6.

46 An-Na`im AA, "Islam, Islamic Law and the Dilemma of Cultural Legitimacy for Universal Human Rights" in An-Na`im AA ed, *Human Rights in Cross-Cultural Perspective: A Quest for Consensus* (1992) p 31 at 47.

47 Afkhami M and Vaziri H, *Claiming Our Rights: A Manual for Women's Human*

Today, Islamic *law* is confined to "personal" matters of family and inheritance in many States, but Islamic philosophy continues to shape the world view of a significant proportion of the world's population.[48]

Many Islamic advocates of human rights have adopted the strategy of reading human rights protections into Islam's doctrines through radical reinterpretation, in an attempt to achieve consistency with universal human rights standards and ensure their cultural legitimacy within Islam.[49] One outcome of these efforts is the 1981 Universal Islamic Declaration of Human Rights which states that human rights have always been guaranteed by Islam.[50] Even so, the notion that human reason, as distinct from God's word, might underlie the notion of human dignity is specifically rejected in the Declaration as fundamentally anathema to the tradition.[51]

The strategy of synthesising dissimilar traditions has been adopted by human rights proponents in other non-European traditions[52] and is a important pragmatic attempt to legitimate local human rights struggles against various authoritarian, fundamentalist, patriarchal and otherwise repressive States. But the problem with this strategy is that it also assumes that neutral universal knowledge is possible and that it can be realised as a result of bringing disparate knowledges into commensurability with modernity. The dangers of this process are that the universal claims of modernity are confirmed and the specificities of human diversity which are inconsistent with modernity continue to be erased. As Pannikar has said, "[t]here are no trans-cultural values, for the simple reason that a value exists as such only in a given cultural context".[53] However, as he goes on to say, "there may be cross-cultural values, and cross-cultural critique is indeed possible".[54] It follows that human rights law would be more appropriately imagined as a perpetually developing conversation across

Rights Education in Muslim Societies (1996) pp v–vi.

48 An-Na`im, "Human Rights in the Muslim World: Socio-Political Conditions and Scriptural Imperatives", n 43 above, at 14.

49 An-Na`im, "Islam, Islamic Law and the Dilemma of Cultural Legitimacy for Universal Human Rights", n 46 above, pp 46–50, who draws on the work of the Sudanese Muslim reformer Ustadh Mahmoud Mohamed Taha; Tibi B, "The European Tradition of Human Rights and the Culture of Islam" in An-Na`im AA and Deng FM eds, *Human Rights in Africa: Cross-Cultural Perspectives* (1990) p 104 at 119–121; Afkhami and Vaziri, n 47 above.

50 Tibi, *ibid*, p 118 quotes from the Universal Islamic Declaration of Human Rights: "Fourteen centuries ago Islam rendered human rights legal in full depth and extent. Islam attached to these rights all necessary guarantees to protect them" from the Declaration reprinted in Muhammad Salim al-`Awwa, *fi al-nizam al-siyasi li al-dawla al-islamiyya*, p 307. For an English translation see Weeramantry CG, *Islamic Jurisprudence: An International Perspective* (1988) pp 176–83.

51 Al-`Awwa, n 50 above, "human reason is incapable of finding the right path for a proper life without the guidance of God", pp 308–9.

52 Gangjian D and Gang S, "Relating Human Rights to Chinese Culture: The Four Paths of the Confucian Analects and the Four Principles of a New Theory of Benevolence" in Davis MC ed, *Human Rights and Chinese Values* (1995) p 35.

53 Pannikar, n 38 above, at 87.

54 *Ibid*, at 87–88.

different traditions and viewpoints, rather than as a universal, trans-cultural Truth.

(b) The relationship between individual and society

Flowing from its foundational assumptions about human dignity, international human rights law makes further European and masculinist presumptions about the relationship between the individual and her/his society. I will highlight three of these presumptions: the theorisation of the subject of human rights as an autonomous and masculine individual; the notion that rights are distinct from and prioritised over obligations; and that civil and political rights are paramount.

First, the UDHR is premised on modernity's assumption that the pre-constituted, autonomous, self-interested individual is the fundamental unit of society and the sole subject of international human rights law,[55] despite the communitarian orientation of most, if not all, philosophical traditions outside modernity.[56] The provisions of the UDHR make no mention of group or collective rights and the single reference to cultural rights is expressed in individual terms.[57] Further, although the UDHR's anti-discrimination provisions prohibit distinctions of any kind, making explicit reference to "race, colour, sex, language, religion, political or other opinion, national or social origin, property, birth or other status", these distinctions are conceived as affecting individuals, not groups.[58] Even the prohibition of discrimination on the basis of the international standing of a person's country is articulated in individual terms.[59]

In contrast, subjectivity and identity in the communal traditions of indigenous African societies rely on relational concepts,[60] while in the ancient

55 The right of peoples to self-determination was included in the first article of the ICCPR and the ICESCR and the "third" and "fourth" generations of human rights also encompassed collective or group rights. However, the hierarchical ordering of the categories of human rights ensures that the primary emphasis on the individual as the subject of human rights law remains by virtue of the "higher" generational status of individual rights.

56 Howard, n 33 above, p 85.

57 UDHR, n 12 above, Article 27(1) "*Everyone* has the right freely to participate in the cultural life of the community, to enjoy the arts and to share in scientific advancement and its benefits" (my emphasis). However, it should be recognised that the ICCPR, Article 27, does expand this formulation to oblige States not to deny members of ethnic, religious or linguistic minorities the right *"in community with the other members of their group*, to enjoy their own culture ..." (my emphasis).

58 UDHR, n 12 above, Article 2, "*Everyone* is entitled to all the rights and freedoms set forth in the Declaration, without distinction ..." (my emphasis).

59 *Ibid*, "no distinction shall be made on the basis of the political, jurisdictional or international status of the country or territory to which a *person* belongs ..." (my emphasis). The framers of this article specifically had in mind the discrimination that may attend the foreign administration of trust or non-self-governing territories.

60 Kenyatta J, *Facing Mount Kenya: The Tribal Life of the Gikuyu* (1965) ch 5; Obiora LA, "Feminism, Globalisation, and Culture: After Beijing" (1997)

tradition of Confucianism being human is understood as only one aspect of an interdependent cosmos.[61] In these traditions, the individual has no privileged status. Instead, identities are understood in terms of reciprocal social and legal obligations involving family, community, tribe, and may even include non-sentient things and the physical and spiritual universe. In a context where individuals understand themselves as fundamentally connected with others, extending perhaps to aspects of their environment, the concept of the individual having autonomous pre-emptive human rights is, as Cover says in relation to the tradition of Judaism, simply the "wrong" category.[62] It casts non-individualist traditions as subordinate, outside or Other to the universal claims of modern Europe. The Kantian injunction to treat others as we would wish to be treated becomes coercive when it results in the imposition of the values of one tradition trans-culturally.[63]

It is also clear that the trans-national individual of human rights law is constructed on a masculinist model. In fact, male domination appears to be coextensive with modernity. The UDHR refers throughout to the beneficiary of universal human rights as "he", which is not simply an outmoded generic language convention which can be updated by the substitution of gender-inclusive terminology, as illustrated by the 1989 Convention on the Rights of the Child.[64] The gendered orientation of the UDHR goes to its very core. Its subject is assumed to be the breadwinner for "his family"[65] which presumes heterosexuality as well as masculinity; the rights outlined are focused on protecting violations in the *public* sphere of human activity where men predominate and ignore violations in *private* where women are mainly harmed;[66] and the protective arrangements which entitle mothers to "special care and assistance"[67] indicate that a person who mothers falls outside the masculinist standard. Feminist critiques of the paternalism of human rights instruments towards women as mothers[68] raise, from a different perspective, the

---

4 *Global Legal Studies Journal* 355 at 397. It should be noted that in communal traditions the dignity of individuals results from the collective welfare.

61 Davis MC, "Chinese Perspectives on Human Rights" in Davis MC ed, *Human Rights and Chinese Values* (1995) p 3 at 13; Little R and Reed W, *The Confucian Renaissance* (1989) p 54–55.

62 Cover, n 34 above, 65.

63 Derrida J, "Force Of Law: The 'Mystical Foundation of Authority'" (1990) 11 *Cardozo Law Review* 921 at 1003.

64 CRC, n 14 above. Despite its gender inclusive language, the Convention does not recognise or address the gendered dimensions of children's human rights violations. For example, it makes no reference to a minimum marriage age or to education about reproduction and family planning. Nor does the Convention acknowledge the systemic dimensions of many girls' unequal access to such basics as food, education, leisure and, in some States, to life itself.

65 UDHR, n 12 above, Articles 23(3) and 25(1).

66 Charlesworth H and Chinkin C, "The Gender of *Jus Cogens*" (1993) 15 *Human Rights Quarterly* 63.

67 UDHR, n 12 above, Article 25(2).

68 Zearfoss S, "The Convention for the Elimination of All Forms of Discrimination Against Women: Radical, Reasonable, or Reactionary?" (1991) 12 *Michigan Journal of International Law* 903 at 916. For further discussion of the problems

same absence of relational values as do the critiques from the stand-point of communitarian traditions. Together these critiques present a fundamental challenge to the universal Truth claims of human rights law.

A second constitutive assumption that human rights law makes about the relationship between the individual and her/his society is implicit in the concept of *rights* as distinct from obligations. Rights discourse is deeply rooted in the liberal tradition of modernity and is concomitant with the prioritisation of individual liberty over collective interests.[69] Modern democratic society is conceived as a contractual association between sovereign individuals and the State. As Howard observes, this paradigm marks a "radical rupture" with most human traditions which are organised according to communal obligations[70] and reliant on principles of solidarity and interdependence to express dignity with no separation of public and private realms — for example *dharma* (social custom regarded as duty) in the "Indian" tradition[71] and *mitzvoth* ("incumbent obligation") in the Jewish tradition.[72] Rights, if their equivalence exists at all, are not understood in many societies as abstracted from duties or other relational obligations necessary to ensure cohesiveness, survival, maintenance of a specific moral or spiritual order, or harmony of the cosmos.

The UDHR is clear in its prioritisation of rights over duties or responsibilities. The one reference to duties, in Article 29(1) states that "[e]veryone has duties to the community in which alone the full and free development of his [or her] personality is possible". In this formulation, duties are understood as correlative to individual rights rather than as owed relationally. The former Soviet Union, as well as Saudi Arabia, protested the absence of social obligations in the UDHR in 1948.[73] What results, as critical legal theorist Nigel Purvis observes about liberalism's shaping of international law generally, is that the only substantive commitment made is to the modern value of the liberty of preconstituted sovereign individuals[74] which is promoted as a neutral universal value. This outcome is anathema to many human traditions.

A third constitutive assumption of the primacy of civil and political rights is illustrated by the prioritising of these rights in the UDHR. While the UDHR does include so-called *positive*[75] economic, social and cultural rights as well as

---

associated with "special" treatment in human rights law, see nn 143–147 below.

69 Waldron J, "Nonsense Upon Stilts? A Reply" in Waldron J ed, *Nonsense Upon Stilts: Bentham, Burke and Marx on the Rights of Man* (1987) p 183–190; Taylor C, "Atomism" in Taylor C, *Philosophy and Human Sciences* (1985) pp 29–50.

70 Howard, n 33 above, p 84.

71 Pannikar, n 38 above, at 95–96. By the "Indian" tradition, Pannikar means Hindu, Jain and Buddhist conceptions of reality.

72 Cover, n 34 above, pp 69–70.

73 Lazreg, n 41 above, pp 35–36.

74 Purvis N, "Critical Legal Studies in Public International Law" (1991) 32 *Harvard International Law Journal* 81 at 94.

75 Waldron J, "Rights In Conflict" in Waldron J, *Liberal Rights: Collected Papers 1981–1991* (1993) p 203 at 214. Waldron argues that it is impossible to argue that any given right is purely positive or purely negative in character once you start to

negative civil and political rights, this was an outcome due to the influence of Latin American States and the Eastern bloc during the drafting process.[76] Articles 22–27 enumerate the right to social security, to work and equal pay, to rest and leisure, to an adequate standard of living, to education and to the right to participate in the cultural life of the community. Human rights lawyer Virginia Leary has argued, like Henkin, that the inclusion of economic, social and cultural rights saves the UDHR from being an exclusively Western production.[77] But the Declaration is clear in the preference it gives to civil and political rights as evidenced by their numerical majority and their positioning in the preceding Articles 3–21. This emphasis was one reason that the communist States abstained from voting for the adoption of the UDHR in 1948.[78]

The argument that the inclusion of social and economic rights indicates the broad applicability of the UDHR overlooks several things: its individualist approach to those rights; that socialism as well as liberalism was a modern European production; and that both types of rights were consistent with the social democratic camp within liberalism which was well established by 1948.[79] In any event, the later production of the separate ICCPR and ICESCR confirmed both the split and hierarchy between these two categories of rights in human rights discourse.

(c) Rejecting universal "innocence"

From a poststructural perspective, all knowledge is understood as shaped by the historical, political and economic particularities of its context.[80] Therefore human dignity, while it can be accepted as a universal aspiration, can have no innocent universal philosophical content. Furthermore, the idea that a universally applicable formulation of the relationship between an individual and her/his society can be rationally and neutrally determined is rejected. That human rights law is able to envisage both liberal and socialist systems of governance, as Henkin argues, does not make it universally applicable. Humankind is a plurality of "universes" outside Europe, as well as within it, and cannot be understood, without domination, as a single essence or a rational and coherent whole.

Yet the way in which international human rights normativity is currently understood depends on the foundational belief that absolute, value-free universal knowledge is possible. The result is that European rationality

---

think about what duties are associated with it.

76 Leary, "The Effect of Western Perspectives on International Human Rights", n 2 above, p 22.

77 *Ibid*, p 21.

78 Lazreg, n 41 above, p 37.

79 Donnelly J, "Human Rights and Western Liberalism" in An-Na`im AA and Deng FM eds, *Human Rights in Africa: Cross-Cultural Perspectives* (1990) p 31 at 34. Donnelly argues that even Locke's minimalist conception of liberalism had within it the germ of the more radical social democratic tradition which was to later emerge.

80 Foucault M, "Truth and Power" in Gordon C ed, *Power/Knowledge* (1980) p 109 at 131–2; Foucault, n 10 above, p 93.

masquerades as universal knowledge in the form of human rights law, erasing context and specificity, and privileging heterosexual European male likeness in a world of enormous diversity. The erasure of human connectedness, contingency and diversity by human rights law is not an empirical oversight, but is deeply embedded in the structures of European thought. Acknowledging the European positionality of human rights law is an essential step towards reconceiving it. Once the camouflage of universal innocence is exposed and the present human rights regime is understood as a specific and contested way of giving meaning to human dignity, the potential for transformative rethinking of human rights law opens.

This analysis of the specificity of the UDHR does not invalidate it within the context of the 1948 configuration of world power from which it emerged. Nor do I want to suggest that the world can be understood without foundational assumptions. As Butler puts it, "theory posits foundations incessantly, and forms implicit metaphysical commitments as a matter of course, even when it seeks to guard against it".[81] The task is to bring transparency to foundational claims, "to interrogate what the theoretical move that establishes foundations *authorizes*, and what precisely it excludes or forecloses".[82] Further, it is important to understand how one tradition comes to predominate in a world of immense diversity. Such an understanding can only emerge from continually questioning the claims to Truth of foundational knowledges and exposing the political purposes they serve. In particular, it requires rejection of the modern project of decontextualising the individual in order to make innocent universal assessments.

Thus a transformative framework for the realisation of human dignity, which is concerned to recognise difference and promote diversity, is a context-dependent, discursively negotiated project. While human diversity and contingency remain concealed and disciplined in the modern human rights production of dignity as a preconstituted universal, the egalitarian categories of Europe hold vast potential to produce homogenising and dominating outcomes. Taking account of the political and economic allegiances of the present human rights paradigm challenges us to rethink the way universality is understood in the quest to realise non-domination as a cross-cultural value, and to translate it into international legal discourse.

II. Human Rights as a Technology of Difference

Of course there have been many developments since the adoption of the UDHR in 1948, including the expansion of the constituency of the UN with the emergence of post-colonial States, and the growth of local, sometimes transnational and cross-cultural movements for women's, sexuality, cultural, racial and indigenous peoples' rights. At the same time as finding human rights discourse a powerful means of expressing inequalities and subjugation, these new developments have inspired attempts to address the European and

81 Butler, n 32 above, p 7.
82 *Ibid.*

masculinist specificity of the UDHR and its progeny. This activity has led to the articulation of "third" and "fourth" generation rights and the proliferation of specialised human rights Conventions and Declarations. While human rights discourse has displayed a considerable degree of flexibility and dynamism in responding to issues of diversity, I will argue that the resulting expansion of the human rights heartland has occurred on the terms of the dominant framework. In this way, radical challenges from those excluded or marginalised by human rights orthodoxy have served to entrench the foundational assumptions of modernity. Among the many discursive technologies that this consolidation has relied upon are the deployment of dualistic, hierarchical concepts of "difference" and comparative notions of "equality" which continue to reproduce, as universal, the standards of Europe.

In this section I will explore how the trope of difference operates in human rights law to shape global and local knowledges and arranges them in hierarchical categories and relationships. I examine, first, in a general way, how political and legal boundaries are drawn between the standard of Europe and the many versions of its Other by notions of difference and equality which purport to be neutral. I then illustrate how these boundaries have operated to produce two outcomes: the hierarchical development of generational categories of human rights and the exclusionary effects of the operation of equality discourse. I argue that the many radical contestations of human rights boundaries have been restrained by the dominant paradigm and I highlight the need for transformative strategies to find ways to reject dualistic and hierarchical constructions of meaning.

(a) The standard of Europe

Addressing the issue of the world's diversity is not just a question of what gets included in the catalogue of recognised universal human rights, although this is a critical practical problem in itself and a good starting point for analysis. Taking what Foucault calls a "genealogical" approach,[83] the content of human rights law can be understood as dependent on a multiplicity of micro power relations at the local level which are ordered, included/excluded and transformed through many processes of contestation to produce, eventually, the appearance of a global unity. This "ascending analysis of power"[84] inverts modern theories of power which seek to explain local phenomena by reference to universal indices and centralised forms of juridical power. An ascending analysis starts with diverse local knowledges, not with the assumption of an overarching unity. Viewed in this way, the local possibilities for contesting or resisting the dominant paradigm are immense. However, resistance requires challenging the disqualification of local knowledges within the global framework of modernity which bases inclusion on notions of similarity with Europe rather than diversity, despite liberalism's rhetoric of pluralism and tolerance.[85]

---

83 Foucault, n 10 above, p 83.

84 *Ibid*, p 99.

85 Morgan W, Otto D and Walker K, "Rejecting (In)Tolerance: Critical Perspectives

For example, as incontrovertibly fundamental as the right to life is, its content can be understood as dependent on local histories and knowledges: as an individual political and civil right related to personal security and safety; as a social and economic right to adequate food, health care and housing; as an aspect of the collective right to a clean, unpolluted environment; as a group right to cultural and spiritual survival; as the prevention of the death of 500,000 women annually from pregnancy and labour;[86] and so on. Further, there is intense controversy about the boundaries to the right to life — whether it is infringed by capital punishment,[87] or by making available the choices of voluntary euthanasia[88] or abortion.[89] Foucault sees the State's modern power over life lying in its disciplinary mechanisms, in "the administration of bodies and the calculated management of life",[90] which in his view has largely superseded the pre-modern sovereign power to impose the death penalty.[91] From a Foucauldian perspective the right to life would therefore entail anti-disciplinary rights or protections from State power. These diverse views illustrate in a simple way how the content of a universal human right is, in practice, highly controversial and contingent.

As I have been arguing, the view that currently prevails as universal is consistent with the dominant regimes of European power which, in the case of the right to life, give priority to the conception of life as a civil and political right which obligates States to maximise individual liberty and security.[92] Thus, despite the multitudinous possibilities and priorities at the local level some unity emerges on the global plane, although it would be a mistake to think of this outcome as predetermined or inevitable, as Foucault's analysis of local power reminds us. Understanding how dominant regimes of power achieve the

---

on the United Nations Year for Tolerance" (1995) 20 *Melbourne University Law Review* 190.

86 Cook R, WHO/DGH/93.1, Geneva 1993, quoted in Leary VA, "The Right to Health in International Human Rights Law" (1994) 1 *Health and Human Rights* 24 at 51.

87 Second Optional Protocol to the International Covenant on Civil and Political Rights, Aiming at the Abolition of the Death Penalty, adopted 15 December 1989, entered into force 11 July 1991, GA Res 44/128, preamble para 6 notes the differing views of States about whether imposing the death penalty is a human rights violation.

88 Schneider CE, "Rights Discourse and Neonatal Euthanasia" (1988) 76 *California Law Review* 151 at 153.

89 Shelton D, "Abortion and the Right to Life in the Inter-American System: The Case of 'Baby Boy'" (1981) 2 *Human Rights Law Journal* 309; Cook R, "International Protection of Women's Reproductive Rights" (1992) 24 *New York University Journal of International Law and Politics* 645 at 703–711.

90 Foucault M, *The History of Sexuality* (1976) vol I, p 140.

91 As Foucault explains, the rationale for capital punishment changed from one of justifiable defence of the sovereign's power to an invocation of "the monstrosity of the criminal, his incorrigibility, and the safeguard of society", *ibid*, p 138.

92 UDHR, n 12 above, Article 3. The relevant article in the ICCPR, n 14 above, Article 6, obligates States to provide protection against arbitrary deprivation of life, restricts the circumstances in which the death penalty can be carried out and specifies that its provisions do not derogate from the provisions of the Genocide Convention.

appearance of global unity is a central focus of poststructural inquiry. It is also important to understand how the global discourse, in turn, has an effect on how the right to life is understood locally. Foucauldian Alan Hunt usefully suggests the Gramscian concept of "hegemony" is an important supplement to Foucault's paradigm.[93] The descending, hegemonic effect is not just due to the impact of judicial determinations and domestic laws which result directly from States fulfilling their international legal obligations, to the extent that they do. The effect of global knowledges on local knowledges is also produced by the disqualification of other (False) knowledges by the discursive hegemonic assertion of the content of human rights law as universal Truth.

In its construction of True and False, human rights law erects boundaries, between what is and is not fundamental and therefore universal and, as a consequence, defines what is and is not normal or standard or within human dignity.[94] What lies inside the boundaries of Truth not only "trumps" other interests according to law,[95] but is constitutive of universal dignity. The inside view is presented as an unquestionable, rationally self-evident "point-of-viewlessness"[96] around which legal standards, claims and arguments are then organised. Thus the claim to a clean environment is not cognisable as a right to life because it is outside the boundaries of protecting individual liberty and security. Many would claim it does not qualify as a human right at all.[97] A related example is the exclusion of groups as bearers of human rights by the assumption of the autonomous individual as the basic normative unit. This relegates group identity and interests to a form of difference which, as with other outsider characteristics, is contrasted as secondary to the individualist standard. To argue for group rights, then, is to argue a special case, or for expansion (some would say dilution) of the heavily policed human rights heartland, unless of course the relevant group is a State, which has privileged status in international law.[98]

The boundaries of the universal rely on dualistic and hierarchised notions of difference which, as Swiss linguist Ferdinand de Saussure describes it, contrast

---

93 Hunt A, "Rights and Social Movements: Counter-Hegemonic Strategies" (1990) 17 *Journal of Law and Society* 309.

94 Pannikar, n 38 above, at 86.

95 Dworkin R, *Taking Rights Seriously* (1978) p xi. I employ Dworkin's concept of a trump card to illustrate the apparent unbeatable winning position of knowledges that are constructed as True by dominant discourses.

96 MacKinnon CA, "Feminism, Marxism, Method and the State: Toward Feminist Jurisprudence" (1983) 8 *Signs* 635 at 638–9.

97 Alston P, "Conjuring Up New Human Rights: A Proposal for Quality Control" (1984) 78 *American Journal of International Law* 607 at 613; Gibson N, "The Right to a Clean Environment" (1990) 54 *Saskatchewan Law Review* 5 at 15. Contra, Kiss A and Shelton D, *International Environmental Law* (1991) pp 21–31.

98 Kingsbury B, "Claims By Non-State Groups In International Law" (1992) 25 *Cornell International Law Journal* 481 at 488 notes that Article 27 of the ICCPR, which is narrow in its scope, "remains the only express and legally binding minority rights provision of general application" in international human rights law.

positive and negative "signs" in the processes of creating meaning.[99] The Sausseurean insight is that a particular meaning or sign results from its binary contrast with Other signs which are its antithesis. In other words, the dualistic interplay of difference is fundamental to the way that modern knowledge is constructed. For example, the meaning of the tradition of "modernity" as universal knowledge is dependent on the contrasting meanings attributed to "underdeveloped", "uncivilised" or "backward" traditions. Further, as the poststructural analysis of Jacques Derrida reveals, the binaries which create meaning/knowledge are invested with a hierarchical power relationship of domination and subordination.[100] Therefore an affirmative or inclusionary definition relies on the negative or repressed status of its antithetical sign(s). There is nothing self-evident about the "fact" of difference which these dualisms rely upon as feminist poststructuralist Joan Scott explains.[101] Rather, deciding what counts as sameness or difference, or determining "the differences that make a difference", is a political act.[102] Therefore to contest the boundaries between sameness and difference which determine what qualifies as universal, is to challenge a hierarchical relationship of power. The dualities of difference locate and normalise the power of dominance with the modern standard (insider) and the corresponding subordinate position lies with the less advanced Other (outsider).[103]

(b) The generations of human rights

The generational development of the human rights corpus provides one example of the way that difference is utilised as a means of justifying and naturalising what is actually the highly politicised and hierarchical valuation of different epistemological viewpoints and not the outcome of neutral humanitarian principles. I have already made reference to the first generational hierarchy which prioritises civil and political rights over social, economic and cultural rights. This hierarchy was an early product of the Cold War which gave the long-running debate over the status of economic and social rights new significance.[104] Clearly, in 1941 Roosevelt was not confining his post-War vision to civil and political rights and the US did support the inclusion of social

99 de Saussure F, *Course In General Linguistics* (1959). Saussure's concept of the "sign" consists of both the "concept" which he calls the "signified" and the "sound-image" which he calls the "signifier". The relationship between any particular sign and signifier is the result of convention and not determined by a prior system. See also Davies, n 8 above, pp 229–240.

100 Derrida J, *Positions* (1981) p 41.

101 Scott JW, "Deconstructing Equality-Versus-Difference: or, the Uses of Poststructuralist Theory for Feminism" (1988) 14 *Feminist Studies* 33 at 44.

102 Nicholson LJ, "Introduction" in Nicholson LJ ed, *Feminism/Postmodernism* (1990) p 4 at 10.

103 MacKinnon CA, "Difference and Dominance: On Sex Discrimination" in MacKinnon CA, *Feminism Unmodified* (1987) p 32 at 36.

104 Steiner HJ and Alston P, *International Human Rights in Context: Law, Politics, Morals* (1996) p 257 locate some of historical origins of this debate in the work of Enlightenment philosophers including Kant and Marx.

and economic rights in the UDHR.[105] Despite the prioritisation of civil and political rights in the UDHR, Henkin's observation that it represented "a remarkable juncture of political-civil and economic-social rights",[106] takes on a new significance in the light of the present post-Cold War experience of economic and social rights disappearing altogether from the main agendas of States, in the rush to globalise free market capitalism.[107]

Earlier, with the deepening of the Cold War, the distinctions between the two categories of rights became increasingly represented as absolute, despite the spurious nature of many of these claims[108] and the continuing statements in UN forums about their indivisibility.[109] The fundamental differences posited included, for instance, that civil and political rights are absolute and immediately realisable as against the variable and progressive obligations associated with economic and social rights; and that the negative character of the former category of rights involves non-interference by the State which distinguishes them from the rights in the latter category which require positive State action. These distinctions overstate differences in a highly politicised manner and, further, ignore the positive State action required for the realisation of many civil and political rights[110] such as, for example, the right to a fair trial. In the early years of the Cold War, Western States used such difference arguments to justify their insistence on the drafting of two human rights Covenants, rather than the single instrument that was originally envisaged.[111]

The result was not simply an affirmation that there were fundamental differences between the two sets of human rights, but the production of two opposing narratives of universality which represented the interests of two versions of Europe and gave precedence to the capitalist/liberal view as the "first" generation. This human rights production assisted in Europe's Cold War division of the entire globe into two oppositional camps in its own dualistic image. In this context, diversity came to be understood as inclusive of both socialist and liberal perspectives, as in Henkin's view, which confirmed the

105 *Ibid*, p 260.

106 Henkin, *The International Bill of Rights*, n 4 above, p 8.

107 Cossman B, "Reform, Revolution or Retrenchment? International Human Rights in the Post-Cold War Era" (1991) 32 *Harvard International Law Journal* 339 at 345.

108 Van Hoof GJH, "The Legal Nature of Economic, Social and Cultural Rights: A Rebuttal of Some Traditional Views" in Alston P and Tomasevski K eds, *The Right To Food* (1984) p 97, extracted in Steiner and Alston, *International Human Rights in Context*, n 104 above, pp 279–283.

109 GA Res 543, 6 GAOR Supp 20, UN Doc A/2119 at 36 (1952) which approved the development of two Covenants but emphasised their interdependence and required that they be simultaneously adopted by the General Assembly; Statement to the World Conference on Human Rights on Behalf of the Committee on Economic, Social and Cultural Rights, UN Doc E/1991/22, Annex III.

110 Waldron, "Rights in Conflict", n 75 above.

111 Pechota V, "The Development of the Covenant on Civil and Political Rights" in Henkin L ed, *The International Bill of Rights: The Covenant on Civil and Political Rights* (1981) p 32 at 42.

difference of non-European traditions as inferior to modernity and excluded them from the universal Occidental frame of reference for human rights.

The exclusionary effects of the Cold War formulation of rights did not go unchallenged by the newly independent decolonised States, whose influence gathered momentum during the long drafting period of the Covenants as their numerical majority in the General Assembly grew.[112] One result of their efforts, despite strong resistance from Western States, was the assertion in the first Articles of both Covenants of the collective right of all peoples to self-determination and to sovereignty over their natural wealth and resources.[113] This was the beginning of the Third World "non-aligned" movement's (NAM)[114] exploration of the potential of human rights discourse to address their concerns and was a precursor to the emergence of the "third" generation of human rights, also known as "solidarity" or "peoples" rights.

The highly controversial grouping of the "third" generation includes the right to peace, to a clean environment, to the common heritage of mankind [sic] and, perhaps most currently significant, to development. [115] Judge Mohammed Bedjaoui of the International Court of Justice argues that the right to development should be regarded as *jus cogens* or a peremptory norm. As he explains,

> [it is] a fundamental right, the precondition of liberty, progress, justice and creativity ... [its] international dimension ... is nothing other than *the right to an equitable share in the economic and social well-being of the world.*[116]

Debate about the veracity of this and other "third" generation human rights highlights important questions of difference left unresolved by the modern framework of the first and second generations, especially the relationship between individual and collective rights, and between human rights and issues of global redistributive justice and equity. The General Assembly's adoption of the Declaration on the Right to Development in 1986[117] lends this particular right a measure of moral legitimacy, but its normativity and utility is hotly disputed,[118] and implacably opposed by the US.[119] It also must be noted that, in

---

112 *Ibid*, p 45.

113 Cassese A, "The Self-Determination of Peoples" in Henkin L ed, *The International Bill of Rights: The Covenant on Civil and Political Rights* (1981) p 92.

114 The Non-Aligned Movement (NAM) also known as the Group of 77 (G77) formed in the early 1970s as a lobby group of Third World States united in their goal to challenge global European economic domination.

115 Alston, "Conjuring Up New Human Rights", n 97 above.

116 Bedjaoui M, "The Right To Development" in Bedjaoui M ed, *International Law: Achievements and Prospects* (1991) p 1177 at 1182.

117 Declaration on the Right to Development (DRD) GA Res 41/128, UN Doc A/Res/41/128 (4 December 1986) was adopted by 146 votes to one against, with 8 abstainers. The US cast the only vote against adoption. Abstainers were Denmark, Finland, Germany, Iceland, Israel, Japan, Sweden, UK. Both Canada and Australia voted for the resolution.

118 Donnelly J, "In Search of the Unicorn: The Jurisprudence and Politics of the Right to Development" (1985) 15 *California Western International Law Journal* 473.

119 Alston P, "Revitalising United Nations Work on Human Rights and Development"

its current formulation, the right to development reads more like a right that Nation-States hold and exercise rather than a collective right of people(s) to be asserted against the Nation-State.[120]

The primary political cleavage that spawned the emergence of solidarity rights was between the NAM and the West, with Eastern European States prevaricating. The "third" generation of human rights has assumed a new importance in the post-Cold War context as a marker of difference between the North and the South, producing the most recent version of discursive difference between Europe and its Other. While raising critical issues of diversity, global economic justice and transnational responsibilities, the relegation of solidarity rights to "third" generational status attributes to them a *relative* or questionable universality. Despite considerable agreement that solidarity rights occupy a place within general human rights discourse, the generational trope ensures that their universal status remains in doubt, and consequently reconfirms the unquestionable universality, and superiority, of the European norms of the first generation.

The characterisation of the rights of indigenous peoples as constituting a "fourth" generation of human rights confirms a further difference which has enormous political and legal significance: the distinction between "colonised" peoples who have a right to self-determination and indigenous peoples who do not. The effect of this classification repeats, in the egalitarian form of human rights discourse, the colonial narrative of indigenous peoples as "too low in the scale of social organisation to be acknowledged as possessing [sovereign] rights and interests in land".[121] This denial reveals the deeply exclusionary paradigm of human rights discourse and has led to the sleight of hand whereby self-determination as it applies to indigenous peoples has come to mean *internal* self-determination.[122] International lawyer Benedict Kingsbury aptly describes this as the dominant norms shifting just as indigenous peoples think they are gaining access to them.[123]

(1991) 18 *Melbourne University Law Review* 216 at 219.

120 DRD, n 117 above, Article 2(3): "States have *the right and the duty* to formulate appropriate national development policies" (my emphasis).

121 *Mabo v Queensland* (No 2) (1992) 175 CLR 1 at 58 (Brennan J) referring to this view as out of step with contemporary standards of justice and human rights.

122 Otto D, "A Question of Law or Politics? Indigenous Claims to Sovereignty in Australia" (1995) 21 *Syracuse Journal of International Law and Commerce* 65 at 92.

123 Kingsbury B, "Whose International Law? Sovereignty and Non-State Groups", *Proceedings*, American Society of International Law, 88th Annual Meeting (1994). The statement by Canada at the 2nd meeting of the Human Rights Commission's Working Group on the draft Declaration on the Rights of Indigenous Peoples bears this out:

> The Government of Canada accepts a right of self-determination for indigenous peoples which respects the political, constitutional and territorial integrity of democratic states.

Coles S, "UN Working Group on the Draft Declaration on the Rights of Indigenous Peoples, Second Meeting, October 21–November 1, 1996" (1996) 4 *International Law News* 3 at 4.

At the same time, the international discourse on indigenous peoples has, at least, moved on from its earlier assimilationism[124] to a rights approach,[125] and some openings have been created for dialogue between the local knowledges of indigenous peoples and international human rights discourse.[126] While Foucault has observed that one function of the discourse of rights is to mask domination,[127] it also provides a language[128] and a legal framework for challenging dominating power. As indigenous peoples have shown in the negotiation of a draft Declaration on the Rights of Indigenous Peoples, dominating global discourses *can* be influenced by coalitions and alliances of local networks of power.[129] However on the other hand, the cost is the acceptance of the terms of the dominant discourse which, ultimately, reconfirm the interests of the modern Nation-State which is premised on the denial of indigenous sovereignty. As feminist Carol Smart expresses this dilemma in the domestic context of UK law, it is "the problem of challenging a form of power without accepting its own terms of reference and hence losing the battle before it has begun".[130]

Thus the normative content of human rights, and the current hierarchical divisions and classifications, reflect and reproduce dominant regimes of global power. As international lawyer Martti Koskenniemi observes:

> much of rights discourse is no more than the transformation of substantive political goals into human rights language, perhaps most evident in the perennial argument about whether economic and social rights and, *a fortiori*, the so-called third generation or solidarity rights are 'real' human rights.[131]

At the centre of this argument is the technology of difference which assists the naturalisation of politically determined distinctions by reproducing the superiority of European standards as a progressivist inevitability, in contradistinction to the secondary status of the many forms that Europe's Other can take. The struggles over diversity are disciplined and contained in the

---

124 International Labour Organisation Convention, No 107, The Protection and Integration of Indigenous and Other Tribal and Semi-Tribal Populations in Independent Countries (1957) in ILO, *International Labour Conventions and Recommendations 1919–1981* (1996) p 99.

125 Dodson M, "Towards The Exercise of Indigenous Rights: Policy, Power and Self-Determination" (1994) 35 *Race and Class* 65; Langton M, "The United Nations and Indigenous Minorities: A Report on the United Nations Working Group on Indigenous Populations" in Hocking B ed, *International Law and Aboriginal Human Rights* (1988) p 83; Anaya J, *Indigenous Peoples and International Law* (1996).

126 Barsh RL, "Indigenous Peoples: An Emerging Object of International Law" (1986) 80 *American Journal of International Law* 369; Langton, n 125 above.

127 Foucault, "Two Lectures", n 10 above, p 95.

128 Williams P, *The Alchemy of Race and Rights: Diary of a Law Professor* (1991) p 163.

129 Williams RA, "Encounters on the Frontiers of International Human Rights Law: Redefining the Terms of Indigenous Peoples' Survival in the World" (1990) *Duke Law Journal* 660.

130 Smart C, *Feminism and the Power of Law* (1989) p 5.

131 Koskenniemi M, "The Future of Statehood" (1991) 32 *Harvard International Law Journal* 397 at 399.

interests of the elites of Nation-States through international human rights discourse, which is one way of accounting for the wide State acceptance of human rights instruments. Expressions of commitment to diversity, understood in this context, are minimalist concessions to a pluralism that is ordered hierarchically so as to protect the global *status quo* of modernity.

(c) The exclusions of equality

The exclusionary operation of the human right to equality provides a second example of how modernity's dualistic construction of difference shapes the substantive content of human rights. Equality is one of the foundational Truths of modernity and, as such, of international human rights law. The UDHR emphasises that human rights apply without distinction across all differences, yet even in its drafting processes double-standards were apparent. For example, a draft article suggested by India, making specific reference to the prevention of discrimination against minorities, was rejected with most participants expressing assimilationist views.[132] Indeed the preceding century of the European practice of equality had been fraught with contradictions. Within Europe the exclusion of women from the political realm was justified[133] and beyond Europe the practices of slavery and colonialism were endorsed as hallmarks of modernity,[134] unimpeded by the rhetoric of inherent human dignity and equality.

It is the hierarchisation of difference that makes such blatant inconsistencies appear natural, defensible and incontestable. The equality of modernity is a formal standard which, as Henkin observes, makes "no direct injunction towards equality in fact".[135] Rather, equality is constructed as a comparative standard which has no autonomous substantive content.[136] Equality, meaning equal treatment or equality of opportunity, is mandated only when compared subjects are assessed as "the same". Difference, then, is a technique for justifying unequal treatment and naturalising discriminatory actions on the basis that subjects are not the same. The standard against which sameness and difference are assessed is, as I have argued, not a neutral disembodied abstraction but the privileged figure of Europe's masculinist heterosexual elites.

In practice, then, a claim to equality (inclusion), which brings with it human rights protections, relies on satisfying the criterion of sameness with the standard. For example, women's experiences of violation and injury are included only to the extent that they are commensurable with men's. As feminists have shown, dominant understandings of human rights abuses like

---

132 Leary, "The Effect of Western Perspectives on International Human Rights", n 2 above, p 22.

133 Pateman C, *The Disorder of Women: Democracy, Feminism and Political Theory* (1989).

134 Locke J, *Two Treatises of Government: Second Treatise* (Laslett P ed, (1960) ch IV, "Of Slavery" paras 23–24.

135 Henkin, n 3 above, p 20.

136 Otto D, "Holding Up Half the Sky but for Whose Benefit? A Critical Analysis of the Fourth World Conference on Women" (1996) 6 *Australian Feminist Law Journal* 7 at 13–15.

"torture" and "persecution" largely exclude women's gendered experience[137] and the individualism of the framework denies the web of relationships that constitute the realities of many women's daily lives.[138] The paradigm of sameness/difference has the effect of excluding rights violations associated with women's corporeality from the universal category of human rights. It also perpetuates subordinating and essentialist ideas about women[139] and presumes that the Woman[140] of international human rights discourse, to the extent that she does appear, is European[141] and heterosexual.[142]

If the test of sameness is not satisfied, the alternative made available in human rights discourse is to argue that "difference" justifies special treatment. There is a crucial distinction between special treatment and the recognition of additional universal human rights, as the specialised Conventions outlawing discrimination on the basis of race and gender illustrate.[143] These Conventions do not expand the human rights heartland. They do not achieve a more inclusive standard by identifying gender or race-specific rights violations, such as domestic violence, racial harassment, or the denial of indigenous relationships with land, as human rights abuses. They merely prohibit the denial of equal (the same) treatment on the basis of racial or gender difference.

Further, although both Conventions envisage that special measures (unequal treatment) may be necessary, for "securing the adequate advancement of certain racial or ethnic groups or individuals"[144] or for "accelerating *de facto* equality between men and women",[145] the need is assumed to be temporary. That is, ultimately, it is presumed that equality will be satisfied by treating everyone the same despite huge disparities in wealth and power, and enormous diversities in cultural, sexuality, racial, gender and other identities. In the few instances where different treatment *is* authorised by human rights instruments, such as

---

137 Copelon R, "Intimate Terror: Understanding Domestic Violence As Torture" in Cook RJ ed, *Human Rights of Women* (1994) p 116; Holt R, "Women's Rights and International Law: The Struggle for Recognition and Enforcement" (1991) 1 *Columbia Journal of Gender and the Law* 117; Greatbach J, "The Gender Difference: Feminist Critique of Refugee Discourse" (1989) 1 *International Journal of Refugee Law* 518.

138 Bunch, n 39 above, at 492.

139 Peterson, n 39 above; Binion G, "Human Rights: A Feminist Perspective" (1995) 17 *Human Rights Quarterly* 509; Cain PA, "Feminism and the Limits of Equality" (1990) 24 *Georgia Law Review* 803.

140 Smart C, "The Woman of Legal Discourse" (1992) 1 *Social and Legal Studies* 29.

141 Mohanty C, "Under Western Eyes: Feminist Scholarship and Colonial Discourses" (1988) 30 *Feminist Review* 61; Amos V and Parmar P, "Challenging Imperial Feminism" (1984) 17 *Feminist Review* 4.

142 Miller A, Rosga AJ and Satterthwaite M, "Health, Human Rights and Lesbian Existence" (1994) 1 *Health and Human Rights* 428; Otto D, "Questions of Solidarity and Difference: Transforming the Terms of Lesbian Interventions in International Law" in Robson R and Brownworth V eds, *Seductions of Justice: Lesbian Legal Theories and Practices* (forthcoming).

143 CERD, n 14 above; CEDAW n 14 above.

144 CERD, *ibid*, Article 1(4).

145 CEDAW, n 14 above, Article 4(1).

protective workplace measures for pregnant women and mothers,[146] the effects are paternalistic and demeaning rather than consistent with substantive equality.[147]

Both the strategies of basing equality claims on sameness or difference leave the masculine, heterosexual, European standard unquestioned and therefore confirmed. This is the conundrum that feminist Martha Minow calls the "dilemma of difference"[148] and Scott refers to as "structur[ing] an impossible choice",[149] because both options of either highlighting difference or ignoring it tend to reconfirm difference as a secondary, non-universal characteristic which justifies inequality. This interdependence of sameness and difference, of the standard and its other as in the Derridaean analysis, explains how radical challenges have been contained by the dominant human rights discourse and coopted to the service of its consolidation, rather than to its reinvention. This insight, as Scott observes, is

> [t]he brilliance of so much of Foucault's work [which is] to illuminate the shared assumptions of what seemed to be sharply differing arguments, thus exposing the limits of radical criticism and the extent of power of dominant ideologies or epistemologies.[150]

The various local and global human rights movements, which have sought inclusion in the human rights paradigm on the basis of sameness *or* difference, are thus limited and disciplined by modernity's dichotomies of True and False.

In this way, human rights arguments about equality in terms of sameness and difference function as a technology of power. The allegiance of equality discourse to dominating regimes of power is disguised by the characterisation of inequality as an issue of non-discrimination rather than empowerment.[151] The language of anti-discrimination obscures relations of power by normalising privilege as "the way things are"[152] and awards remedies for discrimination only in relation to a highly politicised and closely monitored set of differences. It does not lead to the recognition of new human rights, nor to a reassessment of the underlying standards, nor to a recognition of the multiplicity of difference.

In sum, dualistic and hierarchised conceptions of difference are a central technique of European domination through the egalitarian narratives of modernity. Human rights law engages these technologies of difference as illustrated by its generational development and its understanding of inequality in terms of comparative sameness and difference with the standards of

---

146 *Ibid*, Article 11(2).

147 Zearfoss, n 67 above.

148 Minow M, "Learning To Live With the Dilemma of Difference: Bilingual and Special Education" (1984) 48 *Law and Contemporary Problems* 157.

149 Scott, n 101 above, at 43.

150 *Ibid*, at 36.

151 Coomaraswamy R, "To Bellow Like A Cow: Women, Ethnicity and the Discourse of Rights" in Cook RJ ed, *Human Rights of Women: National and International Perspectives* (1994) p 39 at 40.

152 Wildman SM with Davis AD, "Language and Silence: Making Systems of Privilege Visible" in Delgado R ed, *Critical Race Theory: The Cutting Edge* (1995) p 573 at 574.

modernity. Of critical importance to transformative change is understanding how the multiplicity of global difference might replace the dualistic hierarchies of modernity. This involves, among other things, a deeper understanding of the relationship between local and global knowledges and how local knowledges might organise to resist the hegemony of European modernity. Some insights are offered by Foucault's notion of "governmentality" which I will explore in the following section.

III. Governmentality and the Cooperation Between Legal and Disciplinary Power

The extension of international law by the UN Charter to include the promotion and protection of universal human rights was championed by the Great Powers in the context of the 1945 balance of world power. This expanded role was indeed a "unique and revolutionary purpose"[153] for international law, despite lacking the innocent humanitarian motivations attributed to it by Henkin. By including the advancement and regulation of economic and social development in the UN's mandate, the way was opened for unprecedented levels of international intervention in the domestic affairs of States.[154] It fostered the emergence of an institutional framework for global governance which would promote "social progress and better standards of life".[155] I will argue that, in this endeavour, both law and the social sciences have assumed key and complementary roles in promoting the universal reach of disciplinary European knowledges. This promotion is evident in the governmental activities of Nation-States which are fostered by the UN Charter.

In this section, I will explore the interplay between law and the discipline of the social sciences in the promotion of international human rights and build on Foucault's genealogical analysis of the relationship between local micro knowledges and global regimes of power. First, I critically examine the emergence of the modern Nation-State as a universally legitimate entity using Foucault's notion of "governmentality". I show how modern disciplinary knowledges, like law, dualise and hierarchise difference in the production of a discourse of governmental Truth that is globalised through UN institution-building. Second, I examine the cooperative links between human rights law and the science of governmentality in order to argue that, while law remains an important site for transformative struggle, human rights strategies need to take account of the interpenetration of law by discipline. Finally, I suggest that Foucault's typology of ascending power, augmented by a parallel and interconnected *descending* analysis of power, suggests new possibilities for transformative, grass roots human rights strategies.

153 Henkin, *The International Bill of Rights*, n 4 above, p 7.
154 UN Charter, n 1 above, Articles 55–72.
155 *Ibid*, preamble.

(a) Universalising the Nation-State and governmentality

Human rights law, like all international law, assumes that the social, political and legal form of the modern Nation-State has global legitimacy. The institution of the Nation-State envisages a relatively homogeneous citizenry,[156] relies on centralised government and asserts the primacy of imagined national identification and loyalty. [157] The focus of human rights law is on preserving the rights of the individual as against this type of State. In assuming Nation-Statehood as universal, human rights instruments assist the erasure of diverse associations and multiplicitous identities, repeating the earlier "civilising mission" of colonialist Europe — this time by the global imposition of a modern State-based governmental framework, in the name of progress, order and freedom. The Kantian view takes this mission a step further by asserting that the only *legitimate* States are liberal-democracies because they are the only States that respect human rights.[158]

In reality, the postcolonial Nation-State has violently disrupted and displaced earlier political arrangements.[159] The universalisation of Statehood has enforced the transfer of locally negotiated obligations and power, formerly residing in communal groupings, to central State institutions making the "radical rupture" with communitarian traditions referred to by Howard.[160] This transfer of power serves the interests of post-colonial elites and not, as promised in the anti-colonial self-determination struggles, the democratic interests of the people themselves.[161] The African Charter on Human and People's Rights,[162] often cited as a paradigm example of the flexibility and cross-cultural legitimacy of human rights discourse, illustrates this well in its neo-colonial emphasis on protecting the imperialist-designed territorial entities that became postcolonial Nation-States. As Tanzanian law professor Issa Shivji argues, the African Charter asserts the principles of non-interference and territorial integrity over the self-determination of peoples.[163] By presupposing the Nation-State as the primary locus of identification for all humanity, the discourse of human rights functions as a strategy of recolonisation wherein the importance of local or transnational identities is denied,[164] as is the possibility of multiple identities.

---

156 Belvisi F, "Rights, World-Society and the Crisis of Legal Universalism" (1996) 9 *Ratio Juris* 60 at 61.

157 Anderson B, *Imagined Communities: Reflections on the Origin and Spread of Nationalism* (1991).

158 Tesón, n 30 above, at 82–84, referring to Immanuel Kant's work *To Perpetual Peace: A Philosophical Sketch* (1795).

159 Pollis A and Schwab P, "Human Rights: A Western Construct with Limited Applicability" in Pollis A and Schwab P eds, *Human Rights: Cultural and Ideological Perspectives* (1979) p 1 at 9.

160 Howard, n 33 above, p 84.

161 Guha R, "On Some Aspects of the Historiography of Colonial India" in Guha R and Spivak GC eds, *Selected Subaltern Studies* (1988) p 37 at 38.

162 African Charter on Human and Peoples' Rights, n 14 above.

163 Shivji IG, *The Concept of Human Rights in Africa* (1989) p 99.

164 Note "Constructing the State Extraterritorially: Jurisdictional Discourse, the National Interest, and Transnational Norms" (1990) 103 *Harvard Law Review*

The UN Charter promotes a world-wide system of governance by Nation-States in its fostering of global economic and social development. This system sets out to strengthen the power of the Nation-State by advancing the development of modern institutions and practices of government within States. The UN's sponsoring of State-centred modern government promotes globally what Foucault calls "government rationality" or "governmentality".[165] He locates the origins of governmentality in the early modern recognition that a State's power and wealth lies with its population rather than its territory.[166] Therefore, establishing a government requires

> set[ting] up an economy at the level of the entire state, which means exercising towards its inhabitants, and the wealth and behaviour of each and all, a form of surveillance and control as attentive as that of the head of a family over his [sic] household and his goods.[167]

In Foucault's view, the aim of modern government is to develop and harness the individual capacities of a State's citizens so that they ultimately foster the strength of the Nation-State.[168]

Foucault identifies "discipline" as a new form of modern power, which first emerged during the seventeenth and eighteenth centuries and came to represent the interests of Europe's elites.[169] His work traces the development and exercise of disciplinary power in prisons, schools, factories and other newly emerging modern institutions. He describes discipline as becoming embedded in daily life, resulting in an extensive "carceral network"[170] which operates to exclude subversive or resistant knowledges and anatomies. Foucault emphasised the multiple origins and localised operation of the social sciences and their productivity in creating detailed knowledges designed to respond to an endless variety of circumstances.[171]

In response to criticism that his analysis was too localised and failed to address macro issues of global power and politics, Foucault argued that the methods he had developed to examine the local operation of disciplinary power could also be applied to the study of governmental practices involved in the political management of populations.[172] According to Foucault, in the realm of politics,[173] the science of governmentality developed in response to the tension in the democratic idea of simultaneously governing for the good of all and

1273 at 1287.

165 Foucault M, "Governmentality" in Burchell G, Gordon C and Miller P eds, *The Foucault Effect: Studies in Governmentality* (1991) p 87 at 102–3.

166 *Ibid*, p 103.

167 *Ibid*, p 92.

168 Gordon, n 11 above, p 10.

169 Foucault, n 90 above.

170 *Ibid*, p 303.

171 Gordon, n 11 above, p 10.

172 *Ibid*, p 4.

173 *Ibid*, p 2. Foucault talks about "government" on a number of levels besides the political, including of one's self, of interpersonal relationships, and of institutional and community relationships.

governing in a way that is responsive to each individual.[174] Thus liberal ideas grew from the necessity to forge new relations of power between the divergent interests of the emerging Nation-State and the autonomous individual of the Enlightenment. What ensued was the modern disciplinary relationship between the government and the governed.

Further, the disciplines of modernity mapped human behaviour in universal humanist categories which were utilised in the processes of colonisation and of normalising other forms of domination. The concrete arrangements of government relied on knowledges which regulated the social body of a population,[175] such as demography, statistics, birth control regulation and the psychiatrisation of sexual activity which resisted discipline.[176] In Foucault's view, disciplinary regulation was indispensable to the development of capitalism which required "methods of power capable of optimizing forces, aptitudes, and life in general without at the same time making them more difficult to govern".[177] Although Foucault is sceptical of meta-theory, his notion of governmental macro-management of the population comes close to suggesting how one discursive formation comes to be dominant. As he says, social science knowledges "acted as factors of segregation and social hierarchization ... guaranteeing relations of domination and effects of hegemony".[178] That is, the dualisms and hierarchies of modernity became central techniques of domination in political as well as legal discourse.

One example of the new technologies of rational government was the collection of statistics.[179] The development of modern institutions, laws, policies and representative forms of government all rely on statistics, which utilise social science categories to quantify, but also to produce, contain, erase and hierarchise, various aspects or phenomena of population.[180] Subaltern Studies[181] scholar Dipesh Chakrabarty illustrates the constitutive power of statistics in the colonial context of India, with reference to the categories of Religion and Caste which were introduced in the regular census undertaken by the British.[182] These categories sorted and ordered people into absolute and

174 *Ibid*, pp 3 and 22.
175 Foucault, n 165 above, p 99.
176 Foucault, n 90 above, p 147.
177 *Ibid*, p 141.
178 *Ibid.*
179 Foucault, n 165 above, p 96.
180 Hacking I, "How Should we do the History of Statistics?" in Burchell G, Gordon C and Miller P eds, *The Foucault Effect: Studies in Governmentality* (1991) p 181.
181 The Subaltern Studies Collective is a group of Indian historiographers whose work is informed by critical Marxist and poststructural perspectives. The initial focus of their work was to understand how, in the formation of the independent Nation-State of India, the nationalists came to represent an Indian elite that was closely allied to the British colonialists, rather than with the mass of the Indian people. This work quickly became multidimensional, producing critiques of modernity and nationalism, and addressing complex epistemological questions. See Guha R and Spivak GC eds, *Selected Subaltern Studies* (1988).
182 Chakrabarty D, "Modernity and Ethnicity in India" in Bennett D ed, *Multicultural*

hierarchical classifications which made the population "knowable" to the colonisers by bringing them into a relationship of commensurability with Europe. The colonial categories eventually predominated as "factual" Truth, denying the previous multi-layered and contingent understandings of difference and identity.[183]

Chakrabarty's analysis makes the connection between the local processes which colonised India and the hierarchising techniques promoted by the UN Charter system as follows:

> My point is that the social assumptions on which the classification and organization of census figures rested were fundamentally modern: they showed India to be a collection of 'communities' whose 'progress' or 'backwardness' could be measured by the application of some supposedly 'universal' indices. This is exactly how the modern world of nation states is structured — it is a united but internally hierarchized world where some countries are described as measurably — or should I say immeasurably — more 'advanced' than others...[184]

Implicit in the way in which the UN Charter promotes social and economic development is the idea that non-European peoples need to go through a kind of re-education process whereby governmentality is embraced, before they can emerge from "underdevelopment" and legitimately claim sovereign equality with the Nation-State members of the UN.[185]

Foucault stresses the point that governmentality is reliant more on Truth than pure violence and posits an interdependence between the power to govern and the control over Truth.[186] The science of modern government produces a discourse of Truth in much the same way as law, by dualising and hierarchising difference and by disqualifying incommensurable knowledges. The disciplinary distinction between "normal" (civilised) and "abnormal" (uncivilised) is a social sciences version of the boundaries of inclusion and exclusion propounded by human rights law. The trope of difference thus operates as a disciplinary, as well as a legal, technique of domination. As in the legal paradigm of equality where inclusion can be negotiated or attained on the basis of sameness in the name of justice, so too in the governmental paradigm is inclusion available on the condition that normalisation (civilisation) is embraced in the name of progress.

(b) Human rights law and governmentality

Foucault draws a distinction between legal and disciplinary power. He characterises law as a monolithic and menacing form of power reliant on "the

States: Rethinking Difference and Identity (forthcoming) pp 8–10.

183 *Ibid*, p 19.

184 *Ibid*, p 15.

185 UN Charter, n 1 above, Article 55. See also Articles 57(1) and 61(1) which set up intergovernmental specialised agencies and the Economic and Social Council respectively. The latter "may make or initiate studies and reports with respect to international economic, social, cultural, educational, health, and related matters"; Article 62(1).

186 Gordon, n 11 above, p 8.

sword"[187] that contrasts with the local and dispersed operation of disciplinary power, especially in his earlier work. He saw the rise of discipline as gradually colonising or absorbing the premodern sovereign power of law, forcing law to operate increasingly as a normalising discourse. In his view law is not capable of encoding the continuous surveillance that governmentality requires:

> it is a question not of imposing law on men, but of ... employing tactics rather than laws, and even of using laws themselves as tactics ... [t]he instruments of government, instead of being laws, now come to be a range of multiform tactics.[188]

Yet Foucault also said that when confronted with disciplinary power, law attempts to recode it in legal form.[189] Therefore his proposition about law's absorption by discipline was not unequivocal.

In fact, in Foucault's conception of governmentality, both legal and disciplinary discourses play a role in the production of dominating, universal knowledges. He refers to the triangle of sovereignty-discipline-government, [190] in which the interests of government are clearly linked with both sovereign legal rights and disciplinary regulation. Further, Foucault identifies the expansion and increasing influence of rights discourses as contributing to the management and normalisation of populations.[191] For example, he suggests that the constitutions of modernity, framed in the egalitarian terms of the French Revolution, were the legal forms that made an essentially disciplinary State palatable.[192] Although Foucault uses this as an illustration of how law comes to operate more as a form of discipline, it is more usefully understood as a cooperative enterprise between law and discipline.[193] Rights come to be accepted as an essential element of "good government" in their own right as law, rather than in the service of discipline. This cooperation can be seen in the way that the right to liberty becomes an idea that is critical to effective government; "disrespect of liberty is not simply an illegitimate violation of rights, but an ignorance of how to govern".[194]

The UN Charter's promotion of universal human rights, as a component of economic and social development, is unequivocal. In empowering the Economic and Social Council to set up mechanisms to assist in the performance of its functions, the only explicit direction given is to establish a *human rights* commission.[195] The snowballing of universal human rights law since its inauguration in the UN Charter, and the proliferation of claimants, have been

187 Foucault, n 90 above, p 144.
188 Foucault, n 165 above, p 95.
189 Foucault, n 90 above, p 109.
190 Foucault, n 165 above, p 102.
191 Foucault, n 90 above, p 144.
192 *Ibid.*
193 Smart, *Feminism and the Power of the Law*, n 130 above, p 17; Hunt A, "Foucault's Expulsion of Law: Toward a Retrieval" (1992) 17 *Law and Social Inquiry* 1 at 23.
194 Gordon, n 11 above, p 20.
195 UN Charter, n 1 above, Article 68.

breathtaking.[196] In the universal production of dignity, of the relationship between the individual and her/his society, and of the hierarchies of equality discourse and human rights generations, human rights law is both supportive of and supported by the disciplinary discourse of the social sciences. Both systems of power/knowledge affirm and normalise the subordinating universal indices of a masculinist, civilising Europe.

The complementarity of legal and disciplinary power is perhaps most evident in the categories of human rights claimants. The disciplines have produced groupings for the purposes of social regulation, like the categories of homosexuals, prisoners, mothers and indigenous peoples, and hierarchies like those of Race, Gender, Caste, Sexuality and Religion. These categories have been embraced by human rights law and used to extend its own "protective" powers in the form of rights. The attendant cost of the attainment of more rights, as Smart has astutely observed, is the increased information that claimants must provide to the State in establishing their entitlements, which enlarges the potential for surveillance, regulation and the enforcement of conformity.[197]

Legal categories utilise disciplinary knowledges in setting the identities of claimants and determining which injuries qualify for redress. Pheng Cheah points to aboriginal tribes in South-East Asia who are compelled by the universal human rights paradigm to "go ethnic" to defend their rights by "staging a collective identity and demanding rights in the name of that identity".[198] Likewise, feminist and sexuality claims tend to reproduce the gender and sexual difference they seek to do away with, as a condition of their inclusion in the dominant discourse.[199] Although, in Foucault's view, the new discourse of rights[200] was a political response to the demands of governmental power which he thought the juridical system incapable of comprehending,[201] it is significant that this response nevertheless took the form of law because it attests to the ongoing efficacy of legal discourse. Thus law remains an important site of transformative struggle, contrary to Foucault's predictions of its demise. Further, it is important to understand that human rights law, despite

196 Alston P, "Appraising The United Nations Human Rights Regime" in Alston P ed, *The United Nations and Human Rights: A Critical Appraisal* (1992) p 1 at 2.

197 Smart, *Feminism and the Power of the Law*, n 130 above, p 162.

198 Cheah P, "Posit(ion)ing Human Rights in the Current Global Conjuncture" (1997) 9 *Public Culture: Society for Transnational Studies* 233 at 256, with reference to Anderson B, "Introduction", *Southeast Asian Tribal Groups and Ethnic Minorities* (1987) p 1 at 11.

199 Scott JW, "Universalism and the History of Feminism" (1995) 7 *Differences: A Journal of Feminist Cultural Studies* 1 at 7; Smart, *Law, Crime and Sexuality*, n 9 above, pp 105–7 discussing Judith Butler's views.

200 Foucault refers directly to "the 'right' to life, to one's body, to health, to happiness, to the satisfaction of needs, and beyond all the oppressions or 'alienations', the 'right' to rediscover what one is and all that one can be", n 90 above, p 145.

201 *Ibid.*

its disciplinary and protective dimensions, also generates and shapes possibilities for resistance[202] which I will now explore.

(c) Power in ascending and descending analyses

The importance of Foucault's ascending analysis of power is its insistence that local knowledges are forms of power which are able to contest dominating knowledges despite, or perhaps because of, being subjugated or disqualified by them. Although Foucault emphasises the local operation of discipline on individual bodies and identities, disciplinary power clearly comes to produce global effects through the universal knowledges of the social sciences and the practices of governmentality. In order to understand better how local knowledges come to be reorganised, coordinated, condensed and coded into global, dominating discourses, it is crucial also to acknowledge the reverse effect that global knowledges have on the local, which I have called a *descending* analysis of power. As I have outlined, the content of the global discourses of dignity and of the relationship between the individual and her/his society have had constitutive, subjugating effects on local meanings. Also as Chakrabarty observes, the European categories of Caste and Religion came eventually to predominate locally in India, with terrible consequences in India's enduring problems of racial and ethnic conflict.[203]

A descending analysis of power is not to be mistaken for a reassertion of modern theories of monolithic, unified power but rather as the addition of a further dimension to Foucault's paradigm which maintains his emphasis on the importance of the local. A descending analysis seeks to understand how global knowledges come to influence, reorganise and shape local knowledges and, alternatively, how global knowledges are themselves disqualified or brought into a relationship of commensurability with the local. How, for example, does the denial of a group's spiritual and cultural associations with land become experienced locally as a violation of the universal rights of indigenous peoples? It is necessary to understand the hegemonic effects of global knowledges in order to realise the potential of local knowledges to resist and reshape them.

A further important point is that neither law nor the disciplines are unitary discourses.[204] While they interact with each other in multiple ways locally and globally, they also intersect with other discourses and practices. This produces multiple sites of power and therefore also of resistance. So, before rushing to forecast a superdisciplinary, carceral global society, we need to recognise, as Hunt suggests, that the interaction between different regulatory discourses and practices is seldom, if ever, complete.[205] This recognition opens many possibilities for local resistance which, if we can better understand how they might be linked and coordinated, could mount powerful challenges to the prevailing dominating discourses of universality and difference.

---

202 Hunt, "Rights and Social Movements", n 93 above.

203 Chakrabarty, n 182 above, p 19.

204 Smart, *Feminism and the Power of the Law*, n 130 above, p 87; Hunt, "Foucault's Expulsion of Law", n 193 above, at 32.

205 Hunt, *ibid*, at 38.

This returns to Pannikar's point that, while there can be no transcultural values, "there may be cross-cultural values, and cross-cultural critique is indeed possible".[206] To explore these possibilities we need to learn to engage in critical conversations in which differences in power are acknowledged and addressed, difference itself is understood as politically determined, and the modern Nation-State is reconstructed. We need to learn to speak in multiplicities rather than dualities and to continually engage diverse local knowledges in our efforts to understand and resist the hegemonic effects of all global discourses. At the same time, we must learn how to speak about and defend human value across differences and not allow our diversities to muffle or silence common pursuit of a world in which non-domination is the principle value.

In sum, the UN Charter promotes a global regime of governmentality by its privileging of the modern Nation-State as universal and its measurement of social and economic development according to European indices. In this endeavour, legal and disciplinary powers operate in tandem rather than, as Foucault suggests, discipline increasingly colonising law. The cooperative enterprise of producing universal Truths is highly effective in shaping local and global knowledges and in restraining and recoding resistance. However, its hegemonic effects are rarely complete and, with a better understanding of the operations of power in modernity, in both its ascending and descending movements, the hegemony of modern forms of power can be more effectively challenged.

Transformative human rights strategies need to forge alliances and coalitions between local and global knowledges, across the many divisions and hierarchies produced by the dualistic arrangements of difference of the dominant discourse. Such strategies need to reimagine the classic European ideals of liberty, democracy, equality, fraternity and self-determination so that they disrupt global regimes of dominating power rather than reinforce them. This task has a new imperative in the context of the balance of global power precipitated by the conclusion of the Cold War, in which the UN is championing, with renewed vigour, the universal cause of human rights.

IV. Conclusions

Examination of the constitutive assumptions of human rights law reveals that it is not based on innocent humanitarian, timeless and universal Truth. Rather, it is a situated, contingent and contested knowledge that is discursively produced by multiple dominating and resistant discourses. In its current form, human rights law naturalises and legitimises the subjugating and disciplinary effects of European, masculinist, heterosexual and capitalist regimes of power.

The techniques of dualising and hierarchising difference assist in the global legitimation of modernity as evidenced by the generational narrative of categories of human rights and in the exclusionary operation of the concept of equality. Differences like those of gender, race, sexuality, indigeneity, culture,

206 Pannikar, n 38 above, at 87.

class and nation are defined and contained by dichotomous language structures so as to confirm and normalise the supremacy of Europe's elites.

The global system of the UN Charter can be analysed as a means of promoting the science of governmentality that engages both legal and disciplinary power in instituting the modern form of the Nation-State as universal. Human rights law provides an example of the complementarity of these two forms of power. Foucault's ascending analysis of power, and his genealogies of the operation of law and discipline in modernity, open space for reassessing the potential of legal strategies to promote transformative change. His analysis suggests that reexamining modern categories with a view to revealing the loyalties and relations of power they support can open transformative non-dominating and anti-disciplinary possibilities. This provides a starting point for understanding how dispersed local knowledges might be coordinated and coded into global human rights movements that are able to challenge the hegemony of Europe.

Rethinking, from the margins of human rights orthodoxy, the way in which universality and difference are conceived is a project that is potentially both dangerous and liberating. Finding ways to understand dignity in the context of differences and of contested meanings has important implications for global regimes of power. Rethinking universality may further entrench dominating forms of power at the same time as it may open transformative possibilities. In any event, human rights law remains a critical site for deepening our understanding of the relationship between local and global knowledges, for learning to converse across differences without erasure and domination, for contesting the disciplinary hegemonic Truths of modernity, and for realising a world in which non-dominating discourses are powerful.

[9]

Toward a Multicultural Conception of Human Rights

Boaventura de Sousa Santos

Zusammenfassung: Der Artikel legt dar, daß Menschenrechtspolitik, wenn sie ein genuin emanzipatorisches Projekt mit weltweiter Reichweite werden soll, mit der Wahrnehmung des falschen Universalismus beginnen muß, der der konventionellen Konzeption der Menschenrechte unterliegt. Ein Versuch wird unternommen, auf der Basis einer diatopischen Hermeneutik eine mehr kosmopolitische, multikulturelle Konzeption der Menschenrechte zu entwickeln, die auf das Verbinden gleichgerichteter Besorgnisse um Menschenwürde in den westlichen, islamischen und hinduistischen Kulturen gerichtet ist.

Summary: The paper argues that in order to become a genuine emancipatory project with a worldwide reach, human rights politics must start by recognizing the false universalism that underlies the conventional conception of human rights. An attempt is made to develop a more cosmopolitan, multicultural conception of human rights on the basis of a diatopical hermeneutics aimed at bridging isomorphic concerns about human dignity in the Western, Islamic and Hindu cultures.

Introduction

For the past few years I have been puzzled by the extent to which human rights have become the language of progressive politics. Indeed, for many years after the Second World War human rights were very much part and parcel of cold war politics, and were so regarded by the Left. Double standards, complacency towards friendly dictators, the defense of tradeoffs between human rights and development – all this made human rights suspect as an emancipatory script. Whether in core countries or throughout the developing world, the progressive forces preferred the language of revolution and socialism to formulate an emancipatory politics. However, with the seemly irreversible crisis of these blueprints of emancipation, those same progressive forces find themselves today resorting to human rights to reconstitute the language of emancipation. It is as if human rights were called upon to fill the void left by socialist politics. Can in fact the concept of human rights fill such a void? My answer is a qualified yes. Accordingly, my analytical objective here is to specify the conditions under which human rights can be put at the service of a progressive, emancipatory politics.

The specification of such conditions leads us to unravel some of the dialectical tensions which lie at the core of western modernity.[1] The crisis now affecting these tensions signals better than anything else the problems facing western modernity today. In my view, human rights politics at the end of the century is a key factor to understand such crisis.

I identify three such tensions. The first one occurs between social regulation and social emancipation. I have been claiming that the paradigm of modernity is based on the idea of a creative dialectical tension between social regulation and social emancipation, which can still be heard, even if but dimly, in the positivist motto of "order and progress." At the end of this century this tension has ceased to be a creative tension. Emancipation has ceased to be the other of regulation to become the double of regulation. While until the late sixties the crisis of social regulation was met by the strengthening of emancipatory politics, today we witness a double social crisis. The crisis of social regulation, symbolized by the crisis of the regulatory state, and the crisis of social emancipation, symbolized by the crisis of the social revolution and socialism as a paradigm of radical social transformation. Human rights politics, which has been both a regulatory and an emancipatory politics, is trapped in this double crisis, while attempting, at the same time, to overcome it.

The second dialectical tension occurs between the state and civil society. The modern state, though a minimalist state, is potentially a maximalist state, to the extent that civil society, as the other of the state, reproduces itself through laws and regulations which emanate from the state and for which there seems to be no limit, as long as the democratic rules of law making are respected. Human rights are at the core of this tension: while the first generation of human rights was designed as a struggle of civil society against the state, considered to be the sole violator of human rights; the second and third generations of human rights resort to the state as the guarantor of human rights.

Finally, the third tension occurs between the nation-state and what we call globalization. The political model of Western modernity is one of sovereign nation-states coexisting in an international system of equally sovereign states, the interstate system. The privileged unit and scale both of social regulation and social emancipation is the nation-state. The interstate system has always been conceived of as a more or less anarchic society, run by a very soft legality, and even working class internationalism has always been more an aspiration than a reality. Today, the selective erosion of the nation-state due to the intensification of globalization raises the question whether both social regulation and social emancipation are to be displaced to the global level. We have started to speak of global civil society, global governance, global equity. Worldwide recognition of human rights politics is at the forefront of this process. The tension, however, lies in the fact that in very crucial aspects human rights politics is a cultural politics. So much so that we can even think of human rights as symbolizing the return of the cultural and even of the religious at the end of the century. But to

1 Elsewhere, I deal at length with the dialectical tensions in western modernity Santos (1995).

speak of culture and religion, is to speak of difference, boundaries, particularity. How can human rights be both a cultural and a global politics?

My purpose here is, therefore, to develop an analytical framework to highlight and support the emancipatory potential of human rights politics in the double context of globalization, on the one hand, and cultural fragmentation and identity politics, on the other. My aim is to establish both global competence and local legitimacy for a progressive politics of human rights.

On Globalizations

I shall start by specifying what I mean by globalization. Globalization is very hard to define. Most definitions focus on the economy, that is to say, on the new world economy that has emerged in the last two decades as a consequence of the globalization of the production of goods and services, and financial markets. This is a process through which the transnational corporations have risen to a new and unprecedented preeminence as international actors.

For my analytical purposes I prefer a definition of globalization that is more sensitive to the social, political, and cultural dimensions. I start from the assumption that what we usually call globalization consists of sets of social relations; as these sets of social relations change, so does globalization. There is strictly no single entity called globalization; there are, rather, globalizations, and we should use the term only in the plural. Any comprehensive concept should always be procedural, rather than substantive. On the other hand, if globalizations are bundles of social relations, the latter are bound to involve conflicts, hence, both winners and losers. More often than not, the discourse on globalization is the story of the winners as told by the winners. Actually, the victory is apparently so absolute that the defeated end up vanishing from the picture altogether.

Here is my definition of globalization: it is the process by which a given local condition or entity succeeds in extending its reach over the globe and, by doing so, develops the capacity to designate a rival social condition or entity as local. The most important implications of this definition are the following. First, in the conditions of western capitalist world system there is no genuine globalization. What we call globalization is always the successful globalization of a given localism. In other words, there is no global condition for which we cannot find a local root, a specific cultural embeddedness. Indeed, I can think of no entity without such a local grounding. The only possible but improbable candidate would be airport architecture. The second implication is that globalization entails localization. In fact, we live in a world of localization, as much as we live in a world of globalization. Therefore, it would be equally correct in analytical terms if we were to define the current situation and our research topics in terms of localization, rather than globalization. The reason why we prefer the latter term is basically because hegemonic scientific discourse tends to prefer the story of the world as told by the winners. Many examples of how globalization entails localization can be given. The English language, as *lingua franca*, is one such example. Its expansion as global language has entailed the localization of other potentially global languages, namely, the French language.

Therefore, once a given process of globalization is identified, its full meaning and explanation may not be obtained without considering adjacent processes of relocalization occurring in tandem and intertwined with it. The globalization of the Hollywood star system may involve the ethnicization of the Hindu star system produced by the once strong Hindu film industry. Similarly, the French or Italian actors of the 60's-from Brigitte Bardot to Alain Delon, from Marcello Mastroianni to Sofia Loren – which then symbolized the universal way of acting, seem today, when we see their movies again, as rather ethnic or parochially European. Between then and now, the Hollywoodesque way of acting has managed to globalize itself.

One of the transformations most commonly associated with globalization is time-space compression, that is to say, the social process by which phenomena speed up and spread out across the globe. Though apparently monolithic, this process does combine highly differentiated situations and conditions, and for that reason it cannot be analyzed independently of the power relations that account for the different forms of time and space mobility. On the one hand, there is the transnational capitalist class, really in charge of the time-space compression and capable of turning it to its advantage. On the other hand, the subordinate classes and groups, such as migrant workers and refugees, that are also doing a lot of physical moving but not at all in control of the time-space compression. Between corporate executives and immigrants and refugees, tourists represent a third mode of production of time-space compression. There are also those who heavily contribute to globalization but who, nonetheless, remain prisoners of their local time-space. The peasants of Bolivia, Peru and Colombia, by growing coca, contribute decisively to a world drug culture, but they themselves remain as "localized" as ever. Just like the residents of Rio's favelas, who remain prisoners of the squatter settlement life, while their songs and dances are today part of a globalized musical culture.

Finally and still from another perspective, global competence requires sometimes the accentuation of local specificity. Most of the tourist sites today must be highly exotic, vernacular and traditional in order to become competent enough to enter the market of global tourism.

In order to account for these asymmetries, globalization, as I have suggested, should always be referred to in the plural. In a rather loose sense, we could speak of different modes of production of globalization to account for this diversity. I distinguish four modes of production of globalization, which, I argue, give rise to four forms of globalization.

The first one I would call *globalized localism*. It consists in the process by which a given local phenomenon is successfully globalized, be it the worldwide operation of TNCs, the transformation of the English language in *lingua franca*, the globalization of American fast food or popular music or the worldwide adoption of American copyright laws on computer software.

The second form of globalization I would call *localized globalism*. It consists of the specific impact of transnational practices and imperatives on local conditions that are thereby destructured and restructured in order to respond to transnational imperatives. Such localized globalisms include: free-trade enclaves; deforestation and massive depletion of natural resources to pay for the foreign debt; touristic use of historical treasures, religious sites or ceremonies, arts and crafts, and wildlife; ecological dumping; conversion of sustainability oriented agriculture into export oriented agriculture as part of the "structural adjustment"; the ethnicization of the workplace. The international division of globalization assumes the following pattern: the core countries specialize in globalized localisms, while the choice of localized globalisms is imposed upon the peripheral countries. The world-system is a web of localized globalisms and globalized localisms.

However, the intensification of global interactions entails two other processes which are not adequately characterized either as globalized localisms or localized globalisms. The first one I would call *cosmopolitanism*. The prevalent forms of domination do not exclude the opportunity for subordinate nation-states, regions, classes or social groups and their allies to organize transnationally in defense of perceived common interests and use to their benefit the capabilities for transnational interaction created by the world-system. Cosmopolitan activities involve, among others, South-South dialogues and organizations, worldwide labor organizations (the World Federation of Trade Unions and the International Confederation of Free Trade Unions), North-South transnational philanthropy, international networks of alternative legal services, human rights organizations, worldwide women's groups networks, transformative advocacy NGOs, networks of alternative development and sustainable environment groups, literary, artistic and scientific movements in the periphery of the world-system in search of alternative, non-imperialist cultural values, engaging in postcolonial research, subaltern studies, and so on.

The other process that cannot be adequately described either as globalized localism or as localized globalism is the emergence of issues which, by their nature, are as global as the globe itself and which I would call, drawing loosely from international law, the *common heritage of humankind*. These are issues that only make sense as referred to the globe in its entirety: the sustainability of human life on earth, for instance, or such environmental issues as the protection of the ozone layer, the Amazon, the Antarctica, biodiversity or the deep seabed. I would also include in this category the exploration of the outer space, the moon and other planets, since the interactions of the latter with the earth are also a common heritage of humankind. All these issues refer to resources that, by their very nature, must be administered by trustees of the international community on behalf of present and future generations.

The concern with cosmopolitanism and the common heritage of humankind has known great development in the last decades; but it has also elicited powerful resistances. The common heritage of humankind in particular has been under steady attack by hegemonic countries, specially the United States (Santos 1995, pp. 365-373). The conflicts, resistances, struggles and coalitions clustering around cosmopolitanism and the common heritage of humankind show that what we call globalization is in fact a set of arenas of cross-border struggles.

For my purpose in this paper, it is useful to distinguish between globalization from above and globalization from below, or between hegemonic and counter-hegemonic globalization. What I called *globalized localism* and *localized globalism* are globalizations from above; *cosmopolitanism* and the *common heritage of humankind* are globalizations from below.

Human Rights as an Emancipatory Script

The complexity of human rights is that they may be conceived either as a form of globalized localism or as a form of cosmopolitanism or, in other words, as a globalization from above or as a globalization from below. My purpose is to specify the conditions under which human rights may be conceived of as a globalization of the latter kind. In this paper I will not cover all the necessary conditions but rather only the cultural ones. My argument is that as long as human rights are conceived of as universal human rights, they will tend to operate as a globalized localism, a form of globalization from above. To be able to operate as a cosmopolitan, counter-hegemonic form of globalization human rights must be reconceptualized as multicultural. Conceived of, as they have been, as universal, human rights will always be an instrument of Samuel Huntington's "clash of civilizations", that is to say, of the struggle of the West against the rest. Their global competence will be obtained at the cost of their local legitimacy. On the contrary, multiculturalism, as I understand it, is a precondition for a balanced and mutually reinforcing relationship between global competence and local legitimacy, the two attributes of a counter-hegemonic human rights politics in our time.

We know, of course, that human rights are not universal in their application. Four international regimes of human rights are consensually distinguished in the world in our time: the European, the Inter-American, the African and the Asian regime.[2] But are they universal as a cultural artifact, a kind of cultural invariant, a global culture? All cultures tend to define ultimate values as the most widespread. But only the western culture tends to focus on universality. The question of the universality of human rights betrays the universality of what it questions by the way it questions it. In other words, the question of universality is a particular question, a Western cultural question.

The concept of human rights lies on a well-known set of presuppositions, all of which are distinctly Western, namely: there is a universal human nature that can be known by rational means; human nature is essentially different from and higher than the rest of reality; the individual has an absolute and irreducible dignity that must be defended against society or the state; the autonomy of the individual requires that society be organized in a non-hierarchical way, as a sum of free individuals (Panikkar 1984, p. 30). Since all these presuppositions are clearly Western and liberal, and easily distinguishable from other conceptions of human dignity in other cultures, one might

2 For an extended analysis of the four regimes, see Santos (1995, pp. 330-337), and the bibliography cited there.

ask why the question of the universality of human rights has become so hotly debated, why, in other words, the sociological universality of this question has outgrown its philosophical universality.

If we look at the history of human rights in the post-war period, it is not difficult to conclude that human rights policies by and large have been at the service of the economic and geopolitical interests of the hegemonic capitalist states. The generous and seductive discourse on human rights has allowed for unspeakable atrocities and such atrocities have been evaluated and dealt with according to revolting double standards. Writing in 1981 about the manipulation of the human rights agenda in the United States in conjunction with the mass media, Richard Falk spoke of a "politics of invisibility" and of a "politics of supervisibility" (1981). As examples of the politics of invisibility he spoke of the total blackout by the media on news about the tragic decimation of the Maubere People in East Timor (taking more than 500,000 lives) and the plight of the hundred million or so "untouchables" in India. As examples of the politics of supervisibility Falk mentioned the relish with which post-revolutionary abuses of human rights in Iran and Vietnam were reported in the United States. Actually, the same could largely be said of the European Union countries, the most poignant example being the silence that kept the genocide of the Maubere people hidden from the Europeans for a decade, thereby facilitating the ongoing smooth and thriving international trade with Indonesia.

But the Western and indeed the Western liberal mark in the dominant human rights discourse could be traced in many other instances: in the Universal Declaration of 1948, which was drafted without the participation of the majority of the peoples of the world; in the exclusive recognition of individual rights, with the only exception of the collective right to self-determination which, however, was restricted to the peoples subjected to European colonialism; in the priority given to civil and political rights over economic, social and cultural rights, and in the recognition of the right to property as the first and, for many years, the sole economic right.

But this is not the whole story. Throughout the world, millions of people and thousands of nongovernmental organizations have been struggling for human rights, often at great risk, in defense of oppressed social classes and groups that in many instances have been victimized by authoritarian capitalistic states. The political agendas of such struggles are often either explicitly or implicitly anti-capitalist. A counter-hegemonic human rights discourse and practice has been developing, non-Western conceptions of human rights have been proposed, cross-cultural dialogues on human rights have been organized. The central task of emancipatory politics of our time, in this domain, consists in transforming the conceptualization and practice of human rights from a globalized localism into a cosmopolitan project.

What are the premises for such a transformation? The first premise is that it is imperative to transcend the debate on universalism and cultural relativism. The debate is an inherently false debate, whose polar concepts are both and equally detrimental to an emancipatory conception of human rights. All cultures are relative, but cultural relativism, as a philosophical posture, is wrong. All cultures aspire to ultimate concerns and values, but cultural universalism, as a philosophical posture, is wrong. Against universalism, we must propose cross-cultural dialogues on isomorphic concerns. Against relativism, we must develop cross-cultural procedural criteria to distinguish progressive politics from regressive politics, empowerment from disempowerment, emancipation from regulation. To the extent that the debate sparked by human rights might evolve into a competitive dialogue among different cultures on principles of human dignity, it is imperative that such competition induce the transnational coalitions to race to the top rather than to the bottom (what are the absolute minimum standards? the most basic human rights? the lowest common denominators?). The often voiced cautionary comment against overloading human rights politics with new, more advanced rights or with different and broader conceptions of human rights (Donnelly 1989, pp. 109-124), is a latter day manifestation of the reduction of the emancipatory claims of Western modernity to the low degree of emancipation made possible or tolerated by world capitalism: low intensity human rights as the other side of low intensity democracy.

The second premise is that all cultures have conceptions of human dignity but not all of them conceive of it as human rights. It is therefore important to look for isomorphic concerns among different cultures. Different names, concepts and *Weltanschauungen* may convey similar or mutually intelligible concerns or aspirations.

The third premise is that all cultures are incomplete and problematic in their conceptions of human dignity. The incompleteness derives from the very fact that there is a plurality of cultures. If each culture were as complete as it claims to be, there would be just one single culture. The idea of completeness is at the source of an excess of meaning that seems to plague all cultures. Incompleteness is thus best visible from the outside, from the perspective of another culture. To raise the consciousness of cultural incompleteness to its possible maximum, is one of the most crucial tasks in the construction of a multicultural conception of human rights.

The fourth premise is that all cultures have different versions of human dignity, some broader than others, some with a wider circle of reciprocity than others, some more open to other cultures than others. For instance, Western modernity has unfolded into two highly divergent conceptions and practices of human rights – the liberal and the Marxist – one prioritizing civil and political rights, the other prioritizing social and economic rights.[3]

Finally, the fifth premise is that all cultures tend to distribute people and social groups among two competing principles of hierarchical belongingness. One operates through hierarchies among homogeneous units. The other operates through separation among unique identities and differences. The two principles do not necessarily overlap and for that reason not all equalities are identical and not all differences are unequal.

These are the premises of a cross-cultural dialogue on human dignity which may eventually lead to a *mestiza* conception of human rights, a conception that instead of resorting to false universalisms, organizes itself as a constellation of local and mutually intelligible meanings, networks of empowering normative references.

But this is only a starting point. In the case of a cross-cultural dialogue the exchange is not only between different knowledges but also between different cultures, that is

3 See, for instance, Pollis/Schwab (1979); Pollis (1982); An-na'im (1992).

to say, between different and, in a strong sense, incommensurable universes of meaning. These universes of meaning consist of constellations of strong *topoi*. These are the overarching rhetorical commonplaces of a given culture. They function as premises of argumentation, thus making possible the production and exchange of arguments. Strong *topoi* become highly vulnerable and problematic whenever "used" in a different culture. The best that can happen to them is to be moved "down" from premises of argumentation into arguments. To understand a given culture from another culture's *topoi* may thus prove to be very difficult, if not at all impossible. I shall therefore propose a *diatopical hermeneutics*. In the area of human rights and dignity, the mobilization of social support for the emancipatory claims they potentially contain is only achievable if such claims have been appropriated in the local cultural context. Appropriation, in this sense, cannot be obtained through cultural cannibalization. It requires cross-cultural dialogue and diatopical hermeneutics.

Diatopical hermeneutics is based on the idea that the *topoi* of an individual culture, no matter how strong they may be, are as incomplete as the culture itself. Such incompleteness is not visible from inside the culture itself, since aspiration to the totality induces taking *pars pro tote*. The objective of diatopical hermeneutics is, therefore, not to achieve completeness – that being an unachievable goal – but, on the contrary, to raise the consciousness of reciprocal incompleteness to its possible maximum by engaging in the dialogue, as it were, with one foot in one culture and the other in another. Herein lies its *diatopical* character.[4]

A diatopical hermeneutics can be conducted between the *topos* of human rights in Western culture and the *topos* of *dharma* in Hindu culture, and the *topos* of *umma* in Islamic culture. According to Panikkar, *dharma* "is that which maintains, gives cohesion and thus strength to any given thing, to reality, and ultimately to the three worlds (triloka). Justice keeps human relations together; morality keeps oneself in harmony; law is the binding principle for human relations; religion is what maintains the universe in existence; destiny is that which links us with future; truth is the internal cohesion of a thing ... Now a world in which the notion of Dharma is central and nearly all-pervasive is not concerned with finding the 'right' of one individual against another or of the individual vis-à-vis society but rather with assaying the dharmic (right, true, consistent) or adharmic character of a thing or an action within the entire theantropocosmic complex of reality" (1984, p. 39).[5] Seen from the *topos* of *dharma*, human rights are incomplete in that they fail to establish the link between the part (the individual) and the whole (reality), or even more strongly in that they focus on what is merely derivative, on rights, rather than on the primordial imperative, the duty of individuals to find their place in the order of the entire society, and of the entire cosmos. Seen from *dharma* and, indeed from *umma* also, the Western conception of human rights is plagued by a very simplistic and mechanistic symmetry between rights and duties. It grants rights only to those from whom it can demand duties. This explains why according to Western human rights nature has no rights: because

4 See also Panikkar (1984, p. 28).

5 See also K. Inada (1990); K. Mitra (1982); R. Thapar (1966).

it cannot be imposed any duties. For the same reason, it is impossible to grant rights to future generations: they have no rights because they have no duties.

On the other hand, seen from the *topos* of human rights, *dharma* is also incomplete due to its strong undialectical bias in favor of harmony, thereby occulting injustices and totally neglecting the value of conflict as a way toward a richer harmony. Moreover, *dharma* is unconcerned with the principles of democratic order, with freedom and autonomy, and it neglects the fact that, without primordial rights, the individual is too fragile an entity to avoid being run over by whatever transcends him or her. Moreover, *dharma* tends to forget that human suffering has an irreducible individual dimension: societies don't suffer, individuals do.

At another conceptual level, the same diatopical hermeneutics can be attempted between the *topos* of human rights and the *topos* of *umma* in Islamic culture. The passages in the Qur'an in which the word *umma* occurs are so varied that its meaning cannot be rigidly defined. This much, however, seems to be certain: it always refers to ethnical, linguistic or religious bodies of people who are the objects of the divine plan of salvation. As the prophetic activity of Muhammad progressed, the religious foundations of *umma* became increasingly apparent and consequently the *umma* of the Arabs was transformed into the umma of the Muslims. Seen from the topos of *umma,* the incompleteness of the individual human rights lies in the fact that on its basis alone it is impossible to ground the collective linkages and solidarities without which no society can survive, and much less flourish. Herein lies the difficulty in the Western conception of human rights to accept collective rights of social groups or peoples, be they ethnic minorities, women, or indigenous peoples. This is in fact a specific instance of a much broader difficulty: the difficulty of defining the community as an arena of concrete solidarity, and as an horizontal political obligation. Central to Rousseau, this idea of community was flushed away in the liberal dichotomy that set asunder the state and civil society.

Conversely, from the *topos* of the individual human rights, *umma* overemphasizes duties to the detriment of rights and, for that reason, is bound to condone otherwise abhorrent inequalities, such as the inequality between men and women and between Muslims and non-Muslims. As unveiled by the diatopical hermeneutics, the fundamental weakness of Western culture consists in dichotomizing too strictly between the individual and society, thus becoming vulnerable to possessive individualism, narcissism, alienation, and anomie. On the other hand, the fundamental weakness of Hindu and Islamic cultures consists in that they both fail to recognize that human suffering has an irreducible individual dimension, which can only be adequately addressed in a society not hierarchically organized.

The recognition of reciprocal incompletenesses and weaknesses is a *condition-sine-qua-non* of a cross-cultural dialogue. Diatopical hermeneutics builds both on local identification of incompleteness and weakness and on its translocal intelligibility. As mentioned above, in the area of human rights and dignity, the mobilization of social support for the emancipatory claims they potentially contain is only achievable if such claims have been appropriated in the local cultural context, and if a cross-cultural dialogue and diatopical hermeneutics are at all possible. A good example of a diatopical hermeneutics between Islamic and Western culture in the field of human rights is given by Abdullahi Ahmed An-na'im (1990; 1992).

There is a long-standing debate on the relationships between Islamism and human rights and the possibility of an Islamic conception of human rights.[6] This debate covers a wide range of positions, and its impact reaches far beyond the Islamic world. Running the risk of excessive simplication, two extreme positions can be identified in this debate. One, absolutist or fundamentalist, is held by those for whom the religious legal system of Islam, the Shari'a, must be fully applied as the law of the Islamic state. According to this position, there are irreconcilable inconsistencies between the Shari'a and the Western conception of human rights, and the Shari'a must prevail. For instance, regarding the status of non-Muslims, the Shari'a dictates the creation of a state for Muslims as the sole citizens, non-Muslims having no political rights; peace between Muslims and non-Muslims is always problematic and confrontations may be unavoidable. Concerning women, there is no question of equality; the Shari'a commands the segregation of women and, according to some more strict interpretations, even excludes them from public life altogether.

At the other extreme, there are the secularists or the modernists, who believe that Muslims should organize themselves in secular states. Islam is a religious and spiritual movement, not a political one and, as such, modern Muslim societies are free to organize their government in whatever manner they deem fit and appropriate to the circumstances. The acceptance of international human rights is a matter of political decision unencumbered by religious considerations. Just one example, among many: a Tunisian law of 1956 prohibited polygamy altogether on the grounds that is was no longer acceptable and that the Qur'anic requirement of justice among co-wives was impossible for any man, except the Prophet, to achieve in practice.

An-na'im criticizes both extreme positions. The via *per mezzo* he proposes aims at establishing a cross-cultural foundation for human rights, identifying the areas of conflict between Shari'a and "the standards of human rights" and seeking a reconciliation and positive relationship between the two systems. For example, the problem with historical Shari'a is that it excludes women and non-Muslim from the application of this principle. Thus, a reform or reconstruction of Shari'a is needed. The method proposed for such "islamic Reformation" is based on an evolutionary approach to Islamic sources that looks into the specific historical context within which Shari'a was created out of the original sources of Islam by the founding jurists of the eighth and ninth centuries. In the light of such a context, a restricted construction of the other was probably justified. But this is no longer so. On the contrary, in the present different context there is within Islam full justification for a more enlightened view. Following the teachings of *Ustadh* Mahmoud, An-na'im shows that a close examination of the content of the Qur'an and Sunna reveals two levels or stages of the message of Islam, one of the earlier Mecca period and the other of the subsequent Medina stage. The earlier message of Mecca is the eternal and fundamental message of Islam

6 Besides An-na'im (1990; 1992), see Dwyer (1991); Mayer (1991); Leites (1991); Afkhami (1995). See also Hassan (1982); Al Faruqi (1983). On the broader issue of the relationship between modernity and Islamic revival, see, for instance, Sharabi (1992), and Shariati (1986).

and it emphasizes the inherent dignity of all human beings, regardless of gender, religious belief or race. Under the historical conditions of the seventh century (the Medina stage) this message was considered too advanced, was suspended, and its implementation postponed until appropriate circumstances would emerge in the future. The time and context, says An-na'im, are now ripe for it.

It is not for me to evaluate the specific validity of this proposal within Islamic culture. This is precisely what distinguishes diatopical hermeneutics from orientalism. What I want to emphasize in An-na'im's approach is the attempt to transform the Western conception of human rights into a cross-cultural one that vindicates Islamic legitimacy rather than relinquishing it. In the abstract and from the outside, it is difficult to judge whether a religious or a secularist approach is more likely to succeed in an Islamic based cross-cultural dialogue on human rights. However, bearing in mind that Western human rights are the expression of a profound, albeit incomplete process of secularization which is not comparable to anything in Islamic culture, one would be inclined to suggest that, in the Muslim context, the mobilizing energy needed for a cosmopolitan project of human rights will be more easily generated within a enlightened religious framework. If so, An-na'im's approach is very promising.

Diatopical hermeneutics is not a task for a single person writing within a single culture. It is, therefore, not surprising that An-na'im's approach, though a true *exemplar* of diatopical hermeneutics, is conducted with uneven consistency. In my view, An-na'im accepts the idea of universal human rights too readily and acritically. Even though he subscribes to an evolutionary approach and is quite attentive to the historical context of Islamic tradition, he becomes surprisingly ahistorical and naively universalist as far the Universal Declaration goes. Diatopical hermeneutics requires not only a different kind of knowledge, but also a different process of knowledge creation. It requires a production of knowledge that must be collective, interactive, inter-subjective, and networked.

The diatopical hermeneutics conducted by An-na'im, from the perspective of Islamic culture, and the human rights struggles organized by Islamic feminist grassroots movements following the ideas of "Islamic Reformation" proposed by him, must be matched by a diatopical hermeneutics conducted from the perspective of other cultures and namely from the perspective of Western culture. This is probably the only way to embed in the Western culture the idea of collective rights, rights of nature and future generations, and of duties and responsibilities vis-à-vis collective entities, be they the community, the world, or even the cosmos.

More generally, the diatopical hermeneutics offers a wide field of possibilities for debates going on, in the different cultural regions of the world-system, on the general issues of universalism, relativism, cultural frames of social transformation, traditionalism, and cultural revival.[7] However, an idealistic conception of cross-cultural dialogue will easily forget that such a dialogue is only made possible by the temporary simultaneity of two or more different contemporaneities. The partners in the dialogue

7 For the African debate, see O. Oladipo (1989); Oruka (1990); K. Wiredu (1990); Wamba dia Wamba (1991a, 1991b); H. Procee (1992); M.B. Ramose (1992). A sample of the rich debate in India is in A. Nandy (1987a, 1987b, 1988); P. Chatterjee (1984); T. Pantham (1988). A bird's eye view of cultural differences can be found in Galtung (1981).

are only superficially contemporaneous; indeed each of them feels himself or herself only contemporaneous with the historical tradition of his or her respective culture. This is most likely the case when the different cultures involved in the dialogue share a past of interlocked unequal exchanges. What are the possibilities for a cross-cultural dialogue when one of the cultures *in presence* has been itself molded by massive and long lasting violations of human rights perpetrated in the name of the other culture? When cultures share such a past, the present they share at the moment of starting the dialogue is at best a *quid pro quo* and at worst a fraud. The cultural dilemma is the following: since in the past the dominant culture rendered unpronounceable some of the aspirations of the subordinate culture to human dignity, is it now possible to pronounce them in the cross-cultural dialogue without thereby further justifying and even reinforcing their unpronounceability?

Cultural imperialism and epistemicide are part of the historical trajectory of Western modernity. After centuries of unequal cultural exchanges, is equal treatment of cultures fair? Is it necessary to render some aspirations of Western culture unpronounceable in order to make room for the pronounceability of other aspirations of other cultures? Paradoxically – and contrary to hegemonic discourse – it is precisely in the field of human rights that Western culture must learn form the South, if the false universality that is attributed to human rights in the imperial context is to be converted into the new universality of cosmopolitanism in a cross-cultural dialogue.

The emancipatory character of the diatopical hermeneutics is not guaranteed *a priori* and indeed multiculturalism may be the new mark of a reactionary politics. Suffice it to mention the multiculturalism of the Prime Minister of Malaysia or Chinese gerontocracy, when they speak of the "Asian conception of human rights." To preempt this move, two transcultural imperatives must be accepted by all social groups engaging in diatopical hermeneutics. The first one goes like this: of the different versions of a given culture, that one must be chosen which represents the widest circle of reciprocity within that culture, the version that goes farthest in the recognition of the other. As we have seen, of two different interpretations of the Qur'an, An-na'im chooses the one with the wider circle of reciprocity, the one that involves Muslims and non-Muslims men and women alike. I think this must be done within Western culture as well. Of the two versions of human rights existing in our culture – the liberal and the Marxist – the Marxist one must be adopted for it extends to the economic and social realms the equality that the liberal version only considers legitimate in the political realm.

The second transcultural imperative goes like this: since all cultures tend to distribute people and groups according to two competing principles of hierarchical belongingness, and thus to competing conceptions of equality and difference, people have the right to be equal whenever difference makes them inferior, but they also have the right to be different whenever equality jeopardizes their identity. This is a very difficult imperative to attain and to sustain. Multinational constitutional states such as Belgium approximate it in someway. There is much hope that South Africa will do the same.

Conclusion

As they are now predominantly understood, human rights are a kind of esperanto which can hardly become the everyday language of human dignity across the globe. It is up to the diatopical hermeneutics sketched above to transform them into a cosmopolitan politics networking mutually intelligible and translatable native languages of emancipation.

This project may sound rather utopian. But, as Sartre once said, before it is realized an idea has a strange resemblance with utopia. Be it as it may, the important fact is not to reduce realism to what exists, in which case we may be constrained to justify what exists, no matter how unjust or oppressive.

References

Afkhami, Mahnaz (ed.), 1995: Faith and Freedom: Women's Human Rights in the Muslim World, Syracuse: Syracuse University Press.

Al Faruqi, Isma'il R., 1983: Islam and Human Rights, in: The Islamic Quarterly 27(1), pp. 12-30.

An-na'im, Abdullahi A. (ed.), 1992: Human Rights in Cross-Cultural Perspectives. A Quest for Consensus, Philadelphia: University of Pennsylvania Press.

An-na'im, Abdullahi A., 1990: Toward an Islamic Reformation, Syracuse: Syracuse University Press.

Chatterjee, Partha, 1984: Gandhi and the Critique of Civil Society, in: *Ranajit Guha* (ed.), Subaltern Studies III: Writings on South Asian History and Society, Delhi: Oxford University Press, pp. 153-195.

Donnelly, Jack, 1989: Universal Human Rights in Theory and Practice, Ithaca: Cornell University Press.

Dwyer, Kevin, 1991: Arab Voices. The Human Rights Debate in the Middle East, Berkeley: University of California Press.

Falk, Richard, 1981: Human Rights and State Sovereignty, New York: Holmes and Meier Publishers.

Galtung, Johan, 1981: Western Civilization: Anatomy and Pathology, in: Alternatives 7, pp. 145-169.

Guha, Ranajit (ed.), 1984: Subaltern Studies III: Writings on South Asian History and Society, Delhi: Oxford University Press.

Hassan, Riffat, 1982: On Human Rights and the Qur'anic Perspective, in: Journal of Ecumenical Studies 19(3), pp. 51-65.

Inada, Kenneth K., 1990: A Budhist Response to the Nature of Human Rights, in: *Claude Welsh, Jr.* and *Virginia Leary* (eds.), Asian Perspectives on Human Rights, Boulder: Westview Press, pp. 91-101.

Leites, Justin, 1991: Modernist Jurisprudence as a Vehicle for Gender Role Reform in the Islamic World, in: Columbia Human Rights Law Review 22, pp. 251-330.

Mayer, Ann Elizabeth, 1991: Islam and Human Rights: Tradition and Politics, Boulder: Westview Press.

Mitra, Kana, 1982: Human Rights in Hinduism, in: Journal of Ecumenical Studies 19(3), pp. 77-84.

Nandy, Ashis, 1987a: Cultural Frames for Social Transformation: A Credo, in: Alternatives XII, pp. 113-123.

Nandy, Ashis, 1987b: Traditions, Tyranny and Utopias. Essays in the Politics of Awareness, Oxford: Oxford University Press.

Nandy, Ashis, 1988: The Politics of Secularism and the Recovery of Religious Tolerance, in: Alternatives XIII, pp. 177-194.

Oladipo, Olusegun, 1989: Towards a Philosophical Study of African Culture: A Critique of Traditionalism, in: Quest 3(2), pp. 31-50.

Oruka, H. Odera, 1990: Cultural Fundamentals in Philosophy, in: Quest 4(2), pp. 21-37.

Panikkar, Raimundo, 1984: Is the Notion of Human Rights a Western Concept?, in: Cahier 81, pp. 28-47.

Pantham, Thomas, 1988: On Modernity, Rationality and Morality: Habermas and Gandhi, in: The Indian Journal of Social Science 1(2), pp. 187-208.

Pollis, Adamantia, 1982: Liberal, Socialist and Third World Perspectives of Human Rights, in: *P. Schwab* and *A. Pollis* (eds.), Toward A Human Rights Framework, New York: Praeger, pp. 1-26.

Pollis, Adamantia/Schwab, P., 1979: Human Rights: A Western Construct with Limited Applicability, in: *A. Pollis* and *P. Schwab* (eds.), Human Rights. Cultural and Ideological Perspectives, New York: Praeger, pp. 1-18.

Procee, Henk, 1992: Beyond Universalism and Relativism, in: Quest 6(1), pp. 45-55.

Ramose, Mogobe B., 1992: African Democratic Traditions: Oneness, Consensus and Openness, in: Quest 6(1), pp. 63-83.

Santos, Boaventura de Sousa, 1995: Toward a New Common Sense. Law, Science and Politics in the Paradigmatic Transition, New York: Routledge.

Sharabi, Hisham, 1992: Modernity and Islamic Revival: The Critical Tasks of Arab Intellectuals, in: Contention 2(1), pp. 127-147.

Shariati, All, 1986: What is to be done: the Enlightened Thinkers and an Islamic Renaissance. Edited by Farhang Rajaee, Houston: The Institute for Research and Islamic Studies.

Thapar, Romila, 1966: The Hindu and Buddhist Traditions, in: International Social Science Journal 18(1), pp. 31-40.

Wamba dia Wamba, Ernest, 1991a: Some Remarks on Culture Development and Revolution in Africa, in: Journal of Historical Sociology 4, pp. 219-235.

Wamba dia Wamba, Ernest, 1991b: Beyond Elite Politics of Democracy in Africa, in: Quest 6(1), pp. 28-42.

Welsh, Jr., Claude/Leary, Virginia (eds.), 1990: Asian Perspectives on Human Rights, Boulder: Westview Press.

Wiredu, Kwasi, 1990: Are there Cultural Universals?, in: Quest 4(2), pp. 5-19.

Part II
Applying Human Rights Concepts

[10]

THE GLOBAL MARKET AND HUMAN RIGHTS: TRADING AWAY THE HUMAN RIGHTS PRINCIPLE

*Frank J. Garcia**

I. INTRODUCTION

The task set for this Article is to consider the impact which the globalization of markets may have on the effectiveness of international human rights law. But what *is* globalization? By comparison, the term "international human rights" is relatively easier to categorize,[1] and in this Article shall be used principally in the positive sense to denote the basic legal rights enumerated in the first twenty articles of the Universal

---

* Associate Professor, Florida State University College of Law. This Article is based on a paper delivered at Brooklyn Law School as part of a symposium entitled "The Universal Declaration of Human Rights at 50 and the Challenge of Global Markets," November 5, 1998. The author would like to thank Sam Murumba for his invitation to participate in the symposium and for his enthusiastic support, and fellow panelists Mark Warner, Steve Charnovitz, and Jeffrey L. Dunoff for their helpful comments. The author also wishes to thank Paolo Annino for his thoughtful critique of the manuscript, as well as participants in the Florida State University Faculty Workshop Series and members of his International Legal Theory Seminar for their many contributions. The author gratefully acknowledges the excellent research assistance of Ani Majuni and Sandra Upegui. Research for this Article was supported by a grant from the Florida State University College of Law.

1. In saying this, I do not mean to suggest that the concept of international human rights is simple, uncontroversial, and has precise limits—that is far from the case. *See generally* Joy Gordon, *The Concept of Human Rights: The History and Meaning of its Politicization,* 23 BROOK. J. INT'L L. 689 (1998) (reviewing the concept, and asserting its oddness, political history and inconsistency); Anthony D'Amato, *The Concept of Human Rights in International Law,* 82 COLUM. L. REV. 1110 (1982). Commentators have objected to the uncertain boundaries of the concept, as well as to inherent gender and culture biases. *See, e.g.,* Philip Alston, *Conjuring Up New Human Rights: A Proposal for Quality Control,* 78 AM. J. INT'L L. 607, 607 (1984) (criticizing the "haphazard" expansion of the term); Celina Romany, *Women as Aliens: A Feminist Critique of the Public/Private Distinction in International Human Rights Law,* 6 HARV. HUM. RTS. J. 87, 88 (1993) (arguing that the concept of human rights rests on discredited public/private distinction); Sompong Sucharitkul, *A Multi-Dimensional Concept of Human Rights in International Law,* 62 NOTRE DAME L. REV. 305, 305 (1987) (discussing European bias of basic human rights instruments). I mean only that it is relatively easier to have some assurance that we know what the term is referring to in discourse, at least when employed in a positive sense, in comparison to the term "globalization," as I discuss below. *See infra* note 4 and accompanying text.

Declaration of Human Rights.[2] Such rights include the right to life, liberty and the security of one's person; the right to freedom from slavery or servitude; the right to freedom from torture or cruel, inhuman or degrading treatment; the right to equality before the law; and the right to own property.[3] But globalization? As many commentators have pointed out, "globalization" is a rather vague, "loose and overstretched" term which can be used to mean many things or, perhaps, nothing at all.[4] And why think about the impact of *globalization,* in particular the globalization of *markets*, on human rights law, rather than the impact of some other international trend? Is it

2. Universal Declaration of Human Rights, G.A. Res. 217A, U.N. GAOR, 3d Sess., pt. I, 183d plen. mtg., U.N. Doc. A/810 (1948) [hereinafter UDHR]. An alternative list of "core" rights might consist, for example, of the rights listed in Section 702 of the Restatement. RESTATEMENT (THIRD) OF THE FOREIGN RELATIONS LAW OF THE UNITED STATES § 702 (1986) (customary international law recognizes prohibitions against, *inter alia*, genocide, slavery, murder or disappearance of individuals, torture, prolonged arbitrary detention, and systematic racial discrimination). International human rights includes other rights, of course, such as those enumerated in the two U.N. covenants, often referred to as "second-generation" rights. These are set forth in and enforced through other instruments and mechanisms, such as regional human rights conventions, specialized tribunals, national courts, and state initiatives such as international diplomacy, and economic coercion.

The term "international human rights" can also be used in a normative sense to refer to the bundle of related concepts in moral and political theory used to justify positive legal rights, such as natural law, natural rights and moral rights. This Article shall endeavor in its use of the term to distinguish the positive law from its normative justification. *See infra* notes 74-82 and accompanying text. The term can also be used in a historical or sociological sense with reference to the post-war human rights movement, and in an aspirational sense as representing an ideal of human dignity protected through law. *See generally* Burns Weston, *Human Rights, in* 20 NEW ENCYCLOPAEDIA BRITANNICA (15th ed. 1993).

3. UDHR, *supra* note 2, arts. 3-5, 7, 17.

4. Rudolph Dolzer, *Global Environmental Issues: The Genuine Area of Globalization*, 7 J. TRANSNAT'L L. & POL'Y 157, 157 (1998) ("Behind the loose and overstretched notion of globalization are both quantitatively and qualitatively different phenomena in economic, cultural, and environmental international relations."). *See also* Alfred C. Aman, Jr., *Introduction,* 1 IND. J. GLOBAL LEGAL STUD. 1, 1 (1993); S. Tamer Cavusgil, *Globalization of Markets and its Impact on Domestic Institutions,* 1 IND. J. GLOBAL LEGAL STUD. 83, 84 (1993); Jost Delbrück, *Globalization of Law, Politics, and Markets—Implications for Domestic Law—A European Perspective,* 1 IND. J. GLOBAL LEGAL STUD. 9, 9-10 (1993); Miguel de la Madrid H., *National Sovereignty and Globalization*, 19 HOUS. J. INT'L L. 553, 555-60 (1997); Alberto Tita, *Globalization: A New Political and Economic Space Requiring Supranational Governance*, 32 J. WORLD TRADE 47 (1998). For a thorough review of the history and uses of the term, see Tahirih V. Lee, *Swallowing the Dragon? Some Directions for Research on Globalization Theory and Legal and Economic Restructuring in East Asia,* AM. J. COMP. L. (forthcoming 1999).

simply because we presume that "human rights," being in some non-trivial way about "human beings," are therefore likely to be influenced by any important change in human self-understanding and social activity, such as market globalization may represent? Or do we intuit that there is something particular about market globalization which leads us to suspect that it will have a unique and important impact on the effectiveness of human rights law, one that is worth examining carefully?

Taking the last question first, this Article begins with the premise that something unique and important with respect to human rights *is* in fact going on in the process of globalization, in particular when one distinguishes between the economic facts of market globalization and its regulatory infrastructure.[5] While market globalization may represent in some aspects a unique opportunity for human rights law, the globalization of the market economy may also pose a threat to the continued effectiveness of human rights law, just as the rise of the market economy itself has been blamed for leading to conditions requiring the formal development of human rights law.[6] The regulatory framework which international economic law provides for globalization operates according to a view of human nature, human values and moral decision-making fundamentally at odds with the view of human nature, human values and moral decision-making which underlies international human rights law. The human rights movement could thus find in market globalization the ultimate victory of a regulatory system that, by nature and operation, cannot properly take into account what the human rights movement holds most dear: that underlying positive human rights laws are moral

5. *See infra* notes 22-25 and accompanying text.

6. "Modern markets also created a whole new range of threats to human dignity and thus were one of the principal sources of the need and demand for human rights." JACK DONNELLY, UNIVERSAL HUMAN RIGHTS IN THEORY AND PRACTICE 64 (1989). It may be, for example, that the globalization of markets erodes the social and normative preconditions for human rights protection, as well as for the market itself. Hausman & McPherson point out that core trade and economic values such as economic efficiency depend upon ethical values which paradoxically may be undermined by market economies. *See* Daniel M. Hausman & Michael S. McPherson, *Taking Ethics Seriously: Economics and Contemporary Moral Philosophy*, 31 J. ECON. LITERATURE 671 (1993). Hausman & McPherson list honesty, trust and goodwill as three values critical to the efficient function of markets, which may in fact be undermined by appeals to rational self-interest, at least in certain forms. *Id.* at 673.

entitlements that ground moral, political, and legal claims of special force,[7] claims which must be morally and legally prior to society and the state.[8] They are "[u]nalienable."[9] It is this inalienability and priority of human rights which this Article refers to as the "human rights principle" justifying international human rights law, and it is this principle which is at risk of being "traded away," if you will, when human rights laws and the claims and values they presuppose, come into conflict with trade law and trade values in the new tribunals of globalization, in particular the World Trade Organization's (WTO) dispute settlement mechanism.[10]

In proposing that the effects of market globalization on human rights law be analyzed as a normative conflict in WTO dispute resolution, I am suggesting that this sort of problem is in fact a problem of justice.[11] In other words, the legal and institutional mechanisms created to facilitate and respond to market globalization, and the legal and institutional mechanisms created to define and protect human rights, both involve

---

7. DONNELLY, *supra* note 6, at 9.

8. *Id.* at 70.

9. *See* THE DECLARATION OF INDEPENDENCE (U.S. 1776).

10. Understanding on Rules and Procedures Governing the Settlement of Disputes, Dec. 15, 1993, Final Act Embodying the Results of the Uruguay Round of Multilateral Trade Negotiations, 33 I.L.M. 112 (1994) [hereinafter DSU]; *See generally* Ernst-Ulrich Petersmann, *The Dispute Settlement System of the World Trade Organization and the Evolution of the GATT Dispute Settlement System Since 1948,* 31 COMMON MKT. L. REV. 1157 (1994) (reviewing the structure and function of the WTO dispute settlement process).

11. Globalization has a recognized normative aspect. *See* Alex Y. Seita, *Globalization and the Convergence of Values*, 30 CORNELL INT'L L.J. 429, 431 (1997) ("globalization is an important source of common economic and political values for humanity"); Delbrück, *supra* note 4, at 11 (the term globalization itself is often used as a normative term, in that it presupposes a value judgement "that the common good is to be served by measures that are to be subsumed under the notion of globalization"). In particular, the conflicts which globalization can engender between trade law and other bodies of law, such as environmental law and labor law are inescapably normative. *See* Philip M. Nichols, *Trade Without Values*, 90 NW. U. L. REV. 658, 672-73, 680 (1996). On the applicability of normative theory to international relations, see CHARLES R. BEITZ, POLITICAL THEORY AND INTERNATIONAL RELATIONS 5 (1979); STANLEY HOFFMANN, DUTIES BEYOND BORDERS: ON THE LIMITS AND POSSIBILITIES OF ETHICAL INTERNATIONAL POLITICS 1 (1981); Anthony D'Amato, *International Law and Rawls' Theory of Justice*, 5 DENV. J. INT'L L. & POL'Y 525, 525 (1975); Frank J. Garcia, *Trade and Justice: Linking the Trade Linkage Debates*, 19 U. PA. J. INT'L ECON. L. 391, 395-406 (1998); Alfred P. Rubin, *Political Theory and International Relations*, 47 U. CHI. L. REV. 403 (1980) (review of BEITZ 1979).

public order decisions as to the allocation of social benefits and burdens, and the correction of improper gain.[12] The fundamental normative goal of every such public order decision is justice, which is to say that such decisions are to be made in accordance with, and their outcomes must reflect, our basic moral and political principles.[13]

Considered broadly, globalization has the potential to promote broad, if not universal, international consensus on the basic principles of Western liberalism: free markets, democratic government, and human rights.[14] However, within this broadly framed liberalism the various components can themselves come into conflict through the very process of globalization which brings them into the ascendant.[15] Moreover, international problems of justice such as the market-globalization/human rights conflict present unique difficulties, in that they reflect a central feature, if not defect, of the international governance system, namely that the pursuit of global justice is splintered into a myriad of treaties and institutions, in this case into two distinct regimes, one concerned with economic justice and one with human dignity. Therefore, the inquiry into the effects of market globalization on human rights law becomes an inquiry into how the economic facts and regulatory infrastructure of globalization enhance, or interfere with, the contributions which international human rights law seeks to

---

12. This is Aristotle's classic subdivision of Plato's general concept of justice as Right Order into its main constituent parts, which distinction continues in influence to the present day. *See* ARISTOTLE, NICHOMACHEAN ETHICS, bk. V., chs. 2, 4, *in* INTRODUCTION TO ARISTOTLE 400, 404-07 (Richard McKeon ed., 1947); Alan Ryan, *Introduction*, *in* JUSTICE 1, 9 (Alan Ryan ed., 1993) (citing the continuing influence of this categorization).

13. *See* Garcia, *supra* note 11, at 395-96.

14. *See* Seita, *supra* note 11, at 431.

15. Commentators recognize the inevitability of conflict between the various elements of a globalized liberalism, such as free markets and human rights. *See, e.g.*, Seita, *supra* note 11, at 470 ("[T]he basic values that globalization spreads can sometimes be at odds with each other and with other important values."); Nichols, *supra* note 11, at 672-73 ("At any given point in time a society will possess more than one value. These values may, in fact, conflict with one another. Thus, it is possible for a country to hold a value of enhancing wealth through international trade and at the same time hold values that conflict with the precepts of free trade.") (footnotes omitted). Moreover, where a market is dominated by ethnic minorities, globalization may lead an anti-democratic and anti-market backlash by impoverished ethnic majorities, with disasterous human rights consequences. *See generally* Amy L. Chua, *Markets, Democracy, and Ethnicity: Toward a New Paradigm for Law and Development*, 108 YALE L.J. 1 (1998).

make towards the attainment of justice. The conflicts engendered by this bifurcation, particularly in view of the preeminence of international economic law,[16] must be addressed in order that we may avoid undoing with the tools of economic liberal justice what we have accomplished with the tools of rights-based liberal justice.

After a brief discussion of globalization introducing a distinction between "transactional" and "regulatory" globalization and their differing impact on human rights, this Article turns in Part III to a discussion of the normative conflict underlying globalization/human rights disputes, which this Article characterizes as reflecting the conflict between consequentialist and deontological forms of moral decision-making and justification. This Article then turns to an analysis of the disposition of globalization/human rights disputes in the WTO, illustrating how the trade-oriented nature of such an institution, coupled with the underlying normative conflict in such disputes, work to disadvantage laws based on human rights claims in that forum. Finally, this Article offers some suggestions as to how WTO doctrine could be amended or interpreted so as to resolve trade-human rights disputes in a manner more in keeping with the human rights principle.

II. GLOBALIZATION

As was indicated above, the term "globalization" can have many meanings.[17] Taken most broadly, globalization represents the sum total of political, social, economic, legal and symbolic processes rendering the division of the globe into national boundaries increasingly less important for the purpose of individual meaning and social decision.[18] "Globalization" thus in fact contains many smaller "globalizations," which

---

16. *See, e.g.*, Joel P. Trachtman, *The International Economic Law Revolution*, 17 U. PA. J. INT'L ECON. L. 33, 35-36 (1996).

17. *See supra* note 4 and works cited therein.

18. *See, e.g.*, Seita, *supra* note 11, at 429 ("Globalization . . . is a multifaceted concept encompassing a wide range of seemingly disparate processes, activities, and conditions . . . connected together by one common theme: what is geographically meaningful now transcends national boundaries and is expanding to cover the entire planet. Globalization has led to an awareness that international issues, not just domestic ones, matter."); Aman, *supra* note 4, at 1-2 ("In our view, 'globalization' refers to complex, dynamic legal and social processes . . . . Today, the line between domestic and international is largely illusory.").

can both "reinforce *and clash with* one another."[19]

Globalization is often defined principally in economic terms, namely as the globalization of markets.[20] Since we are also concerned in this context with the globalization of markets, a good starting point is to begin with the idea of a market. In this Article, the term "market" shall be used in the rather traditional sense of a series or system of private interactions involving voluntary exchanges of goods, services, labor and capital, the four basic economic factors of production.[21] What we are concerned with, then, is to understand what is meant by the "globalization" of mechanisms for the private exchange of the factors of production, and the effects of this globalization on human rights.

In considering the globalization of the market, one can distinguish between the geographic facts of globalization, and the regulatory predicates and consequences of such globalization. One definition of market globalization, which this Article terms "transactional globalization," views the globalization of markets as an increase in the number of transactions involving goods, services, labor and capital which cross national boundaries, such that they come to resemble in operation a single market spanning the globe.[22] This definition assumes that there has always been a certain amount of transboundary economic activity, but that such activity is increasing both in scope and scale such as to warrant the tag "globalization," thus saying in essence that globalization is a quantitative rather than a qualitative change.[23]

---

19. Seita, *supra* note 11, at 429 (emphasis added).

20. *See* Seita, *supra* note 11, at 429-30. However, other commentators point out that globalization involves significant non-economic processes, and Seita himself points out that "[d]emocracy and human rights are, for example, as much a part of globalization as are free market principles." Aman, *supra* note 4, at 1; Delbrück, *supra* note 4, at 9-10; Seita, *supra* note 11, at 429.

21. I will not be addressing "markets" in the specialized or analogic sense, as the term is employed in analyzing such phenomena as the "market for control" in private firms, or the "regulatory market."

22. *See, e.g.*, Seita, *supra* note 11, at 439 (discussing economic globalization as the "expansion of markets for goods, services, financial capital, and intellectual property"); Cavusgil, *supra* note 4, at 83 ("Globalization of markets involves the growing interdependency among the economies of the world; multinational nature of sourcing, manufacturing, trading, and investment activities; increasing frequency of cross-border transactions and financing; and heightened intensity of competition among a larger number of players.").

23. *See* Dolzer, *supra* note 4, at 157 (stating that "[i]n the economic sphere,

This common approach to defining economic globalization, however, represents only one aspect of economic globalization. Another definition, which shall be termed "regulatory globalization," includes the quantitative changes identified in transactional globalization, but emphasizes a qualitative change in the nature of our regulation of markets. In particular, regulatory globalization focuses on the complex social processes which have led to the regulation of markets for goods, labor, capital and services at new levels, levels which require formalized interstate cooperation through new and powerful institutions like the WTO, and which may, in certain cases, transcend nation-state control to a significant degree, as in the case of the European Community.[24]

The question before us, then, can be framed as an inquiry into the ways in which each of these "market globalizations" affects the vitality and effectiveness of human rights law. Before turning to the possible adverse effects of regulatory globalization on human rights law, which is the principal focus of this Article, a few words about the effects of transactional globalization, and the *positive* effects of regulatory globalization, are in order. To begin with, globalization of both types may in certain respects represent an unparalleled opportunity for enhancing the exercise and protection of human rights. For example, transactional globalization can contribute directly to the enjoyment of economic rights, due to the relationship between economic activity and the human freedom and dignity we express in our decisions as producers and consumers.[25] Indirectly, transactional globalization may enhance the effectiveness of human rights law by contributing to the attainment of the economic preconditions for socioeconomic rights through

globalization is not a novel phenomenon, but relates to the *pace* of change that has increased dramatically") (emphasis added).

24. *See* Trachtman, *supra* note 16, at 46-55 (reviewing history of regulatory changes in international economic law); Delbrück, *supra* note 4, at 10-11, 17 (explaining globalization as signifying changes in the locus of regulation); Aman, *supra* note 4, at 2 (emphasizing change in dynamics of law formation wrought by globalization).

25. As the trade liberalization attendant to globalization reduces governmental barriers to private economic decision-making, individuals have an increased scope for realizing such economic rights. *See* Robert W. McGee, *The Fatal Flaw in NAFTA, GATT and All Other Trade Agreements,* 14 NW. J. INT'L L. & BUS. 549, 560-61 (1994) (criticizing protectionist unfair-trade remedies as impermissibly restricting consumer rights).

the significant increases in global welfare which trade theory predicts should follow such globalization.[26] Furthermore, transactional globalization can contribute to the enforcement of human rights, through the effects which increased contact between the citizens of oppressive regimes and the citizens and products of rights-protective regimes may have on the continuing viability of oppressive regimes.[27] Participation in the market itself may increase domestic pressure for increased political and social rights.[28] Finally, there is the possibility, at least, that the significant economic power unleashed through transactional globalization and the interdependent economies it encourages, might be marshaled in the form of economic sanctions against human rights violations.[29]

---

26. Transactional globalization represents at least an apparent vindication on a global level of basic free trade principles. This should mean that, as imperfections in the market are worked out and the regulatory system strengthened, we should be poised to witness significant improvements in global welfare, as individuals gain in economic liberty and material prosperity as a result of the operation of free trade principles globally. *See* Nichols, *supra* note 11, at 661-67 (summarizing the contributions which free trade can make to human well-being). Such improvements enhance the conditions for the attainment of socioeconomic rights, such as the right to employment and the right to a decent standard of living, and the conditions for human rights protection generally. *See* UDHR, *supra* note 2, art. 22 ("Everyone, as a member of society, . . . is entitled to realization, through national effort and international cooperation and in accordance with the organization and resources of each state, of the economic, social and cultural rights indispensable for his dignity . . . .").

27. The revolution in information and communications technologies involved in globalization has brought people in rights-protective regimes face to face with human rights crises thousands of miles away. *See* Seita, *supra* note 11, at 455-60 (surveying links between communication technology and democracy and human rights). Globalization can thus make it more difficult for persistent violators to maintain the cloak of secrecy and deniability. Also, oppressive regimes are finding it increasingly difficult to control the access to and spread of "subversive" information and ideas in the information age. *See, e.g.,* Upendra Baxi, *Voices of Suffering and the Future of Human Rights,* 8 TRANSNAT'L L. & CONTEMP. PROBS. 125, 160-61 (citing the use of "cyberspace solidarity").

28. Liberalization in economics may lead to liberalization in politics as well, as the economic liberalization required by globalization has a favorable spillover effect on liberalization of domestic policies on speech, democratic participation, etc. *See* Seita, *supra* note 11, at 453-54 (reviewing indirect impact of transactional globalization on democratic and human rights values).

29. *See* Philip Alston, *International Trade as an Instrument of Positive Human Rights Policy*, 4 HUM. RTS. Q. 155, 168-70 (1982); Robert W. McGee, *Trade Embargoes, Sanctions and Blockades: Some Overlooked Human Rights Issues*, 32 J. WORLD TRADE 139, 142 (1998); Patricia Stirling, *The Use of Trade Sanctions as an Enforcement Mechanism for Basic Human Rights: A Proposal for Addition to the World Trade Organization*, 11 AM. U. J. INT'L L. & POL'Y 1, 42-45 (1996). On the

Regulatory globalization can also have several positive effects on human rights. First, there is the fact that globalization has been facilitated and managed by an increase in the rule of law in international economic relations.[30] Therefore, since a commitment to the rule of law is integral to human rights law as well as the international economic law system, regulatory globalization has contributed in a significant way towards establishing a key regulatory goal of human rights law as well.

Second, there has been some recognition at the regulatory level of the importance of considering human rights in connection with the operation of trade and integration rules and systems. At the mulilateral level, for example, both GATT 1947 and GATT 1994[31] contain an exception to the most-favored-nation (MFN) and national treatment principles[32] recognizing a state's right to ban the importation of products of prison labor.[33] The WTO has publicly, albeit weakly, affirmed the importance of observance of international labor standards, while pushing the onus of the development of appropriate standards to the ILO.[34] Regionally, one can point to the formation of the NAFTA Labor Commission, charged with monitoring the national enforcement of state labor laws.[35]

---

use of economic sanctions generally, see Raj K. Bhala, *MRS. WATU: Seven Steps to Trade Sanctions Analysis*, MICH. J. INT'L L. (forthcoming 1999) (proposing eponymous algorithm for evaluating sanctions measures).

30. *See* Seita, *supra* note 11, at 430 (stating that "[l]aw has been important in managing economic globalization and may become as important with respect to political globalization"); John H. Jackson, *International Economic Law: Reflections on the "Boilerroom" of International Relations*, 10 AM. U. J. INT'L L. & POL'Y 595, 596 (1995) (stating that "it is plausible to suggest that ninety percent of international law work is in reality international economic law in some form or another").

31. General Agreement on Tariffs and Trade, Oct. 30, 1947, 61 Stat. A-11, T.I.A.S. No. 1700, 55 U.N.T.S. 194; General Agreement on Tariffs and Trade-Multilateral Trade Negotiations (The Uruguay Round): Final Act Embodying the Results of the Uruguay Round of Trade Negotiations, Apr. 15, 1994, 33 I.L.M. 1125 (1994) (GATT 1947 was incorporated into the WTO as GATT 1994 in Annex IA to the WTO Agreement) [hereinafter GATT].

32. GATT, arts. I, III. *See infra* notes 109-10 and accompanying text.

33. *Id.* art. XX(e). *See infra* notes 116-18 and accompanying text.

34. *See* World Trade Organization, *Singapore Ministerial Declaration*, WTO Doc. WT/MIN(96)/DEC/W, Dec. 13, 1996, 36 I.L.M. 218 (1996) (WTO affirms commitment to international labor standards but considers ILO to be appropriate forum for trade and labor issues) [hereinafter *Singapore Declaration*].

35. North American Agreement on Labor Cooperation, Sept. 8, 1993, Can.-Mex.-U.S., 32 I.L.M. 1499 (entered into force Jan. 1, 1994); *see, e.g.*, Elizabeth M. Iglesias, *Human Rights in International Economic Law: Locating Latinas/os in the*

Finally, there has been some recognition at the regulatory level of the powerful leverage which transactional globalization places at the service of human rights reform and enforcement, at least at the level of conditions on entry into regional trading systems. For example, participation in the European Community is contingent upon membership in and observance of treaty-based human rights norms.[36] This link has also been observed, at least at the rhetorical level, in this hemisphere, in the fact that the agreements launching the Free Trade Area of the Americas cite the importance of democratic values and human rights for hemispheric integration.[37]

For these reasons, human rights advocates could view both transactional and regulatory globalization as unreservedly advancing the cause of human rights on a global level. However, due to the bifurcated nature of the international governance system into separate trade and human rights regimes, and the fact that trade law and institutions are increasingly called upon to resolve disputes involving areas outside of trade law, the globalization of markets, at least in its regulatory form, may in fact retard the effectiveness of human rights law. Disputes between trade law and other bodies of law such as human rights law which come before the institutions of regulatory globalization involve normative conflicts, in that they represent disputes between trade values and non-trade values, such as those values underlying human rights law.[38] The degree to which the law and institutions of regulatory globalization can or cannot effectively take into account these non-trade values, such as those values at stake in human rights claims and enforcement measures, is therefore going to determine to a

Linkage Debates, 28 U. MIAMI INTER-AM. L. REV. 361, 369-71 (1997) (briefly describing treaty structure and shortcomings).

36. The link between European Community membership and participation in the European Convention on Human Rights and Fundamental Freedoms is an historic and effective example. *See* James F. Smith, *NAFTA and Human Rights: A Necessary Linkage*, 27 U.C. DAVIS L. REV. 793, 793, 817-23 (1994). This form of conditionality is a part of EC expansion doctrine as well. *Id.*; Frank J. Garcia, *"Americas Agreements"—An Interim Stage in Building the Free Trade Area of the Americas*, 35 COLUM. J. TRANSNAT'L L. 63, 63, 92-93, 102-03 (1997).

37. Garcia, *supra* note 36, at 103. However, in our hemisphere the dominant economic unit, the United States, has exerted a restraining rather than an activist impulse in this regard. *See* Smith, *supra* note 36, at 806-17.

38. *See* Nichols, *supra* note 11, at 671-89 (analyzing linkage conflicts as value conflicts).

large extent the degree to which globalization is a friend or foe to human rights.

III. Regulatory Globalization: Utility over Rights

Understanding the adverse effects which market globalization may have on human rights requires an understanding of the changes in the way trade is now regulated through law. An increasingly globalized economy has brought many new aspects of global economic life into the ambit of trade law and trade institutions, which in turn has facilitated the further globalization of the marketplace.

A. *Changes in the Global Regulation of Markets*

The globalization of markets in transactional terms has been facilitated by, and has in turn facilitated, a significant change in the nature of the international regulation of economic activity. From its imperfect beginnings in the GATT 1947 to its current apotheosis in the WTO, the revolution in international economic law means that more aspects of the international economy are regulated through treaty-based rules than at any previous time, rules with less room for state discretion and unilateral action than at any prior time, and under the adjudicative supervision of stronger institutions than at any other time.[39]

One might at first, therefore, think that globalization has been an unmitigated boon for international economic law. After all, what regulatory system would not want to see the scope of its jurisdiction vastly enlarged, and the effectiveness of its norms enhanced? Because of this globalization, however, trade law is now a more complicated business. In practice, the revolution in international economic law has meant that institutions created to adjudicate trade disputes are increasingly being asked to resolve policy issues which involve not only trade law, but other issues and values as well. There have always been so-called trade linkage problems, which in practice raise questions about appropriate conditions under which states may pursue non-trade domestic policy goals such as

---

39. *See generally* John H. Jackson, *Reflections on International Economic Law*, 17 U. PA. J. INT'L ECON. L. 17, 21-23 (1996) (assessing Uruguay Round as "watershed shift" in international economic regulation).

national security and economic development, despite their short or long-term adverse effects on trade.[40] Now, however, trade law and trade institutions are impacting more and more areas of traditional domestic concern, such as environmental protection,[41] labor and employment standards,[42] and cultural identity.[43]

In the absence of an effective global legislative forum, trade law and institutions will, for the time being and by default, be charged with resolving difficult linkage issues involving trade values and other values, and resolving them in an adjudicative setting. The degree to which trade law and institutions are capable of adequately taking into account other non-trade interests and values at the point of conflict, will serve as the determining factor in the effect regulatory globalization has on the viability and vigor of human rights law in a global market.

B. *The Normative Conflict Between International Economic Law and Human Rights Law*

International human rights law and international economic law each have an important role in the implementation of a just global order, and yet the principal normative foundations of each regime are, if not incompatible, then at least in fundamental tension. The primary discipline for the analysis of international economic relations, economics, and the dominant

---

40. *See* Frieder Roessler, *Domestic Policy Objectives and the Multilateral Trade Order: Lessons From the Past*, *in* THE WTO AS AN INTERNATIONAL ORGANIZATION 213 (Anne O. Krueger ed., 1998), *reprinted in* 19 U. PA. J. INT'L ECON. L. 513 (1998) (discussing antecedents of current linkage issue).

41. *See, e.g.*, World Trade Organization Appellate Body Report on United States—Import Prohibition of Certain Shrimp and Shrimp Products, WT/DS58/AB/R, *available in* 1998 WL 720123 [hereinafter Shrimp Case]; Robert Howse, *The Turtles Panel: Another Environmental Disaster in Geneva*, 32 J. WORLD TRADE 73 (1998).

42. *See Singapore Declaration*, *supra* note 34 (reviewing WTO position on trade and international labor standards); Virginia Leary, *Workers' Rights and International Trade: The Social Clause (GATT, ILO, NAFTA, U.S. Laws)*, *in* 2 FAIR TRADE AND HARMONIZATION: PREREQUISITES FOR FAIR TRADE? 175 (Jagdish Bhagwati & Robert E. Hudec eds., 1996).

43. *See* World Trade Organization Appellate Body Report on Canada—Certain Measures Concerning Periodicals, WT/DS31/AB/R, *available in* 1997 WL 398913; W. Ming Shao, *Is There No Business Like Show Business? Free Trade and Cultural Protectionism*, 20 YALE J. INT'L L. 105, 105 (1995).

model of international economic relations law, the Efficiency Model, are based on a set of values and an approach to normative issues which are in conflict with the values and normative approach underlying contemporary human rights law.

1. The Normative Underpinnings of Trade Law

Trade law is not simply about the exchange of goods. As is the case with all human interaction which is structured by law, trade law embodies a particular vision of justice, a theory of what constitutes the Right Order as it applies within the scope of economic law.[44] Therefore, as with any particular account of justice, a normative account of trade law presupposes a certain view of human nature, and favors a particular approach to moral reasoning.

The dominant normative account of trade law is an economic one, which Jeffrey Dunoff has termed the "Efficiency Model." In the Efficiency Model, trade law is exclusively concerned with the twin values of economic efficiency and welfare.[45] The goal of trade law is to improve the economic wellbeing of human beings through the facilitation of efficient exchanges.[46] This approach has several important implications for the viability of human rights law within a trade-based regulatory regime.

---

44. I have elsewhere outlined the arguments in favor of this view, in an essay drawn from a larger work in progress on the problem of justice in contemporary international economic law. *See* Garcia, *supra* note 11.

45. *See* Jeffrey L. Dunoff, *Rethinking International Trade*, 19 U. PA. J. INT'L ECON. L. 347, 349-50 (1998). *See also* G. Richard Shell, *Trade Legalism and International Relations Theory*, 44 DUKE L.J. 829, 877-85 (1995) (discussing what Shell calls the "Efficient Market Model" of trade law).

46. *See, e.g.*, DAVID RICARDO, PRINCIPLES OF POLITICAL ECONOMY AND TAXATION 93 (3d ed. 1996).

> Under a system of perfectly free commerce, each country naturally devotes its capital and labor to such employments as are most beneficial to each. This pursuit of individual advantage is admirably connected with the universal good of the whole. By stimulating industry, by rewarding ingenuity, and by using most efficaciously the peculiar powers bestowed by nature, it distributes labor most effectively and most economically: while by increasing the general mass of productions, it diffuses general benefit and binds together, by common ties of interest and intercourse, the universal society of nations throughout the civilized world.

Id.; JOHN H. JACKSON, THE WORLD TRADING SYSTEM: LAW AND POLICY OF INTERNATIONAL ECONOMIC RELATIONS 8-9 (2d ed. 1989) (efficiency-based increases in general welfare are the preeminent goal of trade law).

First, there is a marked tendency for other values besides efficiency and welfare to be viewed as outside the scope of trade law, and even inimical to its purposes.[47] From the viewpoint of Efficiency Model adherents, advocates of non-trade values and issues are seen as trying to complicate the trade law system with what are at best extraneous concerns such as human rights or environmental protection,[48] and what may be at worst simply disguised protectionism.[49] In adopting this stance, Efficiency Model adherents fail to recognize that, while efficiency and welfare are undeniably important values in trade, their pursuit is necessarily part of an overarching effort to establish a just global order, an order in which other values are also central, values which are implicated and quite properly considered in trade law decisions.[50] In other words, there is no such thing as a pure trade issue.

Second, economic analysis and methodology will exert a dominant, if not overweening, influence on trade and non-trade policy formed or implemented within trade institutions operating on an Efficiency Model. In noting this consequence, I do not mean to question the relevance of economics for the purposes of trade and trade law and policy. Economics will play a critical role in trade law under *any* model, since economics involves the study of resource decision-making, and trade law

47. *See* Nichols, *supra* note 11, at 700 ("That the trade regime gives primacy to trade is evidenced throughout the history of GATT dispute settlement, as well as in the writings of officials and scholars closely allied with the General Agreement and the nascent World Trade Organization.").

48. *See* Steve Charnovitz, *The World Trade Organization and Social Issues*, 28 J. WORLD TRADE 17, 23 (1994) [hereinafter Charnovitz, *Social Issues*] (citing objection by GATT and WTO members to efforts in 1991 and 1994 to begin work on labor and environment issues on the basis that such issues were not trade issues); Robert E. Hudec, *GATT Legal Restraints on the Use of Trade Measures Against Foreign Environmental Practices*, *in* 2 FAIR TRADE AND HARMONIZATION: PREREQUISITES FOR FAIR TRADE?, 95, 108 (arguing that GATT has a good reason to be skeptical of linkage claims).

49. *See* Charnovitz, *Social Issues*, *supra* note 48, at 32 ("Simplistic demands for drastic trade remedies against so-called eco-dumping or social dumping sometimes bear a striking similarity to more conventional forms of protectionist rhetoric . . . .") (quoting then-GATT Director General, Peter Sutherland).

50. *See* Robert Howse & Michael J. Trebilcock, *The Fair Trade-Free Trade Debate: Trade, Labor and the Environment*, *in* ECONOMIC DIMENSIONS IN INTERNATIONAL LAW (Jagdeep S. Bhandari & Alan O. Sykes eds., 1997) (observing that "[a] visceral distrust of any or all demands for trade restrictions has impeded a careful analysis of the kinds of normative claims at issue and has allowed fair traders to characterize free traders as moral philistines").

is a powerful engine for resource allocation. However, due to the range of interests and values affected by the contemporary international economic law system, other disciplines and models are unquestionably relevant to trade policy analysis and formulation.

Moreover, in order to properly evaluate trade law's impact on human rights and other non-trade areas, it is important to remember that economics is not a value-free method of analysis.[51] Trade arguments are generally founded on some form of welfare economics, and standard welfare economics rests on strong and contestable moral presuppositions.[52] To begin with, economics employs, both descriptively and prescriptively, models and concepts which adopt a position on the nature of human beings, i.e., *homo economicus*,[53] and the appropriate ends of moral decision-making, preference satisfaction,[54] which calls into question the suitability of economics for the definitive evaluation of non-economic values.[55]

---

51. In the discussion which follows, I rely heavily on Hausman & McPherson, *supra* note 6, for their analysis of the metaethics of economics.

52. Welfare economics typically translates normative questions into questions of efficiency and equity. The traditional emphasis in welfare economics on efficiency over equity may in fact reflect the perceived intractability of evaluating distributive fairness economically, rather than a clear analysis of the moral priority of efficiency over equity. Moreover, the moral implications of analysis of welfare questions into equity and efficiency issues need to be addressed from a normative perspective. *Id.* at 675.

53. Economics presupposes a model of human beings as *homo economicus*, as rational self-interest maximizers. *Id.* at 688. In the words of John Stuart Mill, political economy "is concerned with [man] solely as a being who desires to possess wealth . . . . It makes entire abstraction of every other human passion or motive." John Stuart Mill, *On the Definition of Political Economy; and On the Method of Investigation Proper to It,* 26 LONDON & WESTMINSTER REV. 1 (1836), *cited in* DOUGLAS A. IRWIN, AGAINST THE TIDE: AN INTELLECTUAL HISTORY OF FREE TRADE 180 n.1 (1996). On this view, trade is about maximizing self-interest through economic exchange, and trade law is about facilitating conditions which lead to the maximization of self-interest, by eliminating state-imposed barriers to efficient exchanges.

54. In terms of the ends of moral decision-making, economists speak in terms of individual well-being, and tend to equate well-being with preference satisfaction, and therefore the morality of an act is equated with its ability to satisfy individual preferences. *See* Hausman & McPherson, *supra* note 6, at 689.

55. However useful as an economic construct, the *homo economicus* model of human behavior is troubling when viewed as an account of moral behavior, in that it most closely resembles egoism, a much-criticized moral theory. *Id.* at 686-88. Moreover, this model does not provide a rich enough picture of individual choice to fully analyze moral behavior, for the reason that such a model precludes true altruistic reasoning and tends to assimilate moral choice into preference satisfac-

Perhaps most importantly for the purposes of this Article, the *method* of moral reasoning which normative economics adopts is a type that is fundamentally at odds with the dominant mode of moral reasoning underlying human rights law. Economic moral reasoning is consequentialist in nature, in that it focuses on outcomes, and not on procedures or acts on their own terms.[56] Consequentialism is the term for ethical theories which evaluate the rightness or wrongness of an act solely in terms of its consequences.[57] On this view, an act will be morally right if its consequences are better than those of any alternative acts.[58] Different types of consequentialist theory differ on what precisely better consequences consist of.[59]

The dominant normative account of trade law and policy is utilitarian in nature.[60] Utilitarianism is a particular form of consequentialism, which in its classical form determines the morality of an act according to its consequences for the aggregate of individual utility.[61] Forms of utilitarian ethics can be distinguished according to whether they focus on the justification of acts, which is classical or act-utilitarianism,[62] or the justification of rules which in turn justify or constrain acts,

---

tion. *See id.* at 687.

56. As Hausman and McPherson put it, "[t]he standard definition of a social optimum compares social alternatives exclusively in terms of the goodness of their outcomes (rather than the rightness of their procedures), and identifies the goodness of outcomes with satisfaction of individual preferences." *Id.* In defining positive outcomes with individual preferences, it is therefore also liberal, and not communitarian. *Id.* at 675.

57. For a good introduction to consequentialism in general, see G.E.M. Anscombe, *Modern Moral Philosophy*, 33 PHIL. 1 (1958); Germain Grisez, *Against Consequentialism*, 23 AM. J. JURIS. 21 (1978).

58. *See* ALAN DONAGAN, THE THEORY OF MORALITY 52 (1977).

59. For example, welfarist moral theories take the view that consequences for aggregate individual well-being matter, with other notions such as rights or virtues serving as means to promoting welfare. *See* Hausman & McPherson, *supra* note 6, at 704. Egoism is a form of consequentialism, focusing on the outcome for the individual decision-maker. *See* R.G. Frey, *Introduction: Utilitarianism and Persons, in* UTILITY AND RIGHTS 3, 5 (R.G. Frey ed., 1984).

60. *See* RAJ BHALA, INTERNATIONAL TRADE LAW 36 (1996) (economic foundation of trade law furnishes utilitarian justifications for free trade regime); McGee, *supra* note 25, at 549 ("vast majority" of trade scholarship analyzes trade from a utilitarian perspective).

61. Put in economic terms, utilitarianism takes morality as the maximizing of some function of the welfare of individual members of society. *See* Hausman & McPherson, *supra* note 6, at 689.

62. Act utilitarianism is the classical utilitarianism of Bentham and Mills. *See* sources cited *infra* note 65.

which is rule-utilitarianism.[63] For the purposes of this article, both forms shall be taken together, and generally referred to as utilitarianism.[64] Utilitarianisms can also be distinguished on the basis of their particular theory of value, or utility. Historically, utility was defined in hedonic terms involving individual pleasure.[65] Modern utilitarianism and the economists who deploy it are more likely to define utility in terms of preference satisfaction,[66] or more generally as a form of welfarism, in which the sum or average of resulting individual welfare levels determines the correctness of an act, principle or policy.[67]

Thus from a normative perspective, the Efficiency Model of trade law asserts, explicitly or implicitly, the utilitarian argument that free trade is good *because of its consequences,* namely the maximization of aggregate individual welfare from effi-

63. Under rule utilitarianism, a particular rule is justified along utilitarian lines, which rule must then be followed with regard to individual acts without undertaking a further utilitarian calculation for each act, unless and until the utilitarian calculus underlying the rule itself changes. *See* DONAGAN, *supra* note 58, at 193, 196-99.

64. While an oversimplification for many purposes, such treatment is defensible with regard to the subject of this article, which focuses on the effects of either utilitarianism's inherent consequentialism for human rights. *See* Frey, *supra* note 59, at 5 and *infra* note 96-97 and accompanying text.

65. Jeremy Bentham, *An Introduction to the Principles of Morals and Legislation, in* THE ENGLISH PHILOSOPHERS FROM BACON TO MILL 791, 792 (Edwin A. Burtt ed., 1967) ("By the principle of utility is meant that principle which approves or disapproves of every action whatsoever, according to the tendency which it appears to have to augment or diminish the happiness of the party whose interest is in question: or, what is the same thing in other words, to promote or oppose that happiness."); JOHN STUART MILL, UTILITARIANISM 10 (Oskar Piest ed., 1957) ("The creed which accepts as the foundation of morals 'utility' or the 'greatest happiness principle' holds that actions are right in proportion as they tend to promote happiness; wrong as they tend to produce the reverse of happiness. By happiness is intended pleasure and the absence of pain; by unhappiness, pain and the privation of pleasure.").

66. *See* Frey, *supra* note 59, at 5 ("In recent years, however, numerous writers have moved away from a mental-state view of utility and value, on the ground that it is too confining to restrict utility to a concern with states of mind, to an interest-satisfaction view, in which 'interests' is a generic term covering a multiplicity of desires or preferences. Thus, construed as I have done here, preference-utilitarianism is classical utilitarianism with an expanded value theory."); Hausman & McPherson, *supra* note 6, at 705 ("[N]o prominent theorist now defends a hedonistic conception of utility. All of the other specifically utilitarian theorists . . . join economists in taking utility not as an object of reference, but as an index of preference satisfaction.").

67. *See* Hausman & McPherson, *supra* note 6, at 704.

ciency gains and the operation of comparative advantage.[68] Trade maximizes welfare for many reasons, including lower prices, increased consumer choice, increased employment, enhanced economies of scale, specialization, increased competition and the accelerated diffusion of the fruits of innovation.[69]

In the case of conflicts between trade-liberalizing rules and trade-restrictive measures advocated on non-trade grounds, one will find arguments in favor of free trade expressed in utilitarian consequentialist terms. For example, embargoes based on moral or national security grounds may be attacked on the utilitarian ground that it may be in a nation's best interest to trade with its enemies, because doing so will have more good effects than bad in the economic sense.[70] Trade restrictions justified on environmental grounds may encounter arguments in favor of a utilitarian evaluation of their merits, leading to a preference for market-oriented compromises with trade values.[71] In each case, the relative trade costs and regulatory benefits of a particular law or policy are weighed, and the best policy is determined to be that which, on balance, has the least trade cost or promises the greatest trade benefit.

2. The Normative Underpinnings of Human Rights Law

In contrast, human rights law is built on a fundamentally different approach to human nature and moral reasoning, which puts it in tension with the normative underpinnings of trade law. The human rights movement has undertaken to establish through human rights law a different aspect of a just global order than that undertaken in trade law, namely the protection of human dignity.[72]

The dominant contemporary discipline for the critical analysis and justification of human rights law is moral and political philosophy. While human rights in positive law can be

---

68. *See supra* notes 45-46 and works cited therein.

69. *See, e.g.*, JACKSON, *supra* note 46, at 10-13; McGee, *supra* note 25, at 552-54.

70. *See* McGee, *supra* note 25.

71. Richard B. Stewart, *International Trade and Environment: Lessons From the Federal Experience,* 49 WASH. & LEE L. REV. 1329, 1332, 1371 (1992).

72. "Human rights represent a social choice of a particular moral vision of human potentiality, which rests on a particular substantive account of the minimum requirements of a life of dignity." DONNELLY, *supra* note 6, at 17.

derived from and justified by a variety of theological and philosophical moral theories of human nature,[73] at the core of the concept of human rights is the notion of a transcendental standard of justice by which particular acts of the state can be judged.[74] The dominant contemporary normative justification of human rights law is some variety of Western liberalism.[75] International human rights law is essentially rooted in the liberal commitment to the equal moral worth of each individual, regardless of their utility,[76] and human rights themselves embody the minimum standards of treatment necessary in view of this equal moral worth. Moreover, human rights, the very concept of a right, and the closely associated natural rights tradition,[77] are all linked to a particular strand of liberalism, the

---

73. Traditionally, there have been three approaches to establishing the existence and basis of human rights: they can be derived from God; they can be grounded in human nature and what is necessary for human beings to attain their natural end through perfection of their nature; and they can be argued to be self-evident, i.e., they can be discerned through reflection on the nature of human beings and the concept of a moral right. The latter, the so-called natural rights approach, has emerged as the most promising and widely-accepted rationale of the three, and is the rationale attributed to the UN Declaration of Human Rights and credited with their widespread acceptance. *See* H.J. McCloskey, *Respect for Human Moral Rights Versus Maximizing Good, in* UTILITY AND RIGHTS 121, 126 (R.G. Frey ed., 1984).

74. Gordon, *supra* note 1, at 694.

75. Despite this foundation, human rights advocates generally claim some form of universalism for human rights. Henkin and others claim a form of positivist universalism on the grounds that human rights instruments have been ratified by the vast majority of the states of the world. *See, e.g.,* LOUIS HENKIN, THE AGE OF RIGHTS ix (1990); Pieter van Dijk, *A Common Standard of Achievement: About Universal Validity and Uniform Interpretation of International Human Rights Norms,* 2 NETH. HUM. RTS. Q. 105, 109-10 (1995). Others claim a normative universalism for some or all human rights, either on philosophical or empirical grounds. *See* Fernando Tesón, *International Human Rights and Cultural Relativism,* 25 VA. J. INT'L L. 869, 873 (1985) (arguing that the liberal theory of justice underlying human rights is demonstrably correct across cultural lines); Christopher C. Joyner & John C. Dettling, *Bridging the Cultural Chasm: Cultural Relativism and the Future of International Law,* 20 CAL. W. INT'L L.J. 275, 297 (1990) (positing that universalism is assertable where it can be empirically shown that cultural practice does *not* in fact vary with respect to a given principle, such as the prohibition against arbitrary killing and violence).

76. DONNELLY, *supra* note 6, at 68 (following Dworkin).

77. *See* JOHN FINNIS, NATURAL LAW AND NATURAL RIGHTS 198 (1980) ("Almost everything in this book is about human rights ('human rights' being a contemporary idiom for 'natural rights': I use the terms synonymously)."); *but see* S. Prakash Sinha, *Freeing Human Rights From Natural Rights*, 70 ARCHIV FÜR RECHTS- UND SOZIALPHILOSOPHIE 342, 343 (1984) (disputing necessity or adequacy of natural rights as basis for human rights).

non-utilitarian liberalism[78] of Locke[79] and Kant,[80] which provides the normative basis for the rights set out in the various UN instruments.[81]

This model inevitably affects the human rights approach to human nature and moral decision-making, and distinguishes it from a utilitarian economic approach. The *Homo Economicus* Model of human beings presupposed in trade law places little emphasis on the precise end of human activity, assuming it to be individual well-being through the satisfaction of individually determined preferences.[82] In contrast, the Human Rights Model of human nature is obsessed with ends, in particular with the status of the human person as an end in themselves.[83] What is central about human beings is not their ability or tendency to rationally maximize their self-interest, but their intrinsic human dignity and worth. Human dignity and worth are not matters of individual preference or utility, but matters of moral duty and principle.[84] The normative arguments advanced for the protection of human rights are deontological in nature, in that they focus on principles about

78. Millsian utilitarianism, though it is a liberal theory, is a problematic theory for human rights because it is consequentialist in nature. While such a theory can illuminate the moral importance of the consequences of an act for human dignity, the theory is an inadequate justification for human rights in that it countenances consequential approaches to rights questions themselves. *See infra* notes 94-104 and accompanying text.

79. For an overview of Locke's contribution and the Enlightenment roots of contemporary international human rights law generally, see Gordon, *supra* note 1, at 711-20.

80. On the Kantian basis for international human rights, see Fernando Tesón, *The Kantian Theory of International Law*, 92 COLUM. L. REV. 53, 60-70 (1992).

81. McCloskey, *supra* note 73, at 121.

82. Instead, the inquiry concerning *homo economicus* focuses on the range of means available towards attainment of this end, and the effects of particular choices on the conditions for the satisfaction of preferences.

83. *See* Tesón, *supra* note 80, at 64 (observing that the Kantian view of international law is based on our duty to treat human beings as ends in themselves, which requires that the state incorporate respect for human rights); Baxi, *supra* note 27, at 166 (stating that "[t]he diverse bodies of human rights found their highest summation with the Declaration on the Right to Development, insisting that the individual is a *subject* of development, not its *object*.") (footnotes omitted) (emphasis added).

84. Frey notes that while the preservation of human life can be advocated on utilitarian grounds, there is no absolute bar to a change in circumstances such that killing could subsequently be justifiable on the same utilitarian calculus, thus demonstrating the unfitness of utilitarian theory as a grounds for human worth and dignity. *See* Frey, *supra* note 59, at 8-9.

how people are and are not to be treated, regardless of the consequences.[85] Deontological moral reasoning determines the rightness or wrongness of an act by the nature of the act itself, specifically whether it is in accord with or violation of certain moral principles, and regardless of the personally favorable or unfavorable consequences of the act itself. Rights are things that are valued chiefly in themselves, and not for their consequences.[86] For example, the widely-recognized international prohibition against torture[87] is justified on the ground that torture is wrong as a direct violation of human dignity, *despite* its utility, despite the fact that it might lead to information of value to the state, or deter conduct which threatens the state.[88] This is in direct contrast to the consequential form of moral reasoning which predominates in trade and in economics generally, and which at least in theory could determine torture, slavery and other human rights violations to be economically advantageous or justifiable, and hence appropriate.

The deontological nature of human rights principles also has important implications for situations in which different competing claims or values are at stake. Human dignity and moral worth, which are at the core of human rights, are expressed in absolute terms: human beings have a dignity and worth which are not subject to compromise on the basis of consequential justifications. Human rights claims "ordinarily

---

85. *See* Tesón, *supra* note 80, at 71 ("Kant's international ethics follow from the categorical imperative. Just as individuals may not use human beings as mere means to an end, so foreigners, and specially foreign governments, may not use the persons that form another state . . . .").

The deontological approach is reflected in the nature of human rights themselves, and in the language of human rights instruments. For example, the Universal Declaration of Human Rights states these rights are based on the "inherent" dignity of the human person. *See* UDHR, *supra* note 2. Our constitutional tradition also echoes the sense that these rights are inalienable, that is, they cannot be separated from the human person. Regarding the U.S. approach to human rights as constitutional rights, see HENKIN, *supra* note 75, at 83-108.

86. Hausman & McPherson, *supra* note 6, at 694.

87. *See* UDHR, *supra* note 2, art. 5; Convention Against Torture and Other Cruel Inhuman or Degrading Treatment or Punishment, Dec. 10, 1984, 23 I.L.M. 1027 (entered into force June 26, 1987) [hereinafter Convention Against Torture]; Filártiga v. Peña-Irala, 630 F.2d 876, 884 (2d Cir. 1980) (torture prohibited by "law of nations").

88. Convention Against Torture, *supra* note 87, art. 2.2 ("No exceptional *circumstances* whatsoever, whether a state of war or a threat of war, internal political instability or any other public emergency, may be invoked as a *justification* of torture.") (emphasis added).

trump utility, social policy, and other moral or political grounds for action."[89] A human rights-based claim should therefore take priority over counterclaims based in utility, and other consequentialist appeals.[90] Where human rights claims are in conflict with other sorts of claims, human rights theory dictates that human rights claims receive a very high, if not trumping, value in such processes.

3. International Economic Law and Human Rights: Normative Approaches in Conflict

What we find, then, when we examine international economic law and international human rights law, are two attempts to identify and implement the obligations which a broadly liberal theory of justice place on us in international relationships. We find the international economic law system attempting to establish a liberal view of the Right Order with regard to economic well-being, along utilitarian lines. We find the international human rights system attempting to establish a liberal view of the Right Order with regard to human dignity and worth, along deontological lines. And we find that, due to two salient facts of contemporary international life, namely globalization and a defective international governance system, these two powerful mechanisms for global justice are brought into conflict.

At the practical level, the conflict between trade law and human rights law is not, at first glance, an obvious one. Short of a trade treaty providing directly for trade in the products of prison or slave labor,[91] it is hard to imagine a direct conflict between trade law and core human rights, for example rights involving life, liberty and the security of one's person.[92] If one

---

89. DONNELLY, *supra* note 6, at 10 (citing Dworkin TRS 90).

90. As Donnelly puts it, "[a]s the highest moral rights, [human rights] regulate the fundamental structures and practices of political life, and in ordinary circumstances they take priority over other moral, legal and political claims." *Id.* at 1.

91. Unfortunately, history reveals that such international economic arrangements are quite possible, and theory suggests they are fully justifiable on an Efficiency Model of trade, however reprehensible they are on other terms. *See* Nichols, *supra* note 11, at 703 (referring to trade in human beings).

92. In fact, the GATT contains a provision explicitly permitting bans on trade in the products of prison labor, thus arguably reducing an incentive for the exploitation of prisoners. *See infra* notes 116, 118 and accompanying text. Of course,

considers human rights more broadly to include property rights and the rule of law,[93] it would appear that in many cases trade law is in fact working in favor of human rights, as for example when investment and intellectual property protection and increased transparency are negotiated as part of a trade agreement.

Rather, one is more likely to encounter a conflict between international trade law and measures taken at the *national* level *to protect* human rights, usually by imposing some form of economic sanction on a state engaged in rights-violating practices. When instituted between parties to a trade-liberalizing treaty such as the GATT, such measures are likely to be challenged as unlawful trade restrictions. Given the ascendancy of international economic law and its institutions, this challenge is most likely going to be brought in a trade forum, such as the WTO dispute settlement process. This interaction between regulatory globalization and the normative conflict outlined above therefore results in the prospect of a deontologically justified human rights law being challenged in, and perhaps declared invalid by, utilitarian-oriented international trade institutions.

At the meta-ethical level, there is reason for concern that in the contest suggested above, it is the human rights law which will lose. The deontological morality underlying human rights law has traditionally been recognized as difficult to reconcile with the utilitarian and other consequentialist forms of moral reasoning predominating in trade law.[94] The deontological nature of human rights render it difficult for human rights law to operate successfully within a system like the trade law system that is consequentialist in nature, because in the hypothetical conflict identified above, the trade institution will follow a normative approach committed to the possibility of sacrificing human rights protection on the basis

---

here there is a strong economic rationale as well, in that it is difficult for firms employing free, compensated labor to compete with the products of unpaid prisoners.

93. *See* UDHR, *supra* note 2, arts. 6-8, 17.

94. *See* Frey, *supra* note 59, at 10 (stating that "[classical utilitarianism] is, without refinement, inimical to some claim that there are incommensurable values (such as human life)"). While preference-satisfaction utilitarianism ameliorates some of the unpleasant effects of classical utilitarianism, it is subject to the same basic criticisms. *Id.* at 13.

of the human rights measure's adverse *effects* on trade. Utilitarian theory in fact *presupposes* that determinations of human worth will involve the trading-off of one life against another.[95] To a pure act-utilitarian, the fact that a particular trade policy or trade decision violates or undercuts the effectiveness of a human right is of no consequence in itself,[96] and rule-utilitarianism is not an improvement in this respect.[97] Even if human rights are justified on rule-utilitarian grounds as useful for increasing utility, there is always the possibility that human rights as a utilitarian-based set of rules will be cast off if the utility calculus changes.[98] This must be so because utilitarianism is committed to denying the possibility of natural human rights, which people hold simply by virtue of their status as persons.[99]

In contrast, human rights law resists such tradeoffs, because the concept of a right functions to privilege certain claims against other competing claims, claims which in other contexts might overcome rights claims. It is in fact a distinctive feature of a right that it can be pressed this way.[100] Human rights by their very nature and justification are not subject to compromise in the pursuit of good consequences, and it is precisely such compromises that international economic law excels in. For this reason,[101] a utilitarian approach to trade

---

95. *Id.* at 8.

96. Rights violations are of no concern to a pure act utilitarian. *Id.* at 11.

97. Though consequentialist arguments can be framed for rights, such as rule-utilitarian arguments, there remains a core content to rights that is not exhausted by their usefulness. *See* Hausman & McPherson, *supra* note 6, at 695-96. Moreover, the criticisms which apply in this regard to act utilitarianism also apply to more sophisticated forms of rule-utilitarianism. *See* McCloskey, *supra* note 73, at 124; Frey, *supra* note 59, at 4.

98. Frey, *supra* note 59, at 11 ("[F]ar from providing a persuasive case over the wrongness of killing, classical utilitarianism . . . seems perpetually to place persons and their vital interests at risk, a risk that will be realized if the contingencies fall out one way rather than another."); *see also* McCloskey, *supra* note 73, at 124 (incorporation of a rights-principle into a rule-utilitarian system, while normatively more attractive, does not insulate it from criticism). There is reason to fear that the human rights principle reaches that cast-off point precisely when enforcement would interfere with the powerful economic benefits at stake in trade decisions, when human rights are at their most vulnerable.

99. McCloskey, *supra* note 73, at 121.

100. DONNELLY, *supra* note 6, at 11-12.

101. Other critiques include the concern that utility theory is inadequate to measure gains and losses. *See* McGee, *supra* note 25, at 555, as well as the libertarian argument that there is no public interest or public good, only individuals.

cannot adequately incorporate human rights concerns based on deontologically justified rights.[102] Consequentialist, trade-off based approaches to the evaluation of trade and human rights conflicts are, in their very method of analysis, biased against human rights and place human rights at risk, in the fact that they are unwilling to accord human rights claims the sort of privilege which human rights advocates consider essential.[103] Hausman and McPherson point out that strictly deontological approaches to rights are disturbing to contemporary economists,[104] precisely because such approaches view rights as absolutely not to be violated, essentially foreclosing the sort of analysis which economists engage in when evaluating a policy or course of conduct. Yet this absolute quality which economists find disturbing about rights, is the absolute quality which human rights advocates find essential in the human rights principle.

C. *Trade-based Decisions on Trade/Human Rights Conflicts: Doctrinal Approaches to Normative Conflicts*

The theoretical risk posed to human rights law from the differing approaches to moral decision-making adopted by trade law and human rights law is borne out at the doctrinal level when one examines the approach the WTO dispute settle-

---

Id. at 559.

102. *See* Frey, *supra* note 59, at 11.

> Since utilitarian reasoning can justify trade-offs . . . whenever contingencies so dictate, and since there are no person-relative principles that bar utilitarian sacrifice of persons and their vital interests within the unconstrained theory, there seems no way to deflect the risk to persons. And constraints that might deflect the risk, for example, *that a life is of inherent worth irrespective of its pleasure or capacity for pleasure, that life is an incommensurable value and so beyond the compass of utilitarian trade-offs, that this or that person-relative principle could secure persons and their vital interests from such trade-offs*, do not obviously form part of the classical theory.

Id. (emphasis added). The same basic criticism holds true for preference-satisfaction forms of utilitarianism. *Id.* at 15.

103. *Id.* at 17 (questioning whether any consequential theory can adequately account for the wrongness of fundamental rights violations such as killing).

104. Historically, arguments for capitalism were often rights-based, in that they lauded capitalism less for its efficiency-enhancing capability than for the protection of individual freedom offered by the separation of economic and political power. *See* Hausman & McPherson, *supra* note 6, at 693. However, with respect to modern economics, rights-oriented moral theories are more difficult to link to traditional forms of economic analysis. *Id.* at 672.

ment system would actually take to conflicts involving trade and non-trade values, including trade-human rights conflicts. Returning to the example first posed above of domestic trade-restrictive measures adopted at the national level against an egregious rights-violating state, this Article now assumes that such a measure has in fact been enacted. Examples of such measures might include a national-level decision to suspend GATT-obligated MFN treatment as a response to particular human rights violations,[105] the imposition by a sub-federal unit of a government procurement ban as a response to human rights violations,[106] or the imposition of a trade ban on the products of indentured child labor, either unilaterally[107] or perhaps in response to a future ILO convention prohibiting such practices.[108] The common denominator here is state action imposing a trade sanction on human rights violators, as a mechanism to both punish the state and to encourage compliance with international human rights law.

---

105. For example, the much-debated Helms-Burton legislation, Title I of which is aimed at trade in goods. For a recent overview of the arguments concerning the legality of the Helms-Burton legislation under WTO law, including citations to the extensive literature on the matter, see John A. Spanogle, Jr., *Can Helms-Burton Be Challenged Under WTO?*, 27 STETSON L. REV. 1313, 1313 & n.1 (1998). For a review of the history of U.S. sanctions against Cuba, see Andreas F. Lowenfeld, *The Cuban Liberty and Democratic Solidarity (Libertad) Act*, 90 AM. J. INT'L L. 419 (1996). For an interesting analysis of the Helms-Burton legislation and its furor from an international relations perspective, see David P. Fidler, *LIBERTAD v. Liberalism: An Analysis of the Helms-Burton Act from Within Liberal International Relations Theory,* 4 IND. J. GLOBAL LEGAL STUD. 297 (1997).

106. The Massachusetts government procurement statute sanctioning Myanmar (formerly Burma) was recently declared unconstitutional as an impermissible infringement on the federal government's power to regulate foreign affairs. *See* National Foreign Trade Council v. Baker, 26 F. Supp. 2d 287, 1998 U.S. Dist. LEXIS 17789 (D. Mass. 1998). Massachusetts plans a similar law against Indonesia. *See* David R. Schmahmann et al., *Off the Precipice: Massachusetts Expands Its Foreign Policy Expedition from Burma to Indonesia*, 30 VAND. J. TRANSNAT'L L. 1021 (1997). On the matter of federal and sub-federal relations in trade law generally, see Matthew Schaefer, *Searching for Pareto Gains in the Relationship Between Free Trade and Federalism: Revisiting the NAFTA, Eyeing the FTAA,* 23 CAN.-U.S. L.J. 441 (1997).

107. The United States enacted such a ban in 1997, forbidding the importation of products "mined, produced or manufactured by forced or indentured child labor." Treasury, Postal Service, and General Government Appropriations Act of 1998, § 634, Pub. L. No. 105-61, 111 Stat. 1272, 1316 (1997).

108. The United States, among others, has been calling for such a convention. *See* President William Jefferson Clinton, State of the Union Address (Jan. 19, 1999).

1. Human Rights Trade Sanctions in the WTO

In any of these cases, the target state would challenge such actions in a WTO dispute settlement proceeding, assuming all states-parties are WTO Member States. The most likely basis for such a challenge would be that the measure violates the most-favored-nation and national treatment rules contained in GATT Articles I and III. The challenged measure would be determined a *prima facia* Article I violation, because the like products from other WTO Member States which are not targets are not subject to the trade restriction.[109] The measure is also likely to be determined a *prima facia* Article III violation, because like domestic products are also not subject to the same trade restriction.[110] Therefore, the sanctioning state is going to have to find a GATT-authorized exception applicable in such cases, or face a judgement that the measure nullifies or impairs the target state's expected trade benefits, and the likelihood of being itself subject to WTO-authorized sanctions if it fails to amend or withdraw the measure.

As the GATT treaty stands today, there is no single clearly applicable exception for such a human rights-oriented measure. There are, however, several exceptions which might apply if interpreted with human rights concerns in mind. One possible avenue is that the sanctioning state would seek the shelter of the national security exception in Article XXI. Article XXI permits states to unilaterally enact trade-restrictive measures when the state judges such measures to be "necessary for the protection of its essential security interests" during a time of "emergency in international relations."[111] However, this is a controversial provision much disliked and distrusted by the majority of WTO Member States, in that it is not justiciable as it has been interpreted.[112] Therefore, states would be reluc-

109. *See* Philip M. Nichols, *GATT Doctrine,* 36 VA. J. INT'L L. 379, 437 & nn.333-35, panel proceedings cited therein and accompanying text (discussing elaboration and application of most-favored-nation test).

110. *See id.* at 436 nn.327, 332, the panel proceedings cited therein and accompanying text (discussing elaboration and application of national treatment test). In certain cases, the product may be so closely linked to the human rights violation that the same products are prohibited domestically. This may be the case, for example, with trade involving body parts or organs of prisoners. In such cases, there may be no underlying national treatment violation.

111. *See* GATT, *supra* note 31, art. XXI(b)(iii).

112. *See* Raj K. Bhala, *Fighting Bad Guys with International Trade Law,* 31

tant to invoke this provision absent at least a plausible national security risk, and the WTO would be very likely to oppose any effort to read that exception broadly enough to include general human rights-based trade sanctions.

A more likely candidate is Article XX, whose exceptions are intended to permit GATT violations, including Articles I and III violations, in pursuit of several categories of non-trade policy goals.[113] Three Article XX exceptions in particular, the public morals, human life and health, and prison labor exceptions, may be relevant in connection with human rights measures. Article XX(a) permits measures "*necessary* to protect human morals."[114] Article XX(b) permits measures "*necessary* to protect human, animal or plant life or health."[115] Finally, Article XX(e) permits measures "relating to the products of prison labour."[116]

The availability of these exceptions turns on two sorts of interpretive problems. First, each presents at the outset a similar textual issue, namely whether the scope of the exemption can be interpreted to accommodate human rights-based measures.[117] The prison labor exception is least likely to

U.C. DAVIS L. REV. 1, 6-20 (1997) (critically assessing Article XXI); Spanogle, *supra* note 105, at 1328-35 (reviewing problems raised by invoking Article XXI exception).

113. As a preliminary matter, it should be noted that the availability of any of the Article XX exceptions is limited by the *chapeau* test prohibiting that measures otherwise justifiable under that article be applied so as to be "a means of arbitrary or unjustifiable discrimination . . . or a disguised restriction on international trade." GATT, *supra* note 31, art. XX; Shrimp Case, *supra* note 41 (interpreting and applying the *chapeau* test).

114. GATT, *supra*, note 31, art. XX(a) (emphasis added) (highlighting the "necessity" test). *See infra* notes 125-26 and accompanying text. *See generally* Steve Charnovitz, *The Moral Exception in Trade Policy*, 38 VA. J. INT'L L. 689 (1998) [hereinafter Charnovitz, *Moral Exception*] (discussing the legislative history and policy issues of this provision).

115. GATT, *supra* note 31, art. XX(b) (emphasis added) (highlighting the "necessity" test); *infra* notes 125-26 and accompanying text. Much has been written about the Article XX(b) exception in connection with trade/environment linkage problems. *See, e.g.*, DANIEL C. ESTY, GREENING THE GATT (1994); Steve Charnovitz, *Free Trade, Fair Trade Green Trade: Defogging the Debate*, 27 CORNELL INT'L L.J. 459 (1994) [hereinafter Charnovitz, *Green Trade*] (reviewing the history of trade and environmental issues).

116. GATT, *supra* note 31, art. XX(e). *See* Christopher S. Armstrong, *American Import Controls and Morality in International Trade: An Analysis of Section 307 of the Tariff Act of 1930*, 8 N.Y.U. J. INT'L L. & POL. 19 (1975) (reviewing legislative history and policy issues relating to this exception).

117. In approaching an issue of textual interpretation, the WTO Appellate Body

serve in this case, despite the fact that arguably it is the clearest case of a human rights exception in the GATT, for the very reason that it is so clearly drafted to refer to a single category of products, namely those produced by prison labor.[118] The public morality exception should apply in at least a subset of human rights-related claims,[119] but its broader applicability turns on whether the provision can be interpreted to encompass a wide range of human rights concerns beyond traditional "public morals" issues.[120] Finally, interpreting Article XX(b) to include human rights violations as threats to "human . . . life or health," would run counter to existing, albeit limited, GATT jurisprudence on this issue.[121] Second, availability of both the public morals and human life and health exceptions depends upon whether Articles XX(a) and XX(b) would be in-

---

will follow the "customary rules of interpretation of public international law," DSU, *supra* note 10, art. 3.2, which the Appellate Body has determined are set out in Articles 31 and 32 of the Vienna Convention. Vienna Convention on the Law of Treaties, May 23, 1969, 1155 U.N.T.S. 311 (entered into force Jan. 27, 1988); World Trade Organization Appellate Body Report on United States—Standards for Reformulated and Conventional Gasoline, WT/DS2/AB/R, *available in* 1996 WL 227476; World Trade Organization Appellate Body Report on Japan—Taxes on Alcoholic Beverages, WT/DS8/AB/R, *available in* 1996 WL 738800. This strategy promises to improve upon the uneven pattern of interpretive approaches taken by GATT panels historically. *See* Nichols, *supra* note 11, at 422-30 (reviewing panel approaches). However, the Appellate Body has itself been criticized for its uneven application of this approach. *See* Rambod Behboodi, *Legal Reasoning and the International Law of Trade: The First Steps of the Appellate Body of the WTO*, 32 J. WORLD TRADE 55, 77-78, 92 (1998).

118. GATT, *supra* note 31, art. XX(e); *but see* Stirling, *supra* note 29, at 33-39 (arguing it would be a "logical extension" of Article XX(e) to apply it to a broad range of human rights violations).

119. *See* Charnovitz, *Moral Exception*, *supra* note 114, at 729-30 (suggesting claims involving slavery, trade in weapons, narcotics, liquor and pornographic materials, religion, and compulsory labor).

120. *Id.* at 742-43 (suggesting that international human rights law be used to interpret the vague scope of the exception).

121. This author is not aware of any GATT panel in which the issue is directly raised. However, the approach taken by the panel in the Thai Cigarettes case, for example, would suggest that the provision only exempts measures aimed at products which *themselves* pose a threat to human life or health, such as cigarettes. Thailand—Restrictions on Importation of and Internal Taxes on Cigarettes, Nov. 7, 1990, GATT B.I.S.D. (37th Supp.) at 200 (1991) [hereinafter Thai Cigarettes case]. This is consistent with the approach taken by the first Tuna panel regarding the "process/product" distinction in Article III violations, in which a measure aimed at the *process* by which a product was made would not be eligible for consideration under more favorable GATT provisions involving measures aimed at the product itself. GATT Dispute Panel Report on United States Restrictions on Imports of Tuna, 33 I.L.M. 1594 (1991) [hereinafter Tuna I].

terpreted as available for "outward-oriented" measures designed to influence the human rights policies of another jurisdiction,[122] which existing GATT jurisprudence calls into question.[123]

If none of these exceptions are available on scope or territoriality grounds, then the hypothetical human rights measure proposed above would be ruled a GATT violation. If, however, these scope issues could be resolved so as to bring human rights-based domestic measures within the ambit of either Article XX (a) or (b), then adjudication of the GATT claim would ultimately rest on the application of the "necessity" test required by the language of both articles.[124] As the test is applied, the WTO panel would rule that the disputed measure was not in fact necessary, and therefore a GATT violation, if it were to find that another less trade-restrictive measure was "reasonably available."[125]

In conditioning the availability of these Article XX exceptions, and therefore any human rights-favorable resolution of this conflict, on the necessity test, the WTO is applying what has been called a trade-off device, a term encompassing various legal techniques used in trade institutions to relate the trade burden of a given measure against its intended non-trade regulatory benefit.[126] It is in the utilization of trade-off devic-

122. The exception for the products of prison labor does not raise this issue, as by its terms it is drafted to permit importing states to take into account the prison labor practices of other jurisdictions in deciding whether to permit or block the importation of certain products. *See* GATT Dispute Panel Report on United States Restrictions on Imports of Tuna, 33 I.L.M. 839, ¶ 5.16 (1994) [hereinafter Tuna II].

123. *See* Charnovitz, *Green Trade*, *supra* note 115, at 718-24 (discussing the distinction between "inward" and "outward" oriented measures, and disfavor towards outward-oriented measures expressed in the Tuna cases).

124. *See supra* notes 114, 115 and accompanying text. The exception for the products of prison labor does not impose a "necessity" test, requiring merely that the measure in question be one "*relating* to the products of prison labour," thereby incorporating the more lenient "rationality" test. *See infra* notes 161-62 and accompanying text.

125. *See* Thai Cigarettes case, *supra* note 121, ¶ 75 (stating that the measure is not "necessary" if there exists a less trade-restrictive alternative a state could "reasonably be expected to employ" in pursuit of its non-trade objectives); Tuna I, *supra* note 121, ¶ 5.18; Tuna II, *supra* note 122, ¶ 3.72.

126. Joel Trachtman, in his pioneering study of trade-off devices, identifies as potential trade-off devices national treatment rules, simple means-end rationality tests, necessity/least trade restrictive alternative tests, proportionality, balancing, and cost-benefit analysis. Joel P. Trachtman, *Trade and . . . Problems, Cost-Benefit*

es, and in the choice and application of a particular device, that the WTO dispute resolution system embodies the utilitarian approach to normative conflicts in trade, and in so doing raises issues about its compatibility with human rights law.

2. Trade-off Mechanisms in Trade Linkage Disputes

As a preliminary matter, it should be noted that trade-off devices have as a defining feature the willingness to juxtapose, and in many cases to commensurate between, trade values on the one hand and non-trade values on the other. Such an approach is consistent with the consequentialist approach taken by most economists and economically-minded analysts to trade matters.[127] It has in fact been said that utilitarianism is preeminently "a theory about trade-offs."[128] It should not be surprising to find such a market-oriented measure in a trade-based dispute settlement mechanism.[129]

In contrast, the very notion of trade-off devices runs counter to the deontological approach to human rights. Normatively, human rights rest on the *incommensurability* of rights, which is alien to utilitarian theories.[130] In human rights terms, one cannot morally trade a certain amount of human rights violation in exchange for a greater amount of trade welfare benefit, even if the latter is seen as enhancing or embodying other human rights. While it is foreseeable that a trade-based forum may be legally required to engage in some sort of balancing analysis, weighing the trade costs of protection against the human rights costs of acquiescence, such an analysis might be objected to by human rights advocates at the outset as simply inadequate in view of the absolute moral obligation to enforce human rights regardless of the consequences.[131] On this view, the preeminent mechanism for re-

---

Analysis and Subsidiarity, 9 EUR. J. INT'L L. 32, 32 (1998).

127. Trachtman accepts as a general proposition that trade-offs must be made between trade values and other social values. *Id.*; *accord* Hausman & McPherson, *supra* note 6, at 696 (discussing Nozick).

128. Frey, *supra* note 59, at 16.

129. Indeed, Delbrück notes a preference for market-oriented strategies and mechanisms for globalization problems, where "the globalization of trade as a means of maximizing economic welfare for the greatest number constitutes the policy goal." Delbrück, *supra* note 4, at 19.

130. *Id.*

131. *See* Hausman & McPherson, *supra* note 6, at 696 (child torture example).

solving policy disputes in trade institutions by its very nature defeats the fundamental tenet of human rights law.

In thus failing to distinguish a subset of values the trade-off of which is not permitted, some may view any trade analysis as already skewed in favor of trade values over human rights values. However, it may nevertheless be inevitable that a trade-off type of analysis will be carried out in the event of regulatory conflicts, at least under the current international governance regime. Some form of balancing is often involved in policy formation: one compares two options in terms of their mutual effects on identified values, and one decides. In particular, where the dispute is not directly between trade law and human rights law, but trade law and domestic measures enacted to *enforce* human rights, it is conceivable that balancing be used in determining the appropriate or most effective *means* towards achieving the human rights goals when there is a trade cost. Any such approach, however, and in particular the trade-off device actually employed, must be carefully examined and carefully utilized in policy decisions where rights are involved, or the very nature and principle of rights can be violated at the outset. Therefore, it becomes important to evaluate each trade-off device in terms of the degree to which it discriminates against human rights. Trachtman concludes that from a trade perspective certain measures are to be preferred over others, citing in particular the necessity test.[132] It is not surprising, therefore, that from a human rights perspective, a different set of preferences emerges, in fact the opposite one.

3. The WTO Necessity Test as a Trade-off Device

Notwithstanding the argument that some sort of balancing is required in policy-formulation where competing values are at stake, the necessity test is clearly objectionable in human-rights terms as a trade-off device on the ground that it is biased in favor of trade values.[133] In other words, the test evaluates measures favorably precisely insofar as their impact on trade is the least possible, despite the fact that more trade-impacting measures might be more effective in realizing the non-trade value. Not only does this trade-off mechanism fail to

132. Trachtman, *supra* note 126, at 81-82.
133. *See* Nichols, *supra* note 11, at 699-700.

recognize the high priority which rights must hold in any policy determination, but in fact the necessity test turns this on its head, and privileges trade values over all other competing values.[134]

To a limited extent the "reasonably available" qualification invites some consideration of the effectiveness of the disputed measure in accomplishing its non-trade regulatory purpose, since any less trade-restrictive measure, which forms the basis for an invalidation of the chosen measure, must be "reasonably available" in view of the state's non-trade regulatory objectives. The extent of such consideration, however, depends entirely on the interpretation of such language, and the application of the qualification, by the GATT panel. In particular, the language clearly does not require specific consideration of the *effectiveness* of alternative measures in achieving their non-trade goals, in the way that similar language in the Sanitary and Phytosanitary Agreement does refer to the level of protection achievable by the alternative measure.[135]

Therefore, it would be consistent with the language of the necessity test as currently interpreted for a GATT panel to find that a measure significantly less effective in achieving the non-trade purpose would nonetheless be identified by the panel as "reasonably available," and therefore serve as the basis for invalidating the chosen measure. This is disturbing in that, since such a measure was in fact *not* chosen by the sanctioning state, this language would have the effect of substituting the trade forum's opinion of the rationality of alternatives for the opinion of the legislating forum.[136] If one considers that do-

134. Thomas J. Schoenbaum has argued that the current GATT/WTO interpretation of the Article XX(b) necessity test turns the provision "on its head" in a literal sense, in that "necessary" refers syntactically to the need for protection of life and health, and not to the trade effects of the measure, and is thus wrong on textual grounds. Thomas J. Schoenbaum, *International Trade and Protection of the Environment: the Continuing Search for Reconciliation*, 91 AM. J. INT'L L. 268, 276 (1997).

135. "[A] measure is *not* more trade-restrictive than required unless there is another measure, reasonably available taking into account technical and economic feasibility, *that achieves the appropriate level of sanitary or phytosanitary protection* and is significantly less restrictive to trade." Agreement on the Application of Sanitary and Phytosanitary Measures, Dec. 15, 1993, Final Act Embodying the Results of the Uruguay Round of Multilateral Trade Negotiations, 33 I.L.M. 9, art. 5 n.3 (1994) (emphasis added). *See infra* notes 168-69 and accompanying text.

136. Also, if the test is interpreted, as it has been, to require justification not of the entire regulatory scheme but of each specific trade restrictive component,

mestic legislatures may, in principle and at least in certain cases, produce legislative outcomes "on the merits," then it is clear that the language of Article XX(a) and (b) invites the questionable substitution by a panel of trade experts, with a built-in bias favoring trade values, of a less effective human rights measure in the place of a more effective, democratically-selected, human rights measure on the basis of the measure's effects on trade.[137]

IV. Protecting Human Rights in the Institutions of the Global Market: Doctrinal Solutions for Normative Conflicts

As a matter of justice, our society is committed to both markets and rights. Therefore, it is inevitable that there will be conflict between the rationality of markets and the rationality of rights. In many respects, the challenge facing the global community is akin to the challenge facing any society based on both markets and rights—how to carve out the respective spheres for rights and for free market choices, and how to regulate or limit the range of market choices when they threaten fundamental rights. This comes down to institutional decisions, of both a norm-creating and adjudicative nature. In other words, how do we incorporate both trade values and human rights values in comprehensive policies respecting both markets and rights, and what rules do we apply when these values, and the laws incorporating these values, conflict?[138]

The resolution of globalization/human rights conflicts in a manner which enhances the effectiveness of human rights law is going to require a mechanism for the recognition within

---

then the burden is much more difficult to meet. Trachtman in fact concedes that the alternative would be much more favorable to non-trade values. Trachtman, *supra* note 126, at 69.

137. *Accord* Schoenbaum, *supra* note 134, at 277 ("this interpretation of 'necessity' constitutes too great an infringement on the sovereign powers of states to take decisions (one hopes) by democratic means so as to solve problems and satisfy their constituents"). Trachtman concedes that in this approach the characterization of the measure to be evaluated introduces "a certain degree of outcome-determinative discretion." Trachtman, *supra* note 126, at 69. This discretion is, of course, in the hands of trade policy experts.

138. The importance of mechanisms to balance the conflicts which can occur between fundamental normative elements of a globalized liberalism, such as the conflict between free markets and human rights, is recognized as one of the central challenges of globalization. *See* Seita, *supra* note 11, at 484-85.

international economic law of the priority, which at least certain fundamental human rights must enjoy. In other words, there must be some mechanism for a constitutional level of deference within international economic law toward at least certain elements of the International Bill of Human Rights, such as the core rights involving life, freedom, security and bodily integrity, and the recognition within international economic law of rights-enforcement techniques such as trade sanctions, which make such rights effective, and which cannot be balanced or traded off in international economic law dispute resolution decisions. Where some sort of trade-off is inevitable, there must be clear recognition of the priority which human rights claims must have in any value conflict.

A. *Pre-empting Conflicts Among Different Sets of Rules*

At the global level, resolution of the trade/human rights conflict is complicated by the defects, from a constitutional viewpoint, of international governance.[139] It is a fundamental feature of the landscape of global social policy in the late 20th century that no one institution has the effective jurisdiction to create and adjudicate norms in all aspects of global social concern.[140] Instead, we find separate treaty regimes and separate institutions, built and justified according to conflicting normative principles, yet both ultimately reflecting critical aspects of a liberal vision for global social life.

As a result, it is likely that norms affecting both human rights and trade will continue to be negotiated in the context of a treaty or treaty-making conference predominantly oriented towards one or the other of these areas of social concern. And it is likely that disputes involving both human rights and trade law will, absent modification of the existing governance mechanism, continue to be resolved in dispute resolution fora which will be constrained by treaty law and institutional paradigm to give priority to one set of concerns over another. Therefore, a natural question to consider first would be whether one solu-

139. In fact, national measures are more likely to be used in absence of international government. *See* Charnovitz, *Social Issues*, *supra* note 48, at 19.

140. For an excellent discussion of the problems which this institutional fragmentation creates in the trade/environment area, see Jeffrey L. Dunoff, *Institutional Misfits: The GATT, the ICJ & Trade-Environment Disputes*, 15 MICH. J. INT'L L. 1043 (1994).

tion might be some mechanism to either expand the scope of the WTO to include human rights norms themselves, thus bridging the regulatory chasm, or concede the institutional disjunction and limit the jurisdiction of trade institutions over human rights measures.

1. Include Human Rights Rules in Trade Agreements

It has been suggested that one approach would be the incorporation of certain human rights norms into the WTO agreements.[141] Modifying the WTO to include human rights concern is of course more attractive than the reverse, namely adding trade issues to the scope of existing human rights treaties and institutions, since the WTO is the preeminent global economic institution, with a newly strengthened enforcement system and immense international prestige. Moreover, the GATT treaty does recognize to a certain extent certain important social policy concerns based in values other than trade.[142] This approach would add to that foundation by interpreting Article XX(e) as a broad human rights exception,[143] modifying the WTO agreements to add a core list of recognized human rights,[144] and creating a specialized human rights body within the structural framework of the WTO, with authority to hear human rights related complaints and to impose trade sanctions.[145]

This approach has the benefit of reversing the current trend of institutional specialization which complicates the trade-human rights and other trade linkage issues. However, it is precisely for this reason that such an approach is unlikely to succeed, in that there does not appear to be the requisite degree of political support that such a sweeping overhaul would require. In fact, the trend seems in the opposite direction, as the majority of the world's trading nations have decided that

141. *See* Stirling, *supra* note 29, at 33.

142. However, the adequacy of the measures adopted can be questioned, as can the extent to which such concerns are recognized. Moreover, the underlying normative source of the conflict is not recognized explicitly, principally because the GATT adopts a trade values-based regulatory system. *See* Charnovitz, *Social Issues*, *supra* note 48, at 23-24.

143. *See supra* notes 117-19 (discussing the Article XX(e) exception).

144. *See* Stirling, *supra* note 29, at 39-40.

145. *Id.* at 40-45.

the WTO is not the appropriate institution to articulate human rights norms, leaving that to other specialized agencies such as the ILO.[146]

2. Limiting Trade Jurisdiction Over Human Rights Measures

Alternatively, the jurisdiction of the WTO could be limited such that the legitimacy of any human rights-related trade actions would not be adjudicated in the WTO.[147] The broadest across-the-board restriction on the WTO's jurisdiction over human rights measures would be a general exception added to either the GATT, the WTO Charter or the WTO Dispute Settlement Understanding, excluding national measures taken in response to violations of treaty-based or customary human rights from WTO review.[148] However, contrary to existing Article XX exceptions, which incorporate some form of trade-off mechanism presupposing panel review, such an exception would have to be drafted more along the lines of the national security exception in Article XXI, vesting in the sanctioning state some form of unilateral discretion in the face of human rights violations. Otherwise, human rights-based measures are not really excluded from WTO review, but privileged according to some form of trade off mechanism.[149]

An alternative approach, more limited in scope, would only apply to human rights treaties involving products which themselves embody or are the fruits of human rights violations, such as pornography and the products of indentured child labor; or to any human rights treaties negotiated in the future to expressly provide for the use of economic sanctions in response to human rights violations.[150] In such cases, the WTO

146. *See Singapore Declaration*, *supra* note 34.

147. This is the approach Philip Nichols advocates for linkage issues in general. *See* Nichols, *supra* note 11, at 709-12.

148. *Cf.* Kevin C. Kennedy, *Reforming U.S. Trade Policy to Protect the Global Environment: A Multilateral Approach*, 18 HARV. ENVTL. L. REV. 185, 204 (1994) (arguing that amending GATT to draft new environmental exception is the best approach to the trade/environment linkage problems).

149. Nichols seems to blur this point, in that the operation of his exemption would still require an investigation by a dispute settlement panel into the measure's purpose. Nichols, *supra* note 11, at 709-12 (positing implementation of human rights measures through modification or interpretation of the DSU).

150. This might resemble the practice under certain environmental treaties to provide for trade-restrictive measures to be taken with regard to delineated products which harm the environment. *See* Protocol on Substances that Deplete the

should be required to recognize the legitimacy of sanctions imposed within the constraints of such a treaty, and such measures should not have to undergo the necessity test as applied through the Article XX exceptions.[151] Such recognition could take the form of a pure hierarchy of norms provision, ensuring that in the event of a conflict between a trade measure and a measure taken pursuant to an obligation under such an enumerated treaty, the obligations of that treaty should prevail.[152]

There are several benefits to adopting either of these variants. First, this approach would represent the decision by the international community at the *political* or legislative level[153] that trade-related human rights measures are appropriate despite their potentially adverse trade effects. Second, either amendment eliminates the interpretive problems attendant to including human rights measures within the scope of existing exceptions.[154] Third, in its Article XXI-like form, such an exception would grant the broadest possible scope for state action, including both economic measures taken pursuant to a

---

Ozone Layer, Sept. 16, 1987, 26 I.L.M. 1550, art. 4 (entered into force Jan. 1, 1989) [hereinafter Montreal Protocol]; Convention on International Trade in Endangered Species of Wild Fauna and Flora, Mar. 3, 1973, arts. III-V, VIII 12 I.L.M. 1085 (entered into force July 1, 1975) [hereinafter Wild Fauna Convention] (both providing for the total ban of unlawful trade in covered substances, even with non-parties to the agreement). Of course, in the case of these treaties, the restrictions apply to products which themselves produce the harm.

151. The GATT already recognizes this principle in its exception for economic sanctions implemented in response to a U.N. Security Council Resolution. GATT, *supra* note 31, art. XXI(c). Particularly when one considers that such a measure would still be subject to multilateral review and constraint within its own system, such an exclusion may not be too broad for advocates of the trade system.

152. The "purity" of this proposed hierarchy of norms lies in the fact that it does not incorporate a trade-off mechanism requiring panel review, in contrast to the actual NAFTA hierarchy of norms provision, which in the case of environmental treaties imposes a necessity test on measures taken pursuant to the listed treaties. Article 104 of NAFTA states that, where there is an inconsistency between NAFTA obligations and the obligations imposed by certain listed treaties, including the Montreal Convention and the Wild Fauna Convention, *supra* note 150, the obligations under the listed treaties shall prevail to the extent of the inconsistency, provided that the Party has chosen the least inconsistent means of complying with the conflicting obligation, where the party in fact has a choice among "equally effective and reasonably available" means of compliance. North American Free Trade Agreement, Dec. 1992, Can.-Mex.-U.S., 32 I.L.M. 605 (1993).

153. On the distinction between legislative and adjudicatory approaches to the problem, see Nichols, *supra* note 11, at 691-99.

154. *See supra* notes 118-24 and accompanying text.

human rights treaty authorizing sanction, and economic measures taken unilaterally by a state in response to violations of rights which, while they are the subject of binding international custom or treaty law, are not expressly contained within instruments authorizing economic sanctions. In its narrower, hierarchy-of-norms form, such an amendment would still grant a very high level of deference to at least treaty-based human rights measures.

In granting to human rights measures an automatic exclusion from review according to trade values and trade principles, such a general exception would be quite congenial to the philosophic approach of the human rights movement, which seeks recognition of the priority of human rights claims.[155] However, the very breadth of such an approach, coupled with its preference for human rights over trade values, would make such an amendment difficult to enact in the face of concerted opposition from WTO Member States committed to a higher priority for trade values. Moreover, an Article XXI approach, or a pure hierarchy of norms, would be unpopular for its very nonjusticiability, already a concern with the existing Article XXI exception. This nonjusticiability would be resisted on formal grounds, in view of the strong preference in the WTO for rule-based adjudicative dispute resolution, and by Member States reluctant to open themselves to such broad unreviewable use of economic sanctions. Finally, such an approach would raise quite legitimate concerns over the invitation to protectionist abuse that such a blanket exception would invite.[156]

---

155. Moreover, the conflict at the norm-creation stage remains less constraining, in that states are free to reach negotiated compromises between different sets of values in the creation of a treaty, in a way that treaty-based dispute settlement mechanisms are not.

156. Such an exception could still be conditioned on the *chapeau* test for arbitrary discrimination or disguised restrictions on trade, and thus would not be a blanket invitation to protectionist legislation. Adding a *chapeau*-style test would change the nature of the exception from a limitation of jurisdiction to an amendment altering the nature of the trade-off device. It may also be possible to determine a rule or metric for distinguishing "authentic" from "protectionist" invocations of such a human rights exception, as Jeffrey Atik has proposed regarding linkage issues generally. *See* Jeffrey Atik, *Identifying Anti-democratic Outcomes*, 19 U. PA. J. INT'L ECON. L. 229 (1998).

B. *Rights-deferential Trade-off Mechanisms Where Conflicts Must Arise*

Absent the implementation of a preclusionary approach such as those discussed above, one must then face the existing problem of how to adjudicate trade disputes involving human rights, where measures based on the obligations of customary or treaty-based human rights norms are at issue within trade fora which are treaty-bound to consider only trade-based factors. Therefore, the remainder of this section will focus on ways to avoid or minimize such conflicts as they might arise in trade dispute settlement fora, attempting to reconcile trade and human rights claims in a way that more accurately reflects the preeminent status which human rights claims must be afforded in policy disputes.

1. Amending the GATT to Apply a Different Trade-off Mechanism

To the extent that trade-human rights conflicts are going to be adjudicated within trade institutions, it becomes critical to revise the trade-off mechanisms which will be applied in trade dispute resolution mechanisms to better take into account human rights law and principles, while permitting the trade panel to identify and rule against disguised protectionism.

a. National Treatment

The principle of national treatment is a basic tradeoff mechanism employed by most trade agreements, including the WTO. The national treatment rule is not inherently objectionable for human rights, since it merely requires a level of consistency between foreign and domestic treatment of goods or producers with regard to any legislation, including one addressing human rights violations.[157] To begin with, in appropriate cases national treatment may be the only requirement,

---

157. Interestingly enough, however, Trachtman characterizes national treatment as in fact biased in favor of non-trade values and is critical on this basis. *See* Trachtman, *supra* note 126, at 72. However, from the perspective of human rights, one would expect that any trade-off mechanism employed *should* be biased in favor of human rights.

as in a ban on trade in obscene materials, in which the product itself embodies the violation. If such products are banned domestically as well, then there is no national treatment violation, and the inquiry should stop there. However, in the hypothetical case we are considering involving trade sanctions, national treatment would not be an appropriate mechanism. The measure in question would almost certainly be a *prima facie* violation of the national treatment rule, since the measure is addressed at a rights-oppressive practice that in many cases will not even be connected to the process, let alone the product, targeted by the sanction.[158] For the same reason,. domestic products will not be subject to any analogous restriction. In this case, if national treatment alone were the dispositive test, then it would in fact operate as a complete rejection of non-trade values, contrary to Trachtman. Thus, while a national treatment test may be friendly or even biased in favor of non-trade values where an aspect of the product or process is in question, this rule would not work so favorably towards non-trade values in a general sanctions situation, which is likely to be more common.

In such cases, a modified form of national treatment may be indicated, focusing on the sanctioned conduct and not on the products which are the targets of the sanctions.[159] In such a case, one would want to know if the conduct which forms the basis of the sanction is also prohibited domestically.[160] For sanctions which are applied pursuant to a human rights treaty, or which have been approved by a multilateral human rights treaty-based organ, this should be enough from a trade point of view. The legitimacy of the sanction itself, if challenged, should be challenged in the applicable human rights

158. In the child labor example, however, there is a link between the embargoed product and the suspect process. Nevertheless, the product/process distinction, if carried forward into WTO jurisprudence, would be fatal to measures addressing human rights violations which arise in the production of certain products. *See* Tuna I, *supra* note 121; Tuna II, *supra* note 122.

159. The panel report in Tuna I may not be an insurmountable obstacle in this regard, in that it has been much-criticized and, in any event, was not adopted. *See* Tuna I, *supra* note 121; Charnovitz, *Green Trade*, *supra* note 115, at 723.

160. This approach would be consistent with an early draft of the predecessor to Article XX in the Draft ITO Charter, as noted by the panel in Tuna I: "exception (b) read: 'For the purpose of protecting human, animal or plant life or health, *if corresponding domestic safeguards under similar conditions exist in the importing country.*'" (emphasis added). Tuna I, *supra* note 121, ¶ 5.26.

forum, not the trade forum.

b. Rationality

Assuming human rights can come under Article XX (a) or (b) or Article XX is amended to create an additional, express human rights exception, the nature of human rights will require a more rights-deferential test than the necessity test. In the case of unilateral sanctions that are not aimed at specific products tied to the human rights abuse, it may be appropriate at the trade level to apply a simple rationality test, as a safeguard against blatantly protectionist measures.[161] Thus if there is a rational, means-end relationship between the sanction and the targeted conduct, the inquiry should stop there.[162] A trade sanction imposed against a vital export of the abusive country, with conditions for its removal clearly tied to changes in human rights practices, should satisfy such a test. A trade sanction imposed against a less significant export, but one which has a powerful domestic producer lobby, or where the conditions for removal cannot be met or have been met without the lifting of the sanction, should not meet this test.

c. Proportionality

It may be that the trade community would consider a mere rationality test inadequate, because of the omnipresent danger of disguised discrimination, and would press for a still-more trade deferential form of trade-off device such as proportionality. The proportionality test requires that the trade cost be proportionate with reference to the non-trade benefits. Trachtman cites this as deferential to a degree to non-trade values, in that it requires only that the burden be proportionate.[163] But this test seems quite biased in favor of trade values, at least in the case of conflicting human rights values, in that human rights law places a supreme value on human

161. This would be consistent to the approach taken to measures restricting trade in the products of prison labor, which face only a rationality test.

162. This would bring the language of Article XX(b) into line with the existing language of Article XX(e), which merely imposes a rationality test. *See supra* note 124 and accompanying text.

163. Trachtman, *supra* note 126, at 81.

rights, which might in fact *require* a "disproportionate" level of deference or protection. At least, it could easily appear disproportionate to trade policy experts charged with applying these rules, particularly given the bias in trade fora against deontological forms of moral reasoning. The very inalienability of human rights might suggest a disproportionality to some.[164]

2. Modifying the Necessity Test Through Judicial Interpretation

For the reasons discussed above, the necessity test as applied fails to take into account the priority which human rights-related claims must be accorded, and in fact is biased against non-trade values including human rights. However, the political factors attendant to WTO amendment and the strong, if not overwhelming, pro-trade bias of the institution and its dominant Member States, may preclude any sort of amendment substituting a potentially more human-rights deferential trade-off mechanism, leaving the necessity test in place. Therefore, if some sort of necessity test must perforce be utilized, it should be modified to grant increased deference to human rights values.

One approach would be to simply introduce such modifications into the jurisprudence of Article XX through a decision by the WTO Appellate Body. This is less formally protective than an explicit amendment of the language, but is certainly procedurally more readily attainable.[165] A logical place to consider

---

164. Ultimately, such measures would not be ruled disproportionate if the forum recognizes the priority of human rights to a sufficient degree that the resulting trade burden would be considered appropriate. But this depends entirely on the trade forum's characterization of the importance of the value being protected by the legislation in conflict. Is it appropriate for democratically-enacted human rights laws to be subject to this sort of evaluation by an independent body of trade policy experts? *See generally* Robert F. Housman, *Democratizing International Trade Decision-making*, 27 CORNELL INT'L L.J. 699 (1994) (presenting a critique of the anti-democratic nature of trade institutions).

165. The effectiveness of these approaches would, of course, depend on the precedential effect of WTO appellate body rulings. To the extent that the emerging doctrine of *stare decisis* in WTO decisions continues to evolve, such approaches may be equally as effective as formal amendments, and more readily attainable. *See* Raj K. Bhala, *The Myth About Stare Decisis and International Trade Law*, 14 AM. U. J. INT'L L. & POL. (forthcoming 1999); Raj K. Bhala, *The Precedent Setters: De Facto Stare Decisis in WTO Adjudication*, 9 J. TRANSNAT'L L. & POL'Y (forth-

an interpretive amendment would be in the application of the existing "reasonably available" qualification. The most rights-protective interpretation would stipulate that, in order for the existence of a less trade restrictive alternative to invalidate a human rights measure, it must be shown that the less restrictive alternative is *equally effective* in terms of its impact on the human rights abuse in question. So interpreted, the WTO necessity test would resemble the necessity test embodied in the NAFTA's hierarchy of norms provision.[166]

A somewhat less rights-protective approach would be to interpret the necessity test in Article XX to conform to the necessity test as established in the Sanitary and Phytosanitary Agreement, which requires that a less restrictive measure be both "significantly" less restrictive, and disqualify the challenged measure only if it meets the "appropriate" level of protection.[167] This is clearly not as strong as the NAFTA test, since an "appropriate" level may be somewhat less than the "equally effective" level. However, it is still an improvement over the necessity test as currently interpreted, and should be the minimum standard applied to any less effective but more trade-friendly human rights measure at the panel level, since to find such a measure reasonably available without any consideration of such effects would be to utterly subvert both the judgement and the regulatory aim of the state. If coupled with procedural reforms allowing amicus briefs, panelists with non-trade expertise, or other forms of participation by the human rights community,[168] such an amendment would put non-trade values more on a par with trade values in any Article XX (a) or (b)-based proceeding.

V. CONCLUSION

The linkage debates currently underway in trade law and policy reveal to us that international economic law is funda-

coming 1999); Rutsel Silvestre J. Martha, *Precedent in World Trade Law*, 64 NETH. INT'L L. REV. 346 (1997).

166. *See supra* note 152.

167. *See supra* note 135 and accompanying text.

168. *See* Shrimp Case, *supra* note 41, ¶¶ 89-91; Philip M. Nichols, *Extension of Standing in World Trade Organization Disputes to Nongovernment Parties*, 17 U. PA. J. INT'L ECON. L. 295, 328-29 (1996) (arguing that panel composition should be changed to include appropriate non-trade experts).

mentally about justice, as are human rights law and other linkage issues. Therefore, conflicts between the regulatory infrastructures of globalization and international human rights must be analyzed and approached as justice questions. In practice this means paying attention to the decision-making process employed in such conflicts, in that it reflects a process of moral reasoning about issues of justice, and is not simply an exercise in identifying trade-liberalizing and trade-restrictive practices.

Ultimately, the effect of globalization on the recognition, protection and enforcement of human rights is going to depend on the relationship between international economic law, which provides the institutional and regulatory framework for globalization, and the international law of human rights. The issue is complicated by the overlapping jurisdiction of both international economic law and international human rights law over the same geographic and social space. Each regulatory system has been built according to, and operates on, fundamentally different, even conflicting, normative assumptions. Thus the institutional mechanisms developed to establish norms and resolve disputes in the context of overlapping jurisdictions and conflicting values will in practice determine whether globalization proves to be a friend or foe to human rights. From the above it is evident that absent significant reforms, trade law, and the forms of economic analysis underlying it, are inadequate for the just resolution of conflicts involving human rights law in a global market, at least if one considers human rights to hold a privileged position in law and policy. The changes suggested above, while they undeniably reflect a social decision in favor of the human rights principle over, or at least on a par with, conflicting trade interests, are in line with our domestic stance on such issues. If we have taken a position in our domestic constitutional orders that fundamental rights are not subject to unfettered balancing and compromise, then there is no principled reason to reach a different conclusion in the international arena. Of course, one can still differ as to the best means towards this end, and consequential forms of analysis are useful in identifying favorable approaches. However, the end must be clear, and not open to accommodation.

It has been suggested that, paradoxically, the greater the potential threat to human beings and their vital interests posed by utilitarian reasoning, the greater the perceived need for rights-based theories.[169] If so, this might lead one to be optimistic that some version or combination of the reforms outlined above might be adopted in the next stage of WTO evolution. Absent such changes, market globalization, in its institutional and regulatory form as the international economic law of today, could mean the triumph of utilitarian approaches to values over deontological ones, and therefore the triumph of trade over human rights. The trade system as it is now constituted is normatively incapable of properly evaluating linkage decisions because its very approach signals a defeat of fundamental non-trade values. At a minimum, this means that to the extent that trade institutions are called upon to resolve issues involving trade values and other values such as those underlying human rights law, the utilitarian approach underlying trade values will lead to decisions which are fundamentally skewed in favor of trade over other values at stake. This is not a victory for trade, but a defeat for our efforts to establish a just global order.

169. Frey, *supra* note 59, at 18.

[11]

The Attack on Human Rights

Michael Ignatieff

FROM WITHIN AND WITHOUT

SINCE 1945, human rights language has become a source of power and authority. Inevitably, power invites challenge. Human rights doctrine is now so powerful, but also so unthinkingly imperialist in its claim to universality, that it has exposed itself to serious intellectual attack. These challenges have raised important questions about whether human rights norms deserve the authority they have acquired: whether their claims to universality are justified, or whether they are just another cunning exercise in Western moral imperialism.

The cultural challenge to the universality of human rights arises from three distinct sources—from resurgent Islam, from within the West itself, and from East Asia. Each of these challenges is independent of the others, but taken together, they have raised substantial questions about the cross-cultural validity—and hence the legitimacy—of human rights norms.

The challenge from Islam has been there from the beginning. When the Universal Declaration of Human Rights was being drafted in 1947, the Saudi Arabian delegation raised particular objection to Article 16, relating to free marriage choice, and Article 18, relating to freedom of religion. On the question of marriage, the Saudi delegate to the committee examining the draft of the declaration made

---

MICHAEL IGNATIEFF is Director of the Carr Center for Human Rights at the Kennedy School of Government at Harvard University. This essay is adapted from his latest book, *Human Rights as Politics and Idolatry*.

an argument that has resonated ever since in Islamic encounters with Western human rights, saying that

> the authors of the draft declaration had, for the most part, taken into consideration only the standards recognized by Western civilization and had ignored more ancient civilizations which were past the experimental stage, and the institutions of which, for example, marriage, had proved their wisdom through the centuries. It was not for the Committee to proclaim the superiority of one civilization over all others or to establish uniform standards for all the countries of the world.

This was a defense of both the Islamic faith and patriarchal authority. The Saudi delegate in effect argued that the exchange and control of women is the very raison d'être of traditional cultures, and that the restriction of female choice in marriage is central to the maintenance of patriarchal property relations. On the basis of these objections to Articles 16 and 18, the Saudi delegation refused to ratify the declaration.

There have been recurrent attempts, including Islamic declarations of human rights, to reconcile Islamic and Western traditions by putting more emphasis on family duty and religious devotion and by drawing on distinctively Islamic traditions of religious and ethnic tolerance. But these attempts at fusion between the Islamic world and the West have never been entirely successful: agreement by the parties actually trades away what is vital to each side. The resulting consensus is bland and unconvincing.

Since the 1970s the relation of Islam to human rights has grown more hostile. When the Islamic Revolution in Iran rose up against the tyrannical modernization imposed by the shah, Islamic figures began to question the universal writ of Western human rights norms. They have pointed out that the Western separation of church and state, of secular and religious authority, is alien to the jurisprudence and political thought of the Islamic tradition. And they are correct. The freedoms articulated in the Universal Declaration of Human Rights make no sense within the theocratic bias of Islamic political thought. The right to marry and establish a family, to freely choose one's partner, is a direct challenge to the authorities in Islamic society that enforce the family choice of spouse, polygamy, and other restrictions on women's freedom. In Islamic eyes, universalizing rights discourse implies a sovereign and discrete individual, which is blasphemous from the perspective of the Koran.

In responding to this challenge, the West has made the mistake of assuming that fundamentalism and Islam are synonymous. But in fact Islam speaks in many voices, some more anti-Western or theocratic than others. National contexts may be more important in defining local Islamic reactions to Western values than are broad theological principles in the religion as a whole. Where Islamic societies have managed to modernize, create a middle class, and enter the global economy—Egypt and Tunisia being examples—a constituency in favor of basic human rights can emerge. Egypt, for instance, is now in the process of passing legislation to give women the right to divorce, and although dialogue with Egypt's religious authorities has been difficult, women's rights will be substantially enhanced by the new legislation. In Algeria, a secular human rights culture is more embattled. The governing elite, which rode to power after a bloody anticolonial revolution failed to modernize the country, faces an opposition, led by Islamic militants, that has taken an anti-Western, anti–human rights stance. And in Afghanistan, where the state itself has collapsed and foreign arms transfers have aggravated the nation's decline, the Taliban explicitly rejects all Western human rights standards. In these instances, the critical variant is not Islam itself but the fateful course of Western policy and economic globalization.

A second challenge to the universality of human rights comes from within the West itself. For the last 20 years, an influential current in Western political opinion has been maintaining, in the words of the radical scholars Adamantia Pollis and Peter Schwab, that human rights are a "Western construct of limited applicability," a twentieth-century fiction dependent on the rights traditions of the United States, the United Kingdom, and France and therefore inapplicable in cultures that do not share this historical matrix of liberal individualism.

This current of thought has complicated intellectual origins: the Marxist critique of the rights of man, the anthropological critique of the arrogance of late-nineteenth-century bourgeois imperialism, and the postmodernist critique of the universalizing pretensions of Enlightenment thought. All of these tendencies have come together in a critique of Western intellectual hegemony as expressed in the language of human rights. Human rights are seen as an exercise in the cunning of Western reason: no longer able to dominate the world through direct imperial rule, the West now masks its own will to power in the impartial, universalizing language of human rights and seeks to impose its own narrow agenda on a plethora of world cultures that do not actually share the West's conception of individuality, selfhood, agency, or freedom. This postmodernist relativism began as an intellectual fashion on Western university campuses, but it has seeped slowly into Western human rights practice, causing all activists to pause and consider the intellectual warrant for the universality they once took for granted.

This challenge within has been amplified by a challenge from without: the critique of Western human rights standards by some political leaders in the rising economies of East Asia. Whereas the Islamic challenge to human rights can be explained in part by the failure of Islamic societies to benefit from the global economy, the Asian challenge is a consequence of the region's staggering economic success. Because of Malaysia's robust economic growth, for example, its leaders feel confident enough to reject Western ideas of democracy and individual rights in favor of an Asian route to development and prosperity—a route that depends on authoritarian government and authoritarian family structures.

The same can be said about Singapore, which successfully synthesized political authoritarianism with market capitalism. Singapore's Senior Minister Lee Kuan Yew has been quoted as saying that Asians have "little doubt that a society with communitarian values where the interests of society take precedence over that of the individual suits them better than the individualism of America." Singaporeans often cite rising divorce and crime rates in the West to illustrate that Western individualism is detrimental to the order necessary for the enjoyment of rights themselves.

An "Asian model" supposedly puts community and family ahead of individual rights and order ahead of democracy and individual freedom. In reality, of course, there is no single Asian model: each of these societies has modernized in different ways, within different political traditions, and with differing degrees of political and market freedom. Yet it has proven useful for Asian authoritarians to argue that they represent a civilizational challenge to the hegemony of Western models.

TRADES AND COMPROMISES

LET IT BE CONCEDED at once that these three separate challenges to the universality of human rights discourse—two from without and one from within the Western tradition—have had a productive impact. They have forced human rights activists to question their assumptions, to rethink the history of their commitments, and to realize just how complicated intercultural dialogue on rights questions becomes when all cultures participate as equals.

But at the same time, Western defenders of human rights have traded too much away. In the desire to find common ground with Islamic and Asian positions and to purge their own discourse of the imperial legacies uncovered by the postmodernist critique, Western defenders of human rights norms risk compromising the very universality they ought to be defending. They also risk rewriting their own history.

Many traditions, not just Western ones, were represented at the drafting of the Universal Declaration of Human Rights—for example, the Chinese, Middle Eastern Christian, Marxist, Hindu, Latin American, and Islamic. The members of the drafting committee saw their task not as a simple ratification of Western convictions but as an attempt to delimit a range of moral universals from within their very different religious, political, ethnic, and philosophical backgrounds. This fact helps to explain why the document makes no reference to God in its preamble. The communist delegations would have vetoed any such reference, and the competing religious traditions could not have agreed on words that would make human rights derive from human beings' common existence as God's creatures. Hence the secular ground of the document is not a sign of European cultural domination so much as a pragmatic common denominator designed to make agreement possible across the range of divergent cultural and political viewpoints.

It remains true, of course, that Western inspirations—and Western drafters—played the predominant role in the drafting of the document. Even so, the drafters' mood in 1947 was anything but triumphalist. They were aware, first of all, that the age of colonial emancipation was at hand: Indian independence was proclaimed while the language of the declaration was being finalized. Although the declaration does not specifically endorse self-determination, its drafters clearly foresaw the coming tide of struggles for national independence. Because it does proclaim the right of people to self-government and freedom of speech and religion, it also concedes the right of colonial peoples to construe moral universals in a language rooted in their own traditions. Whatever failings the drafters of the declaration may be accused of, unexamined Western triumphalism is not one of them. Key drafters such as René Cassin of France and John Humphrey of Canada knew the knell had sounded on two centuries of Western colonialism.

Western defenders of human rights have traded too much away.

They also knew that the declaration was not so much a proclamation of the superiority of European civilization as an attempt to salvage the remains of its Enlightenment heritage from the barbarism of a world war just concluded. The declaration was written in full awareness of Auschwitz and dawning awareness of Kolyma. A consciousness of European savagery is built into the very language of the declaration's preamble: "Whereas disregard and contempt for human rights have resulted in barbarous acts which have outraged the conscience of mankind ..."

The declaration may still be a child of the Enlightenment, but it was written when faith in the Enlightenment faced its deepest crisis. In this sense, human rights norms are not so much a declaration of the superiority of European civilization as a warning by Europeans that the rest of the world should not reproduce their mistakes. The chief of these was the idolatry of the nation-state, causing individuals to forget the higher law commanding them to disobey unjust orders. The abandonment of this moral heritage of natural law and the surrender of individualism to collectivism, the drafters believed, led to the catastrophes of Nazi and Stalinist oppression. Unless the disastrous heritage of European collectivism is kept in mind as the framing experience in the drafting of the declaration, its individualism will appear to be nothing more than the ratification of Western bourgeois capitalist prejudice. In fact, it was much more: a studied attempt to reinvent the European natural law tradition in order to safeguard individual agency against the totalitarian state.

THE POWER OF ONE

IT REMAINS TRUE, therefore, that the core of the declaration is the moral individualism for which it is so reproached by non-Western societies. It is this individualism for which Western activists have become most apologetic, believing that it should be tempered by greater emphasis on social duties and responsibilities to the community. Human rights, it is argued, can recover universal appeal only if they soften their individualistic bias and put greater emphasis on the communitarian parts of the declaration, especially Article 29, which says that "everyone has duties to the community in which alone the free and full development of his personality is possible." This desire to water down the individualism of rights discourse is driven by a desire both to make human rights more palatable to less individualistic cultures in the non-Western world and also to respond to disquiet among Western communitarians at the supposedly corrosive impact of individualistic values on Western social cohesion.

But this tack mistakes what rights actually are and misunderstands why they have proven attractive to millions of people raised in non-Western traditions. Rights are meaningful only if they confer entitlements and immunities on individuals; they are worth having only if they can be enforced against institutions such as the family, the state, and the church. This remains true even when the rights in question are collective or group rights. Some of these group rights—such as the right to speak your own language or practice your own religion—are essential preconditions for the exercise of individual rights. The right to speak a language of your choice will not mean very much if the language has died out. For this reason, group rights are needed to protect individual rights. But the ultimate purpose and justification of group rights is not the protection of the group as such but the protection of the individuals who compose it. Group rights to language, for example, must not be used to prevent an individual from learning a second language. Group rights to practice religion should not cancel the right of individuals to leave a religious community if they choose.

Rights are inescapably political because they tacitly imply a conflict between a rights holder and a rights "withholder," some authority against which the rights holder can make justified claims. To confuse rights with aspirations, and rights conventions with syncretic syntheses of world values, is to wish away the conflicts that define the very content of rights. Individuals and groups will always be in conflict, and rights exist to protect individuals. Rights language cannot be parsed or translated into a nonindividualistic, communitarian framework; it presumes moral individualism and is nonsensical outside that assumption.

Moreover, it is precisely this individualism that renders human rights attractive to non-Western peoples and explains why the fight for those rights has become a global movement. The language of human rights is the only universally available moral vernacular that validates the claims of women and children against the oppression they experience in patriarchal and tribal societies; it is the only vernacular that enables dependent persons to perceive themselves as moral agents and to act against practices—arranged marriages, purdah, civic disenfranchisement, genital mutilation, domestic slavery, and so on—that are ratified by the weight and authority of their cultures. These agents seek out human rights protection precisely because it legitimizes their protests against oppression.

> Rights doctrines challenge powerful religions, tribes, and authoritarian states.

If this is so, then it is necessary to rethink what it means when one says that rights are universal. Rights doctrines arouse powerful opposition because they challenge powerful religions, family structures, authoritarian states, and tribes. It would be a hopeless task to attempt to persuade these holders of power of the universal validity of rights doctrines, since if these doctrines prevailed, their exercise of authority would necessarily be abridged and constrained. Thus universality cannot imply universal assent, since in a world of unequal power, the only propositions that the powerful and powerless would agree on would be entirely toothless and anodyne. Rights are universal because they define the universal interests of the powerless—namely, that power be exercised over them in ways that respect their autonomy as agents. In this sense, human rights represent a revolutionary creed, since they make a radical demand of all human groups that they serve the interests of the individuals who compose them. This, then, implies that human groups should be, insofar as possible, consensual, or at least that they should respect an individual's right to exit when the constraints of the group become unbearable.

The idea that groups should respect an individual's right of exit is not easy to reconcile with what groups actually are. Most human groups—the family, for example—are blood groups, based on inherited kinship or ethnic ties. People do not choose to be born into them and do not leave them easily, since these collectivities provide the frame of meaning within which individual life makes sense. This is as true in modern secular societies as it is in religious or traditional ones. Group rights doctrines exist to safeguard the collective rights—for example, to language—that make individual agency meaningful and valuable. But individual and group interests inevitably conflict. Human rights exist to adjudicate these conflicts, to define the irreducible minimum beyond which group and collective claims must not go in constraining the lives of individuals.

CULTURE SHOCK

ADOPTING THE VALUES of individual agency does not necessarily entail adopting Western ways of life. Believing in your right not to be tortured or abused need not mean adopting Western dress, speaking Western languages, or approving of the Western lifestyle. To seek human rights protection is not to change your civilization; it is merely to avail yourself of the protections of what the philosopher Isaiah Berlin called "negative liberty": to be free from oppression, bondage, and gross physical harm.

Human rights do not, and should not, delegitimize traditional culture as a whole. The women in Kabul who come to human rights agencies seeking protection from the Taliban do not want to cease being Muslim wives and mothers; they want to combine their traditions with education and professional health care provided by a woman. And they hope the agencies will defend them against being beaten and persecuted for claiming such rights.

The legitimacy of such claims is reinforced by the fact that the people who make them are not foreign human rights activists or employees of international organizations but the victims themselves.

In Pakistan, for example, it is poor rural women who are criticizing the grotesque distortion of Islamic teaching that claims to justify "honor killings"—in which women are burned alive when they disobey their husbands. Human rights have gone global by going local, empowering the powerless, giving voice to the voiceless.

It is simply not the case, as Islamic and Asian critics contend, that human rights force the Western way of life on their societies. For all its individualism, human rights rhetoric does not require adherents to jettison their other cultural attachments. As the philosopher Jack Donnelly argues, human rights assume "that people probably are best suited, and in any case are entitled, to choose the good life for themselves." What the declaration does mandate is the right to choose, and specifically the right to exit a group when choice is denied. The global diffusion of rights language would never have occurred had these not been authentically attractive propositions to millions of people, especially women, in theocratic, traditional, or patriarchal societies.

Human rights should not delegitimize traditional culture.

Critics of this view would argue that it is too "voluntaristic"; it implies that individuals in traditional societies are free to choose the manner of their insertion into the global economy and free to choose which Western values to adopt and which to reject. In reality, these critics argue, people are not free to choose. Economic globalization steamrolls local economies, and moral globalization—human rights—follows behind as the legitimizing ideology of global capitalism. "Given the class interest of the internationalist class carrying out this agenda," law professor Kenneth Anderson writes, "the claim to universalism is a sham. Universalism is mere globalism and a globalism, moreover, whose key terms are established by capital."

This idea that human rights represent the moral arm of global capitalism falsifies the insurgent nature of the relationship between human rights activism and the global corporation. The activists of nongovernmental organizations (NGOs) who devote their lives to challenging the labor practices of global giants such as Nike and Royal Dutch/Shell would be astonished to discover that their human rights agenda has been serving the interests of global capital all along.

Anderson conflates globalism and internationalism and mixes up two classes, the free market globalists and the human rights internationalists, whose interests and values are in conflict.

Although free markets do encourage the emergence of assertively self-interested individuals, these individuals seek human rights in order to protect themselves from the indignities and indecencies of the market. Moreover, the dignity such individuals seek to protect is not necessarily derived from Western models. Anderson writes as if human rights were always imposed from the top down by an international elite bent on "saving the world." He ignores the extent to which the demand for human rights comes from the bottom up.

Indeed, what makes human rights demands legitimate is that they emanate from the bottom, from the powerless. Instead of apologizing for the individualism of Western human rights standards, activists need to attend to another problem, which is how to create conditions in which individuals on the bottom are free to avail themselves of such rights. Increasing the freedom of people to exercise their rights depends on close cultural understanding of the frameworks that often constrain choice.

The much debated issue of female circumcision illustrates this point. What may appear as mutilation in Western eyes is, in some cultures, simply the price of tribal and family belonging for women. Accordingly, if they fail to submit to the ritual, they lose their place in that world. Choosing to exercise their rights, therefore, may result in social ostracism, leaving them no option but to leave their tribe and make for the city. Human rights advocates should be aware of what it really means for a woman to abandon traditional practices under such circumstances. And activists have an equal duty to inform women of the medical costs and consequences of these practices and to seek, as a first step, to make them less dangerous for those who choose to undergo them.

As for the final decision, it is for women themselves to decide how to adjudicate between tribal and Western wisdom. The criteria of informed consent that regulate medical patients' choices in Western societies are equally applicable in non-Western settings, and human rights activists must respect the autonomy and dignity of agents. An activist's proper role is not to make the choices for the women in question but to enlarge those women's knowledge of what the choices entail. In traditional societies, harmful practices can be abandoned only when the whole community decides to do so. Otherwise, individuals who decide on their own face ostracism and worse. Consent in these cases means collective or group consent. Yet even group consent must be built on consultation with the individuals involved.

Sensitivity to the real constraints that limit individual freedom in different cultures is not the same thing as deferring to these cultures. It does not mean abandoning universality. It simply means facing up to a demanding intercultural dialogue in which all parties come to the table under common expectations of being treated as moral equals. Traditional society is oppressive for individuals within it, not because it fails to afford them a Western way of life, but because it does not accord them a right to speak and be heard. Western activists have no right to overturn traditional cultural practice, provided that such practice continues to receive the assent of its members. Human rights are universal not as a vernacular of cultural prescription but as a language of moral empowerment. Their role is not in defining the content of culture but in trying to enfranchise all agents so that they can freely shape that content.

The best way to face the cultural challenges to human rights coming from Asia, Islam, and Western postmodernism is to admit their truth: rights discourse is individualistic. But that is precisely why it has proven an effective remedy against tyranny, and why it has proven attractive to people from very different cultures. The other advantage of liberal individualism is that it is a distinctly "thin" theory of the human good: it defines and proscribes the "negative"—that is, those restraints and injustices that make any human life, however conceived, impossible; at the same time, it does not prescribe the "positive" range of good lives that human beings can lead. The doctrine of human rights is morally universal because it says that all human beings need certain specific freedoms "from"; it does not go on to define what their freedom "to" should comprise.[1] In

[1] These distinctions—negative liberty, positive liberty, freedom from, freedom to—are suggested by Isaiah Berlin, "Two Concepts of Liberty," in *The Proper Study of Mankind*, ed. Henry Hardy (London: Chatto and Windus, 1997), pp. 191–243; on "thin" theories of the good, see John Rawls, *A Theory of Justice* (Cambridge: Harvard University Press, 1970).

this sense, it is a less prescriptive universalism than the world's religions: it articulates standards of human decency without violating rights of cultural autonomy.

THE WEST AGAINST ITSELF

IN THE MORAL DISPUTE between the "West" and the "rest," both sides make the mistake of assuming that the other speaks with one voice. When the non-Western world looks at human rights, it assumes—rightly—that the discourse originates in a matrix of historical traditions shared by all the major Western countries. But these Western nations interpret the core principles of their own rights tradition very differently. A common tradition does not necessarily result in common points of view on rights. All of the formative rights cultures of the West—the English, the French, and the American—give a different account of such issues as privacy, free speech, incitement, the right to bear arms, and the right to life.

In the 50 years since the promulgation of the Universal Declaration of Human Rights, these disagreements have become more salient. Indeed, the moral unanimity of the West—always a myth more persuasive from the outside than from the inside—is breaking up and revealing its unalterable heterogeneity. American rights discourse once belonged to the common European natural law tradition and to British common law. But this awareness of a common anchorage now competes with a growing sense of American moral and legal exceptionalism.

American human rights policy in the last 20 years has been increasingly distinctive and paradoxical: it is the product of a nation with a great national rights tradition that leads the world in denouncing the human rights violations of others but refuses to ratify key international rights conventions itself. The most important resistance to the domestic application of international rights norms comes not from rogue states outside the Western tradition or from Islamic and Asian societies. It comes, in fact, from within the heart of the Western rights tradition itself, from a nation that, in linking rights to popular sovereignty, opposes international human rights oversight as an infringement on its democracy. Of all the ironies in the history of human rights since the signing of the Universal Declaration of Human

Rights, the one that would most astonish Eleanor Roosevelt is the degree to which her own country is now the odd one out.

In the next 50 years, the moral consensus that sustained the declaration in 1948 will continue to splinter. For all the rhetoric about common values, the distance between the United States and Europe on issues such as abortion and capital punishment may grow, just as the distance between the West and the rest may also increase. There is no reason to believe that economic globalization entails moral globalization. Indeed, there is some reason to think that as economies have unified their business practices, ownership, languages, and networks of communication, a countermovement has developed to safeguard the integrity of national communities, national cultures, religions, and indigenous and religious ways of life.

Disagreements within the competing Western rights traditions have become more salient over the last 50 years.

This is a prophecy not of the end of the human rights movement but of its belated coming of age, its recognition that we live in a world of plural cultures that have a right to equal consideration in the argument about what we can and cannot, should and should not, do to human beings. Indeed, this may be the central historical importance of human rights in the history of human progress: it has abolished the hierarchy of civilizations and cultures. As late as 1945, it was common to think of European civilization as inherently superior to the civilizations it ruled. Today many Europeans continue to believe this, but they know that they have no right to do so. More to the point, many non-Western peoples also took the civilizational superiority of their rulers for granted. They no longer have any reason to continue believing this. One reason for that is the global diffusion of human rights talk—the language that most consistently articulates the moral equality of all the individuals on the face of the earth. But to the degree that it does this, it simultaneously increases the level of conflict over the meaning, application, and legitimacy of rights claims.

Rights language states that all human beings belong at the table in the essential conversation about how we should treat each other. But once this universal right to speak and be heard is granted, there is bound to be tumult. There is bound to be discord. Why? Because the

European voices that once took it upon themselves to silence the babble with a peremptory ruling no longer take it as their privilege to do so, and those who sit with them at the table no longer grant them the right to do so. All this counts as progress, as a step toward a world imagined for millennia in different cultures and religions: a world of genuine moral equality among human beings. But a world of moral equality is a world of conflict, deliberation, argument, and contention.

We need to stop thinking of human rights as trumps and begin thinking of them as part of a language that creates the basis for deliberation. In this argument, the ground we share may actually be quite limited—not much more than the basic intuition that what is pain and humiliation for you is bound to be pain and humiliation for me. But this is already something. In such a future, shared among equals, rights are not the universal credo of a global society, not a secular religion, but something much more limited and yet just as valuable: the shared vocabulary from which our arguments can begin, and the bare human minimum from which differing ideas of human flourishing can take root.

[12]

International Humanitarian Law and Human Rights Law

by **Louise Doswald-Beck**
and Sylvain Vité

Introduction

International humanitarian law is increasingly perceived as part of human rights law applicable in armed conflict. This trend can be traced back to the United Nations Human Rights Conference held in Tehran in 1968[1] which not only encouraged the development of humanitarian law itself, but also marked the beginning of a growing use by the United Nations of humanitarian law during its examination of the human rights situation in certain countries or during its thematic studies. The greater awareness of the relevance of humanitarian law to the protection of people in armed conflict, coupled with the increasing use of human rights law in international affairs, means that both these areas of law now have a much greater international profile and are regularly being used together in the work of both international and non-governmental organizations.

However, as human rights law and humanitarian law have totally different historical origins, the codification of these laws has until very recently followed entirely different lines. The purpose of this paper is to consider the philosophy of these two branches of law in the light of their origins, how in many essential respects they nevertheless coincide, how they have influenced each other in recent developments and, finally, to consider how their similarities and differences could influence their future use.

---

[1] Resolution XXIII "Human Rights in Armed Conflicts" adopted by the International Conference on Human Rights, Tehran, 12 May 1968.

Origin and nature of human rights law and humanitarian law

The philosophy of humanitarian law

Restrictions on hostile activities are to be found in many cultures and typically originate in religious values and the development of military philosophies. The extent to which these customs resemble each other is of particular interest and in general their similarities relate both to the expected behaviour of combatants between themselves and to the need to spare non-combatants.[2] Traditional manuals of humanitarian law cite the basic principles of this law as being those of military necessity, humanity and chivalry.[3] The last criterion seems out of place in the modern world, but it is of importance for an understanding of the origin and nature of humanitarian law.

The first factor of importance is that humanitarian law was developed at a time when recourse to force was not illegal as an instrument of national policy. Although it is true that one of the influences on the development of the law in Europe was the church's just war doctrine,[4] which also encompassed the justice of resorting to force, the foundations of international humanitarian law were laid at a time when there was no disgrace in beginning a war. The motivation for restraint in behaviour during war stemmed from notions of what was considered to be honourable and, in the nineteenth century in particular, what was perceived as civilized.[5] The law was therefore in large part based on the appropriate respect that was due to another professional army. We will use here as a good illustration of the philosophy underlying the customary law of war the Lieber Code of 1863,[6] as this code was

---

[2] For an interesting survey of these customs from different parts of the world, see Part 1 of *International Dimensions of Humanitarian Law*, UNESCO, Paris, Henry Dunant Institute, Geneva, 1988.

[3] See, for example, L. Oppenheim, *International Law*, Volume II, *Disputes, War and Neutrality*, Seventh edition, Longmans and Green, London, 1952, pp. 226-227.

[4] For a good summary of these doctrines, see S. Bailey *Prohibitions and Restraints in War*, Oxford University Press, 1972, Chapter 1.

[5] There are frequent references in the preambles of nineteenth century humanitarian law instruments to civilization requiring restraints in warfare, for example, the Declaration of St. Petersburg of 1868 to the effect of prohibiting the use of certain projectiles in war time: "*Considering that the progress of civilization should have the effect of alleviating as much as possible the calamities of war...*" ; 1899 Hague Convention II with Respect to the Laws and Customs of War on Land: "*Animated by the desire to serve... the interests of humanity and the ever increasing requirements of civilization...*".

[6] *Instructions for the Government of Armies in the Field*, 24 April 1863,

used as the principal basis for the development of the Hague Conventions of 1899 and 1907 which in turn influenced later developments.

The relevance of war being a lawful activity at the time is reflected in Article 67 of the Lieber Code:

"The law of nations allows every sovereign government to make war upon another sovereign state, and, therefore, admits of no rules or laws different from those of regular warfare, regarding the treatment of prisoners of war, although they may belong to the army of a government which the captor may consider as a wanton and unjust assailant".

The law was therefore based on what was considered necessary to defeat the enemy and outlawed what was perceived as unnecessary cruelty:

"Military necessity, as understood by modern civilized nations, consists in the necessity of those measures which are indispensable for securing the ends of the war, and which are lawful according to the modern law and usages of war" (Art. 14).

"Military necessity does not admit of cruelty — that is, the infliction of suffering for the sake of suffering or for revenge, nor of maiming or wounding except in fight, nor of torture to extort confessions. It does not admit of the use of poison in any way, nor of the wanton devastation of a district..." (Art. 16).

Two basic rules of international humanitarian law, namely the protection of civilians and the decent treatment of prisoners of war, are described in the following terms:

"Nevertheless, as civilization has advanced during the last centuries, so has likewise steadily advanced, especially in war on land, the distinction between the private individual belonging to a hostile country and the hostile country itself, with its men in arms. The principle has been more and more acknowledged that the unarmed citizen is to be spared in person, property, and honour as much as the exigencies of war will admit" (Art. 22).

The importance of respectful treatment of prisoners of war is referred to as follows:

---

prepared by Francis Lieber during the American Civil War, and promulgated by President Lincoln as General Orders N° 100. Reproduced in Schindler and Toman, eds., *The Laws of Armed Conflicts*, Martinus Nijhoff Publishers, Dordrecht, Henry Dunant Institute, Geneva, 1988.

"A prisoner of war is subject to no punishment for being a public enemy, nor is any revenge wreaked upon him by the intentional infliction of any suffering, or disgrace, by cruel imprisonment, want of food, by mutilation, death, or any other barbarity" (Art. 56).

"Honorable men, when captured, will abstain from giving to the enemy information concerning their own army, and the modern law of war permits no longer the use of any violence against prisoners in order to extort the desired information or to punish them for having given false information" (Art. 80).

On the protection of hospitals the Lieber Code states:

"Honorable belligerents often request that the hospitals within the territory of the enemy may be designated, so that they may be spared..." (Art. 116).

"It is justly considered an act of bad faith, of infamy or fiendishness, to deceive the enemy by flags of protection..." (Art. 117).

The chapter relating to occupied territory specifies the action that an occupier may take for military purposes, in particular levying taxes and similar measures, but is very clear about the types of abuses that are prohibited:

"All wanton violence committed against persons in the invaded country, all destruction of property not commanded by the authorized officer, all robbery, all pillage or sacking, even after taking a place by main force, all rape, wounding, maiming, or killing of such inhabitants, are prohibited under the penalty of death, or such other severe punishment as may seem adequate for the gravity of the offense.

A soldier, officer or private, in the act of committing such violence, and disobeying a superior ordering him to abstain from it, may be lawfully killed on the spot by such superior"[7] (Art. 44).

Finally, in this small selection of articles, mention should be made of Lieber's caution to States in their resort to reprisals which were still generally considered lawful at that time:

"Retaliation will ... never be resorted to as a measure of mere revenge, but only as a means of protective retribution, and moreover, cautiously and unavoidably; that is to say, retaliation shall only be

[7] Needless to say, this punishment would these days be a violation of the right to fair trial of the accused, which is reflected in Article 75 of 1977 Protocol I and equally applies to the treatment of a party's own soldiers.

resorted to after careful inquiry into the real occurrence, and the character of the misdeeds that may demand retribution.

Unjust or inconsiderate retaliation removes the belligerents farther and farther from the mitigating rules of regular war, and by rapid steps leads them nearer to the internecine wars of savages" (Art. 28).

The Lieber Code was regarded at the time as generally reflecting customary law although in places it particularly stressed the importance of respecting humanitarian treatment which, in practice, was not always accorded. The Code was used as the basis for the first attempted codification of these customs at the Brussels Conference of 1874. Although the conference was not successful in adopting a treaty, the declaration which was adopted is very similar to the Hague Regulations of 1899 and 1907. Those Regulations are considerably less complete than the Lieber Code, and, like later treaties, do not expressly include the explanation for the rules as does the Lieber Code.

The fundamental concepts of the laws of war have remained essentially unchanged and are still based on the balance between military necessity and humanity, although less reference is now made to chivalry. The major characteristic of humanitarian law which first tends to strike a human rights lawyer is the fact that the law makes allowance in its provisions for actions necessary for military purposes. Much of it may therefore not seem very "humanitarian", and indeed many lawyers and military personnel still prefer to use the traditional name, "the law of war" or "the law of armed conflict." The way in which humanitarian law incorporates military necessity within its provisions is of particular interest when comparing the protection afforded by this branch of law and human rights law.

Military necessity has been defined as:

"Measures of regulated force not forbidden by international law which are indispensable for securing the prompt submission of the enemy, with the least possible expenditure of economic and human resources".[8]

The Lieber Code describes military necessity as follows:

"Military necessity admits of all direct destruction of life or limb of armed enemies, and of other persons whose destruction is incidentally

---

[8] *U.S. Air Force Law of War Manual.* There are similar definitions published in the United States Manual FM 27-10 and in the German Manual ZDv 15/10.

unavoidable in the armed contests of the war; it allows of the capturing of every armed enemy, and every enemy of importance to the hostile government, or of peculiar danger to the captor; it allows of all destruction of property, and obstruction of the ways and channels of traffic, travel, or communication, and of all withholding of sustenance or means of life from the enemy; of the appropriation of whatever an enemy's country affords necessary for the subsistence and safety of the army, and of such deception as does not involve the breaking of good faith either positively pledged, regarding agreements entered into during the war, or supposed by the modern law of war to exist. Men who take up arms against one another in public war do not cease on this account to be moral beings, responsible to one another and to God" (Art. 15).

The fact that military necessity is included in the rules of humanitarian law is well explained in the German Military Manual as follows:

"Military necessity has been already taken into consideration by the conventions on the law of war, because the law of war constitutes a compromise between the necessities to obtain the aims of war and the principles of humanity".[9]

This balance between military necessity[10] and humanity is broadly speaking achieved in four different ways.[11] First, some actions do not have any military value at all and are therefore simply prohibited, for example, sadistic acts of cruelty, pillage and other private rampages by soldiers which, far from helping the military purpose of the army, tend to undermine professional disciplined behaviour. In this respect it is worth recalling that many of the early customs of war, which were set down in written instructions to armies,[12] were motivated by a desire to encourage discipline.

Secondly, some acts may have a certain military value, but it has been accepted that humanitarian considerations override these. On this basis, the use of poison and toxic gases has been prohibited.

---

[9] ZDv 15/10.

[10] For a very good analysis of the concept of military necessity, see E. Rauch, "Le concept de nécessité militaire dans le droit de la guerre", *Revue de droit pénal militaire et de droit de la guerre*, 1980, p. 205.

[11] See G. Schwarzenberger, *International Law as applied by International Courts and Tribunals*, Volume II, *The Law of Armed Conflict*, Stevens, London, 1968, pp. 10-12. These are not legal categories, but rather a conceptual way of grouping the different methods used for this purpose.

[12] *Ibid.* at pp. 15-16.

Thirdly, some rules are a true compromise in that both the military and the humanitarian needs are accepted as important to certain actions and consequently consideration of both is limited to some extent. An example is the rule of proportionality in attacks, which accepts that civilians will suffer "incidental damage" (the limitation with respect to humanitarian needs), but that such attacks must not take place if the incidental damage would be excessive in relation to the value of the target (the limitation with respect to military needs).

Finally, some provisions allow the military needs in a particular situation to override the normally applicable humanitarian rule. Conceptually, these provisions resemble more closely the limitation clauses commonly found in human rights treaties. Some provisions introduce the limitation within the body of the protective rule, for example, medical personnel cannot be attacked unless they engage in hostile military behaviour. Secondly, certain protective actions required by the law are restricted by the military situation. For example, parties to a conflict are to take "all possible measures" to carry out the search for the wounded[13] and dead, and "whenever circumstances permit" they are to arrange truces to permit the removal of the wounded. There are also a number of limitation clauses that refer directly to military necessity. For example, immunity may in *"exceptional cases of unavoidable military necessity"* be withdrawn from cultural property under special protection.[14] Other examples are Article 53 of the Fourth Geneva Convention which prohibits the destruction of property by occupying authorities in occupied territory *"except where such destruction is rendered absolutely necessary by military operations"*, and Article 54 of 1977 Protocol I which allows the destruction of objects indispensable to the survival of the civilian population in a party's own territory when this is *"required by imperative military necessity"*.

Unlike human rights law, however, there is no concept of derogation in humanitarian law. Derogation in human rights law is allowed in most general treaties in times of war or other emergency threatening the life of the nation.[15] Humanitarian law is made precisely for those

---

[13] Article 15, First Geneva Convention of 1949.

[14] Article 11, 1954 Hague Convention for the Protection of Cultural Property in the Event of Armed Conflict.

[15] Article 4 of the International Covenant on Civil and Political Rights, 1966; Article 15 of the European Convention on Human Rights, 1950; Article 27 of the American Convention on Human Rights, 1969. Curiously, the African Charter on Human and Peoples' Rights contains no derogation clause, but in general it has more far-reaching limitation clauses.

situations, and the rules are fashioned in a manner that will not undermine the ability of the army in question to win the war. Thus in order to cease respecting the law an army cannot, for example, invoke the fact that it is losing for such violation of the law will not be of sufficient genuine military help to reverse the situation.

The philosophy of human rights law

Turning now to the nature of human rights law, we see that the origin of this law is actually very different and that this has affected its formulation.

The first thing that is noticed when reading human rights treaties is that they are arranged in a series of assertions, each assertion setting forth a right that all individuals have by virtue of the fact that they are human. Thus the law concentrates on the value of the persons themselves, who have the right to expect the benefit of certain freedoms and forms of protection. As such we immediately see a difference in the manner in which humanitarian law and human rights treaties are worded. The former indicates how a party to a conflict is to behave in relation to people at its mercy, whereas human rights law concentrates on the rights of the recipients of a certain treatment.

The second difference in the appearance of the treaty texts is that humanitarian law seems long and complex, whereas human rights treaties are comparatively short and simple.

Thirdly, there is a phenomenon in human rights law which is quite alien to humanitarian law, namely, the concurrent existence of both universal and regional treaties, and also the fact that most of these treaties make a distinction between so-called "civil and political rights" and "economic, social and cultural" rights. The legal difference between these treaties is that the "civil and political" ones require instant respect for the rights enumerated therein, whereas the "economic, social and cultural" ones require the State to take appropriate measures in order to achieve a progressive realization of these rights. The scene has been further complicated by the appearance of so-called "third generation" human rights, namely, universal rights such as the right to development, the right to peace, etc.

We have seen that humanitarian law originated in notions of honourable and civilized behaviour that should be expected from professional armies. Human rights law, on the other hand, has less clearly-defined origins. There are a number of theories that have been used as a basis for human rights law, including those stemming from religion (i.e. the law of God which binds all humans), the law of nature which is permanent and which should be respected, positivist utilitarianism and socialist movements.[16] However, most people would point to theories by influential writers, such as John Locke, Thomas Paine or Jean-Jacques Rousseau, as having prompted the major developments in human rights in revolutionary constitutions of the eighteenth and nineteenth centuries. These theorists of the natural law school pondered on the relationship between the government and the individual in order to define the basis for a just society. They founded their theories on analysis of the nature of human beings and their relationships with each other and came to conclusions as to the best means of assuring mutual respect and protection. The most commonly cited "classical" natural lawyer is Locke, whose premise is that the state of nature is one of peace, goodwill, mutual assistance and preservation. In his opinion the protection of private rights assures the protection of the common good because people have the right to protect themselves and the obligation to respect the same right of others. However, as the state of nature lacks organization, he saw government as a "social contract" according to which people confer power on the understanding that the government will retain its justification only if it protects those natural rights. He generally referred to them as "life, liberty and estate". Positivist human rights theorists,[17] on the other hand, do not feel bound by any overriding natural law but rather base their advocacy for human rights protection on reason which shows that cooperation and mutual respect are the most advantageous behaviour for both individuals and society. The other important factor to be taken into account in the development of human rights is the existence of various cultural traditions and advocates for social development.[18] Although coming from different starting points, these influences stressed the importance of providing means to maintain life as well as assuring protection from economic and social exploitation. A particularly important development which influenced later human rights law was the creation of the International Labour Organization in 1919

[16] For a good presentation of the different human rights theories, see J. Shestack, "The Jurisprudence of Human Rights" in T. Meron, ed., *Human Rights in International Law*, Oxford University Press, London, 1984, Volume 1, p. 69.

[17] In particular J. Bentham and J. Austin, in T. Meron, ed., *ibid.* p. 79.

[18] Marx is commonly cited as the origin of this social development, but he was not the only theorist of that period to speak of the importance of social and economic rights. We may refer in particular to Thomas Paine who proposed, in *The Rights of Man*, a plan which resembles a type of social security system, including children's allowances, old-age pensions, maternity, marriage and funeral allowances, and publicly endowed employment for the poor.

which made major efforts, through the development of treaties and the installation of supervisory mechanisms, to improve economic and social (including health) conditions for workers.[19]

As the development of human rights progressed from theories of social organization to law, it is not surprising that lawyers began to analyse the nature of these rights from the legal theory point of view. Thus there is a plethora of articles arguing over whether human rights are really legal rights if the beneficiary cannot insist on their implementation in court.[20] The focus of this argument is on the nature of economic and social rights, which many legal theorists argue cannot therefore be described as legal rights.

However, the first major international instrument defining "human rights", namely the 1948 Universal Declaration of Human Rights, contains not only civil and political but also economic and social rights. In drafting it a conscious effort was made to take into account the different philosophies as to the appropriate content of human rights. It was only when the attempt was made to transform this document into international treaty law that the legal difficulties outlined above made themselves felt. The International Covenant on Civil and Political Rights (CP Covenant), 1966, requires each State Party to *"respect and to ensure to all individuals ...the rights recognized in the present Covenant..."*.[21] On the other hand, the International Covenant on Economic, Social and Cultural Rights (ESC Covenant),1966, requires each State Party to *"take steps, individually and through international assistance and co-operation, especially economic and technical, to the maximum of its available resources, with a view to achieving progressively the full realization of the rights recognized in the present Covenant..."*.[22] The main difference is that civil and political rights are perceived as not requiring any particular level of economic development, as for the most part they consist in individual freedoms. Yet it would not be accurate to say that respect for the CP Covenant does not involve the creation of certain State structures. In particular, the right to fair trial calls for certain infrastructures and professional training, and the same is true as regards the political

[19] For a general article on the work of the ILO, see F. Wolf, "Human Rights and the International Labour Organization" in T. Meron, ed., *Human Rights and International Law, op.cit.*, No. 16 above, Volume II, p. 273.

[20] See in particular M. Cranston, *What Are Human Rights?*, 1973. Also, Dowrick, *Human Rights, Problems, Perspectives and Texts*, Saxon House, Farnborough, 1979.

[21] Article 2.

[22] Article 2.

rights listed in Article 25. However, it is a fact that the implementation of most of the economic rights does necessitate some resources and thought as to the best economic arrangement in order to achieve the best standard of living possible. The genuine difficulty thus created in giving a proper interpretation to the ESC Covenant in the particular circumstances of each State has a direct effect on the nature of the individual's economic rights.[23] In 1987 a committee was created in order to examine the reports submitted by States under the Covenant. Such a committee was not originally provided for, and although its creation would appear to show a willingness to examine the implementation of this instrument more carefully, the committee is finding that States are still somewhat reticent about having their economic policies carefully analysed by an international body in order to assess whether they are compatible with the Covenant.[24]

A further development of importance in the philosophy underlying human rights law is the appearance of what are commonly referred to as "third generation" rights.[25] Third World States have in particular pointed out that in order to be able to show proper respect for economic and social rights, the appropriate economic resources are required, and that for this purpose they have a right to development. Other rights in this category are, for example, the right to peace or to a decent environment. It is clear that these factors have a direct effect on the quality of individuals' lives or even their very existence, but legal purists again indicate here that it is not possible to categorize these as human rights as they cannot be implemented by a court and also because the specific corresponding legal duties are unclear.

What is certain, however, is that these doctrinal differences with regard to economic and social rights and third generation rights have resulted in seriously divergent interpretations of human rights obligations, in terms both of what they really entail (economic and social) and of the extent to which they exist, if at all (third generation). Some doubt has even been expressed recently as to the universality of civil and political rights.[26] Although it is true that there are some differ-

---

[23] Illustrative of this problem is the extensive discussion of how the right to food should be implemented in P. Alston and K. Tomasevski, eds., *The Right to Food*, SIM, Utrecht, 1984.

[24] See P. Alston, "The Committee on Economic, Social and Cultural Rights" in P. Alston, ed., *The United Nations and Human Rights*, 1992.

[25] For a general article on this subject see K. Drzewicki, "The Rights of Solidarity — the Third Revolution of Human Rights", 53 *Nordisk Tidsskrift for International Ret*, 1984, p. 26.

[26] There are various articles on the subject in Interculture, Volume XVII,

ences in the terms of the United Nations Covenant, the European Convention, the Inter-American Convention and the African Charter, it is the opinion of these authors that their similarities are far more evident, and that they are essentially the same in their protection of basic civil rights and freedoms. Further, the extent to which the United Nations now investigates certain human rights violations, irrespective of whether the State concerned is a party to one of these treaties, indicates that it considers the rights concerned to be customary.

Conceptual similarities in present-day humanitarian law and human rights law

Having looked at the origins and formulation of these two areas of law, we can now turn to their present method of interpretation and implementation.

The most important change as far as humanitarian law is concerned is the fact that recourse to war is no longer a legal means of regulating conflict. In general, humanitarian law is now less perceived as a code of honour for combatants than as a means of sparing non-combatants as much as possible from the horrors of war.[27] From a purist human rights point of view, based as it is on respect for human life and well-being, the use of force is in itself a violation of human rights. This was indeed stated at the 1968 Human Rights Conference in Tehran as follows:

"Peace is the underlying condition for the full observance of human rights and war is their negation".[28]

However, the same conference went on to recommend further developments in humanitarian law in order to ensure a better protection of war victims.[29] This was an acknowledgement, therefore, that

---

Nos. 1-2 1984. An interesting address on "The universality of human rights and their relevance to developing countries" was also given by Dr. Shashi Tharoor at the Friedrich Naumann Stiftung Conference on Human Rights, Sintra, Portugal, 14-16 November 1988 (available from UNHCR).

[27] The main justification of the continued applicability of humanitarian law is that most of the rules have as their aim the protection of the vulnerable in armed conflicts and that these rules can be applied in practice only if they are applicable to both sides. Further, as with human rights philosophy, humanitarian law has as its major premise the applicability of protection to all persons, irrespective of whether the individuals are perceived as "good" or "bad".

[28] Note 1 above.

[29] *Ibid.*

humanitarian law is an effective mechanism for the protection of people in armed conflict and that such protection remains necessary because unfortunately the legal prohibition of the use of force has not in reality stopped armed conflicts.

A conceptual question of importance is whether human rights law can be applied at all times, thus in armed conflict as well, given that the philosophical basis of human rights is that by virtue of the fact that people are human, they always possess them. The answer in one sense is that they do continue to be applicable. The difficulty as regards human rights treaties is that most of them allow parties to derogate from most provisions in time of war, with the exception of what are commonly termed "hard-core" rights, i.e., those which all such treaties list as being non-derogable. These are the right to life, the prohibition of torture and other inhuman treatment, the prohibition of slavery and the prohibition of retroactive criminal legislation or punishment. However, the other rights do not thereby cease to be applicable, but must be respected in so far as this is possible in the circumstances. Recent jurisprudence and the practice adopted by human rights implementation mechanisms have stressed the importance of this, and also, in particular, the continued applicability of certain judicial guarantees that are essential in order to give effective protection to the "hard-core" rights.[30] However, the major difficulty of applying human rights law as enunciated in the treaties is the very general nature of the treaty language. Even outside armed conflict situations, we see that the documents attempt to deal with the relationship between the individual and society by the use of limitation clauses. Thus the manner in which the rights may be applied in practice must be interpreted by the organs instituted to implement the treaty in question. Although the United Nations Human Rights Committee, created by the CP Covenant, has made some general statements on the meaning of certain articles,[31] the

[30] See in particular:
- For the Human Rights Committee: *Lanza de Netto, Weismann and Perdomo v. Uruguay*, Com. No. R.2/8, A/35/40, Annex IV, paragraph 15; *Camargo v. Colombia*, Com. No. R.11/45, Annex XI, paragraph 12.2.
- European Court of Human Rights: *Lawless Case (Merits)*, Judgment of 1st July 1961, paragraph 20 ff.; *Ireland v. United Kingdom*, Judgment of 18 January 1978, Series A No. 25, paragraph 202 ff.
- For the Inter-American Court of Human Rights: *Habeas corpus in emergency situations*, Advisory opinion OC-8/87 of 30 January 1987; *Judicial guarantees in states of emergency*, Advisory opinion OC-9/87 of 6 October 1987.

[31] See in particular the following general observations:
5(13) on Article 4 of the Covenant, A/36/40, Annex VII;
7(16) on Article 7 of the Covenant, A/37/40, Annex V;

normal method of interpretation by both the United Nations and regional systems has been through a decision or an opinion on whether a particular set of facts constitutes a violation of the article in question. A study of this jurisprudence shows that although at first sight an assertion of an individual right may seem very favourable to the individual, its interpretation in practice reduces its implementation considerably in order to take into account the needs of others.[32] Now, if we transfer this to a situation of armed conflict, we can appreciate straight away the inconvenience of having to wait for decisions as to whether every action that takes place is justifiable or not, as the protection of people in armed conflict is usually literally a matter of life or death at that very moment. What is needed, therefore, is a code of action applicable in advance. Human rights lawyers have consequently turned to humanitarian law because, despite its different origins and formulation, compliance with it has the result of protecting the most essential human rights both of the "civil" and the "economic and social" type. The major legal difference is that humanitarian law is not formulated as a series of rights, but rather as a series of duties that combatants have to obey. This does have one very definite advantage from the legal theory point of view, in that humanitarian law is not subject to the kind of arguments that continue to plague the implementation of economic and social rights.

As space does not allow us to go into a detailed assessment of the similarities between human rights law and humanitarian law, we shall limit ourselves here to an impressionistic overview of the most important provisions of humanitarian law that help to protect the most fundamental human rights in practice.

The most important general observation to be made is that, like human rights law, humanitarian law is based on the premise that the protection accorded to victims of war must be without any discrimination. This is such a fundamental rule of human rights that it is specified not only in the United Nations Charter but also in all human rights treaties. One of many examples in humanitarian law is Article 27 of the Fourth Geneva Convention of 1949:

"...all protected persons shall be treated with the same consideration by the Party to the conflict in whose power they are, without

---

8(16) on Article 9 of the Covenant, A/37/40, Annex V;
13(21) on Article 14 of the Covenant, A/39/40, Annex VI.

[32] See Higgins, "Derogations under Human Rights Treaties", *British Yearbook of International Law*, 1976-1977, 281.

any adverse distinction based, in particular, on race, religion or political opinion".

Given the obvious risk to life in armed conflict, a great deal of humanitarian law is devoted to its protection, thus having a direct beneficial effect on the right to life. First and foremost, victims of war, i.e. those persons directly in the power of the enemy, are not to be murdered as this amounts to an unnecessary act of cruelty. These persons are mainly protected by the 1949 Geneva Conventions, with some extension of this protection in 1977 Additional Protocol I. As far as the protection of life during hostilities is concerned, it is obvious that the lives of combatants cannot be protected whilst they are still fighting. However, humanitarian law is not totally silent even here, for the rule that prohibits the use of weapons of a nature to cause superfluous injury or unnecessary suffering is partly aimed at outlawing those weapons that cause an excessively high death rate among soldiers.[33] With regard to civilians, we have seen that the customary law of the nineteenth century required that they be spared as much as possible. Military tactics at the time made this possible, and civilians were less affected by direct attacks than by starvation during sieges, or shortages due to the use of their resources by occupying troops. However, military developments in the twentieth century, in particular the introduction of bombardment by aircraft or missiles, seriously jeopardized this customary rule.

The most important contribution of Protocol I of 1977 is the careful delimitation of what can be done during hostilities in order to spare civilians as much as possible. The balance between military necessities and humanitarian needs that was explained in the Lieber Code continues to be at the basis of this law, and the States that negotiated this treaty had this firmly in mind so as to codify a law that was acceptable to their military staff. The result is a reaffirmation of the limitation of attacks to military objectives and a definition of what this means,[34] but accepting the occurrence of "incidental loss of civilian life" subject to the principle of proportionality.[35] This is the provision

[33] The most recent codification of the prohibition of the use of weapons of a nature to cause unnecessary suffering is in Article 35(b) of 1977 Protocol I. This reasoning, however, is most clearly stated in the St. Petersburg Declaration of 1868: *"...the only legitimate object which States should endeavour to accomplish during war is to weaken the military forces of the enemy... this object would be exceeded by the disabled men, or render their death inevitable..."*

[34] Articles 48 and 52.

[35] Article 52(5)(b).

that probably grates most with human rights lawyers, not only because it in effect allows the killing of civilians but also because the assessment of whether an attack may be expected to cause excessive incidental losses, and therefore should not take place, has to be made by the military commander concerned. On the other hand, the Protocol protects life in a way that goes beyond the traditional civil right to life. First, it prohibits the starvation of civilians as a method of warfare and consequently the destruction of their means of survival[36] (which is an improvement on earlier customary law). Secondly, it offers means for improving their chance of survival by, for example, providing for the declaration of special zones that contain no military objectives[37] and consequently may not be attacked. Thirdly, there are various stipulations in the Geneva Conventions and their Additional Protocols that the wounded must be collected and given the medical care that they need. In human rights treaties this would fall into the category of "economic and social rights".[38] Fourthly, the Geneva Conventions and their Protocols specify in considerable detail the physical conditions that are needed in order to sustain life in as reasonable a condition as possible in an armed conflict. Thus, for example, the living conditions required for prisoners of war are described in the Third Geneva Convention and similar requirements are also laid down for civilian persons interned in an occupied territory. With regard to the general population, an occupying power is required to ensure that the people as a whole have the necessary means of survival and to accept outside relief shipments if necessary to achieve this purpose.[39] There are also provisions for relief for the Parties' own populations, but they are not as absolute as those that apply in occupied territory.[40] Once again, these kinds of provisions would be categorized by a human rights lawyer as "economic and

[36] Article 54.

[37] Articles 14 and 15 of the Fourth Geneva Convention and Articles 59 and 60 of 1977 Protocol I. It should be noted, however, that a non-defended area was protected from bombardment in customary law.

[38] Article 12 of the ESC Covenant recognizes that everyone has the right to "*the enjoyment of the highest attainable standard of physical and mental health*". This goes much further of course than what is provided for in humanitarian law, but it is the only human rights provision under which the right to receive needed medical treatment could be categorized.

[39] Article 55 of the Fourth Geneva Convention and Article 69 of Additional Protocol I.

[40] Article 23 of the Fourth Geneva Convention and Article 70 of Additional Protocol I.

social".[41] Finally in this selection of provisions relevant to the right to life, humanitarian law lays down restrictions on the imposition of the death penalty, in particular, by requiring a delay of at least six months between the sentence and its execution, by providing for supervisory mechanisms, and by prohibiting the death sentence from being pronounced on persons under eighteen or being carried out on pregnant women or mothers of young children. Also of interest is the fact that an occupying power cannot use the death penalty in a country which has abolished it.[42]

The next "hard-core" right is that no one shall be subjected to torture or to cruel, inhuman or degrading treatment or punishment. Humanitarian law also contains an absolute prohibition of such behaviour, and not only states this prohibition explicitly in all the appropriate places[43] but goes still further, since a large part of the Geneva Conventions can be said in practice to be a detailed description of how to carry out one's duty to treat victims humanely.

As far as the prohibition of slavery is concerned, this is explicitly laid down in 1977 Protocol II;[44] the possibility of slavery is furthermore precluded by the various forms of protection given elsewhere in the Geneva Conventions. It is interesting to note in particular that this prohibition was well established in customary law, and is reflected in the Lieber Code's articles on the treatment of prisoners of war, who are not to be seen as the property of those who captured them,[45] and on the treatment of the population in occupied territory.[46]

As mentioned above,[47] human rights bodies are now recognizing the importance of judicial guarantees to protect hard-core rights although, with the exception of the Inter-American Convention, these are unfortunately not expressly listed as non-derogable. If human rights specialists had at an earlier stage taken a close interest in humanitarian law, they would have noted the extensive inclusion of judicial guarantees in the Geneva Conventions. This is because those drawing up humanitarian law treaties had seen from experience the

---

[41] Article 11 of the ESC Covenant recognizes the right of everyone to "an adequate standard of living... including adequate food, clothing and housing".

[42] Articles 68 and 75 of the Fourth Geneva Convention.

[43] For example, Article 3 common to the Geneva Conventions prohibits "violence to life and person, in particular murder of all kinds, mutilation, cruel treatment and torture".

[44] Article 4(2)(f).

[45] Article 74 in particular.

[46] Articles 42 and 43 in particular.

[47] Page 106.

crucial importance of judicial control in order to avoid arbitrary executions and other inhuman treatment.

The protection of children and family life is also given a great deal of importance in humanitarian law. It is taken into account in a number of different ways, such as the provision made for children's education and physical care, the separation of children from adults if interned (unless they are members of the same family), and special provisions for children who are orphaned or separated from their families.[48] The family is protected as far as possible by rules that help prevent its separation by keeping members of dispersed families informed of their respective situation and whereabouts and by transmitting letters between them.[49]

Respect for religious faith is also taken into account in humanitarian law, not only by stipulating that prisoners of war and detained civilians may practise their own religion,[50] but also by providing for ministers of religion who are given special protection.[51] In addition the Geneva Conventions stipulate that if possible the dead are to be given burial according to the rites of their own religion.[52]

This very brief review is by no means an exhaustive list of the ways in which humanitarian law overlaps with human rights norms. However, it should be noted that there are a number of human rights, such as the right of association and the political rights, that are not included in humanitarian law because they are not perceived as being of relevance to the protection of persons from the particular dangers of armed conflict.

The mutual influence of human rights and humanitarian law

The separate development of these two branches of international law has always limited the influence which they might have had upon each other. However, their present convergence, as described above,

---

[48] For further detail, see D. Plattner, "Protection of children in international humanitarian law", *IRRC*, No. 240, May-June 1984, pp. 140-152.

[49] The articles are too numerous to list individually, but the majority are to be found in the Third and Fourth Geneva Conventions and their Additional Protocols.

[50] Article 34, Third Geneva Convention, and Articles 27 and 38(3), Fourth Geneva Convention.

[51] Articles 33 and 35-37, Third Geneva Convention, and Articles 38(3), 58 and 93, Fourth Geneva Convention.

[52] Article 17, First Geneva Convention; Article 120, Third Geneva Convention; Article 130, Fourth Geneva Convention.

makes the establishment of certain closer links between these two legal domains conceivable.

In this connection, Article 3 common to the Four Geneva Conventions is revealing. A real miniature treaty within the Conventions, common Article 3 lays down the basic rules which States are required to respect when confronted with armed groups on their own territory. It thus diverges from the traditional approach of humanitarian law which, in principle, did not concern itself with the relations between a State and its nationals.[53] Such a provision would be more readily associated with the human rights sphere which, in 1949, had just made its entry into international law with the mention of human rights in the 1945 Charter of the United Nations and the adoption of the Universal Declaration of Human Rights in 1948.

The true turning point, when humanitarian law and human rights gradually began to draw closer, came in 1968 during the International Conference on Human Rights in Tehran, at which the United Nations for the first time considered the application of human rights in armed conflict. The delegates adopted a resolution inviting the Secretary-General of the United Nations to examine the development of humanitarian law and to consider steps to be taken to promote respect for it.[54] Humanitarian law thus branched out from its usual course of development and found a new opening within the UN, which had hitherto neglected it — unlike human rights, to which UN attention had been given from the start.

The convergence which began in 1968 slowly continued over the years and is still in progress today. Human rights texts are increasingly expressing ideas and concepts typical of humanitarian law. The reverse phenomenon, although much rarer, has also occurred. In other terms, the gap which still exists today between human rights and humanitarian law is diminishing. Influences from both sides are gradually tending to bring the two spheres together.[55]

The rest of this chapter will give a few examples illustrating the tendency we have just outlined.

---

[53] Although the Lieber Code did make some mention of forms of protection that could be accorded in civil wars, treaty law did not do so until common Article 3 of the Geneva Conventions.

[54] See footnote 1 above.

[55] See: T. Meron, "The protection of the human person under human rights law and humanitarian law", *Bulletin of Human Rights 91/1*, United Nations, New York, 1992.

Some of these illustrations are to be found in the texts of treaties. For example, the adoption in 1977 of the two Protocols additional to the 1949 Geneva Conventions was, in a certain sense, a reflection of what had happened in Tehran nine years earlier. The world of humanitarian law paid tribute to the world of human rights. The subjects and wording of Protocol I's Article 75, entitled "Fundamental guarantees", are in fact directly inspired by the major human rights instruments, for it lays down the principle of non-discrimination, the main prohibitions relating to the physical and mental well-being of individuals, the prohibition of arbitrary detention and the essential legal guarantees. The same could be said of Articles 4, 5 and 6 of Protocol II, which, in situations of non-international armed conflict, are the counterpart to the aforesaid article in Protocol I.

Another example appears in the 1989 Convention on the Rights of the Child. The adoption procedure for this Convention, the substance of the rules which it establishes and the built-in mechanism for its implementation clearly show that it belongs to the family of human rights treaties. That did not prevent it, however, from casting a glance at the law of armed conflicts. It does so in Article 38, on the one hand by making a general reference to the humanitarian law provisions applicable to children (paragraph 1), and on the other hand by laying down rules itself that are applicable in the event of armed conflict.[56]

This tendency can also be seen in international instruments which are legally less binding than the Conventions we have just briefly surveyed. In particular, several United Nations General Assembly resolutions mingle references to humanitarian law and human rights within one and the same text. The General Assembly often states that it is "guided by the principles embodied in the Charter of the United Nations, the Universal Declaration of Human Rights, the International Covenants on Human Rights and accepted humanitarian rules as set out in the Geneva Conventions of 12 August 1949 and the Additional Protocols thereto, of 1977".[57]

A more restricted forum than that of the United Nations, namely the Islamic Conference of Ministers of Foreign Affairs, adopted an Islamic Declaration of Human Rights in April 1990.[58] Although expressly

---

[56] "Convention on the Rights of the Child", *Human rights in international law, Basic texts*, Council of Europe, Strasbourg, 1991.

[57] Resolution 46/136 on the situation of human rights in Afghanistan. See also Resolution 46/135 on the situation of human rights in Kuwait under Iraqi occupation and Declaration 47/133 on the protection of all people against forced disappearances.

[58] This document was published by the UN under reference No. A/CONF. 157/PC/35.

claiming to be a human rights instrument, this declaration contains provisions which derive their inspiration directly from humanitarian law. For instance, it stipulates that "in case of use of force or armed conflict", people who do not participate in the fighting, such as the aged, women and children, the wounded, the sick and prisoners, shall be protected. It also regulates the methods and means of combat.[59]

This declaration is one of the working documents used in preparation for the World Conference on Human Rights to be held in Vienna in June 1993. As such it is a sign that humanitarian law and human rights might again draw a little closer during that conference.

The interlinking of human rights and humanitarian law can also be seen in the work of bodies responsible for monitoring and implementing international law.

In this connection, it is interesting to note that in recent years the Security Council has been citing humanitarian law more and more frequently in support of its resolutions. The latest example of this tendency can be found in Resolution 808 (1993) on the conflict in the former Yugoslavia, in which the Security Council decided to establish an international tribunal "for the prosecution of persons responsible for serious violations of international humanitarian law committed in the territory of the former Yugoslavia since 1991".[60]

A body more specifically concerned with the implementation of human rights, the Commission on Human Rights, likewise no longer hesitates to invoke humanitarian law to back up its recommendations.[61] The "Report on the Situation of Human Rights in Kuwait under Iraqi Occupation" presented at its 48th session is a clear example.[62]

To establish the law applicable to the situation in Kuwait, the Special Rapporteur begins by pointing out, in a chapter entitled "Interaction between human rights and humanitarian law", that "there is consensus with the international community that the fundamental human rights of all persons are to be respected and protected both in times of

---

[59] Islamic Declaration of Human Rights, Article 3.

[60] See also Security Council Resolutions 670 (1990) and 674 (1990) on Iraq's occupation of Kuwait, and Resolution 780 (1992) establishing a Commission of Experts to enquire into breaches of humanitarian law committed in the territory of the former Yugoslavia. See also the Interim Report of the Commission of Experts established pursuant to Security Council Resolution 780 (1992): S/25274.

[61] Among the most recent examples, see in particular the Report of the Working Group on Enforced or Involontary Disappearances (E/CN.4/1993/25 paras. 508-510) and its Addendum on the situation in Sri Lanka (E/CN.4/1993/25/Add.1 paras. 40.42), and the Report on Extrajudicial, Summary or Arbitrary Executions (E/CN.4/1993/46 paras. 60, 61, 664 and 684).

[62] Report on the situation of human rights in Kuwait under Iraqi occupation, prepared by Mr. Walter Kälin (E/CN.4/1992/26).

peace and during periods of armed conflict".[63] Customary international law provides the Rapporteur with some of the rules he seeks to apply. There are, *inter alia*, three fundamental rules of humanitarian law which he singles out as being customary principles of human rights protection. These three principles stipulate: "(i) that the right of parties to choose the means and methods of warfare, i.e. the right of the parties to a conflict to adopt means of injuring the enemy, is not unlimited; (ii) that a distinction must be made between persons participating in military operations and those belonging to the civilian population to the effect that the latter be spared as much as possible; and (iii) that it is prohibited to launch attacks against the civilian population as such."[64] The Rapporteur further considers that the rules of customary law applicable to the occupation of Kuwait include Article 3 common to the 1949 Geneva Conventions, Article 75 of the 1977 Additional Protocol I thereto and the 1948 Universal Declaration of Human Rights. In terms of positive law, he considers that the 1966 International Covenant on Civil and Political Rights, the 1966 International Covenant on Economic, Social and Cultural Rights and the 1949 Geneva Conventions can also be applied.

This brief review of the legal framework thus defined shows that the Commission on Human Rights is no longer concerned with marking an overly clear distinction between human rights and humanitarian law. Although the Commission was set up to promote the implementation of human rights, it does not hesitate to invoke humanitarian law when the situation so requires. It now seems to consider that its mandate is no longer confined to human rights but takes in a larger area comprising "the principles of the law of nations derived from the usages established among civilized peoples, from the laws of humanity and the dictates of the public conscience."[65] This view of its terms of reference thus enables it to draw upon the rules of humanitarian law to make pronouncements on the situations it is asked to examine.

Outside the United Nations, one must look to the Inter-American Commission on Human Rights to find any hint of a similar tendency. In 1983, the organization *Disabled Peoples' International* filed a complaint with the Commission, accusing the United States of violating the right to life guaranteed by Article 1 of the American Declaration of

---

[63] *Ibid*, para. 33.

[64] *Ibid*, para. 36.

[65] As in Articles 63, 62, 142 and 158 common to the four 1949 Geneva Conventions. The Rapporteur considers that the principles set out in these articles are relevant to the case he is examining and that they belong both to human rights and to humanitarian law.

the Rights and Duties of Man. During its invasion of Grenada that year, the United States had bombed a mental asylum, killing several patients. In its petition, the organization asked the Commission to interpret Article 1 of the American Declaration on the basis of the principles of humanitarian law. The Commission declared the petition to be admissible. In dealing with the fundamental aspects of the issue, therefore, the Commission had to base its decision on a provision drawn up in the spirit of human rights in order to apply that provision to an armed conflict.[66]

Outside official circles as well, the convergence of human rights law and humanitarian law is increasingly apparent in the form of private initiatives. Law specialists are concerning themselves more and more with situations involving widespread violence but which cannot be said to have reached the point where they could be described as armed conflicts and where humanitarian law could be applied. Such situations often induce the State concerned to declare a state of emergency and to suspend most of the human rights that it has undertaken to respect.[67] Though, as we have seen, such derogations must remain the exception and are in any case excluded for certain rights, there is a risk of a gap in the law appearing in that area. In order to fill it, a new approach is needed to protection of the individual. It is becoming apparent that legal instruments should be drawn up combining elements of both humanitarian and human rights law in order to provide rules that can be applied in peacetime as well as in wartime.

This objective was behind the adoption in 1990 of the Declaration of Minimum Humanitarian Standards, the so-called Turku Declaration.[68] This text makes it clear from the outset that its drafters are determined not to take a position on any dichotomy between humanitarian law and human rights law. It proclaims principles "which are applicable in all situations, including internal violence, disturbances, tensions and public emergency, and which cannot be derogated from under any circumstances".[69] That determination finds expression in a succession of provisions based alternately on the spirit of human rights law (for example

[66] For further details on the Grenada affair, see D. Weissbrodt and B. Andrus, "The Right to Life During Armed Conflict: Disabled Peoples' International v. United States" 29, *Harvard Int. L.J.*, 1988, p. 59.

[67] See Article 4(2) of the International Covenant on Civil and Political Rights, Article 15(2) of the European Convention on Human Rights and Article 27(2) of the American Convention on Human Rights.

[68] For the text of the Declaration of Minimum Humanitarian Standards, see E/CN.4/Sub.2/1991/55 or the *International Review of the Red Cross*, No. 282, May-June 1991, pp. 330-336.

[69] *Idem*, Article 1.

the prohibition of torture and the principle of *habeas corpus*) and on the spirit of humanitarian law (for example the prohibition on harming individuals not taking part in hostilities and the obligation to treat wounded and sick persons humanely).

The Turku Declaration is the work of a group of experts who met privately for the purpose. It therefore lacks the force in law that it would have if it had been adopted by an international body. But it is not meaningless; for one thing, some of its provisions have long been part of general international law. For another, it was drawn up by qualified specialists in order to meet a need acknowledged by the international community. It can thus not be ruled out that the Declaration will gradually gain recognition by a number of international legal institutions. A first step in this direction has already been taken by the Sub-Commission on Prevention of Discrimination and Protection of Minorities which referred to it in its Resolution 1192/106 on the human rights situation in Iraq.[70]

Conclusion

It is very likely that the present trends will continue in future. The obvious advantage of human rights bodies using humanitarian law is that humanitarian law will become increasingly known to decision-makers and to the public who, it is hoped, will exert increasing pressure to obtain respect for it. On the other hand, one concern could be that the growing politicization of human rights by governmental bodies could affect humanitarian law. However, there are several reasons why this is unlikely. First, humanitarian law treaties are all universal and there are no regional systems which could encourage a perception that the law varies from one continent to another. Secondly, we have seen that humanitarian law does not present the kind of theoretical difficulties encountered by human rights law as regards "first", "second", and "third" generation rights. Thirdly, the most politically sensitive aspect of human rights law, namely, political rights and mode of government, is totally absent from humanitarian law. What will probably not be avoided, however, are the political influences that lead States to insist

[70] Other initiatives comparable to the Turku Declaration have been taken in recent years. Examples are:

Hans-Peter Gasser, "Code of Conduct in the event of internal disturbances and tensions", *International Review of the Red Cross*, No. 262, January-February 1988, pp. 51-53.

Theodor Meron, "Draft Model Declaration on Internal Strife", *International Review of the Red Cross*, No. 262, January-February 1988, pp. 59-76.

on the implementation of the law in some conflicts whilst ignoring others. This, however, is not new and it is to be hoped that a greater interest in humanitarian law will tend to bring about more demands for it to be respected in all conflicts.

There can be no doubt that the growing prominence of human rights law in recent decades is largely due to the activism of non-governmental human rights organizations. Several have now begun to use humanitarian law in their work[71] and may well exert a considerable influence in the future. Such an interest could encourage both the implementation and the further development of the law. As one of the major factors in the development of humanitarian law, namely the perception of honour in combat, has lost influence in modern society, there is a need for a motivating force to fill this void. A perception of human rights has in effect done so, and will continue to be of importance in the future. Another area in which interest in human rights could help further develop humanitarian law is that of internal armed conflicts. Common Article 3 and 1977 Protocol II are much less far-reaching than the law applicable to international armed conflicts and yet internal conflicts are more numerous and are causing untold misery and destruction. Given that human rights law is primarily concerned with behaviour within a State, it is possible that resistance to further responsibility in internal armed conflicts will be eroded by human rights pressure. We have already seen how there are moves towards further regulation in states of emergency[72] which have been influenced by humanitarian law although they are outside its sphere of action.

It may well be, however, that States will recognize their own interest in respecting humanitarian law and will not in future perceive themselves as being induced to show such respect solely because of human rights activism. The benefits of respecting humanitarian law are self-evident, in particular the prevention of extensive destruction and bitterness so that a lasting peace is more easily established.[73] If the chivalry of earlier times cannot be resurrected, it would be a positive development if the military could be encouraged to take a certain pride

---

[71] In particular Human Rights Watch, which has used humanitarian law in a number of its reports, e.g. *Needless Deaths*, issued in 1992, on the Second Gulf War.

A large number of these organizations have recently begun a campaign to reduce the severe problems caused by the indiscriminate use of land mines, by calling for better respect for existing humanitarian law and for the eventual ban of the use of anti-personnel mines.

[72] See pp. 116-117 above.

[73] The importance of humanitarian law for facilitating the return to peace was already indicated in nineteenth century instruments, including the Brussels Declaration of 1874.

in the professionalism shown when behaving in accordance with humanitarian law.[74] As this law is still largely rooted in its traditional origins, it is not alien to military thinking and has the advantage of being a realistic code for military behaviour as well as protecting human rights to the maximum degree possible in the circumstances. It is to be hoped that continued recognition of the specific nature of humanitarian law, together with the various energies devoted to implementation of human rights law, will have the effect of enhancing the protection of the person in situations of violence.

Louise Doswald-Beck
and Sylvain Vité

Louise Doswald-Beck, LLM (London), a barrister, was a lecturer in international law at Exeter University and University College London, where her special subjects were the law of recourse to force, international humanitarian law and human rights law. She is a legal adviser at the ICRC; she has specialized in particular on questions relating to the conduct of hostilities and advises the ICRC on international human rights law. She has published numerous articles, including an article on "The development of new anti-personnel weapons" written together with Gérald C. Cauderay, which appeared in the November-December 1990 issue of the *Review*.

Sylvain Vité holds a law degree from Geneva University. He continued his studies at the Graduate Institute of International Studies, Geneva, and has just obtained an advanced diploma in international relations with specialization in international law, for which he wrote a dissertation on the International Fact-Finding Commission. He is an assistant lecturer on constitutional law at Geneva University and is currently doing a traineeship with the ICRC's Legal Division.

[74] Modern teaching methods of humanitarian law stress the importance of inculcating correct behaviour during military exercises, rather than separate lessons that appear to have nothing to do with practicalities.

[13]

A "Violations Approach" for Monitoring the International Covenant on Economic, Social and Cultural Rights[1]

Audrey R. Chapman

I. INTRODUCTION

If economic, social, and cultural rights are to be taken seriously, there needs to be a change in the paradigm for evaluating compliance with the norms established in the International Covenant on Economic, Social and Cultural Rights[2] (hereinafter the Covenant). "Progressive realization," the current standard used to assess state compliance with economic, social, and cultural rights, is inexact and renders these rights difficult to monitor. Monitoring the major international human rights covenants is central to the development of a meaningful international human rights system. Otherwise, countries that ratify or accede to specific human rights instruments cannot assess their own performance in promoting effective realization of the enumerated rights. Further, without effective monitoring, states cannot be held accountable for implementation of, or be made liable for violation of, these rights.

To assist states parties in fulfilling their obligations and to enable international monitors to evaluate a country's performance, each of the

1. This article is part of a larger study developing a "violations approach" for monitoring economic, social, and cultural rights. For an article applying a violations approach to women's right to health, see Audrey R. Chapman, *Monitoring Women's Right to Health Under the International Covenant on Economic, Social and Cultural Rights*, 44 Am. U. L. Rev. 1157 (1995). The author is grateful to Virginia Dandan, Bruno Simma, Scott Leckie, Miloon Kothari, and Allan McChesney for their comments on an earlier draft of this article. The author would also like to thank A. Tikhanov for making available the reports of the Committee on Economic, Social and Cultural Rights, as well as Eben Friedman for his assistance in editing this article.
2. International Covenant on Economic, Social and Cultural Rights, *adopted* 16 Dec. 1966, 993 U.N.T.S. 3 (*entered into force* 3 Jan. 1976), G.A. Res. 2200 (XXI), 21 U.N. GAOR Supp. (No. 16) at 49, U.N. Doc. A/6316 (1966).

major international human rights covenants requires the regular submission of reports by states parties for review by UN established committees of experts. However, these requirements do not ensure necessarily that effective monitoring will take place. Monitoring state compliance is a complex and exacting process with numerous political and methodological prerequisites. Although effective monitoring requires the systematic collection and analysis of appropriate data, the determination of which data are relevant depends on translating the abstract legal norms, in which the various human rights covenants are framed, into operational standards. To accomplish this operationalization, specific enumerated rights (for example, the right to education) need to be adequately conceptualized and developed to measure implementation or to identify potential violations. These indicators, some of which may be based on statistical data, can then provide yardsticks to evaluate state compliance. Otherwise, the preparation and review of reports can be little more than a formality.

This article reviews the problems that the current performance standard of "progressive realization" entails for monitoring economic, social, and cultural rights, and proposes a "violations approach" as a more feasible and effective alternative. The violations approach advocated here focusses on three types of violations: (1) violations resulting from actions and policies on the part of governments; (2) violations related to patterns of discrimination; and (3) violations taking place due to a state's failure to fulfill the minimum core obligations contained in the Covenant. In order to illustrate examples of violations of the rights enumerated in the Covenant, this article analyzes several years of reports by the UN Committee on Economic, Social and Cultural Rights.

II. CURRENT ABSENCE OF EFFECTIVE MONITORING

At first glance, the assertion that little effective or systematic monitoring of the Covenant is taking place seems to be at variance with the current international human rights system. The principle that the two major categories of rights, civil and political rights on the one hand and economic, social, and cultural rights on the other, are interrelated, interdependent, and indivisible constitutes one of the fundamental underpinnings of the international consensus on human rights norms. This principle has been endorsed on numerous occasions by the General Assembly, the Economic and Social Council, the Commission on Human Rights, and international conferences, the most recent being the 1993 World Conference on Human Rights.[3] In

3. Paragraph five of the *Vienna Declaration and Programme of Action* adopted by the World Conference on Human Rights on 25 June 1993 states that "[a]ll human rights are universal, indivisible and interdependent and interrelated." However, the rest of the text

addition to the Covenant, several other international human rights instruments enumerate economic, social, and cultural rights. These include the International Convention on the Elimination of All Forms of Racial Discrimination,[4] the Convention on the Elimination of All Forms of Discrimination Against Women,[5] and the Convention on the Rights of the Child.[6] Countries which become states parties to these instruments also assume the international obligation to submit periodic reports to the United Nations on the measures that they have adopted and the progress made in achieving compliance. As of March 1995, 130 countries had become states parties to the Covenant.[7]

Currently, states parties to the Covenant are requested to submit an initial report dealing with the entire Covenant within two years of the Covenant's entry into force and to submit a periodic report every five years thereafter. These reports are reviewed by the UN Committee on Economic, Social and Cultural Rights, a body of experts (hereinafter the Committee). According to a General Comment by the Committee, these reporting obligations fulfill seven objectives:

> (1) to ensure that a state party undertakes a comprehensive review of national legislation, administrative rules and procedures, and practices in order to assure the fullest possible conformity with the Covenant;
>
> (2) to encourage the state party to regularly monitor the actual situation with respect to each of the enumerated rights in order to assess the extent to which the various rights are being enjoyed by all individuals within the country;
>
> (3) to provide a basis for government elaboration of clearly stated and carefully targeted policies to implement the Covenant;
>
> (4) to facilitate public scrutiny of government policies with regard to the Covenant's implementation, while encouraging the involvement of a multiplicity

---

virtually ignores issues related to the realization of economic, social, and cultural rights. *See Vienna Declaration and Programme of Action*, World Conference on Human Rights, U.N. Doc. A/CONF.157/23 (1993).

4. International Convention on the Elimination of All Forms of Racial Discrimination, *adopted* 21 Dec. 1965 (*entered into force* 4 Jan. 1969), 660 U.N.T.S. 195.
5. Convention on the Elimination of All Forms of Discrimination Against Women, *adopted* 18 Dec. 1979, G.A. Res. 34/180, 34 U.N. GAOR Supp. (No. 46) at 193, U.N. Doc. A/34/36 (1980), *reprinted in* 19 I.L.M. 33 (1980) (*entered into force* 3 Sept. 1981).
6. Convention on the Rights of the Child, *adopted* 20 Nov. 1989, G.A. Res. 44/25, 44 U.N. GAOR Supp. (No. 49) at 165, U.N. Doc. A/44/736 (1989), *reprinted in* 28 I.L.M. 1448 (1989).
7. *States Parties to the International Covenant on Economic, Social and Cultural Rights and the Status of the Submission of Reports in Accordance with the Programme Established by the Economic and Social Council in Resolution 1988/4 and Rule 58 of the Rules of Procedure of the Committee*, Committee on Economic, Social and Cultural Rights, 12th Sess., ¶ 2, U.N. Doc. E/C.12/1995/2 (1995).

of sectors of society in the formulation, implementation, and review of relevant policies;

(5) to offer a basis on which both the state party and the Committee can effectively evaluate progress toward the realization of Covenant obligations;

(6) to enable the state party to develop a better understanding of problems and shortcomings impeding the realization of economic, social, and cultural rights; and

(7) to facilitate the exchange of information among states parties and to develop a fuller appreciation of both common problems and possible solutions affecting the realization of each of the rights contained in the Covenant.[8]

Initial appearances notwithstanding, the fundamental preconditions for effective monitoring of economic, social, and cultural rights are largely absent. At the very least, monitoring requires three things. First, a sustained commitment on the part of the relevant country to assessing and improving its performance is necessary. Second, international human rights bodies must provide resources and standards. Third, the ongoing attention of nongovernmental organizations is required, particularly where the other preconditions are lacking. Currently, neither the political will nor the methodological capabilities required for effective monitoring is present.

Despite a rhetorical commitment to the indivisibility and interdependence of human rights, the international community, including the international human rights movement, has consistently treated civil and political rights as more significant, while consistently neglecting economic, social, and cultural rights. As the Statement to the World Conference on Human Rights on Behalf of the Committee on Economic, Social and Cultural Rights observes, the principle of the indivisibility of human rights has been honored more in the breach than in the observance.[9] As the Committee anticipated, the ritualistic affirmations in the Vienna Declaration and Programme of Action at the World Conference were followed by near-silence regarding specific issues or concerns. Despite the fact that a large proportion of the issues on the agenda of the March 1995 World Summit for Social Development overlapped with the domain of economic, social, and

8. *General Comment 1: Reporting by States Parties*, Committee on Economic, Social and Cultural Rights, 3rd Sess., *reprinted in Compilation of General Comments and General Recommendations Adopted by Human Rights Treaty Bodies*, at 36–38, (the comments have been paraphrased and are not as they are in the original document) U.N. Doc. HRI/GEN1 (1992) [hereinafter *Compilation of General Comments*].

9. *Draft Report of the Committee on Economic, Social and Cultural Rights to the Economic and Social Council in accordance with Economic and Social Council Resolution 1985/17*, Committee on Economic, Social and Cultural Rights, 7th Sess., ¶ 2, U.N. Doc. E/C.12/1992/CRP.2/Add.1 (1992).

cultural rights, the Copenhagen Declaration on Social Development and Programme of Action[10] used the vocabulary of development rather than rights, thus further marginalizing the Covenant.

For reasons that will be made clearer below, the international community has invested little attention and few resources in the realization or monitoring of economic, social, and cultural rights. Despite the complexity of, and problems related to, implementing and monitoring these rights, the Human Rights Commission has appointed only one special rapporteur with a mandate to study such issues. At the recommendation of the special rapporteur, Danilo Türk, the UN Human Rights Centre in 1993 convened an expert Seminar on Appropriate Indicators to Promote Progressive Realization of Economic, Social and Cultural Rights. In its conclusions, the Seminar

> expressed its concern about the continued neglect of economic, social and cultural rights within the United Nations System and by states parties to the International Covenant on Economic, Social and Cultural Rights. Failure to invest sufficient attention and resources in economic, social and cultural rights has resulted in their conceptual underdevelopment and a lack of progressive realization of specific rights in many countries.[11]

Despite the Human Rights Commission's acceptance and affirmation of these conclusions, the recommendations of the Seminar for follow-up action have not been implemented yet.[12]

Although the Covenant has been ratified by 130 countries, few states parties take their responsibilities seriously enough to attempt to comply with the standards of the Covenant in a deliberate and carefully structured way. The Committee has had to remind the international community that the full realization of economic, social, and cultural rights cannot be achieved as a direct consequence of, or flow automatically from, the enjoyment of civil and political rights, but rather that it requires the development and implementation of specific policies and programs. According to the Committee,

---

10. U.N. Department of Public Information, *The World Summit for Social Development, 6–12 March 1995: The Copenhagen Declaration and Programme of Action* (1995) [hereinafter *Copenhagen Declaration*].
11. *Report on Other Meetings and Activities, Report of the Seminar on Appropriate Indicators to Measure Achievements in the Progressive Realization of Economic, Social and Cultural Rights*, World Conference on Human Rights, ¶ 157, U.N. Doc. A/CONF.157/PC/73 (1993) [hereinafter *Report of the Seminar on Appropriate Indicators*].
12. *Question of the Realization in All Countries of the Economic, Social and Cultural Rights Contained in the Universal Declaration of Human Rights and in the International Covenant on Economic, Social and Cultural Rights: A Study of Special Problems which the Developing Countries Face in Their Efforts to Achieve These Rights, Draft Report of the Commission*, Commission on Human Rights, 51st Sess., Agenda Item 28, U.N. Doc. E/CN.4/1995/L.11/Add.1 (1995).

> [j]ust as carefully targeted policies and unremitting vigilance are necessary to ensure that respect for civil and political rights will follow from, for example, the holding of free and fair elections or from the introduction or restoration of an essentially democratic system of government, so too is it essential that specific policies and programs be devised and implemented by any Government which aims to ensure the respect of the economic, social and cultural rights of its citizens and of others for whom it is responsible.[13]

A majority of states parties do not even comply with the reporting requirements set out in the Covenant. Of the 130 states parties, seventy-six had reports that were overdue in 1995, and several states, among them a few ratifying the Covenant as early as 1976, have never submitted even an initial report.[14] Most of the reports that are submitted are very superficial and appear to be designed to camouflage rather than to reveal problems and inadequacies. In addition, virtually all the reports ignore the request found in the Covenant's reporting guidelines for specific types of disaggregation in reporting the data. Thus, the Committee rarely receives data that differentiate between the sexes or that identify disadvantaged groups and minorities. Instead, countries present national averages that cloak gender differences and the problems of disadvantaged and vulnerable groups.

Because governments almost never voluntarily admit to violations of human rights, the integrity and vitality of any human rights review process depends on alternative sources of information. During the past thirty years, the international human rights movement has played a major role in monitoring human rights and in promoting compliance with international human rights standards. Despite the Committee's openness to receiving information from nongovernmental organizations and to having such groups attend and contribute to its proceedings, very few human rights groups have taken advantage of these opportunities for participation. There is a major discrepancy between the number of groups that participate in the work of the UN Human Rights Commission and the number participating in some of the other treaty-monitoring bodies, particularly the Human Rights

13. *Committee on Economic, Social and Cultural Rights, Report on the Seventh Session (23 Nov.–11 Dec. 1992), Economic and Social Council, Official Records, 1993, Supplement No. 2, Annex III, Statement to the World Conference on Human Rights on Behalf of the Committee on Economic, Social and Cultural Rights*, Committee on Economic, Social and Cultural Rights, ¶ 4, U.N. Doc. E/1993/22 (1993); E/C.12/1992/2 (1992) [hereinafter *Report on the Seventh Session*].
14. These figures were compiled by the author from tables in *States Parties to the International Covenant on Economic, Social and Cultural Rights and Status of the Submission of Reports in Accordance with the Programme Established by the Economic and Social Council in Resolution 1988/4 and Rule 58 of the Rules of Procedure of the Committee*, Committee on Economic, Social and Cultural Rights, 12th Sess., U.N. Doc. E/C.12/1995/2 (1995).

Committee which monitors the International Covenant on Civil and Political Rights,[15] and the Committee on Economic, Social and Cultural Rights. One reason for this discrepancy is that violations of civil and political rights attract far greater attention within the UN system than noncompliance with economic, social, and cultural rights. Another reason is that international human rights organizations that have full consultative status in the UN system and access to various UN human rights bodies have focussed primarily on civil and political rights. Because national and local groups are not eligible for full consultative status, few of the organizations interested in economic, social, and cultural rights are encouraged to attend the sessions of UN human rights bodies. Specialized nongovernmental organizations, such as those interested in health and education, are generally even less connected to this review process. Another important factor is the lack of methodologies and resources to facilitate the monitoring of economic, social, and cultural rights. Many of the academic and nongovernmental organizations interested in specific economic, social, and cultural rights do not know how to monitor the performance of their own governments. Monitoring of economic, social, and cultural rights has also been hampered by conceptual and methodological problems that other categories of human rights have not experienced.

Systematic monitoring of these rights has five methodological preconditions: (1) conceptualization of the specific components of each enumerated right and the concomitant obligations of states parties; (2) delineation of performance standards related to each of these components, including the identification of potential major violations; (3) collection of relevant data, appropriately disaggregated by sex and a variety of other variables; (4) development of an information management system for these data to facilitate analysis of trends over time and comparisons of the status of groups within a country; and (5) the ability to analyze these data in order to determine patterns and trends. For reasons that will be discussed below, none of these five preconditions is currently being fulfilled.

III. CONCEPTUAL AND METHODOLOGICAL REQUIREMENTS FOR MONITORING PROGRESSIVE REALIZATION

The implementation and monitoring of the rights articulated in the Covenant have been hampered by conceptual and methodological difficulties.

15. International Covenant on Civil and Political Rights, *adopted* 16 Dec. 1966, 999 U.N.T.S. 171 (*entered into force* 23 Mar. 1976), G.A. Res. 2200 (XXI), 21 U.N. GAOR, Supp. (No. 16) at 52, U.N. Doc. A/6316 (1966).

Much has been written about the lack of intellectual clarity as to the definition and scope of these rights.[16] Understanding of the full implications of economic, social, and cultural rights is far less advanced than is the case with civil and political rights. In contrast with civil and political rights, the rights contained in the Covenant, with the exception of the labor-related rights, are not grounded in significant bodies of domestic jurisprudence. Most of these rights were first recognized in the Universal Declaration of Human Rights[17] and then given greater specificity in the Covenant. Additionally, the international community has not engaged in systematic norm clarification. Thus far, the Committee has developed only one General Comment setting forth the scope of a specific right and the resultant obligations of states parties: General Comment 4 on the right to adequate housing, which is a component of Article 11.[18] The different nature of economic, social, and cultural rights; the vagueness of many of the norms; the absence of national institutions specifically committed to the promotion of economic, social, and cultural rights *qua* rights; and the range of information required in order to monitor compliance effectively all present challenges.[19] It often is not appreciated sufficiently that this conceptual underdevelopment also has an adverse effect on the monitoring of these rights.

Further complicating matters is that the evaluation of the performance of states parties thus far has focussed on assessments of progressive realization rather than on the identification of violations. Article 2(1) of the Covenant mandates states parties

> to take steps, individually and through international assistance and co-operation, especially economic and technical, to the maximum of its available resources, with a view to achieving progressively the full realization of the rights recognized in the present Covenant by all appropriate means, including particularly the adoption of legislative measures.[20]

16. *See, e.g.*, Philip Alston, *Out of the Abyss: The Challenges Confronting the New U.N. Committee on Economic, Social and Cultural Rights*, 9 Hum. Rts. Q. 332–81 (1987).
17. Universal Declaration of Human Rights, *adopted* 10 Dec. 1948, G.A. Res. 217A (III), 3 U.N. GAOR (Resolutions, part 1) at 71, U.N. Doc. A/810 (1948), *reprinted in* 43 Am. J. Int'l L. Supp. 127 (1949).
18. *General Comment 4: The Right to Adequate Housing (Art. 11(1))*, Committee on Economic, Social and Cultural Rights, 6th Sess., *reprinted in Compilation of General Comments, supra* note 8, at 48–54.
19. On these problems, see Philip Alston, *The Committee on Economic, Social and Cultural Rights, in* The United Nations and Human Rights: A Critical Appraisal 490–91 (Philip Alston ed., 1992) [hereinafter The United Nations and Human Rights].
20. International Covenant on Economic, Social and Cultural Rights, *supra* note 2, art. 2(1).

This differs considerably from the standard enumerated in Article 2 of the International Covenant on Civil and Political Rights, which specifies an immediate obligation to respect and ensure all enumerated rights.[21]

Evaluating progressive realization within the context of "the maximum of available resources" considerably complicates the methodological requirements. Under this formulation, monitoring requires generating operational standards based, not only on "the maximum of available resources," but also on what it means to be "achieving progressively the full realization of the rights." The progressive realization benchmark assumes that valid expectations and concomitant obligations of states parties under the Covenant are not uniform or universal, but instead relative to levels of development and available resources. This necessitates the development of a multiplicity of performance standards for each enumerated right in relationship to the varied social, developmental, and resource contexts of specific countries.

Moreover, the standard of progressive realization cannot be used as a measuring tool for evaluating compliance without first clarifying what the phrase "maximum of its available resources" entails in specific circumstances. In a recent article in the *Human Rights Quarterly,* Robert E. Robertson observes that the phrase has little more definition today than when it was first written, commenting that the resources issue is so complicated that universal agreement on standards seems unattainable. "It is a difficult phrase—two warring adjectives describing an undefined noun. 'Maximum' stands for idealism; 'available' stands for reality. 'Maximum' is the sword of human rights rhetoric; 'available' is the wiggle room for the state."[22] Despite his considerable efforts, Robertson is unable to put forward a methodology that provides a comprehensive method for analyzing resource availability and usage, and he concludes that such a comprehensive method would itself require significant resources and constant fine-tuning to keep pace with new thinking in human rights, economics, and other fields.[23]

The Committee's own problems in interpreting and rendering operational "progressive realization" are indicative of the underlying dilemmas this standard raises. Its General Comment on "The Nature of States Parties Obligations" attempts both to acknowledge the constraints imposed by limitations on available resources and to maintain the rigor of a standard of

---

21. *See* International Covenant on Civil and Political Rights, *supra* note 15, art. 2.
22. Robert E. Robertson, *"Measuring State Compliance with the Obligation to Devote the 'Maximum Available Resources' to Realizing Economic, Social and Cultural Rights,"* 16 Hum. Rts. Q. 694 (1994).
23. *Id.* at 713.

full implementation. According to the language of the General Comment on this subject,

> The concept of progressive realization constitutes a recognition of the fact that full realization of all economic, social and cultural rights will generally not be able to be achieved in a short period of time. . . . It is on the one hand a necessary flexibility device, reflecting the realities of the real world and the difficulties involved for any country in ensuring full realization of economic, social and cultural rights. On the other hand, the phrase must be read in the light of the overall objective, indeed the *raison d'être*, of the Covenant which is to establish clear obligations for States parties in respect of the full realization of the rights in question.[24]

However, because the Committee has not defined what moving expeditiously and effectively entails, it lacks concrete standards for evaluating the performance of governments and their compliance with the Covenant. Given these problems, it should come as no surprise that the Committee itself does not use progressive realization as the standard by which it reviews the performance of states parties.

The Committee's guidelines for reporting under the Covenant,[25] which are intended to assist states parties in preparing their reports, do not constitute a "how-to guide" for monitoring these rights. Because the reporting requirements were developed without reference to performance standards or indicators, the conceptual adequacy, relevance, and coverage of much of the requested data is also questionable.[26] The general part of the report has four sections: (1) a country profile (discussing physical characteristics of the land; the population; the general political structure of government; economic, social, and cultural factors at work in the county; and the general legal framework within which human rights are protected); (2) information and publicity concerning the Covenant and the country's reports to the Committee; (3) the legal status and specific implementation of the Covenant within that country; and (4) the role of international cooperation in the implementation of the Covenant. There are specific guidelines, structured on an article-by-article basis, for reporting on the substantive

---

24. *General Comment 3: The Nature of States Parties Obligations (Art. 2(1))*, Committee on Economic, Social and Cultural Rights, 5th Sess., *reprinted in Compilation of General Comments, supra* note 8, at 45, ¶ 9 [hereinafter General Comment 3].
25. *Committee on Economic, Social and Cultural Rights. Report on the Fifth Session. Annex IV. Revised Guidelines Regarding the Form and Content of Reports to be Submitted by States Parties under Articles 16 and 17 of the International Covenant on Economic, Social and Cultural Rights*, Committee on Economic, Social and Cultural Rights, 5th Sess., U.N. Doc. E/1991/23 (1991) [hereinafter *Report on the Fifth Session*].
26. Thomas B. Jabine & Denis F. Johnston, *Socio-Economic Indicators and Human Rights*, Occasional Paper, Science and Human Rights Program (American Association for the Advancement of Science ed., 1991).

provisions, and the information requested generally consists of a mix of descriptive information and statistical data. For several articles, the reporting guidelines specify that information provided should be based on "time-related goals and benchmarks," but no instructions or details are provided as to how these goals and benchmarks might be established or used. Realizing that an assessment of performance requires disaggregated data about the enjoyment of rights in specific sectors of the population, the reporting guidelines frequently ask for information about "particularly vulnerable or disadvantaged groups." However, the reporting guidelines infrequently define or identify these groups. When the guidelines do so, the list of groups is inconsistent from one article to the next.

Monitoring the progressive realization of economic, social, and cultural rights is extremely complicated and requires an enormous amount of good-quality data. The list of data requested by the reporting guidelines for specific articles of the Covenant sometimes continues for several pages, and the guidelines stipulate that much of this data be disaggregated into relevant categories, including gender, race, region, socioeconomic group, linguistic group, and urban/rural divisions. Such requests for data stem from the Committee's recognition that national averages reveal little about the situation of specific groups and communities within a country. Because of the Committee's concern with the status of vulnerable and disadvantaged communities, the list of requested data with regard to some of the rights, for example the right to adequate food, is quite extensive. It specifies that detailed information, including statistical data broken down in terms of different geographical areas, also should be provided for landless peasants, marginalized peasants, rural workers, rural unemployed, urban unemployed, urban poor, migrant workers, indigenous peoples, children, elderly people, and other especially affected groups.[27]

Measuring progressive realization not only requires an assessment of current performance, but also a determination of whether a state is moving expeditiously and effectively towards the goal of full implementation. The reporting guidelines frequently ask for changes that have taken place over the past five years. Five years, however, is too short a period; it would be fairer and more accurate to have time series data, perhaps at five year intervals, for all of the years since a particular country ratified the Covenant. In principle, then, the disaggregated data for specific societal groups detailed above should be presented in time series, with the status of each group profiled in relationship to the data requested under each right and at five year intervals since the state party ratified the Covenant.

---

27. Philip Alston, *The International Covenant on Economic, Social and Cultural Rights, in* MANUAL ON HUMAN RIGHTS REPORTING 60, U.N. Doc. HR/PUB/91/1 (1991), U.N. Sales No. E.91.XIV.1 (1991).

The problem with the data requirements outlined above is that they are unrealistic and virtually impossible to handle. Few states parties have either the requisite data or the willingness to share such detailed data with a UN supervisory body or with nongovernmental organizations. The preparation of a report that followed the guidelines fully and that was sensitive to the need for consistent disaggregation of data and presentation in time series would be a major undertaking, involving an enormous investment of time and resources. Further, members of the Committee lack the time, staff, and analytical abilities to deal with such detailed reports—the Committee currently has problems reviewing the present flow of shorter and often quite superficial reports. Moreover, analysis of these data to evaluate performance, were such data to be available, would require statistical expertise that members of the Committee, staff of the UN Centre on Human Rights, and nongovernmental organizations generally do not possess.

The volume of statistical data that would be generated if states parties provided appropriately disaggregated data as requested in the Committee's guidelines also would require a sophisticated computerized information system, something that the UN Centre for Human Rights currently lacks and that very few nongovernmental organizations have. At present, the Committee uses a League of Nations-style filing system, in that information from previous reports has to be recovered manually. Despite repeated calls from the chairs of the various human rights treaty-monitoring bodies for the establishment of a computerized information system,[28] the UN Centre for Human Rights is still at the early stages of installing computers even for the simplest word processing. Current plans of the Coordinator for Office Automation do not include the creation of a comprehensive and integrated information and documentation system that would facilitate the retrieval and analysis of complex statistical data, and the establishment and management of such an information system seems beyond the capabilities of most nongovernmental organizations.

Attempting to circumvent some of the problems outlined above, the Sub-Commission on the Prevention of Discrimination and Protection of Minorities and the Human Rights Commission appointed Danilo Türk as a Special Rapporteur in 1988, giving him a mandate to prepare a study of the problems, policies, and practical strategies relating to the more effective realization of economic, social, and cultural rights. In his reports, the Special Rapporteur discussed the potential use of economic and social indicators for assessing progress in the realization of these rights. He

---

28. *Improving the Operation of the Human Rights Treaty Bodies. Report of the Secretary General*, Fifth Meeting of Chairpersons of Treaty Bodies, Provisional Agenda Item 6, ¶ 14–16, U.N. Doc. HRI/MC/1994/2 (1994).

identified the following roles for indicators: to provide a quantifiable measurement device of direct relevance to the array of economic, social, and cultural rights; to measure the progressive realization of these rights over time; and to determine difficulties or problems encountered by states in fulfilling these obligations. In addition, the Special Rapporteur found that use of indicators can assist the development of a "core content" for this category of rights and can offer a yardstick whereby countries can compare their progress with that of other countries.[29] Therefore, he recommended that the United Nations convene a seminar for the discussion of appropriate indicators to measure achievements in the progressive realization of economic, social, and cultural rights, offering an opportunity for a broad exchange of views among experts.[30]

In January 1993, the UN Centre for Human Rights convened such an expert seminar on indicators, with this author serving as rapporteur. After an extensive review the members of this seminar concluded that, far from being a shortcut to defining and monitoring economic, social, and cultural rights, the development of appropriate indicators is an end product. Proper indicator development necessitates an initial identification of the scope of each enumerated right, as well as the obligations of states parties. Accordingly, it is not yet possible to formulate indicators to assess the progressive realization of these rights. The seminar concluded that additional work is required, in particular to:

> (a) Clarify the nature, scope and contents of specific rights enumerated in the Covenant;
>
> (b) Define more precisely the content of the specific rights, including the immediate core obligations of States parties to ensure the satisfaction of, at the very least, minimum essential levels of each of these rights; and
>
> (c) Identify the immediate steps to be taken by States parties to facilitate compliance with their legal obligations toward the full realization of these rights, including the duty to ensure respect for minimum subsistence rights for all.[31]

In addition, the seminar stated the need to improve evaluation and monitoring of progressive realization, to identify and address violations, to institute improved cooperation within the UN system, to facilitate the

29. *The New International Economic Order and the Promotion of Human Rights. Realization of Economic, Social and Cultural Rights. Progress Report Prepared By Mr. Danilo Türk, Special Rapporteur,* Sub-Commission On Prevention of Discrimination and Protection of Minorities, 42nd Sess., Provisional Agenda Item 7, ¶ 96, U.N. Doc. E/CN.4/Sub.2/1990/19 (1990).
30. *Id.* ¶ 220.
31. *Report of the Seminar on Appropriate Indicators, supra* note 11, ¶ 159.

participation of nongovernmental organizations and affected communities in each of the tasks outlined above, and to apply scientific statistical methodologies.[32]

The seminar repeatedly cautioned about the use of indicators to assess the progressive realization of economic, social, and cultural rights. It emphasized that human rights indicators are not necessarily identical to the statistical indicators utilized by specialized agencies to measure economic and social development. Monitoring states parties' performance in the progressive realization of economic, social, and cultural rights, therefore, requires new approaches in data collection, analysis, and interpretation, focussing on the status of the poor and disadvantaged groups while disaggregating the data for a number of variables, including gender.[33] At a minimum, use of existing statistical indicators to evaluate human rights compliance requires a reanalysis from a human rights perspective.[34] Finally, the seminar concluded that it might be premature or inappropriate at times to apply quantifiable indicators; because not all indicators can be expressed in numerical terms, it is important to develop qualitative criteria, principles, and standards for evaluating performance.[35]

IV. THE ALTERNATIVE: A "VIOLATIONS APPROACH"

Given all of the limitations outlined above, there is a need for a new approach to monitoring economic, social, and cultural rights. Instead of attempting to evaluate compliance with some notion of progressive realization, it seems more fruitful and significant to focus on identifying violations of the rights enumerated in the Covenant. What is being advocated here is the open and explicit adoption of a review process for evaluating compliance with the Covenant which is consistent with the review processes used for other international instruments. While not labeling it as such, the Committee's current format for its concluding observations on states parties' reports approximates a "violations approach," detailing the Committee's concerns and suggestions/recommendations. The Committee does not and cannot assess progressive realization; if effective and systematic monitoring of economic, social, and cultural rights is to take place, then nongovernmental organizations, governments, and human rights-monitoring bodies need to reorient their work to identifying and rectifying violations. This is

32. *Id.* ¶ 181.
33. *Id.* ¶ 160.
34. *Id.* ¶ 171.
35. *Id.* ¶ 170.

not to diminish the importance of continuing with efforts to conceptualize the content of the constituent rights in the Covenant and to develop indicators, but rather to separate these initiatives from the monitoring process.

It also might be argued that the identification of violations in order to end and rectify abuses constitutes a higher priority than does promoting progressive realization. The monitoring of human rights is not an academic exercise; it is intended to be a means of reducing the human suffering that results from serious violations of international standards. The Committee's own "Statement to the World Conference on Human Rights" provides an eloquent testimony to the importance of addressing what were termed "massive and direct denials of economic, social and cultural rights."[36] According to the Committee:

> The shocking reality, against the background of which this challenge must be seen, is that States and the international community as a whole continue to tolerate all too often breaches of economic, social and cultural rights which, if they occurred in relation to civil and political rights, would provoke expressions of horror and outrage and would lead to concerted calls for immediate remedial action. In effect, despite the rhetoric, violations of civil and political rights continue to be treated as though they are far more serious, and more patently intolerable, than massive and direct denials of economic, social and cultural rights.[37]

The identification of violations as a means to ending and rectifying abuses also might be a more effective path to conceptualizing the positive content of economic, social, and cultural rights than the more abstract legal or philosophical analyses attempted thus far. Henry Shue's conception of "standard threats" is useful here. Shue argues that a fundamental purpose of acknowledging any basic rights is to prevent or eliminate, insofar as possible, the degree of vulnerability that leaves people at the mercy of others. Hence,

> one fundamental purpose served by acknowledging basic rights at all is, in Camus' phrase, that we "take the victim's side," and the side of the potential victims. The honoring of basic rights is an active alliance with those who would otherwise be helpless against natural and social forces too strong for them.[38]

Historically, the positive content of key security rights, such as the rights not to be subjected to murder, torture, rape, and assault, was defined in relationship to the relevant "standard threats," in particular the powers of an

---

36. *Report on the Seventh Session, supra* note 13, Annex III, ¶ 5.
37. *Id.*
38. Henry Shue, Basic Rights: Subsistence, Affluence, and U.S. Foreign Policy 33 (1980).

unlimited or absolute state. Thus, civil and political rights were first articulated in order to provide protection against the acknowledged "standard threats," or actual and potential violations of these rights.

There would be many advantages to adopting a violations approach. Such an approach offers a greater possibility of promoting and protecting the economic, social, and cultural rights of individuals, while providing greater incentives for states parties to furnish means of redress. After all, the goal of any approach to human rights is to enhance the enjoyment of rights of individual subjects and to bring them some form of redress when the rights are violated, not to abstractly assess the degree to which a government has improved its level of development on a range of statistical indicators. A violations approach, therefore, returns the focus to the tangible domain in which it belongs. Moreover, the stigma of being labeled a human rights violator is one of the few "weapons" available to human rights monitors. A violations approach offers the possibility of wielding that weapon more effectively and fairly.

A more limited and focussed emphasis on violations is also more consistent with the tenure of the times than is an approach based on progressive realization. The language of progressive realization is predicated on the assumption that states parties would take their obligations seriously and move steadily toward full implementation of the rights covered by the Covenant. Such language reflects the optimistic belief of the early post–World War II period that the United Nations would establish an effective international system promoting human rights and world peace. A half century later, it is clear that the rhetoric of support for international human rights has not translated into implementation or into the investment of resources and mandates to develop effective international monitoring mechanisms. Despite frequent affirmations that all human rights are universal and indivisible, the international community generally treats economic, social, and cultural rights more as aspirations than as full-fledged rights. That the 1995 Copenhagen Declaration on Social Development contains only one explicit reference to the Covenant is indicative of the cavalier manner in which these rights are treated.[39] Despite the fact that the mandate of the World Conference on Social Development substantially overlapped with the subject matter of the Covenant, delegates to the Conference refrained from utilizing the language of rights.

A violations approach is both more feasible and more manageable than the pursuit of progressive realization alone. While still requiring further definition and specification at this point, violations are more easily defined and identified, particularly for nongovernmental organizations and perhaps

39. *Copenhagen Declaration, supra* note 10.

for governments and international bodies as well. The work of the Committee attests to the fact that it is possible to identify violations of enumerated rights without first conceptualizing their full scope or the states parties' concomitant obligations with respect to them. To date, the Committee has not formulated General Comments setting parameters for interpreting each of the constituent rights of the Covenant. Nevertheless, the Committee's concluding observations detail a wide range of concerns and problems with the performance of states parties.

A violations approach does not necessarily require access to extensive statistical data. Despite the considerable inadequacies, superficiality, and lack of good-quality statistical data in states parties' reports, the Committee has been able to identify violations of economic, social, and cultural rights. While the availability of extensive, appropriate, and reliable statistical data, disaggregated for major subgroups and organized in time series, would certainly facilitate the assessment of performance, such data are not indispensable for identifying many types of violations. Thus, monitoring economic, social, and cultural rights utilizing a violations approach does not depend on major improvements in states' statistical systems or on the public release of large quantities of data. Such an approach, therefore, is more feasible than efforts to assess progressive realization, particularly given grass roots organizations' limited access to official statistical data, as well as their likely lack of methodological sophistication.

Many of the Committee's arguments in support of drafting an optional protocol to the Covenant, which would permit the submission of complaints by individuals and groups, are also relevant for understanding the advantages of a violations approach. According to the Committee, an optional protocol would enhance the practical implementation of the Covenant as well as the dialogue with states parties. The Committee also anticipates that an optional protocol would focus public opinion to a greater extent on economic, social, and cultural rights.[40]

According to the analytical paper adopted by the Committee at its seventh session, a complaints procedure would render issues concrete and tangible.[41] The existence of a potential "remedy" at the international level would provide an incentive to individuals and groups to formulate economic and social claims in more precise terms and in relation to specific provisions of the Covenant.[42] Despite the fact that the Committee's opinions would not be binding, the possibility of an adverse "finding" by an

40. *Report on the Seventh Session, supra* note 13, Annex IV, *Toward an Optional Protocol to the International Covenant on Economic, Social and Cultural Rights,* ¶ 2.

41. *Id.* ¶ 33.

42. *Id.* ¶ 36.

international committee would give economic and social rights greater political salience than they presently enjoy.[43] In addition, a complaints procedure would produce a tangible result that is far more likely than existing procedures to generate interest in and understanding of the Covenant.[44] The adoption of a more explicit violations approach would have many of the same benefits.

As the Committee has noted, there are a number of long-standing procedures and precedents for addressing complaints in relationship to economic, social, and cultural rights. These include the International Labor Organization's procedure for responding to alleged violations of trade union rights and working conditions (comparable to Articles 6–8 of the Covenant); the United Nations Educational, Social and Cultural Organization's procedure for dealing with alleged violations of rights related to education, science, and culture (comparable to Articles 13–15 of the Covenant); and the procedure established under Economic and Social Council Resolution 1503 (27 May 1970).[45] On a regional level, there is a provision in the Inter-American system under the Additional Protocol to the American Convention on Human Rights in the area of social, economic, and cultural rights (the Protocol of San Salvador) for complaints to be filed relating to infringements of the right to organize trade unions and the right to education.[46] In addition, the Council of Europe has drafted an additional protocol to the European Social Charter that includes a complaints procedure.[47]

If the Committee is to go forward with the development of an optional protocol, it will be important to elucidate the nature of actual and potential violations under the Covenant. To this end, a catalogue of recognized violations should be developed. The Committee has proposed that complaints be admissible in so far as they relate to acts or omissions and the individual or group submitting a communication is able to demonstrate that a clear "detriment" has been suffered.[48] In light of this proposal, it seems unlikely that complaints alleging failure to achieve progressive realization of specific enumerated rights will be pursued; more likely complaints will focus on serious violations of the kind cited in this article. The prior definition of potential violations, therefore, would contribute to the effectiveness of a complaints procedure to be established in the future.

As noted above, the Committee's current evaluation process, while

43. *Id.* ¶ 37.
44. *Id.* ¶ 38.
45. *Id.* ¶ 9.
46. *Id.* ¶ 11.
47. *Id.* ¶ 10.
48. Id. ¶¶ 82, 85.

sparing in the use of violations terminology, focusses on problems and concerns. Furthermore, the openness of the Committee to the involvement of nongovernmental organizations is likely to accentuate even further the emphasis on infringements and violations. The present working methods of the Committee invite the participation of nongovernmental organizations in a variety of ways. First, nongovernmental organizations may submit relevant and appropriate documentation to the secretariat in preparation for the presessional working group that identifies in advance the questions that most usefully might be discussed with the representatives of the reporting states. Second, in order to ensure that the Committee is well informed, it provides opportunities for nongovernmental organizations to submit written reports at any time. Third, the Committee sets aside part of the first afternoon at each of its sessions for nongovernmental organizations to present information verbally.[49] Although the subject matter of this oral testimony was formerly confined to matters related to the states parties being reviewed at the session, the Committee agreed at its eleventh session to open the procedure to nongovernmental organizations wishing to address the performance of any state party. Nongovernmental organizations can also participate as experts during days of general, noncountry-specific discussions. Initially, only a few human rights organizations took advantage of these opportunities to participate, but the numbers of nongovernmental organizations represented has increased at each of the Committee's most recent sessions. In the 1994 regular and supplementary sessions of the Committee, nongovernmental organizations from Panama, Argentina, Hong Kong, and the Dominican Republic attended to communicate violations related to their respective countries' implementation of the Covenant. In the future, more nongovernmental organizations are likely to take advantage of this opportunity.

Nongovernmental organizations motivated to submit reports or to send representatives to Geneva to provide evidence undoubtedly will do so because they perceive problems and hope that the Committee can help rectify them. Although the Committee is reluctant to use explicit violations terminology, preferring to express its "principal subjects of concern" and to make "suggestions and recommendations," nongovernmental organizations need not adhere to such diplomatic niceties. Nongovernmental organizations can and should call a violation a violation, both in issuing their own performance evaluations and in reporting on the Committee's concluding observations.

---

49. *Committee on Economic, Social and Cultural Rights. Report on the Tenth and Eleventh Sessions (2–20 May and 21 Nov.–9 Dec. 1994). Economic and Social Council. Official Records, 1995. Supplement No. 3,* ¶¶ 26–27, U.N. Doc. E/1995/22 (1995); U.N. Doc. E/C.12/1994/20 (1994) [hereinafter *Report on the Tenth and Eleventh Sessions*].

In advocating that monitors of economic, social, and cultural rights utilize a violations approach, this article is not claiming that the identification and prevention of violations of these rights should be the sole thrust of efforts by nongovernmental organizations and the international community. Efforts to improve the implementation of these rights also require the conceptualization of their content (particularly the core minimum of each right), the formulation of indicators of performance, and the establishment of various types of advisory services that can assist states parties in developing plans of action. However, in the current environment, where the Committee and nongovernmental organizations have scarce resources and capabilities, a violations approach seems the most feasible and productive.

V. TYPES OF VIOLATIONS

The Limburg Principles on the nature and scope of the obligations of states parties to the Covenant, define a "violation" of the Covenant as a failure by a state party to comply with an obligation articulated therein. These failures may be acts of either commission or omission. Like the rights classified as civil and political rights, many economic, social, and cultural rights consist of requirements for states parties to both desist from particular kinds of activity and to fulfill specific requirements. According to the Limburg Principles, a state party will be in violation of the Covenant if:

- it fails to take a step which the Covenant requires it to take;
- it fails to remove promptly obstacles which it is obligated to remove in order to permit the immediate fulfillment of a right;
- it fails to implement without delay a right which the Covenant requires it to provide immediately;
- it willfully fails to meet a generally accepted international minimum standard of achievement, which is within its powers to meet;
- it applies a limitation to a right recognized in the Covenant in a manner not in accordance with the Covenant;
- it deliberately retards or halts the progressive realization of a right, unless it is acting within a limitation permitted by the Covenant, or it does so because of a lack of available resources or due to *force majeure*; or
- it fails to submit reports as required under the Covenant.[50]

---

50. The Limburg Principles on the nature and scope of the obligations of states parties to the International Covenant on Economic, Social and Cultural Rights were developed by a group of distinguished experts in international law convened by the International Commission of Jurists, the Faculty of Law of the University of Limburg, and the Urban

To provide a more meaningful categorization of violations and to make it more feasible to identify violations of the Covenant, this article proposes a tripartite scheme. In monitoring economic, social, and cultural rights, it is useful to distinguish among three types of violations: (1) violations resulting from actions and policies on the part of governments; (2) violations related to patterns of discrimination; and (3) violations related to a state's failure to fulfill the minimum core obligations of enumerated rights. Here, it should be noted that, while the Committee has identified violations in all three categories in its examination of states parties' reports, the typology given here is the author's own.

Violations resulting from state actions (type 1) comprise the type of violation most comparable to violations of civil and political rights. Many are acts of commission or activities of states or governments that contravene standards set in the Covenant. Others are policies or laws that create conditions inimical to the realization of recognized rights. In categorizing these failures of state policy as violations of the Covenant, the language of Article 5 should be borne in mind. Article 5 states that "[n]othing in the present Covenant may be interpreted as implying for any State, group or person any right to engage in any activity or to perform any act aimed at the destruction of any of the rights or freedoms recognized herein. . . ."[51]

Violations related to patterns of discrimination (type 2) also represent a fundamental breach of the Covenant. According to the Covenant, states parties have the immediate obligation to ensure nondiscrimination. Article 2(2) calls on states parties to guarantee that the rights enumerated in the Covenant "will be exercised without discrimination of any kind as to race, color, sex, language, religion, political or other opinion, national or social origin, property, birth or other status."[52] Article 3 further amplifies that states parties are required "to undertake to ensure the equal rights of men and women to the enjoyment of all economic, social, and cultural rights set forth in the present Covenant."[53] Obligations under Articles 2(2) and 3 ensure that nondiscrimination is not subject to progressive realization. These provisions have been interpreted as requiring both negative measures to prevent discrimination and positive "affirmative action"-type initiatives to compensate for past discrimination.[54] Moreover, the Committee has indicated that

---

Morgan Institute for Human Rights (University of Cincinnati) meeting in Maastricht on 2–6 June 1986. The principles and a series of related papers are found in *The Limburg Principles on the Implementation of the International Covenant on Economic, Social and Cultural Rights*, 9 Hum. Rts. Q. 122, 131, ¶¶ 37–40 (1987).

51. International Covenant on Economic, Social and Cultural Rights, *supra* note 2, art. 5.
52. *Id.* at art. 2(2).
53. *Id.* at art. 3.
54. The United Nations and Human Rights, *supra* note 19, at 47.

the positive measures needed to give effect to Article 2(2) go beyond the mere enactment of legislation.[55]

While "discrimination" is not defined in the Covenant itself, the section on the Covenant in the United Nations *Manual on Human Rights Reporting,* written by Philip Alston, the current Chair of the Committee, observes that its meaning may be ascertained by reference to the usage developed in the references and interpretation of other international human rights instruments, particularly Article 2(1) of the International Covenant on Civil and Political Rights, Article 1 of the International Convention on the Elimination of All Forms of Racial Discrimination, and Article 1 of the Convention on the Elimination of All Forms of Discrimination Against Women. When considered in relationship to these provisions, according to Alston, discrimination for purposes of the Covenant

> may be understood to cover any distinction, exclusion, restriction or preference which is based on any ground such as race, colour, sex, language, religion, political or other opinion, national or social origin, property, birth or other status, and which has the purpose or effect of nullifying or impairing the recognition, enjoyment or exercise by all persons, on an equal footing, of all of the rights set forth in the Covenant.[56]

As interpreted in the Limburg Principles, the obligations for states parties to ensure nondiscrimination under the Covenant are quite comprehensive. Upon becoming a party to the Covenant, states are under an obligation to eliminate both *de jure* and *de facto* forms of discrimination. It is expected that each state party will rescind without delay all discriminatory laws, regulations, and practices (including acts of omission as well as commission) that adversely affect the realization of the rights covered by the Covenant. States parties also are called upon to end all forms of discrimination occurring as a result of the unequal enjoyment of economic, social, and cultural rights as quickly as possible. In addition, Article 2(2) demands that states parties "prohibit private persons and [groups] from practicing discrimination in any field of public life."[57]

There is a general consensus among interpreters of various international and regional human rights instruments that some, but not all, distinctions or differential treatment constitute discrimination. In the *Belgian Linguistic Case,*[58] for example, the European Court of Human Rights developed criteria

---

55. *Id.* at 48.
56. *Id.* at 47.
57. *The Limburg Principles on the Implementation of the International Covenant on Economic, Social and Cultural Rights, supra* note 50, at 127.
58. *Belgian Linguistic Case,* 1968 *Y.B. Eur. Conv. on Hum. Rts.* 832 (*cited in* Yvonne Klerk, *Working Paper on Article 2(2) and Article 3 of the International Covenant on Economic, Social and Cultural Rights,* 9 Hum. Rts. Q. 250, 255 (1987)).

useful for determining when differential treatment amounts to a violation of the principle of nondiscrimination. According to this judgment, discrimination in the sense of Article 2(2) of the Covenant exists if:

> (a) the facts found disclose a differential treatment;
>
> (b) the distinction does not have a legitimate aim, i.e.[,] it has no objective and reasonable justification having regard to the aim and effects of the measure under consideration; and
>
> (c) there is no reasonable proportionality between the means employed and the aim . . . to be realized.[59]

The third category of violations consists of those resulting from the failure to fulfill minimum core obligations. In its third General Comment, the Committee declared itself to be "of the view that a minimum core obligation to ensure the satisfaction of, at the very least, minimum essential levels of each of the rights is incumbent upon every state party."[60] According to the General Comment, "a State party in which any significant number of individuals is deprived of essential foodstuffs, of essential primary health care, of basic shelter and housing, or of the most basic forms of education is, *prima facie*, failing to discharge its obligations under the Covenant."[61] While recognizing that resource constraints impose limitations, the Committee emphasized that the obligation remains for each state party to strive to ensure the widest possible enjoyment of the relevant rights. "Moreover, the obligations to monitor the extent of the realization, or more especially of the non-realization, of economic, social and cultural rights, and to devise strategies and programmes for their promotion, are not in any way eliminated as a result of resource constraints."[62] Similarly, the Committee underscored that, even in times of severe resource constraints, the vulnerable members of society "can and indeed must be protected by the adoption of relatively low-cost targeted programs."[63]

At this point, the Committee has neither defined the core minimum obligations of states parties related to specific rights nor delineated the minimum core content of each enumerated right. Therefore, it could be anticipated that identifying violations of omission (type 3) would be especially problematic. Nevertheless, examination of the section entitled "Suggestions and Recommendations" in the Committee's concluding observations indicates that the Committee has in fact been able to identify such violations. The Committee's suggestions and recommendations usually

59. *Id.*
60. *General Comment 3, supra* note 24, ¶ 10.
61. *Id.*
62. *Id.* ¶ 11.
63. *Id.* ¶ 12.

include a list of enumerated rights that a given state party is not implementing, as well as advice on how to improve compliance with the Covenant's standards in relationship to specific rights. In this manner, the Committee already seems to have adopted something of a violations approach.

VI. VIOLATIONS OF ECONOMIC, SOCIAL, AND CULTURAL RIGHTS IDENTIFIED BY THE COMMITTEE

Compiling an inventory of specific examples of each of the three types of violations for each of the rights enumerated in the Covenant is a first step toward developing improved monitoring capabilities. By anticipating the kinds of violations that monitors are likely to encounter, an inventory can provide the foundation for formulating instructions and guides as to what monitors should consider in relation to specific rights. Through a better understanding of the most significant violations, it also will be possible to develop standards and indicators for evaluating compliance with the Covenant. Improving the capabilities of nongovernmental organizations to monitor violations and better linking them to relevant UN and regional monitoring bodies also will help to make the Committee more effective.

The remainder of this article examines reports of the Committee as a resource for identifying specific violations related to each of the three categories described above. The present piece of research is one component of a larger project that also will review existing literature and survey grass roots organizations to develop an inventory of violations. This inventory then will be used to develop methodologies and resources to enable nongovernmental organizations to better monitor these rights. This article, thus, is intended as an invitation to other human rights advocates, international lawyers, researchers, and nongovernmental organizations to contribute to the development of a fuller cataloguing of actual and potential violations of all rights enumerated in the Covenant.

The following inventory of violations is based on a review of the official records of the Committee supplemented by the author's observation and discussions with Committee members and staff. It includes the following sessions:

- Sixth Session (25 November through 13 December 1991);[64]
- Seventh Session (23 November through 11 December 1992);[65]

64. *Committee on Economic, Social and Cultural Rights. Report on the Sixth Session (25 Nov.–13 Dec. 1991). Economic and Social Council. Official Records, 1992. Supplement No. 3.*, Committee on Economic, Social And Cultural Rights, U.N. Doc. E/1992/23 (1992); U.N. Doc. E/C.12/1991/4 (1992) [hereinafter *Report on the Sixth Session*].

65. *Report on the Seventh Session, supra* note 13, ¶ 264.

- Eighth Session (10 through 28 May 1993);[66]
- Ninth Session (22 November through 10 December 1993);[67]
- Tenth Session (2 through 20 May 1994);[68] and the
- Eleventh Session (21 November through 9 December 1994).[69]

While these reports review a wide range of countries and examples of violations, the inventory is meant to be exemplary, not exhaustive.

In evaluating the inventory compiled here, the limitations under which the Committee operates need to be borne in mind. To date, the Committee has been dependent on a limited range of information, consisting primarily of states parties' reports, documents submitted by a small number of nongovernmental organizations, and some data from other UN agencies. As noted above, reports submitted by states parties rarely conform to the reporting guidelines and tend, almost without exception, to be superficial and inadequate, designed more to camouflage than to illuminate problems and inadequacies. Moreover, governments frequently do not comply with the Committee's requests for supplementary data. Only one UN agency, the International Labour Organization, regularly compiles data for the Committee. With only one staff member, who has other responsibilities as well, the Committee simply does not have adequate research capabilities. Fact-finding missions also are difficult for the Committee to undertake because they require an invitation from the prospective host government.

In addition to these data limitations, the volume of reports that the Committee must cover at each session makes it difficult to undertake a thorough examination. According to the Committee's procedures, a presessional working group reviews the written state party report and requests supplementary information, also identifying in advance the questions that might be most usefully discussed with representatives of each reporting state. The Committee usually devotes three sessions, each three hours in length, to its review of a state party report. Representatives of the reporting states are both entitled and strongly encouraged to be present at the sessions. The formal review begins with introductory comments by the representative of the state party and then proceeds to a question and answer exchange between Committee members and the state party's representative(s). However, it is not unusual for state party representatives, even those from Western democratic governments, to be defensive and unhelpful, refusing

66. *Committee on Economic, Social and Cultural Rights. Report on the Eighth and Ninth Sessions (10–28 May 1993 and 22 Nov.–10 Dec. 1993). Economic and Social Council. Official Records, 1994. Supplement No. 3,* Committee on Economic, Social and Cultural Rights, U.N. Doc. E/1994/23 (1994); U.N. Doc. E/C.12/1993/19 (1994) [hereinafter *Report on the Eighth and Ninth Sessions*].
67. *Id.*
68. *Report on the Tenth and Eleventh Sessions, supra* note 49.
69. *Id.*

to answer specific questions or to provide requested data. Even under the best of circumstances, when the state party seeks to be cooperative and conscientious, there is insufficient time to explore more than a few issues in any depth. Thus, the interchange is often unsatisfactory.

The types of violations detected in particular countries frequently are correlated with the involvement of nongovernmental organizations in monitoring relevant rights and either sending reports to the Committee or attending its sessions. For example, among countries reviewed in the Committee's eleventh session, the catalogue of Committee concerns regarding the United Kingdom and its dependent territories is far greater than those noted for Mali. This situation has less to do with the objective reality than with the Committee's access to data. Whereas a large contingent of nongovernmental organizations was present from the United Kingdom (particularly Hong Kong), the Committee did not have the benefit of either a government report or information from nongovernmental organizations in Mali. Similarly, the type and incidence of violations noted also often reflects the interests of the reporting groups. For example, the abundant cataloguing of violations relating to infringements of the right to housing bears testament to the exemplary collaboration between nongovernmental organizations working on this subject (particularly the International Habitat Coalition) and the Committee, but only partially reflects the serious problems that exist in many countries.

Two further caveats should be kept in mind. The first involves the relation between the language used by the Committee and that used by the author. Like many other actors within the UN system, the Committee is inclined to diplomatic formulations and disinclined to label inadequacies and problems as violations. In the Committee's early years, its reports focussed primarily on the relative inclusiveness of the states parties' reports and on the subjects discussed in the oral review, and the concluding observations contained little in the way of actually evaluating the performance of the countries being examined. At its seventh session, the Committee decided to broaden criteria for summary observations to focus not only on the extent to which the report and the supplementary information that were submitted were satisfactory, but also on the situation with regard to the realization of the rights in the Covenant. In conjunction with this decision, the Committee adopted a new format for its concluding observations similar to that of many of the other human rights treaty-monitoring bodies.[70] Beginning with its eighth session, the Committee describes "positive aspects," goes on to note "factors and difficulties affecting the implementation of the Covenant," then identifies "principal

70. *Report on the Seventh Session*, *supra* note 13, ¶¶ 263–64.

subjects of concern" and makes "suggestions and recommendations." While the Committee comes close to using the language of violations, it is reluctant to use it explicitly. In compiling the inventory used here, some of these "concerns" and "recommendations" have been translated into violations and it should be noted that Committee members do not necessarily concur with the judgment of this author.

The final caveat concerns the provisional nature of the categorization of specific violations. When the Covenant articulates a positive obligation and a government refrains from fulfilling its obligations, it is particularly difficult to determine whether this inaction should be considered a type 1 or a type 3 violation. For example, Article 13 of the Covenant recognizes that primary education should be compulsory and free to all,[71] and Article 14 mandates that each state party which does not provide compulsory primary education, free of charge, at the time of accession develop a detailed plan of action to do so within two years.[72] Many countries do not fulfill this duty and in this era of IMF-dictated austerity plans it is more common than not for educational investments and rates of school attendance to be declining rather than improving in poor countries. There are good arguments for labeling these failures as both direct acts of state policy and the results of states' inability or refusal to implement a core minimum. In the inventory below, egregious examples of nonimplementation are considered to be deliberate state policies and therefore to fall under the first category of violations.

A. Type 1: Violations Deriving from Governmental Actions, Laws, and Policies

Right to self-determination (Article 1):

The government of Morocco has not allowed the Western Sahara to exercise the right to self-determination.[73]

Progressive full realization of the enumerated rights, including the adoption of legislative measures (Article 2(1)):

(1) In a number of countries, the Covenant does not have full legal status under domestic legislation, and individuals are circumscribed in invoking the Covenant before the courts. Countries which have been so criticized by the

71. International Covenant on Economic, Social and Cultural Rights, *supra* note 2, at art. 13.
72. *Id.* at art. 14
73. *Report on the Tenth and Eleventh Sessions, supra* note 49, ¶ 110.

Committee include Sweden[74] and Belgium.[75] In several cases, the Committee has noted the contrast with the International Covenant on Civil and Political Rights, which can be directly invoked by complainants before national courts and tribunals.

(2) In the case of Hong Kong, the Committee found unacceptable the view expressed by the government that the rights in the Covenant were "different in nature" from civil and political rights and therefore not capable of being incorporated into domestic law.[76]

(3) The Committee has noted a contradiction between the obligations set forth under the Covenant and various provisions relating to the civil law status governed by the Moroccan *Code of Personal Status,* which is partly based on religious precepts.[77]

(4) The rights enumerated in the Covenant are contained neither in the Constitution of Kenya nor in a separate bill of rights, and have not been incorporated into Kenyan national law. Further, there is no "institution or national machinery with responsibility for overseeing implementation of human rights in the country[,]" as the courts do not "play an effective role in the enforcement of human rights."[78]

(5) "In some [Canadian] court decisions and in recent [Canadian] constitutional discussions, social and economic rights have been described as mere 'policy objectives' of governments rather than as fundamental human rights."[79] "[P]rovincial human rights legislation has not always been applied in a manner which would provide improved remedies against violations of social and economic rights."[80]

(6) In Iran, the enjoyment of universally recognized human rights is subject to such restrictions as "provided it is not against Islam," "in conformity with . . . Islamic criteria," and not "detrimental to fundamental principles of Islam." "[T]hese restrictive clauses negatively affect the application of the Covenant, in particular . . . [A]rticle 2(2) (non-discrimination), [A]rticle 3 (equality of rights of men and women), [A]rticle 6 (right to work), [A]rticle 12 (right to health), [A]rticle 13 (right to education), and [A]rticle 15 (right to take part in cultural life)." The Committee concluded that authorities in Iran are using religion as a pretext to abuse these rights.[81]

---

74. *Report on the Sixth Session, supra* note 64, ¶ 258.
75. *Report on the Tenth and Eleventh Sessions, supra* note 49, ¶ 146.
76. *Id.* ¶ 285.
77. *Id.* ¶ 109.
78. *Report on the Eighth and Ninth Sessions, supra* note 66, ¶ 76.
79. *Id.* ¶ 110.
80. *Id.* ¶ 113.
81. *Id.* ¶ 125.

Rights to work, to enjoyment of just and favourable conditions of work (Articles 6 and 7):

Employers' and workers' representatives were not consulted in setting the national minimum wage for agricultural workers and public sector employees in Uruguay.[82]

Right to form trade unions (Article 8):

(1) Provisions of Zairian law which make permanent staff of the State public service automatically members of the National Union of Zairian Workers are inconsistent with the freedom of the individual to join the trade union of his/her choice.[83]

(2) Although the Moroccan constitution guarantees the right of association, the right to form labor unions, and the right to strike, these rights are violated in practice.[84]

(3) In several countries, among them Uruguay[85] and Mauritius,[86] there are restrictions on the right to strike. This has the effect of making most strikes illegal and provides grounds for the dismissal of striking workers.

(4) "The domination of the Central Organization of Trade Unions (COTU) by KANU [in Kenya] appears to contravene the letter and spirit of the Covenant."[87] There is a similar absence of an independent and pluralized trade union movement, with the right to strike, in Vietnam.[88]

Right to social security (Article 9):

(1) There are "reports of large-scale mismanagement of the National Social Security Fund" in Kenya.[89]

(2) Recent, extensive reforms in the social security and labor relations system in New Zealand might affect negatively the enjoyment of enumerated rights.[90]

Rights to protection of and assistance to the family (Article 10):

(1) Despite legislation to the contrary, child labor is still prevalent in a number of countries, among them Mali.[91]

82. *Id.* ¶ 19.
83. *Report on the Sixth Session, supra* note 64, ¶ 328.
84. *Report on the Tenth and Eleventh Sessions, supra* note 49, ¶ 115.
85. *Id.* ¶ 70.
86. *Id.* ¶ 175.
87. *Report on the Eighth and Ninth Sessions, supra* note 66, ¶ 79.
88. *Id.* ¶ 139.
89. *Id.* ¶ 80.
90. *Id.* ¶ 191.
91. *Report on the Tenth and Eleventh Sessions, supra* note 49, ¶ 348.

(2) Hong Kong's immigration laws result in split families (i.e., forced separation of spouses; children living apart from parents).[92]

Right of everyone to an adequate standard of living, including food, clothing, and housing (Article 11):

(1) On several occasions, the Committee has reminded states parties that "instances of forced evictions are *prima facie* incompatible with the requirements of the Covenant and can only be justified in the most exceptional circumstances, and in conformity with relevant principles of international law." Nicaragua was so reminded when the Committee requested precise information on the expulsion of persons from occupied land.[93]

(2) During a five year period (1986 through 1991), the massive expulsion of nearly 15,000 families took place in the Dominican Republic, resulting in deplorable living conditions for the expelled families.[94] The Committee also has expressed concerns about forced evictions in the Dominican Republic and about the ease with which the government is prepared to authorize or undertake demolition of homes, even when such dwellings are capable of being repaired or renovated.[95]

(3) Panama was severely criticized for forcibly removing over 5,000 people from their homes following the U.S. military action and for failing to rehouse those made homeless, including up to 20,000 persons who lost their homes due to bombing.[96]

(4) In the United Kingdom and its dependent territories, a large number of households have experienced harassment or illegal eviction.[97]

(5) Mexico was criticized for "the prevalence of forced evictions in both urban and rural areas."[98]

Right to health (Article 12):

The Committee has expressed profound concern about the prevalence of the traditional practice of female genital mutilation in some countries. Mali, for instance, was criticized for not enforcing 30-year-old legislation prohibiting this practice.[99]

---

92. *Id.* ¶ 289.
93. *Report on the Eighth and Ninth Sessions, supra* note 66, ¶ 209 (emphasis added).
94. *Report on the Sixth Session, supra* note 64, ¶ 330 (*referring to Report on the Fifth Session, supra* note 25, ¶ 250).
95. *Report on the Tenth and Eleventh Sessions, supra* note 49, ¶¶ 319–20.
96. *Report on the Sixth Session, supra* note 64, ¶ 135.
97. *Report on the Tenth and Eleventh Sessions, supra* note 49, ¶ 274.
98. *Report on the Eighth and Ninth Sessions, supra* note 66, ¶ 235.
99. *Report on the Tenth and Eleventh Sessions, supra* note 49, ¶ 351.

Right to education (Articles 13 and 14):

(1) The failure of the government in Finland to authorize the necessary certificates and to provide sufficient financial support has resulted in the disappearance of private educational institutions.[100]

(2) In the United Kingdom, there is a growing reliance in the context of education reform on voluntary contributions by parents instead of free education.[101]

(3) There are reports of the infringement of academic freedom in Iraq[102] and the drainage programs that the Iraqi government has initiated affecting the areas inhabited by the "Marsh Arabs" has impacted that community's ability to exercise its right to education.[103]

(4) Freedoms of debate and choice are restricted in Iranian universities.[104]

(5) In Kenya, academic freedom is still curtailed through intimidation and a variety of measures, such as the requirement for academics to obtain official research and travel clearance.[105]

(6) Budgetary cutbacks carried out in the educational sector under the program of structural adjustment will result in much lower school enrollment in a number of countries, including Senegal.[106]

Right to take part in cultural life and to enjoy the benefits of scientific progress (Article 15):

(1) The government of Iraq is destroying the cultural heritage of religious communities and minorities.[107] Another violation of this right in Iraq consists of government policies that control the choice and broadcast of minority language programs.[108] Further, drainage programs in areas inhabited by "Marsh Arabs" have an adverse impact on that community's ability to conserve its culture and traditional lifestyle.[109]

(2) The two languages spoken by a large majority of the population in Mauritius are not used in the educational system, are banned in the national assembly, and are actively discouraged in all government institutions.[110]

---

100. *Report on the Sixth Session, supra* note 64, ¶ 219.
101. *Report on the Tenth and Eleventh Sessions, supra* note 49, ¶ 276.
102. *Id.* ¶ 135.
103. *Id.* ¶ 138.
104. *Report on the Eighth and Ninth Sessions, supra* note 66, ¶ 126.
105. *Id.* ¶ 85.
106. *Id.* ¶ 261.
107. *Report on the Tenth and Eleventh Sessions, supra* note 49, ¶ 136.
108. *Id.* ¶ 138.
109. *Id.* ¶¶ 136, 138.
110. *Id.* ¶¶ 181–82.

(3) Kenya was criticized for government intervention in "cultural life, [as] through . . . the banning of plays and the prohibition of certain books and periodicals."[111]

(4) The government of Iran persists in the violation of the right of the Baha'i community to take part in cultural life.[112]

Responsibility to submit periodic reports (Articles 16, 17, and 18):

The Committee has noted the failure of many countries to submit periodic reports. Several of the countries ratifying or acceding to the Covenant as early as 1976 have failed to submit even a single report. While the failure to report initially exempted a government from being examined by the Committee, the Committee decided at its seventh session to evaluate the performance of states parties even in the absence of reports. Reviews of Mali, Mauritius, the Gambia, Kenya, and Guinea have been conducted in the absence of reports, with members of the Committee relying on other sources of data. This has motivated several malingerers to send representatives for the session and then to prepare reports. Other countries have submitted reports very late; Belgium[113] and Senegal,[114] for instance, were criticized for being nearly ten years late with their reports.

B. Type 2: Violations Based on Acts or Policies Reflecting Discrimination

Responsibility to guarantee that the rights enunciated in the Covenant be exercised without discrimination of any kind (Article 2(2)):

(1) The Committee has criticized a number of countries for the failure of legislation to provide protection against discrimination consistent with the requirements of Article 2 of the Covenant. Another type of fundamental violation is for legislation to be written in a manner that allows for exclusions and exemptions that have the effect of discriminating against women. In various of its concluding observations, the Committee has expressed concerns about policies that have the effect of discriminating against the following: women, poor/disadvantaged regions, the homeless, disabled, indigenous peoples, the elderly, asylum seekers/illegal immigrants, foreigners, and domestic helpers. It is notable that in a world which offers few protections for "illegal immigrants," the Committee has disagreed with the interpretation of at least one government (the government of Hong

111. *Report on the Eighth and Ninth Sessions, supra* note 66, ¶ 85.
112. *Id.* ¶ 126.
113. *Report on the Tenth and Eleventh Sessions, supra* note 49, ¶ 145.
114. *Report on the Eighth and Ninth Sessions, supra* note 66, ¶ 260.

Kong) that asylum seekers are not entitled to enjoy the right to education or other rights in view of their status as "illegal immigrants."[115]

(2) In Morocco, a "dual" society persists, characterized by disparities in the level of modernization and the enjoyment of economic, social, and cultural rights which particularly affect persons living in the rural regions. For example, the rate of school attendance in urban areas is double that of rural regions.[116]

(3) Iran systematically discriminates against the Kurdish population in education, work, travel, housing, and cultural activities.[117]

(4) Gypsies in Romania continue to suffer many forms of unofficial discrimination which the government is unable to prevent and/or unwilling to redress; since the Revolution of 1989, there has been no appreciable improvement in the Roma's situation.[118]

(5) "[T]here has been practically no progress in ensuring greater respect and protection for [the] rights of . . . non-Muslim religious communities in . . . Iran."[119]

Responsibility to ensure the equal rights of men and women (Article 3):

(1) The Committee gives special consideration to issues relating to the rights of women and strictly interprets this provision of the Covenant. For example, the Committee has informed several Islamic countries, including Afghanistan[120] and Iran,[121] that Islamic law is not a sufficient ground to impede full application of the principle of equality of treatment between the sexes. Afghanistan was criticized for its failure to assure women equal rights under the law.

(2) The government of Iran fails to fulfill its responsibility to ensure the equality of women with men. Women are limited in the subjects that they can study and must seek their husband's permission to work or travel abroad.

(3) As in Iran, the Committee noted that women still occupy a subordinate role in Mauritian society and that discrimination and violence against women are serious social problems affecting women's enjoyment of their economic, social, and cultural rights.[122]

---

115. *Report on the Tenth and Eleventh Sessions, supra* note 49, ¶ 291.
116. *Id.* ¶ 111.
117. *Report on the Eighth and Ninth Sessions, supra* note 66, ¶ 126.
118. *Id.* ¶ 94.
119. *Id.* ¶ 126.
120. *Report on the Sixth Session, supra* note 64, ¶ 93.
121. *Report on the Eighth and Ninth Sessions, supra* note 66, ¶ 125.
122. *Report on the Tenth and Eleventh Sessions, supra* note 49, ¶ 172.

Right to work, to enjoyment of just and favourable conditions of work (Articles 6 and 7):

(1) Women in several countries, among them Morocco, do not enjoy equal rights as regards matters arising under Articles 6 and 7, such as employment opportunities and equal remuneration for equal work.[123] This inequality continues despite the efforts of some governments, that of Iceland for example, to address the problem through legislation.[124] In other countries, such as Mauritius, women in specific sectors are paid lower wages for the same work done by men on the (stated) assumption that their productivity is lower than that of men.[125]

(2) The Committee has noted that, particularly in developed countries, "insufficient proportions of women [work] in certain areas of the economy." Finland provides a prime example of this phenomenon.[126]

(3) In the United Kingdom, women are still employed disproportionately in lower paid occupations.[127]

(4) The government of Mauritius has not assured that foreign workers, employed mainly in the textile and construction industries, are treated in accordance with the provisions of Article 7.[128]

(5) Hong Kong does not allow domestic workers from abroad to bring their families into the territory, yet permits professional migrant workers from developed countries to do so.[129]

(6) In Austria, there are persistent inequalities in the remuneration of women as compared with men, particularly in the private sector. Despite the existence of legislation mandating that women be treated as the equals of men, there are inequalities between the sexes in practice, particularly in the matter of promotion, and sometimes in the provision of social benefits.[130]

(7) Discrimination was shown in the German government's pattern of dismissal of teachers and other public sector employees of the former German Democratic Republic.[131]

Right to form trade unions (Article 8):

In Austria, workers in small businesses seem not to enjoy adequate protection against the threat of dismissal or termination for participating in trade union activities.[132]

123. *Id.* ¶ 112.
124. *Report on the Eighth and Ninth Sessions, supra* note 66, ¶ 222.
125. *Report on the Tenth and Eleventh Sessions, supra* note 49, ¶ 174.
126. *Report on the Sixth Session, supra* note 64, ¶ 219.
127. *Report on the Tenth and Eleventh Sessions, supra* note 49, ¶ 273.
128. *Id.* ¶ 174.
129. *Id.* ¶ 292.
130. *Id.* ¶ 254.
131. *Report on the Eighth and Ninth Sessions, supra* note 66, ¶ 249.
132. *Report on the Tenth and Eleventh Sessions, supra* note 49, ¶ 256.

Right to social security (Article 9):

Women in Kenya "whose husbands are in taxable employment cannot participate in the [program] of the National Hospital Insurance Fund."[133]

Rights to protection of and assistance to the family (Article 10):

(1) Children born out of wedlock are the objects of discrimination in many societies, among them Moroccan society.[134]

(2) There are persistent gender differences in the regulation of marriage and family relations in many countries, including Morocco.[135]

(3) Traditional practices as well as existing laws in Mali place women at a disadvantage with regard to family and property rights.[136]

(4) In a number of societies, parents or guardians arrange marriages for women without their full and free consent. One country in which this occurs is the Gambia.[137]

Right of everyone to an adequate standard of living, including food, clothing and housing (Article 11):

In Canada, there is "widespread discrimination in housing against people with children, people on social assistance, people with low incomes," and people with outstanding debts.[138]

Right to health (Article 12):

(1) The Committee has noted that the geographical distribution of the limited health services available in Mali continues to show a heavy urban bias.[139]

(2) The island of Rodrigues is disadvantaged relative to the island of Mauritius in enjoying the rights to health and to education.[140]

Right to education (Articles 13 and 14):

(1) Many countries, including Iraq, do not give equal priority to the education of women.[141] Similarly, although the constitution of Mali states that there shall be no discrimination, economic and educational opportunities for women are still disproportionately limited; females in Mali receive only 29

---

133. *Report on the Eighth and Ninth Sessions, supra* note 66, ¶ 80.
134. *Report on the Tenth and Eleventh Sessions, supra* note 49, ¶ 116.
135. *Id.* ¶ 112.
136. *Id.* ¶ 344.
137. *Id.* ¶ 200.
138. *Report on the Eighth and Ninth Sessions, supra* note 66, ¶ 107.
139. *Report on the Tenth and Eleventh Sessions, supra* note 49, ¶ 350.
140. *Id.* ¶ 183.
141. *Id.* ¶ 133.

percent as much schooling as males and the adult literacy rate among women is only half that of the rate among men.[142]

(2) Women in Iran are not permitted to become magistrates, or "to study engineering, agriculture, mining, or metallurgy."[143]

(3) In the United Kingdom, there are regional disparities in the quality of education, as well as grave disparities which appear to prevail in the level of education depending on the social origins of the pupil.[144]

(4) Gypsies in Romania face discrimination in schools.[145]

(5) In Iran, the education provided to children belonging to the Kurdish minority is insufficient and members of the Baha'i faith are not allowed to attend university.[146]

(6) Children born out of wedlock in Morocco do not fully enjoy the right to education.[147]

C. Type 3: Violations Resulting from the Failure to Implement a Core Minimum

Progressive full realization of enumerated rights, including the adoption of legislative measures (Article 2(1)):

(1) The Committee has criticized countries, the United Kingdom[148] and Iceland,[149] for example, on the grounds that judges and other members of the legal profession give insufficient consideration to the Covenant within domestic law.

(2) The failure to promote awareness of the rights enumerated in the Covenant, as in Kenya, constitutes another violation or deficiency.[150]

(3) The Committee has expressed concern that particular governments, for example, Kenya[151] and Hong Kong,[152] are opposed to establishing a human rights commission or other body that would be able to adjudicate complaints of the infringement of rights under the Covenant.

142. *Id.* ¶ 344.
143. *Report on the Eighth and Ninth Sessions, supra* note 66, ¶ 127.
144. *Report on the Tenth and Eleventh Sessions, supra* note 49, ¶ 275.
145. *Id.* ¶ 94.
146. *Report on the Eighth and Ninth Sessions, supra* note 66, ¶ 126.
147. *Report on the Tenth and Eleventh Sessions, supra* note 49, ¶ 116.
148. *Id.* ¶ 271.
149. *Report on the Eighth and Ninth Sessions, supra* note 66, ¶ 224.
150. *Id.* ¶ 77.
151. *Id.* ¶ 76.
152. *Report on the Tenth and Eleventh Sessions, supra* note 49, ¶ 288.

(4) The text of New Zealand's recently adopted Bill of Rights contains no reference to economic, social, and cultural rights.[153]

(5) The government of Senegal failed to "undertake a systematic and comprehensive review of . . . relevant legislation, administrative procedures, and policies" in order to ensure that they conform to the requirements of the Covenant.[154]

Responsibility to guarantee the enumerated rights will be exercised without discrimination (Article 2(2)):

(1) There is no law on minorities in Romania, a country with large Gypsy, Hungarian, German, and other minority populations.[155] The Committee consequently recommended that the state party implement an active nondiscrimination policy with respect to its minorities.[156]

(2) Several countries, among them Iraq, were informed that they do not pay sufficient attention to the implementation of Article 2 of the Covenant as it relates to nondiscrimination in respect of the policies and measures adopted to promote and protect economic, social, and cultural rights. The Committee recommended, in particular, that Iraq address implementation of the rights provided for under Articles 13 to 15, particularly with respect to women and persons belonging to various cultural groups.[157]

Rights to work and to just and favourable conditions of work (Articles 6 and 7):

(1) The incidence of child labor has been an issue of recurring concern to the Committee. Morocco is an example.[158]

(2) In Morocco, labor laws and regulations are largely ignored or disregarded in the informal and traditional sectors of the economy and the absence or limited presence of labor inspectors has impeded the effective implementation of regulations relating to just and favorable conditions of work.[159]

(3) Ineffective enforcement of health and safety standards is a common problem. In Mauritius, it has resulted in fatal industrial accidents.[160]

---

153. *Consideration of Reports Submitted By States Parties Under Articles 16 and 17 of the Covenant. Concluding Observations of the Committee on Economic, Social and Cultural Rights. New Zealand,* Committee on Economic, Social and Cultural Rights, ¶ 190, U.N. Doc. E/C.12/1993/13 (1994).
154. *Report on the Eighth and Ninth Sessions, supra* note 66, ¶ 263.
155. *Report on the Tenth and Eleventh Sessions, supra* note 49, ¶ 93.
156. *Id.* ¶ 97.
157. *Id.* ¶ 139.
158. *Id.* ¶ 116.
159. *Id.* ¶ 114.
160. *Id.* ¶ 174.

(4) Failure to create employment means that only a small proportion of persons leaving school can expect to find work. Kenya is an example of a country in which the labor force participation rate is decreasing.[161] The Committee also recommended that Lebanon immediately address the problem of unemployment.[162]

(5) Despite the legal prohibition on forced labor in the new constitution of Mali, debt bondage still exists in the salt mining communities north of Timbuktu. Although Mali has a detailed labor code, most people earn their living in the informal sector and, thus, remain unprotected by such legislation. Due to a lack of inspectors, legal provisions on occupational safety remain insufficiently enforced.[163]

(6) Hong Kong does not set maximum working hours for domestic helpers.[164]

Right to form trade unions (Article 8):

(1) Several countries, among them Belgium, were informed that the right to strike needs to be explicitly inscribed in law.[165]

(2) The government of the Gambia has not ratified any of the ILO conventions.[166]

Right to social security (Article 9):

(1) In Hong Kong, the present level of social security payments to the elderly is insufficient to permit them to enjoy the rights set forth under the Covenant.[167]

(2) A number of countries, including Western democracies such as Belgium, do not take adequate measures to protect vulnerable groups or to assure their social benefits.[168]

(3) Despite the persistence of poverty in Canada, particularly among women and children, the federal government reduced the ratio of its contributions to cost-sharing agreements for social assistance.[169]

(4) The situation of children, particularly abandoned street children or children in extremely difficult circumstances, has been of concern to the Committee (in Mexico,[170] for example) and governments have been asked to do more to address the situation of these children.

161. *Report on the Eighth and Ninth Sessions, supra* note 66, ¶ 78.
162. *Id.* ¶ 176.
163. *Report on the Tenth and Eleventh Sessions, supra* note 49, ¶¶ 345–46.
164. *Id.* ¶ 292.
165. *Id.* ¶ 155.
166. *Id.* ¶ 199.
167. *Id.* ¶ 294.
168. *Id.* ¶ 153.
169. *Id.* ¶ 102.
170. *Report on the Eighth and Ninth Sessions, supra* note 66, ¶ 232.

Rights to protection of and assistance to the family (Article 10):

Mauritius was criticized for its lack of a comprehensive system of family benefits and for its failure to implement child labor laws.[171]

Right of everyone to an adequate standard of living, including food, clothing, and housing (Article 11):

(1) There is a shortage of housing in relationship to demand in Uruguay, where high rents disadvantage the most vulnerable groups in society.[172]

(2) Because a large number of households (particularly private tenants who are single parents, have low income, or are in general among the most vulnerable groups in society) were experiencing harassment or illegal evictions, the Committee concluded that the United Kingdom did not have an adequate housing policy. It also criticized the government's failure to make improvements to unsafe housing in England and Wales, as well as the failure of authorities to deal with the growing problems of the homeless. Hong Kong was cited for the failure of the government, despite the abundant financial resources at its disposal, to deal with the plight of persons, most of whom are elderly, living in subhuman conditions in "cage homes."[173]

(3) The minimum wage in a number of countries, among them Kenya[174] and Mexico,[175] is "too low to allow even a . . . modest standard of living."[176]

(4) While the Committee acknowledged the initiatives taken by the government of Argentina to overcome the housing shortage, it noted that there is no indication that the Argentine government's policies are adequate to meet the current need.[177]

(5) The government of New Zealand does not keep statistical information on the extent of malnutrition, hunger, or homelessness.[178]

(6) The Committee has recommended that several states parties, among them Belgium, undertake appropriate measures to promote and encourage the construction of low-cost rental housing.[179]

(7) The Committee has expressed concern about the persistence of poverty in a number of countries, particularly those where there are resources to address this issue. One example was Canada, where the Committee noted that there

171. *Report on the Tenth and Eleventh Sessions, supra* note 49, ¶ 177.
172. *Id.* ¶ 72.
173. *Id.* ¶ 293.
174. *Report on the Eighth and Ninth Sessions, supra* note 66, ¶ 78.
175. *Id.* ¶ 231.
176. *Id.*
177. *Report on the Tenth and Eleventh Sessions, supra* note 49, ¶ 235.
178. *Report on the Eighth and Ninth Sessions, supra* note 66, ¶ 193.
179. *Report on the Tenth and Eleventh Sessions, supra* note 49, ¶ 157.

was no progress in the past decade "in alleviating the severity of poverty among . . . vulnerable groups."[180]

(8) The Committee has expressed concerns with measures that many governments have taken under structural adjustment programs or for purposes of budget reduction. For example, the government of Mauritius abolished subsidies on rice and flour without replacing them with a system that would guarantee food security for the most vulnerable groups of the population.[181]

(9) In a number of instances, the Committee has reminded states parties of "the need to ensure that structural adjustment programmes are . . . formulated and implemented . . . to provide adequate safety nets for the vulnerable sectors of society." Both Nicaragua[182] and Morocco[183] have been so reminded.

(10) To protect vulnerable groups, the Committee has recommended the reallocation of national budgets. Mexico is an example.[184]

Right to health (Article 12):

(1) The Committee has expressed concerns that child, infant, and maternal mortality rates in Mali are still among the highest in the world. The average rate of access to water country-wide is 50 percent, but is as low as 4 percent in some areas.[185]

(2) The Committee has expressed profound concern about the prevalence of the traditional practice of female genital mutilation. It has criticized some governments, for example that of Mali,[186] for failing to enforce legislation prohibiting such practices.

(3) Government expenditures on health care appear to be constantly decreasing in Kenya and the introduction of fees for treatment in hospitals has had negative effects, particularly on those most vulnerable.[187]

Right to education (Articles 13 and 14):

(1) A number of countries were criticized for failure to develop a plan for the introduction of free and compulsory education as required under the Covenant. One such country is Zaire;[188] another is Kenya.[189]

---

180. *Report on the Eighth and Ninth Sessions, supra* note 66, ¶ 101.
181. *Report on the Tenth and Eleventh Sessions, supra* note 49, ¶ 178.
182. *Report on the Eighth and Ninth Sessions, supra* note 66, ¶ 214.
183. *Report on the Tenth and Eleventh Sessions, supra* note 49, ¶ 119.
184. *Report on the Eighth and Ninth Sessions, supra* note 66, ¶ 236.
185. *Report on the Tenth and Eleventh Sessions, supra* note 49, ¶ 350.
186. *Id.* ¶ 351.
187. *Report on the Eighth and Ninth Sessions, supra* note 66, ¶ 83.
188. *Report on the Sixth Session, supra* note 64, ¶ 328.
189. *Report on the Eighth and Ninth Sessions, supra* note 66, ¶ 84.

(2) The Committee has noted with concern the failure of many countries, among them Vietnam, to introduce a program to guarantee free primary education.[190]

(3) Despite high overall levels of school attendance, disadvantaged groups in many countries do not attend school. One country so characterized is Australia, where certain aboriginal communities have high illiteracy rates.[191] Australia also was criticized for "the lack of opportunities . . . to persons with disabilities [to] fully . . . enjoy their rights to education[, and] the effects of funding accorded to non-government schools on the quality of education" were noted with concern.[192]

(4) Kenya was reminded that the obligation to provide free and compulsory primary education to all "applies in all situations, including those in which local communities are unable to furnish buildings, or individuals are unable to afford any costs associated with school attendance."[193] Mexico also was so reminded and was asked to undertake vigorous steps toward compliance with this Article.[194]

(5) With regard to Mali, the Committee has expressed concern about the high rate of illiteracy and about the fact that the country has shown only modest progress in improving educational standards over the past twenty years. Over the past ten years, educational opportunities actually have been regressing. The rate of school enrollment in Mali is among the lowest in the world.[195]

(6) Deficiencies noted with regard to the United Kingdom are the failures to take sufficient measures toward the development of universal preschool education, to deal with the large number of children not completing school, to provide sufficient opportunities to enable persons with disabilities to pursue the right to education within the mainstream, and to address regional disparities in the quality of education.[196]

(7) It was recommended that the government of Romania pay more attention to the problem of street and abandoned children, and that it assure such children access to all forms of primary and secondary education.[197]

---

190. *Id.* ¶ 140.
191. *Id.* ¶ 150.
192. *Id.* ¶¶ 151–52.
193. *Id.* ¶ 84.
194. *Id.* ¶ 240.
195. *Report on the Tenth and Eleventh Sessions, supra* note 49, ¶ 352.
196. *Id.* ¶¶ 275–76.
197. *Id.* ¶ 98.

Right to take part in cultural life (Article 15):

(1) A number of countries do not undertake sufficient measures to help preserve the cultural identities of minorities. One example was Sweden not doing enough to help promote the cultures of the Sami and the Gypsies.[198]

(2) The Committee has recommended that a number of countries, Mexico for instance, do more to preserve the culture of indigenous groups.[199]

Responsibility to submit periodic reports (Articles 16, 17, and 18):

(1) Many countries were criticized for deficiencies in their reports. A common inadequacy was that the reports were too general and legalistic in nature, and that they placed "too much emphasis upon a recital of legislative decrees[,] rather than [providing] details of the practical measures taken for the implementation of the Covenant." Shortcomings of this kind were noted in the reports of Panama,[200] the Democratic People's Republic of Korea,[201] and Syria.[202] Other reports, for example a report from Finland, were considered to be "too short and not sufficiently informative."[203] Another frequent complaint relates to the absence of statistical and other data that would enable the Committee to evaluate the implementation of specific rights, such as the availability of educational opportunity for various sectors of the population in Iraq.[204]

(2) Several countries, including the United Kingdom, have been criticized for the failure to make reports easily available to the public and to include in the reports the concerns and views expressed by nongovernmental organizations and the public.[205]

(3) Governments criticized for omissions in their reports include Argentina, where the Committee expressed surprise at the absence of information about specific programs adopted by the government to guarantee the economic, social, and cultural rights of ethnic minorities.[206]

(4) Consistent with their frequent and justified criticisms of the inadequacies in reports, the Committee often requested additional data from particular governments. These requests were sometimes quite specific and detailed. In 1993, Nicaragua was asked "to provide detailed statistical information on the distribution of income and wealth among groups living in rural and urban areas of the country, disaggregated by linguistic and ethnic character-

198. *Report on the Sixth Session, supra* note 64, ¶ 259.
199. *Report on the Eighth and Ninth Sessions, supra* note 66, ¶ 233.
200. *Report on the Sixth Session, supra* note 64, ¶ 134.
201. *Id.* ¶ 157.
202. *Id.* ¶ 194.
203. *Id.* ¶ 218.
204. *Report on the Tenth and Eleventh Sessions, supra* note 49, ¶ 134.
205. *Id.* ¶ 271.
206. *Id.* ¶ 239.

istics. . . . Similar statistical information [was] also required on the mortality rates, birth rates, life expectancy[,] and the rates of school attendance up to [the] university level."[207]

VII. CONCLUSION

This article has argued that there needs to be a change in the paradigm for evaluating compliance with the norms in the Covenant if these rights are to be taken seriously. It has shown why "progressive realization," the current standard used to assess implementation, renders economic, social, and cultural rights difficult to monitor. It is time for nongovernmental organizations, governments, and human rights monitoring bodies to reorient their work toward identifying and rectifying violations. All of this, however, is not to diminish the importance of continuing with efforts to conceptualize the content of the constituent rights in the Covenant and to develop indicators to measure implementation, but rather to separate these efforts from the monitoring process.

Although it pays continual lip service to progressive implementation, the Committee evaluates problems and concerns with the performance of countries rather than the countries' success in achieving progressive realization of the enumerated rights. The preceding inventory of violations drawn from the concluding observations of the Committee testifies to the feasibility and fruitfulness of a violations approach. Despite the many limitations under which the Committee functions—superficial and inadequate state party reports, lack of cooperation from most of the governments being reviewed, insufficient staff, severe time constraints, and the failure of nongovernmental organizations in many of the countries to share their data—the Committee has been able to identify serious violations of the Covenant.

As important as it might be, this inventory is just a beginning. The constraints under which the Committee operates and the sources on which it has relied have made it difficult for the Committee to detect many types of violations. For example, there is little in the inventory relating to violations of the right to health, despite serious problems in many countries. The greater availability of data about countries at both ends of the human rights spectrum—gross abusers of human rights at one end and democratic countries with active human rights monitors at the other—enables the Committee to be more specific in identifying human rights violations in

207. *Report on the Eighth and Ninth Sessions, supra* note 66, ¶ 212.

these states parties. Most of the states parties that do not fall at either of the extremes, but which still fail to comply with the Covenant, receive a more cursory review. Further, the inventory is inadequate for purposes of evaluating the extent to which particular countries are violating economic, social, and cultural rights.

The next steps in ensuring that economic, social, and cultural rights are taken seriously should be to compile a fuller catalogue of types of violations of each of the constituent rights in the Covenant and to use this catalogue to develop resources for monitoring these rights. One potential source for examples of violations is to be found in the development, topical, and country literatures. A "bottom-up" approach that utilizes the experience of human rights monitors and nongovernmental organizations would be even more valuable. This article is meant as an invitation to other researchers and monitors to join with this author and the American Association for the Advancement of Science in the development of such a violations approach.

[14]

Freedoms and Needs

By Amartya Sen

At the southern edge of Bangladesh and West Ben gal in India, bordering on the Bay of Bengal, is the Sundarban, which literally means "beautiful forest." It is the natural habitat of the so-called Royal Bengal Tiger. Few of the tigers are left, but they are now protected by a hunting ban. The Sundarban is famous also for the honey that it produces in large clusters of natural bee hives. The people bordering that region, many of whom are desperately poor, go into the forests to collect the honey, but they also have to escape the tigers. In a good year, only about fifty or so honey gatherers are killed by tigers, but the number can be much higher when things do not go so well.

The tigers are protected, but nothing protects the human beings who make a living in those deep and lovely and perilous woods: this is just one illustration of the force of economic needs in many Third World countries. It is not hard to feel that this force can outweigh other claims, including the claims of liberty and political rights. If poverty drives human beings to take terrible risks, and sometimes to suffer terrible deaths, for a dollar or two of honey, it might well be odd to insist on discussing their liberty and their political rights.

A concept such as habeas corpus, for example, might not seem very relevant, or even at all communicable, in such a context. Priority must surely be given, or so the argument runs, to fulfilling economic needs, even if it involves compromising political liberties; political rights are a "luxury" that a poor country cannot afford." This skepticism about the primacy of political rights, including civil rights, is heard very frequently in international discussions. Why bother about the finesse of democracy given the over powering grossness of material need?

Such a question reflects a deep agnosticism about the urgency of political freedoms, an agnosticism that loomed large at the conference on human rights in Vienna earlier this year, where delegates from several countries argued against a general endorsement of basic political rights across the globe, in particular in the Third World. The focus, it was argued, should be rather on "economic rights" and the satisfaction of elementary economic needs. The declaration that emerged from the Vienna conference was very much a compromise, to which the United States was a leading party; it left many ambiguities in demanding civil and political rights, but it did acknowledge them in a general way, along with economic rights.

The place of political rights also has been under active debate in many other international forums, including various organs of the United Nations, even spilling into the recent meetings of the International Olympic Committee. It has become a particularly urgent question facing sub-Saharan Africa, as democracy begins to regain some of the ground it has lost fairly comprehensively since the 1960s. Indeed, there are few general issues more central to the contemporary, and especially the developing, world.

But is a dichotomous view of economic needs and political rights a sensible way of approaching the problem? Do needs and rights represent a basic contradiction? Do the former really undermine the latter? I would argue that this is altogether the wrong way to understand, first, the force of economic needs and, second, the salience of political rights. The real issues that have to be addressed lie elsewhere, and they involve taking note of extensive interconnections between the enjoyment of political rights and the appreciation of economic needs. Political rights can have a major role in providing incentives and information toward the solution of economic privation. But the connections between rights and needs are not merely instrumental; they are also constitutive. For our conceptualization of economic needs depends on open public debates and discussions, and the guaranteeing of those debates and those discussions requires an insistence on political rights.

The attack on political rights (which include civil rights) on the grounds of the force of economic needs contrasts starkly with a broad current of modern political philosophy that tends to assert, in one form or another, what John Rawls has called "the priority of liberty." That priority takes a particularly sharp form in modern libertarian theory, some formulations of which claim (for example, in Robert Nozick's first book, *Anarchy, State and Utopia*) that extensive classes of rights—varying from personal liberties to property rights—have nearly complete political precedence over the pursuit of social goals, including the removal of deprivation. In less demanding liberal formulations, most notably in the writings of Rawls, the rights that receive precedence are much less extensive, and essentially consist of various personal liberties. But the precedence that these more limited rights receive is complete; and while they cover much less than the rights championed in libertarian theory, they, too, cannot be in any way compromised by the force of economic needs.

The case for such a complete priority of liberty can be disputed by demonstrating the force of other considerations, including those of economic needs. Why must a society get all excited about making the desperately poor honey-gatherer in the Sundarban free from the interference of his neighbors or the state, while leaving him forced by economics to take the risk of being eaten by a tiger? This issue was raised, in a general form, by H. L. A. Hart in 1973, in a famous article in the *University of Chicago Law Review* disputing in particular the plausibility of presuming "a preference for liberty over other goods which every self-interested person who is rational would have." Rawls, too, has acknowledged the force of Hart's argument, and in his new book, *Political Liberalism*, he has suggested ways of accommodating it.

If the priority of liberty is to be made plausible in general, and particularly in the context of countries that are intensely poor, the nature of the claim would need, I would argue, to be considerably modified. It is possible to distinguish between Rawls's strict proposal that liberty should receive overwhelming precedence in the case of a conflict, and his general procedure of separating out personal liberty from other types of advantages, for special treatment. The second claim is a more general one, concerning the relative importance to be attached to liberties compared with individual advantages of other kinds. The real issue is not the absolute precedence of personal liberty, but whether a person's liberty should be given more importance than other types of personal advantages, such as incomes.

Is the significance of liberty for a society adequately reflected by the weight that an individual would tend to give to it in judging his or her own overall advantage? This may be disputed; and the issue of the pre-eminence of liberty relates to that challenge. The political significance of rights can far exceed the personal utility of rights; that is, it can exceed the extent to which the personal advantage of the holders of these rights is enhanced by having these rights. In this respect, political rights are not symmetrical with other sources of individual advantage; and the safeguarding of political rights would have the procedural priority that follows from this asymmetry.

Consider an illustration from India. The outrage that was felt across the country at the killing of helpless Muslims by a small but organized group of Hindu extremists in Bombay last winter did not simply reflect the tragedy of human deaths. While the number of people who perished in Bombay was large, perhaps as large as 1,000, in the scale of deaths this magnitude is outweighed many times over by the number of people who die from preventable illnesses every single day in that huge and needy country. What was outrageous was not only the unnecessary deaths, but also the violation, by means of targeted attacks on one particular community, of the liberty to live.

The people who died in those riots might or might not have themselves held a view as to whether, if they were to die, they would prefer to die of a painful illness or in an accident or at the hands of a communal rioter. That is not the issue here. The violation of their basic liberty to live, resulting from the homicidal actions of extremists, involved some thing much more terrible; and the nature of the outrage across India confirms the fact that this distinction is widely understood and seen to be important. It even had an impact, among other factors, on the recent electoral reverses suffered by the BJP, the Hindu activist party, in its contest with its secularist opponents, even though the BJP itself had not been directly involved in the murders.

This is not a matter of complicated deontology, which only a person steeped in high Kantianism can be expected to grasp. There are deep and fundamental and intuitively understood grounds for rejecting the view that confines itself merely to checking the parity of outcomes, the view that matches death for death, happiness for happiness, fulfillment for fulfillment, irrespective of how all this death, happiness and fulfillment comes about.

Those who are skeptical of the relevance of political rights to poor countries would not necessarily deny the basic importance of political rights. Some of them would not even deny my contention that the nastiness of the violation of liberty can go well beyond other forms of disadvantage. Instead their arguments turn on the impact of political rights on the fulfillment of economic needs, and they take this impact to be firmly negative and overwhelmingly important.

The belief abounds that political rights correlate negatively with economic growth. Indeed, something of a "general theory" of this relationship between political liberty and economic prosperity has been articulated recently by that unlikely theorist Lee Kuan Yew, the former prime minister of Singapore; and the praise of the supposed advantages of "the hard state" in promoting economic development goes back a long way in the development literature. Even the sagacious Gunnar Myrdal's extensive skepticism, in *Asian Drama*, of what he called "the soft state" has sometimes been interpreted (rather unfairly to Myrdal) as a celebration of political toughness in the cause of good economics.

It is true that some relatively authoritarian states (such as Lee's Singapore, South Korea under military rule and more recently China) have had faster rates of economic growth than some less authoritarian states (such as India, Costa Rica and Jamaica). But the overall picture is much more complex than such isolated observations might suggest. Systematic statistical studies give little support to the view of a general conflict between civil rights and economic performance. In fact, scholars such as Partha Dasgupta, Abbas Pourgerami and Surjit Bhalla have offered substantial evidence to suggest that political and civil rights have a *positive* impact on economic progress. Other scholars find divergent patterns, while still others argue, in the words of John Helliwell, that on the basis of the information so far obtained "an optimistic interpretation of the overall results would thus be that democracy, which apparently has a value independent of its economic effects, is estimated to be available at little cost in terms of subsequent lower growth."

There is not much comfort in all these findings for the "Lee Kuan Yew hypothesis" that there exists an essential conflict between political rights and economic performance. The general thesis in praise of the tough state suffers not only from casual empiricism based on a few selected examples, but also from a lack of conceptual discrimination. Political and civil rights come in various types, and authoritarian intrusions take many forms. It would be a mistake, for example, to equate North Korea with South Korea in the infringement of political rights, even though both have violated many such rights; the complete suppression of opposition parties in the North can hardly be taken to be no more repressive than the roughness with which opposition parties have been treated in the South. Some authoritarian regimes, both of the "left" and of the "right," such as Zaire or Sudan or Ethiopia or the Khmer Rouge's Cambodia, have been enormously more hostile to political rights than many other regimes that are also identified, rightly, as authoritarian.

Thus, broader empirical coverage as well as greater discrimination and precision are needed to re-examine the common generalizations in favor of the repressive state, and these generalizations do not survive much scrutiny. It is also necessary to examine more rigorously the *causal* process that is supposed to underlie these generalizations about the impact of authoritarianism on prosperity. The processes that led to the economic success of, say, South Korea are now reasonably well understood; a variety of factors played a part, including the use of international markets, an openness to competition, a high level of literacy, successful land reforms and the provision of selective incentives to encourage growth and exports. There is *nothing* to indicate that these economic and social policies were inconsistent with greater democracy, that they had to be sustained by the elements of authoritarianism actually present in South Korea. The danger of taking *post hoc* to be *propter hoc* is as real in the making of such political and strategic judgments as it is in any empirical reasoning.

Thus the fundamental importance of political rights is not refuted by some allegedly negative effect of these rights on economic performance. In fact, the instrumental connections may even give a very positive role to political rights in the context of deprivations of a drastic and elementary kind: whether, and how, a government responds to intense needs and sufferings may well depend on how much pressure is put on it, and whether or not pressure is put on it will depend on the exercise of political rights (such as voting, criticizing, protesting and so on).

Consider the matter of famine. I have tried to argue elsewhere that the avoidance of such economic disasters as famines is made much easier by the existence, and the exercise, of various liberties and political rights, including the liberty of free expression. Indeed, one of the remarkable facts in the terrible history of famine is that no substantial famine has ever occurred in a country with a democratic form of government and a relatively free press. They have occurred in ancient kingdoms and in contemporary authoritarian societies, in primitive tribal communities and in modern technocratic dictatorships, in colonial economies governed by imperialists from the north and in newly independent countries of the south run by despotic national leaders or by intolerant single parties. But famines have never afflicted any country that is independent, that goes to elections regularly, that has opposition parties to voice criticisms, that permits newspapers to report freely and to question the wisdom of government policies without extensive censorship.

Is this historical association between the absence of famine and the presence of political freedom a causal one, or is it simply an accidental connection? The possibility that the Connection between democratic political rights and the absence of famine is a "bogus correlation" may seem plausible when one considers the fact that democratic countries are typically rather rich, and thus immune to famine for other reasons. But the absence of famine holds even for those democratic countries that happen to be poor, such as India, Botswana and Zimbabwe. There is also what we might call "intertemporal evidence," which we observe when a country undergoes a transition to democracy. Thus India continued to have famines right up to the time of independence in 1947; the last famine, and one of the largest, was the Bengal famine of 1943, in which it is estimated that between 2 million and 3 million people died. Since independence, how ever, and the installation of a multiparty democratic system, there has been no substantial famine, even though severe crop failures and food scarcities have occurred often enough (in 1968, 1973, 1979 and 1987).

Why might we expect a general connection between democracy and the nonoccurrence of famines? The answer is not hard to seek. Famines kill millions of people in different countries in the world, but they do not kill the rulers. The kings and the presidents, the bureaucrats and the bosses, the military leaders and the commanders never starve. And if there are no elections, no opposition parties, no forums for uncensored public criticism, then those in authority do not have to suffer the political consequences of their failure to prevent famine. Democracy, by contrast, would spread the penalty of famine to the ruling groups and the political leadership.

There is, moreover, the issue of information. A free press, and more generally the practice of democracy, contributes greatly to bringing out the information that can have an enormous impact on policies for famine prevention, such as facts about the early effects of droughts and floods, and about the nature and the results of unemployment. The most elementary source of basic information about a threatening famine is the news media, especially when there are incentives, which a democratic system provides, for revealing facts that may be embarrassing to the government, facts that an undemocratic regime would tend to censor. Indeed, I would argue that a free press and an active political opposition constitute the best "early warning system" that a country threatened by famine can possess.

The connection between political rights and economic needs can be illustrated in the specific context of famine prevention by considering the massive Chinese famines of 1958-61. Even before the recent economic reforms, China had been much more successful than India in economic development. The average life expectancy, for example, rose in China much more than it did in India, and well before the reforms of 1979 it had already reached something like the high figure—nearly seventy years at birth—that is quoted now. And yet China was unable to prevent famine. It is now estimated that the Chinese famines of 1958-61 killed close to 30 million people—ten times more than even the gigantic 1943 famine in British India.

The so-called "Great Leap Forward," initiated in the late 1950s, was a massive failure, but the Chinese government refused to admit it, and continued dogmatically to pursue much the same disastrous policies for three more years. It is hard to imagine that this could have happened in a country that goes to the polls regularly and has an independent press. During that terrible calamity, the government faced no pressure from newspapers, which were controlled, or from opposition parties, which were not allowed to exist.

The lack of a free system of news distribution even misled the government itself. It believed its own propaganda and the rosy reports of local party officials competing for credit in Beijing. Indeed, there is evidence that just as the famine was moving toward its peak, the Chinese authorities mistakenly believed that they had 100 million more metric tons of grain than they actually did. Interestingly enough, Mao himself, whose radical beliefs had much to do with the initiation of, and the perseverance with, the Great Leap Forward, identified the informational role of democracy, once the failure was belatedly acknowledged. In 1962, just after the famine had killed so many millions, he made the following observation, to a gathering of 7,000 cadres:

> Without democracy, you have no understanding of what is happening down below; the situation will be unclear; you will be unable to collect sufficient opinions from all sides; there can be no communication between top and bottom; top-level organs of leadership will depend on one-sided and incorrect material to decide issues, thus you will find it difficult to avoid being subjectivist; it will be impossible to achieve unity of understanding and unity of action, and impossible to achieve true centralism.

Mao's defense of democracy here is quite limited. The focus is exclusively on the informational side, ignoring the incentive role of democracy, not to mention any intrinsic importance that it may have. Still, it is significant that Mao himself acknowledged the extent to which disastrous official policies were caused by the lack of the informational links that a more democratic system could have provided.

These issues remain relevant in China today. Since the economic reforms of 1979, official Chinese policies have been based on the acknowledgment of the importance of economic incentives with out a similar acknowledgment of the importance of political incentives. When things go reasonably well, this disciplinary role of democracy might not be greatly missed; but when big policy mistakes are made, this lacuna can be quite disastrous. The significance of the democracy movements in contemporary China has to be judged in this light.

Another set of examples comes from sub-Saharan Africa, which has been plagued by persistent famine since the early 1970s. There are many factors underlying the susceptibility of this region to famine, from the ecological impact of climatic deterioration—making crops more uncertain—to the negative effects of persistent wars and skirmishes. But the typically authoritarian nature of many of the sub-Saharan African polities also has something to do with the frequency of famine.

The nationalist movements were all anti-colonialist, but they were not all pro-democratic, and it is only recently that the assertion of the value of democracy has achieved some political respectability in many of the countries of sub Saharan Africa. And in this political milieu the cold war did not help at all. The United States and its allies were ready to support undemocratic governments if they were sufficiently anti-Communist, no matter how anti-egalitarian they might be in their domestic policies. (The Soviet Union and China, of course, also did not recoil from authoritarian regimes.) When opposition parties were banned and newspapers were suppressed, there were very few international protests.

One must not deny that there were African governments even in one-party states that were deeply concerned about averting disasters and famine. Examples of this range from the tiny country of Cape Verde to the politically experimental nation of Tanzania. But quite often the absence of opposition and the suppression of free newspapers gave the respective governments an immunity from social criticism and political pressure that translated into thoroughly insensitive and callous policies. Often famines were taken for granted, and it was common to put the blame for the disasters on natural causes and the perfidy of other countries. In various ways, Sudan, Ethiopia, Uganda, Chad, several of the Sahel countries and others provide glaring examples of how badly things can go wrong without the discipline of opposition parties and the news media. The present problem of Somalia seems to be a lack of political and economic order, of an effective national government; but the way toward this crisis was prepared by decades of intolerance, authoritarianism and a general undermining of orderly political processes.

This is not to deny that famines in these countries were often associated with crop failures: when a crop fails, it not only affects the food supply, it also destroys employment and the means of livelihood. But the occurrence of crop failures is not independent of public policies (such as governmental fixing of relative prices, policy regarding irrigation and agricultural research and so on). Moreover, even when crops fail, a famine can be averted by a careful redistribution policy. Botswana, for example, experienced a fall in food production of 17 percent, and Zimbabwe a fall of 38 percent, between 1979-81 and 1983-84, in the same period in which the decline in food production amounted to a relatively modest 11 percent or 12 per cent in Sudan and Ethiopia. Sudan and Ethiopia, with comparatively smaller declines in food output, had major famines. Botswana and Zimbabwe had none. This splendid outcome was owed largely to timely and extensive famine prevention policies by these latter countries. And democracy, which included a relatively uncensored press, made such policies imperative. For had the governments in Botswana and Zimbabwe failed to do this, they would have come under severe criticism from the political opposition. The Ethiopian and Sudanese governments, by contrast, did not have to reckon with such democratic inconveniences.

The role of electoral processes is sometimes underestimated even in the rich, developed countries. Thus, in understanding the deprivation of immigrants in Germany, who are often subjected to severe attacks by right-wing groups, more emphasis may have to be placed on the absence of voting rights for noncitizens and their corresponding lack of political power. In Britain, by contrast, where special electoral laws give resident Commonwealth citizens full voting rights whether or not they are British citizens, immigrants from the West Indies or from such countries as India, Bangladesh, Nigeria or Ghana acquire a measure of political clout immediately, which is particularly important in local elections. This tends to weaken the political exploitation of anti-immigrant sentiments in an extremist direction. The sharp contrast between the recent experiences of immigrants in Britain and in Germany owes something to the respective reach of a democratic political culture in the two countries.

In making such arguments, of course, there is the danger of exaggerating the effectiveness of democracy. Political rights and liberties are permissive advantages, and their effectiveness depends on how they are exercised. Democracies have been particularly successful in preventing disasters that are easy to understand, in which sympathy can take an especially immediate form. Many other problems are not quite so accessible. Thus India's success in eradicating famine is not matched by a similar success in eliminating non-extreme hunger, or in curing persistent illiteracy or in relieving inequalities in gender relations. While the plight of famine victims is easy to politicize, these other deprivations call for deeper analysis, and for greater and more effective use of mass communication and political participation—in sum, for a fuller practice of democracy.

A similar observation may be made about various failings in more mature democracies as well. For example, the extraordinary deprivations in health care, education and social environment of African Americans in the United States make their mortality rates exceptionally high; as I tried to show in *Scientific American* in May 1993, American blacks have low survival chances not only compared with American whites, but also compared with the citizens of China, Sri Lanka or the Indian state of Kerala, who are better provided with these public goods (despite being immensely poorer in per capita income). And some American blacks are even more deprived than others: the male residents of Harlem not only have lower survival chances than the corresponding groups in Kerala or Sri Lanka or China, they even fall behind Bangladeshi men by their late 30s.

But, again, the remedy of these failures in the practice of democracy turns, to a great extent, on the fuller use of political and civil rights, including more public discussion, more accessible information and more concrete proposals. To be sure, the difficulties in deciding on the means of eradicating these hardened deprivations remain, and they have become quite perspicuous in the sphere of health care in recent months. Still, the fact that the lack of medical care for many has become so prominent in the politics of the United States is what lends the matter its urgency, what directs new energy toward the solution of the problem. And the same grounds for hope would be true in the case of the poorer countries as well.

It is important to acknowledge, however, the special difficulty of making a democracy take adequate notice of some types of deprivation, particularly the needs of minorities. One factor of some importance is the extent to which a minority group in a particular society can build on sympathy rather than alienation. When a minority forms a highly distinct and particularist group, it can be harder for it to receive the sympathy of the majority, and then the protective role of democracy may be particularly constrained.

Consider the ineffectiveness of electoral politics in ensuring sensitivity to the rights and the welfare of separatist groups, particularly those groups that are tainted with some use of terrorist methods, and with receiving assistance from beyond the border. Illustrations are not hard to find in India, particularly in the case of Kashmir, where there is increasing evidence of the violation of civil rights and personal liberties by the Indian police and military. The frustration of the Kashmiris does not seem to influence the political behavior of the majority of Indians. Even India's large Muslim population, which numbers well over 100 million, does not appear to have much interest in working for the rights of the relatively tiny Muslim population of Kashmir. There is also a basic tension between the separatism of Kashmiri Muslim activists and the deep seated integrationist beliefs of the immensely larger Muslim population in the rest of the country.

In the rather straitjacketed models of so-called "rational choice theory," which tend to characterize human beings as narrowly self-interested, it is hard to incorporate the satisfaction of minority needs through majority votes. To some extent this skepticism is justified. Even the plight of African Americans has something to do with the fact that blacks constitute a relatively small minority of the American population. And yet politics does not always operate in this way. Much depends on which issues are identified and politicized and made into a concern of those who are not directly involved. Potential famine victims form a small minority in any country (a famine rarely affects more than 5 percent, and at most 10 percent, of a population), and the effectiveness of democracy in the prevention of famine has tended to depend on the politicization of the plight of famine victims, through the process of public discussion, which generates political solidarity. Outrage at famine deaths moves vast numbers of people who are in no way threatened by starvation themselves. In the United States, similarly, the plight of the medically uninsured, who really are a deprived minority, seems to have become politicized at last, and there is some real hope that the political process will lead to remedial arrangements, which are much overdue. The reach of political rights is deeply influenced by the way in which they are used.

The examples that I have been discussing so far illustrate the practical and instrumental linkages between political liberty and sensitivity to economic needs; but we must not overlook, in the practical discussion of these matters, the constitutive importance of political rights. I have already argued that the importance of such rights goes beyond the personal advantages that the holders of these rights derive from them, that there is an asymmetry between political rights and other types of advantages, including economic ones. But there is, in addition, a deeper connection. The comprehension and the conceptualization of economic needs themselves may require the exercise of political and civil rights, open discussion and public exchange.

Human lives suffer from miseries and deprivations of various kinds, some more amenable to alleviation than others. The totality of the human predicament would be an undiscriminating basis for the social analysis of needs. There are many things that we might have good reason to value if they were feasible, maybe even immortality; yet we do not see them as needs. Our conception of needs relates to our analysis of the nature of deprivations, and also to our understanding of what can be done about them. Political rights, including freedom of expression and discussion, are not only pivotal in inducing political responses to economic needs, they are also central to the conceptualization of economic needs themselves.

Sometimes it is hard to determine what is, or is not, an economic need. Take the controversial subject of population policy. Much depends on how we count the pressure on the world's resources, a subject on which scientific opinion varies. No less importantly, the conceptualization of the problem depends on what view we take of the willingness of people to reduce the birth rate on a voluntary basis, as the opportunity of family planning is extended and the reduction in the death rate makes it less important to have many children to ensure some survivors when the parents are old.

The international politics of population policy is rife with pressure groups. Their views vary from a general hostility toward birth control (and more specifically toward abortion) to an advocacy of population control so forceful that it would override what the people themselves would voluntarily do. These issues are bound to receive considerable attention and scrutiny in the coming decade. Among the developing countries, China has distinguished itself in its use of coercion to cut down the growth rate of its population, in some regions by means of such measures as a 'one-child policy," and more generally by the conditioning of social security and economic rights (such as housing) on adherence to the government's rules about the number of births, the terrible predicament of children in larger families notwithstanding. There are many admirers of such harsh policies. And the birth rate in China has certainly come down; the last systematic estimate put it around twenty-one per 1,000, which is considerably lower than India's thirty per 1,000 and the average figure of thirty-eight per 1,000 for poor countries other than India and China.

Within India, however, there are wide variations in the birth rate, and these variations relate both to rates of mortality and to education, especially to female education. Consider the state of Kerala, which, with its population of 29 million people, is rather larger than Canada. Kerala has the highest life expectancy in India (more than seventy years, a little higher than that of China's), the highest rate of literacy in general, and the highest rate of female literacy (higher than that of China as a whole and higher, for corresponding rural populations, than that of every province in China). The birth rate in Kerala has fallen sharply over the last few decades, from forty-four per 1,000 in the 1950s to twenty per 1,000 in the late 1980s. In making comparisons, it is important to observe that the Keralan figure of twenty per 1,000, which is no higher than the Chinese birth rate of twenty-one per 1,000 in the corresponding period, has not been achieved by compulsory birth control or by the violation of the individual's freedom to decide on these matters, but by the voluntary exercise of the family's right to family planning. And subsequent provisional statistics suggest that China's further fall in birth rate in very recent years—it is now down to nineteen per 1,000—has continued to be matched by Kerala's declining birth rate, which was estimated to be eighteen per 1,000 in 1991.

The change in Kerala is owed in part to the operation of economic and social incentives toward smaller families, as the death rate has fallen and family planning opportunities have been combined with health care. But it is owed also to a general perception that the lowering of the birth rate is a real need of a modern family; and this perception would not have been possible without public education and enlightened discussion. The emergence of a resolute desire by Keralan women to be less shackled by continuous child rearing is part of the process of the free formation of values and priorities.

The temptation to impose compulsory birth control arises when the government's view of needs differs from the views of the families themselves. Such a disjunction can lead to deeply disturbing results. Thus, while China has ended up with a birth rate similar to the birth rate of Kerala, one result of official coercion in China has been a much higher level of mortality among female children, quite unlike the situation in Kerala. The traditional "son preference" seems often to have led to extreme responses in China to compulsory birth control measures, including an increase in female infanticide and in the differential neglect of female children. These horrors must be counted among the consequences of a closed society in which the reduction in the birth rate is achieved without an open and educated discussion of personal and economic needs.

Political rights are important not only for the fulfillment of needs, they are crucial also for the formulation of needs. And this idea relates, in the end, to the respect that we owe each other as fellow human beings. In *Taking Leave*, William Cobbett observed that "we now frequently hear the working classes called 'the population,' just as we call animals upon a farm 'the stock."' The importance of political rights for the under standing of economic needs turns ultimately on seeing human beings as people with rights to exercise, not as parts of a "stock" or a "population" that passively exists and must be looked after. What matters, finally, is how we see each other.

AMARTYA SEN is Lamont University Professor of Economics and Philosophy at Harvard University and the president of the American Economic Association.

[15]

THE PUBLIC/PRIVATE DISTINCTION AND THE RIGHT TO DEVELOPMENT IN INTERNATIONAL LAW

HILARY CHARLESWORTH*

> Women do two thirds of the world's work .... Yet ... women earn no more than one tenth of the world's income and own less than one per cent of the world's property.[1]

Why has gender not been an issue in international law? Although international lawyers have been forced to confront the challenge made to the traditional canons of international law by developing nations, the deeply gendered nature of their discipline has remained uncontroversial and unexplored. In this paper I argue that international law is built on paradigms which privilege a male perspective, one of which is a distinction between public and private spheres of life.[2] I first outline the theoretical basis of the public/private distinction and the feminist critique of the dichotomy. I then examine the operation of the public/private distinction in one particular area of international law: the right to development.

The Public/Private Distinction

The dichotomy between public and private activities and spheres is central to liberalism – the dominant political, and legal, philosophy of the West.[3] Thus John Locke, one of the most influential architects of modern liberal thought, drew distinctions between reason and passion, knowledge and desire, mind and body. The first of each of these dualisms was associated with the public sphere of rationality, order and political authority; the latter with a private sphere of subjectivity and desire.[4]

How did the dichotomy between the public and private spheres become gendered? Women had no place in the public order and became associated with irrational desire. Locke viewed women as naturally inferior to men, a condition

---

* Law School, University of Melbourne

The author thanks Philip Alston, Christine Chinkin and Jenny Morgan for their very helpful comments on a draft of this paper.

1 UN Doc E/CN.4/AC.39/1988/L.2 para 59.

2 See generally Charlesworth H, Chinkin C, and Wright S, "Feminist Approaches to International Law" (unpublished paper 1990).

3 For a historical account of the distinction in Western thought see Elshtain JB, *Public Man, Private Women* (1981).

4 Locke J, *Two Treatises of Government* (Laslett P (ed) 1965). See Elshtain JB, above n 2, pp 116–127.

which was the result of God's punishment of Eve by making her bear children.[5] So although he regarded authority in the public, political sphere as based on consent, and natural differences irrelevant to the equality of men with one another, Locke could argue that the basis of men's authority over women in the private, familial sphere was nature.[6] The work of John Stuart Mill two centuries later continued this tradition of applying different standards to the two spheres of life. In his work *On the Subjection of Women*,[7] Mill argued strongly for equal rights for women in the public, political sphere. He nevertheless regarded a division of labour assigning women to the world of home and hearth as the most suitable and appropriate.[8]

The centrality of the public/private distinction in liberal thought continues today. And it is a dominant feature of the organisation of Western society. As Sandra Harding has said, the distinction "cannot be shucked off by mental hygiene and willpower alone."[9] But the division into public and private spheres is not a simple, monolithic construct.

First, there is great debate among liberals as to where precisely the boundary between the two spheres lies. Secondly, as Carole Pateman has pointed out, notions of public and private are often used in quite different ways than those identified by Locke. Locke distinguished a private, domestic world from that of civil society, the world of politics and men. In modern liberalism the purely domestic sphere is ignored as an area of concern and "[t]he separation between private and public is ... re-established as a division *within* civil society itself, within the world of men."[10] Thus references to a dichotomy between the public and private can refer to the distinction between politics and economic and social life or between state and society. The western legal classifications of public law, which concerns the state, and private law, which regulates relationships between individuals,[11] rest on precisely this type of public/private distinction. Unlike Locke's public/private scheme, here the private sphere, in which the pursuit of individual interests and enterprise takes place, is regarded as central.[12]

---

5 Locke J, above n 4, 209–210. See Clark LMG, "Women and Locke: Who owns the apples in the Garden of Eden?" in Clark LMG & Lange L (eds), *The Sexism of Social and Political Theory* (1979) pp 6, 17–18.

6 Locke J, above n 4, p 82.

7 Reprinted in Rossi A (ed), *Essays on Sex Equality* (1970) p 125.

8 See O'Donovan K, *Sexual Divisions in Law* (1985) pp 8–9.

9 Harding S, "The instability of the analytical categories of feminist theory" (1986) 11 Signs 646 quoted in Stivens M, "Why Gender Matters in Southeast Asian Politics" (1989) Asian Stud Rev 4, 5.

10 Pateman C, "Feminist Critiques of the Public/Private Dichotomy" in Benn SI & Gaus GF (eds), *Public and Private in Social Life* (1983) pp 281, 285.

11 See Tay A & Kamenka E, "Public Law – Private Law" in Benn SI & Gaus GF, above n 10, pp 67, 82–83.

12 Pateman C, above n 10, p 285.

Another function of the dichotomy in liberal jurisprudence is to demarcate areas appropriate for legal regulation from those which come within the sphere of personal autonomy. A well known passage from the 1957 Wolfenden Committee's Report on Homosexual Offences and Prostitution illustrates this well: "... there must remain a realm of private morality and immorality, which is, in brief and crude terms, not the law's business."[13]

The Feminist Critique of the Public/Private Distinction

Challenging the separation and opposition of the public and private domains, in the original Lockean sense, in liberal theory and practice is regarded by many western feminists as a crucial aspect of their project.[14] Liberalism asserts that it pays equal concern and respect to all individuals and because of this lays claim to the qualities of objectivity, abstractness and neutrality. As described by liberal theorists, the distinction between public and private realms operates generally and neutrally with respect to individuals. However, in Western society women are relegated to the private sphere of home, hearth and family. The public sphere of workplace, law, economics, politics, intellectual and cultural life is regarded as the province of men. This phenomenon is explained as a matter of nature (Locke), convenience (Mill) or individual choice.

The feminist response to these claims is that the public/private distinction in fact operates both to obscure and legitimate men's domination of women. Feminists link the western identification of women with the domestic sphere with the separation of production from the household and the "privatisation" of the family in the Eighteenth Century together with the growth of capitalism and deeply held beliefs about gender.[15] The public/private dichotomy is gendered: it is a "metaphor for the social patterning of gender, a description of sociological practice, and a category grounded in experience."[16] It is also a normative distinction, for greater significance and power attaches to the public, male world. The assignment of women to the domestic sphere entrenches their inequality with men, for women are regarded as dependent on men for subsistence. Moreover the privacy of domestic life makes women's concerns invisible and ensures the preservation of the status quo.

Feminist legal scholars have only recently begun to examine the significance of the public/private distinction in law. It is deeply embedded in western legal structures and the vocabulary of the distinction is built into the language of the law itself. Law lays claim to rationality, neutrality and authority, qualities associated with the public sphere, and is defined in opposition to supposed

13 (1957) para 61. See O'Donovan K, above n 8, pp 8–9.

14 See eg Garmanikow E & Purvis J, "Introduction" in Garmanikow E et al (eds), *The Public and the Private* (1983) pp 1, 3; Pateman C, above n 10, p 281.

15 Pateman C, above n 10, p 286.

16 Garmanikow E & Purvis J, above n 14, p 5.

characteristics of women and the private sphere, feeling, subjectivity and emotion.[17]

The distinction between public and private law is familiar to all western lawyers. The feminist concern however is with the public/private dichotomy in law in two different senses: the way that the law has been used to exclude women from the public sphere – from professions, from the marketplace, from the vote;[18] and a more basic form of the dichotomy, between what is considered the business of law and what is left unregulated. Analyzing the distinction in this latter sense can be particularly useful in the area of international law.

In her book *Sexual Divisions in Law*, Katharine O'Donovan defines the private realm in the same way as some modern liberal philosophers: the area of life into which the law will not intrude, which is "not the law's business."[19] Because there is a large coincidence of the legally unregulated areas of social, economic and moral life and issues such as the family, home and sexuality, which are associated with women, O'Donovan argues that the legal translation of the public/private distinction plays a major role in the modern subordination of women. She goes further than the liberal notion of privacy, however, by recognising a distinction between "areas of privacy that are unrecognised and invisible [e.g. lesbianism] and those that are specifically delimited as private [e.g. homosexuality (at least in some jurisdictions)]."[20] This notion of the private, then, includes all unregulated activities whether legally designated as private or not. The law is both central to concepts of public and private and crucial in constructing the distinction between them.[21]

Why is lack of regulation of particular areas of social life significant for women? Some feminist jurists argue that "law's absence devalues women and their functions: women are simply not important enough to merit legal regulation."[22] But it is important also to recognise that a deliberate policy of non-intervention[23] by the state does not signify non-control or neutrality.[24] Thus lack of regulation of rape in marriage supports and legitimates the power of husbands over wives. Further, regulation of areas such as employment, taxation,

17 See Olsen F, "Feminism and Critical Legal Theory: An American Perspective" (1990) 18 Int J of the Sociology of Law 199, 201.

18 See, eg, Polan D, "Toward a Theory of Law and Patriarchy" in Kairys D (ed), *The Politics of Law* (1982) pp 294, 298; Taub N & Schneider E, "Perspectives on Women's Subordination and the Role of Law" ibid 117, pp 118–120.

19 O'Donovan K, above n 8, p 3.

20 Ibid p 7.

21 Ibid p 7.

22 Taub N & Schneider E, above n 18, p 122.

23 Frances Olsen points out the incoherence of the term "intervention": particular activities can be characterised as intervention or non-intervention depending on the perspective taken. "The Myth of State Intervention in the Family" (1985) 18 U of Mich J of L Reform 835.

24 O'Donovan K, above n 8, p 7.

social security and crime have significant, if indirect, impact on the private sphere and reinforce a particular sort of family unit – a nuclear family in which there is a division of labour between men and women.[25] Lack of direct state intervention in the name of protection of privacy can thus disguise the inequality and domination exercised in the private sphere.[26]

The Public/Private Distinction and International Law

Distinctions between spheres of public and private define the scope of international law. One such distinction is between public international law, the law governing the relations between nation states, and private international law, the rules about conflicts between national legal systems. Another is the distinction between matters of international (public) concern and matters "private" to states, considered within their domestic jurisdiction, and in which the international community has no recognised legal interest.[27] Yet another is the line drawn between law and other forms of private knowledge, such as morality.[28]

Like national legal systems, international law is constructed within a "public" world, although national and international "public" spheres are often differently defined. International law operates in the most public of all public worlds, that of nation states. One consequence of this has been, until recently, the invisibility of individual or group concerns in international law. The development of human rights law in the second half of this century has altered one set of boundaries between public and private in international law to allow the law to address violations of designated individual and group rights. This development, however, has not challenged the much deeper public/private dichotomy based on gender.[29]

The Right to Development

Many principles of international law rest on and reproduce a public/private distinction. I focus here on a particular principle of international law, the right to development, and argue that it is an example of how the international legal order privileges a male perspective and fails to accommodate the realities of women's lives. The problematic nature of current development practice for Third World women goes of course much deeper than the international legal formulation of

25 Ibid pp 14–15. See also Thornton M, "Feminist Jurisprudence: Illusion or Reality?" (1986) 3 AJLS 5, 6.

26 See O'Donovan K, above n 8, p 12; Taub N & Schneider E, above n 18, pp 121–122; Thornton M, above n 25, p8.

27 Article 2 (7), United Nations Charter.

28 Eg, *South West Africa* cases, ICJ Rep 1966, p 6. Cf *Western Sahara* case, ICJ Rep 1975, p 12 at 69: "economics, sociology and human geography are not law" (Judge Gros sep op).

29 See Byrnes A, "A Feminist Analysis of International Human Rights Law" and Wright, S, "Economic Rights and Social Justice: A Feminist Analysis of Some International Human Rights Conventions", both in this volume.

the right to development. But the rhetoric of international law both reflects and reinforces a system that contributes to the subordination of women.

The right to development is of relatively recent legal formulation and its status in international law is controversial.[30] It was an important aspect of the New International Economic Order promoted, ultimately unsuccessfully, in the 1970s and 80s by Third World countries. The proponents of the right present it as both an individual and a collective right which responds to the phenomenon of global interdependence,[31] while its critics argue that it is vague and unenforceable.[32]

The 1986 United Nations Declaration on the Right to Development[33] describes the content of the right as the entitlement "to participate in, contribute to and enjoy economic, social, cultural and political development, in which all human rights and fundamental freedoms can be fully realised."[34] Primary responsibility for the creation of conditions favourable to the right is placed on States:

> States have the right and the duty to formulate appropriate national development policies that aim at the constant improvement of the well-being of the entire population and of all individuals, on the basis of their active, free and meaningful participation in development and in the fair distribution of the benefits resulting therefrom.[35]

The right is apparently designed to apply to all individuals within a State and is assumed to benefit men and women equally: the preamble of the UN Declaration twice refers to the Charter exhortation to promote and encourage respect for human rights for all without distinction of any kind such as race or sex. Moreover, Article 8 of the Declaration places an obligation on States to ensure equality of opportunity for all in access to basic resources and the fair distribution of income. It states that "effective measures should be undertaken to ensure that women have an active role in the development process." Such a specific reference to women in a generally applicable international formulation of rights is unusual and indicates an apparent sensitivity to issues of gender equality. Why, then, is the Declaration nevertheless unsatisfactory from a feminist perspective?

---

30 Alston P,"Making Space for New Human Rights: the Case of the Right to Development" (1988) 1 Harv Hum Rts YB 3; Rich R, "The Right to Development: A Right of Peoples" in Crawford J (ed), *The Rights of Peoples* (1988) p 39.

31 Eg M'Baye K, "The Right to Development as a Human Right" (1972) 5 Rev des Droits de l'Homme 503.

32 Eg Donnelly J, "In Search of the Unicorn: The Jurisprudence and Politics of the Right to Development" (1985) 15 Cal W Int L J 473; Brownlie I, "The Rights of Peoples in Modern International Law" in Crawford J (ed), above n 30, p 1 at 14–15.

33 GA Res 41/128.

34 Article 1(1).

35 Article 2(3).

First, the acknowledgement of the need to involve women in the development process is only token in the context of the Declaration as a whole. Other provisions of the Declaration indicate that discrimination against women is not seen as a major obstacle to development, nor to the fair distribution of its benefits. For example, one aspect of the right to development is the obligation on States to take "resolute steps" to eliminate "massive and flagrant violations of the human rights of peoples and human beings." The examples given of such massive and flagrant violations include apartheid and race discrimination but do not include sex discrimination.[36] The lack of attention paid to inequality between men and women as an issue in development is a feature of influential writing on the topic[37] and of precursor resolutions to the Declaration on the Right to Development.[38] Although subsequent United Nations deliberations have given more regard to gender implications of the right to development,[39] these concerns are presented as quite discrete, soluble by the application of special protective measures, rather than as central to the issue of development.[40]

A second, more fundamental, objection to the Declaration is that the model of development on which it is built exacerbates the inequality of Third World women. While the formulation of the right to development does not rest on a simple economic model of development, and includes within it a synthesis of all recognised human rights, redress of economic inequality is at its heart.[41] An assumption of the international law of development is that underdevelopment is

---

36 Article 5.

37 Eg, Independent Commission on International Development Issues, North–South: A programme for survival (1990) (the "Brandt Report") pp 59–62.

38 Eg, Declaration on Social Progress and Development GA Res 2542 (1969); Declaration on the Establishment of a New International Economic Order GA Res 3201 (1974); Programme of Action on the Establishment of a New International Economic Order GA Res 3202 (1974); Charter of Economic Rights and Duties of States GA Res 3281 (1975).

39 Eg, Analytical compilation of comments and views on the implementation of the Declaration on the Right to Development prepared by the Secretary General UN Doc E/CN.4/AC.39/1988/L.2 paras 59–63; Report prepared by the Secretary General on the Global Consultation on the Realization of the Right to Development as a Human Right UN Doc E/CN.4/1990/9 paras 15, 42, 51, 52, 59.

40 The section of the Secretary General's report dealing with "Obstacles to the implementation of the right to development as a human right", for example, mentions failure to respect the right of peoples to self determination, racial discrimination, apartheid, foreign occupation, restrictions on transfers of technology and the consumption patterns of industrialised countries as serious barriers to the realisation of the right to development, but contains no reference to sex discrimination. Ibid paras 27–35. Compare the detail of Article 14 of the Convention on the Elimination of All Forms of Discrimination Against Women 1979 UN Doc A/Res/34/180.

41 See Bulajic M, *Principles of International Development Law* (1986) 49–50, 333; Turk D, "The Human Right to Development" in van Dijk P et al (eds), *Restructuring the International Economic Order* (1987) p85; Schachter O, "The Evolving International Law of Development" (1976) 15 Col J of Transnational L 1.

caused by a failure to meet the model of a capitalist economy. Development means industrialisation and westernisation.[42]

Three major paradigms dominate theories of the causes of underdevelopment: shortages of capital, technology, skilled labor and entrepreneurship; exploitation of the wealth of developing nations by richer nations; and economic dependence of developing nations on developed nations.[43] Modernisation is assumed to have the same impact on women as on men. The domination of women by men within the family and in society generally does not enter the traditional development calculus: "development" as economic growth above all is not concerned with the lack of benefits or disadvantageous effects this growth may have on half of the society it purports to benefit.[44]

Over the last twenty years, considerable research has been done on the role of women in Third World development.[45] This research has documented the crucial role of women in the economies of developing nations, particularly in agriculture. It has highlighted the significant inequality of women within Third World households.[46] It has also pointed to the often adverse impact of "development" on Third World women's lives. The international legal order, like many international and national development policies, has not taken this research into account in formulating the right to development. "Human persons" may be declared the central subject of development, but the practice of development has exacerbated women's inequality in developing countries.[47] How can this asymmetry in the effects of development on women and men be explained? One reason is that the theory and practice of development depends on a distinction between public and private spheres.

Some feminist scholars have cautioned against universal explanations of the universally observed[48] domination of women by men. Particular cultural and

42 Bulajic M, above n 41, 42–46; de Waart P, "State Rights and Human Rights as Two Sides of One Principle of International Law" in de Waart P et al (eds), *International Law and Development* (1988); Kwakwa E, "Emerging International Development Law and Traditional International Law – Congruence or Cleavage?" (1987) 17 Georgia J of Int and Comp L 431.

43 Thomas P & Skeat H, "Gender in Third World Development Studies: An Overview of an Underview" (1990) 28 Aust Geographical Stud 5, 11. See also Henshall-Momsen J & Townsend J, *Geography of Gender in the Third World* (1987) p 16; Jacquette J, "Women and Modernization Theory: A Decade of Feminist Criticism" (1982) 34 World Politics 267.

44 See generally Thomas P & Skeat H, above n 43.

45 The first major study was Boserup E, *Women's Role in Economic Development* (1970). For a valuable survey of this literature see Thomas P & Skeat H, above n 43.

46 Eg, Dreze J & Sen A, *Hunger and Public Action* (1989) Chapter 4.

47 Henshall-Momsen J & Townsend J, above n 43, p 15; United Nations, World Survey on the Role of Women in Development (1986) pp 19–20.

48 Henshall-Momsen J & Townsend J, above n 43, 28: "in the history and geography of humanity, women's subordination is omnipresent. ...The forms of subordination differ greatly, but, all over the world, women's work tends to be defined as of less value than men's and women tend to have far less access to all forms of social,

social contexts, they argue, must be taken into account and "universal" analytic categories such as the public/private distinction run the risk of simply being shorthand for biological explanations of women's subordination.[49] Maila Stivens, for example, points out that it is very difficult to specify what the private domain is in agrarian societies in South East Asia. She observes the complete gendering of all levels of social life right across the traditional public/private division and argues that we should expand our notion of politics rather than analyse all societies within the confines of a particular western construction of the public/private distinction.[50]

The distinction remains a western one only if the content of each sphere is defined by western experience – if women are regarded as always opposed to men in the same ways in all contexts and societies, for example if women's social inferiority is universally attributed to their role in bearing and raising children.[51] What *is* important to observe universally is that it is not the activity which characterises the public and the private, but rather the actor:[52] that is, women's subordination to men is mediated through the public/private dichotomy. What is "public" in one society may well be "private" in another, but women's activities are consistently devalued by being construed as private.

In the context of the international law of development, the particular distinction between public and private observed in western societies still has explanatory force. The international law and practice of development allows the ideology and practical consequences of the distinction to be exported from the developed to the developing world. In this way the law functions in a manner parallel to that of colonial administrators whose "reforms" often weakened the position of women in colonial societies.[53]

One implicit aspect of the international right to development is development assistance and aid. International and national efforts are to be aimed at eliminating "economic deprivation, hunger and disease in all parts of the world without discrimination" and international co-operation should be aimed, *inter alia*, at "maintenance of stable and sustained economic growth", increasing concessional assistance to developing countries, building world food security and

---

economic and political power." See also Rosaldo MZ, "Women, Culture and Society: a Theoretical Overview" in Rosaldo MZ & L. Lamphere (eds), *Women Culture and Society* (1974) p 19.

49 H. Moore, *Feminism and Anthropology* (1988) 25–30; H. Eisenstein, *Contemporary Feminist Thought* (1986) pp 20–6; Rosaldo MZ, "The use and abuse of anthropology: reflections on feminism and cross-cultural understanding" (1980) 5 Signs 389; Stivens M, above n 9, 4; Pateman C, above n 10.

50 Stivens M, above n 9, 7.

51 Imray L & Middleton A, "Public and Private: Marking the Boundaries" in Garmanikow E et al (eds), above n 14, pp 12, 13–14. Cf Rosaldo MZ, above n 48.

52 Imray L & Middleton A, above n 51, p 16; Thomas P & Skeat H, above n 43, p 9. See also Moore H, above n 49, pp 54–9.

53 See Boserup E, above n 45; Moore H, above n 49, p 44.

resolving the debt burden.[54] Women and children are generally the primary victims of poverty and malnutrition.[55] Women, therefore, should have much to gain from an international right to development. Proponents of modernisation theories assert that the active intervention of developed nations through aid will have a positive effect on women in developing countries.[56] The generality and apparent universal applicability of the right to development as formulated in the UN Declaration is undermined, however, by the fundamentally androcentric nature of the international economic system and its reinforcement of the public/private distinction.

The distinction between the public and the private spheres of existence operates to make the work and needs of women invisible. Economic visibility depends on working in the public sphere and unpaid work in the home or community is categorised as "unproductive, unoccupied, and economically inactive."[57] Marilyn Waring has recently argued that this division, which is institutionalised in developed nations, has been exported to the developing world in part through the UN System of National Accounts (UNSNA) and operates as another tool of colonialism.[58] The invisibility of women's work thus retards *their* right to development.

The UNSNA, developed largely by Sir Richard Stone in the 1950's, allows States' financial position to be monitored, trends in national development to be tracked and one nation's economy to be compared with that of another. It will therefore influence the categorisation of nations as developed or developing and the style and magnitude of the required international aid. The UNSNA measures the value of all goods and services that actually enter the market and of other non-market production such as government services provided free of charge.[59] The UNSNA designates some activities as outside the "production boundary"

54 GA Res 41/133 (1986). See also Rich R, above n 30, pp 46–8; Schachter O, above n 41, 9–13.

55 See Dreze J & Sen A, above n 46, Ch 4; Waring M, *Counting for Nothing* (1988) p 34.

56 Many international aid programmes have a "Women in Development" [WID] component. These have been of limited success. Some at least have suffered from lack of institutional support and have remained outside the mainstream of development work. More importantly, WID projects have generally done little more than integrate women into a narrowly defined notion of development. They have not challenged the assumptions of the modernisation approach to development, particularly the sexual division of labour. New productive roles for women, which do not disrupt patterns of domestic labour, have been identified. As Elizabeth Reid commented at the Gender and International Law Conference, at which this paper was first presented, WID projects have assumed that women are unemployed or underemployed and ignore the economic value of women's unpaid labour. See also Parpart JL, "Introduction" in Parpart JL (ed), *Women and Development in Africa* (1989) pp 3, 4; Thomas P & Skeat H, above n 43, pp 11–3.

57 Dreze J & Sen A, above n 46, 57; Waring M, above n 55, 13.

58 Waring M, above n 55, 83.

59 Ibid 27.

and thus they are not measured. Economic reality is constructed by the UNSNA's "production boundaries" in such a way that reproduction, child care, domestic work and subsistence production are excluded from measurement of production and economic growth.[60] This view of women's work as non-work is nicely summed up in a report in 1985 by the UN Secretary General to the General Assembly on the "Overall Socioeconomic Perspective of the World Economy to the Year 2000". It said: "Women's productive and reproductive roles tend to be compatible in rural areas of low income countries, since family agriculture and cottage industries keep women close to the home, permitting flexibility in working conditions *and require low investment of the mother's time*."[61]

The devaluation of "private" women's work is one explanation for the observation that "in general, the process of development appears to increase the burdens of Third World women".[62] The effects of the assignment of the work of women to a different sphere than the work of men, and their consequent categorisation as "non-producers", are detrimental to women in developing countries in many ways and make a woman's right to development considerably less attainable than a man's.

The invisibility of women's work has, first of all, serious consequences in an immediate physical sense, in that the overwork of many women in developing countries reduces their life expectancy.[63] In many Third World countries women work a "double day" – as agricultural workers and as homemakers and mothers.[64] Moreover, women may not have equal claim to basic necessities of life. For example, Dreze and Sen have identified the significance of perceptions of relative economic contributions in the familial division of food, resources and health care in some Third World countries. They observe that "[i]n determining how the family benefits should be divided, importance seems to be attached ... to who is 'contributing' how much to the joint prosperity of the family. ... [In] the accounting of respective 'contributions', paid employment and outside 'gainful' activities seem to loom particularly large."[65]

Secondly, the endorsement of the public/private distinction in international economic measurement excludes women from many aid programs because they are not considered workers, or because they are regarded as less productive than

60 Ibid 25. Many national measures omit unpaid family workers entirely from measurement of women in the labour force: Henshall–Momsen J & Townsend J, above n 43, 56.

61 UN Doc. A/40/5198/23/1985 quoted in Waring M, above n 55, 177 (italics added).

62 Henshall–Momsen J & Townsend J, above n 43, p 16.

63 Waring M, above n 55, pp 144–145. See also Henshall–Momsen J & Townsend J, above n 43, pp 58–59.

64 Moore H, above n 49, p 43; Rathberger EM, "Women and Development: An Overview" in Parpart JL (ed), above n 56, pp 19, 21.

65 Dreze J & Sen A, above n 46, 52.

men.[66] If aid is provided to women, it is often to marginalise them: foreign aid may be available to women only in their guise as mothers[67] although at least since 1967 it has been recognised that women are responsible for as much as 80 per cent of food production in developing countries as well as most "domestic" work.[68] The non-recognition of women's significant role in agriculture and the lack of concern with the impact of development on women means that the potential of any right to development is jeopardised from the start. The recent lengthy evaluation by the World Bank of its twenty-one years in rural development simply noted that "lack of information and focus on women farmers as a sub-category of beneficiary groups has had serious consequences for achieving project goals."[69]

Growing food crops is generally subsistence agricultural activity and is usually considered the task of women.[70] But because it is not seen as an activity contributing to the market economy, support from aid programs is minimal. For example in a World Bank Agriculture and Development Program in Sierra Leone, women were regarded as ineligible for financial and technical aid because their land holdings were too small.[71] Priority given to export crops may also mean that local elites and transnational companies acquire significant land holdings, further reducing land available for women.[72]

"Development" and cash crops may bring the illusion of prosperity but this is very often at the expense of the autonomy of women and a fall in overall nutritional and environmental standards. The report, *The State of the World's Women 1985* prepared for the UN World Conference on Women in Nairobi provides telling examples of the practical effect of the public/private distinction on women's lives in developing countries and the failure of development programs to take account of this. In the Ivory Coast food staple shortages arose from men claiming some of the best agricultural land for food crops where

---

66 Ruth Pfanner gives an example of an official Australian aid programme in the Pacific where supervision and training in beef cattle production was directed exclusively at men, ignoring Melanesian women's traditional role in animal husbandry. Pfanner R, "Australian Foreign Aid and Women in the Third World" in Grieve N & Burns B (eds), *Australian Women: New Feminist Perspectives* (1986) pp 305, 307.

67 A World Bank report on development projects it had sponsored acknowledged that it had supported women's projects almost exclusively in the areas of "health, hygiene, nutrition and infant care." World Bank, World Bank Experience with Rural Development 1965–1986 (1987) 89. See generally Rogers B, *The Domestication of Women: Discrimination in Developing Societies* (1980).

68 Charlton S, *Women in Third World Development* (1984) 61.

69 Above n 67.

70 Columbo-Sacco D & Lopez-Morales G, *The Missing Half* (1975) p 11. Dixon R, "Land, Labour and the Sex Composition of the Agriculture Labour Force: An International Comparison" (1983) 14 Development and Change 347.

71 World Bank, above n 67, 89.

72 Thomas P & Skeat H, above n 43, 7.

women had been growing food.[73] And even investment in development aid for food production can be useless if given to men who are not involved in this work rather than to women who are. Thus the Nairobi Report notes that planners had aimed to make Gambia self-sufficient in rice by 1980. A disastrous 300 per cent increase in rice imports between 1966 and 1979 occurred because although women grew 84 per cent of Gambia's rice, agricultural advice and investment was only given to men.[74] Women may also be excluded from the benefits of development programs and innovations because information about them is disseminated through male communication networks.[75]

A third consequence of the relegation of women's work to a private, unmeasured sphere is that women may not be seen as full bearers of a right to development on the assumption that they are supported by male household heads and that the low level of their economic activities is inevitable and appropriate.[76] This in turn may justify giving less priority to the education and training of women than is given to men. Thus ECOSOC reported in 1986 that in developing countries girls formed up to 75% of children who were not enrolled in primary education. It went on to observe that "[e]fforts to achieve equality of educational opportunity for women have been hampered by the need to make difficult choices among competing demands for limited and even declining resources."

In other words, the education of women is seen as of little immediate economic return and dispensable in times of economic crisis. Women have no role in the public world and thus need no education or training. Moreover aid programs may often replicate sex stereotypes in training schemes, providing training in agriculture, mechanics, carpentry and business for men, while offering domestic training to women.[77] The reproduction of the public/private distinction in the international economic system thus reinforces patterns of unequal social relations between men and women by supporting the notion of a woman as the property of a man.

Fourthly, the distinction drawn between the public and private sphere means the benefits obtained from improvement or development of work methods may offer little relief to women. Women are routinely assigned the most tedious, time consuming and arduous tasks. Marilyn Waring cites a UN case study in Gambia which showed that women's working time in agriculture rose from nineteen to twenty hours when improved methods were introduced, while men's working time fell from eleven to nine hours.[78] Also, the premium placed on the growth of the market economy as a measure of development can mean that food availability is lessened as subsistence farmland is taken for cash crops and men

73 United Nations, *The State of the World's Women 1985* (1985) 8.

74 Id.

75 Thomas, P & Skeat, H, above n 43.

76 Waring, M, above n 55, 10.

77 Thomas P & Skeat H, above n 43, pp 8–9; Rathberger EM, above n 64, pp 22–23.

78 Waring M, above n 55, p 16. See also Rathberger EM, above n 64, p 22.

are paid an income.[79] Although the increased industrialisation of the Third World has meant greater employment opportunities for women, this has not increased their economic independence or social standing and has had little impact on women's equality. Women are found in the lowest paid and lowest status jobs without career paths and their working conditions are often discriminatory and insecure.[80] There is little difference in the position of women in developing nations with a socialist political order.[81] The dominant model of development assumes that any type of paid employment is better than unpaid work[82] and the potential for increased inequality for women and decline in their economic position is not taken into account.

Yet another consequence of women's invisibility as workers in the domestic sphere is that even when they do work in the public area, little attention is paid to their work conditions and possible exploitation. As Waring notes, "[s]ince housework is seen as a women's primary activity, and is not defined, anything else that she does is not work either, because it is secondary to housework."[83] Pervasive poverty is a widespread result of the invisibility of women's work. Households headed by women (1984 ILO figures for developing countries show that three out of ten households were headed by women) must combine income earning and home and family maintenance. Yet women in this position are less likely to be employed than their male counterparts and, if working, are likely to be less skilled and with a consequently reduced earning capacity.[84]

Conclusion

The operation of the public/private distinction in international law is one reason why gender has not been an issue in international law: this discipline, as many others, has defined gender out of existence. Despite the claim of international law to abstract, general principles of universal applicability, it is in fact constructed on the silence of women. Newly emerging principles of international law continue this silence.

The controversy about the right to development among international lawyers has not extended to the skewed notion of development on which it is based. The international formulation of the right draws no distinction between the economic position of men and women. In using the neutral language of development and

79 See Marilyn Waring's account of the effects of commercial agriculture in Colombia. Waring M, above n 55, p 192.

80 Thomas P & Skeat H, above n 43, p 8; Parpart JL, above n 56, pp 5–6.

81 See Molyneux M, "Women's Emancipation under Socialism: A Model for the Third World?" (1982) 9 World Development 1019.

82 Thomas P & Skeat H, above n 42, p 11.

83 Waring M, above n 55, p 70. See also Bennholdt-Thomsen V, "Why Do Housewives Continue to be Created in the Third World, too?," in Mies M et al (eds), *Women: The Last Colony* (1988) p 159.

84 Waring M, above n 55, pp 189–190.

economics, it does not challenge the pervasive, and detrimental, assumption that women's work is of a lesser order than men's. The right thus rests on and reinforces a public/private distinction based on gender. The effect is not only to deny the fruits of development to Third World women, but also to exacerbate their already unequal position.

If the rhetoric of international law is currently part of the problem of development for Third World women, could it eventually contribute to changing inappropriate models of development so that the position of women is improved? While international law cannot work immediate social change, its symbolic and long term force is significant. The international legal structure needs to accommodate the reality that pursuit of narrowly defined economic growth can deliver increased inequality for half of the population of developing nations: in this sense at least the "private" sphere requires recognition in the international legal order.

[16]

HUMAN RIGHTS AND SUSTAINABLE DEVELOPMENT IN CONTEMPORARY AFRICA: A NEW DAWN, OR RETREATING HORIZONS?

J. Oloka-Onyango

I. A Background Note

More than at any other point in time, the start of the third millennium of modern Western history[1] heralds both significantly new and radically different challenges and opportunities for the overall human rights situation on the African continent. On the one hand, a new African "renaissance" has been proclaimed in which the peoples of the continent are being called upon to assume their rightful place in the community of nations and to put the turmoil and tragedy of their past behind.[2] On the other, internal and regional conflicts appear to grow not simply in frequency and magnitude, but also in intensity, viciousness and complexity. This is true even in countries such as Namibia and Senegal that have been relatively stable and sanguine.

International wars, such as those in the Democratic Republic of Congo (DRC) and the one between Eritrea and Ethiopia, do not bode well for the observation and respect of human rights. Explanations for the ferocity and morbid depths of the civil conflagration that engulfed Sierra Leone will preoccupy psychologists of armed conflict for decades to come.[3] The 1994 genocide in Rwanda will stand as vivid testimony to the horrid evils of which human kind is capable of inflicting on its own kith and kin. Despite the opening of some democratic space in countries as diverse as Algeria and Nigeria, the problems have not gone away; they have simply assumed different forms of expression. In a nutshell, the human rights situation on the African continent today can only be described as being in a state of considerable flux.

---

1 Given that the millennium that was commemorated at the end of 1999 is one that relates to the supposed birth of Jesus Christ, it is quite clearly a commemoration that does not have universal validity for all the peoples of the world.

2 The notion of an African "renaissance" has been frequently invoked by South African President Thabo Mbeki, and taken up by numerous other leaders on the continent.

3 A vivid description of the kinds of abuse that became the norm in Sierra Leone is provided by Abdul Tejan-Cole. *See* Abdul Tejan-Cole, *Human Rights under the Armed Forces Revolutionary Council (AFRC) in Sierra Leone: A Catalogue of Abuse*, 10 Afr. J. Int'l & Comp. L. 481 (1998).

At the same time, Africa remains a continent marginalized from the tremendous technological, economic, and developmental achievements that the world has made over the last few decades. Rigorous measures of economic and social reform have resulted in marginal improvement over what conditions were before the "shock therapy" measures were applied. Moreover, this is true for only some countries on the continent.[4] For the ten years that the Human Development Report has been produced, African countries have dominated the lower quartile of the UNDP's Index.[5] It goes without saying that Africa's human development situation is in dire need of attention.[6]

However, when discussing the issue of human rights from a continental perspective, it is important to remember that the internal dynamics of individual countries are crucial to an understanding of the overall human rights context. Each of Africa's over fifty countries has distinct political economies and historical backgrounds that need to be taken into account in any analysis that seeks to draw broad conclusions of general conceptual veracity. Thus, countries that enjoy stable political systems will differ from

---

4 As Mkandawire and Soludo have pointed out: "It is remarkable to observe how Africa, over the decades, has been the pawn of international interests experimenting with development models. Most countries have followed passively; at each turn, previous policies implemented with all the technical assistance and massive support of the donor agencies have been berated as Africa's mistakes, and new policies are recommended. Africa's problem has not been its failure to learn but its learning too well from all and sundry." *See* THANDIKA MKANDAWIRE & CHARLES C. SOLUDO, OUR CONTINENT, OUR FUTURE: AFRICAN PERSPECTIVES ON STRUCTURAL ADJUSTMENT 37 (CODESRIA/IDREC 1999).

5 The last ten countries in both the 1998 and the 1999 Human Development Indices were African. Only one of those in the last 10 in 1998—the Gambia—left the list, with a marginal improvement of its ranking from 165 to 163. The African country with the highest ranking HDI in 1999 was Mauritius which was ranked at 59, followed by the Libyan Arab Jamahiriya at 65 and Seychelles at 66. Only these three countries make it to the top 100, with South Africa standing at 101. *See* UDNP, HUMAN DEVELOPMENT REPORT 1998 21 (1998); UDNP, HUMAN DEVELOPMENT REPORT 1999 45-48 (1999).

6 Part of the problem is that developmental discussions and strategies are still dominated by the World Bank and the IMF to the neglect of alternative prescriptions that place an emphasis elsewhere than on production for the external market. Indeed, even in discussing the market, the orthodoxy that continues to prevail in the international financial institutions (IFIs) adopts what Giovanni Cornea has described as a "reductionist" role for the state with little attention to the need to equalize economic opportunities. *See* Giovanni Cornea, *Convergence on Governance Issues, Dissent on Economic Policies*, 29 IDS BULL. 33 (1998).

those facing irredentist and secessionary movements. States undergoing political transition will manifest distinct problems from those engaged in internal armed conflict.[7] States struggling against collapsed social and political systems are faced with unique issues, including for some like Somalia the questioning of their very raison d'être and viability as states.[8] The myriad social, religious, cultural, political and even idiosyncratic distinctions between the countries of the continent all need to be taken into account. Thus, making broad prognostications and drawing sweeping conclusions for a continent as diverse and complex as Africa may be an exercise in futility.

There is little doubt that external regional and international forces will impact upon domestic country contexts in numerous ways. Thus, external conditions driven by the forces of the contemporary global political economy, compounded by cultural factors, will also be of significance in assessing the overall human rights situation. The influence of global arms-dealers will be as significant as that of the international broadcast media and of transnational corporations (TNCs). Alexandr Kalashnikov's AK-47 assault rifle will vie for domination alongside Ted Turner's Cable News Network (CNN) and cultural/corporate phenomena such as Madonna and Nike.[9] Major questions of accountability and social responsibility are

---

7 For a discussion of the impact of conflict on the protection of human rights and the broader issue of reconstruction, *see* Yashushi Yakashi, *Development Foregone: The Negative Impact of Crisis and Conflict in West Africa*, in UNDP, BACK TO BASICS, POST-CONFLICT PEACE-BUILDING IN WEST AFRICA: POLITICAL AND DEVELOPMENT INITIATIVES 22 (1997).

8 The phenomenon of statehood and its collapse is an issue that has once again emerged to capture intellectual imagination and discourse following the 1970s debates that took the state as a given, stable and unchanging entity in the African reality. *See, e.g.*, Julius Ihonvbere, *The 'irrelevant' State, Ethnicity and the Quest for Nationhood in Africa*, 17 ETHNIC & RACIAL STUD. 42 (1994). *See also* LYNNE RIENNER, COLLAPSED STATES: THE DISINTEGRATION AND RESTORATION OF LEGITIMATE AUTHORITY (I. William Zartman ed. 1995); Herbert Dittgen, *World Without Borders? Reflections on the Future of the Nation-State*, 34 GOV'T & OPPOSITION 161 (1999).

9 Recent developments on the African continent have seen the emergence of a new non-state actor which has significant implications for the situation of human rights in conditions of armed conflict, viz., mercenary companies—the so-called new "dogs of war." *See* Juan Carlos Zarate, *The Emergence of a New Dog of War: Private International Security Companies, International Law, and the New World Disorder*, 34 STAN. J. INT'L L. 75 (1998).

raised by the dominance of such actors in the economic scene.[10] What is also apparent from the preceding is that no external factor is likely to have as telling an impact on the overall human rights condition in the African continent than the phenomenon of globalization.[11] Although traditionally conceived in its economic manifestations, globalization has significant implications for the social, political, and cultural evolution of humankind in Africa in the coming century.[12] Moreover, the human rights implications of the phenomenon are only just beginning to be critically engaged and comprehensively understood.[13] As United Nations Secretary General Kofi Annan has pointed out: "Globalization has an immense potential to improve people's lives, but it can disrupt and destroy them as well. Those who do not accept its pervasive, all-encompassing ways are often left behind."[14]

In analyzing the human rights context from either the broad continental level, or from a narrower country-specific perspective, concern must invariably be focused on the situation of the individual and the manner in which the protection of his or her individual human rights is enhanced. This is the essential remit of the human rights text that is just over 50 years of age: protecting the individual against unwarranted and unjustified state interference to body and mind. Needless to say, the contemporary African situation presents wholly new and different contexts, within which the realization of such rights extend beyond individual concern and must be expanded to encompass the family and community. It is also crucially important not to forget the fact that traditional conceptions of human rights in the African context subsume the interests of the individual to those of the community at large and raise the correlation between human rights and

---

[10] On the issue of accountability, *see* Christopher G. Weeramantry, *Human Rights and the Global Market place*, 25 BROOK. J. INT'L L. 27, 41 (1999).

[11] For an analysis of the nexus between human rights and globalization, *see* Philip Alston, *The Universal Declaration in an Era of Globalization, in* REFLECTIONS ON THE UNIVERSAL DECLARATION OF HUMAN RIGHTS: A FIFTIETH ANNIVERSARY ANTHOLOGY 29 (Barend van der Heijden & Bahia Tahzib-Lie, eds., 1998).

[12] Joseph Oloka-Onyango, *Globalization in the Context of Increased Incidents of Racism, Racial Discrimination and Xenophobia*, U. N. Sub-Commission on the Promotion and Protection of Human Rights, 51st Sess., Agenda Item 3, E/CN.4/Sub.2/1999/8 (1999).

[13] A good initial engagement is undertaken by Frank J. Garcia, Symposium: The Universal Declaration of Human Rights at 50 and the Challenge of Global Markets and Human Rights: Trading Away the Human Rights Principle, 25 BROOK. J. INT'L L. 51 (1999).

[14] KOFI A. ANNAN, PARTNERSHIPS FOR GLOBAL COMMUNITY: ANNUAL REPORT OF THE WORK OF THE ORGANIZATION 59 (1998).

human duties or obligations.[15] In my opinion, critical to the understanding of the extent to which the protection and promotion of such rights will actually be enhanced is the degree to which the realization of two essentially group rights will be guaranteed. These group rights are the right to peace and security (or freedom from conflict)[16] and the right to sustainable human development (or freedom from want, deprivation and marginalization).[17] Ultimately, we are also speaking of the right to self determination. These rights are critical because they provide a holistic context in which more traditional individual human rights can be given articulate and wholesome expression. It is meaningless to focus on the right to free expression and association in a situation rife with marauding armed combatants, as is the case in Sierra Leone, Burundi or Liberia. The point made by Kofi Annan in his report to the 52nd Session of the General Assembly graphically illustrates this conundrum:

> Since 1970, more than 30 wars have been fought in Africa, the vast majority of them intra-State in origin. In 1996 alone, 14 of the 53 countries of Africa were afflicted by armed conflicts, accounting for more than half of all war-related deaths worldwide and resulting in more than 8 million refugees, returnees and displaced persons. The consequences of those conflicts have seriously undermined

---

[15] For an analysis of this issue from the perspective of refugee law, *see* Isabelle Gunning, *Expanding the International Definition of Refugee: A Multicultural View*, 13 FORDHAM INT'L L. J. 35, 73-75 (1989-1990).

[16] The question of conflict—particularly of the ethnic kind—and those who instigate them (Ethnic Engineers or Conflict Manufacturers) has led some observers to target the phenomenon as the main human rights issue of the contemporary era. According to Bill Berkeley, "They (ethnic conflicts) are all provoked from on high. In Africa, as elsewhere, the role of states and political leaders in fomenting ethnic and sectarian conflicts is the paramount human rights issue in the post-Cold War era." Bill Berkeley, *Judgment Day*, WASH. POST MAG., October 11, 1998, at 11.

[17] The right to development of course has a whole declaration dedicated to its realization. Unfortunately, very little progress has been made in ensuring its global enforcement. *See The Declaration on the Right to Development*, G.A. Res. 41/128, U.N. GAOR, 41st Sess., 97th plen. mtg., Annex 1, Agenda Item 101, U.N. Doc. A/41/128 (1986). For an analysis, see Richard Kiwanuka, *Developing Rights: The UN Declaration on the Right to Development*, 35 NETH. INT'L L. REV. 257 (1988); *see also* James C.N. Paul, *Symposium: The United Nations Family: Challenges of Law and Development: The United Nations and the Creation of an International Law of Development*, 36 HARV. INT'L L. J. 307 (1995).

Africa's efforts to ensure long-term stability, prosperity and peace for its peoples.[18]

It is just as futile to speak of the right of participation in conditions where basic human necessities, such as food, shelter, and water are beyond the reach of the majority of the population. What is the meaning of the 'right to vote' when the voter may be too weak from disease and hunger to effectively exercise his or her franchise? Conversely, unless freedom of expression is guaranteed, the hungry voter is unable to articulate the cause of his or her malnourishment and deprivation. In sum, for a human to be considered whole, he or she must be able to enjoy both civil and political rights and economic, social and cultural rights as well. Moreover, such enjoyment must be exercised in a generalized context that ensures that daily physical existence is not under a threat of predictable extermination by hunger, disease, or conflict. Conceived in this fashion, human rights then becomes the bedrock of a wholesome and integrated approach to sustainable human development. An inordinate focus on one category at the expense of another will obviously produce a truncated human reality.[19]

The primary focus of this study is the regional protection of human rights on the African continent. It provides a short historical backdrop before moving on to an examination of the normative framework that currently prevails on the continent. Included in this section are issues such as cultural relativism or reductionism,[20] the structure and content of the African Charter on Human and Peoples' Rights (hereinafter "the Charter),[21] the

---

[18] Kofi Annan, *The Causes of Conflict and the Promotion of Durable Peace and Sustainable Development in Africa: Report of the Secretary-General*, U.N. SCOR 52nd Sess., Agenda Item 10, ¶4 (1998), *reprinted in* 10 AFR. J. INT'L & COMP. L. 549, 549-50 (1998).

[19] Scott and Macklem put the point succinctly when they argue that, "A constitution containing only civil and political rights projects an image of truncated humanity. Symbolically, but still brutally, it excludes those segments of society for whom autonomy means little without the necessities of life." Craig Scott & Patrick Macklem, *Constitutional Ropes of Sand or Justiciable Guarantees?: Social Rights in a New South African Constitution,* 141 U. PA. L. REV. 1, 29(1992).

[20] For a good discussion of the background and content of the relativism or reductionism debate, *see* Samuel K. Murumba, *Cross-Cultural Dimensions of Human Rights in the 21st Century,* in LEGAL VISIONS OF THE 21ST CENTURY: ESSAYS IN HONOUR OF JUDGE CHRISTOPHER WEERAMANTRY 207-240 (Kluwer Law International, The Hague, 1998).

[21] OAU Doc. CAB/LEG/67/3/Rev.5 (1981), *reprinted in* 21 ILM 59 (1982). Otherwise known as the Banjul Charter—after the Gambian capital in which it was promulgated—the African Charter came into existence in 1981. It came into force

human rights of women, and the phenomenon of forced displacement experienced by refugees and internally displaced persons (IDPs). In the following and most crucial section of the paper, I examine the existing institutional mechanisms that have been established to enforce human rights on the continent. This section focuses on the Commission established by the Charter and on the African Court on Human & Peoples' Rights, the protocol for which has only recently been promulgated.[22] Consideration is also paid to human rights enforcement at the national level, the level at which human rights must ultimately find concrete expression, and the role of civil society therein. The last section of the paper examines the challenges for sustainable human development that lie ahead and the opportunities available for the enhancement of the human rights situation on the African continent.

II. Human Rights In Africa: An Historical Resume

A. *Comprehending the Effects of the Colonial Legacy*

Any analysis of the contemporary situation of human rights on the African continent must approach the issue against the backdrop of a fairly broad socio-historical perspective. Such a perspective is essential due to the transmutation of various forms of social organization and expression as a result of both indigenous and external forces, and the fact that history continues to exert its influence on the continent. Pre-colonial historical forms can be seen in the resilience of cultural (so-called "traditional") norms that govern domestic relations and the family. Colonial influences are apparent in contemporary political systems and economic relations. Nearly half a century after most countries on the continent attained independence, many of them continue to utilize colonial laws governing political association, public health, education and free expression. The consequence is that the claim by African nations' of having made a difference in the

---

in 1986, and to date almost all African countries—with the exception of Ethiopia and Morocco—have ratified the instrument. *See* Jean-Marie Bernard, *International Instruments Relating to Human Rights*, 18 Hum. Rts. L. J. 79 (1997).

22 Protocol to the African Charter on Human and Peoples' Rights on the Establishment of an African Court on Human and Peoples' Rights by the Assembly of Heads of State and Government (ASHG) of the Organization of African Unity, OAU/LEG/MIN/AFCHPR/PROT.(l)Rev.2 (1997). The Protocol was adopted by the ASHG at its 34th session held in Ouagadougou, Burkina Faso. By the end of December 1998, twenty-four states had signed the Protocol. Article 34 of the Protocol stipulates that the instrument shall come into force thirty days after ratification by fifteen OAU member states. *See* Makau Mutua, *The African Human Rights Court: A Two-Legged Stool*, 21 Hum. Rts. Q. 342 (1999).

human rights reality of the people they govern is effectively negated. Laws continue to exist on African statute books outlawing the defamation of a foreign "potentate," the barracking of persons with contagious disease, the establishment of civic associations, and a host of penal sanctions that stem from the Victorian era and clearly violate contemporary notions of human rights.[23]

We need not restate the fact that the colonial epoch in Africa represented the negation of all categories of human rights from the basic right of self-determination to the freedoms of expression and association. Despite the altruistic, moralistic and religious veneer in which the phenomenon was clothed, colonialism was primarily concerned with how much could be extracted from the territories and peoples it brought under its control.[24] Based on a system of extra-economic coercion, colonialism had little time for the recognition and protection of rights that would threaten or undermine its primary economic objective. This explains why resources expended on coercion (the police, gendarmarie, the armed forces, and prison services) were far in excess of those devoted to any social service in any colony on the continent. It also explains the apartheid-like differentials based primarily on race but reinforced by class, that resulted in highly stratified social formations and critically impacted the ethnic frameworks of the colonized territories.[25] In the words of Jalali and Lipset, "Over time such (colonial) policies created widespread economic and social disparities between ethnic groups. Certain ethnic groups were selected as collaborators or channels for the transmission of government patronage."[26] Many such disparities have

---

[23] Prof. Welch puts the matter in proper perspective: "Freedom of expression was subjected to significant restraints when Africa was divided among various colonial powers. The limits imposed in the colonial period were in many respects enhanced following independence, rather than relaxed or abolished. The veneer of democratization that accompanied the achievement of self-government was rapidly stripped away by leaders anxious to preserve their version of national unity, and/or by military elites who shot their way into power." Claude E. Welch Jr., *The African Charter and Freedom of Expression in Africa* 4 BUFF. HUM. RTS. L. REV. 105 (1999).

[24] *See* Theophilus Maranga, *The Colonial Legacy and the African Common Market: Problems and Challenges Facing the African Economic Community,* 10 HARV. BLACKLETTER J. 105(1993).

[25] For an analysis of how racial and economic considerations designed by colonial powers affected conceptions of inclusion and exclusion, *see* Mahmood Mamdani, CITIZEN AND SUBJECT: CONTEMPORARY AFRICA AND THE LEGACY OF LATE COLONIALISM 285-286 (1996).

[26] Rita Jalali & Seymour Martin Lipset, *Racial and Ethnic Conflicts: A Global Perspective in* Michael W. Hughey (ed.), NEW TRIBALISMS: THE RESURGENCE OF RACE AND ETHNICITY, 321 (1998).

persisted into the post-colonial era, resurfacing to wreak havoc with a vengeance.

B. Human Rights in the Organization of African Unity (OAU)

Ironically, in the field of human rights independent African states have performed little better than their colonial predecessors. The first attempt at a continental approach to Africa's myriad problems was pursued under the rubric of the Organization of African Unity (OAU) established in 1963.[27] The Charter delineated the focus of the OAU as being 1) the right to self-determination and 2) the protection of the incipient and fragile foundations of states that had only just regained their independence.[28] Preoccupied with these two major concerns, it is of little surprise that the Charter contained only scant reference to human rights and focused inordinately on state sovereignty and its accompanying concordat of non-interference in the internal affairs of other states.[29] Although noble objectives at the time—given the continued existence of colonies compounded by apartheid in South Africa and Rhodesia, and the debacle of UN intervention in the Congo. The net effect may, in the words of the Commonwealth Human Rights Initiative, "actually have damaged the cause of human rights."[30] The OAU Charter, the quintessential instrument governing the conduct of relations between African states, ignored the fact that states were merely a conglomeration of people to whom human rights protection should have been logically extended. The reference in the Charter to the Universal Declaration of Human Rights reinforced opposition to the policies of colonialism and apartheid. However, scant attention was paid to broad or specific human rights principles.[31]

Unfortunately, the damage done to the concept of human rights in the early years of independence meant that it remained on the back burner of political debate and activity through two bitter decades of African his-

---

27 The Charter of the OAU is reprinted *in* 58 AM. J. INT'L L. 873 (1964).

28 *Id.*

29 *See* Solomon Gomes, Sensitivity to the Principle of Non-interference in the Internal Affairs of States: A Political Imperative (Feb. 17-19, 1993) (paper presented at the International Negotiation Network (INN) Consultation held at the Carter Centre, Emory University).

30 *See* COMMONWEALTH HUMAN RIGHTS INITIATIVE, PUT OUR WORLD TO RIGHTS: TOWARDS A COMMONWEALTH HUMAN RIGHTS POLICY 59 (1991).

31 For a more comprehensive background analysis to the place of human rights in the establishment and evolution of the OAU, see J. Oloka-Onyango, *Beyond the Rhetoric: Reinvigorating the Struggle for Economic and Social Rights in Africa*, 26 CAL. W. INT'L L.J 1, 42-44 (1995).

tory. As a consequence, single party states and military dictatorships assumed the dominant forms of governance on the continent. Characterized in the extreme by leaders such as Uganda's Idi Amin and the Central African Republic's Jean Bedel Bokassa, it was also a period in which the Cold War stalemate between the United States and the Soviet Union allowed for the almost unfettered assault on the human rights of the African peoples. Essential aspects of the right to development, such as health, education, and just conditions of work, were also relegated to oblivion. It was against this background, in 1981, that the OAU promulgated the African Charter that has evolved to become the principal human rights instrument on the continent.[32] Tokunbo Ige has pointed out that there was a sense of urgency that attended the drafting and adoption of the Charter. This resulted in a number of compromises and weaknesses being incorporated into the instrument.[33] Others have dismissed the African Charter outright. We now turn to a consideration of the substance of the Charter to examine the concrete dimensions of its practical operation on the continent.

III. The Normative African Framework: Radical Departure or 'Business as Usual?'

A. *Revisiting the Debate about African Cultural "Relativism"*

Most debates about the human rights framework on the African continent begin from an analysis of the relationship between the international instruments that have evolved over time: the Universal Declaration of Human Rights (UDHR), the ICCPR and ICESR, and the regional body of normative standards.[34] Implicated immediately in this debate is a tension that has come to be characterized as the phenomenon of "Cultural Relativ-

---

[32] The impression should not be given that over this time there were no attempts to address the issue of human rights from a continental perspective. Indeed, the first attempts were commenced in 1961—pre-dating even the debate and promulgation of the OAU Charter. *See* Robert H. Kisanga, *Fundamental Rights and Freedoms in Africa: The Work of the African Commission on Human and Peoples' Rights,* in Fundamental Rights and Freedoms in Tanzania 25, 25-26 (Chris Maina Peter & Ibrahim Hamisi Juma eds., 1998). For more background to the evolution of the Charter, see generally Tokunbo Ige, The African Charter on Human and Peoples' Rights (1998) (unpublished manuscript on file with the author).

[33] *Id.*, at 2-4.

[34] For a recent exposition of this approach see generally Satvinder Juss, *The Coming of Communitarian Rights: Are 'Third-Generation' Human Rights Really 'First-Generation' Rights?*, 3 Int'l J. Discrimination L. 159 (1998).

ism."[35] This is an argument about the extent to which ostensibly universal standards of human rights observance should be tempered and conditioned by the local cultural situation that prevails in distinct regions of the world.[36] That tension is apparent in the text of the African Charter on Human and Peoples' Rights.[37] The African Charter marks itself out as a distinctive human rights instrument while it simultaneously draws inspiration from the UDHR and other international human rights instruments.[38] This is evident from the preamble to the African Charter and from the emphasis on the family, the community, the state, and the concept of duties.[39] In this way, the instrument does indeed mark some conceptual distance from its international precursors.[40] The Charter is definitely an instrument that is married to the socio-cultural context in which it was given birth.[41]

This fact is also reflected in its adoption of the term "peoples"[42] to complement "human" and through its constant references back to the phe-

---

[35] *See* Muramba, *supra* note 20.

[36] Yash Ghai points to at least four assumptions that underlie the phenomenon of cultural relativism: (a) that the world's cultures can be divided into distinct categories; (b) that each state has a homogenous culture; (c) that culture is unchanging, and (d) that culture provides a state with its values. *See* Yash Ghai, *The Critics of the Universal Declaration*, in 12 INTERIGHTS BULL. 45, 45 (1998/9),

[37] Nana K.A. Busia Jr., *The Political Economy of the African Charter on Human and Peoples' Rights*, 7 MENNESKER OG RETTIGHETER [M.R.] 68 (1989).

[38] *See* Bertrand G. Ramcharan, *The Universality of Human Rights*, 53 THE REVIEW 105, 112 (1994). *See also* African Charter on Human and Peoples' Rights, *adopted* 26 June 1981, O.A.U. Doc. CAB/LEG/67/3, Rev.5 (*entered into force* 12 Oct. 1986), *reprinted in* 21 I.L.M. 58 (1982).

[39] Preambular paragraph 7 of the African Charter stipulates that: "Considering that the enjoyment of rights and freedoms also implies the performance of duties on the part of everyone." A recent study on the phenomenon of duties in International Human Rights Law pointed out that the African Charter contains a total of three articles and eleven paragraphs devoted to the issue of individual duties. *See* DANIEL PETRASEK, INTERNATIONAL COUNCIL ON HUMAN RIGHTS POLICY, TAKING DUTIES SERIOUSLY: INDIVIDUAL DUTIES IN INTERNATIONAL LAW (A COMMENTARY) 33 (1999).

[40] For a comparative analysis with other regional instruments, see B. Obinna Okerre, *The Protection of Human Rights in Africa and the African Charter on Human and Peoples' Rights: A Comparative Analysis with the European and American Systems of Human Rights* 6 HUM. RTS. Q. 141 (1984).

[41] *See* Mohamed Komeja, *The African System of Human and Peoples' Rights: An Annotated Bibliography*, 3 E. AFR. J. PEACE & HUM. RTS. 262, 263-65 (1996).

[42] For a detailed discussion of the various meanings of the term 'peoples' as used in the African Charter, *see generally* Richard Kiwanuka, *The Meaning of "People"*

nomenon of "African civilization." Thus, the fifth paragraph of the Charter's preamble stipulates as follows:

> Taking into consideration the virtues of their historical tradition and the values of African civilization which should inspire and characterize their reflection on the concept of human and peoples' rights."

Although the question of culture is certainly an important and relevant one in the discussion about human rights today, much of the debate on the subject is, as Yash Ghai has pointed out, unproductive.[43] This is because it adopts concepts from both Universalists and relativists. The "Universalists" assert that the Universal Declaration and the corpus of norms that have evolved around it constitute a truly universal ethos over which there can be no debate.[44] At the other end of the spectrum are the "relativists" who assert that there can be no universalities; *all* human rights standards must be subjected to the local conditions specific to the country, the culture, or the religion in question. The relativists erect culture as a barrier to criticism or challenge of practices that clearly violate fundamental human rights. Conversely, the universalists have transformed human rights discourse into an intellectual battering ram, chanting the mantra of universalism even when deference to the local norms will produce a solution that is more enduring and ultimately enhances the protection of human rights in that community. Not only is the universalist approach insensitive to the reality of genuine cultural nuances that exist on the ground, but it negates one of the most fundamental tenets on which a truly universalist human rights ethos is grounded: inclusion and dialogue.

In most instances, relativists are politicians from the south whose human rights practices are at a minimum questionable, and often extremely violative on a host of fronts. Regarding the situation of women in particular, relativists seek to retain the dominance of patriarchal structures of social ordering and to resist what would amount to a diminution of traditionally exercised power and control within the family, and its attendant implications to the community and the state.[45]

---

in the African Charter on Human and Peoples' Rights, 82 AM. J. INT'L L. 80 (1988).

43 Ghai, *supra* note 36.

44 *See* JACK DONNELLY, UNIVERSAL HUMAN RIGHTS IN THEORY AND PRACTICE (1989).

45 Arati Rao makes an incisive analysis of how and why this takes place. Arati Rao, *The Politics of Gender and Culture in International Human Rights Discourse*,

Between the two there is no middle ground. In scholarly debate, the relativist argument is the one most often easily dismissed. Unfortunately, the Universalists often premise their debunking of cultural relativism and reaffirmation of the universalist ideal on an ahistorical, and near-missionary, conception of the development and contemporary application of human rights.[46] In the first instance, it is impossible to run away from the fact that the human rights instruments are culturally, politically, and historically rooted in forms of state/individual structuring that have their roots in Western liberal democracy. Very few of the states that make up the international community today were at the table when the Universal Declaration was debated.[47] Moreover, many of the most important promulgators of the instrument, including both Britain and France, were colonial powers. This partly explains why the Declaration fails to mention the right to self determination, a fundamental democratic right of all peoples.[48]

At the time the UDHR was adopted, the United States had yet to recognize the equality of people of colour. On its part, the Soviet Union violently suppressed the rights of numerous peoples forcibly incorporated within its ambit. The same country also housed several thousand in virtual concentration camps. It was quite ironic that these four countries were the most prominent in the promulgation of an instrument whose basic principles they breached in both letter and spirit. Current universalist rhetoric notwithstanding, it is quite evident that the UDHR assumed the shape and character most familiar to Judeo-Christian conceptions of democratic governance and individual autonomy.[49] To compound the problem, the vision

---

in WOMEN'S RIGHTS, HUMAN RIGHTS: INTERNATIONAL FEMINIST PERSPECTIVES 167, (Julie Peters & Andrea Wolper eds., 1995).

[46] *See also* Kofi Kumado, *Africa and the Universal Declaration*, in 60 THE REVIEW 41-46 (1998).

[47] For a good discussion of who made the UDHR and its implications for the contemporary debate about human rights, *see* Dianne Otto, *Rethinking the "universality" of Human Rights Law*, 29 COLUM. HUM. RTS. L. REV. 1, 18-30 (1997).

[48] *See* Issa Shivji, *Human Rights and Development: A Fragmented Discourse, in* FUNDAMENTAL RIGHTS AND FREEDOMS IN Tanzania, *supra* note 32, at 9. For an extensive examination of the glaring loopholes in self-determination theory and practice as it has evolved over the ages, see J. Oloka-Onyango, *Heretical Reflections on the Right to Self-Determination: Problems and Prospects for the Twenty First Century Future*, 15 AM. U. INT'L L. REV. (forthcoming 1999).

[49] In fact, we could describe these conceptions as essentially white and essentially male, regardless of the ideological divide between the capitalist and socialist models that vied for supremacy at the UDHR debating table. As Shelly Wright points out, the terms of debate were the control of property—whether accumulated capitalist, or redistributed socialist—and in this sense it was the language of control and

of human rights that most universalists accept and pursue with single-minded devotion is one that has consistently failed to recognize economic, social and cultural rights, and rights to peace, development and the environment as "genuine" human rights.

In the same way that many of the relativists are pursuing a political agenda designed to retain their hegemony over local political space by utilizing the veneer of culture, the universalists are pursuing an equally politicized agenda of extending global hegemony by using the rubric of human rights. The disparities in the human rights regime have not remained as atavistic relics from a contested and distant past. They are omnipresent even within contemporary struggles over the meaning and the content of human rights. Take the arena of women's human rights as one example. One would imagine that, due to its more recent conceptual development, there would be considerably more comity of perspective between women of different cultures. Nevertheless, significant tension is still manifest on a variety of issues; from reproductive health rights[50] to the debate over the eradication of female genital mutilation (FGM),[51] to the contention that the Convention on the Elimination of All Forms of Discrimination Against Women (CEDAW)[52] did not adequately address the situation of rural women.[53]

---

ownership. That language clearly did not resonate with African conceptions of rights or even of property. *See* Shelly Wright, *Economic Rights and Social Justice: A Feminist Analysis of Some International Human Rights Conventions*, 12 AUSTL. Y.B. OF INT'L L. 241, 255 (1992).

[50] Khawar Mumtaz has argued that at the World Conference on Population and Development in Cairo in 1994 women from the so-called "north" did not reciprocate with the same degree of solidarity over issues that were of concern to their "southern" sisterhood when the latter had initially supported them. *See* Khawar Mumtaz, *Bringing Together the Rights to Livelihoods and Reproductive Health*, in 42 DEV. 15 (1999).

[51] *See* Asma Mohamed Abdel Halim, *Tools of Suppression*, *in* Centre for Women's Global Leadership (ed.) GENDER VIOLENCE AND WOMEN'S HUMAN RIGHTS IN AFRICA 27 (1994); Hope Lewis, *Between Irua and Female Genital Mutilation": Feminist Human Rights Discourse and the Cultural Divide*, 8 HARV. HUM. RTS. J. 1 (1995).

[52] Convention on the Elimination of All Forms of Discrimination Against Women, *adopted* 18 Dec. 1979, G.A. Res. 34/180, U.N. GAOR, 34th Sess., Supp. No.46 at 193, U.N. Doc. A/34/36 (1980) (*entered into force* 3 Sept. 1981), *reprinted in* 19 I.L.M. 33 (1980).

[53] Celestine Itumbi Nyamu, *Rural Women in Kenya and the Legitimacy of Human Rights Discourse and Institutions*, *in* LEGITIMATE GOVERNANCE IN AFRICA 263, 265-66 (Edward Kofi Quashigah & Obiora Chinedu Okafor eds., 1999).

Engaging in an extensive deconstruction of the normative elements enshrined within the existing human rights corpus is not the intention of this article. Nevertheless, it is critical to an understanding of the issues under examination that we remain cognizant of the limitations of the universalist discourse and its dominance in the human rights debate. This is because that dominance has particular implications for several aspects of contemporary human rights discourse and for their linkage to sustainable human development. For example, the under-emphasis of economic and social rights, and the debate over their alleged non-justiciability. Further examples include the discussion about the right to development and its stalled implementation, the issue of the debt burden as a human rights question, and the question of non-state actors - particularly transitional corporations (TNC) and their relevance to the international respect for and enforcement of human rights. All of these issues are implicated in the relativism/universalism discussion. Unfortunately, they tend to be relegated to the background once the bogeyman of culture is erected to trump all alternative or contending argument. Nevertheless, as Anne Orford appropriately warns us:

> Whatever definition of rights and democracy we adopt, it remains necessary to question the assumption that the powerful international institutions operating in the economic and security areas are the bearers of even these limited liberal versions of democracy and rights in the post-Cold War era. To what extent is that idealization of the international realm based in turn upon selective erasures or motivated forgetting?[54]

Regardless of the distinctions entailed by an approach that is rooted in the particularities of the African cultural experience, important consequences flow from the connection of the African normative framework to the obligations concerning human rights under the United Nations Charter and the Universal Declaration. According to Radhika Coomaraswamy, UN Special Rapporteur on Violence Against Women, there is an element of rights discourse and practice that extends beyond geographical location or cultural specificity:

> Thus human rights discourse has resonance in the everyday experiences of individuals. Otherwise it would not have developed so dynamically and have become used by such

---

[54] Anne Orford, *Locating the International: Military and Monetary Interventions after the Cold War*, 38 HARV. INT'L L.J. 443, 464 (1997).

> different groups throughout the world. In other words—yes, perhaps human rights in its present day incarnation is a product of the Enlightenment, but its general thrust has resonance in diverse spiritual and cultural experiences. In terms of political values like the concept of democracy it is an important step forward for all human beings and all cultures.[55]

Contemporary international standards of human rights and the international machinery erected for their protection are rooted in the obligations established under the UN Charter that promote universal respect for and observance of human rights and fundamental freedoms for all, without distinction as to race, sex, language or religion.[56] The essential point is that, despite the distinctive African "cultural fingerprint"[57] that is implicit in several of its provisions, several aspects of the Charter provide evidence of a general acceptance of normative standards (such as non-discrimination, equality of all persons, fundamental freedoms and liberties, for example) enshrined in the international instruments. Having retraced the conceptual issues relating to the African Charter, we now turn to a more critical consideration of the specific provisions and the structure of the instrument.

B. Breaking New Ground? The Structure and Content of the African Charter

The African Charter can generally be divided into five distinct parts: the provisions on civil and political rights; those on economic, social and cultural rights; the group or collective rights; the provisions which elaborate the duties in the Charter; and those governing the enforcement mechanisms in the instrument.[58] The first category of rights is fairly straightforward. It includes non-discrimination (Article 2), equality before the law (Article 3), the right to life (Article 4), and the inherence of human

---

[55] RADHIKA COOMARASWAMY, REINVENTING INTERNATIONAL LAW: WOMEN'S RIGHTS AS HUMAN RIGHTS IN THE INTERNATIONAL COMMUNITY 7.

[56] *See* Chaloka Beyani, *Toward A More Effective Guarantee of Women's Rights in the African System*, *in* HUMAN RIGHTS OF WOMEN: NATIONAL AND INTERNATIONAL PERSPECTIVES 289-290 (Rebecca J. Cook ed. 1994).

[57] Makau wa Mutua, *The Banjul Charter and the African Cultural Fingerprint: An Evaluation of the Language of Duties*, 35 VA. J. INT'L L. 339 (1995).

[58] *see generally* EVELYN A. ANKUMAH, THE AFRICAN COMMISSION ON HUMAN AND PEOPLES' RIGHTS: PRACTICE AND PROCEDURES (1996) (providing a good discussion of the structure of the Charter and of the operation of the Commission created under it).

dignity (Article 5). Articles 6 to 13 specify the rights that are similarly covered in the Universal Declaration or in the International Covenant on Civil and Political Rights (ICCPR). Striking omissions from the Charter include the prohibition against being subjected, "without free consent, to medical or scientific experimentation." This provision appears in Article 7 of the ICCPR. The African Charter also lacks more elaborate guarantees against arbitrary detention. Similarly, although the right to a fair trial is covered by Article 7 of the Charter, it does not speak about trial in absentia, the issue of legal aid, or the right to an interpreter. Also omitted are compensation for the miscarriage of justice and protection against double jeopardy, all of which are covered by Article 14 of the ICCPR.[59]

Perhaps the issue in the African Charter that has attracted most criticism is its extensive deployment of clawback clauses, phrases that could effectively remove (or at a minimum severely curtail) the right ostensibly guaranteed. In each of the provisions referred to above, clauses such as ". . . except for reasons and conditions previously laid down by law. . ." (Article 6), ". . .subject to law and order. . ." (Article 8) and ". . . provided he abides by the law. . ." (Article 10) abound. Although the grant of the right is supposed to be paramount, the clawback clause may have the effect of taking away the right that is granted. This is especially a problem because in many African states you still have laws and regulations that are directly violative of human rights. For example, some states prohibit the formation of certain types of associations merely at the whim of the registering officer. In other cases, the law to which the right is subjected is so arbitrary that its effect is to completely negate the right ostensibly guaranteed. The clawback, clauses coupled with the omission of certain rights, does not give the African Charter a very prominent position in the pantheon of instruments that seek to extend the parameters of rights, respect, and enforcement.

Arguably the most innovative aspect of the African Charter relates to its provisions on Peoples' rights and the duties of individuals. Among the peoples' rights covered are the right to existence and the right to struggle against colonial domination (Article 20). Of course, the interesting point regarding the question of peoples' rights is how the concept is of such fluidity that it could undermine well established principles in the OAU Charter concerning the inviolability of states and the sacrosanct nature of their borders. The "oppressed peoples" who have the right to free themselves from the bonds of domination, in paragraph 2 of Article 20, do not necessarily have to be under the yoke of a colonial power. The collective rights to development (Article 22), to peace and security (Article 23), and

59 Ige, *supra* note 32, at 6-7.

on the right to a "general satisfactory environment" (Article 24), are all rights which have greatly impacted on the jurisprudence of rights in the international arena.[60] The African Charter was the first international instrument to lay down these rights in a legally binding fashion.[61] Indeed, as we have already argued, these collective rights will become of fundamental importance in the coming millennium.

Final mention must be made of the African Charter's elaborate codification of individual duties. Although the Universal Declaration, ICCPR, and ICESR contain reference to the duties individuals owe to society, none of them are as extensive as the African Charter's elaboration.[62] The duties listed extend from the harmonious development of the family[63] to the promotion and achievement of African unity.[64] Most commentary about these duties has considered them to be too onerous and capable of being used by states to effectively trump the individual rights guaranteed.[65] While there has been little action undertaken to test this aspect of the Charter, it is quite clear that the concept of duties is not necessarily antithetical to the respect of human rights. What is clear is that the overall observation and protection of individual rights is not undermined by an undue emphasis on duties. This is especially true of the aspect of the Charter dealing with Economic, Social and Cultural Rights and their connection to the pursuit of sustainable human development.

C. Economic, Social and Cultural Human Rights: A New Approach to Sustainable Human Development?

It is not erroneous to describe economic, social and cultural rights as the "ugly sister" to the more widely recognized civil and political rights.[66] Not only is there a lackluster approach to their effective realization, but also lingering questions about their conception.[67] Some have even

---

60 On the right to environment, *see* Christine Echookit Akello, *The Right to Environment and Generational Equity*, 4 E. AFR. J. PEACE & HUM. RTS. 125 (1998).

61 *See* Inger Österdahl, *The Jurisdiction Ratione Materiae of the African Court of Human and Peoples' Rights: A Comparative Critique*, 7 REV. AFR. COMMISION ON HUM. & PEOPLES' RTS. 149 (1998).

62 *See* PETRASEK, *supra* note 39, at 19-28.

63 Ige, *supra* note 32, at art. 29(1).

64 *Id.* art. 29(8).

65 Ige, *supra* note 32, at 9.

66 J. Oloka-Onyango, *Economic and Social Rights, the Universal Declaration and the New Millennium*, 12 INTERIGHTS BULLETIN 11(1998/1999).

67 Paul Sieghart, AN INTRODUCTION TO THE INTERNATIONAL COVENANTS ON HUMAN RIGHTS, Commonwealth Secretariat, London, 1988.

gone so far as to argue that economic and social rights are not rights; they are merely unenforceable individual or group entitlements. Frequent objections focus on the issue of justiciability.[68] The argument most often heard is that economic, social and cultural rights are simply not justiciable. In other words, they cannot be enforced through litigation and judicial enforcement in the way that civil and political rights can. The argument goes on to assert that economic, social and cultural rights are "aspirational" or "abstract"; they cannot be the subject of either affirmative state obligation or immediate realization and enforcement. Both the Indian[69] and South African courts have effectively disproved this thesis. Additionally, the 1993 Vienna Declaration explicitly reaffirmed the indivisibility, interdependence, and interrelatedness of the two categories of human rights.[70] Consequently, the question for debate is not so much the conceptual, but the practical: how do we make economic and social rights resonate for the vast majority of the human population for whom these rights are critical?

Several cases from both the aforementioned jurisdictions have affirmed that certain obligations with respect to the realization of the rights such as education, health, and shelter cannot simply be evaded by the state, irrespective of the question of resources or financial ability. This is because, in many instances, what is at stake in the disputation over such rights may be issues such as discrimination (on gender or social status), prioritization (concerning budgetary allocations), or access. A state is not required to expend resources to address any of the above. The South African Constitutional Court has responded to the claim that the enforcement of social and economic rights must be dependent on the capacity of a state to afford the cost entailed (the so-called "afford ability" argument) by stating:

> It is true that the inclusion of socio-economic rights may result in courts making orders that have direct implications for budgetary matters. However, even when a court enforces civil and political rights such as equality, freedom of

---

[68] For a summary of the non-justiciability arguments *see* E. Nii Ashie Kotey, *Some Fallacies About Rights: Of Indivisibility, Priority and Justiciability*, *in* REPORT OF A REGIONAL SEMINAR ON ECONOMIC, SOCIAL AND CULTURAL RIGHTS 101 (1999).

[69] See for example the remarks of former Indian Chief Justice Bhagwati on Public Interest Litigation (PIL) as a necessary tool to foster the enforcement of economic and social rights in the case of People's Union v. Union of India [1983] 1 S.C.R 456, 469.

[70] Shadrack Gutto, *Beyond Justiciability: Challenges of Implementing/Enforcing Socio-Economic Rights in South Africa,* 4 BUFF. HUM. RTS. L. REV. 79, 89-91 (1998).

> speech and the right to a fair trial, the order it makes will often have such implications. A court may require the provision of legal aid, or the extension of state beneficiaries of such benefits. In our view, it cannot be said that by including socio-economic rights within a bill of rights, a task is conferred upon them by a bill of rights that it can result in a breach of the separation of powers.[71]

Indeed, as Shadrack Gutto points out, the incorporation of justiciable rights in the Bill of Rights of a constitutional democracy that respects the Rule of Law, under conditions of social inequalities, ". . . means that such rights and processes of their justiciability is open to all; rich and poor, the advantaged and disadvantaged."[72] The rich and advantaged are entitled to use the rights to defend their position, while the poor and disadvantaged are entitled to do so in pursuit of their interests to enter the camp of the rich and advantaged and to improve their life conditions."[73] Although Gutto argues that the social actions of all social classes tend to "balance out", the more important issue is that social and economic rights are not esoteric entitlements. Such rights can indeed be the subject of rights discourse and enforcement at the domestic level. The judgments of the South African court go a considerable distance in clarifying what has traditionally been extremely murky terrain.[74]

The distinctive character of the African Charter has been extolled by numerous authors,[75] particularly with respect to the recognition of economic, social, and cultural rights.[76] The Charter commences its approach to economic, social, and cultural rights from the Preamble, which stipulates that it was "*henceforth essential*" to pay particular attention to the right to

---

71 Certification Judgment of the South African Constitutional Court, (10) BCLR ¶ 77. *See also* Gutto, *supra* note 70 at 92.

72 Id., at 92.

73 Id.

74 Again, we can also cite the Indian examples where the process of Social Action Litigation (SAL) has considerably expanded the parameters of the judicial enforcement of human rights. *See* P.N. Bhagwati, *Liberty and Security of the Person in India, with a particular emphasis on Access to Courts*, *in* DEVELOPING HUMAN RIGHTS JURISPRUDENCE 203-216 (Commonwealth Secretariat/Interrights ed. 1998).

75 *See, e.g.* Rose D'sa, *Human and Peoples' Rights: Distinctive Feaures of the African Charter*, 29 J. AFR. LAW 72, 72-81 (1985).

76 For a good analysis of the conceptual debates and their African dimensions, see Nana K.A. Busia & Bibiane Mbaye, *Filing Communications on Economic and Social Rights under the African Charter on Human and Peoples' Rights (The Banjul Charter),* 3 E. AFR. J. PEACE & HUM. RTS. 191, 191-193 (1996).

development.[77] Furthermore, it goes on to assert that civil and political rights *"cannot be dissociated"* from economic, social and cultural rights in conception as well as in universality.[78] The preamble concludes, with an affirmation that ". . . the satisfaction of economic, social and cultural rights *is a guarantee* for the enjoyment of civil and political rights."[79]

Some scholars have argued that all that the African Charter accomplished was to place economic, social and cultural rights and group (so-called "third generation") rights on the same footing as civil and political rights.[80] It is my view that the Charter conceptually shifted the emphasis from the traditional focus on civil and political rights to one including economic and social rights. However, the extent to which it adopted a genuinely novel and revolutionary approach to the issue is debatable. Indeed, the conceptual shift was not met by a transition in the practical approach to and application of the basic elements of rights-discourse and implementation of economic and social rights, whether at the continental or the national level of action in Africa. How is this so?

A review of the historical treatment of economic and social rights prior to the drafting of the African Charter is extremely important to understanding why there is a dichotomy between the theory enshrined in the instrument and the practice on the ground in many African states. In the first instance, the situation of civil and political rights on the continent was dismal, thereby attracting the opprobrium of the international community. African states and the leaders who assembled to discuss the Charter at the end of the 1970s were clearly on the defensive. Simultaneously, the debate over the New International Economic Order (NIEO) had wound its way through the United Nations system but produced little by way of tangible results. The conceptual reversal implicit in the African Charter was a reflection of the prevailing belief that an alteration in the existing structures of the international political economy was a matter of priority. Among those structures was the absence of attention to issues such as basic education, health care, and potable water. These issues were central to the prevailing developmental paradigm, which focused on increased aid. In this respect, by focusing on the Right to Development, the Charter was presaging the subsequent debate that was to lead to an international declaration on the same subject. However, the economic and social rights in question (to better health, improved education, and shelter *inter alia*) were seen not so much as rights of individual Africans, but rather as rights of the state. It was rights-

77 African Charter, *supra* note 21 preamble.

78 *Id.*

79 *Id.*

80 *See supra* note 76, at 192.

theory in top-down and paternalistic fashion. The state was viewed as the "people."[81] From such a perspective, obviously *the* "people" could not claim these rights against the state.

At the same time, the drafters of the Charter were cautious about the obligations entailed in a rights-approach towards matters that were traditionally confined to the sphere of political largesse. Thus, a systematic review of what is in the Charter will clearly demonstrate a lackluster approach to the issue of economic and social rights. Coupled with the manner in which civil and political rights were approached and articulated, it becomes clear that the drafters of the document were not genuinely rights-sensitive, with regard to civil and political rights or economic, social and cultural rights. In the Charter, the latter category commence with Article 14 guaranteeing the right to property. Article 15 is on the right to work (incorporating the right to equal pay); Article 16 is on the right to mental and physical health; and Article 17 covers the right to education. Finally, Article 18, which we shall consider more extensively when we turn to the issue of the Charter and women's human rights, concerns itself with the family and the obligations of the state towards what is described as the "natural unit and basis of society."[82] The phraseology adopted for all these rights is very broad and nebulous; this in a document which proclaims such rights as a guarantee to the observance of civil and political rights.

There are additional problems with the approach of the African Charter to this category of rights. The Charter does not make mention of several rights enshrined in the International Covenant on Economic, Social and Cultural Rights (ICESCR);[83] such as the right to social security, an adequate standard of living,[84] freedom from hunger,[85] or the right to strike.[86] Furthermore, there is very little elaboration (as is done in the ICESCR) of the specificity of what the rights mentioned entail. This could be because the drafters were wary of duplication. After all, Article 60 allows the Commission to "draw inspiration" from other international instruments. However, specifically elaborating these rights in an African instrument would have been in consonance with the conceptual spirit laid down in the Preamble to the Charter. Indeed, the very scantiness and number of economic and

---

[81] For a more extensive critique of the African leader's approach to economic and social rights see Oloka-Onyango, *supra* note 31, at 40-41.

[82] *Supra* African Charter, note 21 art. 18.

[83] U.N.G.A. Res. 2200 A (XXI), *adopted* 16 December 1966; *entered into force* 3 January 1976.

[84] *Id.*, art. 11(1).

[85] *Id.*, art. 11(2).

[86] *Id.* art. 8(1)(d).

social rights that the Charter does mention belie the very strong statements of affirmation in the Preamble that refer to the necessity for such rights as a guarantee to the realization of civil and political rights. All in all, the African Charter is a serious let-down in both the formulation and in the reconceptualization of economic and social rights.[87]

If the normative framework is lacking, the contemporary realization of economic and social rights on the African continent has been compounded by the policies of structural adjustment (SAPs) that have been in place since the early 1980s and by the phenomenon of globalization. The basic tenets of these policies are essentially antithetical to the effective realization of economic, social and cultural rights.[88] This is primarily because the basic foundation of structural adjustment policies is a reduction of the role of the state in either guaranteeing, or in simply protecting the individual against the violation (or the progressive non-realization) of his or her economic and social rights. Policies such as privatization, trade liberalization, and deregulation inordinately expose the individual to a variety of practices—particularly by TNCs—that have the effect of minimizing their options and parameters of choice. The "race-to-the-bottom" effect, which has been set in place to attract more investment, and the bidding of international finance capital has made the protection of these rights less likely. A distinct group that is considerably affected by both the realization of economic, social and cultural rights, and by the impact of global policies of economic restructuring, is African women.

D. Women's Human Rights in the African Regional Framework

Opinion on the impact and efficacy of the African Charter with respect to the situation of women on the continent is divided.[89] On the one

---

87 The silence and broadness of the Charter on economic, social and cultural rights must be married to the manner in which the same instrument delimits the ambit of civil and political rights through the claw-back clauses. The claw-back clause in Article 10 (on freedom of association) that allows it provided the individual exercising it "abides by the law" can clearly be linked to the bar on active trade union activity.

88 *See* Fantu Cheru, *Effects of Structural Adjustment on the Full Enjoyment of Human Rights* 10-11(E/CN.4/1999/50).

89 Adetoun Ilumoka considers the issue to be one of interpretation, while Florence Butegwa does not see any contradiction in the Charter provisions—specifically Article 18—relating to the protection of women's human rights. Mutua argues that it is wrong to assert that the Charter ". . . sees itself as the savior of an African culture that is permanent, static, and unchanging." Mutua, *supra* note 57, at 359. Adetoun Ilumoka, *African Women's Economic, Social and Cultural Rights—Toward a Rele-*

hand, the Charter contains several provisions that relate to non-discrimination and equality of treatment. On the other, only one article out of more than sixty makes any specific reference to women. Even then, it is contained in an omnibus clause that covers both the family and upholds tradition, thereby reproducing the essential tension that plagues the realization of the human rights of women. Article 18 of the Charter, the single provision that directly refers to women, has been the subject of considerable debate by commentators on the situation of women on the African continent.[90] Thus, it is trite to point out that the Charter is a document that makes minimal reference to the human rights of women; although, as one scholar has observed, it did, "at some level, contemplate the situation of women."[91] Lisa Kois argues further that there is some proof that the framers of the document were not entirely incognizant of the situation of women:

> The proof of such consideration is found through the implicit and explicit identification of discrimination against women as an obstacle impeding the full enjoyment of the human rights of women. Implicitly, the drafters identified the existence of sex-based discrimination found in both the preamble to the Charter and in Article 2. Additionally, Article 18, which specifically addresses the family, contains a provision directing states to eliminate all existing forms of discrimination against women and to protect the rights of women.[92]

Many commentators have argued that both the type of family and the kind of tradition envisaged in the African Charter can be deployed to inhibit the realm and enjoyment of women's human rights. Outside the Charter, *the Guidelines on State Reportage* that are supposed to provide states with the methodology for their submission to the Commission follow the principles adopted in Article 18 of CEDAW. However, the emphasis continues to be on marriage, motherhood, and child-care; while issues such

---

vant Theory and Practice, *in* HUMAN RIGHTS OF WOMEN: NATIONAL AND INTERNATIONAL PERSPECTIVES, 307, 313 (Rebecca J. Cook, ed., Univ. of Pennsylvania Press, Philadelphia, 1994); *see* Florence Butegwa, *Using the African Charter on Human and Peoples' Rights to Secure Women's Access to Land in Africa*, *in* COOK, *supra*, 495-514 (noting the significance at 504).

90 *See id.* at 290-291.

91 Lisa Kois, *Article 18 of the African Charter on Human and Peoples' Rights: A Progressive Approach to Women's Human Rights*, 3 EAST AFR. J. OF PEACE & HUM. RTS. 97 (1996).

92 *Id.* at 98.

as employment, property rights, and gender violence are given only scant attention. It is not that the former issues are unimportant. However, a focus that is confined only to those spheres of concern is clearly a limited one.[93]

The regional and international framework guaranteeing the rights of women notwithstanding, considerable problems subsist for African women at the national and community levels. Indeed, it is at this level that the full force of discriminatory and exclusionary practices continues to be felt. Different countries have approached the issue of gender-based discrimination in a variety of ways. Mumbi Mathangani states that in practice Courts in Kenya "have completely disregarded the country's commitments to CEDAW and to other international standards."[94] However, in the famous Botswana case *of Attorney General v. Unity Dow*,[95] the Court adopted and used values enshrined in the Bill of Rights of the Constitution of Botswana and the African Charter to override traditional customs of unequal treatment of women in their citizenship rights. *Unity Dow's* case was thus important for the conceptual and normative boost it gave to the domestic application of the African Charter. Although Botswana is a state party to the instrument (as is the case with every other African country), it had not adopted enabling legislation incorporating the provisions of the instrument into the domestic legal regime. Regardless of this fact, the court found no problem in holding that the provisions of the instrument bound Botswana.

But victories such as those represented by the *Unity Dow* case are sometimes counter-acted and even undermined by judicial pronouncements, government policies, and resilient cultural practices that have the effect of turning the clock back. To its credit, the government of Botswana eventually amended its citizenship law to remove the discriminatory provisions.

---

93 According to Women in Law & Development in Africa (WILDAF)—a regional women's human rights organization—the provisions of Article 18 are inadequate precisely because it is confined to discrimination within the family: "In addition, explicit provisions guaranteeing the right of consent to marriage and equality of spouses during and after marriage are completely absent. These omissions are compounded by the fact that the Charter places great emphasis on traditional African values and traditions without explicitly addressing concerns that many customary practices, such as female genital mutilation, forced marriage, and wife inheritance, can be harmful or life-threatening to women. It follows that by ignoring critical issues such as custom and marriage, many believe that the Charter inadequately defends women's human rights." *See* WILDAF, *The African Charter on Human and Peoples' Rights and the Additional Protocol on Women's Rights*, WILDAF NEWS 18 (1991).

94 *See* Mumbi Mathangani, *Women's Rights in Kenya: A Review of Government Policy*, 8 HARV. HUM. RTS. J., 179, 191 (1995).

95 C.A. Civ. App. No.4/91, (Botswana 1991).

However, executive and judicial action in response to discrimination may do the complete reverse. For example, Human Rights activists across the continent were shocked by the recent ruling by the Zimbabwean Supreme Court, in the case of *Venia Magaya v. Nakayi Shonhiwa Magaya.*[96] The main issue in contention was whether a woman could inherit her father's estate if he died without leaving a will. In the first instance, the Court made no reference to CEDAW or to other relevant international instruments, arguing that domestic provisions which discriminate against the human rights of women are "exceptions" that would effectively override the international instruments.[97]

The learned judge went on to observe that, "at the head of the (African) family there was a patriarch, or a senior man, who exercised control over the property and lives of women and juniors. It is from this that the status of women is derived. The woman's status is therefore basically the same as that of any junior male in the family."[98] In other words, women were deemed the equivalent of minors. The Court's use of the African Charter was actually the opposite from that espoused by the Bench in *Unity Dow's* case. Citing with approval a book by a Prof. Bennet, entitled *Human Rights and African Customary Law under the South African Constitution*; the learned judge extracted the following quotation:

> The obligation to care for family members, which lies at the heart of the African social system, is a vital and fundamental value, which Africa's Charter on Human and Peoples' Rights is careful to stress. Paragraph 4 of the Preamble to the Charter urges parties to pay heed to 'the virtues of (the African) historical tradition and the values of African civilisation,' and Ch.2 provides an inventory of the duties that individuals owe their families and society. Article 29(1), in particular, states that each person is obliged to preserve the harmonious development of the family and to work for the cohesion and respect of the family; to respect his parents at all times, to maintain them in case of need.[99]

The *Magaya* decision is important to the issue of the realization of the human rights of women in Africa for several reasons. First, it brings out the resilience of patriarchal forms of control and discrimination, and other

---

[96] Judgment No.S.C.210/98/Civil Appeal No.635/92 of the Supreme Court of Zimbabwe (Unreported).

[97] *See id.* at 5.

[98] *Id.* at 10.

[99] *Id.* at 19.

considerable obstacles that stand in the way of the struggle to achieve gender parity and greater respect for women's human rights on the African continent. Many times, the reasons given for the retention of discriminatory practices relate to the ostensible need to retain social harmony and cohesion. Thus, Justice Muchechetere could justify his judgment in terms of the need to approach such matters with caution:

> Whilst I am in total agreement with the submission that there is a need to advance gender equality in all spheres of society, I am of the view that great care must be taken when African customary law is under consideration. In the first instance, it must be recognised that customary law has long directed the way African people conducted their lives and the majority of Africans in Zimbabwe still live in rural areas and still conduct their lives in terms of customary law. In the circumstances, it will not readily be abandoned, especially by those such as senior males who stand to lose their positions of privilege. . .. In view of the above, I consider it prudent to pursue a pragmatic and gradual change which would win long term acceptance rather than legal revolution initiated by the courts.[100]

The *Magaya* decision is of critical importance to the discussion of the contemporary human rights situation on the African continent for several other reasons, aside from the points we have already noted. Upholding discrimination against women simply on account of their sex has several implications for their enjoyment of human rights, both civil and political and economic, social and cultural. Among the reasons why the *Magaya* decision is important are issues relating to participation in both economic and political life.[101] But even more importantly is that deeming a woman a minor means that actions such as "chastisement," better known as domestic violence, would also be deemed acceptable means of subjecting women to the traditional "discipline" of their husbands *cum* guardians.

In this way, customary law is elevated to a status that negates, not only the constitutional provisions that are enshrined within the bill of rights and other provisions of the basic legal regime of a country, but also the whole content and intent of international provisions. At this point, the tensions we earlier referred to between an international regime that seeks to guarantee rights and a domestic framework in which such rights are taken away come to the fore. It then becomes necessary to engage the specific

---

100 *Id.* at 17-18.

101 Minors are not allowed to contract or to vie for political office.

practice being endorsed in what Abdullahi An-Naim and others have described as a cross-cultural discourse. Secondly, this means that it is essential to interrogate the interests that underpin the continued support for the cultural practice in question. Who is supporting the practice? Why are they doing so? What are its consequences for the particular individual and for the class or group of persons that the practice is being directed against? How can we most effectively convey the point that gender discrimination is not simply a matter of disparate treatment, but that it also affects the realization of sustainable human development? All these questions demonstrate that the African Charter provides an incomplete answer. Not only is there a need to reinforce Article 18 with a more elaborate rendering of the respect for women's human rights, a process being attempted through the drafting of an optional protocol to the Charter,[102] but critical attention must also be paid to the domestic context of each African country.

E. The Phenomenon of Refugees and Internally Displaced Persons (IDPs)

The human rights regime in Africa is also concerned with the situation of people who have been forcibly displaced from their homes and have either fled across the border (as refugees) or are internally displaced. Following a growing prominence of refugee flows after the attainment of independence for most African countries in the 1960s, the OAU promulgated the Convention Governing the Specific Aspects of the Refugee Problem in Africa.[103] Considered among the most liberal regimes governing refugees in the world, the Convention made several significant contributions to the corpus of international refugee law. Among them were its approach to burden sharing, non-rejection at the border, the principle of *non-refoulement*, voluntary repatriation and temporary asylum.[104] In particular, the definition of the term "refugee" employed in the Convention is extremely wide in that it recognizes the objective conditions that may cause flight, rather than the subjective criteria imposed by the international legal regime epitomized by the 1951 Geneva Convention.[105] As the Lawyer's Committee for Human

---

[102] Nyamu *supra*, note 53, at 301, 307. For an examination of the process the draft has undergone since theidea was first mooted in 1995 until the present, and for a look at the draft protocol, see *WILDAF News,supra* note 93.

[103] September 10, 1969, 1001 U.N.T.S. 45 (entered into force on 20 June 1974).

[104] J. Oloka-Onyango, *The Plight of the Larger Half: Human Rights, Gender Violence and the Legal Status of Refugee and Internally Displaced Women in Africa*, 24 DENV. J. INT'L L. & POL'Y 349, 374-5 (1996).

[105] For a background analysis to the OAU Convention and the situation relating to refugees at the time it was promulgated, *see*, J. Oloka-Onyango, *Plugging the*

Rights has pointed out, the adoption of the Convention was prompted ". . . more by a concern with large flows of refugees whose exodus was related to Africa's colonial occupation and wars of national liberation than by concern about persecution on an individual basis."[106]

Despite possession of a liberal refugee regime the continental spirit embodied in the OAU Convention is tempered by existing realities on the ground. In the first instance, there is no continental-wide agency akin to the African Commission exclusively devoted to the situation of refugees. Although forced displacement is a human rights matter, the Commission has its hands full as it is dealing with the myriad other human rights problems it must address. The OAU Bureau for Refugees that is stationed at the OAU headquarters, in Addis Ababa, is almost wholly impotent and has been further subordinated by the establishment of a conflict management and resolution mechanism within the body. Although refugees are indeed a product of conflict, their problems cannot be simply lumped together in omnibus fashion under the overall focus of the question of conflict.[107] The consequence of the lack of an effective institution at the continental level is two-fold; the refugee crisis is dominated by the UNHCR, the global agency concerned with refugees, that sometimes approaches the question of displacement in hot-house fashion, and by individual states. Needless to say, both have their problems. At individual country levels the spirit of the OAU Convention is even less apparent. According to the Lawyers Committee:

> Individual status determination procedures are often labyrinthine and incomprehensible to applicants. Frequently, applicants have no access to independent advice or representation, and no possibility of appealing an unfavorable decision. Collective determination may also carry with it serious restrictions on a refugee's rights. For example, refugees may only be recognized as such while they remain in designated rural settlements or regions. Thus, should they

---

Gaps: Refugees, OAU Policy and the Practices of Member States in Africa, US Committee for Refugees Issue Brief (1986).

106 Lawyers Committee for Human Rights, AFRICAN EXODUS: REFUGEE CRISIS, HUMAN RIGHTS AND THE 1969 OAU CONVENTION 29 (1995).

107 Indeed, as Carlson Anyangwe has pointed out, there is also a security dimension to the refugee issue which also partly informed the debates leading up to the promulgation of the OAU Convention of 1969. Although security is indeed a significant factor, it is important not to reduce the refugee factor to only that dimension. See Carlson Anyangwe, *Obligations of States Parties to the African Charter on Human and Peoples' Rights*, 10 AFR. J. INT'L & COMP. L. 625, 652 (1998).

> attempt to exercise their right to freedom of movement, they may lose their refugee status. They may even risk arrest and detention at the hands of security personnel.[108]

For a refugee that does not have any status whatsoever, the implications are even more dire in both legal and practical terms. The grant of status in many countries is often a prerequisite to a host of additional human rights, extending from freedom of movement to the possibility of accessing gainful employment. Where a refugee is not recognized by the law, they stand wedged between the rock of discrimination in the country in which they have sought solace and the hard place of possible *refoulement* to the place from which they escaped in the first instance. Furthermore, in many African countries there is a growing state of xenophobia, in part provoked by conditions of worsening social and economic hardship. Consequently, the old African maxim about African's being their brother's (or sister's) keepers does not necessarily always apply. A country like Tanzania that had traditionally opened its arms to refugees only recently adopted an extremely restrictive approach to refugee settlement and integration in the wake of the Rwandese crisis.

Finally, the OAU Convention is completely silent on the issue of refugee women, and also on the question of internal displacement (of both sexes). The latter is an issue that has come to the fore as a major humanitarian and human rights crisis not only on the African continent.[109] Internally displaced persons (IDPs) do not have an international regime to cover their specific situation, which is compounded by the fact that there is neither a normative nor institutional mechanism to cater to their situation. And yet, in the words of Cohen and Deng, their condition is appalling:

> Of the world's populations at risk, internally displaced people tend to be among the most desperate. They may be forcibly resettled on political or ethnic grounds or find themselves trapped in the midst of conflicts and the direct path of armed attack and physical violence. On the run and without document, they are easy targets for roundups. Arbitrary detention, forced conscription, and sexual assaults. Uprooted from their homes and deprived of their resource base, many suffer from profound physical and psychological trauma. They are more often deprived of shelter, food

[108] *See* Lawyers Committee, *supra* note 106, at 41.

[109] *See generally* Francis M. Deng, Internally Displaced Persons: Compilation and Analysis of Legal Norms (1998).

and health services than other members of the population.[110]

If the most important mechanism for refugees is recognition of their status and the existence of a regime of legal protection to cover undue assault and discrimination against them, it is easy to appreciate why the lack of a similar framework for IDPs is particularly disconcerting. Moreover, the elaboration of an international legal regime is unlikely to be developed beyond the *Guiding Principles on Forced Displacement* produced by the UN Secretary General's Representative on Internally Displaced Persons, Francis Deng.[111] The connection to the issue of human rights is manifest in the fact that the major reason for forced displacement in Africa, is according to Susanne Schmeidl, ". . . brutally repressive regimes, ethnic conflict, and external destabilization campaigns."[112] The magnitude of the problem is better appreciated if we consider the fact that the population of IDPs in Africa outnumbers that of refugees. The implications for sustainable human development are obvious. In the absence of an effective regime to address the issue in a rights-sensitive fashion, the phenomenon of internal forced displacement will act as a significant impediment to the realization of sustainable human development in Africa. Of course, this issue is directly linked to the question of the institutional mechanisms that exist on the African continent.

IV. Africa's Institutional Enforcement Mechanisms

A. The Role and Place of the African Commission and a Note on the New Court

The African Charter has been ratified by every single African state with the exception of two, which is perhaps the most significant rate of ratification of any international instrument. If ratification *per se* were to be the yardstick by which adherence and implementation of the principles within an instrument were to be judged, then the African human rights situation would be considerably less troubled than it is. Unfortunately, even the most positive reviews of the performance of the major mechanism of implementation of the Charter, the African Commission on Human & Peo-

[110] Roberta Cohen & Francis Deng, Masses in Flight: The Global Crisis of Internal Displacement 2 (1998).

[111] Louise Ludlam-Taylor, *Recent Literature on IDPs, in* Internally Displaced People: A Global Survey 38 (Janine Hampton ed., 1998).

[112] Susanne Schmeidl, *Comparative Trends in Forced Displacement,1964-96, in* Internally Displaced People: A Global Survey 29 (Janine Hampton ed., 1998).

ples' Rights, generally agree that the institution has performed at less than par.[113] Several reasons can be advanced in explanation for this situation, extending from the conceptual and infrastructural to the political. A disillusioned Professor Oji Umozurike, a former member of the Commission, was reported to have made several succinct observations on the problems of the African Commission:

> Most cases of human rights violations filed by individuals and organizations take an average of two years to process. State parties rarely provide prompt answers or any answers at all until threatened with a finding in default. Complainants' costs are prohibitive and, until very recently, little or no publicity could be given to the proceedings and issues. Rules . . . ensure that public embarrassment and shame cannot act to remedy current situations or prevent new occurrences.[114]

Additional problems that plague the Commission relate to the facilitative or infrastructural bottlenecks that it faces as an institution. The question of funding has long been a major problem for the Commission, with member states being extremely lax in meeting their dues and thereby preventing the body from operating effectively. As a consequence, the Commission has been forced to rely on funding sources that mainly emanate from outside the continent. This situation, as Shadrack Gutto points out, is not a sustainable one in the long run.[115] Indeed, calls have been made for the establishment of an African Human Rights Fund to facilitate the operations of the Commission.[116]

Joshua Mzizi has observed that the Charter itself is an obstacle to the more effective realization of human rights on the continent:

> The Charter provides for a broad spectrum of rights and responsibilities, but it is woefully deficient in the enforcement machinery. The Commission has the mandate to

---

[113] *See* Kisanga, *supra* note 32.

[114] *See, The African Commission on Human and Peoples' Rights, Special Harare Conference Issue*, Commonwealth Human Rights Initiative (CHRI) News, 28 (1998).

[115] Shadrack B. Gutto, *Non-governmental Organizations, People's Participation and the African Commission on Human and Peoples' Rights: Emerging Challenges to Regional Protection of Human Rights,* in Bård-Anders Andreassen & Theresa Swinehart (eds.), HUMAN RIGHTS IN DEVELOPING COUNTRIES; 1991 YEARBOOK 49-5 (1992).

[116] *See, Human Rights News*, 16 NETH. Q. HUM. RTS. 97 (1998).

> compile reports on violations for the attention of Heads of State and Governments. The internationally respected norm of non-interference in the domestic affairs of a sovereign state makes timely intervention impossible even when urgent measures have to be taken in order to protect human life.[117]

Mzizi touches upon the most fundamental of the problems faced by the African Commission, the issue of political will. This issue is both internal and external to the institution. Internally, there are questions such as the independence and expertise of the Commissioners, as well as the genuineness of their commitment to the protection and promotion of human rights. There is also a reluctance to make decisions that would displease the appointing authority, the Assembly of Heads of State and Government. Thus far, more than ten years after it commenced operations, the Commission has not even slightly threatened the 'business-as-usual' *modus operandi* that prevails among African states and within the OAU. Its operations do not even marginally affect the status quo. To compound it all, the mechanism of state reportage which is supposed to be the bedrock of the system has proven a dismal failure. New initiatives, such as the appointment of a Special Rapporteur on Summary and Extra-Judicial Executions and another on Prisons, are yet to make any significant inroads on the African human rights scene. Externally, the over-bearing presence of African states will always be a factor to countenance. Odinkalu and Christensen put their finger on the issue when they state: "Whether the Commission will be perceived as an effective institution for the protection of human rights in Africa will largely depend on how far and how much the state parties to the African Charter take seriously, and respect, the Commission's views and recommendations."[118] Thus far, they have not.

Against such a background, the establishment of a Court on Human Rights for Africa is a development that can only be greeted with caution.[119] It is likely that the Court will be plagued by the very same problems that have hampered the work of the Commission. Even if by some miraculous occurrence the infrastructural issues were to be tackled, the paramount issue

---

117 Joshua Bhekinkosi Mzizi, *Human Rights, Peace and the African Charter on Human and Peoples' Rights*, AFR. LEGAL AID Q., July /Sept. 1998, at 37.

118 Chidi Anselm Odinkalu & Camilla Christensen, *The African Commission on Human and People's Rights: The Development of its Non-State Communication Procedures,* 20 HUM. RTS. Q. 279 (1998).

119 Both Österdahl and Mutua welcome the idea, but both assert that it is only workable in the face of a far-reaching reform of the African Charter.

of political will remains an outstanding one. If the Court is to be relevant to the human rights scene on the continent, then it must be able to make decisions that will assist individual African men and women. Otherwise, it will have to adopt a "softly-softly" approach mirroring that of the African Commission. If after more than a decade of existence the Commission has hardly made a dent in the human rights scene, the Court would be doomed to a similar fate. But there are additional institutional mechanisms designed to address aspects of the human rights question in Africa, especially with regard to the issue of conflict.

B. The OAU Mechanism on Conflict Resolution and the Bureau for Refugees

Given that the issue of armed conflict and its impact on human rights has surfaced to the fore so dramatically in the contemporary African context, it is not surprising that the OAU established the Mechanism for Conflict Prevention, Management and Resolution in June, 1993.[120] Designed basically to foster the speedy and peaceful resolution of conflicts on the continent, the Mechanism is the newest institution that attempts to ensure that the situation of human rights violations does not escalate out of hand.[121] Some scholars contend that the Mechanism has met with some success. For example, the OAU brokered an agreement in Congo Brazzaville between rival political groups.[122] However, since its establishment, conflicts have broken out in Rwanda (with the genocide that followed), Burundi, Sierra Leone and a host of other countries around the continent. In both the Democratic Republic of Congo and in the Eritrean/Ethiopian war, Africa's most recent conflagrations, the Mechanism has been largely absent or simply silent. Indeed, in the admission of the officer in charge of the Mechanism, "much of the OAU's time is allocated to dealing with the effects of conflicts, rather than preventing situations of tension from growing into full-blown confrontation."[123]

On its part, the OAU Bureau for Refugees, Displaced Persons and Humanitarian Affairs has always had a minimalist role with respect to the human rights or other issues relating to forced displacement on the conti-

---

[120] On the background to the Mechanism, *see* Bertrand G. Ramcharan, *The Evolving Doctrine of Democratic Legitimacy,* 60 The Review 179, 182-188 (1998).

[121] Chris J. Bakwesegeha, *The Role of the Organization of African Unity in Conflict Prevention, Management and Resolution*, International Journal of Refugee Law, spec. issue 1995, at 207.

[122] Cohen and Deng, *supra* note 110, at 215.

[123] Bakwesegeha, *supra* note 121, at 216.

nent.[124] Even before its mandate was extended to include the issue of forced displacement, it was fairly clear that it had not performed very well on the sole issue of refugees. Like the African Commission, it is hamstrung by infrastructural and financial inabilities. As a matter of fact, the problem relates to the manner in which the bureau was initially conceived and the political framework within which it operates. Cohen and Deng thus understate the problem: "In the case of the internally displaced, it has no specific programs, and in the area of protection, it does little, whether for refugees or internally displaced persons."[125] Cohen and Deng also point to the possibility of developing a joint collaborative role between the Bureau, the Mechanism and the African Commission—a collaboration they believe would greatly enhance the overall protection of the human rights of all the concerned parties on the continent. But it is doubtful whether collectively they would be able to overcome their individual limitations.

Is there a possible role for sub-regional bodies in addressing the human rights situation on the continent? Organizations such as the Economic Community of West African States (ECOWAS), the Southern African Development Community (SADC) and the Inter-Governmental Authority on Development (IGAD) in eastern Africa, are at least geographically well situated to address some of the major issues on the human rights scene in their individual regions. Unfortunately, in many respects these institutions are simply microcosms of the OAU with regard to both financial capacity and the critical factor of political will. None of the organizations have explicitly incorporated matters relating to human rights within the operational frameworks of their mandates. Several have broad statements of commitment to, for example, ". . . encourage the observance of human rights as provided for in the charters and conventions of the Organization of African Unity and the United Nations."[126] This is clearly insufficient and requires to be matched by much more concrete manifestations of action on the issue. But regional institutions can only build on the strengths of their individual membership. Individual countries therefore constitute the building blocks on which regional organizations must rely in order to make a serious impact in the human rights and human development arena.

---

[124] Lawyers Committee, *supra* note 106.

[125] Cohen and Deng, *supra* note 110, at 217.

[126] *See* Objective (h) of the SADC Organ on Politics, Defence and Security; quoted in Ramcharan, *supra* note 38, at 189.

C. Enforcement at the National Level and the Role of Civil Society

Promoting a culture of human rights discourse and practice at the national level is perhaps the real struggle, as opposed to the regional or international one. While there are certainly significant benefits that flow from a regional approach to human rights protection and enforcement, ultimately, human rights must be enforced at the national level. This can only take place through a twofold process. First, individual governments muse be encouraged to establish the necessary frameworks and institutional mechanisms, such as human rights commissions or *ombudspersons*, with the specific function of promoting and protecting human rights. A precusor to doing so must be a process of engagement with national constitutional frameworks in order to review them to ensure that they are broadly reflective of the necessary human rights content. Such content must not simply confine itself to a focus on civil and political rights; but be extended to include economic, social and culutural rights, as well as the so-called Third Generation rights. In the context of constitutionalism, Judiciaries have a critical role to play as both mediators of tensions and conflicts that may emerge between the Executive arm of government and the population at large. They must also effectively and progressively translate international and regional human rights instruments into the domestic context, even where the constitutional regime may not be reflective of a progressive human rights approach.

The role of civil society organizations in pursuing the greater promotion of human rights has traditionally been an important one in Africa, at both the individual country level, and even with respect to the mechanisms established at the continental one.[127] Indeed, since the late 1980s there has been a literal explosion of associational activity in the vast majority of countries around the continent.[128] For civil society to effectively execute its role, an enabling environment must be established in which associations dedicated to the promotion of human rights and civil liberties are actually able to operate. Thus, archaic laws that inhibit the registration and operation of civic associations need to be amended. At the same time, civil society cannot confine itself to the pursuit of civil and political rights alone, as has been the case in almost all African countries to date. There is a need to marry the actions of organizations that are involved in traditional develop-

[127] Wolfgang Benedek, *Enforcement of Human and Peoples' Rights in Africa—The Communication System and State Reporting Under the African Charter*, 15 Studie- en Informatiecentrum Mensenrechten (SIM) 22 (1995).

[128] For a general analysis, *see* Civil Society and Democracy in Africa: Critical Perspectives, (Nelson Kasfir, ed., 1998).

ment work to those who pursue action within a rights framework. There is also a need for such organizations to directly engage economic and social issues from a rights-grounded perspective. Only then will some progress be registered in the struggle to marry human rights to the quest for sustainable human development.

V. The Way Ahead: Meeting the Challenges, Exploiting the Opportunities

As this account demonstrates, Africa faces considerable obstacles in meeting the challenges entailed by the coming of a new century, and by the social, political and economic conditions that prevail on the continent. But there are also numerous opportunities which can be ably exploited in order to ensure that human rights serves the objective of attaining sustainable human development. The issue of education or sensitization in human rights is a fundamental one. As Carlson Anyangwe points out however, most African states have been lacklustre in pursuing an obligation clearly imposed by the African Charter:

> Unfortunately the reality is that in many an African State overall human rights law per se and rights ideology generally are little promoted and continue to have little or no place in teaching (and practice) whether in primary, secondary, or tertiary levels of education. For one thing, in many States the discipline of human right is not yet a recognised subject for generalized education. There are few teaching aids. There is little common methodology. Most of those actively involved in human rights advocacy are not teachers. Information on the Charter, key to teaching about the rights and duties therein contained, is often inaccessible to the general public and generally there is a serious lack of knowledge of the content of that instrument. What is more, African Governments still remain deeply suspicious of the teaching and popularisation of human rights.[129]

But such education must be coupled with active promotion and protection. In this respect the challenge is to marry the theoretical analyses that abound to strategies that lead to the development a culture of human rights respect.

Considerable challenges are also presented by the existence of significant Non-state actors (NSAs) such as the family, arms-dealers, guerrilla

---

129 Carlson Anyangwe, *Obligations of States Parties to the African Charter on Human and Peoples' Rights* 10 African Journal of International & Comparative Law 625, 635 (1998).

groups and transnational corporations. All these impact on the human rights situation in varying ways. A multitude of strategies must be employed to address these challenges. Furthermore, we must expand the network of agencies and persons doing human rights. This is one area which cannot remain the exclusive domain of professionals or experts, if it is to be of any utility. For example, the process of demonstrating that economic, social and cultural rughts are indeed rights and can be made justiciable must be made a popular project. As Shadrack Gutto points out in reference to the South African case to confine the notion of justiciability to the courts "would greatly limit the realization of human rights, or undermine the construction of a culture of human rights in South Africa."[130] This point obviously has continental applicability.

There are still considerable normative challenges that need to be addressed, both with respect to the existing frameworks (in the African Charter and the OAU Convention, for example), as well as where there are lacunae, as in the case of IDPs.

The place of the state in Africa—irrespective of the condition in which it is in—is critical to ensuring that the human rights message (especially concerning economic, social and cultural rights) is not only transmitted, but also becomes popularized. A weak state cannot do much against powerful multinationals; an indifferent state ultimately stands to lose from a labour force that exploits child labour and is paid below the minimum wage; a strong state does not have to seek recourse in military methods to resolve a political conflict. Finally, in none of these instances does the state need to place the choice as one relating to resources. And maybe, in the quest for sustainable human development, that is the biggest challenge of them all.

---

[130] Gutto, *Beyond Justiciability*, *supra* note 70, at 86.

[17]

IS THERE A RIGHT NOT TO BE POOR?

Sigrun I. Skogly *

"Does it help to think of poverty or inadequate health care as violations of basic rights?"[1]

The link between poverty and human rights has been made with increased frequency in the last few years.[2] This attention to both the causal and normative aspects of this link coincides with the deepening of human rights understanding in international circles and the more consistent approach to all of the rights contained in the Universal Declaration of Human Rights[3] (UDHR) since the mid-1980s. The United Nations has carried out several studies, and passed a number of resolutions on this topic[4], and work towards a possible Declaration on (Extreme) Poverty and Human Rights has been initiated in the last few years.[5]

* Senior Lecturer in Law, Lancaster University Law School. Much of the content of this article stems from work I did as a consultant and rapporteur for the Office of the High Commissioner for Human Rights on Extreme Poverty and Human Rights in 2000-2001. I would in particular like to thank Laurent Meillan, Stefanie Grant and Thomas Hammarberg for input in the earlier work. The content of this article reflects my own views and not those of the Office of the High Commissioner for Human Rights.

1 "The Politics of Human Rights," *The Economist*, 18 August 2001.

2 See for instance Alston, "No right to complain about being poor: The Need for an Optional Protocol to the Economic Rights Covenant," in Eide and Helgesen (eds.) *The Future of Human Rights Protection in a Changing World: Fifty years since the Four Freedoms Address. Essays in Honour of Torkel Opsahl* (Oslo: Universitetsforlaget, 1991).

3 Adopted by the UN General Assembly on 10 December 1948. G.A. Res. 217A(III), G.A.OR, 3rd Sess., Part I, Resolutions, 71.

4 Among these documents are: (i) UN Commission on Human Rights: Resolution 2000/12 on Human Rights and Extreme Poverty, E/CN.4/RES/2000/12; Resolution 1999/26 on Human Rights and Extreme Poverty, E/CN.4/RES/1999/26; Resolution 1998/25 on Human Rights and Extreme Poverty, E/CN.4/RES/1998/25; Human Rights and Extreme Poverty, Report of the independent expert, Ms.Lizin, E/CN.4/1999/48; Report of the Independent Expert, Ms. Lizin, E/CN.4/2000/52; Report of the Workshop on Human Rights and Extreme Poverty, E/CN.4/2000/52/Add.1; Follow-up to the 4th World Conference on Women: Review of mainstreaming in organisations of the UN System, E/CN.4/1998/22; (ii) UN Sub-Commission on the Promotion and Protection of Human Rights: Final Report on Human Rights and Extreme Poverty, submitted by Special Rapporteur Mr. Leandro Despouy, E/CN.4/Sub.2/1996/13; Resolution 2001/8 on Implementation of existing human rights norms and standards in the context of the fight against poverty, E/CN.4/Sub.2/RES/2001/8; (iii) General Assembly: Resolution on Human Rights and Extreme Poverty, 8 March 1999, A/RES/53/146; Implementation of the first United Nations Decade for the Eradication of Poverty (1997-2006), Report of the Secretary-General, 7 September 1999, A/54/316; (iv) UN Committee on Economic, Social and Cultural Rights: Statement on Poverty and the International Covenant on Economic, Social and Cultural Rights adopted on 4 May 2001, E/C.12/2001/10.

5 'Extreme' is here put in brackets, as it is not clear whether a distinction between 'poverty' and 'extreme poverty' would be made in a possible future declaration or guiding principles on human rights and poverty.

The attention to this link also coincides with the UN's Decade on Poverty (1997-2006), and Secretary General Kofi Annan's call for mainstreaming human rights in all of the activities of the United Nations and its agencies. Thus, a human rights approach to development is now seen as a convergence with poverty eradication strategies.

There are several interesting questions to be asked in this context. What does the link between poverty and human rights add to the work for poverty alleviation, and to flip the coin – what does it add to the work to guarantee human rights? Is there a value added to approach these two concepts simultaneously, or does it distract attention from the serious core of human rights violations? Does the link between human rights and poverty imply a *right not to be poor?*

In this article I will dwell on some of the topics that arise from the questions asked above. I will start by briefly tracing the work that the human rights bodies of the United Nations have carried out to clarify the link between poverty and human rights. Secondly, I will discuss the existing normative framework for addressing poverty through a human rights approach. Then, I will analyse whether indeed it can be argued that there is a right not to be poor. Finally, I will address the possible effects that a link between human rights and poverty may have on efforts for poverty alleviation.

THE UNITED NATIONS WORK ON POVERTY AND HUMAN RIGHTS

In 1990, the Commission on Human Rights initiated work on a link between poverty and human rights, and requested that the Sub-Commission on Prevention of Discrimination and Protection of Minorities (now the Sub-Commission on the Protection and Promotion of Human Rights) consider this issue.[6] The Sub-Commission subsequently appointed Mr. Leandro Despouy as Special Rapporteur on the issue, and he produced his final report on human rights and extreme poverty in 1996.[7] Following this work, and the proclamation of the United Nations Decade for the Eradication of Poverty, the Commission on Human Rights appointed an independent expert, Ms. A.-M. Lizin, on the question of extreme poverty and human rights.[8] The Independent Expert delivered two reports.[9] In the Commission on Human Rights Resolution 1998/25, she had been requested to make suggestions to the Commission on Human Rights on a possible draft declaration on human rights and extreme poverty. Following her interim report in which she recommended that a meeting be held in order to draw up the basic elements of a preliminary draft declaration on human rights and extreme poverty, the Commission on Human Rights asked the Office of the

6 UN Commission on Human Rights, Resolution 1990/15 on Human Rights and Extreme Poverty, E.CN.4/RES/1990/15.

7 UN Sub-Commission on the Promotion and Protection of Human Rights, Final Report on Human Rights and Extreme Poverty, submitted by Special Rapporteur Mr. Leandro Despouy, supra note 4.

8 UN Commission on Human Rights, Resolution 1998/25 on Human Rights and Extreme Poverty, supra note 4.

9 UN Commission on Human Rights, Human Rights and Extreme Poverty, Report of the Independent Expert Ms. Lizin, supra note 4, and Report of the Independent Expert, Ms. Lizin, supra note 4.

High Commissioner to organize a workshop in 1999 with the Independent Expert on Human Rights and Extreme Poverty, experts of the Sub-Commission and relevant functional commissions of ECOSOC to consult on the main elements of such a draft declaration. The usefulness of a declaration was unanimously confirmed by the workshop.[10] At its session in 2000, the Commission on Human Rights considered the need for an expert meeting aimed at an in-depth analysis of the relationship between human rights and extreme poverty. Therefore, in Resolution 2000/12 the Commission on Human Rights requested the Office of the High Commissioner for Human Rights to 'organize, before the fifty-seventh session of the Commission on Human Rights, a seminar to consider the need to develop a draft declaration on extreme poverty and, if appropriate, to identify its specific points.'[11]

On the basis of this resolution, the Office of the High Commissioner invited government representatives and experts of the United Nations agencies, funds and programmes, the Human Rights Commission and Sub-Commission, the international financial institutions, and academic experts in the field and interested non-governmental organisations to a seminar in Geneva from 7 – 9 February 2001. In this seminar, the participants agreed that guiding principles on poverty and human rights needed to be developed, either through a declaration or in some other form,[12] and 'expressed their hope that the Commission on Human Rights would request the United Nations High Commissioner for Human Rights to continue the work to consider the elements to be included in such guiding principles'.[13] The Commission on Human Rights passed a resolution in which it asked the Sub-Commission to consider the need for guiding principles on the implementation of existing human rights norms and standards in the context of the fight against extreme poverty.[14] This request was subsequently taken up by the Sub-Commission, which passed a resolution in August 2001, in which it reaffirmed that the existence of widespread extreme poverty inhibits the full and effective enjoyment of human rights,[15] and requested that a working paper be undertaken, with the assistance of the secretariat, on the need to develop guiding principles on the implementation of existing human rights norms and standards in the context of the fight against extreme poverty.[16] Finally, the UN Committee on Economic, Social and Cultural Rights adopted a statement on Poverty and the International Covenant on Economic, Social and Cultural Rights (ICESCR) in May 2001.[17]

[10] UN Commission on Human Rights, Report of the Workshop on Human Rights and Extreme Poverty, supra note 4.

[11] UN Commission on Human Rights, Resolution 2000/12 on Human Rights and Extreme Poverty, supra note 4, at para. 8.

[12] UN Commission on Human Rights, Report of the Expert Seminar on Human Rights and Extreme Poverty, 7-10 February 2001, E/CN.4/2001/54/Add.1., at para. 16.

[13] Ibid., at para. 33.

[14] UN Commission on Human Rights, E/CN.4/2001/L.45, at para. 7(a).

[15] UN Sub-Commission on the Promotion and Protection of Human Rights, Resolution 2001/8 on Implementation of Existing Human Rights Norms and Standards in the Context of the Fight Against Extreme Poverty, supra note 4, at para. 1.

[16] Ibid., at para. 3.

[17] UN Committee on Economic, Social and Cultural Rights, Statement on Poverty and the International Covenant on Economic, Social and Cultural Rights, supra note 4.

Thus, the work of the United Nations Human Rights bodies has been going on for more than a decade, although the tangible results are not all that significant. However, in spite of the lack of a declaration or firmer binding principles as a result of the UN's efforts so far, recognition should be given to the impact of this work in indirect ways. In spite of 'poverty' or 'poor' not being used in the language of any of the major human rights instruments, the link is now explicitly being made, by the High Commissioner for Human Rights, the Human Rights Commission and others. There has also been a debate about whether it is pertinent to distinguish between 'poverty' and 'extreme poverty' and commentators have become far more aware of the difficulties in applying this distinction. Finally, in parallel with this work within the UN Human Rights system, attention to poverty has increased in a number of other contexts, not least through the activities of the UNDP,[18] the World Bank,[19] and the IMF through the Poverty Reduction Strategies.[20]

THE EXISTING HUMAN RIGHTS NORMATIVE FRAMEWORK RELEVANT FOR THE ALLEVIATION OF POVERTY

In the documents that resulted from the above mentioned UN work, the philosophical and practical connections between poverty and human rights have been made. It is recognised that the lack of financial resources is only one of the characteristics of life in poverty. The insecurity, the lack of ability to make use of services and opportunities,[21] the humiliation and social and economic exclusion,[22] are other and equally important characteristics. In his work, *Development as Freedom*, Amartya Sen claims that 'poverty must be seen as the deprivation of basic capabilities rather than merely a lowness of incomes, which is the standard criterion of identification of poverty'.[23] To focus on the size of income only is too simplistic and means that the

18 The UNDP has worked on the issues of poverty, development and human rights in a variety of settings. For instance, the *Human Development Report,2000* was subtitled: *Human Development and Human Rights*. For further information, visit UNDP's website at http://www.undp.org.

19 See in particular the work that has been undertaken by the Bank through the major study, *Voices of the Poor*. See below for further discussion.

20 The IMF's poverty reductions strategies are expressed through the Poverty Reduction and Growth Facility, which builds on the member states on Poverty Reduction Strategies. These are expressed through the PRSP – Poverty Reduction Strategy Papers, which member states produce in order to obtain support from the IMF and the World Bank. For further information, see http://www.imf.org and http://www.worldbank.org.

21 Final Report on Human Rights and Extreme Poverty, submitted by Special Rapporteur Mr. Leandro Despouy, supra note 4, at para. 125.

22 Sen explains that

> the difficulties that some groups of people experience in 'taking part in the life of the community' can be crucial for any study of 'social exclusion'. The need to take part in the life of a community may induce demands for modern equipment (televisions, videocassette recorders, automobiles and so on) in a country where such facilities are more or less universal (unlike what would be needed in less affluent countries), and this imposes a strain on a relatively poor person in a rich country even when that person is at a much higher level of income compared with people in less opulent countries: Sen, *Development as Freedom* (Oxford: OUP, 1999) at 89-90.

23 Ibid., at 87.

important aspects of relative poverty for different people based on their ability to function in society is lost. Thus, the capabilities refer to the functions that a person is performing or is able to perform based on the resources available. The functions may be elementary, such as being adequately nourished, or more complex, such as being able to take part in 'the life of the community and having self-respect'.[24] Sen clarifies this by introducing the concept of 'freedom':

> Capability is thus a kind of freedom: the substantive freedom to achieve alternative functioning combinations (or, less formally put, the freedom to achieve various lifestyles). For example, an affluent person who fasts may have the same functioning achievement in terms of eating or nourishment as a destitute person who is forced to starve, but the first person does have a different "capability set" than the second (the first *can* choose to eat well and be well nourished in a way the second cannot).[25]

To introduce this thinking into our discussion on the relationship between poverty and human rights, it is important to view human rights fulfilment as bringing 'capabilities' for people living in poverty. The conditions under which people in extreme poverty live represent violations of human rights. Poverty is not a 'phenomenon'; it is instead an expression of human struggle and human misery. In the words of the High Commissioner for Human Rights, Mary Robinson, poverty in its true light, is 'a denial of a whole range of rights pertaining to the human being, based on each individual's dignity and worth.'[26] The poor are the subjects of poverty, and the poor have rights that are systematically violated. If the human rights violations experienced by poor people are to be addressed, poverty will need to be addressed through the rights of the individual, the family and the social and economic setting in which they live. The rights of the poor and the violations thereof are more significant and complex than what can be captured through statistics of poverty, and particularly statistics based on income alone.

Ever since the early days of human rights development on an international level, the need to address the plight of the poor has implicitly been made. Franklin D. Roosevelt's famous 'Four Freedoms' speech from 1941 included the freedom from want, alongside freedom of expression and speech, freedom to worship and freedom from fear.[27] The comprehensive approach taken in the inclusion of rights in the UDHR expressed this understanding that human rights violations and oppression can occur through material and non-material deprivation. Yet, poverty or poor people are not directly addressed in any of the major human rights instruments, and the special situations that people living in poverty experience are therefore not explicitly taken into account in the current normative human rights regime.

24 Ibid., at 75.

25 Ibid. (Emphasis in original).

26 UN Commission on Human Rights, Summary Records, 41st meeting, "Economic, Social and Cultural Rights," 1 May 2000, E/CN.4/2000/SR.41, at para. 2.

27 President Franklin D. Roosevelt, Address to the Congress, 6 January 1941.

During the 55 years of the UN's existence, the development of a normative framework for human rights has seen legal codification of large number of rights, and provided terms of reference for both individual and collective rights, including within the later category the rights to self-determination and development. Through the adoption and entry into force of human rights instruments (in particular the two International Covenants[28]), the legal framework for a rights-based protection of the poor has implicitly been created. However, this creation of a framework has not necessarily corresponded with a clear attention being paid to the plight of the poor in the implementation and supervision of human rights guarantees.

Qualitatively, the current human rights regime provides the necessary rights to address the structural impediments faced by people living in poverty. Or, in other words, the respect, protection and fulfilment of these human rights would represent a significant step towards the eradication of poverty. All human rights, civil, political, economic, social and cultural, have grown out of a philosophy of ending oppression by the state (or other actors) and of ensuring certain minimum standards for the existence of human beings. It is both about human dignity and about human needs. Human rights provide for the fulfilment of human needs through a respect for human dignity.[29] In many studies on poverty also, the element of human dignity comes forward rather explicitly,[30] often being one of the most common problems that poor people mention. As human rights provide a framework for empowerment and for entitlements[31], the human dignity that results from their advance represents an integral part in relieving the pain of poverty. But not only human dignity. The fact that human rights are rights that every human being possesses by virtue of being born human, the *entitlement* to the material content of the rights cannot be removed. Thus a non-fulfilment of this material content will represent violations, rather than non-existence of rights. This implies a qualitative difference from any provision made through charity or other forms for basic needs assistance, not founded on a rights-based approach. According to the High Commissioner, a rights-based approach to poverty reduction goes further than promoting implicit human rights enjoyment. Such an approach implies that the 'realization of human rights [is] the primary goal of poverty reduction.'[32]

28 The ICESCR and the ICCPR were both adopted in 1966 and both entered into force in 1976.

29 Human dignity as a central element in human rights is confirmed in Article 1 of the Universal Declaration on Human Rights, which reads: 'All human beings are born free and equal in dignity and rights. They are endowed with reason and conscience and should act towards one another in a spirit of brotherhood.'

30 Narayan et al *Voices of the Poor, Vol. I: Can Anyone Hear Us? Voices from 47 Countries* (Washington DC: World Bank, 1999), at 6 ('*Voices of the Poor I*'); Final Report on Human Rights and Extreme Poverty, submitted by the Special Rapporteur Mr. Leandro Despouy, supra note 4; Narayan et al *Voices of the Poor: Crying out for Change* (Washington DC: World Bank, 2000) ('*Voices of the Poor II*').

31 UN Committee on Economic, Social and Cultural Rights, Statement on Poverty and the International Covenant on Economic, Social and Cultural Rights, supra note 4, at para. 14.

32 Supra note 26, at para. 12.

Specific rights affected

More concretely, poor people experience violations of a large range of rights, all of which would – if they were respected, protected and fulfilled – contribute to moving people out of poverty. Part of the problem is a lack of respect for the right to an adequate standard of living,[33] which results in an insecurity for people that implies difficulties in benefiting from services that are being provided for them, or from development projects aimed at improving their situation.[34] In this sense, poverty is a structural problem, the solution of which may lay in respect for and fulfilment of human rights. The ability to exercise one's right to food, to housing, clothing, medical care and education, through the exercise of a right to participation, expression and other civil and political rights, is vital for individuals if they are to move away from being poor, and for society to eradicate poverty. All of these rights are already part of the normative framework of international human rights law, but need to be focused upon in work with poor people.

As the poor are among the most vulnerable to deterioration in their living conditions, the predictability and certainty that comes with respect for and fulfilment of human rights are of utmost importance. Poor people experience nutritional low standards, lack of access to education and to housing, lack of adequate medical treatment, restrictions on their freedom of movement, etc. This implies that in order to remedy the situation, a number of human rights need to be ensured, and a comprehensive approach to this is merited. This comprehensive approach is to be found in a number of human rights instruments, such as the Universal Declaration, the Declaration on the Right to Development,[35] the Convention on the Rights of the Child,[36] and the African Charter on Human and Peoples' Rights.[37] In the following section I will be discussing some of the rights that are crucial in terms of the lives of the poor. This should not be taken as an exhaustive elaboration, but rather as examples both in terms of issues and of rights.

33 ICESCR Article 11 and UDHR Article 25. The Sub-Commission on the Protection and Promotion of Human Rights specifically recalls this latter Article in Resolution 2001/8, supra note 15.

34 Final Report on Human Rights and Extreme Poverty, submitted by the Special Rapporteur Mr. Leandro Despouy, supra note 4, at para. 125.

35 *Declaration on the Right to Development*, Adopted by the UN General Assembly, 10 December 1986.

36 Adopted 20 November 1989, entered into force 2 September 1990.

37 The Preamble to the African Charter on Human and Peoples Rights ('The Banjul Charter') contains the following passage:

> Convinced that it is henceforth essential to pay a particular attention to the right to development and that civil and political rights cannot be dissociated from economic, social and cultural rights in their conception as well as universality and that the satisfaction of economic, social and cultural rights is a guarantee for the enjoyment of civil and political rights.

The Banjul Charter was adopted in 1981 and entered into force in 1986.

Right to adequate food

> *'Poverty for me is the fact that we bought some black flour with our last money, some flour cheaper than the rest. When we baked the bread it was not edible. We were speechless and ate it by force since we did not have anything else.'* [38]

In *Voices of the Poor I,* the authors claim that the lack of adequate food is the 'ultimate criterion of poverty'.[39] Everyone's right to adequate food is firmly established in the relevant international human rights instruments.[40] Article 11 (1) of the ICESCR states that the States Parties to the Covenant 'recognize the right of everyone to an adequate standard of living for himself and his family, including adequate food, ...,' and the right to be free from hunger is recognized in paragraph 2 of the same article.[41] Due to lack of financial and material resources, poor people inevitably face real difficulties in fulfilling their right to food. As food is a basic need for human survival, the struggle to ensure even the very minimum availability of food will for poor people overshadow their efforts to tackle other imminent problems such as health care, housing and education. It will also prevent poor people from participating in communal or other efforts to improve their situation – the struggle for the next meal becomes the immediate and all-consuming activity.

The right to the highest attainable standard of physical and mental health[42]

> *'We watch our children die because we cannot pay the high hospital bills'*.[43]

The lack of adequate health care which is free of charge is often a direct cause of poverty. 'For poor families who are already highly vulnerable, the costs of a sudden illness can be devastating, both because of work income lost and the costs of

[38] Testimony from Macedonia 1998, in *Voices of the Poor I*, supra note 30, at 53.

[39] Ibid.

[40] UDHR Article 25, and ICESCR Article 11.

[41] Article 11(2) reads:
The States parties to the present Covenant, recognizing the fundamental right of everyone to be free from hunger, shall take, individually and through international co-operation, the measures, including specific programmes, which are needed:
(a) To improve methods of production, conservation and distribution of food by making full use of technical and scientific knowledge, by disseminating knowledge of the principles of nutrition and by developing or reforming agrarian systems in such a way as to achieve the most efficient development and utilization of natural resources;
(b) Taking into account the problems of both food-importing and food-exporting countries, to ensure an equitable distribution of world food supplies in relation to need.

[42] As guaranteed by UDHR Article 25, and ICESCR Article 12. For an in-depth analysis of the right to health see Toebes, *The Right to Health as a Human Right in International Law* (Antwerp: Intersentia/Hart, 1999).

[43] Ghana 1995, *Voices of the Poor I,* supra note 30, at 87.

treatment.'[44] In its General Comment on the right to health, the UN Committee on Economic, Social and Cultural Rights have specified, amongst others, the following elements as part of the core obligations pertaining to the right to health:

(a) To ensure the right of access to health facilities, goods and services on a non-discriminatory basis, especially for vulnerable or marginalized groups;

(b) To ensure access to the minimum essential food which is nutritionally adequate and safe, to ensure freedom from hunger to everyone;

(c) To ensure access to basic shelter, housing and sanitation, and an adequate supply of safe and potable water;

(d) To provide essential drugs, as from time to time defined under the WHO Action Programme on Essential Drugs;

(e) To ensure equitable distribution of all health facilities, goods and services;[45]

These elements of the right to health are supposed to be implemented immediately, not progressively, as a 'minimum core obligation to ensure the satisfaction of, at the very least, minimum essential levels of each of the rights is incumbent upon every State party'.[46] Nevertheless, these are rights that poor people regularly experience violations of, both in terms of discrimination (access to health care facilities is often quite unequal for men and women), and lack of access to safe drinking water, shelter, housing and sanitation, and basic health care facilities even if they do exist. The occurrence not only of costs to pay for health care, but also bribes required to receive treatment and corruption is by many poor identified as a major hurdle in their struggle to get access to health care.[47]

The right to education[48]

> *'In Nigeria, if you are not educated, you cannot get a job, and no job determines position in the society. Our parents did not go to school, and so we are poor today. Education can change this*'.[49]

Poor people make distinctions between literacy, education, and acquiring skills.[50] Lack of literacy and numeracy makes poor people vulnerable, and likely to be cheated

44 Ibid.

45 UN Committee on Economic, Social and Cultural Rights, General Comment no. 14 (the Right to the Highest Attainable Standard of Health), 2000, 8 IHRR 1 (2001), at para. 43.

46 UN Committee on Economic, Social and Cultural Rights, General Comment no. 3 (State Obligations), 1990, 1-1 IHRR 6 (1994), at para. 10.

47 *Voices of the Poor I*, supra note 30, at 87 ff.

48 UDHR Article 26, ICESCR Article 13.

49 Testimony from Participant, a group of youths, Dawaki, Nigeria, *Voices of the Poor II*, supra note 30, at 240.

50 Ibid.

in their dealings. This has a direct effect on their immediate situation. Education and the acquisition of skills are necessary for more long-term improvement in their situation. The costs of schooling, both in terms of fees (in many places), but also requirements of buying books, uniforms, etc., are for many poor a direct obstacle to education. Furthermore, the lack of income from children's work while they are in school is often an insurmountable hindrance. There is also a strong element of discrimination, as men are more reluctant to send their daughters to school than their sons. Thus, the right to education needs to be addressed in conjunction with the rights to work, social security, and non-discrimination.

The right to housing[51]

A common plight for poor people is that they almost always live in bad housing or shelter, or without shelter altogether.[52] This situation is precarious in terms of coping on an everyday basis, and to secure the fulfilment of many other human rights, such as the right to adequate food and to health.[53] As was shown in the quote from the Committee on Economic and Social Rights' General Comment on the right to health,[54] access to adequate housing is seen as an integral part in the fulfilment of this right. But housing is not only important for the practical application or enjoyment of these rights. It is also essential in order to get access to social services, since the latter are often only provided to those with a permanent address. People without housing will therefore regularly fall 'outside' the system.

Access to justice[55]

An integral element of human rights guarantees is the entitlement and the ability to bring claims if human rights are violated. This goes to the core of any notion of rights – without the ability to hold obligation-holders accountable, the notion of rights becomes elusive. Access to the justice system is often very expensive, and

[51] UDHR Article 25, ICESCR Article 11. For an elaboration of the content of the right to adequate housing, see UN Committee on Economic, Social and Cultural Rights, General Comment no. 4 (The Right to Adequate Housing), 1991. Reprinted in HRI/GEN/1/Rev.5 26 April 2001 and 1-1 IHRR 9(1994). See also UN Committee on Economic, Social and Cultural Rights, General Comment no. 7 (The Right to Adequate Housing: Forced Evictions), 1997. Reprinted in HRI/GEN/1/Rev.5 26 April 2001 and 5 IHRR 1 (1998).

[52] *Voices of the Poor II*, supra note 30, at 63. According to Miloon Kothari of Habitat International Coalition, now UN Special Rapporteur on the Right to Adequate Housing as a Component of the Right to an Adequate Standard of Living, about 100 million people in the world are homeless, with over one billion subjected to 'insecure and inadequate housing and living conditions:' UN Commission on Human Rights, Summary Records, 41st meeting, "Economic, Social and Cultural Rights," supra note 26, at para. 36.

[53] UN Committee on Economic, Social and Cultural Rights, General Comment no. 4, supra note 51, at paras. 7 and 9.

[54] See supra note 45 and accompanying text.

[55] UDHR Articles 6-11, ICCPR Articles 14-16.

the opportunities for poor people to assert their rights through legal means are greatly hampered. The UDHR and the International Covenant on Civil and Political Rights (ICCPR) contain a number of articles ensuring access to the legal system on an equal basis.[56] Without financial resources to consult and be represented by a lawyer, the justice system is not available to people living in poverty. Therefore, the establishment of a legal aid system that people in poverty can draw upon in order to assert their rights is of utmost importance. This is necessary, not only in terms of ensuring a fair trial, but in order to assert all rights— civil, political, economic, social and cultural – the violation of which directly hampers people's ability to move out of poverty.

Participation

In human rights instruments, participation is often considered to be a separate right. In the Universal Declaration it is stated that 'Everyone has the right to take part in the government of his country, directly or through freely chosen representatives',[57] while the ICCPR states that 'Every citizen shall have the right and the opportunity, without any of the distinctions mentioned in article 2 and without unreasonable restrictions: (a) to take part in the conduct of public affairs, directly or through freely chosen representatives'.[58] This right to take part in a national decision-making process is, however, more far-reaching than it may appear, and it is dependent upon the fulfilment of other rights.[59] The right to participation is part of the current normative framework of human rights, which is crucial for poor people's ability to influence their own situation, including their right to be heard in 'poverty eradication projects'. A rights-based approach to poverty eradication implies working with the poor and developing strategies that support their context for the enjoyment of human rights.[60] Thus, poor people's participation in the identification of their problems, and the design, implementation and evaluation of measures to be taken to solve these problems is imperative. It is encouraging to note that the new strategy on poverty reduction adopted by the World Bank and the IMF through the Poverty Reduction Strategies Paper (PRSP), incorporate an element of participation by civil society.[61] In

56 UDHR Articles 7 – 11, ICCPR Articles 9-10.

57 UDHR Article 21.

58 ICCPR Article 25.

59 Rosas points out that:

> Political rights in the narrow sense cannot thrive without the principle of equality (Articles 1,2,4 and 7), and they presuppose civil rights and liberties, notably liberty and security of person (e.g. articles 3, 5 and 9) and freedom of movement, expression, assembly and association (articles 13, 19, 20). A minimum of social and economic rights also seems crucial (articles 22-26).

See Rosas, "Article 21," in Eide and Alfredsson (eds.) *The Universal Declaration of Human Rights: A Common Standard of Achievement* (The Hague: Martinus Nijhoff Publishers, 1999), at 431.

60 UN Commission on Human Rights, Summary Records, 41st meeting, "Economic, Social and Cultural Rights," supra note 26, at para. 17.

61 Key Features of IMF Poverty Reduction and Growth Facility (PRGF) Supported Programs: http://www.imf.org/external/np/prgf/2000/eng/key.htm.

Voices of the Poor II, the authors suggest the following:

> The framework for grassroots democracy, the right to participate, must be enshrined in law. This has to include rules about public disclosure of information; freedom of association, speech and the press; freedom to form organizations; and devolution of authority and finances to the local level. Institutional rules and incentives are needed to translate laws into effective governance structures. The challenge is to create proper government institutions accountable to the poor.[62]

The extent to which this approach will be incorporated into the PRSP process, and to which the voices of the poor will be heard is still not established.

Non-discrimination

Non-discrimination is one of the most fundamental aspects of human rights. The United Nations Charter provides for human rights protection without distinction as to race, sex language or religion,[63] and non-discrimination clauses are central in all international human rights instruments.[64] People in poverty not only experience poverty, but commonly also suffer from discrimination based on their status. Poor people are often discriminated against in terms of access to housing, education, justice systems, etc. Additionally certain groups, such as minorities and indigenous peoples, suffer from additional discrimination. Highly prevalent, however, is discrimination against women in poverty. Such women face a particularly difficult situation in two regards. First, they are often subject to abuse and oppression, and will not get access to the few resources available.[65] Secondly, women will more often than men end up in poverty due to discriminatory structures in society – lack of access to land, to credit, to inheritance, etc. This reality will often lead to poverty for women and their dependent children. This reality implies that women are more vulnerable in poverty, and that they suffer from more human rights violations than other groups. The discriminatory aspects of poverty need to be addressed from a human rights perspective, in order to alleviate the suffering of all vulnerable groups, including children, indigenous peoples, religious minorities, women, etc.

Indivisibility of rights

This leads us to consider one fundamental part of the problem of poverty, namely the indivisibility of rights. Poverty is often seen to be a material matter only – a lack of financial resources – but, as the testimonies quoted earlier in the paper show,[66]

62 *Voices of the Poor II,* supra note 30, at 282-83.
63 UN Charter, Article 1(3).
64 UDHR Article 2, ICCPR Article 2 and ICESCR Article 2.
65 *Voices of the Poor I,* supra note 30, at 195.
66 See supra notes 38, 39, 43, 44 and 47.

poverty encompasses a large number of aspects of life, many of which involve rights related to personal safety and integrity as well as economic and social safety and well being. Poverty is more than a social or economic problem. Poverty leaves people voiceless and powerless, distancing them from the people and institutions making the decisions that affect their lives. In *Voices of the Poor II*, this problem is clearly identified:

> [The] review of poor peoples' encounters with state institutions is sobering. Dysfunctional institutions do not just fail to deliver services. They disempower - and even silence - the poor through patterns of humiliation, exclusion, and corruption. The process is further compounded by legal and other formal barriers that prevent the poor from trading or gaining access to benefits or trading further compound the problem. Thus, those at society's margins are further excluded and alienated.[67]

This powerlessness makes the poor, in turn, even more vulnerable to abuse and to the cyclical patterns of poverty that could keep the poor and their children in the same state for generations.[68] Thus, one cannot look purely to economic and social rights to address the problems of the poor. This is clearly illustrated in a recent report by the Special Rapportuer on Torture in which he holds:

> It is true that many of the more high-profile cases of torture that come to international attention concern people involved in political activities of various sorts. Such victims of torture may well be of a class or connected with organizations that have international contacts. The experience of missions in several parts of the world has led the Special Rapporteur to observe, however, that the overwhelming majority of those subjected to torture and ill-treatment are ordinary common criminals from the lowest strata of society. They are the ones who cannot afford good lawyers, or who may have access only to less than-diligent lawyers provided, in some instances, by the State, or who may not have access to any lawyer at all; whose families do not have the connections to be taken seriously by the police, prosecutors or judges, or even the means of securing life-saving health care that may be obtained outside the place of detention, or of providing food fit to eat when the detaining authorities and institutions fail to make these available; and who do not have any idea of what their rights are, even the right not to be tortured, or how those rights may be secured. Indeed, they are often members of the lowest level of an underclass that is disconnected from all opportunity of leading decent lives as productive economic citizens.[69]

67 *Voices of the Poor I,* supra note 30, at 85.

68 UN High Commissioner for Human Rights, in UN Commission on Human Rights, Summary Records, 41st meeting, "Economic, Social and Cultural Rights," supra note 26, at para. 6.

69 UN General Assembly, Report by the Secretary General, incorporating Interim Report of the Special Rapporteur of the Commission on Human Rights on the question of torture and other cruel, inhuman or degrading treatment or punishment 11 August 2000, A/55/290, at para. 35.

Similarly, for people living in poverty it will be much harder to assert other rights, including the rights to expression, to assembly, and association.

A comprehensive approach to human rights that reflects this indivisibility of rights is contained in the UDHR, but most prominently in the Declaration on the Right to Development[70]. In Article 1 of the latter Declaration, the 'right to development' is defined as an 'inalienable human right by virtue of which every human person and all peoples are entitled to participate in, contribute to, and enjoy economic, social, cultural and political development, in which all human rights and fundamental freedoms can be fully realized.' In these terms, the right to development is seen both as a synthesis of all human rights, and also an exercise of these rights. The right to development, as expressed through the declaration, is not a new right, but rather something which establishes the individual's right to participate in the process which will lead to the fulfilment of all rights – the aim of the right to development.

To eradicate poverty – to enable poor people to move out of poverty – human rights generally need to be respected, protected and fulfilled for all. This reflects the responsibility of all those whose actions affect the living conditions of poor people: governments, non-governmental organisations, intergovernmental organisations, and private entities, such as transnational - and national - corporations. This does not necessarily imply that states or other entities always need to make provisions for poor people. Due to their difficult living conditions, poor people will often be highly resourceful in terms of surviving.[71] However, many poor people experience obstacles to their own efforts to improve their situation, such as eviction from their homes, or from land where they grow their food, the costs of school uniforms, or the corruption of officials. Much could be done in order to respect poor people's human rights without direct provisions for them, through scrutiny of other elements that affect them in society, or through changes in regulation. Needless to say, however, for people with so few material resources, government action involving monetary expenditure may in many instances be necessary. The building of schools and the provision of basic health care facilities are obvious examples. However, experience shows that people living in poverty find themselves in a complex reality of human rights violations, which, unless directly addressed, will imply that even if schools and hospitals are built, they will not be able to take advantage of these new facilities. The 'trickle-down' model does not work.[72] Therefore, when planning and designing these new facilities, the rights of the poor need to be addressed directly and comprehensively. This should be done through careful analysis of the poor people's situation from a rights based perspective. This would involve analysing where the human rights violations are occurring, and remedying this situation in direct consultation with the affected groups. For example, a rights-based approach to improving the standard of living in the rural area of an African country would involve a process in which the people themselves took an active part in identifying their

[70] Supra note 35.

[71] *Voices of the Poor I*, supra note 30, at 225.

[72] In *Voices of the Poor II*, it is described in great detail how many poor families need to decide whether to eat properly or to send their children to school. Thus the availability of the school is not the only obstacle to education. See *Voices of the Poor II*, supra note 30, at 209.

problems, explaining why the children do not go to school (rather than outsiders observing that the children do not go to school), why so many go hungry, why the local produce is not sold at the regional market, etc. Based on this information, a development scheme would assess the underlying causes of the inability of the people to enjoy the right to education, right to food, and other human rights, and in close cooperation with these people design development plans that address these underlying causes with the express aim of implementing human rights. This may go beyond traditional development work such as building the schools or hospitals, and will also involve working with local and national authorities in improving legislation, administrative practices, infrastructure and accountability.

IS THERE A RIGHT TO BE POOR?

From the above discussion, two central points become clear. First, in the positivist sense of international human rights law, the existing documents do not contain a right not to be poor. Second, the current normative framework in international human rights law contain crucial guarantees that, if fulfilled, would lift poor people out of poverty.

These two central points seem to be somewhat contradictory, and it is of interest to dwell on them briefly from a political/philosophical perspective, before discussing the practical and legal implications of this situation. As to the first point, it was mentioned above[73] that some of the inspiration for the UDHR came from the 'Four Freedoms' speech by President Roosevelt in 1941. One of the freedoms he was advocating was 'freedom from want' – a much more all-embracing approach than what became the result in specific articles in the Universal Declaration. The UDHR, and the Covenants, do not refer to poverty or poor people in any of their articles or in their Preambles. Moreover, the poor have been left out in the implementation of these instruments. As the Special Rapporteur on Torture pointed out in his report quoted above,[74] the vast majority of tortured people are poor people, but their case is not heard due to their lack of ability ('capability') to get the attention of the outside world. Executive Director of FIAN International,[75] Michael Windfuhr, stated in a meeting in Geneva in February 2001[76] that one of the reasons why the United Nations and the human rights community in general have neglected economic and social human rights for so long is that it is poor people that by far most frequently experience violations of these rights, and the poor lack the resources to bring attention to their plight. This unfortunate situation needs to be addressed and could be improved by enhanced participation by the poor in the supervision and implementation of human rights both on a national and international level. Further, the special situation of

73 See supra note 27 and accompanying text.

74 See supra note 69 and accompanying text.

75 *Food First Information and Action Network* - A non-governmental human rights organisation that works on the right to food (or rather 'the right to feed oneself').

76 Seminar on the Justiciability of Economic, Social and Cultural Rights, organised by the Office of the High Commissioner on Human Rights, Geneva, 5-6 February 2001.

people living in poverty needs to be set in focus by the implementation bodies, and not remain a side-issue dependent upon a 'trickle-down' effect.[77]

The second point mentioned above was that that the instruments contain, albeit implicitly, guarantees of human rights that, if fulfilled, would result in great advancements towards lifting people out of poverty. In the section on the existing normative framework, some examples were given indicating how the living conditions experienced by the poor demonstrate violations of a large variety of human rights. If the rights to participation and access to justice and (at least the minimum core obligations of) the rights to food, education, housing, and health were fulfilled for all people (which is what the governments are under a legal obligation to do as a result of ratifying international human rights treaties[78]), a much smaller percentage of people would live in conditions that could be characterised as poverty. Thus, although technically there is no right not to be poor in current international human rights law, these legal provisions contain guarantees that are imperative for people to move out of poverty.

If this is the case, what needs to happen in order for poor people to have their human rights realised? One of the main changes in approach on behalf of the international human rights community that needs to happen is to move from a fragmented to a comprehensive notion of human rights protection. Both NGOs and intergovernmental organisations have for too long worked on a fragmented basis. Not only does the United Nations have six different committees supervising the implementation of its human rights treaties in individual states,[79] but the non-governmental community has also to a large extent focused on one or a handful of rights that have been given their attention, rather than looking towards a comprehensive approach. NGOs have almost exclusively focused on civil and political rights, and within that field, on a few targeted rights.[80] The few NGOs working on

[77] This will be further elaborated in the section 'The linking of human rights and poverty alleviation' below.

[78] As of 1 February 2002, 145 states were parties to the ICESCR while the ICCPR had 147 states parties.

[79] The Human Rights Committee, the Committee on the Elimination of Racial Discrimination, the Committee on the Elimination of Discrimination Against Women, the Committee on the Rights of the Child, the Committee Against Torture, and the Committee on Economic, Social and Cultural Rights.

[80] Amnesty International has for a long time confined its work to torture, disappeared persons and the fight against the death penalty. However, at the organisation's International Council meeting in Dakar in August 2001, a new Mission statement was adopted which implies a somewhat broader mandate:

> 1. Amnesty International's vision is of a world in which every person enjoys all of the human rights enshrined in the Universal Declaration of Human Rights and other international human rights standards.
>
> In pursuit of this vision, Amnesty International's mission is to undertake research and action focused on preventing and ending grave abuses of the rights to physical and mental integrity, freedom of conscience and expression, and freedom from discrimination, within the context of its work to promote all human rights. (http://www.amnesty.org)

Human Rights Watch confines it work to civil and political rights, but with a heavy emphasis on political rights to participation, elections, due process, etc; Article 19 works only on freedom of expression issues.

economic and social rights have again tended to focus on single or limited numbers of issues.[81] There are some organisations that have taken a more comprehensive approach, but they remain small and relatively uninfluential.[82] I am not questioning the effectiveness of these organisations, nor their contribution to the advancement of human rights. Amnesty International was the first mass membership NGO to promote human rights throughout the world, and one should not denigrate or belittle the important work that the organisation has done. But in order to reach and to respond to the needs of people in poverty, a more comprehensive approach is needed. Looking back at the capability approach advocated by Amartya Sen, it becomes clear that to focus on one aspect of poor people's human rights violations will not remedy their situation. In other words, most of the attention given to human rights violations by governmental and non-governmental bodies has been to situations where individual human rights have been violated, for example where somebody has been subjected to torture or has had their correspondence interfered with. Even if these are human rights violations that face the poor as well as others, the individual cases receiving the attention from the human rights community tend to be those faced by people with high levels of 'capabilities', people whose human rights are generally respected, and the attention is drawn to the exceptional circumstances where one single right has been violated. Poor people live in a different reality – a reality where most rights are violated most of the time. This complex situation implies that it is impossible to improve the overall human rights situation by tackling one violation at the time. The right to education can be promoted through the building of schools, the hiring of teachers, and by making primary education compulsory, but unless people have resources sufficient to not have their children work, the right to education will remain elusive for people in poverty. Likewise, free primary health care can be made available, but as long as women need to spend all their time ensuring that the basic subsistence needs of their children are satisfied (such as collecting potable water and growing the family's food) they will not be able to make use of these facilities. Thus, the only way that the current international human rights regime may claim to contain sufficient rights for people in poverty, without adopting a specific right to not be poor, would be if a comprehensive approach to human rights protection was adopted *and* implemented both by the official national organs, the UN bodies, and also NGOs in the field.

THE LINKING OF HUMAN RIGHTS AND POVERTY ALLEVIATION

Having established that there is no recognised right not to be poor per se, the question becomes whether there would be any benefits to advance such a right, or

81 Habitat International Coalition (HIC) works on the right to housing, FIAN International on the right to food.

82 One example is Rights and Humanity based in the United Kingdom, which focuses on all of the rights in the Universal Declaration; another is the Center for Economic, Social and Cultural Rights based in New York, which has a broad economic and social rights mandate.

if an alternative approach would be better. What the above analysis has shown is that not only is there a gap in the law in that the most vulnerable group among the world's population – the poor – do not enjoy specific human rights protection, but also that the implementation machinery largely neglects the special requirements of the poor.[83] Would this be remedied by adopting a new right – the right not to be poor? There are certainly arguments both in favour and in opposition to this proposition. An argument in favour would be that this would finally give the attention to poverty and the situation of poor people that they deserve. On the other hand, others would argue that there is already a large number of rights, both in hard law and in soft law, and that to expand the number would diminish the importance and respect that the current human rights regime enjoys, rather than benefit the intended beneficiaries. I personally will not advocate the adoption of a new right. This would run into the danger of diminishing the regard that the human rights system enjoys, and risks using too much energy on getting something adopted, rather than using the already existing structures that, if implemented, would make a real difference in poverty alleviation. Thus, it is important to look at how these existing structures could be used, and what the benefits would be. There are both material and procedural improvements that can be made in order to ensure that the connection between human rights and poverty moves from being implicit to explicit.

The first important step on the material side would be to get the link between existing human rights and poverty explicitly accepted. The adoption of a declaratory text that makes this connection but without creating a 'new right' would serve an important function in this regard. As discussed above,[84] work is already underway within the United Nations for the drafting of a declaration or guiding principles on human rights and poverty (or extreme poverty).[85] Such a text would serve several purposes. First, much of the work on poverty and human rights has been carried out by the United Nations through the designated human rights bodies (the Charter and Treaty-based bodies), and the Office for the High Commissioner of Human Rights. The danger of keeping this work on the current level of *studies* and *resolutions* is that little attention is paid to it outside the institutions in Geneva. The Commission on Human Rights rarely receives much attention (unfortunately) from outside actors, such as the media, and even human rights NGOs. One of the reasons for starting work on a text would be to *increase public awareness* of the problems of extreme

[83] It should be noted that, on the regional level, the Revised European Social Charter [ETS No. 163; 3 IHRR 726 (1996). Adopted on 3 May 1996, entered into force on 1 August 1999] includes the 'right to protection against social exclusion and poverty' in Article 30:

> The Explanatory Report to the Revised Charter emphasizes that the intention of states was not to repeat existing obligations to tackle poverty .... The obligation is to adopt a coordinated approach involving measures of different kinds that together will tackle the problem of exclusion or poverty: Harris, *The European Social Charter*, 2nd ed. (Ardsley, N.Y: Transnational Publishers, 2001), at 281.

[84] See supra note 4 and accompanying text.

[85] See the list of documents at supra note 4. The current discussions in the UN have been inconclusive in terms of the exact form of a text. Some are in favour of a 'declaration'; others prefer 'guidelines' or 'guiding principles'.

poverty and how it links to human rights. Second, a process of drafting a declaration or guiding principles would provide an opportunity to adopt a participatory approach, whereby the poor may experience that they have a real voice.[86]

Third, a declaration or guiding principles on poverty and human rights would highlight the complex interrelatedness of all human rights,[87] and emphasise that poverty is not only about lack of material well-being, but also an expression of the deprivation of human dignity. The proposed text would add an important dimension to the right to development as expressed through the 1986 Declaration on the Right to Development because it would address the individual's situation, something that is often lacking in a right to development discussion. Although the right to development is considered both an individual and a collective right ('every human person and all peoples'[88]) the individual aspect in the right to development discussion is often lost. Similarly, poverty eradication programmes tend to address poverty in its collectivity rather than the situation as faced by individuals.

Fourth, such a declaration or guiding principles would also provide a tool in the advocacy work of those engaged in poverty eradication from the grass-roots level to large international fora.

Finally, a text on poverty and human rights would provide an opportunity to address and emphasise the responsibility of a variety of actors in poverty alleviation. Emphasising the prime obligations of the state, such a text should consider the role of other actors in society (national as well as international) and stress their shared responsibility in fulfilling all human rights. The World Development Report highlights the poors' bad treatment by state authorities and other segments of society, and calls for 'action to improve the functioning of state and social institutions [which] improves both growth and equity by reducing bureaucratic and social constraints to economic action and upward mobility.' [89]

In these ways, by making a firm link between the current normative framework of human rights and the real life experiences of the poor, a declaration or guiding principles would provide clear added value to the already existing human right instruments.

On the procedural side, an explicit link would have effect on the operation both of human rights bodies and of institutions involved in poverty eradication. First, if a text is adopted, this should be used as a tool to enhance the efficiency of the treaty-

86 The reports that have come out from efforts of engaging the poor in consultation seem to be very positive. See Report of Seminar held from 12–14 October 1994 at the UN Headquarters in New York (in which 20 out of 40 participants were people living in extreme poverty); see *Voices of the Poor I,* supra note 30, based on the 78 Participatory Poverty Assessment reports, which are based on discussions with poor women and men. The importance of the participatory approach to a declaration of guiding principles was also emphasised in the report by the High Commissioner on Human Rights in her report from the Expert Seminar on Poverty and Human Rights, E/CN.4/2000/95, at para. 36.

87 See discussion above under sub-heading 'Indivisibility of rights'.

88 Passage from the Declaration on the Right to Development, Article 1.

89 The World Bank *World Development Report 2000/2001: Attacking Poverty* (Oxford: OUP, 2001), at 9.

based bodies.[90] It should be used as a reference point in their examination of state parties reports to ensure that the situation of the poor people of a state does not remain untargeted. The Committee on Economic, Social and Cultural Rights has already provided important contributions to this through its statement on Poverty and the International Covenant on Economic, Social and Cultural Rights.[91] In this statement the Committee discusses how a poverty approach may be advanced with a view to State Parties' obligations. Reference here is made to the core obligation to 'ensure the satisfaction of, at the very least, minimum essential levels of each of the rights'.[92] The statement explains this 'core obligation' in relationship to poverty in the following manner:

> the core obligations of economic, social and cultural rights have a crucial role to play in national and international developmental policies, including anti-poverty strategies. When grouped together, the core obligations establish an international minimum threshold that all developmental policies should be designed to respect. In accordance with General Comment No. 14, it is particularly incumbent on all those who can assist, to help developing countries respect this international minimum threshold. If a national or international anti-poverty strategy does not reflect this minimum threshold, it is inconsistent with the legally binding obligations of the State party.
>
> For the avoidance of any misunderstanding, the Committee wishes to emphasize three points. First, because core obligations are non-derogable, they continue to exist in situations of conflict, emergency and natural disaster. Second, because poverty is a global phenomenon, core obligations have great relevance to some individuals and communities living in the richest States. Third, after a State party has ensured the core obligations of economic, social and cultural rights, it continues to have an obligation to move as expeditiously and effectively as possible towards the full realization of all the rights in the Covenant.[93]

Thus, in this way, the Committee on Economic, Social and Cultural Rights has shown how the treaty bodies may approach the link between human rights and poverty, and consciously apply it in their work. This approach could be adopted by the other treaty bodies, and used when examining state reports in a comprehensive and integrated manner. Likewise, human rights NGOs could re-examine their strategies and working methods with a view to improving their work with poor people and communities.

Finally, it is pertinent to address the effects that a firm and effective emphasis on the connection between poverty and human rights would have outside the human

90 These are listed at supra note 79.

91 UN Committee on Economic, Social and Cultural Rights, Statement on Poverty and the International Covenant on Economic, Social and Cultural Rights, supra note 4.

92 Ibid., at para. 15.

93 Ibid., at paras. 17 and 18.

rights circles. Indeed, if the effect is only felt within the human rights circles, it could be considered a failure. Thus, it is imperative that the work carried out will penetrate the work done by other international actors involved in poverty alleviation. A text on human rights and poverty should be used by the specialised agencies of the UN, the UN Funds and programmes, as well as non-governmental development organisations in their poverty alleviation strategies. It will be a tool to use in identifying problems and proposing solutions in these strategies. And just like any other tool, if it is left aside and not used, it will not fulfil its purpose. If a text is drafted on the connection between poverty and human rights, this is only a first and preliminary step that needs to be followed up by real implementation activities. The main aim of a declaration or guiding principles would be to make all actors involved in human rights and in poverty alleviation conscious about the connection, so that they will approach the issues from a comprehensive approach.

CONCLUSION

In the introduction, the question was raised whether a link between human rights and poverty would make a difference both to the work for poverty alleviation and to respect for human rights. Based on the above discussion, it would be fair to say that the effect of such a link would be wide ranging. One important consequence would be that a fundamental aspect of poverty would be highlighted, namely that, by virtue of living in poverty, people face systematic and widespread violations of a large number of human rights – violations that are rarely addressed due to the lack of voice that the poor possess in national and international debates and decision-making. This fundamental aspect can only be addressed if poverty is understood in terms of the violations of human rights that result from poverty. It is imperative therefore for both the development and the human rights communities to understand poverty in these terms and to act accordingly. A text – in the form of a declaration or guiding principles – would add a comprehensive approach for the human rights bodies and institutions, while it would add an individual and legal entitlement approach for the development institutions.[94]

In reading *Voices of the Poor*, one of the striking features is the strength that people living in poverty possess. The ability to survive in conditions as harsh as those described in that report does not reflect weakness (or laziness – as some will argue), but rather a tremendous strength and will to survive. A link between human rights and poverty alleviation would empower poor people with the necessary rights, and thus contribute to the elimination the capability deprivation from which people in poverty suffer. This in turn would enable them to move out of poverty while retaining their dignity as human beings. If conditions were conducive to their capabilities, if their human rights were fulfilled, much of the poverty problem that the world currently faces would be solved.

[94] Individuals would be able to enforce their rights and to attain remedies for violations thereof.

Finally, in order to address the question asked by *The Economist* above[95] – does it help to think of poverty as a violation of basic rights? – a rather clear conclusion can be made. It is not a question of whether it helps. Poverty is by its nature a violation of basic rights. It is not a violation of a right not to be poor, but it is a violation of human dignity, and of basic human rights such as the right to equality, to participation, and to food, health, housing and education. A first step towards improving the situation of the poor is to make a conscious recognition of this fact. Only then will we be able to address the problems from the approach of rights, rather than charity, from dignity rather than pity.

95 See supra note 1.

[18]

The International Human Rights Movement: Part of the Problem?

David Kennedy
Henry Shattuck Professor of Law, Harvard Law School[1]

In this second essay in a series of three pieces reflecting on the international legal order and its politics, the author puts forward a critical analysis of the role of the international human rights movement, and questions whether its pre-eminence has not in some respects made it a restriction on the possibilities of emancipation, as well as a force for good. Arguably, the human rights movement has served to legitimate existing power structures, by confining the critique of these structures to the language of human rights. It may also have deflected energies and attention from other strategies of emancipation and critiques of power, which cannot easily be made through the language of human rights. The author stresses the importance of weighing the costs and benefits of human rights discourse and practice, in the interests of a pragmatic approach which ensures the effectiveness of the human rights movement.

There is no question that the international human rights movement has done a great deal of good, freeing individuals from great harm, providing an emancipatory vocabulary and institutional machinery for people across the globe, raising the standards by which governments judge one another, and by which they are judged, both by their own people, and by the elites we refer to collectively as the "international community". A career in the human rights movement has provided thousands of professionals, many of them lawyers, with a sense of dignity and confidence that one sometimes can do well while doing good. The literature praising these, and other, accomplishments is vast. Among well-meaning legal professionals in the United States and Europe—humanist, internationalist, liberal, compassionate in all the best senses of these terms—the human rights movement has become a central object of devotion.

But there are other ways of thinking about human rights. As a well-meaning internationalist and, I hope, compassionate legal professional myself, I thought it might be useful to pull together in a short list some of the questions which have been raised about international human rights by people, including myself, who worry that the human rights movement might, on balance, and acknowledging its enormous achievement, be more part of the problem in today's world than part of the solution. This essay

[1] Let me thank a number of friends who brainstormed with me about this list, often by offering withering criticism of the positions advanced here: Jim Bergeron, Yishai Blanc, Hilary Charlesworth, Janet Halley, Vasuki Nesiah, Joel Ngugi, Pat Macklem, Susan Marks, Scott Newton, Philippe Sands, Hani Sayed, Natalia Schiffrin, Amr Shalakany, Thomas Skouteris, Henry Steiner, Chantal Thomas.

offers an incomplete and idiosyncratic list of such questions which might be of interest to the human rights practitioner.

I should say at the outset that the arguments I have listed are hypotheses. I have stated them as succinctly as I can, at the risk of their seeming conclusive or overly polemical. In fact, although some of them seem more plausible to me than others, to my knowledge none of them has been proven—they are in the air as assertions, worries, polemical charges. They circulate in the background of conversations about the human rights movement. And even if these potential costs *were* demonstrated, it would still be necessary to weigh them against the very real accomplishments of the human rights movement.

I. Thinking Pragmatically About Human Rights

My purpose in pulling these concerns together is to encourage other well meaning legal professionals to adopt a more pragmatic attitude towards human rights. My hope is that we will develop a stronger practice of weighing the costs and benefits of their articulation, institutionalisation and enforcement. Of course, the best human rights practitioners are already intensely strategic and practical in thinking about their work. But it is often tempting (for those within and without the movement) to set pragmatic concerns aside, to treat human rights as an object of devotion rather than calculation. And even the most intense practical evaluations of human rights initiatives too often stop short of considering the full range of potential downsides or negative knock on consequences in their enthusiasm to move forward with efforts whose up side potential seems so apparent.

1) "Pragmatic" always and forever or here and now?

Pragmatic evaluation means specifying the benefits and harms which might attend human rights initiatives in particular cases, under specific conditions, in particular time periods, and so forth. Those cases, conditions, times may be extremely specific (pursuing this petition will make this magistrate less likely to grant this other petition) or very general (articulating social welfare needs as individual "rights" makes people everywhere more passive and isolated) but they need to be articulated, and ultimately demonstrated, in concrete terms. At the same time, concrete does not mean sure or inevitable. The factors which influence policy making are not, by any means, all *proven* empirically. To count as a cost (or benefit), effects must be articulated in terms plausible enough to persuade people seeking to pursue human rights initiatives to take them into account.

Weighing the costs and benefits of "human rights" is difficult because the costs are often articulated in far more general terms than the benefits. The dangers on my list are often expressed as indictments of the entire human rights "idea" and "movement" in all times and places. The benefits are more often cast in immediate and local terms—these people out of this prison, those people provided with housing, this country's political process opened to elections, monitored in this way, these individuals spared the death penalty. It is certainly plausible that thinking about problems in the language of human rights could entail some costs (or benefits) always and everywhere, which would need to be added to each more particularised calculation. More likely, these general costs will be more or less intense in specific places and times. It may turn out that the entire human rights vocabulary or movement suffers from a blindness or works an effect which we should count as a cost. But it is far more likely that the vocabulary is used in different ways by different people, and that the movement is itself split in ways which make blindnesses more acute in some places and times than others. In weighing all this up, it is terribly hard to isolate the effects of "human rights". People in the movement also speak other languages, perhaps using the movement/ vocabulary of human rights to get in the door and then speaking instrumentally or ethically. People in the movement will evaluate risks, costs and benefits in quite different ways. The vocabulary and movement are themselves in flux—many of the open terms are subject to ongoing revision precisely to correct for the sorts of difficulties I have listed here. As a pragmatist, all one can do is take these possibilities into account as best one can, estimating their likelihood and augmenting or discounting risks accordingly. As a movement, one can facilitate open engagement about differing pragmatic assessments.

Imagine, for example, an effort to use the vocabulary and political capital of the international human rights movement to end capital punishment in the Caribbean. It might well turn out that leading corporate lawyers acting *pro bono* in London define the problem and solution differently than lawyers working with non-governmental groups in London, and differently again from lawyers and organisers in the Caribbean. For some the anti-death penalty campaign might seem a distraction from more pressing issues, might occupy the field, might, if the campaign is successful, even legitimate other governmental (in)action or other social conditions which kill more people in the Caribbean. There might be a struggle within the movement about the usefulness of the vocabulary, or within the vocabulary about the conditions and costs of its deployment in particular places. Some people might use the death penalty, and the human rights vocabulary, to leverage interest in other issues or other vocabularies—others might use it to close off broader inquiries. Wherever you are located, if you are thinking pragmatically about devoting scarce institutional resources to furthering or limiting the effort to bring human rights to bear on the instance of Caribbean death penalty, it will be necessary to come to some conclusion, however tentative and general, about how these conflicts and divergent effects will net out. I hope that this list of critical observations about human rights might provide something of a checklist for discussions of this sort.

In assessing costs and benefits, it is as easy to give human rights too much of the blame for costs as it is too much credit for benefits. It is possible, of course, that the potential costs of human rights—as a vocabulary and as a movement—arise when it is *misused, distorted,* or *co-opted*. It is possible that the benefits and burdens of human rights might, in the event, be swamped by the effects of other powers. Human rights may be a drop of liberation in an ocean of oppression, or a fig leaf of legitimisation over an evil collapsing of its own weight. In thinking pragmatically about human rights, all we can do is disaggregate and assess these causes and effects as carefully as possible. At the same time, we should be suspicious if costs are *always* attributed to people and forces outside the movement, just as we should be suspicious of claims that everything bad which happens was somehow always already *inherent* in the vocabulary used by unwitting human rights advocates. In thinking pragmatically about human rights, we will usually find ourselves somewhere in between, evaluating whether the vocabulary or institutional form of the movement, in particular contexts, makes particular types of "misuse" more or less likely. Again, I hope this list will provide a checklist of possible costs which we might think of (in particular circumstances or under certain conditions) as either potential misuses or as outcomes which may be made more likely by the human rights machinery.

Finally, it only makes sense to think pragmatically about human rights in *comparative* terms. How do the costs and benefits of pursuing an emancipatory objective in the vocabulary of human rights compare with other available discourses? How do efforts to work more intently within the human rights vocabulary compare with efforts to develop alternative vocabularies? How do human rights initiatives affect these efforts? Human rights might well discourage focus on collective responsibility, might leach the spiritual from emancipatory projects, but how does this stack up against alternative vocabularies and institutions—of family, kinship, nationhood, religious conviction—or with other political or legal emancipatory rhetorics? Whose hand is strengthened or weakened by each? How do we assess the medium or long-term effort to develop new vocabularies and institutions for emancipation? Again, my hope is that this list will help spark this sort of comparative analysis.

2) Specifying the costs and benefits

To weigh costs and benefits, we will need to be as articulate and concrete about the benefits as about the costs. I have not dwelt on the benefit side here, but it should be clear that people will evaluate the benefits very differently. There will be a struggle, both inside and outside the movement, about what benefits to seek and how to rank gains. Here, I have used the term "emancipation" to capture the broad range of (often conflicting) benefits people of good heart might hope to make of human rights —humanitarian, progressive, internationalist, social welfare enhancing. There might be other benefits—human rights might have aesthetic uses, might stimulate the heart or the imagination, just as they might be psychologically or ethically useful. And, of course, human rights might not be useful only for us, but for all sorts of people pursuing various projects, not all of them good-hearted. I leave the list of benefits to others.

But what about the costs. People who have made the criticisms I have listed here differ about the sorts of costs they feel should be totted up. Some criticisms are ethical, some are political, some are philosophical. For some the problem is aesthetics—the ensemble of characters, identities, vocabularies necessary to achieve what has been achieved by the human rights movement is also an aesthetic blight. Of course, the human rights movement might create bad effects not so much by what it does, as by what it does not do. Costs might include things which happen on the ground to potential victims and violators of human rights, or to other people (innocent bystanders). They might include things which happen to other elites—people doing good things weakened, doing bad things strengthened—or things which happen to participants in the human rights movement itself—professional deformations of various kinds which might be subject to ethical, political or philosophical criticism and then count as a cost of the endeavour.

For some people, it matters (ethically, politically, philosophically, aesthetically) what the human rights movement *expresses*. If the human rights movement increases the incidence of descriptions of women as mothers-on-pedestals or victimised care givers, in legal decisions or institutional documents, that, for some people, is already a cost—ethically, aesthetically, politically. It is bad if women have been represented in too narrow or stereotypical a fashion, even if the only consequence is to pry loose some resources for redistribution to women. A number of the criticisms I have included here are of this type.

For other people, and I must admit, for me, nothing goes in the "costs" column until the human rights movement has a bad *effect*. A bad effect means influencing someone to act (or fail to act) or to think in a way which counts as a cost (again, ethically, politically, philosophically, aesthetically) for the person making the argument. Intensifying stereotypical representations of women might be thought to have an effect on at least some women (perhaps only plaintiffs and women using the human rights movement as a vehicle of self-expression and freedom, and others who learn who they are from what the human rights movement says women are), encouraging them to *become* narrower and more stereotypical or to think of themselves more narrowly than they otherwise might. And, of course, such representations would have an effect if they encouraged people in some positions of authority—judges, men, legislators, other women—to exclude women not meeting this stereotypical profile from benefits they would otherwise receive.

In weighing initiatives pragmatically, it is often more useful to focus on "distributional consequences among individuals or groups" than "costs and benefits". The costs/benefits vocabulary suggests (incorrectly) that one could know at an abstract and general level what to count as a cost or a benefit of the initiative. In fact, of course, the "costs" and the "benefits" will look different and be evaluated differently by different people. For those who feel the death penalty deters, its abolition is a cost, which effects a distribution from victims to criminals. Although I speak here of costs and benefits (or the "problem" and the "solution") as if we shared very vague and general aspirations for a more humanitarian, progressive and egalitarian global society, it would probably be more accurate to think of these "benefits" as distributions of power, status and means towards those who share these objectives and away from those who don't. But let us take this general articulation as a first step. Thereafter we would need to assess, from a more particular point of view, who would win and who would lose from a human rights initiative. In that effort, we would need to recast the criticisms I list here as distributions of power which one might oppose.

3) *Some criticisms left off the list*

In keeping with this focus on usefulness, I have left off the list criticisms of human rights which are not cast in pragmatic terms. For example, the debate about whether human rights "really exist" or are "just" the product of efforts to articulate and use them. Although I find it hard to take too seriously the idea that rights *exist* in some way, let us assume that they do, and that the human rights movement is getting better and better at discovering and articulating them. If it turned out that doing so caused more misery than it alleviated, as a good-hearted legal professional, I would advocate our doing all we can to keep the existence of rights a secret. In a similar way, if it turns out that rights are "just" a fantasy, a social construction, and so forth, that tells us nothing about whether they are useful or not. If they are more useful than not, more power to the society which constructed them.

Traditional debates about whether human rights do or do not express a social consensus, in one society or across the globe, are similarly beside the point. Indeed, we could see them as updated ways of asking whether human rights really exist. Let us say they do express a social consensus—how does this affect their usefulness? Perhaps being able to say they express consensus weakens them, thins them out, skews their usefulness in various ways, perhaps it strengthens them. To decide, as my grandmother used to ask "whether that's a good thing or a bad thing" we still need to know whether once strengthened or skewed or weakened or whatever they are useful, and if so for what and for whom.

Similarly debate about whether human rights "talk" is or is not coherent. Let's say the human rights vocabulary, institutional apparatus, even the soul of the human rights advocate, is riddled with contradictions which would not stand up to logical scrutiny for a minute. Knowing only this does not move us any closer to an understanding of whether they are part of the problem or the solution. Perhaps ambivalent porosity is their secret strength—to the extent human rights is useful, we should then be grateful for the contradictions. Perhaps incoherence is a fatal weakness, but if human rights creates more problems than it solves, this would be all to the good.

I have also left out criticisms which could be answered by intensifying our commitment to the human rights movement—that often rights are not adequately enforced, that the list of rights on which we focus is underinclusive, that participation in the movement—in rights making and enforcing—could be broader, that rights are poorly or unevenly implemented because of opposition from people outside the movement or the movement's own lack of resources, and so forth. This sort of criticism only makes the list when it becomes *structural*—when it appears that deficiencies like this will not be solved by more commitment or resources—and when they also can be said to have bad effects. If what is done is good, but much is left undone, we can only feel more committed to what is precious in that which can be accomplished. But if the combination of doing and not doing makes matters worse, we must weigh that loss against the gain. We might decide, for example, that no matter how strong the human rights movement gets, it will always be disproportionate in its attentions to some rights and some regions. Skewed in this way, it might reinforce ideas and practices of elites which treat these regions, or these rights, differently in other ways—adding to the legitimacy of various other discriminations. If both these things seem plausible—the claimed skew is structural and there are plausible bad consequences—it makes the list. If made out, these consequences would, of course, need to be weighed against the good achieved to see whether either the broad human rights movement or any particular initiative undertaken in its name was *more* part of the problem than the solution.

II. A Short List of Pragmatic Worries and Polemical Charges

This is not a list of things unknown. All of these criticisms have been around for a long time, and the human rights movement has responded to them in a wide variety of ways. Attention is routinely given to previously under-represented rights, regions, modes of enforcement, styles of work. The human rights movement is, in many ways, now moving "beyond" rights, broadening its engagements and terms of reference. In many ways the movement has developed precisely by absorbing waves of criticism, often from those passionate about its possibilities and importance who cast their doubts in one or another of these terms. It would be interesting to list the reactions and reforms which these and other doubts have generated.

Sometimes, of course, reflecting on this sort of criticism can itself become part of the problem. If the costs turn out to be low or speculative, any time spent fleshing them out is time lost to the project of using human rights for emancipation—although having "been through" criticism might also strengthen the movement's ability to be useful. We are all familiar, moreover, with the periodic hand-wringing about possible errors and limits which accompanies the professional practice of human rights. This practice might well do more to stabilise the profession's sense of engagement, entitlement, confidence, than to undermine it, even where it turns out the costs far outweigh the benefits. Nevertheless, I can imagine good-hearted legal professionals coming to these criticisms fresh, in a pragmatic spirit. How, and how adequately, has the movement responded to its critics? Have we done all we can to eliminate these downside costs? Are we right to conclude that overall human rights is more part of the solution than the problem?

1) Human rights occupies the field of emancipatory possibility

Hegemony as resource allocation. The claim here is that this institutional and political hegemony makes other valuable, often more valuable, emancipatory strategies less available. This argument is stronger, of course, when one can say something about what those alternatives are—or might be. But there may be something to the claim that human rights has so dominated the imaginative space of emancipation that alternatives can now only be thought, perhaps unhelpfully, as negations of what human rights asserts—passion to its reason, local to its global, etc. As a dominant and fashionable vocabulary for thinking about emancipation, human rights crowds out other ways of understanding harm and recompense. This is easiest to see when human rights attracts institutional energy and resources which would otherwise flow elsewhere. But this is not only a matter of scarce resources.

Hegemony as criticism. Human rights also occupies the field by implicit or explicit delegitimation of other emancipatory strategies. As an increasingly dominant emancipatory vocabulary, human rights is also a mode of criticism, among people of good will and against people of good will, when pursuing projects which, by comparison, can seem "too" ideological and political, insufficiently universal, objective, and so on. Where this is so, pursuing a human rights initiative or promoting the use of human rights vocabulary may have fully unintended negative consequences for other existing emancipatory projects. Of course this takes us directly to a comparative analysis—how do we compare the gains and losses of human rights to the (potential) gains and losses of these other vocabularies and projects?

Hegemony as distortion. To the extent emancipatory projects must be expressed in the vocabulary of "rights" to be heard, good policies which are not framed that way go unattended. This also distorts the way projects are imagined and framed for international consideration. For example, it is often asserted that the international human rights movement makes an end run around local institutions and strategies which would often be better—ethically, politically, philosophically, aesthetically. Resources and legitimacy are drawn to the centre from the periphery. A "universal" idea of what counts as a problem and a solution snuffs out all sorts of promising local political and social initiatives to contest local conditions in other terms. But there are other lost vocabularies which are equally global—vocabularies of duty, of responsibility, of collective commitment. Encouraging people concerned about environmental harm to rethink their concerns as a human rights violation will have bad consequences if it would have turned out to be more animating, for example, to say there is a duty to work for the environment, rather than a right to a clean environment.

The "right to development" is a classic—and well-known—example. Once concerns about global poverty are raised in these terms, energy and resources are drawn to developing a literature and an institutional practice at the international level of a particular sort. Efforts which cannot be articulated in these terms seem less legitimate, less practical, less worth the effort. Increasingly, people of good will concerned about poverty are drawn into debate about a series of ultimately impossible legal quandaries—right of whom, against whom, remediable how, and so on—and into institutional projects of codification and reporting familiar from other human rights efforts, without evaluating how these might compare with other uses for this talent and these resources. Meanwhile, efforts which human rights does not criticise are strengthened. International economic policy affecting global poverty is taken over by neo-liberal players who do not see development as a special problem.

2) Human rights views the problem and the solution too narrowly

Narrow in many ways. People have made many different claims about the narrowness of human rights. Here are some: the human rights movement foregrounds harms done explicitly by *governments* to individuals or groups—leaving largely unaddressed and more legitimate by contrast harms brought about by governments indirectly or by private parties. Even when addressing private harms, human rights focuses attention on *public* remedies —explicit rights formalised and implemented by the State. One criticises the *State* and seeks *public* law remedies, but leaves unattended or enhanced the powers and felt entitlements of private actors. Human rights implicitly legitimates ills and delegitimates remedies in the domain of private law and non-State action.

Insulating the economy. Putting these narrowings together often means defining problems and solutions in ways not likely to change the economy. Human rights foregrounds problems of *participation* and *procedure,* at the expense of distribution, implicitly legitimating the existing distributions of wealth, status and power in societies once rights have been legislated, formal participation in Government achieved, and institutional remedies for violations provided. However useful saying "that's my right" is in extracting things from the State, it is not good for extracting things from the economy, unless you are a property holder. Indeed, a practice of rights claims against the State may actively weaken the capacity of people to challenge economic arrangements.

Whether progressive efforts to challenge economic arrangements are weakened by the overwhelming strength of the "right to property" in the human rights vocabulary, or by the channelling of emancipatory energy and imagination into the modes of institutional and rhetorical interaction which are described as "public", the imbalance between civil/political and social/economic rights is neither an accident of politics nor a matter which could be remedied by more intensive commitment. It is structural, to the philosophy of human rights, to the conditions of political possibility which make human rights an emancipatory strategy in the first place, to the institutional character of the movement, or to the ideology of its participants and supporters.

Foregrounding form. The strong attachment of the human rights movement to the legal formalisation of rights and the establishment of legal machinery for their implementation makes the achievement of these forms an end in itself. Elites in a political system—international, national—which has adopted the rules and set up the institutions will often themselves have the impression and insist persuasively to others that they have addressed the problem of violations with an elaborate, internationally respected and "state of the art" response. This is analogous to the way in which holding elections can come to substitute for popular engagement in the political process. These are the traditional problems of form: form can hamper peaceful adjustment and necessary change, can be over- or underinclusive. Is the right to vote a floor—or can it become a ceiling? The human rights movement ties its own hands on progressive development.

Backgrounding the background. The effects of a wide array of laws which do not explicitly condone violations but nevertheless affect the incidence of violation in a society are left unattended. As a result, these background laws—which may well be more important in generating the harm than an absence of rights and remedies for victims—are left with clean hands. Moreover, to maintain the claim to universality and neutrality, the human rights movement practices a systematic lack of attention to background sociological and political conditions which will determine the meaning a right has in particular contexts, rendering the evenhanded pursuit of "rights" vulnerable to all sorts of distorted, and distinctly non-neutral outcomes.

Even very broad social movements of emancipation—for women, for minorities of various sorts, for the poor—have their vision blinkered by the promise of recognition in the vocabulary and institutional apparatus of human rights. They will be led away from the economy and towards the State, away from political/social conditions and towards the forms of legal recognition. It has been claimed, for example, that promoting a neutral right to religious expression in Africa without acknowledging the unequal background cultural, economic and political authority of traditional religions and imported evangelical sects will dramatically affect the distribution of religious practice. Even if we limit our thinking to the *laws* which influence the distribution of wealth, status and power between men and women, the number of those laws which *explicitly* address "women's issues", still less "women's rights", would form an extremely small and relatively unimportant percentage. However much the human rights movement reaches out to address other background considerations affecting the incidence of human rights abuse, such "background" norms remain, well, background.

3) Human rights generalises too much

Universal goods and evils. The vocabulary and institutional practice of human rights promotion propagates an unduly abstract idea about people, politics and society. A one-size-fits-all emancipatory practice underrecognises and reduces the instance and possibility for particularity and variation. This claim is not that human rights are too "individualistic". Rather, the claim is that the "person", as well as the "group", imagined and brought to life by human rights agitation is both abstract and general in ways which have bad consequences.

Sometimes this claim is framed as a loss of the pre-existing diversity of experience—as a vocabulary for expressing or representing experience, human rights limits human potential. In this view, limits on pre-existing potentials and experiences are themselves bad consequences. For others who make this argument, the loss of a prior, more authentic, humane, diverse *real* experience is not the issue. Even if it turns out that behind modes of expression there is no authentic experience, much less an edenic one, *this particular vocabulary* is less useful in encouraging possibility or hope or emancipation than others which generalise less or differently.

Becoming free only as an instance of the general. To come into understanding of oneself as an instance of a pre-existing general—"I am a 'person with rights' "—exacts a cost. A loss of awareness of the unprecedented and plastic nature of experience, or a loss of a capacity to imagine and desire alternative futures. We could term this "alienation". The human rights movement proposes itself as a vocabulary of the general good—as knowledge about the shape of emancipation and human possibility which can be "applied" and "enforced". As an emancipatory vocabulary, it offers answers rather than questions, answers which are not only outside political, ideological and cultural differences, but also beyond the human experience of specificity and against the human capacity to hope for more, in denial of the tawdry and uncertain quality of our available dreams about and experience with justice and injustice. Rather than enabling a discussion of what it means to be human, of who is human, of how humans might relate to one another, it crushes this discussion under the weight of moral condemnation, legal adjudication, textual certainty and political power.

Not just bad for victims. The articulation of concrete good and evil in abstract terms is not only limiting for victims. The human rights vocabulary makes us think of evil as a social machine, a theatre of roles, in which people are "victims", "violators" and "bystanders". At its most effective, human rights figures victims as passive and innocent, violators as deviant, and human rights professionals as heroic. Only the bystanders are figured in ambivalent or uncertain terms. To enter the terrain of emancipation through human rights is to enter a world of uncivilised deviants, baby seals and knights errant. There is a narrowing here—other evils and other goods receive less attention. Privileging the baby seals delegitimises the suffering of people (and animals) who are, if anything, more typical in the complexity of their ethical and political posture, and renders the broader political culture less articulate about, and less able to engage, suffering which is embedded in or understood to express a more ambivalent constellation of characters. But this vocabulary also exacts a cost from those who fit most easily into its terms. No number of carefully elaborated "rights" is sufficient to recover a complex sense for a "violator's" human possibility and ambivalent experience. Differences among "victims", the experience of their particularity and the hope for their creative and surprising self-expression, are erased under the power of an internationally sanctified vocabulary for their self-understanding, self-presentation and representation as "victims" of human rights abuse.

Even bad for advocates. To come into experience of oneself as a benevolent and pragmatic actor through the professional vocabulary of legal representation has costs for the human rights advocate, compared with other vocabularies of political engagement or social solidarity. Coming into awareness of oneself as the representative of something else —heroic agent for an authentic suffering elsewhere—mutes one's capacity for solidarity with those cast as victims, violators, bystanders, and stills the habit of understanding oneself to inhabit the world one seeks to affect. This claim is often put in ethical or characterological terms: human rights promotes emancipation by propagating an unbearably normative, earnest, and ultimately arrogant mode of thinking and speaking about what is good for people, abstract people, here and there, now and forever. This is bad for people in the movement—it can demobilise them as political beings in the world while encouraging their sanctimony—as well as those whose sense of the politically possible and desirable is shrunk to fit the uniform size.

4) Human rights particularises too much

Emancipating the "right holders". The specific way human rights generalises is to consolidate people into "identities" on the basis of which rights can be claimed. There are two issues here: a focus on *individuals* and a focus, whether for individuals or groups, on *right-holding identity.* The focus on individuals and people who come to think of themselves as individuals blunts articulation of a shared life. The focus on discrete and insular right holding identities blunts awareness of diversity, of the continuity of human experience, of overlapping identities. Together these tendencies inhibit expression of the experience of being part of a community.

Again we find two types of claims. For some, the key point is that human rights reduces and distorts a more promising *real* experience, of more shifting, less bounded identities, at times fused with a general will or co-participating in identities and social arrangements for which one will turn out to have no corresponding right or privilege. For others, the point is that compared to other vocabularies, human rights renders those who use it inarticulate about and less capable of solidarity and open-ended possibility. Either way, the human rights movement intensifies the sense of entitlement in individuals and groups at great cost to their ability to participate in collective political life and to their understanding of their own lives as part of a more diverse community.

Strengthening the State. Although the human rights vocabulary expresses relentless suspicion of the State, by structuring emancipation as a relationship between an individual right holder and the State, human rights places the State at the centre of the emancipatory promise. However much one may insist on the priority or pre-existence of rights, in the end rights are enforced, granted, recognised, implemented, their violations remedied, by the State. By consolidating human experience into the exercise of legal entitlements, human rights strengthens the national governmental structure and equates the structure of the State with the structure of freedom. To be free is . . . to have an appropriately organised state. We might say that the right-holder imagines and experiences freedom only as a *citizen*. This encourages autochthonous political tendencies and alienates the "citizen" from both his or her own experience as a person and from the possibility of alternative communal forms.

Encouraging conflict and discouraging politics among right holders. Encouraging each person and group wishing to be free to tally the rights he/she/it holds in preparation for their assertion against the State reduces inter-group and inter-individual sensitivity. In emancipating itself, the right holder is, in effect, queue jumping. Recognising, implementing, enforcing rights is distributional work. Encouraging people to imagine themselves as right holders, and rights as absolute, makes the negotiation of distributive arrangements among individuals and groups less likely and less tenable. There is no one to triage among rights and right holders—except the State. The absolutist legal vocabulary of rights makes it hard to assess distribution among favoured and less favoured right holders and forecloses development of a political process for tradeoffs among them, leaving only the vague suspicion that the more privileged got theirs at the expense of the less privileged.

"Refugees" are people too. For fifty years the human rights movement, and the legal departments (often in opposition to the "humanitarian assistance" departments) of the great international institutions have struggled for legal recognition of the status of "refugee", helping to generate millions of people who think of themselves as "refugees", and whose status has often been so certified by one or another institution in the human rights family. Formalising a status of disconnection from the state of "origin", the "host" state and the state in whose location one seeks "settlement", has taken an enormous toll on everyone's ability to think about and affect either the causes or consequences of refugee status. It is a status defined by its detachment from both. The 30-year stillborn effort to codify a "right to asylum" as an entailment of refugee status illustrates the difficulty of addressing solutions as matters of legal entitlement. Illustrates it so strikingly that we should question whether the effort to define the identity and rights of "the refugee" is more part of the problem than the solution.

5) Human rights expresses the ideology, ethics, aesthetic sensibility and political practice of a particular Western 18th–20th century liberalism

Tainted origins. Although there are lots of interesting analogies to human rights ideas in various cultural traditions, the particular form these ideas are given in the human rights movement is the product of a particular moment and place. Post-enlightenment, rationalist, secular, Western, modern, capitalist. From a pragmatist point of view, of course, tainted origins are irrelevant. That human rights *claims* to be universal but *is really* the product of a specific cultural and historical origin says nothing—unless that specificity exacts costs or renders human rights less useful than something else. The human rights tradition might itself be undermined by its origin—be treated less well by some people, be less effective in some places—just as its origin might, for other audiences, accredit projects undertaken in its name. This is the sort of thing we might strategise about—perhaps we should downplay the universal claims, or look for parallel developments in other cultural traditions, etc.

The movement's Western liberal origins become part of the problem (rather than a limit on the solution) when particular difficulties general to the liberal tradition are carried over to the human rights movement. When, for example, the global expression of emancipatory objectives in human rights terms narrows humanity's appreciation of these objectives to the forms they have taken in the 19th–20th century Western political tradition. One cost would be the loss of more diverse and local experiences and conceptions of emancipation. Even within the liberal West, other useful emancipatory vocabularies (including the solidarities of socialism, Christianity, the labour movement, and so forth) are diminished by the consolidation of human rights as the international expression of *the* Western liberal tradition. Other costs would be incurred to the extent the human rights tradition could be seen to carry with it particular downsides of the liberal West.

Downsides of the West. That the emancipations of the modern West have come with costs has long been a theme in critical writing—alienation, loss of faith, environmental degradation, immorality, etc. Seeing human rights as part of the Western liberal package is a way of asserting that at least some of these costs should be attributed to the human rights tradition. This might be asserted in a variety of ways. If you thought secularism was part of what is bad about the modern West, you might assert that human rights shares the secular spirit, that as a sentimental vocabulary of devotion it actively displaces religion, offering itself as a poor substitute. You might claim that the enforcement of human rights, including religious rights, downgrades religion to a matter of private and individual commitment, or otherwise advances the secular project. To the extent human rights can be implicated in the secular project, we might conclude that it leaves the world spiritually less well off. Other criticisms of the modern liberal West have been extended to human rights in a parallel fashion.

In particular, critics have linked the human rights project to liberal Western ideas about the relationships among law, politics and economics. Western enlightenment ideas which make the human rights movement part of the problem rather than the solution include the following: the economy *pre-exists* politics, politics *pre-exists* law, the private *pre-exists* the public, just as the animal pre-exists the human, faith pre-exists reason, or the feudal pre-exists the modern. In each case, the second term is fragile, artificial, a human creation and achievement, and a domain of choice, while the first term identifies a sturdy and natural base, a domain outside human control.

Human rights encourages people to seek emancipation in the vocabularies of reason rather than faith, in public rather than private life, in law rather than politics, in politics rather than economics. In each case, the human rights vocabulary overemphasises the difference between what it takes as the (natural) base and as the (artificial) domain of emancipation, and underestimates the plasticity of what it treats as the base. Moreover, human rights is too quick to conclude that emancipation *means* progress forward from the natural passions of politics into the civilised reason of law. The urgent need to develop a more vigorous human politics is sidelined by the effort to throw thin but plausible nets of legal articulation across the globe. Work to develop law comes to be seen as an emancipatory end in itself, leaving the human rights movement too ready to articulate problems in political terms and solutions in legal terms. Precisely the reverse would be more useful. The posture of human rights as an emancipatory political project which extends and operates within a domain above or outside politics—a political project repackaged as a form of knowledge—delegitimates other political voices and makes less visible the local, cultural and political dimensions of the human rights movement itself.

As liberal Western intellectuals, we think of the move to rights as an escape from the unfreedom of social conditions into the freedom of citizenship, but we repeatedly forget that there is also a loss. A loss of the experience of belonging, of the habit of willing in conditions of indeterminacy, innovating collectively in the absence of knowledge, unchannelled by an available list of rights. This may represent a loss of either the presence of experience itself, experience not yet channelled and returned to the individual as the universal experience of a right holder, or of the capacity to deploy other vocabularies which are more imaginative, open and oriented to future possibility.

The West and the Rest. The Western/liberal character of human rights exacts particular costs when it intersects with the highly structured and unequal relations between the modern West and everyone else. Whatever the limits of modernisation in the West, the form of modernisation promoted by the human rights movement in third world societies is too often based only on a fantasy about the modern/liberal/capitalist west. The insistence on more formal and absolute conceptions of property rights in transitional societies than are known in the developed West is a classic example of this problem—using the authority of the human rights movement to narrow the range of socio-economic choices available in developing societies in the name of "rights" which do not exist in this unregulated or compromised form in any developed western democracy.

At the same time, the human rights movement contributes to the framing of political choices in the third world as oppositions between "local/traditional" and "international/modern" forms of government and modes of life. This effect is strengthened by the presentation of human rights as part of belonging to the modern world, but coming from some place outside political choice, from the universal, the rational, the civilised. By strengthening the articulation of third world politics as a choice between tradition and modernity, the human rights movement impoverishes local political discourse, often strengthening the hand of self-styled "traditionalists" who are offered a common-sense and powerful alternative to modernisation for whatever politics they may espouse.

6) Human rights promises more than it can deliver

Knowledge. Human rights promises a way of knowing—knowing just and unjust, universal and local, victim and violator, harm and remedy—which it cannot deliver. Justice is something which must be made, experienced, articulated, performed each time anew. Human rights may well offer an index of ways in which past experiences of justice achieved have retrospectively been described, but the usefulness of this catalogue as a stimulus to emancipatory creativity is swamped by the encouragement such lists give to the idea that justice need not be made, that it can be found or simply imported. One result is a loss of the habit of grappling with ambivalence, conflict and the unknown. Taken together, belief in these various false promises demobilises actors from taking other emancipatory steps and encourages a global misconception of both the nature of evil and the possibilities for good.

Justice. Human rights promises a legal vocabulary for achieving justice outside the clash of political interest. Such a vocabulary is not available: rights conflict with one another, rights are vague, rights have exceptions, many situations fall between rights. The human rights movement promises that "law"—the machinery, the texts, the profession, the institution—can resolve conflicts and ambiguities in society by resolving those within its own materials, and that this can be done on the basis of a process of "interpretation" which is different from, more legitimate than, politics. And different in a particularly stultifying way—as a looser or stricter deduction from a past knowledge rather than as a collective engagement with the future. In particular, the human rights movement fetishises the judge as someone who functions as an instrument of the law rather than as a political actor, when this is simply not possible—not a plausible description of judicial behaviour—given the porous legal vocabulary with which judges must work and the likely political context within which judges are asked to act.

Many general criticisms of law's own tendencies to over-promise are applicable in spades to human rights. The absoluteness of rules makes compromise and peaceful adjustment of outcomes more difficult. The vagueness of standards makes for self-serving interpretation. The gap between law in the books and law in action, between legal institutions and the rest of life, hollows promises of emancipation through law. The human rights movement suggests that "rights" can be responsible for emancipation, rather than people making political decisions. This demobilises other actors and other vocabularies, and encourages emancipation through reliance on enlightened, professional elites with "knowledge" of rights and wrongs, alienating people from themselves and from the vocabulary of their own governance. These difficulties are more acute in the international arena where law is ubiquitous and unaccompanied by political dialogue.

Community. The human rights movement shares responsibility for the widespread belief that the world's political elites form a "community" which is benevolent, disconnected from economic actors and interests, and connected in some diffuse way through the media to the real aspirations of the world's people. The international human rights effort promises the ongoing presence of an entity, a "community", which can support and guarantee emancipation. This fantasy has bad consequences not only when people place too much hope in a foreign emancipatory friend which does not materialise. The transformation of the first world media audience, as that audience is imagined by the media, into "the international community" is itself an astonishing act of disenfranchisement. We might think the loss as one of "real" politics—such as that available in the context of a legislature, or at the national level. But even if we conclude that these are also fantastic—vocabularies of emancipation and oppression and opportunities for their expression—they are more useful vocabularies, more likely to emancipate, more likely to encourage habits of engagement, solidarity, responsibility, more open to surprise and reconfiguration.

Neutral intervention. The human rights vocabulary promises Western constituencies a politics-neutral and universalist mode of emancipatory intervention elsewhere in the world. This leads these constituencies to unwarranted innocence about the range of their other ongoing interventions and unwarranted faith in the neutral or universalist nature of a human rights presence. They intervene more often than they might otherwise. Their interventions are less effective than they would be if pursued in other vocabularies. Effective or not in their own terms, these interventions-without-responsibility-or-engagement have unfortunate consequences which are neither acknowledged nor open to contestation.

Emancipator as emancipation. Human rights offers itself as the measure of emancipation. This is its most striking—and misleading—promise. Human rights narrates itself as a universal/eternal/human truth and as a pragmatic response to injustice—there was the holocaust and then there was the Genocide Convention, women everywhere were subject to discrimination and then there was CEDAW. This posture makes the human rights movement *itself* seem redemptive—as if doing something *for human rights* was, in and of itself, doing something *against* evil. It is not surprising that human rights professionals consequently confuse work on the movement for emancipatory work in society. But there are bad consequences when people of good will mistake work on the discipline for work on the problem.

Potential emancipators can be derailed—satisfied that building the human rights movement is its own reward. People inside the movement can mistake reform of their world for reform of the world. What seem like improvements in the field's ability to respond to things outside itself may only be improvements in the field's ability to respond to its own internal divisions and contradictions. Yet we routinely underestimate the extent to which the human rights movement develops in response to political conflict and discursive fashion among international elites, thereby overestimating the field's pragmatic potential and obscuring the field's internal dynamics and will to power.

Think of the right to development, born less in response to global poverty than in response to an internal political conflict within the elite about the legitimate balance of concerns on the institutional agenda and to an effort by some more marginal members of that elite to express their political interest in the only available language. The move from a world of "rights" to "remedies" and then to "basic needs" and on to "transnational enforcement" reflected less a changing set of problems in the world than a changing set of attitudes among international legal elites about the value of legal formalism. The result of such initiatives to reframe emancipatory objectives in human rights terms is more often growth for the field—more conferences, documents, legal analysis, opposition and response—than decrease in violence against women, poverty, mass slaughter and so forth. This has bad effects when it discourages political engagement or encourages reliance on human rights for results it cannot achieve.

7) The legal regime of "human rights," taken as a whole, does more to produce and excuse violations than to prevent and remedy them

Treating symptoms. Human rights remedies, even when successful, treat the symptoms rather than the illness, and this allows the illness not only to fester, but to seem like health itself. This is most likely where signing up for a norm—against discrimination—comes to substitute for ending the practice. But even where victims are recompensed or violations avoided, the distributions of power and wealth which produced the violation may well come to seem more legitimate as they seek other avenues of expression.

Humanitarian norms excuse too much. We are familiar with the idea that rules of warfare may do more to legitimate violence than to restrain it—as a result of vague standards, broad justifications, lax enforcement, or prohibitions which are clear but beside the point. The same can often be said about human rights. The vague and conflicting norms, their uncertain status, the broad justifications and excuses, the lack of enforcement, the attention to problems which are peripheral to a broadly conceived program of social justice—all this may, in some contexts, place the human rights movement in the uncomfortable position of legitimating more injustice than it eliminates. This is particularly likely where human rights discourse has been absorbed into the foreign policy processes of the great powers, indeed, of all powers.

Humanitarian norms justify too much. The human rights movement consistently underestimates the usefulness of the human rights vocabulary and machinery for people whose hearts are hard and whose political projects are repressive.

The United States, The United Kingdom, Russia—but also Serbia and the Kosovar Albanians—have taken military action, intervened politically, and justified their governmental policies on the grounds of protecting human rights. Far from being a defense of the individual against the state, human rights has become a standard part of the justification for the external use of force by the state against other states and individuals. The porousness of the human rights vocabulary means that the interventions and exercises of state authority it legitimates are more likely to track political interests than its own emancipatory agenda.

Background norms do the real damages. At the same time, the human rights regime, like the law concerning war, is composed of more than those legal rules and institutions which explicitly concern human rights. The human rights movement acts as if the human rights legal regime were composed only of rights catalogues and institutions for their implementation. In fact, the law concerning torture, say, includes all the legal rules, principles, and institutions which bear on the incidence of torture. The vast majority of these rules—rules of sovereignty, institutional competence, agency, property and contract—facilitate or excuse the use of torture by police and governments.

8) The human rights bureaucracy is itself part of the problem

Professionalises the humanitarian impulse. The human rights movement attracts and demobilises thousands of good-hearted people around the globe every year. It offers many thousands more the confidence that these matters are being professionally dealt with by those whom the movement has enlisted.

Something similar has occurred within academic life—a human rights discipline has emerged between fields of public law and international law, promising students and teachers that work in the public interest has an institutional life, a professional routine and status. Professionalization has a number of possible costs. Absolute costs in lost personnel for other humanitarian possibilities. As the human rights profession raises its standards and status to compete with disciplines of private law, it raises the bar for other pro-bono activities which have not been successful in establishing themselves as disciplines, whose practices, knowledge and projects are less systematic, less analogous to practice in the private interest. Professionalisation strengthens lawyers at the expense of priests, engineers, politicians, soothsayers and citizens who might otherwise play a more central role in emancipatory efforts. At the same time, professionalisation separates human rights advocates from those they represent and those which whom they share a common emancipatory struggle. The division of labour among emancipatory specialists is not merely about efficient specialisation. We need only think of the bureaucratisation of human rights in places like East Timor which have come within the orbit of international governance—suddenly an elaborate presence pulling local elites away from their base, or consigning them to the status of local informants, attention turning like sunflowers to Geneva, New York, to the Centre, to the Commission. To the work of resolutions and reports.

Downgrades the legal profession. Sometimes the concern here is for the legal profession itself. The human rights movement degrades the legal profession by encouraging a combination of overly formal reliance on textual articulations which are anything but clear or binding and sloppy humanitarian argument. This combination degrades the legal skills of those involved, while encouraging them to believe that their projects are more legitimate precisely because they are presented in (sloppy) legal terms. Others have argued that human rights offers the profession, particularly at its most elite sites, a fig leaf of public interest commitment to legitimate the profession's contributions to global emiseration in its daily practice, in part by making all other legal fields, and particularly commercial legal fields, seem outside politics by contrast. For this, the sloppiness of human rights practice is itself useful—marking a line between the political redemptive profession and the a-political workaday world of other legal professionals.

Encourages false solidarity. Of course there are many different types of people in the human rights movement and bureaucracy—different generations, different nationalities, different genders. To be a male human rights lawyer in Holland in your thirties is to live a different life altogether from that of a female human rights lawyer in Uruguay in her sixties. The human rights vocabulary encourages a false sense of the unity among these experiences and projects. As a vocabulary for progressive elite solidarity, human rights is particularly ham-handed, making it more difficult to articulate differences in the projects of male and female Palestinian human rights lawyers, Americans and Nigerians, etc.

Promotes bad faith. One thing these professionals do share, however, is a more or less bad faith relationship to their professional work. Every effort to use human rights for new purposes, to "cover" new problems, requires that they make arguments they know to be less persuasive than they claim. Arguments about their representative capacity—speaking for a consensus, a victim, an international community—and about the decisiveness of the vocabularies they invoke. Professional bad faith accumulates the more the movement tries to torque its tools to correct for its shortcomings—to address background conditions which affect the incidence of abuse as if they were themselves violations, for example. We need only think of the earnest advocate re-describing torture or the death penalty or female genital mutilation as a problem of "public health" to feel the movement's characteristic professional deformations at work.

Speaking law to politics is not the same as speaking truth to power. The human rights professional's vocabulary encourages an overestimation of the distinction between its own idealism and the hard realpolitik motivations of those it purports to address. Professional human rights performances are, in this sense, exercises in de-solidarisation. One intensifies the "legal" marks in one's expression as if one thought this would persuade an actual other person who one imagines, paradoxically, to inhabit an altogether different "political" world. In this, the human rights intervention is always addressed to an imaginary third eye—the bystander who will solidarise with the (unstated) politics of the human rights speaker because it is expressed in an apolitical form. This may often work as a form of political recruitment —but it exacts a terrible cost on the habit of using more engaged and open ended political vocabularies. The result is professional narcissism guising itself as empathy and hoping to recruit others to solidarity with its bad faith.

Perils of "representation.". The professionalism of human rights creates a mechanism for people to think they are working "on behalf of" less fortunate others, while externalising the possible costs of their decision and actions. The representational dimension of human rights work—speaking "for" others—puts the "victims" both on screen and off. The production of authentic victims, or victim authenticity, is an inherently voyeuristic or pornographic practice which, no matter how carefully or sensitively it is done, transforms the position of the "victim" in his or her society and produces a language of victimisation for him or her to speak on the international stage. The injured-one-who-is-not-yet-a-victim, the "subaltern" if you like, can neither speak nor be spoken for, but recedes instead before the interpretative and representational practices of the movement. The remove between human rights professionals and the people they purport to represent can reinforce a global divide of wealth, mobility, information and access to audience. Human rights professionals consequently struggle, ultimately in vain, against a tide of bad faith, orientalism and self-serving sentimentalism

Irresponsible intervention. The people who work within the human rights field have no incentive to take responsibility for the changes they bring about. Consequences are the result of an interaction between a context and an abstraction—"human rights." At the same time, the simultaneously loose and sanctified nature of the vocabulary and the power of the movement itself opens an enormous terrain for discretionary action —intervening here and not there, this way and not that, this time and not that time.

There is no vocabulary for treating this discretion as the responsible act of a person, creating intense psychic costs for human rights professionals themselves, but also legitimating their acts of unaccountable discretion.

Belief in the nobility of human rights places blame for whatever goes wrong elsewhere—on local politicians, evil individuals, social pathologies. This imposes ethical, political and aesthetic costs on people in the movement—but also on those elsewhere in the elite who must abide them, and in those who, as the terrain of engagement and the object of representation, become the mirror for this professional self regard.

9) The human rights movement strengthens bad international governance

Weakest link. Even within international law, the modes of possible governance are far broader than the patterns worn by human rights professionals. The human rights movement is the product of a particular moment in international legal history, which foregrounded rules rather than standards and institutional rather than cultural enforcement. If we compare modes of governance in other fields we find a variety of more successful models—a standards/cultural enforce based environmental regime, an economic law regime embedded in private law, and so forth. The attachment to rights as a measure of authenticity, universality, and above all as the knowledge we have of social justice, binds our professional feet, and places social justice issues under the governance of the least effective institutional forms available.

Clean hands. More generally, international governance errs when it imagines itself capable of governing, "intervening" if you will, without taking responsibility for the messy business of allocating stakes in society—when it intervenes only economically and not politically, only in public and not in private life, only "consensually" without acknowledging the politics of influence, only to freeze the situation and not to improve it, "neutrally" as between the parties, politically/economically but not culturally, and so forth. The human rights movement offers the well-intentioned intervenor the illusion of affecting conditions both at home and abroad without being politically implicated in the distribution of stakes which results, by promising an available set of universal, extra-political legal rules and institutions with which to define, conduct and legitimate the intervention.

Fantasy government. International governance is often asked to do globally what we fantasise or expect national governments to do locally—allocate stakes, constitute a community, articulate differences and similarities, provide for the common good. The human rights movement, by strengthening the habit of understanding international governance in legal rather than political terms, weakens its ability to perform what we understand domestically to be these political functions. The conflation of the law with the good encourages an understanding of international governance—by those within and without its institutions—which is systematically blind to the bad consequences of its own action. The difficulty the human rights movement has in thinking of itself in pragmatic rather than theological terms—in weighing and balancing the usefulness of its interventions in terms like those included in this list—is characteristic of international governance as a whole. The presence of a human rights movement models this blindness as virtue and encourages it among other governance professionals by presenting itself as insurance of international law's broader humanitarian character.

Governing the exception. Human rights shares with the rest of international law a tendency to treat only the tips of icebergs. Deference to the legal forms upon which human rights is built—the forms of sovereignty, territorial jurisdictional divisions, subsidiarity, consensual norms—makes it seem natural to isolate aspects of a problem which "cross borders" or "shock the conscience of mankind" for special handling at the international level —often entrenching the rest of the iceberg more firmly in the national political background. The movement's routine polemical denunciations of sovereignty work more as attestations to its continuity than agents of its erosion, limiting the aspirations of good-hearted people with international and global political commitments. The notion that law sits atop culture as well as politics demobilises people who understand their political projects as "intervention" in a "foreign" "culture." The human rights vocabulary, with its emphasis on the development of law itself, strengthens the tendency of international lawyers more broadly to concern themselves with constitutional questions about the structure of the legal regime itself rather than with questions of distribution in the broader society.

10) Human rights promotion can be bad politics in particular contexts

It may be that this is all one can say—promoting human rights can sometimes have bad consequences. All of the first nine types of criticism suggested that human rights suffered from one or another design defect—as if these defects would emerge, these costs would be incurred, regardless of context. Perhaps this is so. But so long as none of these criticisms have been proven in such a general way (and it is hard to see just how they could be), it may be that all we have is a list of possible down sides, open risks, bad results which have sometimes occurred, which might well occur. In some context, for example, it might turn out that pursuing emancipation as entitlement could reduce the capacity and propensity for collective action. Something like this seems to have happened in the United States in the last twenty years—the transformation of political questions into legal questions, and then into questions of legal "rights", has made other forms of collective emancipatory politics less available. But it is hard to see that this is always and everywhere the destiny of human rights initiatives. We are familiar, even in the United States, with moments of collective emancipatory mobilisation achieved, in part, through the vocabulary of rights. If we come to the recent British Human Rights Act, it seems an open question whether it will liberate emancipatory political energies frozen by the current legislative process and party structure, or will harness those political possibilities to the human rights claims of de-politicised individuals and judges. The point of an ongoing pragmatic evaluation of the human rights effort is precisely to develop a habit of making such assessments. But that human rights promotion can and has had bad consequences in some contexts does seem clear.

Strengthens repressive States and anti-progressive international initiatives. In some places, human rights implementation can make a repressive State more efficient.

Human rights institutions and rhetoric can also be used in particular contexts to humanise repressive political initiatives and co-opt to their support sectors of civil society which might otherwise be opposed. Human rights can be and has been used to strengthen, defend, legitimate a variety of repressive initiatives, by both individuals and states. To legitimate war, defend the death penalty, the entitlements of majorities, religious repression, access to (or restriction of) abortion, and so forth. The recent embrace of human rights by the international financial institutions may serve both functions—strengthening states which will need to enforce harsh structural adjustment policies while co-opting local and international resistance to harsh economic policies, and lending a shroud of universal/rational inevitability to economic policies which are the product of far narrower political calculations and struggles. As deployed, the human rights movement may do a great deal to take distribution off the national and international development agendas, while excusing and legitimating regressive policies at all levels. These difficulties are particularly hard to overcome because the human rights movement remains tone-deaf to the specific political consequences of its activity in particular locations, on the mistaken assumption that a bit more human rights can never make things worse. This makes the human rights movement particularly subject to capture by other political actors and ideological projects. We need only think of the way the move to "responsibilities" signalled by the Universal Declaration on Human Responsibilities of 1998 was captured by neo-liberal efforts to promote privatisation and weaken the emancipatory potentials of government.

Condemnation as legitimation. Finally, in many contexts, transforming a harm into a "human rights violation" may be a way of condoning or denying rather than naming and condemning it. A terrible set of events occurs in Bosnia. We could think of it as a sin and send the religious, as illness and send physicians, as politics and send the politicians, as war and send the military. Or we could think of it as a human rights violation and send the lawyers. Doing so can be a way of doing nothing, avoiding responsibility, simultaneously individualising the harm and denying its specificity. Thinking of atrocity as a human rights violation captures neither the unthinkable nor the banal in evil. Instead we find a strange combination of clinically antiseptic analysis, throwing the illusion of cognitive control over the unthinkable, and hysterical condemnation, asserting the advocate's distance from the quotidian possibility of evil. Renaming Auschwitz "genocide" to recognise its unspeakability, enshrining its status as "shocking the conscience of mankind" can also be a way of unthinking its everyday reality. In this sense, human rights, by criminalising harm and condensing its origin to particular violators, can serve as denial, apology, legitimation, normalisation, and routinisation of the very harms it seeks to condemn.

So that is the list. As I said at the outset, some of these worries seem more plausible to me than others. I would worry about some of these costs more than others. The generation which built the human rights movement focused its attention on the ways in which evil people in evil societies could be identified and restrained. More acute now is how good people, well intentioned people in good societies, can go wrong, can entrench, support, the very things they have learned to denounce. Answering this question requires a pragmatic re-assessment of our most sacred humanitarian commitments, tactics and tools.

Whatever has been the history of human rights, we do not know its future. Perhaps these difficulties will be overcome, avoided. But we will not avoid them by avoiding their articulation, discussion, assessment—by treating the human rights movement as a frail child, in need of protection from critical assessment or pragmatic calculation. At this point these remain suspicions, intuitions, hunches, by people who have seen the human rights movement from one or another point of view. Each person involved in international human rights protection will have his or her own view about which, if any, of these doubts are plausible and worth pursuing. As a profession, it would be good to have a more open conversation about worries of this sort, and to think further about how they should affect our understanding of the human rights project as a whole.

Name Index